THE ATLAS OF
ROYAL BRITAIN

ATLAS
OF
ROYAL BRITAIN

Consultant Editor
Hugh Montgomery-Massingberd

WINDWARD

A QED BOOK

First published in Great Britain in 1984 by
Windward
An imprint owned by WH Smith & Son Limited
Registered No 237811 England
Trading as WHS Distributors,
St John's House, East Street, Leicester, LE1 6NE

ISBN 0-7112-0379-2

This book was designed and produced by
QED Publishing Ltd, 32 Kingly Court,
London W1

Art Director Alastair Campbell
Production Director Edward Kinsey
Editor Nicola Thompson
Designers Nick Clark, Caroline Courtney,
Hilary Krag, Joanna Swindell
Editorial Joanna Edwards, Sabina Goodchild,
Stephen Paul, Jane Walker
Editorial Research Veronique Mott
Design Assistants and Paste-up Jimmy Brewster,
Philip Chidlow, Madeleine Claire-Thompson
Editorial Director Christopher Fagg
Index Richard and Hilary Bird

The publishers wish to express their gratitude for
major contributions by the following people:

Authors
Jenny Barling, Philip Llewellin, Charles
MacLean, Ann Saunders, Simon Scott, James
Tindley

Artists and Photographers
Norman Bancroft-Hunt, Bob Chapman, Simon
Evans, Klim Forster, Edwina Keene, Elly King,
Pavel Kostal, Line & Line, David Mallott, Simon
Roulstone, Don Wood

Filmset in Great Britain by QV Typesetting Ltd, London
Colour origination in Hong Kong by Hong Kong Graphic Arts
Printed in Hong Kong by Leefung Asco Printers Ltd

The pictures in this book were supplied by The
Photo Source Ltd (Colour Library Inter-
national/Fox/Keystone/Central) except for the
following who the publishers wish to thank for
granting permission to reproduce pictures belonging to them:
Aerofilms: 82 (centre), 89 (lower right); Borough of
Brighton: 50 (bottom); British Library: 24, 25, 47
(bottom); British Museum: 43; Foto-Bank: 213;
Ian Howes: 169 (right); Mansell Collection: 34;
Mary Evans Picture Library: 42; National Army
Museum: 50 (top); National Portrait Gallery: 37,
38, 47 (top), 52, 63; Public Records Office, London:
21; Don Wood: 106 (bottom).

Of the many people and organizations who con-
tributed to the preparation of this book, our thanks
are especially due to:
La Ville de Bayeux; Sheldon Marshall, Siobhan
Murphy, Gerry Conrad and George Freston of The
Photo Source Ltd; Jeremy Harwood; Patrick
Deedes-Vincke; Allan MacLean of Dochgarroch;
David Williamson.
While every effort has been made to acknowledge
all copyright holders, we apologize if any omis-
sions have been made.
The specially commissioned maps in this book are
reproduced by permission of the Ordnance Survey
(Crown Copyright Reserved).

Contents

For a substantial proportion of the world's population, to speak of 'the Queen' is to refer specifically to Queen Elizabeth II of Great Britain and the Commonwealth. The continued magnetism of the British Royal Family is attested by front-page headlines, peak-time television news coverage and huge crowds wherever the Queen appears — while media hysteria reached new levels all over the world with the marriage of Prince Charles to Lady Diana Spencer. The birth of Prince William and, more recently, the announcement of the impending arrival of a new member of the Royal Family, were occasions for further excitement. It is strange indeed that monarchy — a supposedly anomalous survival from an earlier age — should remain so potent a symbol.

Most people in Britain recognize the Queen's dual role as both a dedicated servant of state and a symbolic representative of a long history of royal government with its roots in Anglo-Saxon times. But how many people, even in Britain, are aware of the many strands — dynastic, historical, spiritual, political and legal — which are woven into the royal heritage of the British crown? The ceremonial and pageantry which the world associates with our monarchy are not simply costume drama: they represent an institution which has long been deeply involved with the evolution of British political practice and social custom.

The *Atlas of Royal Britain* is an opportunity to tell the full, fascinating story of Britain's royal heritage — a story by turns dramatic, tragic and amusing. Above all, it is a story of individual human beings grappling with great events, echoed in the place names and geography of the land itself. At the same time, the book is designed to satisfy readers' curiosity as to the deeper background and meaning of the romance and pageantry of Britain's royal past and present.

The first main section of the book, *The Royal Story*, follows Britain's monarchy from its origins to the present day, with special features on genealogy, heraldry, Wales, Scotland, civil wars and profiles of the monarchs. The second introductory section, *The Royal Family*, covers the lives and roles of today's royalty, with close looks at the Queen and her relations, the various royal residences, the constitution, the royal routine, the Household, finance, the orders of chivalry and special events. Then comes the third and largest part, which is devoted to a gazetteer of the palaces, castles, houses, villages, towns, cities, churches, cathedrals and battlefields that provide a living backdrop to over 1000 years of royal tradition.

A densely interwoven pattern of blood relationships links the present Queen to rulers of kingdoms in post-Roman Britain and Europe: By way of introduction, this first section explains the genealogy of the royal family

l Heritage

and the development of the royal coat of arms. Here, too, is set out the descent of the crown from Egbert, first King of All England, in the 9th century, to the present Queen, Elizabeth II.

Royal Ancestry and Heraldry

The present royal family descends from Cerdic, who led the West Saxons into England in AD 495. The royal ancestry can be traced with certainty from nearly every dynasty which has reigned in the British Isles — Saxons, Danes, Normans, Angevins, Tudors, Stuarts, Hanoverians and Wettins, all combining to form today's House of Windsor.

Consider the ancestors of an individual as an ever-spreading train or peacock's tail fanning out behind and doubling at each generation; for everybody has two parents, four grandparents, eight great-grandparents, 16 great-great-grandparents and so on. Of course, the number of theoretical ancestors in each receding generation can be drastically reduced by cousin-marriage — more prevalent in royal and noble circles than in those of ordinary people. Nevertheless, if ancestors could be traced *ad infinitum* thousands of different lines of descent would be found from comparatively few individual couples, otherwise the theoretical number of ancestors would far exceed the total world population long before the beginning of Christianity.

The ancestry of Prince William of Wales, for instance, can be traced with certainty from nearly every dynasty which has reigned in the British Isles, Saxons, Danes, Normans, Angevins, Tudors, Stuarts, Hanoverians and Wettins, all of which combine to form today's House of Windsor. Through the ancient Welsh dynasties there are probable lines of descent from Romano-British families and it is quite possible, if slightly far-fetched, to say that Prince William has kinship with Julius Caesar and Claudius.

The present royal family certainly descends from Cerdic, who led the West Saxons into England in AD 495. Beyond Cerdic the legendary pedigree (as recorded in the

Anglo-Saxon Chronicle and by the Venerable Bede and other historians) extends to Woden, a mythical God-King. The kingdom of the West Saxons (or Wessex) finally became predominant and absorbed the other English kingdoms. Egbert, King of Wessex (AD 802-839), was the first to be acknowledged as King of All England.

In 1013 Sweyn, 'Forkbeard', King of Denmark, conquered England and was acknowledged its king, but the 26 years of Danish kings upon the English throne do not break the royal family tree. In fact, both the Queen and the Duke of Edinburgh descend from King Canute's sister, Astrid. William the Conqueror (1066-1087) was no stranger in blood to the royal line; indeed as a maternal

George John Spencer, 2nd Earl Spencer 1758-1834
Lady Lavinia Bingham 1762-1831
— Frederick Spencer, 4th Earl Spencer 1798-1857
Sir Horace Beauchamp Seymour 1791-1851
Elizabeth Malet Palk d. 1827
— Adelaide Horatia Elizabeth Seymour 1825-1877
— Charles Robert Spencer, 6th Earl Spencer 1857-1922
Henry Baring 1777-1848
Cecilia Anne Windham 1803-1874
— Edward Charles Baring, 1st Baron Revelstoke 1828-1897
John Crocker Bulteel 1792/3-1843
Lady Elizabeth Grey 1798-1880
— Louisa Emily Charlotte Bulteel 1839-1892
— Hon Margaret Baring 1868-1906
— Albert Edward John Spencer, 7th Earl Spencer 1892-1975
James Hamilton, 1st Duke of Abercorn 1811-1885
Lady Louisa Jane Russell 1812-1905
— James Hamilton, 2nd Duke of Abercorn 1838-1913
Richard Curzon-Howe, 1st Earl Howe 1796-1870
Hon Anne Gore 1817-1877
— Lady Mary Anna Curzon-Howe 1848-1929
— James Hamilton, 3rd Duke of Abercorn 1869-1953
— John Spencer, 8th Earl Spencer b. 1924
George Charles Bingham, 3rd Earl of Lucan 1800-1888
Lady Anne Brudenell 1809-1877
— George Bingham, 4th Earl of Lucan 1830-1914
Charles Gordon-Lennox, 5th Duke of Richmond 1791-1860
Lady Caroline Paget 1796-1874
— Lady Cecilia Catherine Gordon-Lennox 1838-1910
— Lady Rosalind Bingham 1869-1958
— Lady Cynthia Hamilton 1897-1972
Edward Roche 1771-1855
Margaret Honoria Curtain 1786-1862
— Edmund Burke Roche, 1st Baron Fermoy 1815-1874
James Brownell Boothby 1791-1850
Charlotte Cunningham 1799-1893
— Eliza Caroline Boothby 1821-1897
— James Burke Roche, 3rd Baron Fermoy 1851-1920
John Work 1781-1823
Sarah Boude 1790-1860
— Frank Work 1819-1911
John Wood 1786-1848
Ellen Strong 1802-1863
— Ellen Wood 1831-1877
— Frances Work 1857-1947
— Edmund Maurice Burke Roche, 4th Baron Fermoy 1885-1955
David Gill 1796-1868
Sarah Ogston 1797-1872
— Alexander Ogston Gill 1832-1908
William Smith Marr 1810-1898
Helen Bean 1814/5-1852
— Barbara Smith Marr b. 1842
— William Smith Gill 1865-1957
William Littlejohn 1803-1888
Janet Bentley 1811-1848
— David Littlejohn 1841-1924
James Crombie 1810-1878
Katherine Scott Forbes 1812-1893
— Jane Crombie 1843-1917
— Ruth Littlejohn 1879-1964
— Ruth Gill b.1908
— Hon Frances Burke Roche b. 1936

Diana, Princess of Wales b.1961

cousin of the English King Edward 'the Confessor' (1042-1066), he claimed that he had been promised the English throne.

The Angevin House of Plantagenet was founded by the Conqueror's great-grandson, Henry of Anjou, who became King Henry II of England in 1154. The familiar royal heraldry of England began officially in about 1198 when three lions, then termed leopards, appeared on the second Great Seal of Richard I ('the Lion Heart'). To illustrate his maternal claim to the French throne (the root of the Hundred Years War), Edward III quartered the royal arms of France with the arms of England.

After the Wars of the Roses in the 15th century, the crown passed to a claimant who united the warring Houses of Lancaster and York, Henry Tudor. The future Henry VII (1485-1509), descended from the House of Lancaster, effected this union by marrying the heiress of the House of York, Elizabeth, daughter of Edward IV (1461-1483). This cunning Welshman also laid the foundations for the eventual unification of Scotland with England by negotiating the marriage of his daughter Margaret with James IV (1488-1513). Through his marriage, the House of Stuart succeeded the Tudors on the English throne in 1603.

When James VI of Scotland came to the English throne as James I, the Scottish royal arms had to be incorporated into the royal heraldry and the opportunity was also taken to include a coat of arms for Ireland. Henry VIII had styled himself as 'King of Ireland' in 1542.

The succession in the House of Hanover was regulated by the Act of Settlement of 1701 to ensure a Protestant line. Following Queen Anne (1702-1714), then the heiress presumptive, the scheme was for the crown to be inherited by the Electress Sophia of Hanover, a niece of Charles I (1625-1649), and thence to her Protestant descendants; George I (1714-1727), Sophia's son, duly succeeded to the throne in 1714. It is under the Act of Settlement of 1701 that the present royal family reigns.

When in due time Prince William of Wales ascends the throne (presumably as King William V), he will be the first sovereign since 1714 to descend directly (albeit illegitimately) from Charles I. Through his mother, the former Lady Diana Spencer, there are several lines of descent from illegitimate but acknowledged children of that ill-fated monarch's sons, Charles II (1660-1685) and James II (1685-1688).

The Prince also has descents from Sir Robert Walpole, the first Prime Minister; Earl Grey of the Reform Bill; the 1st Marquess of Anglesey (who lost a leg at Waterloo); the Earl of Lucan of Light Brigade fame (or infamy); and, indeed, from many of the major political and military figures in British history from the 16th century onwards. It is a rich and varied bloodstream, leavened and tempered too by a good admixture of sturdy American pioneer stock through the Princess of Wales's maternal line. The marriages of George VI (1936-1952) and the Prince of Wales to ladies of noble but non-royal birth have provided the royal family with a wider and far more interesting background than that enjoyed by most other European sovereigns who have tended — until recently at least — to marry exclusively within their own ranks. For instance, the universality of genealogy is illustrated by such curiosities as the fact that the Queen Mother's ancestors include a plumber, while the Princess of Wales descends illegitimately from an Armenian lady living in Bombay at the beginning of the 19th century.

BELOW The ancestral table of Prince William.

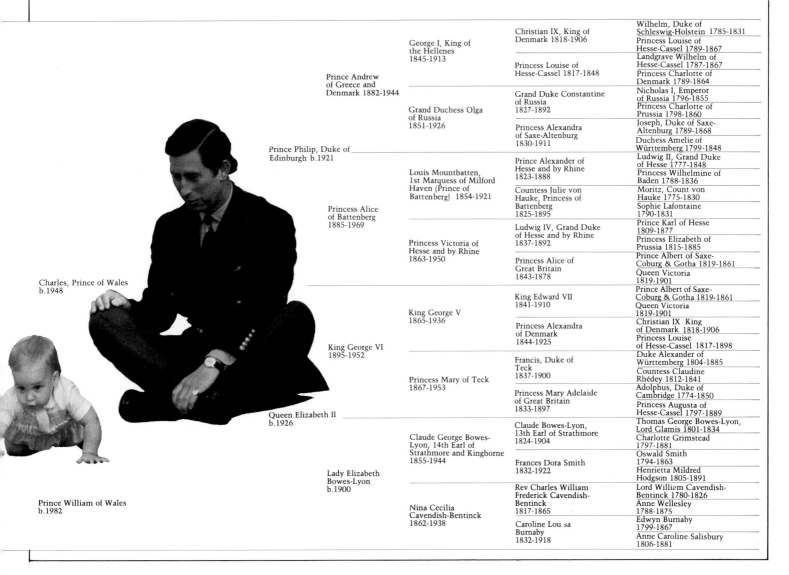

Charles, Prince of Wales b.1948

Prince William of Wales b.1982

Prince Philip, Duke of Edinburgh b.1921	Prince Andrew of Greece and Denmark 1882-1944	George I, King of the Hellenes 1845-1913	Christian IX, King of Denmark 1818-1906
			Wilhelm, Duke of Schleswig-Holstein 1785-1831
			Princess Louise of Hesse-Cassel 1789-1867
		Princess Louise of Hesse-Cassel 1817-1848	Landgrave Wilhelm of Hesse-Cassel 1787-1867
			Princess Charlotte of Denmark 1789-1864
		Grand Duchess Olga of Russia 1851-1926	Grand Duke Constantine of Russia 1827-1892
			Nicholas I, Emperor of Russia 1796-1855
			Princess Charlotte of Prussia 1798-1860
		Princess Alexandra of Saxe-Altenburg 1830-1911	Joseph, Duke of Saxe-Altenburg 1789-1868
			Duchess Amelie of Württemberg 1799-1848
	Princess Alice of Battenberg 1885-1969	Louis Mountbatten, 1st Marquess of Milford Haven (Prince of Battenberg) 1854-1921	Prince Alexander of Hesse and by Rhine 1823-1888
			Ludwig II, Grand Duke of Hesse 1777-1848
			Princess Wilhelmine of Baden 1788-1836
		Countess Julie von Hauke, Princess of Battenberg 1825-1895	Moritz, Count von Hauke 1775-1830
			Sophie Lafontaine 1790-1831
		Princess Victoria of Hesse and by Rhine 1863-1950	Ludwig IV, Grand Duke of Hesse and by Rhine 1837-1892
			Prince Karl of Hesse 1809-1877
			Princess Elizabeth of Prussia 1815-1885
		Princess Alice of Great Britain 1843-1878	Prince Albert of Saxe-Coburg & Gotha 1819-1861
			Queen Victoria 1819-1901
Queen Elizabeth II b.1926	King George VI 1895-1952	King George V 1865-1936	King Edward VII 1841-1910
			Prince Albert of Saxe-Coburg & Gotha 1819-1861
			Queen Victoria 1819-1901
		Princess Alexandra of Denmark 1844-1925	Christian IX King of Denmark 1818-1906
			Princess Louise of Hesse-Cassel 1817-1898
		Princess Mary of Teck 1867-1953	Francis, Duke of Teck 1837-1900
			Duke Alexander of Württemberg 1804-1885
			Countess Claudine Rhédey 1812-1841
		Princess Mary Adelaide of Great Britain 1833-1897	Adolphus, Duke of Cambridge 1774-1850
			Princess Augusta of Hesse-Cassel 1797-1889
	Lady Elizabeth Bowes-Lyon b.1900	Claude George Bowes-Lyon, 14th Earl of Strathmore and Kinghorne 1855-1944	Claude Bowes-Lyon, 13th Earl of Strathmore 1824-1904
			Thomas George Bowes-Lyon, Lord Glamis 1801-1834
			Charlotte Grimstead 1797-1881
		Frances Dora Smith 1832-1922	Oswald Smith 1794-1863
			Henrietta Mildred Hodgson 1805-1891
		Nina Cecilia Cavendish-Bentinck 1862-1938	Rev Charles William Frederick Cavendish-Bentinck 1817-1865
			Lord William Cavendish-Bentinck 1780-1826
			Anne Wellesley 1788-1875
		Caroline Louisa Burnaby 1832-1918	Edwyn Burnaby 1799-1867
			Anne Caroline Salisbury 1806-1881

BELOW RIGHT **The Armorial Bearings of Her Majesty The Queen** In heraldic language, these are described (or 'blazoned') as follows:
Quarterly: 1st and 4th, gules, 3 lions passant guardant in pale, or (for England); 2nd, or a lion rampant within a double tressure flory counter-flory, gules (Scotland); 3rd, azure, a harp or stringed argent (Ireland).
Crown: A circle of gold, issuing therefrom 4 crosses patée and 4 fleurs-de-lys, alternatively: from the crosses patée arise 2 golden arches with pearls, crossing at the top under a mound, surmounted by a cross patée, also gold, the whole enriched with precious stones.

ABOVE **Badges** The Queen has numerous badges (devices used by those who bear arms to mark their servants and property). Here are the badges for England (a rose); Scotland (a thistle) and Ireland (a shamrock); other badges include those for the House of Windsor, Wales and the Union.

Crest: Upon the Royal Helm, the Crown proper, thereon a lion statant guardant or, royally crowned, also proper.
Mantling: Or lined with ermine.
Supporters: On the dexter, a lion guardant or, crowned as the crest; and on the sinister a unicorn argent armed, crined and unguled or, and gorged with a coronet composed of crosses patée and fleurs-de-lys, a chain affixed thereto passing between the forelegs and reflexed over the back, of the last.
Motto: Dieu et mon Droit.

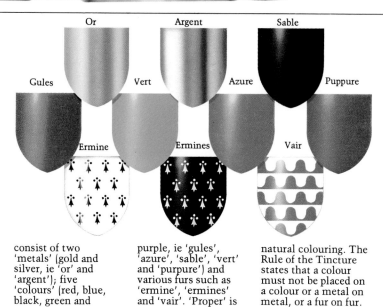

DIEU ET MON DROIT

RIGHT **Key to the Royal Arms** A translation of some of the heraldic terms used:
1. *Arms of England:* The three golden lions with their blue tongues and claws on a red shield — (A) and shown below in the 1st and 4th quarters of the shield — were established as the royal heraldry of England c1198 when they appeared on the second Great Seal of Richard I. Edward III quartered those arms with those of France — fleurs-de-lys on a blue shield (B). This quartered coat of France and England (E)

Heraldry The origins of heraldry were practical rather than aesthetic. Heraldic symbols are known to have been used on shields for the sake of identity on the battlefield at the end of the 12th century. In the 13th century it became the practice to display these 'armorial bearings' on surcoats worn over armour – hence 'coat of arms'. The abbreviation 'arms' is now generally used to describe armorial bearings.

The rules of the game were perfected by the heralds, who marshalled the aristocracy at tournaments in the Middle Ages, and so the study of 'arms' came to be known as heraldry.

Arms are a badge of aristocracy. The herald's definition of a gentleman is a man entitled to bear arms; in other words, a grant of arms is given to a man on the assumption that he is a gentleman already, and does not in itself make him one. Some 150 or so non-corporate grants are now made through the College of Arms in Queen Victoria Street in the City of London every year. In Scotland the armorial authority is the Court of the Lord Lyon King of Arms in Edinburgh.

Once granted, arms are hereditary.

The term 'heraldry' covers a multitude of devices – crests (ie the device modelled on to the top of the helmet), supporters, badges, standards, etc – but the main vehicle for the display of symbols is the shield.

The practice of marshalling more than one coat on a single shield by dividing it into four quarters (repeating the 1st on the last quarter and the 2nd in the 3rd, if only two coats are to be displayed) grew up in the middle of the 13th century.

RIGHT **Tinctures** The principal 'tinctures'

consist of two 'metals' (gold and silver, ie 'or' and 'argent'); five 'colours' (red, blue, black, green and purple, ie 'gules', 'azure', 'sable', 'vert' and 'purpure') and various furs such as 'ermine', 'ermines' and 'vair'. 'Proper' is natural colouring. The Rule of the Tincture states that a colour must not be placed on a colour or a metal on metal, or a fur on fur.

Or   Argent   Sable

Gules   Vert   Azure   Puppure

Ermine   Ermines   Vair

was borne until 1603, though the number of fleurs-de-lys was reduced by three after 1376.

2. *Arms of Scotland:* When James VI of Scotland came to the English throne, the Scottish royal arms — a red lion on a golden shield within a red border of fleurs-de-lys (C) — which had first appeared on a seal of Alexander II *c*1235, had to be incorporated. The royal shield now became: France (modern) and England in the 1st and 4th quarters; Scotland in the 2nd quarter and Ireland in the 3rd (F).

3. *Arms of Ireland:* Henry VIII assumed the style of 'King of Ireland' in 1542 and the coat of arms adopted — a golden harp with silver strings on a blue shield (D) — was based on the badge previously used to symbolize Ireland. Following the Act of Union with Ireland in 1801, the dubious French quartering was banished and the simple quartered shield seen today was marshalled: England in the 1st and 4th quarters; Scotland in the 2nd and Ireland in the 3rd (G). The crowned Hanoverian inescutcheon — a small shield surmounting the main shield — was dropped from the royal arms on the death of William IV in 1837.

4. *The Garter:* Since the reign of Henry VIII, the sovereign has encircled the royal arms with the blue insignia of the Most Noble Order of the Garter (founded by Edward III *c*1348). It is inscribed with the legend 'Honi soit qui mal y pense' (Evil be to him who evil thinks).

5. *Motto:* 'Dieu et mon droit' (My God and my Right) has been used since the reign of Henry V.

6. *The Crown:* The heraldic royal crown is based on St Edward's Crown, made for Charles II's coronation in 1661. It is all of gold; the rim is studded with pearls. A sapphire is shown between two emeralds with a ruby at either end.

7. *The Royal Helm:* The gold barred royal helmet was introduced by Elizabeth I.

8. *The Royal Crest:* Standing upon the crown is a golden lion, looking sideways and himself wearing an arched royal crown. This has been the form of the crest since Henry VIII.

9. *Mantling:* Elizabeth I introduced the gold royal mantling, lined with ermine.

10. *Supporters:* The royal supporters of a crowned lion and a unicorn date back to 1603 when James I substituted the latter from his native Scotland for the red dragon previously used. The silver unicorn, with its golden horn, mane, beard, tuft, hooves, circlet and chain, was established as a Scottish royal beast by the early 15th century.

Heraldic terms:

argent:	silver
armed:	horned
azure:	blue
crined:	bewhiskered
dexter:	right
flory:	flowered with fleurs-de-lys
gules:	red
or:	gold
passant guardant:	walking position, with head full-faced
proper:	natural colouring
rampant:	standing erect on hind legs
sinister:	left
tressure:	inner border
ungules:	hoofed

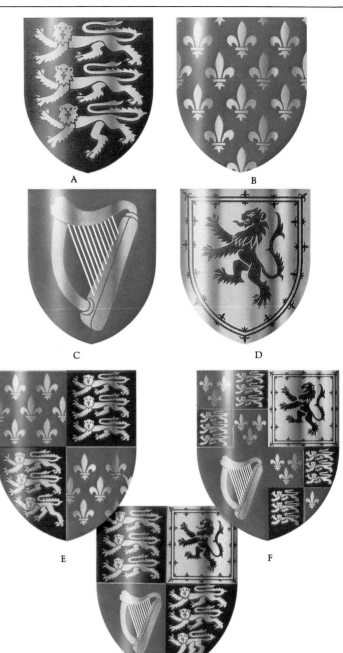

A

B

C

D

E

F

G

BELOW Divisions and Ordinaries The shield is divided into the following points: dexter chief (A); middle chief (B); sinister chief (C); honour point (D); fess point (E); nombril, or navel, point (F); dexter base (G); middle base (H); sinister base (I).

PARTITION LINES These are usually straight (RIGHT), otherwise they tend to be (BELOW from top to bottom): engrailed, invected, wavy; undy; nebuly; indented; dancetty; embattled.

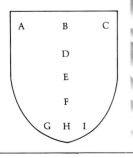

Per Pale

Per Fess

Quarterly

Per Bend

Per Bend Sinister

Per Saltire

Chief

Base

Fess

Pale

Quarterly of Nine

Cross

Bend

Bend Sinister

Saltire

Chequy

Lozengy

Chevron

Through the Ages: the Royal Descent

This family tree shows the descent of the crown from Saxon times to the present day. It is interesting to note how often it has passed to younger sons or other indirect heirs.

The ancestors of the present Queen, Elizabeth II, can be traced back to Egbert, who, in the 9th century, was the first King of All England. In this family tree the monarchs are numbered according to the order they acceded to the throne. The Saxon, Danish, Norman, Plantagenet, Lancastrian, Yorkist, Tudor, Stuart, Hanoverian, Wettin and Windsor dynasties are also indicated.

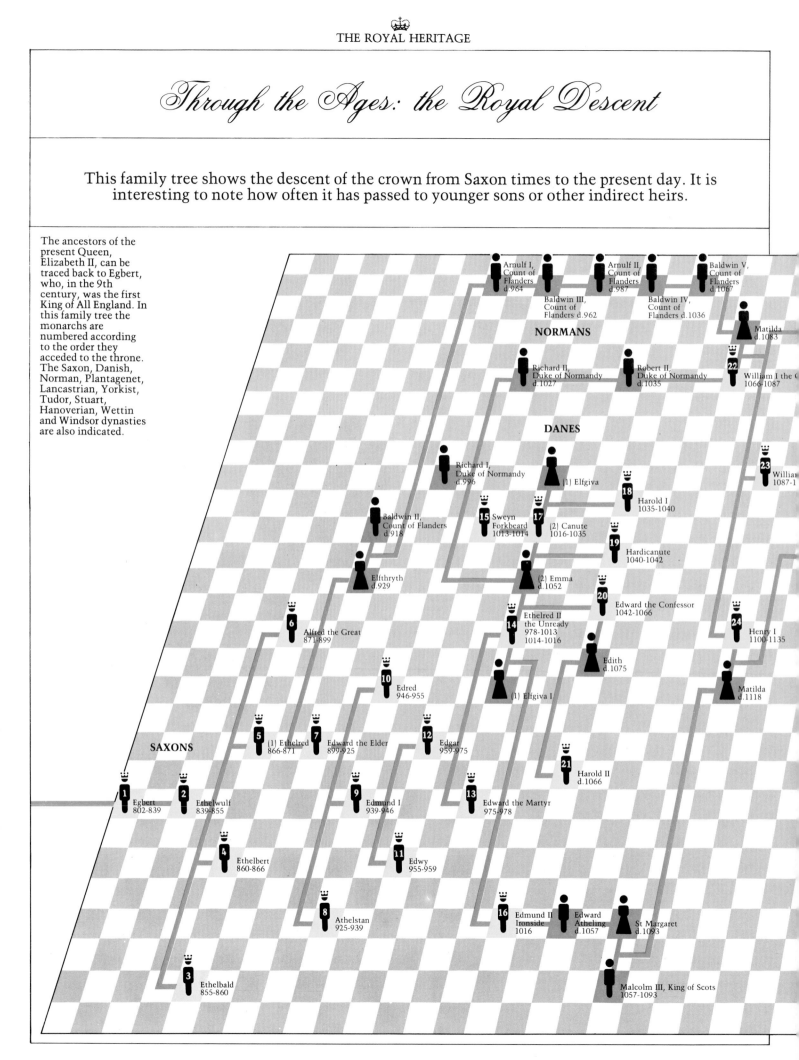

NORMANS

Arnulf I, Count of Flanders d.964

Baldwin III, Count of Flanders d.962

Arnulf II, Count of Flanders d.987

Baldwin IV, Count of Flanders d.1036

Baldwin V, Count of Flanders d.1067

Matilda d.1083

Richard II, Duke of Normandy d.1027

Robert II, Duke of Normandy d.1035

22 William I the C 1066-1087

DANES

Richard I, Duke of Normandy d.996

(1) Elfgiva

18 Harold I 1035-1040

23 Willia 1087-1

Baldwin II, Count of Flanders d.918

15 Sweyn Forkbeard 1013-1014

17 (2) Canute 1016-1035

19 Hardicanute 1040-1042

Elfthryth d.929

(2) Emma d.1052

20 Edward the Confessor 1042-1066

6 Alfred the Great 871-899

14 Ethelred II the Unready 978-1013 1014-1016

24 Henry I 1100-1135

10 Edred 946-955

Edith d.1075

Matilda d.1118

5 (1) Ethelred 866-871

7 Edward the Elder 899-925

12 Edgar 959-975

(1) Elfgiva I

SAXONS

9 Edmund I 939-946

13 Edward the Martyr 975-978

21 Harold II d.1066

1 Egbert 802-839

2 Ethelwulf 839-855

11 Edwy 955-959

4 Ethelbert 860-866

8 Athelstan 925-939

16 Edmund II Ironside 1016

Edward Atheling d.1057

St Margaret d.1093

3 Ethelbald 855-860

Malcolm III, King of Scots 1057-1093

Continued on following page.

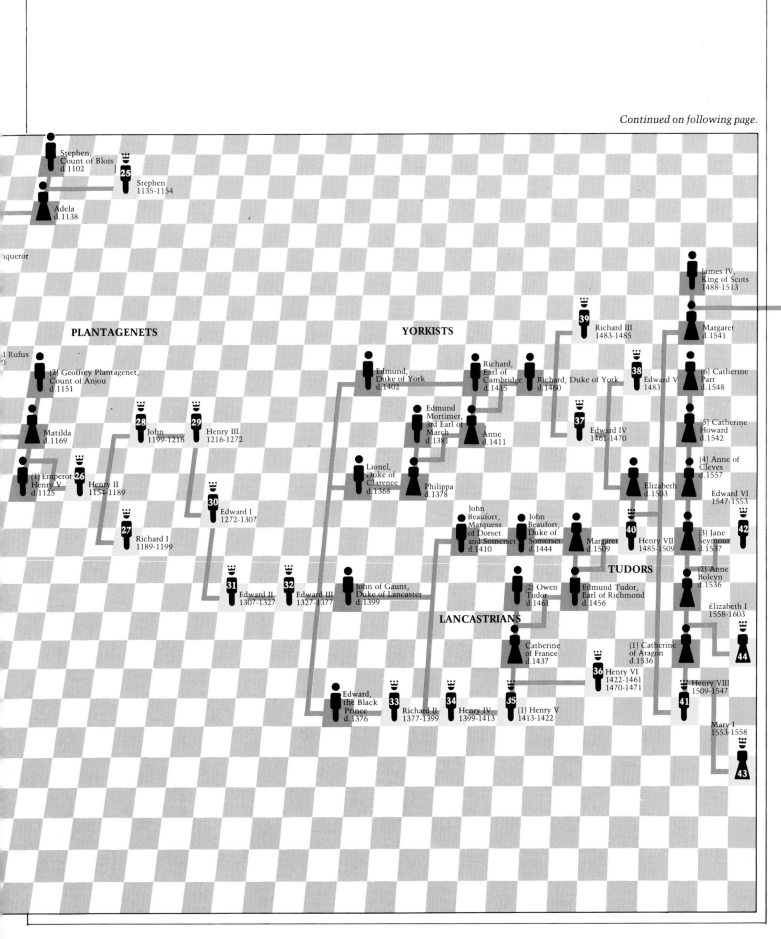

PLANTAGENETS

Stephen, Count of Blois d.1102

25 Stephen 1135-1154

Adela d.1138

I Rufus

(2) Geoffrey Plantagenet, Count of Anjou d.1151

Matilda d.1169

(1) Emperor Henry V d.1125

26 Henry II 1154-1189

27 Richard I 1189-1199

28 John 1199-1216

29 Henry III 1216-1272

30 Edward I 1272-1307

31 Edward II 1307-1327

32 Edward III 1327-1377

John of Gaunt, Duke of Lancaster d.1399

Edward, the Black Prince d.1376

33 Richard II 1377-1399

34 Henry IV 1399-1413

35 (1) Henry V 1413-1422

LANCASTRIANS

Catherine of France d.1437

36 Henry VI 1422-1461 1470-1471

YORKISTS

Edmund, Duke of York d.1402

Edmund Mortimer, 3rd Earl of March d.1381

Anne d.1411

Lionel, Duke of Clarence d.1368

Philippa d.1378

John Beaufort, Marquess of Dorset and Somerset d.1410

John Beaufort, Duke of Somerset d.1444

Margaret d.1509

TUDORS

(2) Owen Tudor d.1461

Edmund Tudor, Earl of Richmond d.1456

Richard, Earl of Cambridge d.1415

Richard, Duke of York d.1460

37 Edward IV 1461-1470

38 Edward V 1483

39 Richard III 1483-1485

Elizabeth d.1503

40 Henry VII 1485-1509

James IV, King of Scots 1488-1513

Margaret d.1541

(6) Catherine Parr d.1548

(5) Catherine Howard d.1542

(4) Anne of Cleves d.1557

Edward VI 1547-1553

42 (3) Jane Seymour d.1537

(2) Anne Boleyn d.1536

Elizabeth I 1558-1603

44

41 Henry VIII 1509-1547

(1) Catherine of Aragon d.1536

Mary I 1553-1558

43

Continued from previous page.

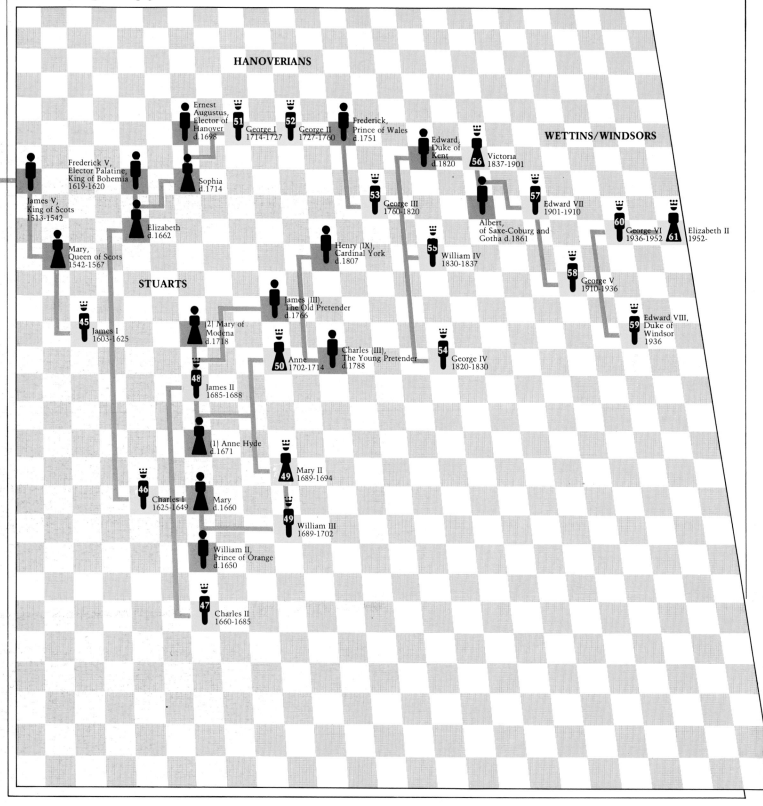

HANOVERIANS

Ernest Augustus, Elector of Hanover d.1698

51 George I 1714-1727

52 George II 1727-1760

Frederick, Prince of Wales d.1751

Edward, Duke of Kent d.1820

56 Victoria 1837-1901

WETTINS/WINDSORS

Frederick V, Elector Palatine, King of Bohemia 1619-1620

Sophia d.1714

53 George III 1760-1820

Albert, of Saxe-Coburg and Gotha d.1861

57 Edward VII 1901-1910

60 George VI 1936-1952

61 Elizabeth II 1952-

James V, King of Scots 1513-1542

Elizabeth d.1662

Henry (IX), Cardinal York d.1807

55 William IV 1830-1837

58 George V 1910-1936

Mary, Queen of Scots 1542-1567

STUARTS

45 James I 1603-1625

James (III), The Old Pretender d.1766

59 Edward VIII, Duke of Windsor 1936

(2) Mary of Modena d.1718

50 Anne 1702-1714

Charles (III), The Young Pretender d.1788

54 George IV 1820-1830

48 James II 1685-1688

(1) Anne Hyde d.1671

49 Mary II 1689-1694

46 Charles I 1625-1649

Mary d.1660

49 William III 1689-1702

William II, Prince of Orange d.1650

47 Charles II 1660-1685

The Royal Story

Between the Dark Ages and the present day, eleven dynasties
have held the English crown: Saxon, Danish, Norman,
Plantagenet, Lancastrian, Yorkist,
Tudor, Stuart, Hanoverian, Wettin and Windsor. This section
deals historically with each in turn, and also includes special
features on the Tower of London, Wales, Scotland, wars
(both at home and abroad) and the changing role of the monarchy.

The First Kingdoms: Saxons and Danes

After the Romans left England early in the 5th century, small kingdoms were established by Angle, Jute and Saxon invaders. In 829, King Egbert of Wessex (the West Saxons) conquered the Mercians and became the first King of All England. The Danes later won the English crown but eventually lost it to William the Conqueror in 1066.

The leaders of the tribes of Britain in pre-Roman times all acted as mini-kings. The Roman occupation, however, despite very strenuous opposition in the east from Boudicca (or Boadicea), Queen of the Iceni, had imposed a national unity in England by the 1st century AD. After the Romans left England, early in the 5th century, the process of kingship developed with Angle, Jute and Saxon invaders establishing small kingdoms. Each king ruled over small tribal communities; there were kings of Kent, Wessex, Bernicia, East Anglia, Essex, Deira, Mercia, Northumbria and Lindsey. The present royal family is descended from the kings of the West Saxons (or Wessex) who became the most powerful leaders, eventually ruling over all the other Kings.

During these early centuries, the 'Age of Settlement', the monarch's main function was to be an active war-leader. Monarchy simply meant supreme power in the hands of one person, the King; the success of kingship depended simply upon the strength, ability and personality of the monarch.

The conversion of England to Christianity in the 7th century was an important unifying factor in the growth of the nation; it also increased the significance of the monarchy's spiritual role. The divine right to be king became a useful concept for consolidating the succession. The first recorded consecration of an English king took place at the end of the 8th century when a religious ceremony was performed on Ecgfrith, son of Offa. The Wessex kings forged closer links with the Church after Egbert (AD 802-839) had conquered the Mercians to establish himself as King of All England.

Egbert's grandson, Alfred 'the Great' (AD 871-899), came to be regarded as the true defender of Christian England after his years of tough campaigning against the Danes. Alfred earned his epithet not only by his military valour but by his administrative reforms ('The Dooms') and his scholarship. He translated Bede, Boethius and Gregory into English from Latin and started a great tradition of popular literature.

The nature of kingship in the late Anglo-Saxon period was epitomized by the oath taken at what is generally regarded as the first actual coronation. Edgar 'the Peaceful' (AD 959-975), who was crowned at Bath on 11 May 973, promised to protect the Church, to

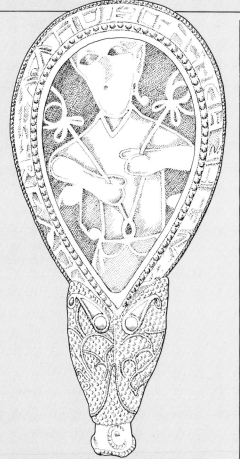

ABOVE Known as 'the Alfred Jewel' this was found near the Island of Athelney in Somerset in 1693. It is thought by some to have belonged to Alfred the Great, who died in 899, because it bears the Anglo-Saxon inscription, 'Alfred had me made'. He may have used it to follow the lines of Latin manuscripts. Decorated with gold and enamel, the jewel is now in the Ashmolean Museum, Oxford.

uphold justice and protect the people against evil-doers. The England of the 10th century is generally portrayed by historians as a territorial kingdom, fully developed out of the early tribal stage.

Despite the Anglo-Saxon unity, the Danes, whose raids began in the 8th century, continued to pose a threat. Alfred obliged the 9th-century invaders to settle in the 'Danelaw', the area of England to the east of the Roman road known as 'Watling Street' where Danish customs remained prominent until after the Norman Conquest. Later in the 9th century, Edgar the Peaceful contained the Danish threat by granting the Danelaw legal autonomy, but during the disastrous reigns of Ethelred 'the Unready' (979-1013 and 1014-16) and his son Edmund II, (who was called 'Ironside' and who reigned during 1016), a fresh Scandinavian invasion and conquest temporarily ousted the dynasty from the English throne.

Despite this apparent setback, it can be argued that no harm was done to the developing institution of the monarchy. The Danish conqueror Cnut (or Canute) (1016-1035), eventually proved to be more English than even the English themselves. His principal achievement was the introduction of an admirable legal system but, just as Alfred is remembered for burning some cakes, Canute is best known for something that probably never happened. The story goes that he tried to halt the incoming tide with a verbal command and was soaked for his pains, but like many fables, it was written many years after the event. The point of the wise ruler's gesture was, in fact, to teach his toadying courtiers that the power of the monarchy could not overcome nature; this is almost invariably lost to those who consider Canute's behaviour to exemplify his arrogant character. In reality, this Anglo-Danish king tried to live by the creed of his close adviser Archbishop Wulfstan of York, who thought that kings should be a comfort to their people, and righteous leaders.

Following a brief interlude under Canute's two sons, the old Wessex dynasty was restored to the English throne in 1042, in the person of Edward 'the Confessor' (1042-1066) whose own formative years had been spent far away from England in Normandy. The Confessor founded Westminster Abbey where he was buried in 1066.

One chronicler described this saintly person, who was canonized in 1161, as having a 'full face and rosy, with hair and beard as white as snow'. His old friend and cousin, William, Duke of Normandy, regarded the Confessor in a different light when he learnt that the King had nominated the powerful Harold, Earl of Godwin as heir to the throne. William believed that the English crown had been promised to him, and that he was a legitimate heir; he was also in no doubt that Harold had sworn to support the Norman succession. Harold was Edward the Confessor's brother-in-law but he was not of royal blood. Even if William's right to succeed was legitimate, it could only be achieved by force.

KING ARTHUR There has been much controversy over the life of 'King' Arthur. His chivalrous reputation has provided possibly unfounded inspiration to poets, musicians and artists through the centuries. Geoffrey of Monmouth, Thomas Malory, John Dryden and Alfred, Lord Tennyson, among many others, wove the mythical tales of the Knights of the Round Table and the wizard Merlin around him. Meanwhile the truth has been distorted and the facts lost. There has even been doubt as to whether he existed.

Most modern historians agree that Arthur was a noble, 6th-century war leader of the Britons against the Saxons. Research is hindered by the lack of any contemporary sources; Nennius's book *Historia Britonum*, written in the early 9th century, contains one of the first known references. According to Nennius, the real Arthur won a great British victory at the Battle of Badon Hill, the exact date and site of which are debatable. It may have been fought in about AD 520 in Wiltshire or Dorset, one of 12 major battles against the Saxons. Arthur is said to have lost his life at the Battle of Camlann, possibly by the River Camel in Cornwall, recorded as taking place either in AD 539 or, more traditionally, in AD 542.

Arthur and his 'Queen' Guinevere are said to be buried at Glastonbury Abbey, where their alleged tomb was 'discovered' in the reign of Henry II. However, the tomb may be an archaeological fake, invented by the monks to bring fame and riches to their abbey.

Glastonbury was known as the 'Isle of Avalon' because, before the Somerset marshes were drained, floods turned the area into an island every winter. Famous also for connections with Joseph of Arimathea, who is said to have brought the Holy Grail here, Glastonbury is a centre of Arthurian legend.

Glastonbury Abbey

ROYAL NAME The Welsh-born Henry VII revived the name of the British hero Arthur by giving it to his eldest son Arthur, Prince of Wales (who never became king). Nearly 400 years later, Queen Victoria named her third son Arthur in honour of his godfather, the great Duke of Wellington, Arthur Wellesley. In his turn, Prince Arthur was godfather to his great-nephew, the future George VI, who was given 'Arthur' as his third Christian name, as was his grandson, the present Prince of Wales. Prince William of Wales, bears 'Arthur' as his second name.

LEFT The Saxon threat was strong at a time when, so the story goes, Arthur rallied the Britons and gained some major victories. Realism would suggest that he was probably a shrewd soldier and courageous leader; legend dictates that his sword, the famous Excalibur, forged in Avalon, possessed strange magical qualities. According to Nennius, he killed as many as 940 men with his sword at the Battle of Badon Hill.

Ben Arthur
Edinburgh
Caerleon
Silchester
Glastonbury
Winchester
Tintagel
Cadbury Castle
Camelford

ABOVE Geoffrey of Monmouth, in the *History of the Kings of Britain*, describes Arthur's conquests not only over the Saxons, or even the Picts in Scotland, but also in Ireland, Iceland, Norway and Gaul. It certainly seems that Arthur travelled widely in Britain, but mostly the stories tell of his exploits in the West Country. He may have been born in Tintagel, in Cornwall, and buried in Glastonbury. A strong contender for the site of Camelot, Arthur's court, is Cadbury Castle, near Yeovil in Somerset. Other possible sites are shown on this map.

The Norman Conquest

After the Saxon King of England St Edward the Confessor (1042-1066) had nominated his Danish brother-in-law Harold as heir to the English throne, Edward's cousin of the Royal Blood, William, Duke of Normandy, decided to establish the 'legitimate' Norman succession by force in 1066. After his victory at Hastings, William the Conqueror brought a harsh new discipline to England.

Harold's brief reign was brought to a violent end at the Battle of Hastings — a single skirmish against some 12,000 Norman invaders that took place in the afternoon of 14 October 1066, and changed the course of history.

BELOW **Harold II**, brother of Edith, St Edward the Confessor's Queen, succeeded his brother-in-law on Edward's death on 5 January 1066.

Although the invasion could not have been completely unexpected in view of William, Duke of Normandy's feelings about Harold's betrayal, the ill-fated English King was engaged in repelling a Norwegian invasion in Yorkshire when the 'Conqueror' landed at Pevensey. Harold moved swiftly south, but his English army was far from complete and lacking a great number of men when it was confronted by William's, just north of Hastings.

The most illuminating, although rather complacent, contemporary account of the saga depicted in the Bayeux Tapestry is given by William of Poitiers in *The History of William, Duke of the Normans and King of the English* (c 1073/4):

'Once he had completed his victory, the Duke rode back to the battlefield to survey the dead. The flower of English youth and nobility littered the ground far and wide. At the King's side they found his two brothers. Harold was recognized, not by any insignia which he wore and certainly not from his features, but by certain distinguishing marks...

We Normans offer you no insult, Harold: rather we pity you and weep to see your fate, we and the pious Conqueror, who was saddened by your fall. You won such measure of success as you deserved, and then, again as you deserved, you met your death, bathed in your own heart's blood. Now you lie there, in your grave by the sea: by

generations yet unborn of English and of Normans you will ever be accursed. So must fall those who in great earthly power seek their own supreme good, who rejoice only when usurping it, who, once that it is seized, strive to retain it by the force of arms... The cataclysm which you caused dragged you down in its wake. You shine no more beneath the crown which you so wrongfully usurped; you sit no longer on the throne to which you proudly climbed. Your last expiring moments proved if it were right or wrong for you to be exalted by this gift made by King Edward as he died. That comet, terror of all kings, which gleamed so bright when you were newly crowned, was but a presage of your own defeat.'

The Norman Conquest certainly progressed smoothly enough to support the view that it was predestined. The 'Bastard', Duke of Normandy (the illegitimate son and successor of Robert *Le Diable*, Duke of Normandy), was duly crowned at Westminster Abbey on Christmas Day, 1066. Later, his strength was not greatly tested when he had to stamp out pockets of resistance in various parts of the country such as in Yorkshire; the Conquest was complete when Hereward the Wake surrendered in the Isle of Ely in 1071.

William I (1066-1087) brought a new discipline and unity to the executive government of the old community. He dispossessed the English nobles and set up a new Norman aristocracy organized feudally. Land became the property of the king and the territorial tenants-in-chief held their estates in return for military service by themselves and their sub-tenants. *The Domesday Book*, compiled under William I's instructions from 1086, provided a detailed record of all the manors of England — a particularly useful document for the tax collector.

When William I died, the *Anglo-Saxon Chronicle* made a summary of his character and achievements. The despotic Conqueror was described as harsh and so stern and relentless that no one dared act against his will. The chronicler conceded that William had achieved good order, but also noted his avarice and greed.

Architecture is the greatest memorial of the Norman Conquest. The formidable range of castles (built to keep subjects in order), the cathedrals and churches, not to mention what remains of the monasteries, stand today as outstanding reminders of a powerful and innovative people.

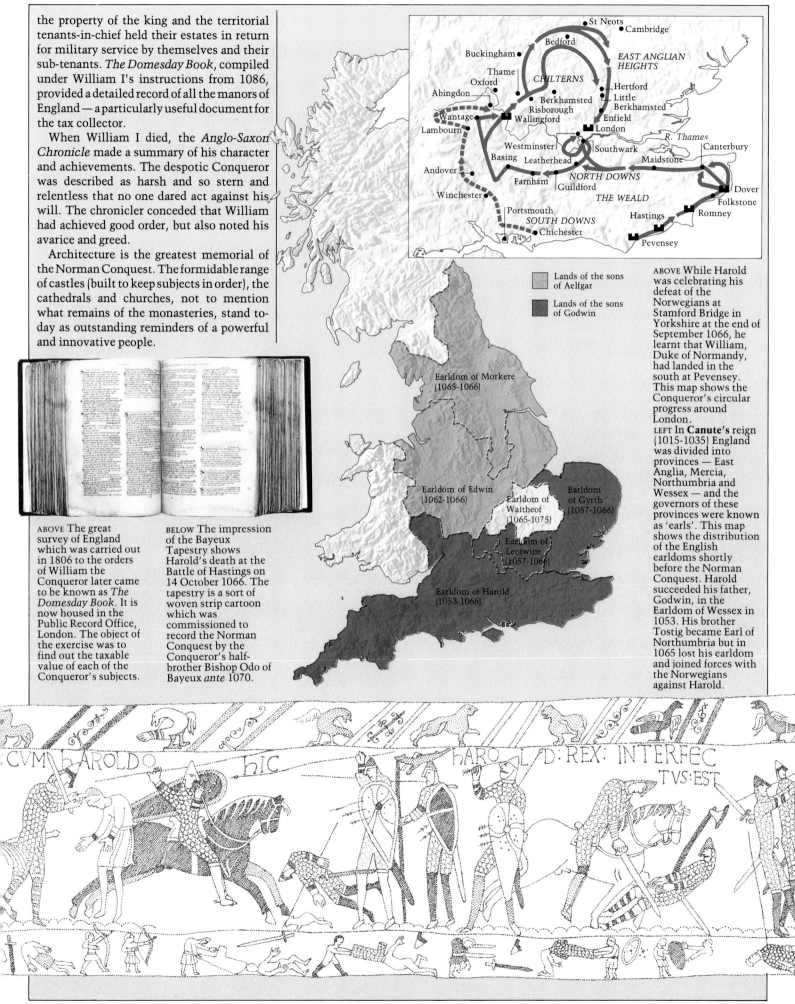

Lands of the sons of Aelfgar

Lands of the sons of Godwin

Earldom of Morkere (1065-1066)

Earldom of Edwin (1062-1066)

Earldom of Waltheof (1065-1075)

Earldom of Gyrth (1057-1066)

Earldom of Leofwine (1057-1066)

Earldom of Harold (1053-1066)

ABOVE The great survey of England which was carried out in 1806 to the orders of William the Conqueror later came to be known as *The Domesday Book*. It is now housed in the Public Record Office, London. The object of the exercise was to find out the taxable value of each of the Conqueror's subjects.

BELOW The impression of the Bayeux Tapestry shows Harold's death at the Battle of Hastings on 14 October 1066. The tapestry is a sort of woven strip cartoon which was commissioned to record the Norman Conquest by the Conqueror's half-brother Bishop Odo of Bayeux *ante* 1070.

ABOVE While Harold was celebrating his defeat of the Norwegians at Stamford Bridge in Yorkshire at the end of September 1066, he learnt that William, Duke of Normandy, had landed in the south at Pevensey. This map shows the Conqueror's circular progress around London.

LEFT In **Canute's** reign (1015-1035) England was divided into provinces — East Anglia, Mercia, Northumbria and Wessex — and the governors of these provinces were known as 'earls'. This map shows the distribution of the English earldoms shortly before the Norman Conquest. Harold succeeded his father, Godwin, in the Earldom of Wessex in 1053. His brother Tostig became Earl of Northumbria but in 1065 lost his earldom and joined forces with the Norwegians against Harold.

Royal Fortress: the Tower of London

The most visited historic building in Britain, the Tower of London remains a royal 'liberty' but it is a long time since a monarch viewed this ancient fortress in the city as a desirable residence. The Norman White Tower was surrounded in the Middle Ages by a ring of stone to form an 18-acre fortress. By Tudor times the Tower was more of a prison than a palace.

There is an old tradition that the mortar used in the building of the White Tower was mixed with blood. In view of the Tower of London's grisly history of imprisonment, torture and execution, this seems appropriate. In fact, the building of the White Tower was begun by William the Conqueror in 1078 and completed by his son William 'Rufus'. The style is no-nonsense Norman.

Henry III (1216-1272) set about converting the Conqueror's keep into a fortress ringed with a curtain wall and 13 bastion towers. The main function of the Tower for Edward III (1327-1377) was as a prison. The list of political prisoners was to stretch to Rudolf Hess in the Second World War. The Black Prince's son, Richard II (1377-1399) kept an elegant court at the Tower, and carried out various elaborate decoration works.

The Tower of London, essentially a medieval fortress, was a far from inviting residen-

and jewels of the crowne, and generall conserver of the most Recordes of the King's Courts of justice at Westminster.'

The Royal Mint was moved to Wales in 1968 but the collection of armoury in the Tower remains a notable feature. The crown jewels on show in the Waterloo Block include St Edward's Crown which was made for the coronation of Charles II in 1661.

It was for this coronation that the sovereign set out for the last time from the Tower, as the next monarch, James II (1685-1688), thought such a tradition (which had grown up from the need to show that the

THE CHAPEL ROYAL OF ST PETER AD VINCULA The chapel of the residents of the royal 'liberty' (rebuilt after a fire in 1512) is the burial place of various personages executed at the Tower, including Lady Jane Grey; her husband, Lord Guildford Dudley, and the last man to lose his head here — the Jacobite Lord Lovat.

TOWER GREEN An old legend has it that when the famous ravens disappear, the White Tower and the British Empire will collapse. These sinister birds, however, are still very much in evidence.

BYWARD TOWER This gatehouse of the outer ward was built by Edward I and added to by Richard II. Parts of a 14th-century wall painting showing the figures of St John the Baptist and St Michael have recently been uncovered.

BEAUCHAMP TOWER This semi-circular tower, begun by Edward I, has some interesting mural inscriptions — the legacy of its many famous prisoners.

MIDDLE TOWER This now gives access to the Tower of London from the modern entrance. It was built by Edward I, who was broadly responsible for the 18-acre stronghold visible today, but largely rebuilt in the 18th century.

QUEEN'S HOUSE The Gunpowder Plot conspirators were interrogated in this timber-framed building of about 1530, now lived in by the resident Governor.

tial palace and its use became increasingly restricted to ceremonial occasions after Henry VII's Queen died here in childbirth in 1503. Further tragic occurrences added to the tradition of doom. As a girl, Elizabeth I 1558-1603) had been a prisoner in the Tower, and even walked through Traitors' Gate, so it is hardly surprising that she did not regard it as a desirable residence. In her reign, the chronicler John Stow defined the Tower's function:

'This tower is a Citadell, to defend or command the Citie: a royal place for assemblies, and treaties. A Prison of estate, for the most dangerous offenders: the onely place for coynage for all England at this time: the armourie for warlike provision: the Treasurie of the ornaments

BELL TOWER Begun by Richard I, this tower housed such prisoners as the Catholic martyr St Thomas More; Charles II's rebellious son, the dashing Duke of Monmouth; and the future Elizabeth I. Her involuntary spell here is commemorated by 'Elizabeth Walk' — the ramparts between the Bell Tower and the Beauchamp Tower.

BLOODY TOWER Said to be named after the suicide here of the 8th Earl of Northumberland in 1585, the Bloody Tower has a gateway built by Henry III and a tower by Richard II. It was long the unwanted home of Sir Walter Raleigh. The 'Princes in the Tower' are also said to have been murdered here.

TRAITORS' GATE The archway under St Thomas's Tower used to give access to the fortress from the River Thames. Here, on their way to the scaffold, passed such figures as St Thomas More, Anne Boleyn, Catherine Howard and the Duke of Monmouth. Anne Boleyn's daughter, Princess Elizabeth, followed her mother's footsteps through the Traitor's Gate, but survived to send others through herself as Elizabeth I.

WAKEFIELD TOWER Built by Henry VIII, this former repository of the national Records has an oratory on the upper floor where Henry VI was found dead, almost certainly by order of Edward IV, in 1471. The alternative explanation was that the wretched Lancastrian had died of 'pure displeasure and melancholy'.

new sovereign commanded the capital from its ancient fortress) was too expensive to maintain. His father and namesake was the last sovereign to keep a proper court at the Tower, entertaining himself and his guests with the pleasures of bear-baiting in the royal menagerie (later transferred to Regent's Park where it formed the basis of the London Zoo).

Even now the Tower is a royal 'liberty' and the Chapel of St John is still a royal chapel, while the fortress is sometimes used as a backdrop to pageantry surrounding the sovereign. Every night at 9.40pm, the Chief Warder of the Yeoman Warders with his escort, locks the West Gate, Middle and Byward Towers, then returns to the Bloody Tower archway, as has been the custom for the last 700 years. He and his escort jangle along in the darkness, overcoming the spoken challenge with the password — 'The Queen's Keys!'. After arms have been presented the Chief Warder cries out: 'God preserve Queen Elizabeth' and the bugler sounds the Last Post.

THE PRINCES IN THE TOWER The grim roll-call of murder in the Tower of London includes such victims as the Duke of Clarence (according to Holinshed 'privately drowned in a butt of malmesie'), brother of Edward IV, and, of course, the King's own sons and heirs, Edward V and the Duke of York — the Princes in the Tower. The Tudors managed to attach the blame for this dastardly deed firmly to the 'wicked uncle' Richard III, but recent research has done much to rehabilitate the character of that greatly maligned monarch and his responsibility for the deaths of the young Princes remains un-proven.

WATERLOO BLOCK Formerly the Waterloo Barracks, this building of 1845 now houses the Oriental Gallery of armour (including Clive of India's 18th-century elephant armour) and, in the west wing, the crown jewels. Apart from the insignia used at coronations, the world famous Koh-i-Noor diamond is on show.

WHITE TOWER This is the original Tower and the most important building in the fortress; begun by William the Conqueror in 1078, it was completed by his son William 'Rufus'. It is 90ft high with walls 15ft thick at the base; the keep is the biggest in the country save for Colchester. There is a stark beauty in the Old Banqueting Hall, the Sword Room and the pristine Chapel of St John the Evangelist (dating from c 1080), as well as the state apartments and the Council Chamber, now used as an impressive museum of armoury.

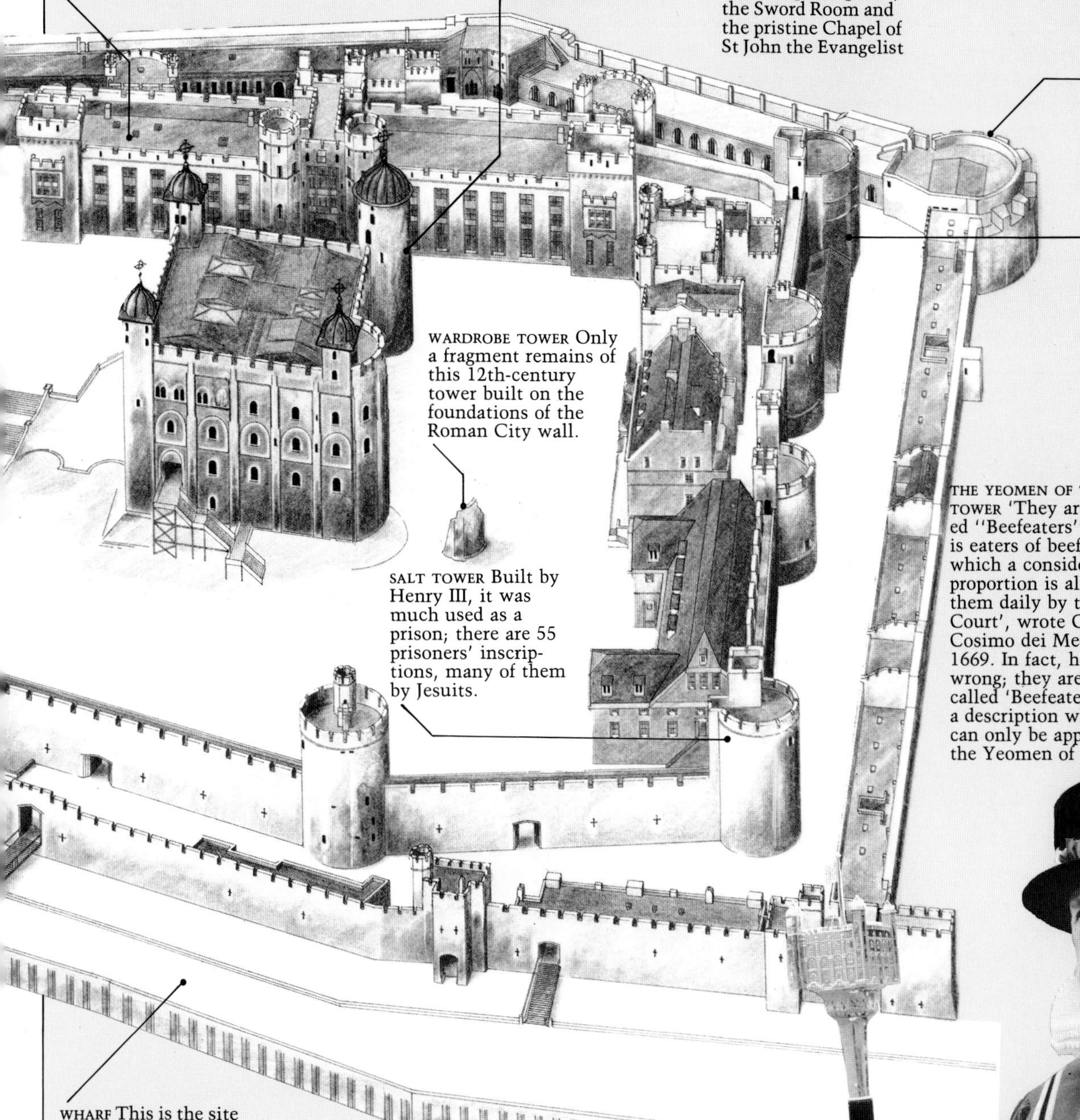

BRASS MOUNT The last of the Tower's fortifications, this artillery bastion was built by Henry VIII.

MARTIN TOWER This tower formerly housed the crown jewels. In 1671 Colonel Thomas Blood, an Irishman, was caught in the act of stealing the insignia, but was later pardoned by Charles II.

WARDROBE TOWER Only a fragment remains of this 12th-century tower built on the foundations of the Roman City wall.

SALT TOWER Built by Henry III, it was much used as a prison; there are 55 prisoners' inscriptions, many of them by Jesuits.

THE YEOMEN OF THE TOWER 'They are called "Beefeaters", that is eaters of beef, of which a considerable proportion is allowed them daily by the Court', wrote Count Cosimo dei Medici in 1669. In fact, he was wrong; they are not called 'Beefeaters' — a description which can only be applied to the Yeomen of the Guard (instituted after Bosworth in 1485), not to the Yeoman Warders of the Tower who became a separate entity in 1509. Their uniform remains as it was in their founder Henry VIII's day, though a thistle was added after the Act of Union in 1707 and a shamrock after 1801.

WHARF This is the site for the salutes fired by the Honourable Artillery Company on special occasions: 62 'guns' sound for a great state event and the anniversaries of the sovereign's birth, accession and coronation; 41 for the Opening of Parliament and for a royal birth.

Mighty Princes: Norman and Angevin Rule

After William the Conqueror's death the House of Normandy continued on the English throne in the persons of his sons William II (1087-1100) and Henry I (1100-1135). Following the struggle over the succession between Henry I's daughter Matilda and his maternal nephew Stephen (1135-1154), it was agreed that the crown would pass to Matilda's son, Henry Plantagenet.

The tradition of strong government established by William the Conqueror was continued by his sons, William II (1087-1100) and Henry I (1100-1135). The former, known as 'Rufus' on account of his ruddy complexion, was an unpopular monarch, notorious for his tyrannical behaviour. It is one of history's ironies that the Great Hall he began at Westminster was later to become the central arena of practised English common law, the progress of which he did so much to hinder by his repressive measures.

Henry I (known as 'Beauclerc'), who brought the old royal blood back into the English ruling stock by marrying the daughter of Queen Margaret of Scotland (a descendant of Ethelred the Unready), now pledged himself to protect the Church, to put down evil customs and to uphold good laws. In a long and well-ordered reign, Henry did much to expurgate his brother's tyranny, and he earned the sobriquet 'lion of justice' through his legal reforms.

At the beginning of the 12th century, responsibility for executive government still rested completely with the monarch. However, as the business administration grew more complex — largely attributable to England's full-scale involvement in continental politics — it was inevitable that new institutions, such as the Exchequer which developed elaborate methods of accounting and of keeping records, would evolve.

Although the Norman kings were naturally often absent in Normandy, it was not this that weakened the power of the feudal government so much as the civil wars during the reign of Stephen (1135-1154). The disputes concerned not only the succession to the monarchy but also to the baronial estates created by the Norman Conquest. Stephen, an agreeable and popular nephew of Henry I, had managed to gain the English crown because the old King's only legitimate child was a girl. Although England did not follow the practice of Salic Law — the rule (supposedly based on the ancient Germanic *Lex Salica*) whereby inheritance could not pass through the female line — Matilda's gender made her unacceptable as a sovereign in the Middle Ages. The compromise adopted was that while Stephen managed to retain the throne for his lifetime, he was eventually succeeded by Matilda's son, the formidable Henry of Anjou, Henry II of England (1154-1189).

The accession of the French dynasty of Anjou, the House of Plantagenet, in 1154 meant that England became part of a huge complex of Angevin lands for some 50 years. The strain of holding such great territorial possessions was obviously considerable for the monarchy. The efficiency of royal government under Henry II and his sons, the largely absent crusader Richard I ('Coeur de Lion') (1189-1199), who was known as 'the Lion Heart', and King John (1199-1216), nicknamed 'Lackland', was characterized by the need for peace and recouping of resources at home so that attempts could be made to stabilize the position on the continent.

King John is generally considered to have been one of England's worst monarchs, but in many respects he was a competent ruler. English legal and financial institutions grew particularly strong, and by the beginning of the 13th century the central organs of government were in a healthy state. His cause, however, was not helped by military fiascos and his abuse of royal power which eventually provoked rebellion. The consequent issue of *Magna Carta* — forced on the King — marks a crucial development in the history of the monarchy. Although no actual machinery was set up for disciplining an unlawful monarch, *Magna Carta* came to stand as a symbol of restriction on royal power. The point had been made that the King governed under law, and that unlawful royal action could not be tolerated.

The next crisis in the development of the monarchy occurred towards the end of the reign of King John's successor, Henry III (1216-1272), when Simon de Montfort tried to establish a government by council as a safeguard against arbitrary royal rule. De Montfort's ultimately unsuccessful efforts between 1258 and 1265 nevertheless included the significant step of summoning a central assembly composed of knights from the shires, burghers and other representatives.

The unsatisfactory Henry III is usually regarded as the last of the Angevin monarchs and his son Edward Longshanks (1272-1307) as the first of the Plantagenets, although actually this dynasty descended from the House of Anjou. Unlike his father, Edward was to become one of the strongest of all English kings.

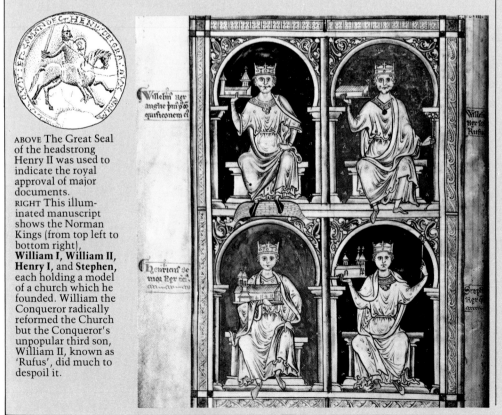

ABOVE The Great Seal of the headstrong Henry II was used to indicate the royal approval of major documents.
RIGHT This illuminated manuscript shows the Norman Kings (from top left to bottom right), **William I, William II, Henry I**, and **Stephen**, each holding a model of a church which he founded. William the Conqueror radically reformed the Church but the Conqueror's unpopular third son, William II, known as 'Rufus', did much to despoil it.

LEFT **King John** is depicted in front of *Magna Carta*, 'the great charter of liberties', which he was made to sign by the barons at Runnymede on 15 June 1215.

ABOVE **Richard the Lion Heart** attacks his former crusading companion, Philip Augustus of France, outside Gisars in 1198 in this picture. Although outnumbered, Richard put the French Army to flight. Earlier Richard had made his reputation as a soldier in the third Crusade to drive the Moslems out of the Holy Land, though he never reached Jerusalem.

BELOW The map shows the extent of the Angevin Empire in the middle of the reign of the first Angevin King of England, Henry II. Henry was the son of the powerful Geoffrey Plantagenet, Count of Anjou and Maine, by his wife Matilda, only surviving child of Henry I of England. From his mother Henry II inherited Normandy; from his father he inherited the lands of Anjou, Maine and Touraine; from his marriage to Eleanor, Duchess of Aquitaine, the former wife of Louis VII of France, in 1152, Henry acquired Aquitaine. He later added Brittany, Auvergne and Toulouse to his dominions, and for a time ruled more of France than the French King.

Held by Henry II

Duchy of Aquitaine

Held by French

BRABANT
FLANDERS
HAINAULT
Vermandois
Rouen
Vexin
Caen
Lisieux
NORMANDY
Paris
CHAMPAGNE
Mortain
BLOIS
MAINE
R. Seine
BRITTANY
R. Loire
Le Mans
ANJOU
Blois
Nantes
Angers
Tours
BURGUNDY
TOURAINE
POITOU
BERRI
Poitiers
La Rochelle
Lusignan
LA MARCHE
THE EMPIRE
SAINTONGE
ANGOUMOIS
Angoulême
LIMOUSIN
PERIGORD
AUVERGNE
Perigueux
R. Dordogne
Bordeaux
AGENAIS
Agen
Montauban
R. Garonne
TOULOUSE
GASCONY
PROVENCE
Toulouse
CASTILE
NAVARRE
ARAGON
BARCELONA

Lion and Dragon: the Conquests of Wales

The great native Prince of Wales, Llywelyn the Last (1246-1282) was conquered by Edward I of England (1272-1307), who consolidated his grip on Wales with a chain of castles in the north of the principality. The last native 'Prince of Wales', Owain Glyndwr, revived Welsh independence briefly at the end of the 14th century.

The Romans had wisely decided to leave the Celtic fringe well alone and, though the Normans set about uniting the Welsh and the English, no other king really seriously contemplated conquering Wales until Edward I (1272-1307).

By 1066 the main Welsh kingdoms were those of Gwynedd in the north, Powys in mid-Wales and Deheubarth in the southwest. The first Norman Earl of Chester, Hugh of Avranches, did much to keep the Welsh under control; by 1090 he had built castles at Aberlleinog in Anglesey, at Caernarvon and Merioneth.

Caernarvon Castle (which was later rebuilt by Edward I) was used by the two most famous native Welsh princes, Llywelyn 'the Great' (Prince of Gwynedd 1194-1240) and his grandson Llywelyn ap Gruffydd, 'the Last' (1246-1282). Although the former was married to King John's bastard daughter, he had a long tussle with the English crown before finally submitting to Henry III (1216-1272) in 1237. Llywelyn the Last was more successful, using skilful diplomacy as well as force to achieve his ambition of an independent principality. He reunited North Wales from the River Dovey to the River Dee and was acknowledged as overlord by the other native princes in 1258. He then took the historic step of assuming the style of 'Prince of Wales' (the first to do so) and, moreover, managed to persuade Henry III to recognize that title at the Peace of Monmouth nine years later. The principality consisted of the following modern shires — Anglesey, Caernarvon and Merioneth.

Henry III's son, Edward I, took a less accommodating view of Llywelyn ap Gruffydd. On his return from the Crusades, Edward saw the Welsh, the Scots and the Jews as elements which interfered with the social and political unification of the 'native state'. A contemporary chronicler described the Welsh as Trojan debris swept into the wooded savagery of Cambria under the guidance of the Devil. It was in the context of attitudes such as this, that Edward announced on 12 November 1276 that he was going against Llywelyn 'as a rebel and disturber of the peace'.

Edward, whose earlier efforts to establish himself in Wales had been an abysmal failure, had some old scores to settle with Llywelyn and this time he made short work

of the native Prince of Wales. Llywelyn was forced to sign humiliating peace terms at the Treaty of Aberconwy in 1277 which reduced the principality to the western part of Snowdonia. Five years later, however, North Wales rose again at the instigation of Llywelyn's turbulent brother Dafydd. Llywelyn himself was blockaded in his mountain stronghold of Snowdonia, but escaped and headed south. On 11 December 1282 Llywelyn the Last is said to have encountered a single English infantryman on a bridge outside Builth Wells who ran him through with his sword.

Welsh independence effectively died with the last native Prince of Wales, although Owain Glyndwr (otherwise known as Owen Glendower) tried to revive the cause at the end of the 14th century. Henry VIII (1509-1547), a member of the Welsh dynasty of Tudor, made Wales a political unity for the first time in the Act of Union in 1536; the medieval principality was extended to include the whole of modern Wales.

The visible legacy of Edward I's conquest is the chain of castles in North Wales. He built eight altogether between 1277 and 1295; Caernarvon, Conwy and Beaumaris are still remarkably complete, Rhuddlan and Harlech only slightly less so. It was at Caernarvon in 1284 that Edward I's Queen, Eleanor, gave birth to the first English Prince of Wales.

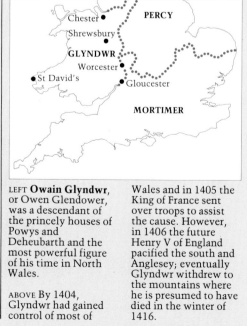

LEFT **Owain Glyndwr**, or Owen Glendower, was a descendant of the princely houses of Powys and Deheubarth and the most powerful figure of his time in North Wales.

ABOVE By 1404, Glyndwr had gained control of most of Wales and in 1405 the King of France sent over troops to assist the cause. However, in 1406 the future Henry V of England pacified the south and Anglesey; eventually Glyndwr withdrew to the mountains where he is presumed to have died in the winter of 1416.

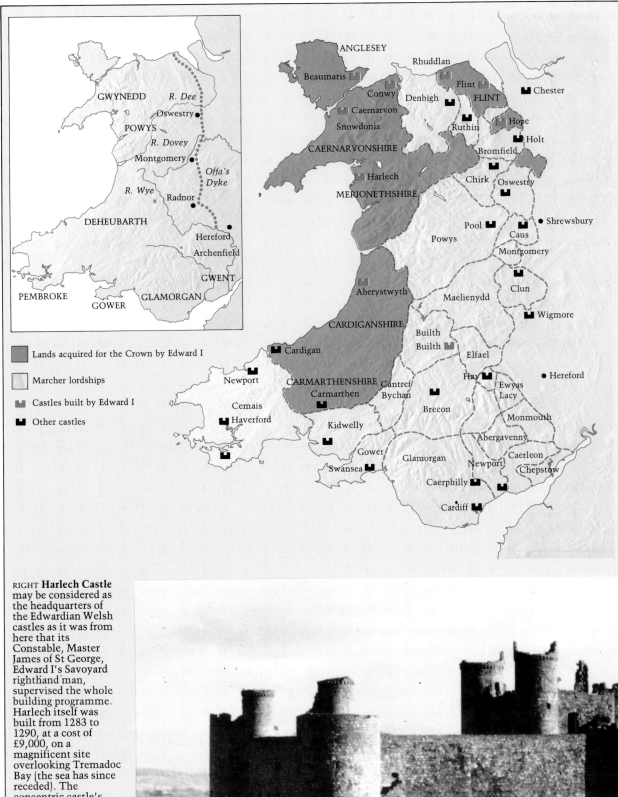

Lands acquired for the Crown by Edward I

Marcher lordships

Castles built by Edward I

Other castles

LEFT To consolidate his conquest of Wales after 1277, Edward I of England built a chain of castles in the north: Caernarvon, Conwy (or Conway), Beaumaris, Rhuddlan, Harlech, Flint, Aberystwyth, Builth and Hope. Built between 1277 and 1295 at a cost approaching £80,000 they constituted an enormous enterprise. Today, the 'Edwardian' architecture of Caernarvon, Conwy and Beaumaris and to a slightly lesser extent, Rhuddlan and Harlech can still be appreciated to the full, whereas Flint, Aberystwyth and Hope have not survived so well. Only the Norman earthworks are now visible at Builth.

In addition to his major building works, Edward I also repaired such stone-built Welsh fortresses as Dolwyddelan (birth-place of Llywelyn the Great in 1194), Criccieth, Dynevor and Dryslwyn.

The map also shows the changing borders of Wales. Until Edward I's conquest in the late 13th century, the division was loose as Wales itself was not so much a united country as a series of small principalities.

RIGHT **Harlech Castle** may be considered as the headquarters of the Edwardian Welsh castles as it was from here that its Constable, Master James of St George, Edward I's Savoyard righthand man, supervised the whole building programme. Harlech itself was built from 1283 to 1290, at a cost of £9,000, on a magnificent site overlooking Tremadoc Bay (the sea has since receded). The concentric castle's architecture has been compared with that of Chillon on the continent. In 1294, the 37 'Men of Harlech' defended the castle against the Welsh army of Prince Madog ap Llywelyn. Owain Glyndwr's assault on Harlech was more successful in the early 1400s and it became the headquarters of his campaign to reassert Welsh independence.

The Princes of Wales

Since Edward I's conquest of Wales there have been 21 'English' Princes of Wales from Edward's heir, the future Edward II, created Prince of Wales in 1301, to the present Prince Charles, created Prince of Wales in 1958 and invested at Caernarvon Castle in 1969. Since the revival of Welsh traditions in the 19th century, the Princes have taken a much greater interest in the principality.

In mythology Edward I (1272–1307) is supposed to have promised to find for his Welsh subjects a prince that was 'born in Wales who speaks no word of English', and then to have duly presented the babe-in-arms to the people from the tower of Caernarvon Castle. Quite apart from the inconvenient detail that the tower in question had not been built in 1284, the story is an Elizabethan fantasy. The fact is that the future Edward II (1307–1327) did not receive the principality of Wales until he was nearly 17, and his birth in Wales was a fluke, merely one of his mother's several 'campaigning' deliveries.

Nevertheless, like many legends, it does convey an element of truth. For Edward I's policy after the death of Llywelyn the Last was clearly to placate the Welsh people. On 17 February 1301 he duly created his son and namesake Prince of Wales and Earl of Chester, granting him the government of the

principality, its lands, administration and revenues. There were two administrative 'capitals' — Caernarvon in the north, Carmarthen in the south — and administrators were specially appointed to govern the principality. The Prince had his own Household, together with a Council to advise him.

There have been 21 English Princes of Wales, all of them heirs apparent to the throne. Seven of the princes were Plantagenets (Edward II, the Black Prince, Richard II, Henry V, Edward of Lancaster, Edward V and Edward of Middleham); two were Tudor (Henry VII's sons Arthur and the future Henry VIII); four were Stuart (James I's sons Henry and the future Charles I, Charles II and the 'Old Pretender'); four were Hanoverian (George II, 'Poor Fred', George III and George IV). Edward III, George V and Edward VIII were all Princes of Wales before acceding to the throne.

Princes of Wales are made, not born. The title does not come automatically (as in the case of the Dukedom of Cornwall) and its bestowal is at the discretion of the sovereign. The age when the title is bestowed has varied considerably: the future George III was made Prince of Wales when only five days old and the Old Pretender (James Francis Edward) merely a month, while the future George II and George V were both into their 30s. The investiture used to be carried out by the monarch from the throne in Parliament, but in 1911 the then Constable of Caernarvon Castle, David Lloyd George, had other ideas.

'With an eye to what would please his constituents', ruefully recalled the Duke of Windsor in his memoirs, '"L.G." proposed that the ceremony be transformed into a spectacular Welsh pageant'. The young Prince was duly fitted up in 'a fantastic costume designed for the occasion, con-

RIGHT This family tree shows some of the descendants of the great Llywelyn, Prince of Gwynedd, down to the present Prince of Wales, Prince Charles.

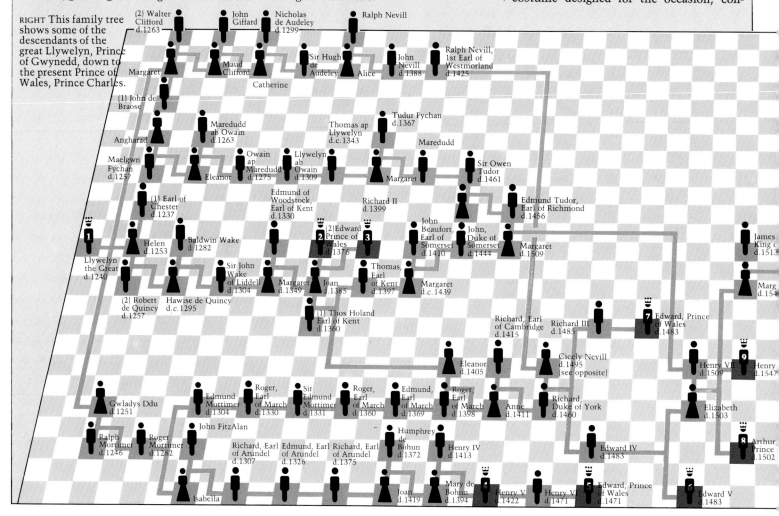

ABOVE The investiture of the future Edward VIII as Prince of Wales took place at Caernarvon Castle on 13 July 1911. It was the first time a reigning sovereign — in this case George V — had been to the greatest of the Welsh castles since Henry IV had led his army there in 1400. The Letters Patent were read by the then Home Secretary, Winston Churchill, and the ceremony was organized by David Lloyd George, then Chancellor of the Exchequer, with assistance from the Bishop of St Asaph.

ABOVE While some 10,000 people watched the 1911 Investiture at Caernarvon, a television audience of millions saw Prince Charles invested by the Queen on 1 July 1969. 'It is my firm intention', declared the Prince in both Welsh and English, 'to associate myself in word and deed with as much of the life of the Principality as possible'. The ceremony followed that of 1911, though Prince Charles's attire was more restrained than the 'preposterous rig' about which his great-uncle complained.

sisting of white satin breeches and a mantle and surcoat of purple velvet edged with ermine'. Matters were slightly more restrained when the present Prince of Wales was invested at Caernarvon in July 1969, although the present Constable, Lord Snowdon, was attired in bottle-green, without a sword to the dismay of the purists. Lord Snowdon had called in his friend Carl Toms, the stage designer, to create 'a kind of theatre in the round so it would read well on television'. The Prince declared that he would become the Queen's 'liege man of life and limb' and would 'live and die against all manner of folk' before going on to make a speech — complete with a reference to Harry Secombe — in Welsh, a language which he had learnt at the University of Aberystwyth.

Until the revival of Welsh traditions in the 19th century, it would not be unfair to say that the English Princes of Wales took little interest in their principality. The present incumbent is, without doubt, the best Prince the Welsh have had; Charles has taken a special interest in Wales through such organizations as the Prince of Wales's Committee and by promoting Welsh Industrial opportunities on his travels. As he has often said, the motto of the Prince of Wales — adopted by the Black Prince at the Battle of Crécy from the King of Bohemia — is singularly appropriate: *Ich Dien* (which means 'I serve').

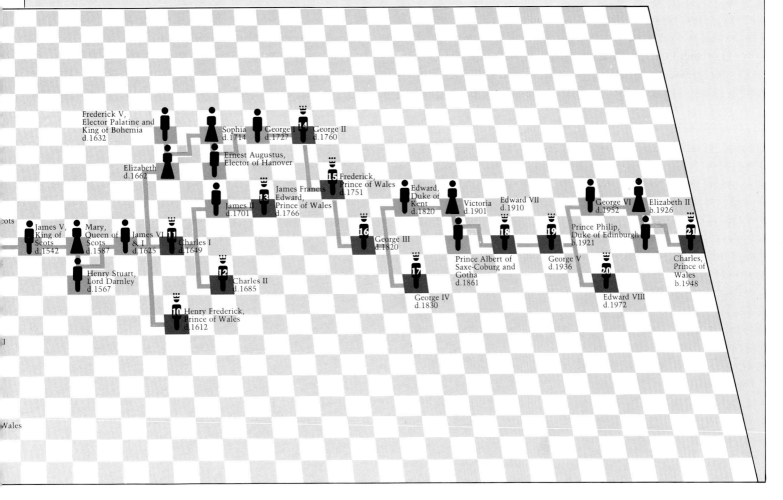

The Kings and Queens of Scotland

The first King of the united Celtic kingdom known as Scotia was Kenneth MacAlpin (844-859). The Royal House of Scotland later intermarried with the Saxons and Normans. David I (1124-1153), a brother-in-law of Henry I of England, introduced the feudal system of land tenure into the Lowlands, while the old clan system persisted in the Highlands.

The Royal House of Scotland descended from Fergus Mor MacErc, himself a descendant of the Irish kings of Dalriada (which is roughly equivalent to modern County Antrim), who came over from Ulster towards the end of the 5th century and established the new Scottish kingdom of Dalriada in Argyll. At this time, following the Roman withdrawal in AD 407, Caledonia (or Alba in Gaelic) was divided between four tribes: the Picts, who ruled from Orkney to the Firth of Forth; the Irish

BELOW **Macbeth** was King of Scotland from 1040, when he murdered Duncan, until 1057, when he was himself dispatched by Duncan's son Malcolm.

Scots; the Britons in Strathclyde and the Angles in Lothian.

The long-established Pictish kingdom had a curious system of succession whereby the throne passed from brother to brother, or from uncle to nephew, and sometimes from cousin to cousin in the female line. In Dalriada the succession, although reckoned in the female line, passed to the *Tanistair* ('appointed successor') of the reigning king, chosen from among his brothers and sisters.

The foundations for the eventual union between the warring Picts and Scots were laid by matrimonial alliances between the two dynasties. The first king of the new united Celtic kingdom of Scotia was Kenneth MacAlpin (844-859), whose great-grandmother was a Pictish heiress. According to a chronicler, Kenneth was a man 'of marvellous astuteness'; he moved his capital to Forteviot in the Pictish east and the remains of the great Christian missionary St Columba from Iona to Dunkeld.

The kingdom of Scotia was not extended

beyond the territories of the Picts and the Scots until the 11th century, when Malcolm II (1005-1034) annexed Lothian after the Battle of Carham (1018) and procured the kingdom of Strathclyde (through a somewhat questionable genealogical claim) for his grandson Duncan I (1034-1040). Duncan, known as 'the Gracious', thus became monarch of a considerably larger Scotland when his grandfather died in 1034. Six years later the throne was usurped by Duncan's murderer, Macbeth (1040-1057), who in fact made a success of his reign. Legitimacy prevailed, however, when Duncan's son, Malcolm III (1058-1093), known as *Ceann Mor* (or 'Bighead'), defeated and killed Macbeth in battle to regain the Scottish throne for his line.

The English-educated Malcolm III married, in about 1069, the English princess, Margaret, a great-niece of Edward the Confessor, who had fled to Scotland after the Norman Conquest. According to the *Anglo-Saxon Chronicle* St Margaret:

RIGHT This family tree shows the 41 Kings and Queens of Scotland from Kenneth MacAlpin, who united the kingdoms of Dalriada and the Picts in AD 844, to Mary Queen of Scots' son, James VI, who became James I of England in 1603.

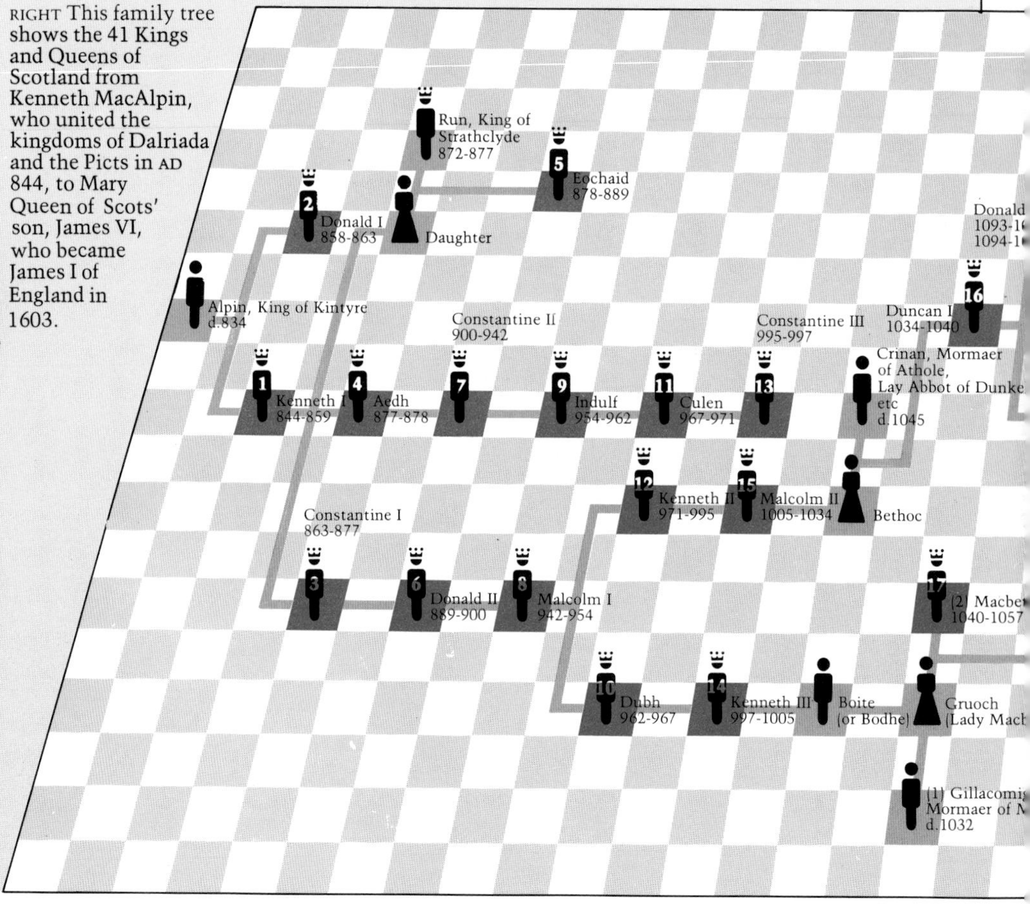

'was destined to increase the glory of God in that land, to turn the King aside from the path of error, to incline him altogether with his people towards a better way of life, and to abolish the vices which that nation had indulged in in the past.'

From now on the affairs of the neighbouring countries became increasingly intertwined; the division of the 'Anglicized' Lowlands and the Celtic North also became more marked.

Malcolm III had an eye for expansion into the northern counties of England, but William the Conqueror resisted this and William II showed scant approval of the attempts by Malcolm's brother, Donald III Bane (1093-1094 and 1094-1097) to revive the Celtic past. David I (1124-1153), a brother-in-law of Henry I (1100-1135), was much more to the Normans' liking; his manners, it was said, had been 'polished from the rust of Scottish barbarity'. He introduced the feudal system of land tenure into the Lowlands, although the old clan system persisted in the Highlands. The latter was based upon the kinship, loose or otherwise, between clansmen and their chief, a patriarchal figure who would protect the clan (generally comprised of his tenants) and lead them in war. The clan system was to survive, at least in spirit, until the crushing of the second Jacobite Rising at Culloden in 1746. In fact, feudal land tenure in the Highlands was organized as in the rest of Scotland much earlier than is popularly supposed, even though the old chieftainship and clan loyalties have lingered to the present day.

LEFT 'Clan' is Gaelic for children and the clan system was based upon the kinship between the clansmen and their chieftain. After the feudal system of land tenure was introduced from the continent into the Lowlands of Scotland by David I, King of Scots, the old clan system persisted in the Highlands; indeed the old chieftainships and clan loyalties have survived to the present day. However, it is a myth that land in the Highlands was held in common by the clansmen until after 1745. A mass of medieval charters prove that the chieftains were in fact granted full territorial rights by the crown. Another popular myth concerning the clan system is that each clan was a single family. In fact a clan was made up of many different families among which the chieftain's family was pre-eminent.

This map shows areas where particular families have historically tended to hold sway.

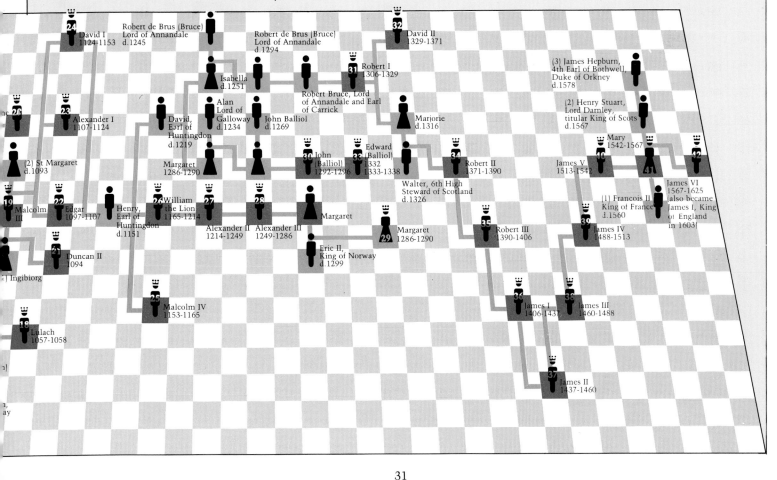

The Two Crowns: England and Scotland

Edward I of England (1272-1307) sought to impose the English overlordship in Scotland, but the Scots battled on for their independence. After the Scottish crown had passed to the Royal House of Stuart in 1371, a dynastic link was forged with England through the marriage of James IV of Scotland (1488-1513) to Margaret, eldest daughter of Henry VII.

The trouble in the Middle Ages between the two kingdoms was based on the way that the English kings tended to treat the Scottish kings as their vassals. In 1301, for instance, Edward I, the 'Hammer of the Scots' (1272-1307), went so far as to tell the Pope that the feudal ties binding Scotland to England originated in the time of the Trojan Wars.

The humiliation of Scotland really began with the Treaty of Falaise in 1174. William I (1165-1214) King of the Scots, known as 'the Lion', had been exiled to Normandy by the English after his great invasion of that year had come to grief at Alnwick. He was compelled to acknowledge Henry II of England (1154-1189) as overlord of Scotland before being allowed to return. Richard the Lion Heart absolved William, 15 years later, from this grovelling allegiance in return for some cash needed for the Crusades. Relations between the two countries then entered a comparatively peaceful period, although the Scottish kings were preoccupied with trying to keep the Norwegians, not to mention the Celtic chieftains, under control.

In the 13th century, Joan, the sister of Henry III (1216-1272), married Alexander II of Scotland (1214-1249) and his daughter Margaret married Alexander III (1249-1286). Despite the uneasiness which is almost inevitably attendant on such family ties, peace seemed assured until the untimely death, in a riding accident, of Alexander III. The heir to the Scottish throne was his young granddaughter, the 'Maid of Norway' (daughter of Margaret of Scotland and Eric II of Norway).

Edward I of England saw his opportunity; a marriage was planned between the Maid and his equally young son, the future Edward II, which would bring about the union of the two kingdoms. In 1290 the still infant bride was sent for from Norway, in a ship stuffed with sweetmeats by Edward I for his prospective daughter-in-law, but she died in Orkney *en route*. Who was now to become the sovereign of Scotland?

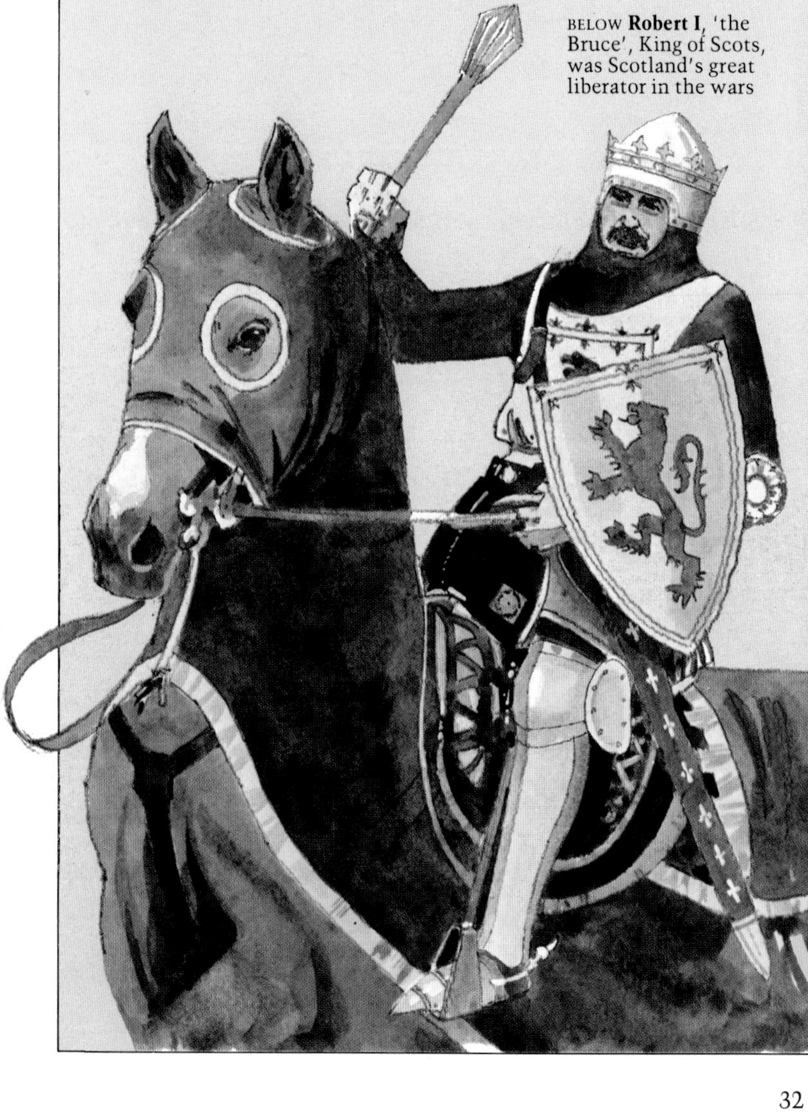

In the Interregnum of 1290-1292, 13 competitors came forward. The two strongest claimants were Robert Bruce (grandfather of the great Robert I (1306-1329), later to be victor of Bannockburn) and John Balliol, who were both descended from William the Lion's brother, David, Earl of Huntingdon. With a civil war in prospect, the Scottish magnates unwittingly played into Edward I's hands by asking the English King to arbitrate at Berwick. Before settling on the unimpressive John Balliol, Edward craftily obtained an assurance from all the competitors that they accepted the English king as lord of Scotland.

Edward duly proceeded to treat John Balliol as his feudal lackey, demanding that the Scottish king come to his aid against France. This was too much even for Balliol, who belatedly attempted to assert his independence by reviving the 'Auld Alliance' with France, the traditional combination against the 'auld enemy' (England) which continued to be invoked until the Scottish Reformation. Balliol began an invasion of northern England early in 1296, but Edward retaliated swiftly and brutally, with the help of Bruce and other Scottish nobles. The Scottish King was trounced at Dunbar and forced to abdicate at Brechin, where Edward later obtained the signatures of some 2,000 Scottish landholders to the 'Ragman's Roll' which recognized him as King.

For 10 years until his death in 1307, during the so-called Second Interregnum, Edward I continued to treat Scotland as a conquered country. His conquest, however, was very far from secure; although known as the 'Hammer of the Scots', his hammering was not nearly so successful as it was in Wales. The Scots battled on for independence, first under Sir William Wallace (who was victorious at Stirling Bridge but vanquished at Falkirk in 1298), and then under Bruce's grandson, Robert I, known as 'the Bruce'.

Robert the Bruce was eventually crowned 'with the consent of. . . the people of the

BELOW **Robert I**, 'the Bruce', King of Scots, was Scotland's great liberator in the wars of independence against Edward I and Edward II of England. He was the grandson of an Anglo Norman noble, Robert de Brus (or Bruce), a competitor for the Scottish crown in the Interregnum between 1290 and 1292, whose own mother was a niece of William I, 'the Lion', King of Scots. Young Robert first came to the fore as the leader of the Scots resistance to Edward I of England after the defeat of John Balliol in 1304. After years on the run and in exile, he won the epic victory of Bannockburn, near Stirling Castle, on 24 June 1314 despite having only some 5,500 men to the English 20,000.

land' in 1306 and went on to drive the English from Scotland in the epic Battle of Bannockburn in 1314 despite being outnumbered by at least three to one. The Treaty of Northampton in 1328 finally recognized Scotland as an independent kingdom and a year later the great Bruce died a Scottish national hero, having begun life as an Anglo-Norman noble.

While Bruce's successors were weak, the successor of the unhappy Edward II (1307-1327), Edward III (1327-1377), was strong. The English again attempted to act as

overlords. David II (1329-1371) was driven into exile after the Battle of Halidon Hill, but strong Scots resistance and Edward III's preoccupation with the Hundred Years' War ensured that the English did not pursue another conquest.

After David II's death in 1371 the Scottish throne passed to the House of Stuart (or Stewart) in the person of Robert II (1371-1390), whose mother, Marjorie, Robert the Bruce's elder daughter, had married Walter, the Hereditary High Steward of Scotland, a noble of Breton descent. Anglo-

Scottish border warfare continued during the 15th and 16th centuries, though Scotland remained independent until the Act of Union in 1707. Family ties still did not prevent bloodshed; James IV (1488-1513), who married Margaret, the eldest daughter of Henry VII, was killed at the Battle of Flodden and his granddaughter, Mary, Queen of Scots (1542-1567), was executed by order of her cousin, Elizabeth I. Mary's son, James VI of Scotland, however, eventually succeeded the Virgin Queen on the English throne in 1603, and became king of both countries.

RIGHT Border warfare between England and Scotland was almost constant between the nations from the 7th to the 18th centuries. There were, however, fairly long gaps of comparative peace — such as the one that followed the Treaty of Falaise in 1174 when William I, 'the Lion', King of Scots, whose

invasion of England had been crushed at Alnwick, had to acknowledge Henry II of England as overlord of Scotland. This Treaty recognized the border line which had officially been in existence for about 100 years. The major Scottish Wars of Independence raged intermittently from

1295, when John Balliol, King of Scots, revived the 'Auld Alliance' with France, to the reign of Edward III of England, who became somewhat distracted by the Hundred Years' War. Some of the key battles and campaigns are indicated in this map.

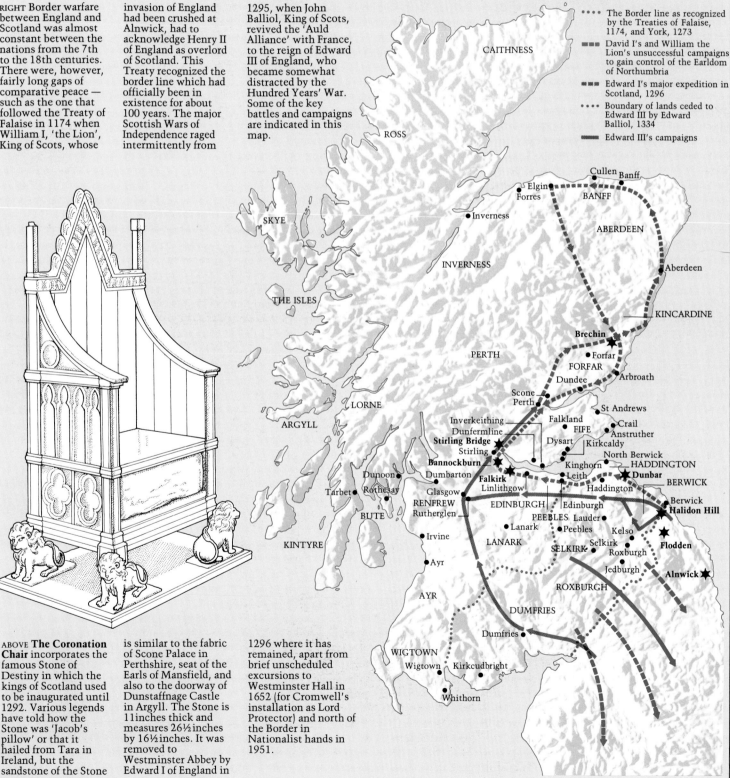

- •••• The Border line as recognized by the Treaties of Falaise, 1174, and York, 1273
- ▬▬▬ David I's and William the Lion's unsuccessful campaigns to gain control of the Earldom of Northumbria
- ▬▬▬ Edward I's major expedition in Scotland, 1296
- •••• Boundary of lands ceded to Edward III by Edward Balliol, 1334
- ▬▬▬ Edward III's campaigns

ABOVE **The Coronation Chair** incorporates the famous Stone of Destiny in which the kings of Scotland used to be inaugurated until 1292. Various legends have told how the Stone was 'Jacob's pillow' or that it hailed from Tara in Ireland, but the sandstone of the Stone

is similar to the fabric of Scone Palace in Perthshire, seat of the Earls of Mansfield, and also to the doorway of Dunstaffnage Castle in Argyll. The Stone is 11 inches thick and measures 26½ inches by 16½ inches. It was removed to Westminster Abbey by Edward I of England in

1296 where it has remained, apart from brief unscheduled excursions to Westminster Hall in 1652 (for Cromwell's installation as Lord Protector) and north of the Border in Nationalist hands in 1951.

The Plantagenet Kings

Edward I (1272-1307), the first of the Plantagenet kings, was a lawgiver as well as a warrior. His foppish son Edward II (1307-1327) was murdered, as (in all probability) was his great-grandson, Richard II (1377-1399). Edward III (1327-1377) claimed the French throne, involving England in the Hundred Years' War.

Edward I (1272-1307), generally regarded as the first and greatest of the Plantagenet monarchs, earned himself the tag of the 'English Justinian'. His notable legislative reforms included the stabilization of land law and the systematization of government. Most important of all, Edward Longshanks continued what de Montfort had begun in summoning representatives of the shires and towns to national assemblies, known as 'parliaments'. It was not until 1325, though, that the presence of an assembly of 'Commons' in Parliament became accepted.

Legends grew about Edward Longshanks as the perfect knightly figure of the Crusades; he had indeed been on a four-year crusade to the Holy Land in the 1270s with the French King, St Louis, and was known as 'the best lance in all the world'. The King was tall and powerful, though he had a drooping eyelid and spoke with a lisp. His achievements display an unbending will, untiring persistence and an unusual skill as an administrator and lawgiver, but he was also a romantic, bequeathing a fine architectural legacy in the form of the Eleanor Crosses (in memory of his Queen, Eleanor of Castile) and all his castles in Wales. Nevertheless, throughout Edward I's reign England remained almost permanently at war and he had much to worry him towards the end.

The position inherited by Edward II (1307-1327) was less enviable than his father's. This should be borne in mind when judging the poor performance of a king generally regarded as a pusillanimous pervert. His notorious favourites, such as Piers Gaveston and Hugh le Despenser, upset the nobles and led eventually to an abdication engineered by his French Queen's lover, the powerful Roger Mortimer, in 1327. Later that year, with barbarous irony, his gaolers at Berkeley Castle thrust a red hot spit into his bowels:

'The shrieks of death thro' Berkeley's roof that ring —
Shrieks of an agonising King. . .'

The inheritance of Edward III (1327-1377), Edward II's 14-year-old son, was to be envied even less, but it has been said that he transformed a fractious wilderness into an English nation. First, he avenged his father's death: he confined his mother to her quarters and had Mortimer executed. Edward III was, however, at the same time content to claim the French throne on account of her French royal birth; so began the first stages of the Hundred Years' War.

The long campaign began well for Edward III with triumphs at Crécy and Poitiers, but these victories could not be repeated; setbacks and severe financial strains ensued as the wars dragged on. At home, virtually a third of the population was destroyed by the appalling Black Death. And yet this was also an age which saw the flowering of chivalry and pageantry under a king who founded the Order of the Garter.

While the panoply of monarchy grew in Edward III's long reign, it seemed clear that Parliament was here to stay. His grandson and successor, Richard II (1377-1399), son of the gallant Black Prince, was to take a more autocratic view (though as a boy-king he had shown a conciliatory and brave face to the Peasants' Revolt of 1381). Like his great-grandfather Edward II, Richard II was considered foppish, was duly deposed and, in all probability, murdered.

The man to take advantage of the restlessness of the barons at Richard II's high-handed behaviour was his own first cousin, Henry, son of the mighty John of Gaunt, Duke of Lancaster. John of Gaunt was the fourth of seven sons of Edward III, a king whose fecundity caused untold problems for the monarchy culminating in the Wars of the Roses. On Richard II's deposition, the Plantagenet House of Lancaster came to the throne, through military success and parliamentary support rather than legal right, in the person of Henry IV (1399-1413). The Lancastrians began well, though the heroic ventures in France of Henry IV's son, Henry V (1413-1422), placed a great strain on the machinery of royal government. The victor of Agincourt's death (from an unknown illness) brought Henry VI (1422-1461) to the throne of both England and France.

The scholarly young Henry was not a military man and his shortcomings spelt disaster for the House of Lancaster. Lamentable political and military failures in the last flickers of the Hundred Years' War, such as the loss of the French territories (save Calais), were coupled with the wretched King's attacks of paralysis and insanity. By 1453 the Hundred Years' War in France had ended, but a long 30 years of civil war in England were soon to begin.

ABOVE **The Battle of Agincourt**, fought on 25 October 1415, was England's most important victory over the French in the Hundred Years' War. Henry V's army was heavily outnumbered en route to Calais, but the French cavalry unwisely charged the English archers on a narrow front near the Somme. The result was that the French, under Constable d'Albret, lost some 6,000 men to Henry's 400.

RIGHT Shakespeare's Henry V rouses his troops before the Battle of Agincourt, fought on St Crispin's Day 1415. Shakespeare's Henry is a true champion. The real Henry V was equally heroic and popular. In 1520 he married Catherine, daughter of Charles VI of France; she later was to marry Owen Tudor, grandfather of Henry VIII.

RIGHT The 'Hundred Years' War' is the name generally given to the long conflict between England and France which began in 1337 — when the English King Edward III invaded Gascony for Aquitaine. Edward was pursuing his claim to the French throne through his mother Isabelle, the eldest daughter of Philip IV of France. His first major success was at the Battle of Crécy in 1346. Edward's son, the 'Black Prince', scored another notable victory at Poitiers 10 years later and the capture of the French

King, John II, marked the nadir of French fortunes. They were later revived, however, by Charles V of France and a truce was sealed by the marriage in 1396 of the Black Prince's son, Richard II to Charles VI of France's daughter, Isabelle. Henry V revived the claim to the French throne and achieved England's most significant success at Agincourt in 1415.

The next swing of the pendulum in the Hundred Years' War owed its momentum to the ill-fated Joan of Arc, who inspired the relief of Orleans in 1429. The French finally asserted their authority to the full under Charles VII who reconquered Normandy and Aquitaine. In 1453 he defeated the English commander, John Talbot, 1st Earl of Shrewsbury, at Castillon; this was the last major battle of the Hundred Years' War. England only retained Calais from its once vast Plantagenet dominions.

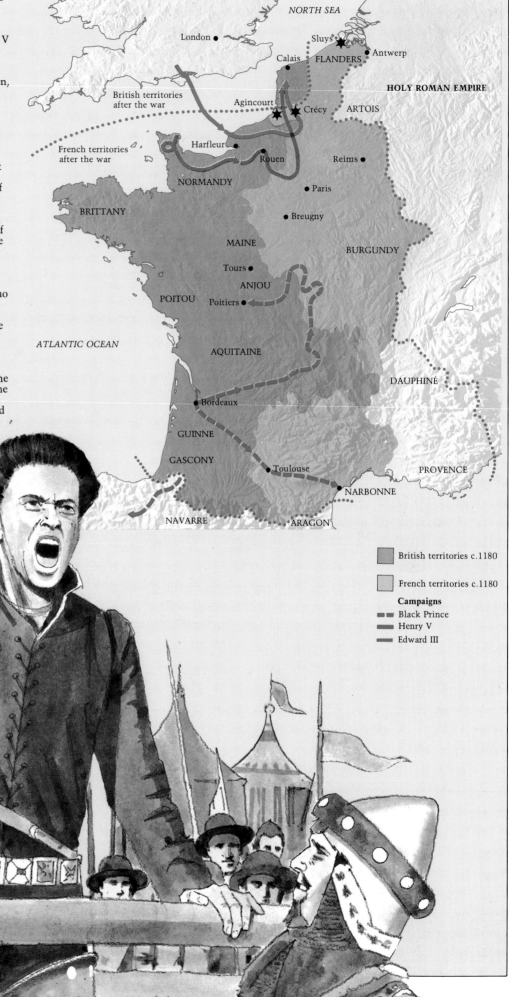

British territories c.1180

French territories c.1180

Campaigns
- - - Black Prince
— Henry V
— Edward III

Divided Realm: the Wars of the Roses

The civil strife between the House of Lancaster (the 'Red Rose') and the House of York (the 'White Rose') erupted in 1455. During the next 30 years, the English crown changed hands half-a-dozen times: Henry VI (deposed 1461); Edward IV (1461-1470); Henry VI again (1470-1471); Edward IV again (1471-1483); Edward V (1483); and Richard III (1483-1485).

In the mid-15th century, failure abroad and the incompetence of Henry VI (1422-1461) had led to factions being formed at home. On one side were the loyal Lancastrians, led by Henry VI's Queen, Margaret of Anjou; on the other, the Yorkists, led by the Duke of York (a grandson of Edward III in the male line and of Roger Mortimer in the female) with the powerful support of Richard Nevill, Earl of Warwick ('Warwick the Kingmaker').

The civil wars that erupted in 1455 were not, in fact, called the 'Wars of the Roses' until 300 years later and, lest it be thought that England was torn apart by civil strife, the battles of the long war only accounted for 13 days' fighting. However, the name neatly sums up the struggle between the Red Rose of Lancaster and the White Rose of York. During 30 turbulent years, the English crown changed hands six times.

First, the Duke of York made a bid for the regency. He captured Henry VI at the first Battle of St Albans in 1455, but the Lancastrians were able to drive the Duke of York and his henchman, Warwick the Kingmaker, into exile at the Battle of Ludlow in 1459. The following year, however, Warwick recaptured Henry VI (who became little more than a symbol of kingship) at Northampton and the Duke of York was declared heir to the throne in October, only to be killed by Margaret of Anjou's northern army at Wakefield on the last day of 1460. In the second Battle of St Albans a few weeks later, the

Queen regained her husband, but failed to recapture London.

York's son, Edward, was now the champion of the White Rose and his objective was no less than the crown. Warwick adopted this aim and the Yorkist claimant was duly declared King Edward IV in Parliament in March 1461; Margaret was routed at Towton in the same month. Edward IV was thanked by the Commons for assuming the crown as the true heir of the murdered Richard II (1377-1399).

Unexpectedly the Red Rose bloomed again nine years later under the ubiquitous Warwick. The scheming Kingmaker had become dissatisfied with his protégé Edward IV and decided to transfer his sympathies to the Lancastrian cause. Warwick drove Edward IV into exile in October 1470 and then dragged the pathetic Henry VI out of the Tower of London to place him on the throne once more. This strange state of affairs lasted only six months after which Edward IV returned with a vengeance. Warwick was killed at Barnet and the Lancastrians under Queen Margaret were soundly defeated at the decisive Battle of Tewkesbury on 4 May 1471.

This time the House of York took no chances: Prince Edward, the Lancastrian heir was killed while his mother, Margaret of Anjou, was imprisoned and Henry VI himself could well have been murdered in the Tower (though it was said that he died 'of pure displeasure and melancholy'). Edward IV

resumed his reign, exploiting conciliar government, restoring the royal coffers, extending the crown lands and feudal rights. He also managed to keep overmighty subjects in their place, with the possible exception of his own brother, Richard of Gloucester.

Upon the death of Edward IV in 1483, his 12-year-old son, Edward V, was proclaimed King, but before he was crowned, the youth and his younger brother were thrown into the Tower, declared bastards and supposedly murdered. Richard of Gloucester, who was crowned Richard III (1483-1485) in July, was long considered the villain of the piece, but defenders of this much-maligned monarch argue that not only was he a distinguished soldier and administrator in the north and a loyal servant of his brother Edward IV, but also that the murderer of the two boys has never been known for certain and probably never will be.

Whatever the verdict of history, Richard III soon found himself faced by opposition from disaffected Yorkists and Lancastrians alike. The death of his only son in 1484 further weakened Richard's position; the following year the exiled Lancastrian heir, Henry Tudor, landed near Milford Haven to begin a campaign which culminated in victory on Bosworth Field. The two Roses were conveniently cross-fertilized following the Battle of Bosworth when the victorious Henry Tudor, of the House of Lancaster, married Elizabeth of York, daughter of Edward IV.

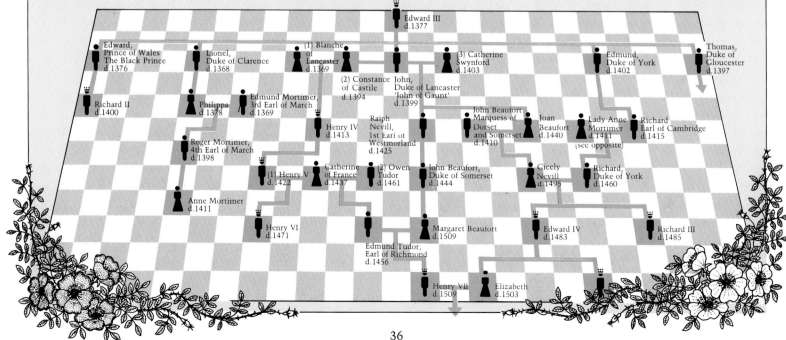

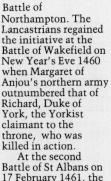

FAMILY WAR The family tree (BELOW LEFT) illustrates the factions and the map (RIGHT) the principal battles in the 30-year struggle from 1455 to 1485, later known as the 'Wars of the Roses'.

At the first Battle of St Albans on 29 May 1455, Richard, Duke of York prevailed over the Lancastrians and took Henry VI prisoner. The Yorkists were, however, routed at Ludlow on 12 and 13 October 1459. Henry VI was captured again, though, by Warwick 'the Kingmaker' at the Battle of Northampton. The Lancastrians regained the initiative at the Battle of Wakefield on New Year's Eve 1460 when Margaret of Anjou's northern army outnumbered that of Richard, Duke of York, the Yorkist claimant to the throne, who was killed in action.

At the second Battle of St Albans on 17 February 1461, the Lancastrians retrieved Henry VI from the clutches of Warwick the Kingmaker. However, the same month, Richard, Duke of York's son, Edward (soon to be Edward IV) defeated the Welsh Lancastrians at the Battle of Mortimer's Cross.

At the decisive Battle of Towton on 29 March 1461, Edward IV crushed the Lancastrians. This was possibly the biggest conflict ever fought on British soil, involving 50,000 people.

At the Battle of Barnet on Easter Sunday, 14 April 1471, the treacherous Kingmaker was killed fleeing from a fiasco in which the Lancastrians scored an 'own goal' by attacking each other in the mist. Edward IV secured his throne by extinguishing the Lancastrian cause at the Battle of Tewkesbury on 4 May 1471, after which Margaret of Anjou was captured and Henry VI put out of his misery.

Finally, the Lancastrian claimant Henry Tudor defeated and killed Richard III at the Battle of Bosworth on 22 August 1485. Tudor became Henry VII and the Middle Ages were over.

▬▬▬	Henry VI's route, June-July 1460
▬ ▬ ▬	Lancastrian movements, Nov 1460-Feb 1461
▬▬▬	Yorkist advance, June-July 1460
▬ ▬ ▬	Duke of York's march north, Dec 1460
▬▬▬	Edward IV's movements, Feb-Mar 1461
▬ ▬ ▬	Henry VII's route to Bosworth, Aug 1485

LEFT The character of **Richard III** was so blackened in the Tudor age, notably by William Shakespeare ('And every tale condemns me for a villain'), that it is difficult to arrive at any clear conclusion. There is no contemporary evidence to suggest that he was a hunchback; Lady Desmond recalled him as 'the handsomest man in the room...very well made'. It has been suggested that Richard murdered the two **Princes in the Tower** (FAR LEFT) but there is no evidence to support this theory.

The Tudor Dynasty

The Tudor kings and queens are among the best monarchs England has ever had. The shrewd Henry VII (1485-1509), the mighty Henry VIII (1509-1547) and the majestic Elizabeth I (1558-1603) were all outstanding rulers. It was an age of national glory and expansion. At the same time, the people's own representatives in Parliament increased their power.

The 15th century had seen constant uncertainty and agitation over long periods as to the nature of monarchy. The very legitimacy of the king had been called into question with no less than five depositions (Henry VI twice, Edward IV once, Edward V and Richard III). By contrast, in the 16th century the English monarchy was at its strongest and most stable. The Tudors were the ablest of all the royal dynasties.

Henry Tudor, crowned Henry VII (1485-1509), is often considered a Renaissance ruler but he looked more of a medieval figure. His face, with its deep-set eyes, is a clue to his character — watchful, secretive, cautious and scheming. The two main preoccupations of this cunning Welshman were money and the survival of his dynasty. Mean and greedy he may have been, but he undoubtedly controlled the nation's finances with great skill. Henry VII's rule was both personal and constitutional.

Henry VII secured the Tudor dynasty by executing Edward, Earl of Warwick (nephew of Edward IV and Richard III), and also dealing harshly with the Yorkist 'pretenders' Lambert Simnel and Perkin Warbeck. He arranged good marriages for his children, planning for England's eventual union with Scotland by marrying his daughter Margaret to James IV, King of the Scots. In 1501 Henry VII's elder son Arthur, Prince of Wales, was married to Catherine of Aragon, who was given away at the service by her brother-in-law and future husband, Henry. The teenaged bridegroom bragged about having been 'in

ABOVE **Henry VII**'s face, with its deep-set eyes, is a clue to his character: watchful, secretive, cautious and scheming. After he had gained the throne at the Battle of Bosworth in 1485, this cunning Welshman united the Houses of York and Lancaster by marrying Elizabeth of York, eldest daughter of Edward IV, and secured the Tudor dynasty by executing his wife's cousin Edward, Earl of Warwick (nephew of both Edward IV and Richard III). He also planned for England's union with Scotland by marrying his daughter Margaret to James IV, King of Scots, in 1501.
RIGHT The six wives of Henry VIII are usually remembered by the mnemonic 'Divorced, Beheaded, Died; Divorced, Beheaded, Survived'. 1. Henry's first marriage to his former sister-in-law, **Catherine of Aragon** (1485-1536), were eventually 'utterly dissolved by Act of Parliament in 1534 because she failed to produce a male heir. Catherine's last letter to Henry ended: 'Lastly, I make this vow, that mine eyes desire you above all things'.

2. **Anne Boleyn** (1507-1536) was the mother of the future Elizabeth I, who was conceived before Anne's marriage. The son she bore the King was stillborn at Greenwich in January 1536. Later that year Anne was obliged to lay her 'very little neck' on the block at Tower Green; the swordsman was paid £23 for his trouble.

3. Henry's favourite Queen was the delicate **Jane Seymour** (c 1509-1537) who died shortly after giving birth to the longed-for male heir, the future Edward VI, in 1537. Her coronation, postponed because of the plague, never took place.

Spain' on his wedding night but the match would not appear to have been consummated before Arthur's death the following year.

The larger-than-life personality of Henry VIII (1509-1547) is famous, or infamous, world-wide. When so much of history has been forgotten, 'Bluff King Hal' is remembered for his vast figure, six wives and despotic rule. With his ruthless egotism he created a lasting image (aided by Holbein's great portraits) of the sovereign who made the monarchy more powerful than ever. Un-

BELOW **Henry VIII** carried through a major constitutional revolution whereby the powers of Church and State were united. He broke with Rome, set up the Church of England and dissolved the monasteries. The athletic young scholar was transformed into a cruel and capricious bully of outsize proportions (judging by his armour, Henry's waist increased by 17 inches in five years), and yet he remained very much in control of the power game until his death, aged 58, from syphilis.

LEFT Henry VIII was effectively the founder of the Royal Navy. In 1545, by which time he was a gross spectacle, the King had himself carried on a chair down to   in Portsmouth in order to direct naval operations against the French. There he witnessed his favourite warship, the *Mary Rose*, pride of the fleet, sink in the Solent and is said to have heard heard the cries of the drowning. A combination of poor handling and overloading seems to have been the cause of the 130ft-long *Mary Rose's* descent into the seabed; as many as 700 soldiers and sailors (almost twice the proper complement) were on board and less than 40 survived.

4. **Anne of Cleves** (1516-1557), Henry VIII's fourth wife, was so unlike her portraits (from which she had been chosen) that the King asked his courtiers if they had brought him the 'Flanders Mare'. The marriage was annulled in 1540 after only seven months.

5. **Catherine Howard** (c 1521-1542), Henry VIII's fifth wife, was the promiscuous niece of the King's righthand man, the Duke of Norfolk. Like her cousin, Anne Boleyn, Catherine was beheaded for adultery.

6. The homely **Catherine Parr** (1512-1548), the sixth wife with whom Henry VIII ended his days in comparative calm, had already had two husbands before she married the King.

4

5

6

fortunately, the popular image held now of Henry VIII is as he was towards the end of his days: syphilitic and so obese that machines with pulleys had to hoist him up into the saddle. In his prime, though, he represented the ideal of a Renaissance prince: he was a scholar, poet, musician (writing *Greensleeves*) and sportsman. He was popular and genial, far from the unpredictable bully he became in later years.

The Pope's refusal to grant Henry VIII a divorce from his Queen Catherine of Aragon caused the King to break with Rome and to declare himself Head of the Church of England. Ironically, he had earlier received the title of Defender of the Faith from Rome in recognition of his learned criticism of Luther. The myth tells how Henry VIII then plunged headlong into despotic tyranny, but

the truth is rather different. Henry VIII was not, in fact, a dictator, rather he was a careful student of the law and constitution. The revolutionary changes whereby the Church was subordinated to the State were effected through Parliament and with an overwhelming measure of parliamentary support. The consequences were to increase the power of the monarchy in the short term, certainly; in the long run, however, it was the efficiency of the state that benefited most.

The Dissolution of the Monasteries (1536) in effect 'nationalized' about one-third of Church land and revenue. Part of the proceeds went on building up the navy and the fortifications round the southern coast; Henry VIII can be regarded as the founder of the Royal Navy. He took a particularly keen interest in military engineering and naval

shipbuilding, finding Greenwich Palace a convenient spot from which to visit burgeoning shipyards.

It was at Greenwich that Henry VIII first met Anne Boleyn whom he married in 1533 in the hope of having a son. He celebrated his new love in verse:

'Now unto my lady
Promise to her I make
From all others only
To her I me betake'

The King's passion for this bewitching creature (born with an extra breast and an extra finger) faded when a son was stillborn in 1536; he promptly sent her to the block on a trumped-up charge of adultery. Henry VIII's third wife, the delicate Jane Seymour, of whom he was especially fond, did produce the son he longed for but she died a few days

LEFT **Elizabeth I**, Henry VIII's daughter by Anne Boleyn, was a highly intelligent woman endowed with scholarship, a taste for music and a gift for statecraft. She staged a splendid regal show (owning 2,000 dresses); during her reign, which saw great naval triumphs and the flowering of the English Renaissance, the monarchy was gloriously popular. The 'Virgin Queen' never married and used the prospect of marriage as a diplomatic lever. She died, aged 69, of infected tonsils, at Richmond Palace.

ABOVE **Sir Francis Drake**, the celebrated Elizabethan 'sea-dog', was knighted by Elizabeth I at Deptford in 1581 following his circumnavigation of the world. Once little more than a pirate on the Spanish Main, he ended up as an admiral and Member of Parliament for Plymouth. His most famous exploits were the 'singeing of the King of Spain's beard' in Cadiz Harbour in 1587 and the defeat of the Spanish Armada in the following year.

ABOVE **Sir Walter Raleigh** was a multi-talented favourite of Elizabeth I. He distinguished himself as a navigator, explorer, military and naval commander and author. He was knighted in 1584, but fell foul of James I who sent him to the Tower.

later. Next Henry VIII married Anne of Cleves, whom he found so unlike her portraits that he asked his courtiers if they had brought him the 'Flanders Mare'. This union was swiftly annulled to enable Catherine Howard, niece of the scheming Duke of Norfolk, to become wife number five. Like Anne Boleyn, Catherine Howard was beheaded on Tower Green and so Henry VIII ended his days in comparative domestic harmony with Catherine Parr.

Throughout his reign Henry VIII was well served by an ambitious breed of 'new men'. These new wealthy magnates, many of them rewarded with monastic lands, were tied to the Tudor monarchy by gratitude and had to be careful to retain royal favour and avoid overreaching themselves. Cardinal Wolsey, originally a butcher's boy from Ipswich, did

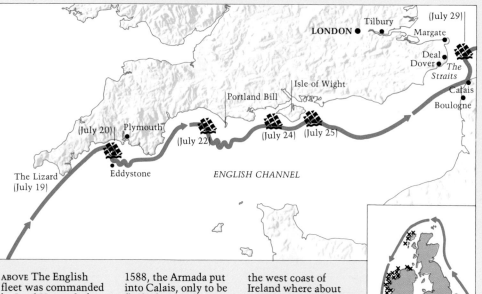

RIGHT **Mary I**, Henry VIII's daughter by Catherine of Aragon, was the first woman to rule England in her own right. In trying to burn out the heresy of Protestantism she succeeded merely in damaging Catholicism.

himself rather too well for the King's taste; his riverside palace at Hampton Court was duly expropriated when the Cardinal failed to secure an annulment of Henry's marriage to Catherine of Aragon. Thomas More, the King's one-time mentor, would not approve of the break with Rome and was executed. Thomas Cromwell, an able manipulator of Parliament, was another of Henry's henchmen of humble origins to outlive his usefulness; the Anne of Cleves fiasco was his final undoing. And even Henry VIII's last righthand man, the Duke of Norfolk, fell foul of the King, only being saved from the block by Henry's death.

ABOVE The English fleet was commanded by Lord Howard of Effingham during the crisis caused by the Spanish Armada. After a running battle along the Channel in July 1588, the Armada put into Calais, only to be flushed out and soundly defeated. The English Navy pursued the Armada north; the Spanish ships were swept by a storm on to the west coast of Ireland where about 10,000 Spaniards were butchered. Only 53 out of the 132 ships returned to Spain.

Henry VIII maintained his grip on power to the end. He kept the factions circling in suspense around his young son, the future Edward VI, as he planned the Protestant succession. Henry finally died at Whitehall on 28 January 1547, aged 58. When the coffin reached Windsor, after being worried by dogs at Syon, it burst open and, according to one witness, 'all the pavement of the church was with the fat and the corrupt and putrefied blood foully imbued'.

The King had wished each of his children in turn to wear the crown — Edward, Mary and Elizabeth — and so it was to be. The precocious Edward VI (1547-1553), however, regarded his sisters as illegitimate and before he died, aged only 16, expressed himself in favour of the scheme to put his cousin Lady Jane Grey (the ill-fated Nine Days Queen) on the throne.

Mary I (1553-1558) was the first woman to rule England in her own right. She was small, determined and stubborn, with a deep voice and an authoritarian manner. A devout Catholic married to the Spanish King, Philip II, she regarded her father's Reformation with loathing; Protestantism was a deviation that literally had to be burnt out. This uncompromising approach was more suited to Spain than England and resulted in her becoming hated; one Shropshire Protestant is said to have died 'through joy' on learning the news of 'Bloody Mary's' death in 1558. Catholicism as the main religion in England died with her. Mary's refusal to bend her principles had resulted in a loss of the crown's authority and power. The damage done to the monarchy, however, was only temporary and swiftly repaired by Mary's successor who was a mistress of the political art.

'Though God hath raised me high,' said Elizabeth I (1558-1603) in her last address to the Commons, 'yet this I count the glory of my crown: that I have reigned with your loves'. Her main task at the outset of her reign was to recover national unity. The return to Protestantism was accepted, but she resisted further changes in the direction of Puritanism. Together with her wise ministers, Lord Burghley and his son Robert Cecil, she thought always in terms of the central well-being of the state and its long-term interests. Despite the pressure put upon her by Parliament, she refused to marry.

'The Virgin Queen' was a splendid sovereign presiding over a glorious chapter of English history which included the defeat of the mighty Spanish Armada in 1588. Spain's power, and the controlling of it, was the key to Elizabethan foreign policy. With Elizabeth I, the cult of monarchy achieved its apotheosis; she was immortalized in Spenser's *Faerie Queene* and by the miniaturist Nicholas Hilliard. The Elizabethan view of monarchy was superbly expressed by Shakespeare, notably in *Henry V* where the hero-king cares for all his people.

When it came to the agonizing affair of Mary, Queen of Scots, though the responsibility remained Elizabeth's, the decision to execute her was virtually taken out of the English Queen's hands by the Council. Under the Tudor dynasty the monarchy was taken a stage further along the path to a strong central government by means of a compact, subservient Royal Council. For all her glory and fame, Elizabeth was bound to leave the monarchy less powerful (and less rich) than it had been under her father and grandfather. Indeed, the Tudor period saw the transition from medieval monarchy, where government was the King's personal affair, to the more modern idea where the role of monarch is to be the representative of society.

The Stuart Monarchy

The priggish James VI of Scotland, son of Mary, Queen of Scots, succeeded his cousin Elizabeth I on the English throne as James I of England in 1603. The Stuart dynasty had many fine qualities but they lacked both luck and money. The 'Divine Right of Kings', exercised by James and his son Charles I (1625-1649), and religious differences led to clashes with Parliament.

Until just before Elizabeth's death at Richmond in 1603, it was not clear who would become the next monarch. She finally chose Mary, Queen of Scots' son, James VI of Scotland, who thus became James I of England (1603-1625) and the country was spared the evils of a disputed succession. Smug, pedantic, ungainly, with a dribbling mouth, stained clothes, soft white hands and a penchant for male favourites, James I may appear an unattractive figure but he was not without ability as a statesman. He wanted a real union with Scotland and was tolerant of Catholics. However the 'Wisest Fool in Christendom' chose to adopt the Divine Right of Kings as a source of power; this conjured up images of monarchical absolutism that provided Parliamentarians with a reason for fighting the Civil War.

The Tudors had strengthened the constitutional position of Parliament by making full use of it as a support; their social, economic, religious and foreign policies had, however, enriched the country gentry and merchant classes, giving a new importance to the House of Commons. These slow changes would inevitably have led to a conflict between the House of Stuart and Parliament, but the conflict might never have assumed the proportions it did — plunging the country into Civil War, sending one King to the scaffold and another into exile — had the Stuarts not been so chronically short of money. Nevertheless, matters were not improved by the Stuart kings and the Commons being on opposite sides in the religious controversy that loomed so large in 17th-century Britain.

Whereas Parliament was theoretically supposed to meet on great occasions only, to vote money for wars (which the Stuarts could not afford) and other national emergencies, the Stuarts were obliged to call it frequently to ask for subsidies towards ordinary expenditure. These sittings gave Parliament plenty of opportunities to criticize the King's government and, in particular, to demand the redress of grievances in the ecclesiastical field. To avoid calling Parliament and being faced with such grievances, the crown looked for ways of increasing its ordinary revenue, which inevitably caused further grievances for Parliament to redress. And so relations with the crown gradually deteriorated.

Sadly, James I's stylish elder son, Prince Henry, predeceased him and the throne passed in 1625 to the younger son, Charles, who was fatally flawed with the weaknesses of being deceitful and obstinate. Moreover, his marriage to the Catholic Henrietta Maria of France proved unpopular with his Protestant subjects, especially as she was prone to interfere in matters of state. For all his faults, Charles I (1625-1649) was a conscientious, dignified, humane monarch.

In 1629 Charles I decided to end his years of wrestling with the House of Commons by dissolving his third Parliament. For the next 11 years, with the help of Archbishop Laud and Thomas Wentworth, Earl of Strafford, Charles I governed without Parliament. This so-called 'Rule of Thorough' involved a number of harsh taxation measures. It finally ground to a halt when Charles I did not have enough money to put down the troubles in Scotland caused by the new prayer book.

In 1640 Charles I was obliged to go begging to Parliament, who took full advantage of their power. Poor Strafford was condemned for treason by a Bill of Attainder and, with the King's lamentable consent, executed. Following the 'Grand Remonstrance' of November 1641, Charles I belatedly agreed to many of the reforms demanded by Parliament but baulked when moves were made to control the army. Foiled in his attempt to arrest the 'Five Members' who headed the opposition to the crown, Charles left London in January 1642. Civil War was inevitable.

LEFT **James I** was fortunate to escape being blown up when he opened Parliament in 1605. The Gunpowder Plot, hatched by Catholics, was foiled when Guido Fawkes was discovered guarding a pile of faggots in the vaults of Parliament on 5 November.

Bates · Robert Winter · Christopher Wright · John Wright · Thomas Percy · Guido Fawkes · Robert Catesby · Thomas Winter

Parlament House

BELOW The diminutive figure of **Charles I**, who was only 4ft 7in tall, is depicted here against the backdrop of Parliament. In 1512 a great fire had consumed most of the Palace of Westminster, sparing the Great Hall where coronation banquets, royal lyings-in-state and state trials — including Charles's own — took place. For 11 years, from 1629 to 1640, Charles I governed without Parliament; when he was financially obliged to call it again, Civil War was inevitable.

Tumbled Crown: the Civil Wars

In the Civil War which began in 1642, the Royalists (or 'Cavaliers') fought for Charles I and for High Anglicanism; the Parliamentarians (or 'Roundheads') for Parliament and for Puritanism. After the Parliamentary victory, Charles I was executed in 1645 and for the first and only time in her history England experimented with republicanism under Oliver Cromwell.

The English Civil War was not the 'class struggle' which has sometimes been depicted, but a conflict over religious and political differences. The Royalists, or 'Cavaliers', fought for Charles I, the Parliamentarians, or 'Roundheads', for Parliament; but few of the King's supporters would have wished to see Parliament abolished and, on the whole, the Roundheads were also monarchists. The Cavaliers fought for High Anglicanism, the Roundheads for Puritanism, but again the difference in beliefs was not very great. It is one of the curiosities of history that both sides in the Civil War claimed to be fighting

LEFT **Oliver Cromwell** made his name leading the cavalry in the Civil War. He assumed the style of 'Lord Protector' of the Commonwealth in 1653 and ruled virtually as a dictator.

for the same thing: to maintain the fundamental laws of England against arbitrary power and to defend the Protestant religion.

While the larger landowners outside the peerage (the class which produced the Parliamentarians Pym and Hampden) tended to be Roundheads, 90 of the 120 peers were for the King. The smaller country squires on the whole supported the King, although Oliver Cromwell — a landowner from Huntingdon — did not count himself among their number. There were paradoxical exceptions to every rule, but the merchants and the urban middle classes were generally staunch Parliamentary supporters. The strongly Protestant eastern counties and London were for Parliament; the north and west were for the King.

When the Civil War began in August 1642, Charles I's objective was to take London. The Parliamentarian Army under Essex failed to stop him at Edgehill in October (the first battle of the Civil War), but the dashing Cavalier Prince Rupert, Charles I's nephew, was held by the London Train Bands at Turnham Green the following month. The King then withdrew to his headquarters at Oxford. Although he failed to take London, the early years of the Civil War went well for Charles I. In 1643 there were Royalist victories in the north, the east and in the west, where the Cornishmen captured Bristol.

The Parliamentarians now decided to go on the offensive, negotiating the Solemn League and Covenant with the Scots to whom they promised the prospect of a strongly Protestant, even Presbyterian England. In the north, with Scots help, the Roundheads gained their first major victory at Marston Moor in 1644. They were less successful in the West, surrendering Lostwithiel, while the Scots Cavaliers, under Montrose, began to make their presence felt in the Highlands.

Until this stage of the Civil War, the Parliamentarians had not benefited from inspiring leadership. The 'Self-Denying Ordinance' of 1644 to 1645 was put into operation in the hope of removing such amateurish and ambitious generals as Lords Exeter and Manchester. A more professional approach was called for, hence the formation of the New Model Army. This body of 20,000 men was under the command of Sir Thomas Fairfax, but Oliver Cromwell was beginning to prove himself as leader.

The New Model Army defeated Charles I at the decisive Battle of Naseby in June 1645 and the Cavaliers suffered more major reverses at Langport in the west and at Philiphaugh in Scotland. The King had no option but to surrender at Newark in May 1646; the 'first' Civil War was at an end. Charles I's only hope was that the Parliamentarians would now fall out among themselves; this they proceeded to do. In 1647, as the King tried to play them against each other, Parliament tried to disband the New Model Army without pay whereupon Cromwell, siding with his soldiers, decided to take matters into his own hands. Charles I became a pawn of the army after being seized at Holdenby (or Holmby) House in Northamptonshire, though he would not accept their proposals. He managed to escape to the Isle of Wight, but he was later imprisoned at Carisbrooke Castle, where he continued to play for time.

The 'second' Civil War (1648) was provoked by Charles's unprincipled attempt to enlist the help of the Scottish Presbyterians. Risings on the King's behalf around the country were soon stamped out, and Cromwell crushed the invading Scots at Preston in August 1648. The King's time was running out; Cromwell had had enough of Parliamentary dalliance and, following a purge, his 'Rump' Parliament proceeded with the trial and execution of Charles I.

For all his weaknesses, the 'Royal Martyr' did not lack courage at the end. On 30 January 1649 Charles I stepped out on to the scaffold through a window of the Banqueting House in Whitehall. He had been charged with treason 'in the name of the people of England', but in reality it was a military junta who sent him to the block. 'And so I die a martyr for my people', the King said, 'and I pray that God will not lay it to their charge'.

After the King's execution, Cromwell set to work unifying Ireland and Scotland, while establishing dictatorial republicanism in the name of the Commonwealth. In 1651, the young Charles II's invading army was routed at Worcester, the Civil War's last battle which was described by Cromwell as 'the crowning mercy'. Afterwards the King escaped abroad, but in the vacuum caused by the formidable Cromwell's death, Charles II was later invited back and crowned. As the German historian Ranke observed, Britain could not be governed save by a monarch.

In August 1642 Charles I raised his standard at Nottingham, following his abandonment of London in January when he had failed in his attempt to arrest Pym, Hampden, Haslerigg, Strode and Holles — the five leading members of the Commons in the 'Long Parliament'. To begin with, the Parliamentary side in the Civil War were hoping for a negotiated settlement but in 1644 Parliament went into the attack, enlisting the help of the Scots Presbyterians, and forming the New Model Army under Fairfax and Cromwell. In May 1646 Charles I surrendered to the Scots at Newark and the 'first' Civil War was at an end. The King enlisted Scottish support in the 'second' Civil War but this was easily won by Cromwell and Fairfax in 1648. After the King's execution in 1649, the Parliamentarians crushed resistance in Ireland, Scotland and, finally, achieved the conclusive victory against the King's son, Charles II, at Worcester in 1651.

THE BATTLE OF PRESTON
Fought from 17 to 19 August 1648, this was a comprehensive defeat of the Royalists by Oliver Cromwell.

THE BATTLE OF NASEBY
Fought on 14 June 1645, this saw the extinction of Charles I's hope of victory in the Civil War. The Royalists, out-numbered two to one, were overwhelmingly defeated by the New Model Army.

THE BATTLE OF WORCESTER
Fought on 3 September 1651, and the last battle of significance in the Civil War, this was described by Cromwell as 'the crowning mercy'. Charles II managed to escape.

THE BATTLE OF EDGEHILL
The first battle of the Civil War was fought on 23 October 1642.

THE BATTLE OF MARSTON MOOR
Fought on 2 July 1644, this was a brief and bloody defeat for the Royalist Army by the Parliamentarians and Scots. The brief battle effectively lost the north for Charles I.

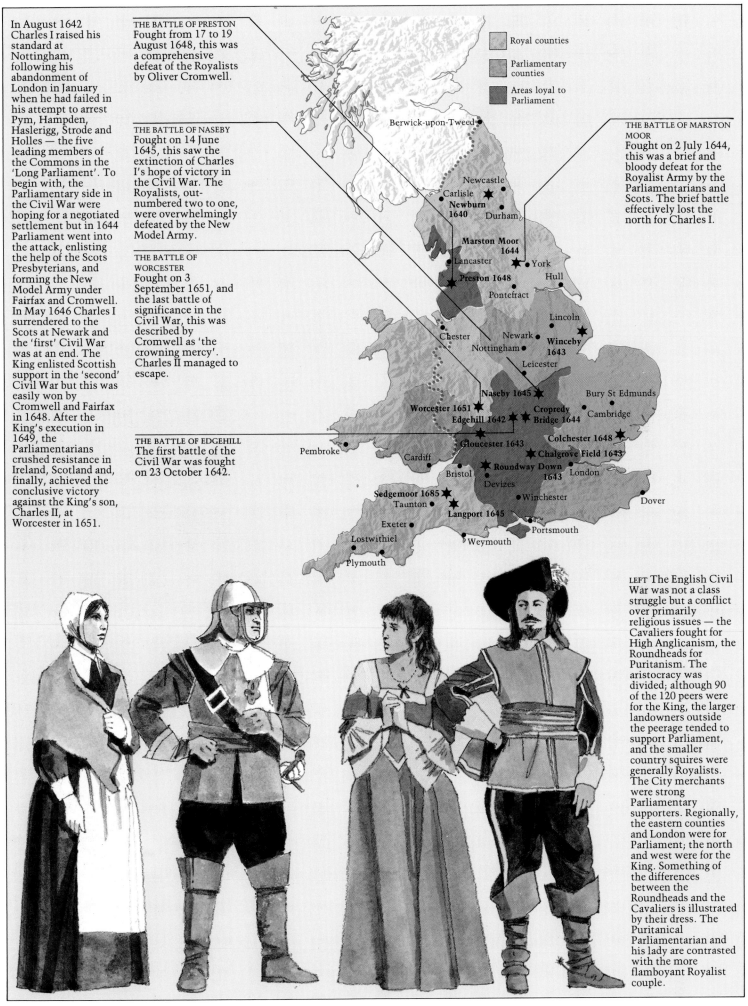

Royal counties

Parliamentary counties

Areas loyal to Parliament

Berwick-upon-Tweed

Newcastle
Carlisle
Newburn 1640
Durham
Marston Moor 1644
Lancaster
Preston 1648
York
Hull
Pontefract
Lincoln
Chester
Newark
Winceby 1643
Nottingham
Leicester
Naseby 1645
Bury St Edmunds
Worcester 1651
Cropredy Bridge 1644
Cambridge
Edgehill 1642
Colchester 1648
Gloucester 1643
Chalgrove Field 1643
Pembroke
Cardiff
Roundway Down 1643
London
Bristol
Devizes
Winchester
Dover
Sedgemoor 1685
Taunton
Langport 1645
Portsmouth
Exeter
Lostwithiel
Weymouth
Plymouth

LEFT The English Civil War was not a class struggle but a conflict over primarily religious issues — the Cavaliers fought for High Anglicanism, the Roundheads for Puritanism. The aristocracy was divided; although 90 of the 120 peers were for the King, the larger landowners outside the peerage tended to support Parliament, and the smaller country squires were generally Royalists. The City merchants were strong Parliamentary supporters. Regionally, the eastern counties and London were for Parliament; the north and west were for the King. Something of the differences between the Roundheads and the Cavaliers is illustrated by their dress. The Puritanical Parliamentarian and his lady are contrasted with the more flamboyant Royalist couple.

The Crown Restored: the Later Stuarts

The Stuarts were restored to the monarchy in 1660 in the attractive person of Charles II (1660-1685), who presided over a charmingly dissolute and talented court. His tactless Catholic brother James II (1685-1688) was swiftly replaced in the 'Glorious Revolution' by his daughter Mary and her staunchly Protestant husband Prince William of Orange.

Charles II (1660-1685) was restored to the throne in May and shrewdly made the best of his opportunities after the long years of exile. The 'Merry Monarch' remains one of the most attractive sovereigns; charming, energetic and cultivated, he brought a stylishness to the monarchy. Physically he was a complete contrast to his diminutive father. Tall, strong and swarthy, Charles II's looks have been likened by the art historian David Piper to those of 'a cynical ageing Hollywood film star'.

Certainly he enjoyed the popularity of a star, whether fighting the Fire of London, going to the races or escorting his famous mistresses. He had no children by his plain Queen, Catherine of Braganza, but a string of bastards by such courtesans as Nell Gwynne, Louise de Kéroualle and Barbara Villiers. His first mistress, Lucy Walters, was the mother of the Duke of Monmouth, the leader of the rebellion in the west against James II (1685-1688) which was crushed at the Battle of Sedgemoor in 1685.

It would be a mistake to regard the Restoration Court as utterly dissolute. If Charles II and his courtiers were sometimes rather too frivolous, it should be remembered that they also helped to found the Royal Society (which elected Isaac Newton as a Fellow). Charles II's contemporaries included such luminaries as Wren and Dryden. For the last time in its history, the society of the British aristocracy was centred on the court. This was held at Whitehall and almost matched the splendour of Versailles in France.

As a ruler, Charles II benefited from the fact that the country, having experienced a republican dictatorship during the Commonwealth, was more ready to tolerate a growth of the royal prerogative after the Restoration than it was before the Civil War. That James II should so quickly throw away the advantage bequeathed to him by his brother remains a historical mystery. Hitherto James had seemed likely to be rather a competent monarch, but he may have depended more than he knew on Charles II's worldly wisdom.

Unfortunately James II was tactless and possessed even more than his father Charles I's share of obstinacy. Appointing Catholics to key positions proved a disastrous policy. The prospect of a Catholic dynasty dismayed his critics further; this arose when James II's Queen, Mary of Modena, bore him a son and heir. In fact, James II was not the Catholic bigot he was popularly supposed to be; he merely wanted to give his Catholic subjects some of their rights. He also suffered from be-

BELOW This charming cultivated, stylish Stuart was one of Britain's most attractive sovereigns. Nicknamed 'Old Rowley', after a procreative royal stallion, **Charles II** sired some 14 or 15 bastards by a string of mistresses. The earthy **Nell Gwynne** was the most popular.

ing regarded as the ally of the Irish — it is significant that *Lillibulero*, the song alleged to have sung him out of his three kingdoms, is about the schemes and machinations of one of his Irish henchman, Richard Talbot, Earl of Tyrconnell.

The settlement of the Glorious Revolution by the Bill of Rights in 1689 effectively extinguished the doctrine of Divine Right. It stated that James II (and VII of Scotland) had abdicated; it settled the succession on William III and Mary II and excluded Roman Catholics from the throne. The royal prerogative, which formed the basis of Stuart absolutism, was very greatly curtailed. Parliaments now had to be summoned at least every three years.

James II had sailed away from England aboard a fishing-smack in December 1688; two months later William III (1689-1702) and Mary II (1689-1694) were proclaimed King and Queen. William III was a Protestant Prince of the House of Orange (the son of Charles I's eldest daughter) who had married his cousin Mary, daughter of James II. As a foreigner who did not bother to understand the British, 'Dutch William', with his cold manner, was not popular. A European statesman of the first magnitude, he regarded his accession to the British throne as an important move on the European chessboard. The warmhearted Queen Mary did much to make up for her husband's lack of popularity with his British subjects, but she died of smallpox in 1694 and William continued to reign alone until his fatal riding accident at Hampton Court in 1702.

The last and least of the Stuarts, Queen Anne (1702-1714) had none of her sister Mary's attractive qualities. She was a tiresome woman: discontented, dull, spoilt, lazy, endlessly playing cards. In fairness, she suffered ill-health, a dreary husband, George of Denmark, and the loss of all her children. Paradoxically, her reign was a period of national glory thanks to the victories of the great Duke of Marlborough over the French, who had replaced the Spaniards as the main threat abroad.

The termagant Duchess of Marlborough was one of the two successive women favourites who strongly influenced Queen Anne. As it turned out, Anne's attachment to the 'Whig' Duchess and the 'Tory' Mrs Masham was instrumental in keeping the Queen and Parliament on speaking terms. In some ways her reign can be seen as a precursor of the modern parliamentary monarchy.

During Queen Anne's reign, Tory opinion swung in favour of the succession of the 'Old Pretender', her Catholic half-brother James Francis Edward. The Whigs, however, ensured that it would be the Protestant House of Hanover that acceded to the throne of Great Britain (as it was known following the Act of Union with Scotland in 1707).

LEFT **Queen Anne** succeeded her brother-in-law William III, who had previously ruled jointly with her sister Mary II. The last and in some ways the least of the Stuart sovereigns, Anne is portrayed here by Sir Godfrey Kneller in about 1654 with her son William, Duke of Gloucester. Young William lived much longer than any of the Queen's four other children but died aged 11 in 1700. Married to her unsatisfactory cousin, Prince George of Denmark, Anne also had no less than 12 stillbirths or miscarriages. The corpulent Queen may have suffered from porphyria; fond of cards, brandy and driving in a post-chaise, she was an unlikely figure to preside over a period of national glory.

BELOW Between 1500 and 1600 the population of London grew from about 40,000 to 300,000 despite such cataclysmic events as the Plague and the Fire. Charles II took charge of the fire-fighting during the fire, but it destroyed much of the City.

The House of Hanover

Although there were several Catholic heirs with a better claim, the succession to the English throne after Queen Anne (1702-1714) was vested in the Protestant House of Hanover descended from Charles I's niece, Sophia. The first two Georges were disliked because they were foreigners; 'Farmer' George III (1760-1820) was more popular than his son, George IV (1820-1830).

Until two months before Queen Anne's death in 1714, the heiress to the British throne was the Electress Sophia of Hanover, the daughter of Charles I's sister, the 'Winter' Queen of Bohemia. Then Sophia died, leaving her boorish and brutish son George to become the first Hanoverian monarch. While the majority of Englishmen gave their allegiance to the 'Illustrious House of Hanover and Protestant Succession', they really wanted the Protestant Succession without the House of Hanover, however illustrious; they had already had enough of foreign kings with Dutch William.

George I (1714-1727) did not make a good impression. Aged 54, heavy and uncouth,

RIGHT **George I** was a 54-year-old German soldier when he ascended the throne of Great Britain. He was a man of few words, all of them German, but in fairness it should be recorded that he was the patron of Handel.

this German soldier could not speak English and never bothered to learn. Instead of a Queen — his wife having been locked up after a sensational scandal involving the murder of her lover — George I brought with him two unprepossessing German mistresses who were christened 'the Maypole' and 'the Elephant' by his subjects. He was under an obligation to the Whigs for his throne and a period of Whig supremacy ensued, with the Tories tainted by the stigma of Jacobitism.

George I's lack of interest in English politics and his perpetual absence from Cabinet meetings (often caused by his sojourns in Hanover) led to a drastic curtailment of the royal prerogative. With the

BELOW Another German soldier, **George II** ('Old Gruff') had no time for 'bainting, blays or boetry', but displayed gallantry in leading his men into battle at the age of 60. 'I have lost my eldest son, but I was glad of it', said George II after 'Poor Fred' (George III's father) died from a cricket injury in 1751.

legitimate Stuart dynasty set aside, less emphasis could be placed on the divine nature of kingship — it is significant that the Georges ceased to 'touch' for the 'king's evil' — previously a custom whereby sufferers from scrofula could receive a laying-on of the royal hands in the hope of a cure. Under George I, in short, the monarchy was brought down to earth. Soon Sir Robert Walpole emerged as the 'Prime Minister' (a term only used opprobriously at first).

When Walpole brought the news of George I's death to the Prince of Wales in 1727, the far from fond son replied: 'Dat is vun beeg lie'. Unlike his father, George II (1727-1760) spoke English fluently (despite a very strong German accent), but he shared his father's passion for the military and was even more attached to his native land, Hanover.

The reign of George II saw further significant steps in the direction of the modern parliamentary monarchy. On more than one occasion, it was Parliament that decided which ministers George II should have, not the King himself, while the latter grumbled about 'that damn'd House of Commons'. For all his concerns in Germany, George II, a perky, peppery, punctilious man, took a lively interest in the spectacular overseas successes of his reign, such as the establishment of English power in India and the winning of Canada. He is always remembered as the last British monarch to lead his troops into battle — at Dettingen in 1743.

Quarrels between the King and the heir to the throne became an unfortunate tradition of the monarchy; there was certainly no love lost between George II and his wretched son 'Poor Fred' who predeceased him. George III

BELOW To quote the present Prince of Wales: 'The vulgar view of King **George III** is quite simply that he was mad, and to make matters worse, that he also succeeded in losing the American colonies. The fact that he ...was a great patron of the arts and sciences ...has been conveniently neglected'.

BELOW **George IV** acted as Prince Regent from 1811 until his father's death. By turns extravagant, selfish, cruel, witty and stylish, George IV was one of Britain's most unpopular monarchs. Queen Victoria, his niece, recollects sitting on his knee: 'Too disgusting, because his face was covered with grease paint'.

BELOW **William IV** George III's third son, failed to produce a surviving heir by his marriage to Adelaide of Saxe-Meiningen, though he had 10 bastards by the actress 'Mrs Jordan', (Dorothy Bland). The eccentric 'Sailor King' was prone to nod off during conversations, waking up with a start and an 'Exactly so, Ma'am'.

ABOVE A painting of George II at the Battle of Dettingen, 27 June 1743. The British, Austrian and Hanoverian armies conquered the French here.

BRIGHTON PAVILION 'It is as though St. Paul's had gone down to the sea and pupped', said Sydney Smith about George IV's multi-domed vision of the East at Brighton. Transformed first by Henry Holland in 1787 and then, in 1815 by John Nash, the exotic pleasure-dome is at once Chinese and Hindu, with a saucy dash of Tartar. This elevation shows Nash's elaboration of Holland's Classicism.

(1760-1820) therefore succeeded his grandfather. Unlike the first two Georges, 'Farmer George' was entirely English in outlook and soon became the most popular monarch since Charles II. Through his rustic habits and tours around the southern counties, George III got to know his humbler subjects in an unprecedented way. He originated the idea of the sovereign being a glorified country squire — a concept of monarchy universally accepted today but strikingly new in 18th-century England.

Although George III could be blamed for losing the American colonies, the policy with which he and Lord North provoked the revolution had the support of the great mass of English public opinion. Another criticism of George III's behaviour is that he attempted to play the absolute monarch. He was influenced by the egregious Bute — the last example in Britain of that extinct species, the royal favourite — who had taught him to

mistrust the Whig magnates. As the Whig party began to disunite once the Jacobite threat had receded, George III was able to build up his own group in Parliament, the 'King's Friends'. With the political situation confused, the King found it easier to impose his will on Parliament. 'The influence of the Crown has increased', declared Dunning in his famous resolution of 1780, 'is increasing and ought to be diminished'.

The rise of the younger Pitt led to the reduction of that influence and the process was accelerated by George III's madness, the result of that cruel hereditary disease, porphyria. After his first attack in 1788 he was never able to exert himself in public life. By the end of 1810, George III's insanity made it necessary for the Prince of Wales to be made Regent. Despite the vicissitudes of its monarchy, however, Britain emerged from the Napoleonic Wars of 1803 to 1815, with victories over the French at Trafalgar and

Organ.

Music Room.

Waterloo, as the world's greatest power.

The pleasure-loving Prince Regent, who became George IV (1820-1830), was too idle to make full use of what remained of the royal power, and so it continued to diminish. To his contemporaries George IV was an extremely unpopular monarch. They looked askance at his extravagance, his private life, his selfishness and petulance, his cruel treatment of his daughter, Charlotte, and the scandal of his attempt to bring a case against Queen Caroline, in Parliament, on the grounds of her alleged infidelities.

Some historians, however, would argue that George IV was the most intelligent and artistic monarch ever to sit upon the British throne. He made some magnificent additions to the nation's cultural heritage, giving the monarchy a suitably splendid background with his improvements to Buckingham Palace and Windsor Castle, the building of the now-vanished Carlton House and exotic Brighton Pavilion. Like another gifted king, Charles II, George IV was supremely stylish and was often the leader of the fashionable world. He also established a new and more informal relationship between the monarchy and the aristocracy. In spite of his shortcomings, the virtuous Mrs Fitzherbert never lost her regard for him, even after the break-up of their marriage. His record as King should also be credited with the first visits by a reigning British sovereign to Scotland and Ireland, since the 17th century.

By his disastrous official marriage to Caroline of Brunswick, George IV had only one child, Princess Charlotte, who died in 1817 after giving birth to a stillborn son. So, although George III had had nine sons and six daughters there was no legitimate grandchild to carry on the line. The ageing, bachelor, royal dukes were told to put aside their mistresses and marry suitable princesses in order to provide an heir to the throne. Of the three who eventually succeeded in having legitimate issue, the eldest was the Duke of Kent, who had a daughter born in 1819 — the future Queen Victoria.

Before the young Victoria could inherit the crown it passed to her elderly and childless uncle, William IV (1830-1837). The bluff 'Sailor King' had a curious past: he was reputed to have sworn like a deckhand, to have been arrested for brawling, frequently in debt and the victim of venereal disease in the West Indies. His lengthy and fruitful liaison with Mrs Jordan, the actress, was described as 'bathing in the river Jordan'. His brief reign, which always seems like an interregnum, was notable in that he gave his consent to Earl Grey, albeit reluctantly, to create enough new peers so that the Reform Bill would pass unchallenged through the House of Lords, and also in that he dismissed the government two years later — the last time a monarch exercised this constitutional right.

Gallery.

Salon.

Victoria: Queen-Empress

Princess Alexandrina Victoria, only child of the Duke of Kent (George III's fourth son) succeeded her uncle William IV (1830-1837), as Queen Victoria. During her reign, Britain became the most powerful nation in the world. The Queen's children intermarried with the Royal Houses of Europe, enabling her to operate an unrivalled intelligence network.

When Victoria became Queen at the age of 18 in 1837, the monarchy was at a low ebb. When she died, more than 60 years later, it stood higher in the affections of the British people than at any time since the reign of Elizabeth I. Her popularity had suffered a setback during the period of her seclusion following the death of the Prince Consort — a period which even saw the brief appearance in Britain of republicanism — but it later revived. To an extent, Victoria's success was due to the fact that she reigned when Britain was the most successful nation in the world, but it was also due to her own personality.

Queen Victoria is one of those figures who grows in stature the more that is known about her. Fresh examples of her kindness, her warm humanity and her good sense are constantly being found. The early 20th-century image of her as the terrifying 'Widow of Windsor', who harassed Mr Gladstone, made her ageing heir apparent metaphorically stand in the corner, and was renowned for the phrase 'We are not amused', now just seems the historian's equivalent of those grime-covered, hard-mouthed statues of the Great Queen visible in industrial towns. Such an image bears little resemblance to the real Victoria, whose smile was unusually sweet, whose voice was musical and whose sense of humour was such that, on solemn occasions, she often had difficulty in preventing herself from laughing. She sketched and painted competently, wrote copiously and dabbled skilfully in European diplomacy.

One of the advantages of a monarchy over a republic, is that a king or queen who has a long reign is able to accumulate political wisdom and experience over the years and pass it on to successive governments. This is particularly true of Queen Victoria, who at the end of her reign could speak with first-hand knowledge of political events which had happened when most of the leading politicians of the day were only schoolboys, or, in the case of Lord Rosebery, her penultimate Prime Minister, before he was born. Even Gladstone, at the time of his death, did not have such a long experience of government as had the Queen. When Campbell-Bannerman (the future Prime Minister) was Secretary of State for War in the 1890s, he took some schemes to the Queen for approval, explaining that they were new ones. 'No, Mr Bannerman', was the reply, 'Lord Palmerston proposed exactly the same thing to me in '52 and Lord Palmerston was wrong'.

As well as being able to impart her wisdom to others, Queen Victoria gained in wisdom herself over the years. Looking back, she realized that, at the beginning of her reign, she had been too strongly prejudiced in favour of the Whigs because of her affection for the avuncular Lord Melbourne. She learnt the lesson of the so-called 'Bedchamber Plot'. After 'Lord M.' had been defeated in Parliament in 1839, Sir Robert Peel was invited to form a Government but the Queen would not have her Whig ladies of the bedchamber replaced by Tories. Peel then refused to form a Government whereupon the Whigs returned to power for another two years. Also in 1839, the tactless young Queen made herself unpopular by her uncharitable treatment of Lady Flora Hastings, a lady-in-waiting whose illness of the stomach made her appear to be pregnant.

These youthful *gaffes*, constitutional or otherwise, were not to be repeated. The spell which Disraeli cast over the Queen naturally made her regret the defeat of the Tories in 1868 and 1880, but she managed to behave with constitutional propriety on each occasion. In 1880, believing Gladstone to be a 'half-mad firebrand' who had usurped the leadership of the Liberal Party, she went as far as she could go within the constitution to get one of the other Liberal leaders to form a Government — only agreeing to send for Gladstone when these attempts had failed.

Some credit for Queen Victoria's constitutional propriety must go to Prince Albert, whose influence over his wife was almost invariably for the good. Though a foreigner, he

ABOVE In the reign of Queen Victoria (1837-1901) Britain became the most powerful nation in the world. Although Britain had lost the American colonies in the 18th century, the Empire still embraced Canada, India, Australasia and most of Southern Africa. The most significant period of expansion followed the opening of the Suez Canal in 1869. Between 1870 and the First World War Britain almost doubled its imperial territories, with acquisitions in Africa, Burma, Malaya, Borneo and the Pacific Ocean. The leader in the 'new imperialism' was Benjamin Disraeli, who had Queen Victoria proclaimed 'Empress of India'.

RIGHT The image of the 'Great White Queen' is nicely expressed by this picture, *The Bible*, by R. Turner after T. J. Barker.

understood the British better than the British were prepared to understand him. He was thought to be an intriguer and was subjected to a campaign of abuse after Palmerston's resignation as Home Secretary at the end of 1853, in the mistaken belief that Albert had been responsible for it. It was ironic that the most virulent attacks came from the Radicals, when the Prince had shown himself to be well in advance of his time in his concern for improving working conditions.

Albert was a remarkable figure: statesman, architect, politician, estates manager and also Cambridge University's greatest Chancellor. His latest biographer, Robert Rhodes James, has pointed out that the Prince Consort was the nearest equivalent to Thomas Jefferson Britain has ever produced. The polymathic Prince's achievements included the Great Exhibition of 1851, the rescue of Cleopatra's Needle from Egypt, the initiation of the Victoria Cross, the prevention of duelling, the popularization of Christmas trees, the creation of the Royal Society of Arts and the reorganization of the Royal Household.

There is a widely-held belief that Albert deliberately goaded Victoria into disliking their eldest son, the Prince of Wales. This belief was probably due to the fact that an indiscretion on Albert's part, that may have been foolish, was followed soon afterwards by his death. Albert told the Queen of the Prince of Wales's first adventure with a woman — not a common occurence within early-Victorian family life — with the result that Victoria believed her husband's death to have been partly caused by her son's conduct. But like so much else about Queen Victoria, her relations with her eldest son have given rise to a great deal of legend. As the Prince of Wales's reputation for being a rake and the Queen's for being strait-laced both became magnified, it was assumed that the Prince must have been in perpetual disgrace.

As well as completing Buckingham Palace, Queen Victoria contributed to the saga of the royal residences by purchasing two estates, one on the Isle of Wight and another in Aberdeenshire, and building a country house on each — the Italianate Osborne and the Scottish Baronial Balmoral. The idea of the monarch leading a simple country life as an escape from the pomp and circumstance was, of course, nothing new, but Osborne and Balmoral were in parts of the country which had no traditional connections with the sovereign.

BELOW 'The Widow of Windsor', in old age, takes the air in the grounds of the castle in a donkey carriage.

The Queen Empress's youngest daughter, Princess Beatrice, looks on from under her parasol.

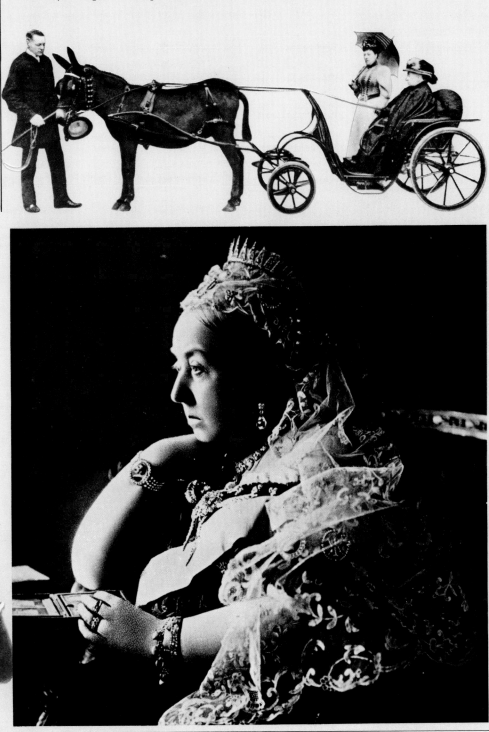

BELOW **Queen Victoria** and her husband, **Prince Albert**, were photographed at Windsor Castle on 1 May 1860. The multi-talented Albert, Prince of Saxe-Coburg and Gotha (1819-1861) was created Prince Consort in 1857. He died of typhoid a year-and-a-half after this photograph was taken.

RIGHT In 1897, when this photograph was taken, the Queen celebrated her Diamond Jubilee. 'I was much moved and gratified', she wrote after being tumultuously cheered to and from St. Paul's Cathedral on 22 June 1897 — 60 years after she had acceded to the throne.

The author of the idea of making Victoria 'Empress of India' was that arch-flatterer Disraeli. This exotic Tory rekindled imperialism in the 1870s, buying a controlling interest in the Suez Canal in 1875 and then piloting the Bill conferring the Imperial title on the Queen through Parliament in the face of violent Liberal opposition. The Empress herself protested in her diaries, underlining for emphasis, that 'it was her wish, as people will have it, that it has been forced upon her!'

Queen Victoria was proclaimed Empress of India on New Year's Day 1877 at the Imperial Assemblage; the ceremony included a Durbar on an unprecedented scale held at Delhi in the presence of 63 ruling Indian princes and some 300 great magnates. The proclamation itself took place on a vast open plain where ornate pavilions with canopies and hangings of red, white, blue and gold, had been erected. The Queen-Empress was not there in person. She always confined her travels to the continent where she rejoiced in the sobriquet of 'Grandmother of Europe'.

The Queen's international intelligence network was second to none. As her voluminous correspondence with her eldest daughter, the German Empress Frederick, shows, Queen Victoria could and would intervene directly with the affairs of many crowned heads of Europe. Her influence on European diplomacy was almost invariably for the good; on several occasions she managed to prevent or postpone major wars thanks to her unrivalled royal connections. As one of her ministers pointed out, the Queen selected throughout Europe the most intelligent member of each royal family, and 'on any question, domestic or foreign, which

arose, she obtained by letter an opinion'. As a diplomatist, she was difficult to equal.

Queen Victoria was least successful in her dealings with the Russians. 'Oh!' she once told Disraeli, 'If the Queen were a man she would like to go and give these Russians, whose word one cannot believe, such a beating!' She never forgave Tsar Alexander III for having brought about the overthrow of the young ruler of Bulgaria, 'dear Sandro' of Battenberg, a particular favourite of hers. 'He may be an Emperor', she remarked, 'but the Queen does not regard him as a gentleman'. There were moments when keeping the peace of Europe proved too much for its 'Grandmother': 'I am sick of all this horrid business of politics, and Europe in general', she once wrote to her eldest daughter, 'and think you will hear of me going with the children to live in Australia, and to think of Europe as the Moon!'

She never went to Australia, but took a lively interest in the responsible expansion of the British Empire. The Victorian age witnessed an enlightened colonial policy. In the year of the Queen's accession there were rebellions in Ontario and Quebec but by 1846 Canada was virtually self-governing. Similarly, the Australian colonies were given self-government a few years later. The new idea was to bind the colonies to the old country by freedom. Disraeli developed the concept of 'trusteeship', whereby more toleration was applied to native traditions. This was particularly significant in the wake of the Indian Mutiny. Queen Victoria took a characteristically humane attitude; she wrote to the first Viceroy of India: 'Lord Canning will easily believe how entirely the Queen shares

his feelings of sorrow and indignation at the un-Christian spirit shown — alas! to a great extent here — by the public towards Indians in general and towards sepoys without discrimination!'

Rudyard Kipling summed up the late-Victorian concept of Empire as 'the white man's burden'. It is nicely expressed in pictorial groups of Queen Victoria presenting the Bible to colonial chieftains. Britain did well out of the partition of Africa in the 1880s; by the end of the 19th century another three million square miles had been added to the Empire, including Nigeria, Kenya, Uganda, Nyasaland and Rhodesia. To the Africans, the Queen was the 'Great White Mother'. When the missionaries told Mutesa I, Kabaka of Buganda, that he would have to give up polygamy if he wished to be baptized, he is said to have replied: 'Give me Queen Victoria's daughter for my wife and I will promise to put away all of my wives'.

If Queen Victoria's Diamond Jubilee of 1897 was the apogee of the British Empire, leaks in the vessel were beginning to show by the end of her reign. The South African War between the British and the Boers was a suitably unsympathetic curtain-raiser to the new century. And lurking in the wings of the Boer War was the erratic figure of the Kaiser. He genuinely liked and admired England, and was intensely proud of being Queen Victoria's grandson. Indeed the 'Grandmother of Europe' died in his arms, but his failure to understand the *Entente Cordiale* between England and France eventually led to the cataclysmic conflict known as the 'Kaiser's War'.

RIGHT This family tree shows why Queen Victoria was known as the 'Grandmother of Europe'. Two of her sons and three of her grandsons became sovereigns.

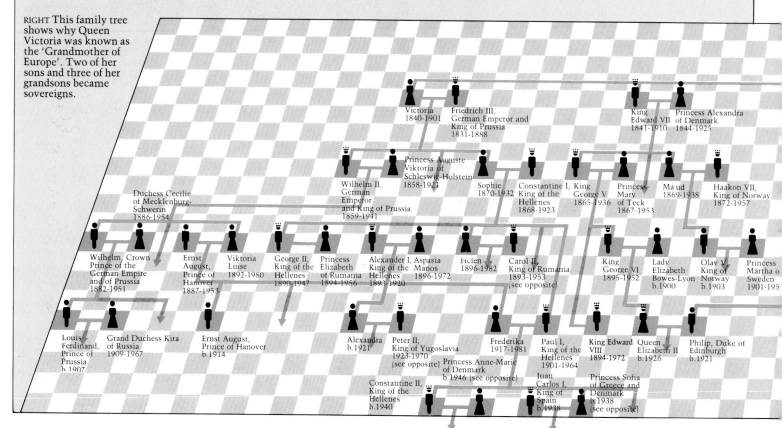

EUROPEAN ROYAL FAMILIES

This map shows 'Royal Europe', in the early 20th century. The **French** monarchy had come to an end in 1870 with the fall of the Second Empire. Emperor Nicholas II of **Russia** remained until the Revolution of 1917. In **Prussia**, Wilhelm II was still **German** Emperor. Until Germany's defeat in the First World War, there were also the German kingdoms of Bavaria, Hanover, Saxony and Wurttemberg.

The mighty **Austro-Hungarian** Empire, then ruled by Emperor Franz Joseph, also survived until the aftermath of the First World War. **Portugal** lost its monarchy in 1910. The Second World War accounted for the monarchies of **Italy, Bulgaria, Rumania, Yugoslavia,** and **Albania**. The **Greek** and **Spanish** monarchies have both had chequered histories; Constantine II was deposed in 1974 while Juan Carlos is on the throne today. Other surviving monarchies are: **Belgium, Denmark, Liechtenstein, Luxembourg, Monaco, the Netherlands, Norway, Sweden** and **the United Kingdom.**

EUROPEAN RELATIONS

This group photograph shows Edward VII with his royal guests and relations at Windsor in November 1907. They include: Kaiser Wilhelm II, his cousin (1); the Prince of Wales (2); Alfonso XIII of Spain (3); Queen Alexandra (4); Grand Duke Vladimir of Russia (4); Queen Victoria Eugenie of Spain, his niece (6); Prince Olav of Norway, his grandson, now Olav V (7); the King himself (8); Queen Amelie of Portugal (9).

Queen Victoria 1819-1901 — **Prince Albert of Saxe-Coburg and Gotha, The Prince Consort** 1819-1861

Prince Henry of Battenburg 1858-1896

Alice 1843-1878 — Ludwig IV, Grand Duke of Hesse & by Rhine d.1892 | Alfred, Duke of Edinburgh, reigning Duke of Saxe-Coburg and Gotha 1844-1900 | Grand Duchess Marie of Russia 1853-1920 | Helena 1846-1923 — Prince Christian of Schleswig-Holstein 1831-1917 | Issue extinct | Louise 1848-1939 — John Campbell, 9th Duke of Argyll 1845-1914 | Arthur, Duke of Connaught 1850-1942 — Princess Louise Margaret of Prussia 1860-1917 | Leopold, Duke of Albany 1853-1884 — Princess Helena of Waldeck and Pyrmont 1861-1922 | Beatrice 1857-1944

Victoria 1863-1950 — Louis Mountbatten, 1st Marquess of Milford Haven 1854-1921 | Alexandra 1872-1918 — Nicholas II, Emperor of Russia 1868-1918 | Marie 1875-1938 — Ferdinand I, King of Rumania 1865-1927 | Others | Gustaf Adolf, Crown Prince (later King Gustaf VI Adolf) of Sweden 1882-1973 | Margaret 1882-1920 | Alexander Cambridge, Earl of Athlone 1874-1957 (brother of Queen Mary) | Alice 1883-1981 | Princess Victoria Adelheid 1885-1970 | Charles Edward, reigning Duke of Saxe-Coburg and Gotha 1884-1954 | Victoria Eugenie 1887-1969 — Alfonso XIII King of Spain 1886-1941

Alice 1885-1969 — Prince Andrew of Greece & Denmark 1882-1944 | Lord Louis Mountbatten, later 1st Earl Mountbatten of Burma 1900-1979 — Hon Edwina Ashley 1901-1960 | Carol II, King of Rumania 1893-1953 — Princess Helen of Greece & Denmark 1896-1982 | Marie 1900-1961 | Alexander I, King of Yugoslavia 1888-1934 | Ingrid b.1910 — Frederik IX, King of Denmark 1899-1972 | Gustaf Adolf, Duke of Västerbotten 1906-1947 — Sibylla 1908-1972 | Juan, Count of Barcelona b.1913 — Princess Maria de las Mercedes

Michael, King of Rumania b.1921 — Princess Anne of Bourbon-Parma b.1923 | Peter II, King of Yugoslavia 1923-1970 — Princess Alexandra of Greece and Denmark b.1921 | Margrethe II, Queen of Denmark b.1940 — Henri de Laborde de Monpezat b.1934 | Constantine II, King of the Hellenes b.1940 (see opposite) — Anne-Marie b.1946 | Carl XVI Gustaf, King of Sweden b.1946 — Silvia Sommerlath b.1943 | Juan Carlos I, King of Spain b.1938 (see opposite) — Sofia b.1938

Alexander, Crown Prince of Yugoslavia b.1945 — Princess Maria da Glória of Orleans and Bragança b.1946

Twentieth-Century Monarchs

After a long wait to succeed his mother, Edward VII (1901-1910) distinguished himself as a diplomatist-king. His more strait-laced son, George V (1910-1936), became a father figure. Following Edward VIII's abdication in 1936, George VI (1936-1952) overcame his lack of training for kingship with the support of the Queen Mother.

ABOVE **George VI** and **Queen Elizabeth**, with the young Princesses Elizabeth and Margaret, on the balcony after the Coronation, 12 May 1937.

The portly, bearded cigar-smoking figure of Edward VII (1901-1910) was, at the time of his accession to the throne, familiar all over Europe — at Newmarket and Biarritz, at Marienbad and Cowes. By refusing to admit her son and heir to the affairs of state, Queen Victoria had given him a lifetime to fill almost as he liked. Although this was a reason for his dissipations, it made Edward also look for ways in which, as heir to the throne, he could be profitably employed.

Thus he took to visiting hospitals, laying foundation-stones and carrying out such engagements as are now recognized royal duties. He was also able to spend more time abroad than would have been possible had he been occupied with state papers and memoranda; although these journeys were undertaken largely for pleasure, they also provided him with an opportunity to attend informal meetings with foreign monarchs and politicians, so that he was able to develop his talent for diplomacy.

It is as a diplomatist that Edward VII is best remembered; he played an important part in creating the *Entente Cordiale* between England and France. He was, in fact, the most respected diplomatist in Europe; by the time he became King, at the age of 59, he was almost as experienced in European diplomacy as his mother had been in English politics. The fact that Edward was something of a newcomer to the business of government would explain why he was more aloof from his ministers than either his mother or his own son. He preferred to make his influence felt through a select group of highly-placed and trusted friends, such as Lord Esher, Sir Ernest Cassel and Sir Charles Hardinge.

In the words of Lord Esher, Edward VII 'had an instinct for statecraft which carried him straight to the core of a great problem without deep or profound knowledge of the subject. He had one supreme gift, and this was his unerring judgement of men and women'. The King, one of the most sociable of monarchs, always took the opportunity of questioning everyone he met about their experiences and asking them their opinions.

George V (1910-1936) was surprisingly unknown when he became King at the age of

BELOW Three naval persons: Edward VII, his son, the Prince of Wales, and grandson, Edward.

44, having been overshadowed by his father and, for some time, by his elder brother who died in 1892. Yet he quickly proved himself to be a king worthy of his great dominions, which were more extensive than those of any monarch either before him or since; it was during his reign that the British Empire and Commonwealth reached its ultimate extent with the addition of the former German colonies in Africa after the victory in the First World War. The process of contraction began with the setting up of the Irish Free State in 1921. At the Delhi Durbar of 1911, George V appeared before his Indian subjects wearing his crown as Emperor of India — as it turned out, the only occasion when this crown was ever worn. Queen Mary stood beside her husband in Delhi. Before his accession, she had been even less known than he, being by nature shy, but she was now beginning to blossom into the superb majestic figure of later years.

When he went to India, George V had already experienced the first crisis of his reign, the political storm caused by the Parliament Bill of 1911 which curtailed the power of the House of Lords. There followed, in quick succession, the crisis over Irish Home Rule and the outbreak of the Great War. After the war there was a struggle for Irish independence, the General Strike and the financial crisis of 1931 which led to the formation of the National Government. In each of these crises, George V acted sensibly,

correctly and patriotically, showing how much he had benefited from the experience in the art of kingship which his father had encouraged him to gain as Prince of Wales. By 1931, the force of his political wisdom was such that he was able to persuade Ramsay MacDonald and other leading members of the Labour Party to join in a coalition with the Conservatives and thus save the country from financial ruin.

Having led a comparatively secluded life before his accession to the throne, George V was old-fashioned in his outlook; it might be said that whereas his father was an Edwardian, he was more a Victorian. Yet he was able to adapt himself to a changing world, and found no difficulty in working with a Labour government or in broadcasting on the wireless. He was, however, less successful as a private individual, particularly in his relations with his own children.

George V's eldest son, Edward, the Prince of Wales, gained wide popularity with his 'Peter Pan' charm, but upset his father by his aggressively modern manners. At one stage the Prince said he would renounce his rights to the throne and settle in one of the dominions unless George V stopped criticizing him. 'After I am dead', shrewdly prophesied the despairing father, 'the boy will ruin himself in 12 months'. It is worth pondering that the King still thought of his 41-year-old heir as 'the boy'.

In 1936 Edward VIII was duly obliged to ab-

dicate after a reign of less than 12 months because he wished to marry a twice-divorced lady, Wallis Warfield from Baltimore, USA, whom his people would not accept as Queen. Since his death in exile in 1972, this immature King's reputation has continued to fall. As things turned out, the monarchy recovered from the shock of the Abdication remarkably smoothly.

Edward VIII's brother 'Bertie', who succeeded him as George VI, was more in the mould of their father: a straightforward ex-naval officer with a love of family life and country pursuits. Like George V, he had not been brought up to be king; but whereas George V had nearly 20 years of preparation between the death of his elder brother and his accession, George VI had no idea that he would ever be king until, at the age of 41, the crown was suddenly thrust upon him. To make this even more daunting, he suffered from chronic ill-health and was also afflicted with a speech impediment.

Queen Mary observed that her second son would be made or marred by his wife and there is no doubt that George VI was fortunate in being very happily married. The new Queen had already won that special place in the affections of the British people which she holds to this day as Queen Mother. With her help and support, George VI embarked on the arduous career of kingship, and made a success of it until his health finally gave way at the early age of 56 in 1952. The strain of leading his country and the Commonwealth through the Second World War, when he and his Queen gave an enormous boost to the morale of their subjects, had clearly taken its toll.

ABOVE **Queen Elizabeth II, Queen Mary** (widow of George V and **Queen Elizabeth, the Queen Mother** (widow of George VI) await George VI's coffin at Westminster Hall in February 1952.

The Monarchy at War

From its earliest days the monarchy has been active in wars. George II (1727-1760) was the last sovereign to lead his troops into battle — at Dettingen in 1743. In modern times, George VI (1936-1952), who had seen action at Jutland in the First World War, proved a fine leader, together with his Queen, in the dark days of the Second World War.

During the darkest days of the Second World War, the calm and courageous bearing of George VI was an inspiration to his people, who were heartened by the words of the song, *The King is Still in London*. As Elizabeth, his Queen, said at the time: 'The children won't leave without me; I won't leave without the King; and the King will never leave'. When Buckingham Palace was bombed she remarked that she could 'now look the East End in the face', and the royal tours of the blitzed areas made a moving impact.

Other members of the royal family served with distinction in the Second World War, including the late Duke of Gloucester (whom one MP, in an excess of zeal, even proposed as Commander-in-Chief), his brother the Duke of Kent (killed on active service in a flying accident) and their cousin, Earl Mountbatten of Burma, who was Supreme Allied Commander in South East Asia. Mountbatten's nautical nephew, Prince Philip, was mentioned in despatches for his part in the Battle of Matapan in 1941. 'Thanks to his alertness and appreciation of the situation', wrote

Prince Philip's captain on HMS *Valiant* in the Mediterranean, 'we were able to sink in five minutes two eight-inch gun Italian cruisers'. The former Edward VIII, the Duke of Windsor, had a staff job at the French Army HQ at the beginning of the war; in the First World War he had been on active service in France. Although present at the Battles of Loos, the Somme and Passchendaele, he was not allowed to participate in trench warfare.

Also during the First World War, George V's second son, the future George VI, saw action at the Battle of Jutland in 1915 on HMS *Collingwood*. Before the ship put out to sea, the young Midshipman (known as 'Mr Johnson') was on the sick list and in bed. A brother-officer, Lieutenant Campbell Tait, recorded the scene:

BELOW George VI and his Queen (now the Queen Mother) in one of their many tours of the blitzed areas in the Second World War. This picture was taken in London, April 1941.

'Suddenly at about 2 p.m. a signal was received that the German High Seas Fleet was out and engaging out battle cruisers only forty miles away and that the battle was coming in our direction. Huge excitement. Out at last. Full speed ahead. Sound of 'Action' — can you imagine the scene! Out of his bunk leaps 'Johnson'. Ill? Never felt better! Strong enough to go to his turret and fight a prolonged action. Of course he was, why ever not?'

The reason usually given as to 'why not' is the danger not so much of being killed as being captured. ('I cannot take the chance of the enemy taking you prisoner', Lord Kitchener told the future Edward VIII in the First World War.) Similarly, in the 1970s, the present Duke of Kent had to forgo his chance of commanding his regiment, the Royal Scots Dragoon Guards (Carabiniers and Greys), in Northern Ireland because of the risk of being kidnapped by the Irish Republican Army (IRA), who later murdered Lord Mountbatten.

However, in 1982, the Queen's second son, Prince Andrew, a helicopter pilot in the

Royal Navy, was allowed to fight in the South Atlantic campaign to recover the Falkland Islands from the Argentine invasion. The Prince, by all accounts, was involved in the thick of some dangerous action. His elder brother, the Prince of Wales, served in all three armed services.

In the early 19th century, the flamboyant George IV used to boast, in his cups, of having led one of the divisions at the Battle of Salamanca in 1812, even having the temerity to ask for corroboration from the Duke of Wellington himself. 'Isn't that so, Duke?' George IV would say, to which the great man is supposed to have sagely replied: 'I have often heard Your Majesty say so'. In fact, the last British monarch to lead his troops into battle was the 60-year-old George II at the Battle of Dettingen (a victory by British, Austrian and Hanoverian troops against the French) in 1743.

George II's youngest son, 'Butcher' Cumberland, smashed the Jacobites at Culloden in 1746. Still further back, notable military monarchs have included James II (though he lost the Battle of the Boyne); Henry VIII; Henry V (victor of Agincourt); Edward III (Poitiers and Crécy); the crusaders Richard I ('the Lion Heart') and Edward I ('the best lance in the world') and, of course, William the Conqueror. After all, the main function of the early monarchs was to be a military commander.

FAR LEFT **George VI** travelled thousands of miles during the Second World War to visit the troops. In June 1943 he was in North Africa where he was a martyr to 'Desert tummy'. Never enjoying robust health, the King showed extraordinary determination on these, in his own words, 'bucking them up' tours.

LEFT The King's cousin, Lord Louis Mountbatten (later **Earl Mountbatten of Burma**) was Supreme Allied Commander in South-East Asia; this photograph was taken in 1944.

ABOVE No.230873, Second Subaltern Elizabeth Alexandra Mary Windsor, Auxiliary Territorial Service, learns how to strip and service an engine in April 1945. 'We had sparking plugs last night all the way through dinner', once remarked the Queen Mother.

RIGHT With a flamboyant gesture, **Prince Andrew**, the Queen's second son, celebrates his return from the victorious Falklands Campaign on HMS *Invincible*; he was welcomed by his parents at Portsmouth on a memorable day in September 1982. The Prince, then aged 22, had seen action as a Naval helicopter pilot.

The Changing Role of Monarchy

The role of the monarch has developed from that of military commander through spiritual leader and administrator to ruler by council and Parliament and, finally, to figurehead and representative of the nation. The doctrine of 'Divine Right' led to republicanism in the 17th century and the 'Glorious Revolution' of 1688 curtailed the 'royal prerogative'.

'I have come amongst you, being resolved in the midst and heat of the battle to live and die amongst you all, to lay down for my God, and for my Kingdom, and for my people, my honour and my blood even in the dust. I know I have the body of a weak and feeble woman, but I have the heart and stomach of a king, and of a king of England too, and think foul scorn that Parma or Spain or any prince of Europe, should dare to invade the borders of my realm; to which, rather than any dishonour shall grow by me, I myself will take up arms, I myself will be your general, judge and rewarder of every one of your virtues in the field.'

Elizabeth I's exhortation to her troops at Tilbury encapsulates the role of the monarch as leader and champion of his or her subjects, and a symbol of the state. The Tudor period saw the transition from the medieval monarchy, where government was the sovereign's personal affair, to the more modern concept in which the role of the monarch is to represent the people.

In the early days, after the Age of Settlement, the responsibilities of kingship were still basically over peoples, rather than territories. The king was an active war leader and would also preside over tribunals at which law was declared. The spiritual aspect of monarchy came later, when England was converted to Christianity in the 7th century. Shakespeare described the religious aura, the sacramental character of the anointing of a

ABOVE **George V** at the microphone making his Christmas broadcast in 1934. Through the powerful new medium of the wireless, he became a 'father figure' to his people all over the Empire. 'It is this personal link between me and my people which I value more than I can say', he told the listeners to his Christmas broadcast of 1935 (the year of the Silver Jubilee celebrations). 'It binds us together in all our common joys and sorrows'. George V's gruff, straightforward and homely chats over the air waves, delivered live, gave considerable solace to his subjects in the crisis-ridden years of his reign. The 'Christmas broadcast', was immediately established as an important institution of modern monarchy but it proved a particular trial for George VI, who suffered from a stammer.

RIGHT On 11 December 1936, 'His Royal Highness Prince Edward', made perhaps the most famous broadcast speech of all. 'At long last', began the former

King **Edward VIII**, who had abdicated the day before, 'I am able to say a few words of my own'.

On the morning of Thursday 10 December 1936, the Instrument of Abdication was signed at Fort Belvedere by 'Edward RI' (the abdicating Edward VIII) and witnessed by his three brothers 'Albert', (who became George VI), 'Henry', (the Duke of Gloucester) and 'George', (the Duke of Kent). The Abdication crisis had arisen in the autumn of 1936 when the King's twice-divorced American mistress, **Mrs Ernest Simpson**, divorced her third husband in Ipswich. When the story broke, Mrs Simpson fled to France. The Prime Minister, Stanley Baldwin, ruled out a compromise solution of a morganatic marriage whereby Mrs Simpson would not have become Queen Consort. There were some displays of support for the King, but it was clear that the Empire would never accept a divorcée as Queen.

'I have found it impossible to carry out the heavy burden of responsibility and to discharge my duties as King as I would wish to do', said Edward in his broadcast, 'without the help and support of the woman I love'.

king:

> 'Not all the water in the rough rude sea
> Can wash the balm from an anointed
> King...'

Contemporaries of Edgar the Peaceful (959-975) and later chroniclers made much of his solemn coronation at Bath in AD 973. In his coronation oath Edgar promised to protect the Church, to put down malefactors and evil-doing and to uphold justice.

The Anglo-Danish King, Canute, introduced law-codes that extended the monarch's role as a special guardian of the law. Canute's laws were still the basis of the English constitution after the Norman Conquest. The Norman kings were careful to stress the legitimacy of their succession and the continuity with the Anglo-Saxon past. In his coronation charter of 1100, Henry I pledged himself to protect the Church, to put down evil customs (such as abuses of the feudal order) and to uphold good laws. The

BELOW **Princess Margaret**, aged 21, is sitting near Group-Captain Peter Townsend among a royal party watching the Olympic Horse Trials at Badminton in 1952. Townsend was a hero of the Battle of Britain, a former equerry and protégé of George VI and Comptroller of the Queen Mother's household, but when the story came out of his romance with the Princess in 1953, all that counted was that he had been through the divorce courts, having sued his wife for adultery. Eventually, in 1955, Princess Margaret announced that she had 'decided not to marry Group Captain Townsend ...mindful of the Church's teaching ...and conscious of my duty to the Commonwealth'.

responsibility for executive government still rested completely with the monarch, but new administrative institutions began to evolve. The monarch's own household was no longer enough. The growth of the Exchequer in the early 12th century was a significant step in the changing role of monarchy. The absence abroad of English kings in Normandy, or, later, in the Crusades, also led to increased delegation of their powers.

Magna Carta, the 'great charter of liberties' which was signed by King John (1199-1216) at Runnymede on 15 June 1215, marks another important stage in the development of the English monarchy. It should be borne in mind that the barons made no real attempt to reduce the authority of the king; they were concerned with the abuse of royal power. The principle behind both the original charter and the re-issue of Henry III in 1225, was that the monarch governed under law and that unlawful royal action could not be tolerated. *Magna Carta* came to be regarded as a symbol of restriction on monarchical power and continued to be cited many centuries later, but, in fact, it did not set up any effective machinery to correct the unlawful actions of a monarch.

Later in the 13th century, as a safeguard against arbitrary royal rule, Simon de Montfort and the barons tried to introduce what was virtually 'government by council'. The attempt failed, but not before de Montfort had summoned representatives to a central assembly of the realm. This parliamentary seedling was nurtured by Edward I (1272-1307), who drew counsel from the assembly and found it a useful place to announce legislation and exercise justice. He and his successors came to rely more and more on Parliament for financial aid, in other words, the benefits of taxation, in extraordinary circumstances.

In the 14th century, the Parliament became accepted as a permanent part of government, though kings still ascended the throne by the grace of God and exercised ex-

tensive powers by royal prerogative. Attempts to substitute government by council for government by king failed, but in 1399 Richard II was deposed not just by faction (as his grandfather Edward II had been in 1327) but by constitutional acts which involved the consent of the realm as expressed by Parliament. The 15th century saw five more depositions (Henry VI twice, Edward IV once, Edward V and Richard III) but somehow the monarchy survived almost unscathed. Whatever the vicissitudes of the Houses of York and Lancaster, the King was still held to govern under law. Practical limitations on prerogative were imposed by Parliament, an institution that was beginning to develop a life of its own.

The weakness of the 15th-century monarchy that led to the Wars of the Roses was in part financial. Henry VII (1485-1509), the first of the Tudors, put a stop to that by being his own finance minister. Under the Tudors strong central government was achieved by means of a small, subservient Royal Council. However, although Henry VIII (1509-1547) increased the power of the monarchy through his changes subordinating the Church to the state, he carried out these 'revolutionary' changes through Parliament, which in fact had the long-term effect of a relinquishment of power.

During the second half of the Tudor period, with a minor (Edward VI) and then two women (Mary I and Elizabeth I) on the throne, more of the day-to-day affairs of government passed to the burgeoning bureaucracy. Bloody Mary's extreme behaviour lost the monarchy some of its authority, which her half-sister Elizabeth had to restore. The latter Queen, apotheosized as 'Gloriana' in the Elizabethan cult of monarchy, zealously guarded her prerogative. 'I am your anointed Queen', she told Parliament who were trying to persuade her to marry. 'I will never be by violence constrained to do anything. I thank God I am endued with such qualities that if I were turned out of the Realm in my petticoat I were able to live in any place in Christendom'. For all the power of her ministers, Lord Burghley and his son, Robert Cecil, and the growing importance of Parliament, the Virgin Queen still had the last word.

The Whigs traditionally blamed the downfall of the House of Stuart in the 17th century on the obstinate determination of James I and Charles I to resist the growth of English parliamentary democracy. Alternatively, the Stuarts can be viewed as conscientious monarchs who were just unable to guide the monarchy through the extremely difficult times in which they were unfortunate and unlucky enough to have to live.

The doctrine of Divine Right, formerly exclusive to popes and emperors, was unwisely taken up by James I (1603-1625) after the Gunpowder Plot; he claimed that his right to the throne came from Heaven. 'That which concerns the mystery of the King's power is not lawful to be disputed', James I told the judges in 1616, 'for that is to wade into the weakness of Princes, and to take away the mystical reverence that belongs unto them that sit in the throne of God'. This implied that the king's power was God's and to disobey him was to disobey God's will. The so-called 'absolute power' of the Stuarts was, in reality, not as despotic as the 'royal prerogative' of the Tudors; whereas the latter was within the framework of the law, however, the former, since it was supposed to derive from Heaven, knew no bounds. As a potential threat to the English parliamentary system, Divine Right provided the Parliamentarians with a reason to fight the Civil War.

The Whigs extinguished the doctrine of Divine Right in the Glorious Revolution of 1688 and replaced it with a vague theory of a contract between king and people, thereby curtailing the royal prerogative quite considerably. Parliaments now had to be summoned at least every three years. The crown could no longer raise and keep a standing army in times of peace.

The advent of the Hanoverians in 1714 brought a further sharp decline in the royal prerogative. With the setting aside of the legitimate Stuart line (the Jacobites), less emphasis could be placed on the divine nature of kingship. George I (1714-1727) ceased to preside over his cabinet, thus leaving the way open for the ascendancy of the first Prime Minister, Sir Robert Walpole. George II (1727-1760) often had to give way to Parliament over the choice of ministers.

Later in the 18th century, George III (1760-1820) had the opportunity to increase the power of the monarchy after the break-up of the Whig party, but he preferred the simple country life. It was 'Farmer George' who began the modern royal practice of moving informally among his people, chatting with them about their lives. The influence of the crown was reduced again by the younger Pitt and, of course, by poor George III's madness; it continued to diminish under the pleasure-loving George IV (1820-1830), who nevertheless lent the monarchy much more style than it had enjoyed in the previous century.

In 1834 William IV (1830-1837) went so far as to dismiss his government. This remains a constitutional right of the monarchy (at least in theory), but the 'Sailor King' was the last sovereign to put it to the test. Queen Victoria (1837-1901) perfected the art of being a constitutional monarch in her long reign, greatly increasing its popularity in the process — even though republicanism of a virulent strain broke out during her interminable period of seclusion after Prince Albert's death. George V (1910-1936) emerged as a father figure to his people through the new invention of the wireless, tackling a number of tricky crises in a straightforward naval manner.

The shock of Edward VIII's Abdication in 1936 caused remarkably few tremors to the position of the monarchy thanks to the purposefulness and quiet strength of George VI (1936-1952). Nothing sums up the modern 'image' of the royal family so well as the conversation piece painted by James Gunn at the Royal Lodge, Windsor, in 1950; in this cosy domestic scene, the Queen (now the Queen Mother) pours tea, the two Princesses wait for a slice of fruit cake, a corgi snoozes behind the tweed-suited King's chair. As Disraeli said, over 100 years ago, the influence of the crown:

'is not confined merely to political affairs. England is a domestic country. Here the home is revered and the hearth sacred. The nation is represented by a family — the Royal Family; and if that family is educated with a sense of responsibility and a sentiment of public duty, it is difficult to exaggerate the salutary influence they may exercise over a nation.'

BELOW *Conversation Piece at Royal Lodge, Windsor,* painted by James Gunn, 1950. George VI, his Queen and their two daughters, Princesses Elizabeth and Margaret at tea. From above the fireplace, George IV gazes down upon a scene of royal life very different from his own.

The Roy

In a wide-ranging survey of the lives, work and roles of the various members of the royal family today, this section includes profiles of the

al Family

Queen, Prince Philip, the Queen Mother, the Prince and Princess of Wales and other members of the royal family.

The House of Windsor

The royal family today consists not only of those in line to the throne but also their husbands and wives. The immediate members of the royal family constantly provide the Queen with invaluable support.

'A *family* on the throne', noted Walter Bagehot in his great work on *The English Constitution*, 'is an interesting idea also'. This 19th-century sage pointed out that 'The women — one half of the human race at least — care fifty times more for a marriage than a ministry...a princely marriage is the brilliant edition of a universal fact, and, as such, it rivets mankind'. In recent times 'the royal family' has come more to resemble a sort of family business carrying on the monarchical trade; indeed George VI used to

refer to himself, his Queen (now the Queen Mother) and their two daughters, Elizabeth and Margaret, as the 'Royal Firm'. Today the 'Royal Firm' has expanded considerably to constitute an invaluable supporting team to the present Queen, performing their royal duties throughout the year on her behalf.

The Court Circular sometimes uses the phrase '...and other members of the Royal Family'. This is a specific definition which applies to members of the royal family whose names appear in the court list. Technically it

does not include those under age — some of whom the commentators often find it difficult to identify at gatherings of the clan, like the Queen's Birthday Parade or Christmas at Windsor.

The 'royal family', as such, does not just include those in line to the throne but also some of their spouses. When Lord Snowdon once remarked that he was not a member of the royal family but was simply 'married to a member of the royal family', he missed the point that the royal family, strictly speaking,

POSING FOR PHOTOGRAPHERS The Queen is frequently seen with other members of the royal family.
LEFT With her on the balcony at Buckingham Palace after the Trooping the Colour ceremony in 1981 are Prince Philip, the Queen Mother, the Prince of Wales and his future Princess, among others.

BELOW LEFT This early photograph taken in about 1901 shows (from left to right) the three eldest children of George V: Prince Albert (later George VI), Princess Mary (later the Princess Royal) and Prince Edward (later Edward VIII).

BELOW Prince William, accompanied his parents on their tour of Australia and New Zealand in 1983.

consists of those that appear on the list of precedence at court.

There are also descendants of Edward VII (1901-1910), Queen Victoria (1837-1901) and even George III (1760-1820), less well known to the general public, who qualify for inclusion on the court list. Thus, the Duke of Fife (whose mother Princess Maud was a younger daughter of Princess Louise, Edward VII's eldest daughter) features on the list; as do Captain Alexander Ramsay of Mar (grandson of the Duke of Connaught, Queen Victoria's third, and favourite, son) and his wife Lady Saltoun; as well as the Marchioness of Cambridge, the Duchess and Duke of Beaufort (she comes first as a niece of the late Queen Mary) and Lady May and Colonel Sir Henry Abel Smith.

In the Anglican church a prayer is read for the Queen, and then one for the royal family: '...we humbly beseech thee to bless Elizabeth, the Queen Mother, Philip, Duke of Edinburgh, Charles, Prince of Wales, and all the royal family...'.

Royal Line of Succession

1.
HRH The Prince of Wales (b. 1948)
2.
HRH The Prince William of Wales (b. 1982)
3.
HRH The Prince Andrew (b. 1960)
4.
HRH The Prince Edward (b. 1964)
5.
HRH The Princess Anne (b. 1950)
6.
Peter Phillips (b. 1977)
7.
Zara Phillips (b. 1981)
8.
HRH The Princess Margaret (b. 1930)
9.
Viscount Linley (b. 1961)
10.
Lady Sarah Armstrong-Jones (b. 1964)
11.
HRH the Duke of Gloucester (b. 1944)
12.
Earl of Ulster (b. 1974)
13.
Lady Davina Windsor (b. 1980)
14.
Lady Rose Windsor (b. 1980)
15.
HRH The Duke of Kent (b. 1935)
16.
Earl of St Andrews (b. 1962)
17.
Lord Nicholas Windsor (b. 1970)
18.
Lady Helen Windsor (b. 1964)
19.
Lord Frederick Windsor (b. 1979)
20.
Lady Gabriella Windsor (b. 1981)
21.
HRH Princess Alexandra (b. 1936)
22.
James Ogilvy (b. 1964)
23.
Marina Ogilvy (b. 1966)
24.
The Earl of Harewood (b. 1923)

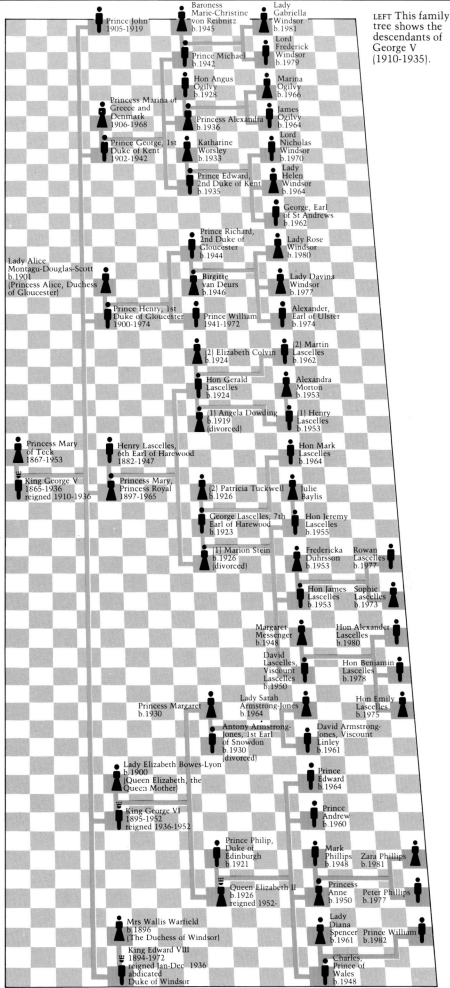

LEFT This family tree shows the descendants of George V (1910-1935).

Prince John 1905-1919

Baroness Marie-Christine von Reibnitz b.1945

Lady Gabriella Windsor b.1981

Lord Frederick Windsor b.1979

Prince Michael b.1942

Hon Angus Ogilvy b.1928

Marina Ogilvy b.1966

Princess Marina of Greece and Denmark 1906-1968

Princess Alexandra b.1936

James Ogilvy b.1964

Prince George, 1st Duke of Kent 1902-1942

Katharine Worsley b.1933

Lord Nicholas Windsor b.1970

Prince Edward, 2nd Duke of Kent b.1935

Lady Helen Windsor b.1964

George, Earl of St Andrews b.1962

Prince Richard, 2nd Duke of Gloucester b.1944

Lady Rose Windsor b.1980

Lady Alice Montagu-Douglas-Scott b.1901 (Princess Alice, Duchess of Gloucester)

Birgitte van Deurs b.1946

Lady Davina Windsor b.1977

Prince Henry, 1st Duke of Gloucester 1900-1974

Prince William 1941-1972

Alexander, Earl of Ulster b.1974

(2) Elizabeth Colvin b.1924

(2) Martin Lascelles b.1962

Hon Gerald Lascelles b.1924

Alexandra Morton b.1953

(1) Angela Dowding b.1919 (divorced)

(1) Henry Lascelles b.1953

Princess Mary of Teck 1867-1953

Henry Lascelles, 6th Earl of Harewood 1882-1947

Hon Mark Lascelles b.1964

King George V 1865-1936 reigned 1910-1936

Princess Mary, Princess Royal 1897-1965

(2) Patricia Tuckwell b.1926

Julie Baylis

George Lascelles, 7th Earl of Harewood b.1923

Hon Jeremy Lascelles b.1955

(1) Marion Stein b.1926 (divorced)

Fredericka Duhrsson b.1953

Rowan Lascelles b.1977

Hon James Lascelles b.1953

Sophie Lascelles b.1973

Margaret Messenger b.1948

Hon Alexander Lascelles b.1980

David Lascelles, Viscount Lascelles b.1950

Hon Benjamin Lascelles b.1978

Princess Margaret b.1930

Lady Sarah Armstrong-Jones b.1964

Hon Emily Lascelles b.1975

Antony Armstrong-Jones, 1st Earl of Snowdon b.1930 (divorced)

David Armstrong-Jones, Viscount Linley b.1961

Lady Elizabeth Bowes-Lyon b.1900 (Queen Elizabeth, the Queen Mother)

Prince Edward b.1964

King George VI 1895-1952 reigned 1936-1952

Prince Andrew b.1960

Prince Philip, Duke of Edinburgh b.1921

Mark Phillips b.1948

Zara Phillips b.1981

Queen Elizabeth II b.1926 reigned 1952-

Princess Anne b.1950

Peter Phillips b.1977

Mrs Wallis Warfield b.1896 (The Duchess of Windsor)

Lady Diana Spencer b.1961

Prince William b.1982

King Edward VIII 1894-1972 reigned Jan-Dec 1936 abdicated Duke of Windsor

Charles, Prince of Wales b.1948

The Queen

Elizabeth II acceded to the throne and the headship of the Commonwealth on 6 February 1952 following the death of her father, George VI (1936-1952). A shy countrywoman, happiest with her family, horses and dogs, Her Majesty has dutifully dedicated herself to an extremely difficult and demanding role which she takes very seriously indeed.

Elizabeth the Second, By the Grace of God, of the United Kingdom of Great Britain and Northern Ireland and of Her Other Realms and Territories, Queen, Head of the Commonwealth, Defender of the Faith — otherwise simply 'The Queen', as she is known the world over, remains a very private person. As if to double the paradox wrapped up in the Elizabethan enigma, the public feel that they understand her character, what she thinks, what she stands for. She is Britain's national conscience as well as her most representative symbol. The Queen is the rock that links the past to the present and the future. And yet her true worth is still underestimated.

Far from being a cipher or a constitutional puppet, the Queen exercises an important influence over affairs of state. She is the most experienced political figure in Britain and the Commonwealth. Although not an intellectual, she is sharply intelligent with an instinct for statecraft and a grasp of essentials. Politicians have testified to her knack of locating the core of a problem. She tackles a vast workload unseen and unappreciated by those who only associate her with pomp and pageantry or holidays in Scotland.

Shy, stiff and unphotogenic as she may appear, the Queen herself is warm, humorous, easy and, to those who have seen her on television or in real life, surprisingly spontaneous and attractive. Emphatically a country person, passionately fond of racing, she does not care for the panoply of monarchy, but duty is her watchword. She has never put a foot wrong. She has shown courage in her reign and she has adapted with the times, but never too much; she has managed to remain aloof from the vulgarity of her times. The Queen does not give interviews. For her the monarchy is a hereditary office with mystical, rational and lasting purpose, not a job from which she can — or would — retire.

It was, of course, never her ambition to become Queen — she is said to have reacted to her status as heiress apparent by praying for a baby brother. When she was born, in fact, there was no reason to suppose she ever would be Queen: the then heir to her grandfather, George V, was her eligible bachelor uncle, Edward, the Prince of Wales.

'The Empire's little Princess', the first child of the Duke and Duchess of York, was born at 17 Bruton Street, Mayfair (the town house of the Duchess's father, the Earl of Strathmore) on 21 April 1926, just before the General Strike. Both on the day of the birth and on the day the strike ended large crowds assembled outside; the reason for the second gathering according to that shrewd royal confidante Lady Airlie, was that the people saw in this child 'something of continuity and of hope in the future'.

The presence of Princess Elizabeth Alexandra Mary (known as 'Lilibet' to the family) cheered George V (1910-1936) ('Grandpa England' to her) during his convalescence at Bognor in the winter of 1928 and 1929. Her early education was entrusted to the Scottish governess Marion Crawford ('Crawfie', whose gushing reminiscences about the 'little Princesses' later embarrassed the royal family) with significant contributions by her mother, the Duchess of

LEFT Christening photograph of Princess Elizabeth with her parents, the Duke and Duchess of York, 29 May 1926. 'Of course, the poor baby cried', noted Queen Mary.

RIGHT Three vignettes of the nine-year-old Princess during her grandfather George V's Silver Jubilee celebrations in 1935. Her cousin George (now the Earl of Harewood) is behind her.

BELOW The two 'little Princesses', Elizabeth and Margaret Rose (as she was then widely known) at a Girl Guides Rally at Windsor Castle in June 1938. Margaret Rose, then nearly eight, had recently become a Brownie, whereas 'Lilibet' was already a Guide.

'Cook, Needlewoman and Child Nurse (badges) are holding me up a bit' the latter once admitted.

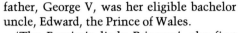

York. Particular stress was laid on languages; the Queen's French still puts many British politicians to shame. After Princess Elizabeth's destiny was altered by the abdication of Edward VIII (who reigned briefly during 1936), she received invaluable grounding in constitutional history and law from Henry Marten, Vice-Provost of Eton, who became a mentor.

The character of the young Princess may be glimpsed in the memoirs of the period: 'dignity and sang froid' was being displayed as early as 1934 in the role of bridesmaid to the Duchess of Kent, while Lady Airlie noted at her confirmation in 1942 that 'The carriage of her head was unequalled and that there was about her that indescribable something which Queen Victoria had'. Princess Elizabeth made her first broadcast in 1940 and her first public engagement (as Colonel of the Grenadier Guards) in 1942, when she also registered as a Sea Ranger. In 1944 the Princess acted for the first time as a Counsellor of State in George VI's absence abroad and began battling with her beloved father to let her do National Service in the ATS. She won, and duly qualified as a driver at the Mechanical Transport Training Centre, covered with oil and axle-grease.

As early as 1939 Princess Elizabeth had met her cousin Prince Philip of Greece and fallen in love. It was as simple as that; she never looked at another man. But the engagement had to wait until after the royal family's trip to South Africa in 1947 where she celebrated her 21st birthday by dedicating her life (in a broadcast) 'to the ser-

ABOVE LEFT The first photograph of Queen Elizabeth II as she arrives back at Heathrow on 7 February 1952 from Kenya after her father's death. The 'young figure in black' descends the gangway to be greeted by her venerable Prime Minister, Winston Churchill.

ABOVE The Queen making her first Christmas radio broadcast in 1952 at Sandringham, where the royal family used to spend Christmas. She had made her broadcasting debut 12 years earlier on *Children's Hour* with 'Uncle Mac'.

ABOVE Princess Elizabeth and the Duke of Edinburgh on honeymoon in Malta in 1947. Here they were to enjoy their only relatively 'normal' period of family life before the Princess's accession to the throne.

RIGHT Princess Elizabeth, holding the infant Princess Anne, and the Duke of Edinburgh, with Prince Charles, in the grounds of Clarence House, their first family home; Princess Anne was born here on 15 August 1950.

vice of our Great Imperial Family to which we all belong'. Field-Marshal Smuts said at her wedding later in the year that the Princess made him sad 'because she is serious and wise beyond her years'.

After an all-too-short period of normal family life with their two young children, Princess Elizabeth and the Duke of Edinburgh set out from London Airport on 31 January 1952 for a Commonwealth tour her father was too ill to undertake. The gaunt King came to wave them goodbye; a week later he died at Sandringham. Thus, at the age of only 25, Princess Elizabeth, then staying in Kenya, became Queen Elizabeth II.

'By the sudden death of my dear father I am called to assume the duties and responsibilities of sovereignty', said the Queen in her Accession Declaration on her return to London on 7 February 1952. 'My heart is too full for me to say more to you today than that I shall always work, as my father did throughout his reign, to uphold constitutional government and to advance the happiness and prosperity of my peoples, spread as they are the world over'. As the politician Oliver Lyttelton (Viscount Chandos) observed, the Privy Councillors to whom this was

LEFT The Queen at her coronation on 2 June 1953 at Westminster Abbey.

BELOW The Queen, Prince Philip, Prince Charles and Princess Anne at lunch in a scene from the 'behind the scenes' documentary, *Royal Family*, shown on both BBC and

Independent Television in 1969.

ABOVE LEFT The Queen visiting an old people's home in the West Indies, February 1983.

ABOVE RIGHT The Queen opening the new set for Granada Television's endless saga of *Coronation Street*, 1982.

addressed 'looked immeasurably old and gnarled and grey' beside the Queen called to carry such a great burden so early in life.

The new reign started in an atmosphere of euphoria, with the youthful Queen symbolizing 'Gloriana' in the so-called New Elizabethan Age. This mood was manifested in the Coronation of June 1953 — the first great event of the television age. This was the first intrusion of this powerful new medium into the British monarchy's life; since then it has had an enormous effect on the relationship between the public and the monarch, helping the Queen's subjects to get to know her much better than any of her predecessors. Since 1957 the Queen's Christmas messages have been transmitted on television; these broadcasts have developed from the formal poses of the Queen sitting in front of the microphone to more relaxed family scenes.

One year the Queen was in the garden at Buckingham Palace, tossing a pebble into the water to illustrate a point; another year her first grandson, Peter Phillips, was on view. The Queen also often introduces film of her travels to stress the point that she is ruler of the Commonwealth and not simply of the United Kingdom.

Another modern invention, jet travel, has enabled the Queen to visit 'all her other realms and territories' both swiftly and frequently. This is one of the important ways in which the present sovereign's reign differs from those of any of her predecessors. When Princess Marie Louise, one of Queen Victoria's granddaughters, visited Nigeria in the 1920s her journey took three weeks. It took the Queen 17 hours 30 years later; today the same flight would take seven. In 1980, for instance, the Queen flew to Australia to open

'Walkabouts' have broken down the formality of royal tours since their success in Australia in 1970. In England the idea was tried and proved successful at the Barbican following the Queen's Silver Wedding Celebrations in 1972. By the time of the Silver Jubilee in 1977 walkabouts were an important part of the royal programme.

The tremendous response to the Silver Jubilee took many people by surprise, not least, perhaps, the Queen herself. From the mid-1950s onwards the monarchy, like other institutions of the 'Establishment', had come under attack for being old-fashioned and, though changes had been made to 'democratize' the monarchy, there were fears about public apathy. They proved to be quite unfounded. The Queen had clearly earned immense popularity through her dedication to duty over 25 years. She continues to represent everything the majority of her subjects still like to think Britain stands for. A grandmother with hair greying at the temples, now often bespectacled, but still far from old, she has been Queen for more than half her life and there is no reason to suppose she will not reign for many years to come.

the new High Court in Canberra, paying one-day visits to Sydney and Melbourne and returning to London four days later.

At the beginning of her reign the Queen became the first sovereign of any nationality to circumnavigate the globe in her Commonwealth Tour of 1953 to 1954. During this voyage she scarcely set foot on any soil not belonging to the Commonwealth. The very survival of the Commonwealth in its present form owes a significant amount to the Queen who is its unifying factor. To keep it together she has shown unflinching determination, as in her visit to Ghana in 1961 when the political climate was highly turbulent.

The Queen also showed considerable courage in visiting Northern Ireland during her Silver Jubilee celebrations. 'All I hoped was that we would get out with honour', one of her advisers was heard to say, 'but we got

out with triumph'. The Queen won further admiration in 1982 for keeping a cool head when, due to a lamentable security lapse, a strange man entered her bedroom at Buckingham Palace. Afterwards she enjoyed mimicking her maid's reaction when this worthy came across the intruder: 'Bloody 'ell ma'am, wot's 'e doin' in 'ere?'

The Queen's lively personality behind her shyness has become increasingly familiar to the public during her reign. The 'image' of royalty went through an almost revolutionary process in the 1969 television film, *Royal Family*, with its glimpses behind the scenes enabling the Queen and her family to spring to life as never before. This unprecedented step was expected to be followed by further insights but, in fact, the years since have witnessed less daylight on the magic than this film led the public to expect.

Prince Philip

Born in 1921, Prince Philip, Duke of Edinburgh, the Queen's husband, is a brash, breezy, forthright, vigorous, plain-spoken and extremely capable naval officer who has been a potent force for change in modern monarchy.

Now well into his 60s, Prince Philip remains one of the most energetic members of the present royal family. To be the husband of a sovereign is not an easy role: constitutionally, for instance, Prince Philip does not exist. He has never been created Prince Consort (like Prince Albert), he sees no state papers, and though he is a member of the House of Lords he has never spoken in the Chamber. None the less, he has carved out a hardworking and rewarding job for himself, never being afraid to say what he thinks — however disagreeable this may occasionally be.

Prince Philip is a more complicated character than is generally understood by his critics or supporters. A Prince of Greece and Denmark he was born in Corfu (on the dining-room table of a villa called 'Mon Repos') in 1921, into a far from affluent or stable background. His parents drifted apart and he was largely brought up by his uncle Lord Milford Haven (whose brother, Lord Louis Mountbatten, did not play quite so

significant a part in Prince Philip's life as has generally been assumed). Prince Philip served in the British Navy but a promising active career had to come to an end on the accession of the Queen to the throne in 1952.

In the early years of the reign, Prince Philip travelled abroad extensively. He seems to have taken the criticisms made about the monarchy in the mid-1950s very much to heart. 'To survive', he said, 'the monarchy has to change' and, as Elizabeth Longford has written: 'He decided that monarchy must make a crash landing into a new age'. The education of the royal children was rigorously planned, presentation parties replaced by informal Palace luncheons for a wider range of 'achievers', and 'men of the world' brought into the Royal Household.

Prince Philip has been associated with many enterprising schemes, such as his own Award Scheme founded in 1956, the Playing Fields Association and the Outward Bound Trust; his formidable number of active appointments includes the Presidency of the Fédération Equestre Internationale.

Remarkably forward-looking for a sexagenarian, he takes a particular interest in technology. His popularity has been enhanced by a breezy nautical manner and the solid, down-to-earth nature of his speeches.

PRINCE PHILIP'S adaptability, common sense and verve are evident in the way he copes with a great variety of situations. BOTTOM He is congratulating the Duke of Edinburgh Gold Award winners at Holyroodhouse, Edinburgh, in 1982.

PRINCE ABROAD Prince Philip has developed many individual interests and patronizes a number of societies and charities in his own right. Here is is visiting Brunette Downs Station, Northern Territory, Australia in 1956 (RIGHT). As President of the World Wildlife Fund, he made a special tour in 1982 (BELOW).

CONSORT TO THE QUEEN At the beginning of 1952 the Duke of Edinburgh was a serving Commander in the Royal Navy; by the following year he was out of active service, Consort to the Queen and an Admiral of the Fleet. Here he is in the uniform of the latter, at the passing out parade of Prince Andrew from the Royal Naval College, Dartmouth in 1980 (LEFT).

The Queen Mother

The Prince's octogenarian mother-in-law, Queen Elizabeth, the Queen Mother, adapted wonderfully to her early widowhood, and continues to be a great support to the Queen as well as an immensely popular 'grandmother figure' to the British people.

Widowed at the early age of 51 in 1952, the Queen Mother had to find a new purpose in a supporting role to her elder daughter. She moved to Clarence House, down the Mall from Buckingham Palace, and was soon undertaking major tours overseas as well as a ceaseless round of engagements at home. Flamboyantly dressed, smiling and giving her much-imitated wave, the Queen Mother is a universally popular figure as the celebrations to mark her 80th birthday in 1980 so very clearly demonstrated.

She has been a member of the royal family for over 60 years. The daughter of the Earl of Strathmore, she was the first Queen since Catherine Parr not to have been of royal birth, though she was prophetically known as 'Princess' when she was a little girl. Her service to the monarchy has been exemplary on all occasions, whether bolstering George VI's self-confidence, providing a natural and happy home for the upbringing of her daughters, supporting Princess Margaret through her

emotional problems or, above all, soldiering on in London through the thick of the Second World War. Her various appointments include being Lord Warden of the Cinque Ports.

The Queen Mother retains a great zest for life. She usually spends her weekends at the Royal Lodge in Windsor Great Park and holidays in the Castle of Mey in Caithness which she restored. Her special interests have included National Hunt racing, gardening and fishing, as well as the arts. Now an octogenarian great-grandmother, she has earned every right to a peaceful retirement, but she continues to serve her eldest daughter.

BELOW An 82nd-birthday wave by Queen Elizabeth the Queen Mother outside her London residence, Clarence House, before setting off for the christening of her great-grandson Prince William of Wales at Buckingham Palace, 4 August 1982.

ABOVE Always a flamboyant dresser, the Queen Mother is seen in some of her celebrated headgear at various recent functions: (from left to right): at Westminster Abbey, at a hospice at West Ham, in Hyde Park and at the Derby.
TOP Norman Parkinson's exotic photograph of the Queen Mother with her daughters, the Queen and Princess Margaret, was taken to mark her 80th birthday in 1980. During the sitting, Parkinson had some problems of communications with his subjects. 'Listen 'Parks', it's absolutely no use you Ma'aming us', said Princess Margaret to the royal photographer. 'We haven't got the slightest idea who you're referring to'.

The Prince and Princess of Wales

Born in 1948 and educated at Gordonstoun and Trinity College, Cambridge, Prince Charles served for five years in the navy before acquainting himself with the workings of government and industry. The heir to the throne takes a particular interest in the Commonwealth which he tours frequently with his immensely popular young Princess, the former Lady Diana Spencer.

BELOW Prince Charles being taken by Nanny Lightbody for a morning outing in Green Park on his second birthday, 14 November 1950.

To those who complain that the Prince of Wales should do a 'proper job', his devoted grandmother, the Queen Mother, answers 'He has a proper job, he is the Prince of Wales'. Indeed from his birth in 1948 Prince Charles has been serving his apprenticeship for sovereignty.

Prince Charles was the first prince to attend a day-school: Hill House in London. Then he followed his father, Prince Philip, to the boarding-schools of Cheam and Gordonstoun. To broaden his education, the Prince was sent to Australia where he spent some time at Geelong Grammar School. A late developer, the Prince's personality burgeoned at Trinity College, Cambridge, where he gained valuable self-confidence and also displayed his 'Goonish' humour. To prepare

for his investiture as Prince of Wales in 1969, Prince Charles was obliged to interrupt his course at Cambridge to learn some Welsh at the University College of Aberystwyth, which he did well enough to acquit himself admirably at the ceremony.

The investiture year of 1969 saw the Prince of Wales swim into the centre of the goldfish bowl where the media have placed the modern royal family. His first radio and television broadcasts revealed him to be a character curiously out of step with many of his contemporaries. The Prince, for all his humour, was a fish out of water in the 'hippy' age; his values and sense of dedication were not those of the Swinging Sixties. When someone remarked on how lucky it was that the heir to the throne was cast in such a

THE YOUNG PRINCE Prince Charles gives a helping hand to his young sister, Princess Anne in 1954 (BELOW LEFT). Standing with his great-uncle (or 'honorary grandfather'), Earl Mountbatten of Burma in 1979 (BELOW). Prince Charles donned diving gear to explore the

Mary Rose on the bed of the Solent (BOTTOM). He is President of the *Mary Rose* Trust.

HONEYMOON The Duke and Duchess of Rothesay (as the Prince and Princess are known in Scotland) on honeymoon at Balmoral ('the best

place in the world') three weeks after their wedding in 1981 (BELOW).

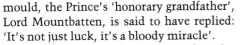

mould, the Prince's 'honorary grandfather', Lord Mountbatten, is said to have replied: 'It's not just luck, it's a bloody miracle'.

Like the Queen, the Prince of Wales believes that an active role in the life of the Commonwealth is one of the most important contributions he can make. He has travelled widely since his University days and there are now few parts of the Commonwealth that he has not visited. Before settling down to acquainting himself with the workings of government and industry in 1978, the Prince pursued an active career in the Services and spent a year running the successful Silver Jubilee Appeal.

For someone not, perhaps, naturally tough the Prince has shown admirable determination in earning the sobriquet of 'Action Man'. He undertook training at RAF Cranwell (winning his wings in 1971) and served in the Royal Navy from 1971 to 1976, ending up as a Commander in charge of HMS *Bronington*. Reluctant to mount a polo pony as a small boy, he went on to play at international level, to ride under National Hunt rules and to be an enthusiastic follower of hounds.

This thirst for the chase is combined with a feeling for the arts, the Service heartiness is blended with a basic sensitivity, maturity with a residual boyishness and broad humour with a deep seriousness and a sense of history. In short, the heir to the throne remains something of an enigma.

He chose his bride, the former Lady Diana Spencer, from a generation younger than his own. Born in 1961 at a house on the Sandringham estate into a family steeped in royal service (her father, Earl Spencer, was an equerry to the Queen, both her grandmothers and four of her great-aunts in the household of the Queen Mother), Lady Diana belonged to a new breed of level-headed girls who calmly managed to avoid the pitfalls of their predecessors from the 1960s and 1970s. Under the glare of publicity focused remorselessly upon her, the Prince's bride was billed as 'Shy Di'; but, happily for everyone, the Princess turned out to be tougher than she looked. The media having built her up to a celestial plane could not find anything new to say about her and so began, inevitably, to criticize her.

The Princess's popularity, however, showed no signs of decline. Her natural behaviour, youth and exceptional beauty brought a welcome breeze of fresh air into the royal family. To her credit she appeared to want to do things in her own way. A former nursery school teacher, she has a special gift with children and has taken on several patronages and presidencies in this connection as well as the Welsh National Opera. After the birth of her son, Prince William of Wales, the Princess broke with precedent by taking him on royal engagements, notably the tour to Australia and New Zealand undertaken by Prince Charles and herself in 1983.

PRINCESS OF WALES 'I am finding it very difficult to cope with the pressures of being Princess of Wales', the Princess confided in 1983 to the Premier of Newfoundland (who duly publicized her remarks), 'but I am learning to cope'. She added that she had 'matured a lot recently and got used to coping with things'.

These pictures illustrate how the Princess has become, in the words of one fashion editor, the best fashion ambassador Britain could have. Her favourite designers include Jasper Conran, Belville Sassoon, Benny Ong, Gina Fratini, Bruce Oldfield, Arabella Pollen, Jan Vanvelden, Caroline Charles and the milliner John Boyd.

Other Members of the Royal Family

Backing up the Queen in the 'family firm' — apart from her husband, mother, eldest son and daughter-in-law — are her younger sons Prince Andrew (born 1960) and Prince Edward (born 1964); her daughter Princess Anne, Mrs Mark Phillips and her sister Princess Margaret, Countess of Snowdon. Other members of the royal family include the Gloucesters and the Kents.

The Queen's two elder and two younger children are divided by a decade: Prince Charles was born in 1948, Princess Anne in 1950 and then Prince Andrew followed in 1960, Prince Edward in 1964. Prince Andrew, who is third in the line of succession to the throne (after his elder brother and his nephew, Prince William of Wales), came to the fore in the Falklands campaign of 1982 in which he served as a helicopter pilot with the Royal Navy. He had followed Prince Charles to Gordonstoun where he indulged in a variety of outdoor activities, notably gliding with the Air Cadet Corps. His education also included stays in France, Germany and Austria. In 1978 he was awarded his 'wings' after a parachute course with the RAF and in the following year he joined the Royal Navy on a 12-year short commission, passing through Dartmouth and a series of testing, challenging courses.

Prince Andrew, a strapping young man, has inherited many of his father's extrovert traits. His boisterous behaviour and his much-publicized girl-friends could be said to recall a much earlier age of royal rumbustiousness. In due course, as the second son of the sovereign, he should be created Duke of York.

Prince Edward is, as yet, less well known than his two elder brothers. He also went to Gordonstoun, where he went gliding with the Air Corps. He is likely to receive as tough a training as his brothers in the Services after he graduates from Jesus College, Cambridge. Like his brother, Prince Edward has spent time in the Commonwealth, teaching at a public school in New Zealand, which convinced him that he did not wish to pursue the profession of schoolmastering, though it also resulted in a published spoof on public schools. The Prince has enjoyed several trips with the Queen and the Duke of Edinburgh, including attending the Commonwealth Games in Canada (1978) and visiting Germany and Liechtenstein. It is not certain

PRINCES ANDREW AND EDWARD Prince Andrew and a friend in a toy bus at the Olympia Fun Fair in 1965 (ABOVE RIGHT). Prince Edward is also shown at an early age going off to kindergarten in 1968 (ABOVE). Prince Andrew is seen here (RIGHT) as a helicopter pilot at the Royal Naval Air Station, Portsmouth. He joined the Royal Navy in 1979, having been awarded his wings with the RAF in 1978. In a 1983 television interview, Prince Andrew said he was 'a recluse' who tried 'to keep out of people's way' and 'to avoid the press'. Prince Edward, photographed at Badminton in 1982 (LEFT), went up to Jesus College, Cambridge in October 1983.

what royal dukedom will eventually be conferred upon Prince Edward, though it will probably be the Dukedom of Sussex which was last in use for the sixth son of George III.

Princess Anne married a fellow equestrian, Captain Mark Phillips, in 1973. Always a keen horsewoman, like her mother, the Princess enjoyed a particularly successful season in the three-day events of 1971, winning the European Championship at Burghley and being voted the BBC's 'Sports Personality of the Year'. In the year of her marriage, Princess Anne took part in the world championship at Kiev and was a member of the British team in 1976 in the Olympic Games at Montreal. Since 1977 the Princess and her family (the children are Peter and Zara) have lived at Gatcombe Park in Gloucestershire in the 'Beaufortshire' country where the royal family are now congregating in numbers.

Here Captain Phillips, a Personal ADC to the Queen and now retired from the Army, farms just over 1,200 acres, half of which is under plough. Woodland takes up 250 acres.

Early in their married life, in March 1974, the Princess and Captain Phillips narrowly escaped injury in a dramatic kidnap attempt in the Mall when their car was held up by a gunman. The Princess's detective, James Beaton, and a gallant journalist, Brian McConnell, were both wounded in the ambush.

Very much her own woman with an individual sense of humour, Princess Anne stepped on to the royal stage at about the same time as her brother, Prince Charles. She has never shown any inclination to be granted the title of 'Princess Royal'. Sensibly she took on comparatively few patronages and presidencies, but the organizations she has adopted have received the benefit of considerable time and effort from the Princess. She has been an outstandingly conscientious President of Save the Children Fund, on whose behalf she has made many overseas visits. Princess Anne takes a full part in the general round of royal duties both at home and abroad. She has recently undertaken a number of important foreign tours.

During the Queen's absences abroad (when she is invariably accompanied by Prince Philip), Princess Anne often acts as a Counsellor of State in conjunction with the Prince of Wales, the Queen Mother and Princess Margaret. The Queen's younger sister was born in 1930 — her birth being the last occasion when, according to a tradition that belongs to the days when babies might have been exchanged in the bedchamber, the Home Secretary was required to attend the delivery. She has had perhaps an unhappy and certainly a difficult life, but still tackles her fair share of royal duties. In 1955 she was placed in the painful position of having to announce publicly that she was not marrying one of her father's equerries, Group Captain Peter Townsend, because he had been married before: 'Mindful of the Church's teaching that Christian marriage is indissoluble, and conscious of my duty to the Commonwealth, I have resolved to put these considerations before others'.

Five years later, in 1960, Princess Margaret married a royal photographer — Antony Armstrong-Jones, who was created Earl of Snowdon — but after they separated in 1976 the marriage ended in divorce. The particular tragedy for the monarchy was that, as a couple, Princess Margaret and her husband had represented a rare contact with the arts, which helped to balance what many see as the tweedy, horsey image of the royal family. The Princess sings, plays the piano and takes a special interest in ballet and modern art. She continues to live at the 'aunt heap' in Kensington Palace. Lord Snowdon has since remarried and has a young daughter by his second marriage.

Both Princess Margaret's children by Lord Snowdon, Viscount Linley and Lady Sarah Armstrong-Jones, were educated at Bedales — a progressive co-educational public shool. Lord Linley went on to do a crafts course at Parham and is now a furniture designer. At the moment, the statuesque Lady Sarah is

PRINCESSES MARGARET AND ANNE Princess Anne and her fellow-equestrian husband Captain Mark Phillips at the Burghley Horse Trials, 1982. She won the trials 11 years earlier (TOP LEFT). Princess Anne with her two children, Peter and Zara Phillips, at Badminton Horse Trials, April 1983. Even though the latter rank high in the order of succession to the throne, they do not have titles; their father refused to accept a peerage which would have given them courtesy styles. (FAR LEFT). Princess Margaret, an honorary Air Commodore, pictured at RAF Lyneham, Wiltshire, April 1983. A talented mimic, musician, arts enthusiast and connoisseur, the Princess is probably the most sophisticated member of the royal family (LEFT).

ROYAL RELATIONS
Prince and Princess
Michael of Kent with
their infant son, Lord
Frederick Windsor, at
the latter's
christening, July 1979
(1). The Duke and
Duchess of Gloucester
at the Murillo
Exhibition at the
Royal Academy, 1983
(2). The Duchess of
Kent talking to
Chelsea pensioners at
the Royal Hospital on
Founder's Day parade,
June 1980 (3). The
Duke of Kent, with
Mother Christmases,
at a Variety Club
lunch, 1982 (4).
Princess Alexandra at
RAF Benson, January
1983 (5). Princess
Alice, Duchess of
Gloucester, at the
service for the Order of
the Bath, Westminster
Abbey, 1978 (6).

1

2

3

4

5

6

best known as a royal bridesmaid, performing that role to Princess Anne in 1973 and the Princess of Wales in 1981.

Another octogenarian in the royal family apart from the Queen Mother is Princess Alice, the widow of the Queen's uncle, the late Duke of Gloucester who died in 1974 after a long illness. Formerly Lady Alice Montagu-Douglas-Scott, daughter of the 7th Duke of Buccleuch, she married Prince Henry, the Duke of Gloucester, in 1935 and they had two sons, Prince William (killed in a flying accident in 1972) and Prince Richard, the present Duke. Since the death of her husband, who was once Governor-General of Australia, Princess Alice has taken on an increased number of Colonelcies of regiments, patronages and presidencies. The present Duke of Gloucester studied architecture at Cambridge, but the pressure of royal duties after his brother's death meant that he was unable to pursue his chosen profession. Nevertheless, he still takes an active interest in the subject as Vice-Chairman of the Historic Buildings Commission and on behalf of the Victorian Society and other organizations. He also produced three books of photographs. In addition to all this, the bespectacled Duke runs the 2,500 acre estate at Barnwell in Northamptonshire, where he

lives with his Danish wife and children.

His cousin, the Duke of Kent, was a serving soldier until the political situation in Northern Ireland cut short his military career, though he had commanded his regiment in Cyprus. Now he travels extensively in his job as Vice-Chairman of the British Overseas Trade Board. The appointments of his Duchess, the former Katharine Worsley (a direct descendant, incidentally, of Oliver Cromwell), include being Controller Commandant of the Women's Royal Army Corps.

Prince Michael of Kent, the Duke's bearded brother, also a military man, was the subject of a religious controversy in 1978 when it became known that he wished to marry a Roman Catholic, Mrs Troubridge (otherwise Baroness Marie-Christine von Reibnitz), whose previous marriage had been dissolved by divorce and then annulled in the ecclesiastical courts. Pope Paul VI refused to allow a religious service and so the couple were married in a civil ceremony in Vienna. Prince Michael surrendered his rights to the throne as his bride is a Roman Catholic but their Protestant children can succeed.

Princess Alexandra has long been one of the most attractive and popular members of the royal family, inheriting the beauty of her mother Princess Marina, the late Duchess of

Kent. Much to the fore in the early and mid-1960s, during a period of transition for the royal family, Princess Alexandra has continued to undertake a full programme of royal duties. Her travels include frequent visits to Hong Kong where she has connections with the University and the Police Force. Princess Alexandra's businessman husband, the Honourable Angus Ogilvy, comes from a family well known in royal service; his father was the Queen Mother's Lord Chamberlain and his grandmother a Lady of the Bedchamber to Queen Mary.

Junior members of the present royal family include the Queen's cousins, the Earl of Harewood and the Honourable Gerald Lascelles (sons of the late Princess Royal) both of whom fathered sons out of wedlock before these children were subsequently legitimized by their father's respective second marriages. Also there are the Duke of Fife, the only great-grandson of King Edward VII residing in the United Kingdom; Captain Alexander Ramsay of Mar, grandson of Queen Victoria's third and favourite son, the Duke of Connaught; and finally, Queen Mary's surviving Teck relations, including the Marchioness of Cambridge, the Duchess and Duke of Beaufort, Lady May and Colonel Sir Henry Abel Smith.

Royal Residences

Special features follow on the five principal residences of
the Queen: Buckingham Palace in London, Windsor
Castle in Berkshire, Sandringham House in Norfolk, the
Palace of Holyroodhouse in Edinburgh and Balmoral
Castle in Aberdeenshire.

Buckingham Palace

Buckingham House, with its spacious gardens, was bought by George III from the Duke of Buckingham in 1762 and later transformed into a palace by George IV to the designs of John Nash. It was further enlarged by Queen Victoria and finally altered by George V in 1913. Divided up into state and private apartments, it is very much the London 'office' of the monarchy.

For countless millions, the name 'Buckingham Palace' immediately suggests the imposing, if not particularly inspiring, grey facade of Portland stone that stands at the end of the Mall. The garden front, however, with its golden Bath stone, is much more attractive. The building that stands today is largely the creation of that great royal builder George IV (1820-1830) who commissioned John Nash to convert the smaller Buckingham House into a palace large enough for entertaining on his accession to the throne.

The site where Buckingham Palace now stands was planted with mulberry trees at the beginning of the 17th century as part of a campaign by James I (1603-1625) to boost the raw silk industry. John Sheffield, Duke of Buckingham, had built the original house at the beginning of the 18th century after Queen Anne (1702-1714) made him the gift of some of St James's Park for him to enlarge his estate. Although the Queen took a dim view of Buckingham building such a fine house looking down the Mall, the Duke delighted in his creation, taking a special pride in the staircase 'with eight and forty steps ten feet broad, each step of one entire Portland stone'. The architects were William Talman (the designer of Chatsworth) and Captain William Winde, a Dutchman.

King George III (1760-1820) bought Buckingham House, which had spacious grounds more like a country house park than a town garden, in 1762. He made various modest improvements and held a celebrated 'house-warming' party, with the grounds lit up by over 4,000 coloured lamps. A vast picture of the 'Farmer' monarch, dispensing peace to all the world, was on show. About 60 years later, George IV managed to extract some £200,000 from Parliament for 'a repair and improvement of Buckingham Palace'. In fact, he spent about three times this in a virtual rebuilding. The 'King's House in Pimlico', as it was known, was constructed around a three-sided courtyard, the open side facing the Mall and approached through a triumphal arch — banished to Tyburn in 1851 where it became familiar to later generations of Londoners as the Marble Arch.

Nash's principal front of Bath stone, incorporating the shell of the original Buckingham House, overlooked the gardens which were landscaped by William Aiton. George IV died

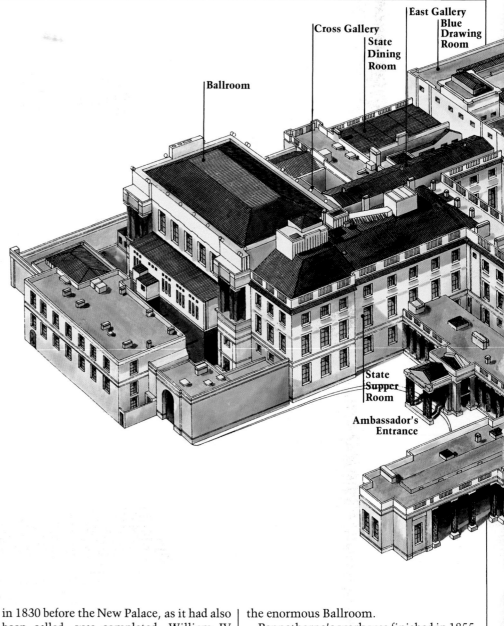

Ballroom

Cross Gallery

State Dining Room

East Gallery

Blue Drawing Room

State Supper Room

Ambassador's Entrance

in 1830 before the New Palace, as it had also been called, was completed. William IV (1830-1837) did not want to live there, suggesting that it might be used as the Houses of Parliament (following a devastating fire at Westminster in 1834) or as army barracks. The building was eventually completed by Edward Blore (who removed Nash's much-derided dome) and in 1847 he provided rooms for Queen Victoria's growing family by enclosing the courtyard with a dull range of Caen stone facing the Mall. Nash's nephew, Sir James Pennethorne, added the south wing which contains the State Supper Room and

the enormous Ballroom.

Pennethorne's work was finished in 1855, but six years later Prince Albert died and the palace was deserted for much of Queen Victoria's long widowhood. In 1873 it was lent to the Shah of Persia for his state visit and there were some bizarre occurrences. Apparently the Shah took his meals on the floor, was reluctant to avail himself of the palace's lavatories and organized a boxing match in the garden. It has even been suggested that he had one of his staff executed with a bowstring and buried in the grounds.

The building did not come into its own as a

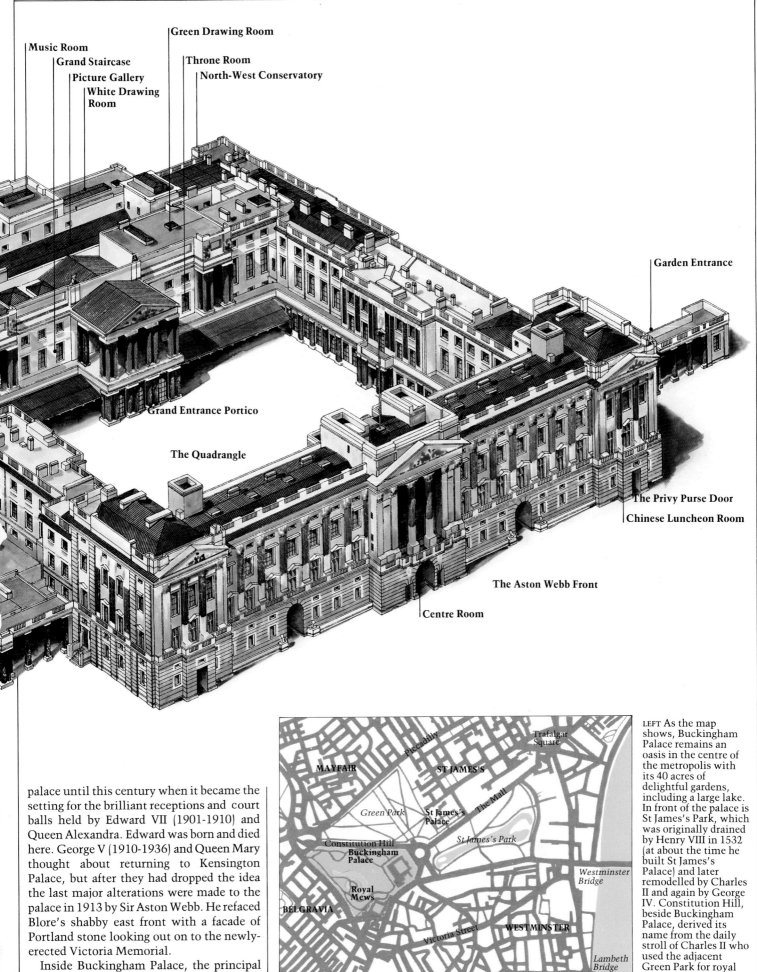

Music Room
Grand Staircase
Picture Gallery
White Drawing Room

Green Drawing Room
Throne Room
North-West Conservatory

Garden Entrance

Grand Entrance Portico

The Quadrangle

The Privy Purse Door
Chinese Luncheon Room

The Aston Webb Front

Centre Room

palace until this century when it became the setting for the brilliant receptions and court balls held by Edward VII (1901-1910) and Queen Alexandra. Edward was born and died here. George V (1910-1936) and Queen Mary thought about returning to Kensington Palace, but after they had dropped the idea the last major alterations were made to the palace in 1913 by Sir Aston Webb. He refaced Blore's shabby east front with a facade of Portland stone looking out on to the newly-erected Victoria Memorial.

Inside Buckingham Palace, the principal rooms on the first floor include the 60ft- long

MAYFAIR
Piccadilly
ST JAMES'S
Trafalgar Square
Green Park
St James's Palace
The Mall
Constitution Hill
St James's Park
Buckingham Palace
Westminster Bridge
Royal Mews
BELGRAVIA
Victoria Street
WESTMINSTER
Lambeth Bridge

LEFT As the map shows, Buckingham Palace remains an oasis in the centre of the metropolis with its 40 acres of delightful gardens, including a large lake. In front of the palace is St James's Park, which was originally drained by Henry VIII in 1532 (at about the time he built St James's Palace) and later remodelled by Charles II and again by George IV. Constitution Hill, beside Buckingham Palace, derived its name from the daily stroll of Charles II who used the adjacent Green Park for royal picnics.

Throne Room, with a ceiling and decoration that followed the designs of Nash. Some of the interior features came from Carlton House, George IV's sumptuous building capriciously pulled down in 1827. The Music Room, with its bold reliefs of *putti* in the spandrels of the domed ceiling, and the Blue Drawing Room are further examples of Nash's surviving designs. The Music Room is where royal christenings take place; the Blue Drawing Room was used for balls until Pennethorne added the largest of all the State apartments, the Ballroom, in the 1850s. Here investitures are held, as well as the occasional state banquet and ball. The throne canopy was designed by Sir Edwin Lutyens out of the Imperial Shimiana used at the Delhi Durbar of 1911.

The highly impressive Picture Gallery is 155 ft long and occupies the whole of the central area of the first floor on the west side of the palace, with an arched glass ceiling. It houses some of the finest pictures in the royal art collections including works by Rembrandt, Hals, Cuyp, Van Dyck and Poussin. Early in her reign Queen Victoria salvaged many of the paintings collected by George IV from store, where they had been placed after the destruction of Carlton House, and hung them in the Picture

LEFT This aerial view of Buckingham Palace shows the attractive, golden garden (or west) front and the grey Portland stone front facing east down the Mall. The adjoining wing nearest the camera, the north front, houses the private apartments of the royal family.

BELOW LEFT The Royal Bodyguard of the Yeomen of the Guard prepare for inspection by the Queen at Buckingham Palace, June 1966. In 1985 the Yeomen of the Guard celebrate 500 years of service to the crown, for this 'private guard of faithful fellowes' was created by Henry VII after his victory at the Battle of Bosworth. At his coronation, Henry declared that the Yeomen were not only for his personal protection but for 'the upholding of the dignity and grandeur of the English crown, in perpetuity, his successors, the kings and queens of England, for all time'.

LEFT The suitably palatial Mall front of Buckingham Palace, designed by Sir Aston Webb in Portland stone, 1913. The Queen Victoria Memorial is on the left.

ABOVE George VI in naval uniform and his Queen, now the Queen Mother, inspect the damage done by the bombing of Buckingham Palace, September 1940. It was, in the King's own words, 'a ghastly experience'; the chapel was destroyed but no one was hurt. 'A magnificent piece of bombing, Ma'am, if you'll pardon my saying so', concluded one policeman.

Gallery. The hanging arrangements were no less of a muddle in Queen Mary's time.

The Chinese Dining Room in the northeast angle of the east front facing the Mall is the most exotic room in the palace. It is a colourful confection made up of parts of the Music and Banqueting Rooms at Brighton Pavilion from where Queen Victoria and Prince Albert decamped in 1847. The old Queen enjoyed lunching in the room, though in modern times it has tended to be used more for meetings. This extraordinary corner room has recently been comprehensively restored, recapturing all its vivid, not to say overwhelming, effects.

The first floor of the east front is known at the palace as the 'principal floor'. Along it are such rooms as the Yellow Drawing Room (with a fantastic Chinese chimney-piece) and the Blue Sitting Room. Also decorated in the Chinese taste is the Centre Room from which, on special occasions, the royal family emerge on to the balcony overlooking the forecourt. It is a surprisingly small room, contrary to the idea of the 'backstage' area in the public imagination.

The semi-state apartments on the ground floor of Buckingham Palace include the 1855 Room (commemorating the occupation of Napoleon III and the Empress Eugénie), the

Bow Room (through which the 20,000 garden-party guests make their way to the lawn every year), the 1844 Room (named because of its occupation by Emperor Nicholas of Russia), and the Belgian Suite where Edward VII used to live. In 1960 Prince Andrew was born in the Orleans Bedroom here. The Garden Entrance on the north front of the palace is the one used by the Queen and her family. After the notorious invasion of the Queen's bedroom in 1982 the layout of the palace became all too familiar.

The Chapel was gutted by the salvo of bombs that fell across Buckingham Palace on 13 September 1940. Queen Elizabeth, the present Queen Mother, said she was glad that the palace had suffered bomb damage because it meant that she could look the people of the blitzed East End in the face. In 1959 her daughter the Queen decided to create an art gallery on part of the bombed site so that the public could see masterpieces from the royal collection. Three years later a spectacular exhibition opened in 'the Queen's Gallery', as it was called, and ever since there has been a rotating series of shows there.

Also open to the public is the Royal Mews where a collection of coaches, including Sir William Chamber's rococo State Coach first used for the opening of Parliament in 1762, is

on display. This is now the coach for coronations; the Irish State Coach is used for the Opening of Parliament and the Glass State Coach for royal weddings. Numerous other coaches, landaus, barouches, broughams, phaetons and sociables can be inspected, together with the Windsor greys themselves, state saddlery and other tack.

Every morning at half past eleven the guard is changed at Buckingham Palace. When the Queen is in residence, her standard flying, there is a guard of four sentries, otherwise there are only two. For herself and the family firm, 'Buck House' is the London office, neatly divided up into apartments for the workings of the Royal Household. The Queen and the Duke of Edinburgh have offices next door to one another on an upper floor. The inside is much more cheerful and interesting than the 'office block' interior one might imagine.

Even if now overlooked by the monstrous skyscrapers which were allowed to disfigure London in the 1960s, the 40 acres of Buckingham Palace gardens, with a lake, form a wonderful oasis in the centre of the metropolis. Visitors can sign their names as a gesture of loyal greetings at the Privy Purse Door (on the right of the Mall front) but the palace itself is not open to the public.

Windsor Castle

Founded by William the Conqueror, Windsor Castle took shape in various royal hands but it really owes its present romantic style to the flamboyant George IV (1820-1830) and his architect Sir Jeffry Wyatville. The extent to which the royal family identifies with Windsor is illustrated by the fact that since 1917 they have taken their surname from the place.

Like Buckingham Palace, Windsor Castle today is largely the creation of George IV (1820-1830). His architect Sir Jeffry Wyatville gave the castle a fairy-tale 'medieval' air, pulling the disparate elements together to give the impression of a composite building. However absurd, and even ugly, Wyatville's Gothic touches may appear close up, from a distance the edifice looks like everything a castle should be.

Windsor Castle was founded by William the Conqueror (1066-1087) as one of a chain of fortresses designed to control the Thames Valley and the environs of London. At first it was a construction of earthwork and timber erected on a hill overlooking an old Saxon palace. The strategic position of this fortress overhanging the river soon offset the greater comfort of the old palace in the valley.

The familiar Round Tower, on top of the mound which the Conqueror had piled up, dates from the reign of the first Plantagenet monarch, Henry II (1154-1189), who began replacing the wooden defences of the castle with stone from Bagshot. By the time of his death Henry II had made a start on a ring of stone around the castle, as well as building the Great Hall in the Lower Ward and the *Domus regis* in the Upper.

Henry III (1216-1272) completed the circuit of stone walls and added 'D'-shaped towers, giving Windsor a stylish air so that one chronicler described it as 'that very flourishing castle, than which, at that time, there was not another more splendid within the bounds of Europe'. Henry III's remodelling marked the advance from just a fortress. However, in the following century Edward III (1327-1377) made Windsor into a magnificent castle, carrying out an ambitious building programme with the help of William of Wykeham. Edward was not amused, however, when Wykeham claimed the credit by having *'Hoc fecit Wykeham'* carved on the wall of a tower.

The old decaying chapel was replaced by Edward IV (1461-1483) with what he wanted to be 'another and altogether more glorious building'. It is said that he wanted St George's Chapel to outshine the glories of the chapel of his predecessor Henry VI (1422-1461) across the river at Eton. Work began in 1472 and the final result was a most noble perpendicular, Gothic edifice, with Henry VII (1485-1509) responsible for the

nave and Henry VIII (1509-1547) for setting the choir roof. As it is the chapel of the Order of the Garter, the banners of the knights are hung above the stalls. The royal pews are separate while the sovereign's stall is marked by the Royal Standard. St George's Chapel contains the tombs of Henry VI (1422-1461), Edward IV, Henry VIII and his beloved Jane Seymour, Charles I (1625-1649), Edward VII (1901-1910) and Queen Alexandra, George V (1910-1936) and Queen Mary. George VI (1936-1952) is buried in the memorial chapel

named after him; whereas George III (1760-1820), Queen Charlotte, George IV and William IV (1830-1837) are buried beneath the chapel at the east end of St George's which Queen Victoria (1837-1901) restored in memory of Prince Albert.

The Albert Memorial Chapel was originally built by Henry VII in memory of Henry VI (1422-1461). Henry VIII rebuilt the entrance to the Lower Ward of the castle (the gatehouse is still named after him) and added the original wooden North Terrace, overlooking

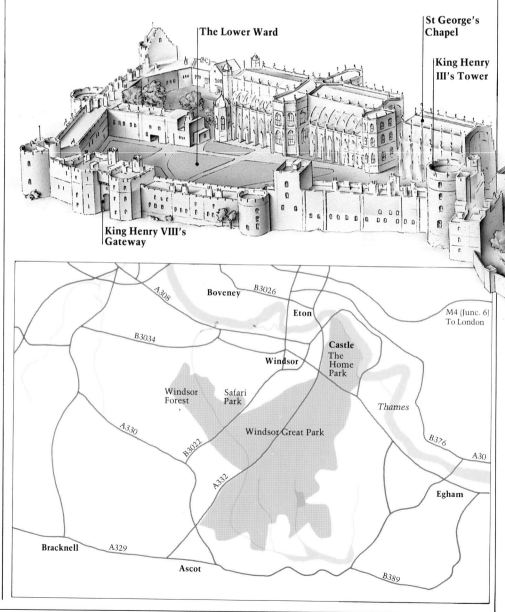

what is now the Home Park, in 1533. At Windsor the energetic young Hal 'exercised himself daily in shooting, singing, dancing, wrestling, casting of the bat, playing at the recorders, flute, virginals; in setting of songs and making of ballads'; but the years of fine living took their toll. His bed at Windsor was 11ft square and eventually he had to be lifted up the stairs by a rope and pulley system.

His daughter Elizabeth I (1558-1603) rebuilt the North Terrace in stone and in 1582 made a pretty garden below, but the castle was too cold for her taste. For her indoor walks she built a long gallery (later adapted into the present Library). She is said to have asked Shakespeare to write *The Merry Wives of Windsor*, which was reputedly first performed in the castle.

We have an idea of what Windsor was like in Elizabeth I's reign from Paul Hentzner's *A Journey in England in the Year 1598*. Hentzner found the castle to be 'a town of proper extent, inexpugnable to any human force', with a view that embraced 'a valley

ABOVE The Lower Ward of Windsor Castle *en fête*, in 1982, for the procession of the Garter Knights down the hill from St George's Hall (where they assemble every June) to the annual service for the Most Noble Order in St George's Chapel. The Order was founded by Edward III about 1348.

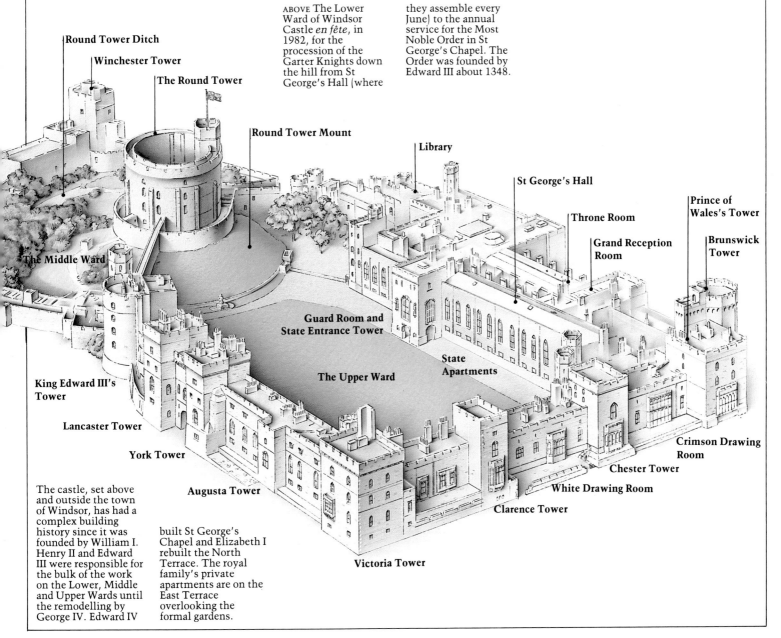

Round Tower Ditch

Winchester Tower

The Round Tower

Round Tower Mount

Library

St George's Hall

Throne Room

Prince of Wales's Tower

Grand Reception Room

Brunswick Tower

The Middle Ward

Guard Room and State Entrance Tower

The Upper Ward

State Apartments

Crimson Drawing Room

King Edward III's Tower

Lancaster Tower

Chester Tower

York Town

White Drawing Room

Augusta Tower

Clarence Tower

Victoria Tower

The castle, set above and outside the town of Windsor, has had a complex building history since it was founded by William I. Henry II and Edward III were responsible for the bulk of the work on the Lower, Middle and Upper Wards until the remodelling by George IV. Edward IV built St George's Chapel and Elizabeth I rebuilt the North Terrace. The royal family's private apartments are on the East Terrace overlooking the formal gardens.

extended every way, and chequered with arable lands and pasture, cloathed up and down with the groves and watered with that gentlest of rivers, the Thames'.

Inexpugnable or not, the royal occupancy of the castle came to an abrupt halt in 1642 when the Parliamentarians took possession after the Battle of Edgehill. Windsor remained the headquarters of Cromwell's army throughout the Civil War and reverted to one of its original functions as a prison. Among the prisoners was Charles I, ignominiously treated without 'the ceremonial of kingship' a few days before his execution and his subsequent return to Windsor in a coffin.

After the Restoration, the diarist John Evelyn recorded that the castle was 'exceedingly ragged and ruinous'. All this was to change under the stylish Charles II (1660-1685). The King had spent much of his youth in France, forming plans to rival the palace of Versailles at Windsor, and the years of exile had increased his leanings towards the Baroque. He reconstructed the Sovereign Apartments to the design of Hugh May and, if the exterior was austerely classical in style, with only an enormous Garter Star for decoration, the interior was a riot of lavish magnificence. There was an abundance of exuberant wood carvings by Philipps and the great Grinling Gibbons. Antonio Verrio painted 20 vast ceilings; unfortunately only three of these survived the redecoration by Wyatville for George IV.

In 1684, Charles II set about constructing a grand avenue stretching away from the south front of the castle up to the top of Snow Hill three miles away in the Great Park. This was the beginning of the Long Walk where, later, Queen Anne (1702-1714) made a road for her chaise in which she enjoyed bowling along often in pursuit of a stag. The avenue which runs for another three miles through the park from Queen Anne's Gate to the Prince Consort's Gate at Windsor is still known as 'Queen Anne's Ride'.

The third Hanoverian monarch, 'Farmer George' (the first king to die at Windsor) decided to change and redecorate the castle in the Gothic manner. He had not made much progress before succumbing to the horrible disease now believed to have been porphyria. Incidents like the one observed by a page called Philip Withers in the Great Park tended to confirm people's worst suspicions that he was mad. While out driving with his Queen, George III suddenly pulled the horses up, descended from the carriage and approached an oak tree, proceeding to shake it by one of the lower branches and carry on an earnest conversation under the impression that the oak was the King of Prussia. Withers was glad to report, however, that 'His Majesty, though under a momentary dereliction of reason, evinced the most cordial attachment to freedom and the Protestant faith'. Sadly, the straitjacket was not long in being applied.

James Wyatt had begun work in the Gothic style at Windsor for George III and his nephew Jeffry Wyatville carried on in earnest for George IV. The name was originally 'Wyatt' but the nephew had asked George IV if he could adopt this rather absurd nomenclature to avoid confusion with the other architects in the family. 'Veal or mutton, call yourself what you like,' the King is said to have replied.

Sir Jeffry Wyatville gave the Upper and Middle Wards of Windsor Castle a Gothic appearance by the romantic additions of curious windows, corbels and crenellations. In his 16 years of work up until 1840, Wyatville also redesigned much of the interior, doubling the length of St George's Hall and building the 550ft-long Grand Corridor joining the east front to the south front. George IV was the first king to use the east front for his private apartments — a tradition begun by Queen Charlotte — leaving the north front as the state apartments.

The best known of the state apartments is the Waterloo Chamber which the King planned towards the end of his reign to commemorate Wellington's mighty victory. It displays a stupendous series of portraits of the monarchs, soldiers and statesmen who contributed to the downfall of Napoleon; some 30 of them are by Sir Thomas Lawrence. The dining table seats 150 and a Waterloo Banquet is held here every year.

George IV's other achievement at Windsor was the completion of the Long Walk. He commissioned an imposing statue of his father, George III, in the unlikely garb of a Roman emperor astride a gigantic copper horse; this was placed as an eye-catcher at the far end of the Long Walk.

Although Windsor acquired its central place in the life of the British monarchy in the Victorian era, the Queen herself was not especially fond of the castle. 'Windsor always appears very melancholy to me,' she wrote at the beginning of her reign, 'and there are so many sad associations with it.' Her beloved Albert died here which did not improve her feelings towards it.

Albert was buried in the Royal Mausoleum at Frogmore in Windsor Park and the Queen's own effigy was added to that of her husband. No one has lived in Queen Charlotte's house at Frogmore since the Second World War, but this pretty place remains a peaceful sanctuary for the royal family. Once a year the public are allowed into the secret garden.

Other royal buildings in the Windsor Park

include the Queen Mother's weekend home, Royal Lodge, where she and her husband, George VI, created a rhododendron garden. In 1932 the small replica of a thatched Welsh cottage *(Y Bwthyn Bach)* was installed in the garden here — a present from the people of Wales to Princesses Elizabeth and Margaret. When Queen Mary came to see her two granddaughters, she found she could not stand up inside.

The little Welsh cottage is a rural complement to Queen Mary's Doll's House, which stands within the castle and was designed by the eminent architect Sir Edwin Lutyens to the scale of one-twelfth. It is a wonderfully elaborate spoof, with the work of noted artists and writers of the day well represented in miniature, and is one of the most popular attractions for the public. The state apartments are open regularly, affording a glimpse of the rich variety of paintings, furniture, armoury, china and other treasures that form part of the fabulous royal heritage.

The royal family enjoys the various equestrian pleasures available in the great expanse of park at Windsor — whether the Horse Show, the polo on Smith's Lawn or racing at Ascot. If Buckingham Palace is their office, Windsor is very much their home.

ABOVE Prince Philip driving down the Long Walk at Windsor which stretches away from the south front of the Castle (in background) to the statue of George III on a copper horse some three miles away on Snow Hill in Windsor Great Park. Begun by Charles II, the Long Walk was continued by Queen Anne, who also enjoyed driving along here, and finally completed by George IV.

LEFT The Queen and the then Dean of Windsor, the Right Reverend Launcelot Fleming, on the steps of St George's Chapel after Christmas Day mattins, 1975. Other members of the royal family seen in the picture include: Princess Margaret, Lady Sarah Armstrong-Jones, the Queen Mother, Prince Andrew and Prince Philip.

Sandringham

The Norfolk seat of the royal family was purchased for the future Edward VII (1901-1910) when he was Prince of Wales in 1862. He rebuilt the house in a sort of 'Jacobethan' style in 1870 and continued to enlarge the structure later in the 19th century. Popular with the royal family for the shooting, Sandringham still provides a rural retreat for the monarchy over the New Year.

It was Prince Albert's idea that his wayward son Albert Edward, Prince of Wales — later Edward VII (1901-1910) — should have a country house, where he could put down rural roots away from the fleshpots of the city, on his coming of age in 1862. Various possibilities were mooted, including the splendid Palladian palace of the Cholmondeleys in Norfolk, Houghton Hall; the wily Lord Palmerston, however, managed to steer the Prince Consort in the direction of Sandringham Hall in the same county, with which the statesman's stepson, Charles Spencer Cowper, was happy to part. Prince Albert died at the end of 1861 before the deal was complete, and Albert Edward himself did not come to inspect the place until February 1862. Its initial attractions for the young Prince were the shooting and the distance from his mother at Windsor.

In keeping with her late husband's wishes, Queen Victoria (1837-1901) adopted the scheme and duly purchased the house and 8,000 acres at Sandringham for £220,000. The house had been built in 1771 by Cornish Henley whose son sold the place to John Motteux; he, in turn, left it to his protégé, Charles Spencer Cowper. To cheer up its plain appearance, Cowper commissioned Samuel Teulon to add a somewhat bizarre Elizabethan porch, as well as a conservatory.

In 1865, after toying with various improvements, Albert Edward decided to pull the building down (apart from the conservatory which he converted into a billiard room) and start again. Prince Albert's architect, A.J. Humbert, who had worked at Osborne and Frogmore, was asked in 1867 to construct a sort of 'Jacobethan' house in red brick with yellowish Ketton stone dressings. 'This

house was built by Albert Edward and Alexandra his wife in the year of Our Lord 1870' is the proud inscription above the door.

Colonel R.W. Edis, perhaps a superior architect to Humbert, added a ballroom in 1881 and was called in again to remodel the house 10 years later after a bad fire just before Albert Edward's 50th birthday celebrations. For the appearance of the house, the fire may be considered a blessing in disguise. Even so, no one could claim that Sandringham is a work of architectural merit; it has been compared, unfavourably, to a hotel in Harrogate.

Sandringham became, however, in Albert Edward's words, 'the house I like best'. George V (1910-1936) also loved 'dear old Sandringham' better than anywhere else in the world. 'I have always been so happy here', wrote George VI (1936-1952) to his mother, 'and I love the place.' When the present

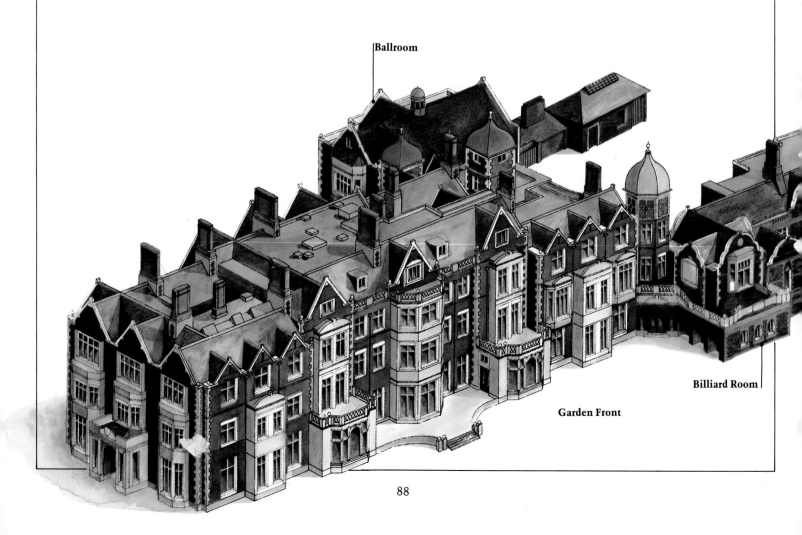

Ballroom

Garden Front

Billiard Room

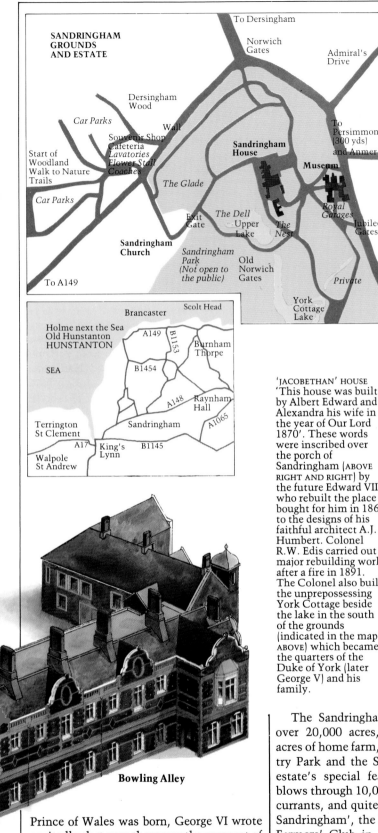

SANDRINGHAM GROUNDS AND ESTATE

Bowling Alley

'JACOBETHAN' HOUSE
'This house was built by Albert Edward and Alexandra his wife in the year of Our Lord 1870'. These words were inscribed over the porch of Sandringham (ABOVE RIGHT AND RIGHT) by the future Edward VII who rebuilt the place bought for him in 1861 to the designs of his faithful architect A.J. Humbert. Colonel R.W. Edis carried out major rebuilding work after a fire in 1891. The Colonel also built the unprepossessing York Cottage beside the lake in the south of the grounds (indicated in the map ABOVE) which became the quarters of the Duke of York (later George V) and his family.

Prince of Wales was born, George VI wrote excitedly that now there was the prospect of five generations at Sandringham. The previous Prince of Wales (briefly Edward VIII in 1936) took a less sympathetic view, describing Sandringham as a 'voracious white elephant' and apparently vowing to 'fix those bloody clocks' on the night of his father's death in 1936. Shooting has always dominated life here and the clocks used to be kept half-an-hour fast in order to fit in an extra half-hour's shooting on dark winter days.

The Sandringham estate today runs to over 20,000 acres, including some 3,200 acres of home farm, the Sandringham Country Park and the Stud. Fruit is one of the estate's special features. 'The wind still blows through 10,000 acres of British blackcurrants, and quite a lot of them…reside at Sandringham', the Prince of Wales told the Farmers' Club in 1977, 'Very few people know all this, but perhaps they will ponder on this rare story as they sip their next Ribena'.

The present royal family often use the six-bedroomed Wood Farm (where the present Queen's epileptic uncle Prince John lived out his 13 years) on the estate when they come to stay and the 'big house', which is open to the public in the summer months, remains much as it was in Queen Alexandra's day.

There are notable collections of Fabergé, Worcester porcelain, knick-knacks, sporting pictures and cases of stuffed game.

The gardens are Sandringham's best feature with two lakes, more than 200 different varieties of rhododendron, as well as daffodils, camellias, azaleas and primulas. One of the lakes, York Cottage Lake, takes its name from the 'most undesirable residence', where Prince George, Duke of York and Princess Mary of Teck (later George V and Queen Mary) brought up their family. Sir Harold Nicolson, George V's official biographer, described York Cottage as being a 'glum little villa'.

For all the criticisms of Sandringham, it expresses the role of the monarch as a simple country squire better than any of the other royal residences.

Holyroodhouse

The Palace of Holyroodhouse, originally an Augustinian abbey, was built by James IV of Scotland (1488-1513) and his son, James V (1513-1542). Although later remodelled (from 1671-1680), it·was not used by British sovereigns again until George IV's visit to Scotland in 1822. Today it remains the official residence of the Queen in Edinburgh.

Holyroodhouse, alone among the ancient royal palaces of Scotland, remains the official residence of the Queen when she goes to Edinburgh every year. A garden party and other state occasions take place here, enhanced by the presence of the Queen's Body Guard, the Royal Company of Archers, in their picturesque green uniforms. State visits to Scotland have recently been paid by the Kings of Norway and Sweden, when the special character of the palace was seen at its best. For all its forbidding aspect, Holyroodhouse is one of the most fascinating of royal palaces, little changed from the time of Charles II (1660-1685) and with a combination of intimacy and grandeur that seems to be particularly Scottish.

Below the cliffs of the brooding, extinct volcano, Arthur's Seat, David I, King of Scots (1124-1153), established a house of Augustinian canons, presenting the community with a reliquary containing a fragment of the True Cross; in consequence the abbey was dedicated to the Holy Cross or Holy Rood. Like other religious houses, Holyrood was used by the kings of Scotland, though their Edinburgh stronghold remained the castle. Of the medieval abbey, all that remains are the ruined nave of the church and the foundations of the transepts and quire. The guest house, west of the main monastic building, was altered and enlarged by James IV (1488-1513), who was determined to make Edinburgh the undisputed capital of Scotland and to give it a suitably magnificent royal palace. James V (1513-1542) carried on the building work at Holyrood and the Great Tower (built between 1529 and 1532) survives from this period.

The time of Mary, Queen of Scots (1542-1587) at Holyrood is overshadowed by the tragic drama that unfolded after her marriage to Darnley. He suspected that Mary was the lover of her secretary David Rizzio, whom he regarded as a Piedmontese upstart. On 9 March 1566 Darnley and some confederates entered the Cabinet where the Queen and her secretary were partaking of a light supper. The intruders asked for a word with Rizzio, then dragged him away to be messily murdered in the Queen's Outer Chamber.

Mary's son James VI (1567-1625) came to live at Holyrood in 1578 at the age of 12 and spent more time here than any other mon-

ABOVE A view of Holyrood royal garden party, 1982. The Queen stays at Holyroodhouse — her official residence in Edinburgh — for a few days every summer.

TOP The shadows from the gates fall across the outer court of Holyrood. The octagonal fountain, on the right, is a Victorian copy of the one at Linlithgow Palace.

arch; after travelling south to become King James I of England he only returned once, in 1617, when some repairs and improvements were carried out to the palace. Holyroodhouse ceased to be regularly occupied for nearly 200 years.

Nevertheless, major building plans were put in hand after the Restoration of Charles II. In works lasting from 1671 to 1680, the great 16th-century tower was remodelled and the rest of the palace rebuilt. Sir William Bruce and Robert Mylne produced a new quadrangle in an austere style, though the

plain walls were relieved in places by typically Scottish turrets. Inside, however, were rich furnishings and tapestries; the Gallery was adorned with 111 portraits, many of them fanciful, of Scottish kings painted by an enterprising Dutch artist called Jacob de Witt. In spite of these elaborate preparations Charles II never stayed here.

During the victorious part of his 1745 campaign, the Stuart 'Young Pretender', Bonnie Prince Charlie held court at Holyrood for five weeks. He touched for the 'King's Evil', dined publicly and gave a state ball in the Gallery, but all the pomp was founded on sadly unrealistic hopes. The following year the Duke of Cumberland stayed here on his way to Culloden. Both Bonnie Prince Charlie and the Butcher stayed in the rooms of the Dukes of Hamilton, Hereditary Keepers of Holyroodhouse who, with other noblemen, occupied much of the palace in the long years of royal absence.

Interest in the palace was revived eventually by the popular visit of George IV (1820-1830) to Scotland in 1822. Inspired by the writer Sir Walter Scott, the ample King donned a kilt, wearing flesh-coloured tights to preserve his modesty. George IV revelled in the ceremonies (including a levée at which 2,000 people were presented to him), being cheered by crowds estimated at one million as he drove in state to and from Holyrood. Scott, who acted as master of ceremonies, reported that 'the visit of the King to Edinburgh...was like the awakening of Abou Hassan to a dream of Sovereignty'. Possibly overcome with emotion, George IV stumbled on the staircase at Holyrood but was saved from a fall by the shoulders of a stout baronet.

The success of the King's adventure can be seen as a prologue to the attachment of Queen Victoria (1837-1901) to Scotland and to Holyrood remaining intact as a royal palace. As early as the 1850s the Queen ordered that the royal apartments should be opened to the public. The Queen was fond of driving round Arthur's Seat, where the impression of being in some desolate place in the Highlands (although still on the edge of a city) is just as striking today as it was then. The route has become known as 'The Queen's Drive'. Queen Victoria started the custom, which has been continued by her successors, of occupying Holyrood for a brief period every year.

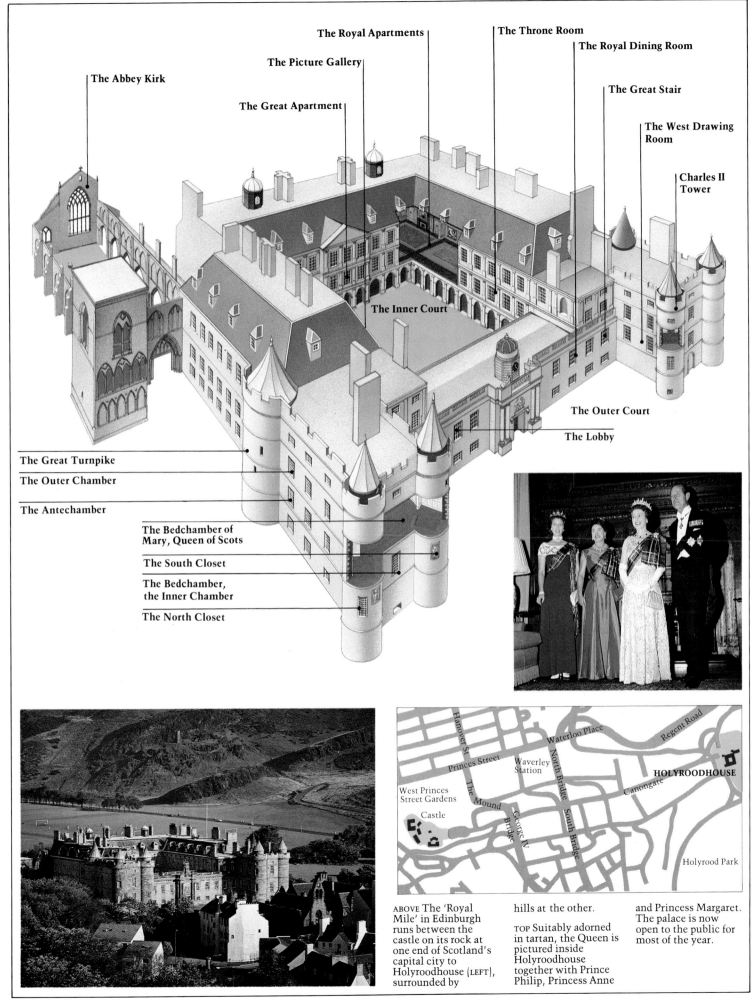

The Abbey Kirk

The Picture Gallery

The Royal Apartments

The Great Apartment

The Throne Room

The Royal Dining Room

The Great Stair

The West Drawing Room

Charles II Tower

The Inner Court

The Great Turnpike

The Outer Chamber

The Antechamber

The Bedchamber of Mary, Queen of Scots

The South Closet

The Bedchamber, the Inner Chamber

The North Closet

The Outer Court

The Lobby

ABOVE The 'Royal Mile' in Edinburgh runs between the castle on its rock at one end of Scotland's capital city to Holyroodhouse (LEFT), surrounded by hills at the other.

TOP Suitably adorned in tartan, the Queen is pictured inside Holyroodhouse together with Prince Philip, Princess Anne and Princess Margaret. The palace is now open to the public for most of the year.

91

Balmoral

Queen Victoria and Prince Albert bought Balmoral Castle underneath Loch-na-Gar in 1852 from the Duff family. Albert promptly rebuilt the castle in 'Scotch Baronial' style. He and the Queen entered enthusiastically into Highland life — a tradition faithfully followed by the present royal family who always spend their summer holidays here.

At breakfast one morning in the autumn of 1847, Sir Robert Gordon, tenant of Balmoral Castle in Aberdeenshire which then belonged to the Duff Earls of Fife, choked to death on a fishbone. This turned out to be convenient for Queen Victoria (1837-1901) and Prince Albert, who had fallen in love with the Highlands and had recently learnt of Balmoral's charms while they were being drenched on the west coast. The unfortunate Sir Robert had had the castle remodelled in 1834 to the designs of 'Tudor Johnny' Smith. 'It is a pretty little castle in the old Scotch style', noted Queen Victoria, '...one enters a nice little hall, and a billiard room and dining-room. A good broad staircase takes one upstairs and above the dining-room is our sitting-room...a fine large room opening into our bedroom, etc'. The Queen and Prince Albert duly took over the lease.

As they settled into their new home in the Highlands, Victoria and Albert set their hearts on buying Balmoral outright, as well as the neighbouring estates of Abergeldie and Birkhall and the forest of Ballockbuie. They had to be content with a lease of Abergeldie from the Gordons, but Birkhall was purchased with 6,500 acres in the name of the Prince of Wales. After protracted negotiations, Balmoral itself, with 17,400 acres, was finally bought in 1852 for 30,000 guineas from the Fife trustees. Whereas previous royal residences had all been crown property, this was a private sale; the purchasing money came out of a bequest from an idiosyncratic old miser, John Camden Neild, who died that year leaving his considerable fortune to the Queen. For Albert, with his passion for architectural projects, this buckshee cash answered a prayer.

As 'Tudor Johnny' had died, Albert promptly sent for his son, William. Together they chose a new site only 100 yards from the old house for a castle to be built in the highly popular Scottish Baronial style. Albert and Smith's idea was to build in such a way that the new castle and gardens would conform with the ranges of foothills rising to the summit of Loch-na-Gar. The landscaping was deputed to James Giles, while William Smith tackled the building.

Smith wasted no time and the new castle was ready for occupation by September 1855, the old having been demolished. Multi-turreted with castellated gables, a *porte-*

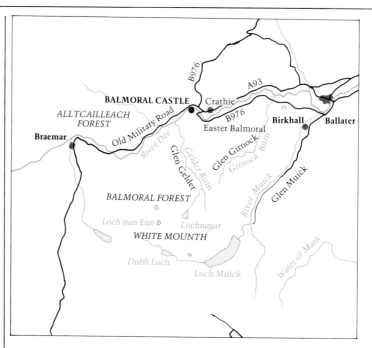

ABOVE The Balmoral estate, purchased by Prince Albert and Queen Victoria in 1852, now extends to some 24,000 acres on 'Royal Deeside', including Birkhall (home of the Queen Mother) and Ballochbuie Forest. The nearest hamlet to the castle, Crathie, to the east, contains the local church (built in 1885) where the royal family worship on their annual Scottish sojourn in August and September. On the first Saturday in September they attend the Highland Gathering at Braemar, to the west. The old railway town of Ballater is to the east of Crathie.

cochère and a 100ft tower, the new castle was built of grey Invergelder granite, had 180 windows, 67 fireplaces (as well as a central heating system), four bathrooms and fourteen water-closets. 'The new house looks beautiful', wrote Queen Victoria in her journal, '...charming; the rooms delightful; the furniture, papers, everything perfection'.

At the end of each summer, Victoria and Albert returned to their beloved Balmoral. Every year, as the Queen wrote in her journal: *'My heart becomes more fixed in this dear Paradise and so much more so now that all has become my dear Albert's own creation, own work, own building, own*

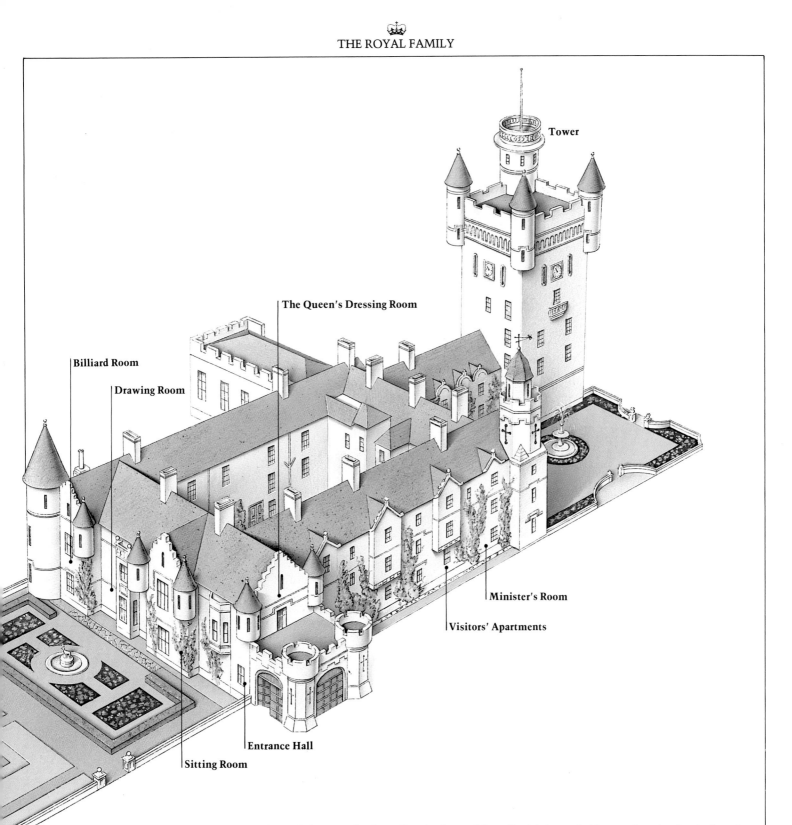

Tower

The Queen's Dressing Room

Billiard Room

Drawing Room

Minister's Room

Visitors' Apartments

Entrance Hall

Sitting Room

laying-out, as at Osborne: and his great taste and the impress of his dear hand, have been stamped everywhere.'
Inside the castle the main effect of this impress was in the ubiquitous tartan and the motif of the thistle.

The Prince Consort designed a special Balmoral tartan of black, red and lavender on a grey background; soon the pattern was literally everywhere. One of the Queen's granddaughters described the decor as 'more patriotic than artistic and had a way of flickering before your eyes and confusing your brain'. Lord Rosebery unkindly remarked that he had considered the drawing room

at Osborne to be the ugliest in the world until he saw the one at Balmoral; while Lord Clarendon observed that 'the thistles are in such abundance that they would rejoice the heart of a donkey if they happened to look like his favourite repast which they don't'.

Sassenach prejudice aside, Victoria and Albert achieved a notable rapport with the Highlanders, relishing the chance to lead an outdoor life. They would repair to 'The Hut' up Glen Muick, travel incognito on excursions to the Cairngorms, where the Queen would jot and sketch, and enjoy sport which was then organized more simply. At the end of the 1861 Scots sojourn, Albert recorded in

his journal: 'Go out shooting for the last time and shoot nothing'. It was indeed the last time he stayed at Balmoral, for he died a few months later.

Queen Victoria, who described herself as 'his broken-hearted widow' in the granite pyramid she erected in memory of 'Albert the Great and Good' on the spot where he had shot his last stag, came slightly less frequently to Balmoral after his death. The Queen's love of the Highlands endured, however, and her devoted servant John Brown (Albert's former gillie) personified what she liked most in upper Deeside. Towards the end of the Queen's life in 1901, the atmosphere at

ABOVE An aerial view of Balmoral in winter. The present castle was built by Prince Albert and his architect, William Smith, in the early 1850s.

RIGHT Well wrapped up for a Scottish summer the Queen and Queen Mother attend a gundog trial at Balmoral, August 1973.

FAR RIGHT A constitutional walk for the corgis at Balmoral.

Balmoral became stiff and formal, giving rise to the expression 'Balmorality'.

Edward VII (1901-1910) and Queen Alexandra had previously spent holidays at Abergeldie but, on his accession, only visited Balmoral for about a month every year. The castle is essentially Victorian, and George V (1910-1936), who was more of a Victorian than his father, had a greater affection for it. He and his son George VI (1936-1952) used to stay for at least two months in the autumn, a practice followed by the present royal family.

Balmoral remains a special private holiday home for the royal family, a world apart.

Here, in the words of Balmoral's historian Ronald Clark, the Queen can still 'take a deep breath on her own property and — with the exception of an unending stream of dispatch boxes — live with her family the life of a Scottish landowner'. Stalking, walking, fishing, picnicking, sketching, interspersed with visits to Crathie Churchyard and the games at Braemar and Ballater nearby, are the order of the day. The Prince of Wales's best-selling book for children (originally written for Prince Edward), *The Old Man of Loch-na-Gar*, was inspired by Balmoral.

The royal family's hereditary love of the

Highlands has, of course, been amplified by the Scots blood of the Queen Mother who has made Birkhall into a charming retreat on the Balmoral estate, adding a bow-fronted wing in the 1950s to the old Scottish 'ha-house'. The Queen Mother's friend, Ruth, Lady Fermoy, who hails from Aberdeenshire, also ensures that there is a high proportion of Scots blood in her granddaughter the Princess of Wales — and hence Prince William. The Prince and Princess of Wales, alias the Duke and Duchess of Rothesay, are to make a Scottish home in another house on the Balmoral estate, Delnadamph Lodge.

The Routine of Royalty

The role of the modern monarchy – the business of what George VI (1936-1952) described as the 'Royal Firm' – involves as much paperwork as pageantry. Special features examine the Queen's constitutional position, the pattern of her days and years, the honours system, the Royal Household, finance, and the meticulous planning which goes into foreign tours and special occasions.

The Queen and the Constitution

As a constitutional monarch Her Majesty has the right to be consulted, the right to encourage and the right to warn. Having been Queen since 1952, she has much wider experience of diplomacy and politics than any of her ministers; already she has dealt with eight prime ministers: Churchill, Eden, Macmillan, Douglas-Home, Wilson, Heath, Callaghan and Thatcher.

Under the British Constitution, which is, of course, unwritten, the Queen is still a highly influential figure, exercising far more power than perhaps many, who only associate the monarch with pageantry, quite realize. In his classic Victorian work, *English Constitution*, Walter Bagehot defined the three rights of a constitutional monarch: 'the right to be consulted, the right to encourage, the right to warn'. He added that:

'a king of great sense and sagacity would want no others. He would find that his having no others would enable him to use these with singular effect. A wise king would gradually acquire a fund of knowledge and experience which few ministers could rival'.

This has certainly been the case with Queen Elizabeth II. After over 30 years on the throne she is without doubt a very experienced political figure, having dealt with eight Prime Ministers — Sir Winston Churchill, Sir Anthony Eden, Harold Macmillan, Sir Alec Douglas-Home, Sir Harold Wilson, Edward Heath, James Callaghan and Margaret Thatcher (who did not even enter Parliament until the Queen had been reigning for over seven years). The Queen has impressed them all with her mastery of crucial issues. Macmillan wrote of an audience which he had on his return from the United States in 1960: 'I was astonished at Her Majesty's grasp of all the details set out in various messages and telegrams'. In the following year, when for security reasons many voices were raised against her visit to Ghana, Macmillan commented that she 'means to be a Queen and not a puppet'.

Lord Esher's description of her great-grandfather Edward VII (1901-1910), is strikingly apt for her too:

'He had an instinct for statecraft which carried him straight to the core of a great problem without deep or profound knowledge of the subject. He had one supreme gift, and this was his unerring judgement of men and women.'

The Queen's knack of going 'straight to the core' of a problem has disconcerted modern politicians. At his farewell dinner in March 1976 Sir Harold Wilson urged his successor, James Callaghan, 'to do his homework before his audience...'

The Queen — unlike, say, the President of the United States — has no veto over Parliament. There has been no example of the use of the veto since the reign of Queen Anne and, according to Bagehot, the Queen 'must sign her own death warrant if the two houses unanimously send it to her'. Certain residual royal 'prerogatives' do, however, remain. For instance she chooses the Prime Minister in the situation when no one party commands a

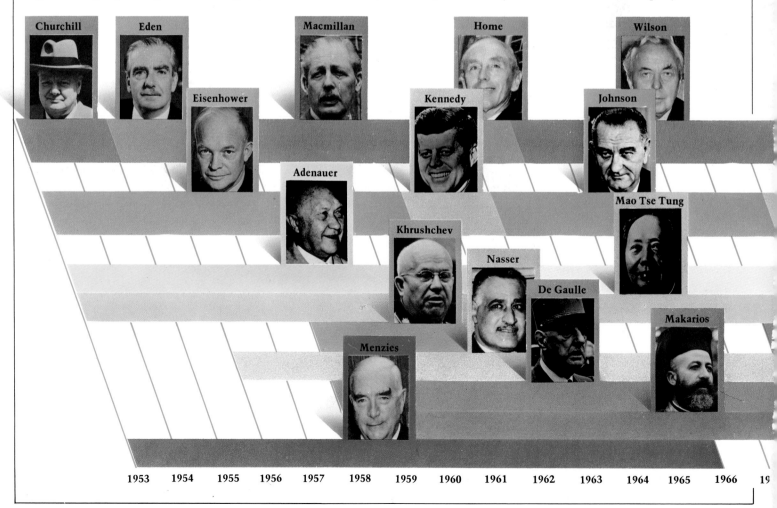

clear majority in the House of Commons. The major British political parties have elective machinery to decide their leaders. However, should an elected leader seem not to be the person best able to command a majority, the Queen could, in theory, step in and suggest a new leader. This is increasingly likely to happen if a 'hung Parliament' arises. The Queen is not afraid of her constitutional responsibilities at home and in the Commonwealth. The dismissal of Mr Whitlam in Australia was a vigorous reminder that the power of the crown is not altogether nominal.

The last monarch to dissolve Parliament without the advice of a Prime Minister was William IV (1830-1837) in 1834, and this aspect of the royal prerogative seems to have lapsed. There remains a slight area of doubt as to whether a constitutional monarch can refuse to grant a dissolution to a Prime Minister. This has not been put to the test for over a century.

The remaining parts of the prerogative concern the creation of peers and the conferment of honours. Only two hereditary peerages and, inexplicably, no baronetcies have been created since 1965 and it will be intriguing to see whether Prince Andrew and Prince Edward are created Duke of York and, say, Duke of Sussex respectively. When the Queen once announced that her government was planning to eradicate the hereditary element from the House of Lords, the irony of this situation seemed lost on almost everyone.

LEFT The Queen is pictured here with the Commonwealth delegation in July, 1977. From left to right, beginning from the back, the delegation leaders are from: Western Samoa, Malaysia, Fiji, Lesotho, Kenya, Singapore, Sri Lanka, Guyana, Swaziland, Trinidad and Tobago, The Gambia, Botswana, Canada, Papua New Guinea, Sierra Leone, Mauritius, Barbados, Granada, Tanzania, Ghana, The Bahamas, Tonga, Malawi, India, Australia, Jamaica, Cyprus, Great Britain, Zambia, Bangladesh, New Zealand and Nigeria.

LEFT Shown here are the British Prime Ministers, American Presidents and other important world leaders who have been in power during the Queen's reign.

Heath

Wilson

Callaghan

Thatcher

Nixon

Ford

Carter

Reagan

Kenyatta

Trudeau

Fraser

1968 1969 1970 1971 1972 1973 1974 1975 1976 1977 1978 1979 1980 1981 1982 1983 1984

The Queen's Day

Even when not 'on show', the Queen tackles a prodigious amount of paperwork, reading government papers from the ubiquitous Red Boxes. She also has to cope with the daily correspondence, audiences with ministers and public figures, meetings of the Privy Council, investitures, garden parties and a programme of official events planned months ahead.

In 1971, when the Queen was requesting an increase in the Civil List, Sir Michael Adeane (her private secretary from 1954 to 1972) drew up a precise account of her actions, her duties and responsibilities. He divided his most important memorandum on 'The Queen's own duties in her capacity as Sovereign of the United Kingdom, and of the 10 other self-governing Commonwealth Monarchies and the remaining colonial Territories, and as Supreme Governor of the Church of England and with her special responsibility to the Established Church of Scotland' into four categories:

'First there is the work arising from the normal operations of Government in the form of information she receives both from Ministers at home and representatives abroad, and submissions which she has to approve and sign. The Queen receives copies of all Government papers — reports from Ambassadors and Ministers abroad, instructions or replies from the Foreign Office, copies of Parliamentary papers, copies of memoranda and minutes of all important conferences such as meetings of Commonwealth Ministers. There is therefore a continuing burden of unseen work involving some hours' reading of papers each day in addition to Her Majesty's more public duties...'

In his memoirs, Edward VIII has left a picture of his father, George V (1910-1936) 'doing his boxes' as 'the relentless grind of the King's daily routine'. What are known as the 'Red Boxes' arrive every day for the Queen; they contain the cream of the official information, not only of all the UK government departments but also all the Commonwealth ones. Thus the Queen's information is as good as any statesman's and, as her reign progresses, so she becomes increasingly knowledgeable. With her retentive brain, this means that her political contribution grows ever more important. The Queen also receives Hansard and a wide selection of newspapers and magazines — even if she is said always to turn first to the *Sporting Life*. Her knowledge is further supplemented by the number of leading world figures she meets, and the wide variety of people in senior positions in the life of the nation with whom she comes in contact. The Queen also has to attend to an enormous daily cor-respondence, assisted by various secretaries, and to numerous internal matters concerning the running of the household. All this has to be fitted into the early part of the morning as well as family life and a walk with the corgis in the garden.

'Secondly', wrote Sir Michael Adeane — or, in other words, later in the morning:

'The Queen receives a large number of important people in audience. These include those about to be appointed to, or retire from, senior public posts and discussions with the Prime Minister and other Ministers. She also holds meetings of the Privy Council and some fourteen investitures each year at which she personally bestows over two thousand orders, decorations and medals...'

During an audience the Queen is invariably alone. She must be knowledgeable and interested in the particular subject of whoever is being received. This may be an Ambassador, a High Court Judge, a Bishop, the Director of Royal Artillery or her stud groom. During a Commonwealth Prime Ministers' Conference, she will see each Prime Minister separately. She must be up to date on the latest developments in the country of each one. The relationship between the Queen and her British Prime Minister is obviously of supreme importance. He or she arrives at Buckingham Palace every Tuesday evening while the Queen is staying in London so that they can talk about recent events. Their discussions can embrace any topic.

The Queen is, of course, apolitical in the sense that she favours no particular party. It would be utterly wrong, for instance, to suppose she leans in any way towards the Conservatives. She is said to have enjoyed a specially harmonious relationship with Labour's Sir Harold Wilson who, when he resigned in 1976, hoped that his successor James Callaghan would enjoy, as he had, the Queen's 'manifold kindness, understanding and trust'. Callaghan also established a rapport with the Queen which is said to have been considerably warmer than that with, say, Edward Heath or Margaret Thatcher. According to Sir Godfrey Agnew, sometime Clerk of the Privy Council, 'The Queen doesn't make fine distinctions between politicians of different parties. They all roughly belong to the same social category in her view'.

Further revelations of the relationship between the Queen and her ministers have been given by the late Richard Crossman and by Barbara Castle in their published diaries. Crossman found the meetings of the Privy Council, which fell within his province as Lord President of the Council, 'the best example of pure mumbo-jumbo you can find';

A DAY IN THE LIFE OF THE QUEEN The Queen discusses her correspondence with her secretary at Buckingham Palace. Note the red despatch boxes and the action baskets (ABOVE). Walking the dogs (RIGHT). Entertaining President Kaunda of Zambia on his State Visit to Britain, 1983 (BELOW). FAR RIGHT The Queen photographed

also, he resented that four busy ministers had to take a day and night off to travel to Balmoral for the two-and-a-half-minute business of a Privy Council meeting during which time 50 or 60 Titles of the Orders in Council were approved by the Queen. Later he conceded that this was necessary to the magic of monarchy. On one occasion, Crossman related, Sir Edward Bridges was introducing four politician Privy Councillors. They knelt on the wrong side of the room and Sir Edward indicated their mistake. They proceeded to crawl across the room on their hands and knees. 'In the process', wrote Crossman, 'they knocked a book off the table and it had to be rescued by the Queen, who looked blackly furious'. Later she revealed that she had been trying desperately not to laugh.

The holding of investitures is one of the most physically exhausting of the Queen's duties. It involves the Queen standing in the Ballroom of the Palace for over an hour and a quarter, during which time she must concentrate continually and maintain a grave dignity. She invests about two hundred citizens, addressing a few words to each one.

The description of a few days in July 1976 can be taken as a random example of how busy the Queen can be. The day after she returned from an onerous tour of the United States and Canada, she was present at St Paul's Cathedral for the annual service of the Order of St Michael and St George. This is a long ceremony in which the procession reforms several times and winds its way up and down the aisle more than once. During the afternoon the Queen hosted a Palace garden party, progressing slowly through the lines of 8,000 invited guests, and, as if that were not enough, the next morning she held an investiture.

Since presentation parties for debutantes were stopped in 1958, informal luncheons for people from varied walks of life have become a feature of the Queen's day. The afternoon may well be taken up with some sort of outside engagement, but on the whole the Queen prefers not to go out in the evening. After an exhausting day she may well be found watching television with her supper on a tray on her lap.

The Queen's official programme is planned months in advance and therefore her life is ruled by endless minor commitments. She cannot suddenly decide to take a holiday or a day off. If a state visit is to be undertaken, she has to spend extra time thoroughly briefing herself, and this has to be fitted into an already arduous schedule.

at her desk at Sandringham to mark the 30th anniversary of her accession in 1982. Her father George VI died here on 6 February 1952.
THE DAY CONTINUES The Queen inspecting Chelsea Pensioners at the Royal Hospital (ABOVE). The Queen unveils the statue of her husband's uncle, Admiral of the Fleet the Earl Mountbatten of Burma (murdered by the IRA in 1979) in London, 1983 (LEFT). The Queen attending the royal film premiere of *Kramer versus Kramer*, 1980 (BELOW).

The Royal Year

A regular pattern emerges: one year the Queen may go to Australia, another to Canada. At home, there is the annual round of such events as Maundy Thursday, the Birthday Parade (Trooping the Colour), the Garter service at Windsor, Ascot, garden parties, the holiday at Balmoral, the State Opening of Parliament, Remembrance Day, Christmas at Windsor, and so on.

One year in the life of the Queen is not unlike the others; they tend to follow a pattern. After Christmas at Windsor, the royal family often migrate to Sandringham for the New Year. Then, back at Buckingham Palace, there are the regular events of the royal diary which come into the category outlined by Sir Michael Adeane in his 1971 Memorandum:

'The Queen attends numerous State occasions such as the State Opening of Parliament, The Queen's Birthday Parade, Remembrance Day, and various services at St Paul's Cathedral and Westminster Abbey. There are many engagements both public and private involving visits to local universities, hospitals, factories and units of the Armed Forces...'

On Maundy Thursday, the day before Good Friday, the Queen distributes the Royal Maundy to as many elderly persons as the years of the monarch's age. This ceremony is said to go back to early medieval times; Edward the Confessor (1042-1066), for instance, used to wash the feet of the poor before handing over the money. The ceremony in its present form was revived, without the feet-washing, by the Queen's grandfather George V (1910-1936). The alms consist of specially minted silver coins. Since 1957, when the Queen distributed the Royal Maundy at St Albans Abbey, the ceremony has been held at various places,

other than the capital itself, for the first time since the days of Charles II (1660-1685).

June and July are particularly busy months. On a chosen Saturday in the middle of June, the Queen celebrates her official birthday; an honours list is published and she rides to Horse Guards Parade where the Household Division are gathered. The colour of one of the five regiments of foot guards (Grenadier, Coldstream, Scots, Irish and Welsh) is then trooped. First performed on the sovereign's birthday for George III (1760-1820), in the reign of Queen Victoria (1837-1901) a Birthday Parade on her actual birthday, 24 May, became a regular feature of the royal year and it has continued to be held around that date ever since.

The Queen, riding side-saddle, wears the uniform of the Guards regiment that owns the colour being trooped. She wears the

ABOVE On both her actual (21 April) and official (mid-June) birthdays, the Queen receives a 41-gun royal salute from the King's Troop of the Royal Horse artillery in Hyde Park.

FAR LEFT The Queen at the Maundy Service in St David's Cathedral in Wales, 8 April 1982. This act of royal charity used to involve the monarch washing the feet of the poor as well as handing over alms and gifts. Since 1957 a custom has grown by which the Royal Maundy is distributed away from Westminster Abbey every other year.

LEFT The Queen, riding side-saddle, takes the salute at the Birthday Parade, the 'Trooping the Colour' ceremony on Horse Guards Parade, June 1979.

ABOVE The Queen, with the Dean of Windsor, the Right Reverend Michael Mann, after Christmas mattins at St George's Chapel, 1982. The royal family have spent Christmas at Windsor since 1964.

Garter ribbon over her red tunic (unless it is the Scots Guards when she wears the dark green ribbon of the Thistle). On the following Monday the Queen and the 24 Garter Knights process down the hill at Windsor Castle for the annual service of the Order of the Garter at St George's Chapel — a sight worth travelling to see for the Queen looks splendid in the blue velvet robes of the Most Noble Order.

Garter Day precedes Ascot Week when the Royal meeting takes place on the course laid out by Queen Anne on the fringes of Windsor Great Park. The tradition of the royal family driving down the course in landaus before racing each day was started by George IV (1820-1830). The landaus are drawn by the Windsor Greys to the entrance of the royal box. A house party is given at Windsor every year for Ascot Week. Another annual racing event that is always attended by members of the royal family is the Derby at Epsom, which is held in early June.

Garden parties are a particular feature of the July calendar and there is also a busy programme of engagements on the more or less annual visits to Holyrood. The late summer to autumn holiday at Balmoral is followed by the return to London in good time for the State Opening of Parliament. In the House of Lords the Queen reads a speech written by her government outlining the forthcoming legislation to be laid before Parliament. In November comes the Festival of Remembrance at the Albert Hall on the Saturday nearest Armistice Day; the following morning the Queen stands by the Cenotaph and lays her wreath of poppies.

Apart from her duties at home, the Queen often travels abroad with her husband. One year she may go to Australia, another to Canada or some smaller Commonwealth countries. Her travels overseas are likely to be even more demanding than her duties at home.

ABOVE Some of the 35,000 people who attend royal garden parties each summer are seen here at Buckingham Palace. The guest list has recently become markedly more 'democratic'.

ABOVE The Queen is pictured at one of her most important engagements, the State Opening of Parliament.

BELOW Laying a wreath of poppies at the Cenotaph during the Remembrance Service in Whitehall, 1978.

The Royal Year

JANUARY	FEBRUARY	MARCH
Sandringham	Investitures, Foreign and Commonwealth Tours	Foreign and Commonwealth Tours

APRIL	MAY	JUNE
Maundy Service	State Visits	Prince Philip's Birthday (10th)
	Founder's Day Royal Hospital (29th)	Derby
Queen's Birthday (21st)		Birthday Parade
	Chelsea Flower Show	Garter Service, Windsor
		Royal Ascot

JULY	AUGUST	SEPTEMBER
	Queen Mother's Birthday (4th)	Balmoral
Buckingham Palace Garden Parties	Holyroodhouse	
	Balmoral	

OCTOBER	NOVEMBER	DECEMBER
Foreign and Commonwealth Tours	State Opening of Parliament	Christmas at Windsor
Investitures	Remembrance Day	
	Prince of Wales's Birthday (14th)	
	Thistle Service, Edinburgh	

Fount of Honour

The Queen's Honours Lists are generally issued on New Year's Day, the Queen's official birthday (on a Saturday in June) and on the dissolution of Parliament. Among the Orders of Chivalry are the Garter (founded by Edward III about 1348) and the Scottish equivalent, the Thistle. The Irish Order of St Patrick is now defunct.

The Queen is the 'fount of honour' but honours, with a few exceptions (ie the Garter, the Thistle, the Order of Merit and the Royal Victorian Order), are conferred on the advice of the Prime Minister.

The most familiar of the British titles, setting aside hereditary peerages and baronetcies (not to mention the life peerages), is the non-hereditary knighthood. Knighthood is conferred either with or without membership of a Knightly Order. Those knights not belonging to any Order are known as 'knights bachelor', a name that originated with the landless warrior knights in the Middle Ages. They constitute the great majority of knights and rank lower than knights who belong to Orders of Knighthood. Unlike the latter, they have no initials after their name; the popular habit of writing 'Kt' after the surname of a knight bachelor is incorrect.

The Orders have their origin in the knightly, monastic orders of the Middle Ages. The most exalted and the oldest is the Order of the Garter founded in about 1348 by Edward III (1327-1377). He was a romantic, obsessed with chivalry, and he founded the Order intending to embody the ideals of the Round Table. The original garter in question is traditionally believed to have dropped from the leg of the 'Fair Maid of Kent' at a dance, whereupon the King picked it up, tied it round his own leg and said *Honi soit qui mal y pense* ('Evil to him who thinks evil'). With an increasing number of exceptions — such as Sir Winston Churchill and Sir Harold Wilson — Knights of the Garter have tended to be peers, members of the royal family or foreign royalties. In fact, until very recently, the Garter resembled some of the more exclusive foreign Orders in that admission to it often depended on who a person was rather than what he had done. Certain old families were known as 'Garter Families' and their successive heads received the Garter almost automatically. This is what Lord Melbourne meant when he said that there was 'no damn-ed nonsense of merit' in the Garter. This phrase has since found its way into almost every letter acknowledging congratulations on receiving the honour — to the extent that etiquette books might be expected to print a standard letter for use in such circumstances, incorporating this well-worn piece of false modesty. Now, however, it seems that there is more 'damned nonsense of merit' in the Garter than there used to be. One is now likely to see a sprinkling of meritocrats — such as Labour life peers — in the colourful procession down the hill at Windsor Castle on the Monday of Ascot week. When Sir Harold Wilson was installed as a Knight in 1976 the congregation included the journalist Bernard Levin, who was heard to observe that he would have been prepared to come a long way to see this politician attired in a floppy feathered hat.

'No damned nonsense of merit' applied until recently to Scotland's equivalent of the Garter, the Order of the Thistle (revived by

LEFT: The temporarily moustachioed Prince of Wales was installed as Grand Master of the Most Honourable Order of the Bath by the Queen in the Henry VII Chapel at Westminster Abbey in 1975 — the 250th anniversary of the founding of this Order of Chivalry by George I. There are over 2,000 military and civilian members of the order; ladies were first admitted in 1971. ABOVE Some of the 16 Knights of the Most Ancient and Most Noble Order of the Thistle seen processing at the annual service held in the Thistle Chapel, St Giles's Cathedral, Edinburgh on St Andrew's Day, 1969.

THE INSIGNIA OF THE MOST NOBLE ORDER OF THE GARTER: the blue and gold garter itself ('*Honi soit qui mal y pense*', 'Evil to him who evil thinks'), worn on the left leg; the gold collar and St George; the 'lesser George' or badge; the Garter star with the St George's cross in the middle.

THE INSIGNIA OF THE MOST ANCIENT AND MOST NOBLE ORDER OF THE THISTLE: the gold collar; the badge showing St Andrew's cross; the star with the green thistle.

THE BADGE OF THE ORDER OF MERIT: red and blue enamel, with the lettering in gold. The most prestigious honour of all (though carrying no title or rank), it was instituted by Edward VII in 1902 and has 24 members.

THE INSIGNIA OF THE MOST DISTINGUISHED ORDER OF ST MICHAEL AND ST GEORGE: gold collar; silver badge; the stars of Knight (or Dame) Grand Cross and Knight (or Dame) Commander. The star shows St Michael trampling on Satan; the motto is *Auspicium Meliori Aevi* ('Token of a Better Age'). Instituted by the Prince Regent in 1818, the order now includes over 2,300 members.

THE MOST EXCELLENT ORDER OF THE BRITISH EMPIRE: the badge of a Knight (or Dame) Grand Cross of the Order, showing the crowned effigies of George V and Queen Mary and the motto 'For God and Empire'. The order was created in 1917 by George V and has been described as 'the Order of Chivalry of the British democracy'; it has over 100,000 members.

Queen Anne (1702-1714) in 1703), and to the now-defunct Irish counterpart, the Order of St Patrick. Although suggestions have been made about a Most Noble Welsh Order, the idea has not been adopted. The most-quoted remark concerning the Thistle is not one which any recipient of the honour would be likely to use when writing to acknowledge congratulations; it is attributed to another Prime Minister, who, when someone suggested that he should give the Thistle to a certain notoriously stolid Scottish peer, replied, 'What's the use? He'd only eat it'.

Apart from a very few Knights of the Garter and the Thistle outside the peerage, those knights who belong to the Orders of Knighthood — as distinct from peers — belong to one or more of six other Orders: the Bath, the Star of India, the St Michael and St George, the Order of the Indian Empire, the Royal Victorian Order and the Order of the British Empire. These orders are mostly given for distinguished service in an official or military capacity; the two Indian Orders, which ceased to be conferred after the end of the British Raj, for service in India; the St Michael and St George, for service overseas, particularly in diplomacy; the Royal Victorian Order, for service to the crown, as distinct from service to the state.

The newest of the Orders, the Order of the British Empire, is the one most freely given now, though its name is anachronistic, not to say misleading, since it is largely given for services within the United Kingdom. It is, in-

cidentally, the Order to which most Dames, female knights, belong.

Several other Orders, apart from the Garter, have an annual service at their own chapels. The Prince of Wales caused a mild sensation in 1975 by being installed as Grand Master of the Order of Bath in the Henry VII Chapel at Westminster Abbey wearing a moustache — not a growth approved of in the Navy in which he was then serving. In the course of the long ceremony he promised 'to honour God above all things' and 'to defend maidens, widows and orphans in their rights'. After the service the Prince returned to the Palace where he whisked off his moustache, before rejoining his ship.

Knights of the Thistle foregather at St Giles Cathedral, Edinburgh. The Order of St Michael and St George, which used to have its treasury in Corfu, holds its service in St Paul's Cathedral. The Chapel of the Royal Victorian Order is the Chapel of the Savoy.

All these Orders — with the exception of the Garter, the Thistle and the Patrick, when it existed — have ranks lower than knighthood such as that of Companion or Commander, Officer or Member. These are only decorations, conferring no title or prefix but just initials after their holder's name.

RIGHT The Queen finely attired in blue velvet as sovereign of the Most Noble Order of the Garter at the Order's Service at Windsor, June 1983. Apart from the sovereign, 24 Knights Companion, as well as certain members of the royal family and foreign monarchs ('Stranger Knights') belong; since the reign of Edward VII, Queen Consorts have been Ladies of the Order.

The Queen entertains the Knights to lunch in the Waterloo Chamber at Windsor Castle, following the Chapter meeting in St George's Hall. The glorious pageantry of the procession from the state apartments down the hill to the Order's magnificent Chapel of St George was revived, after 143 years, by the present Queen's father, George VI, in 1948.

The Royal Household

The Queen's Household consists of five departments: the Lord Chamberlain's office at St James's Palace; the Private Secretary's office, the office of the Privy Purse; the Master of the Household's office; and the Crown Equerry and his staff at the Royal Mews. The Private Secretary, who advises the Queen, plays a particularly important role in constitutional monarchy.

The Lord Chamberlain, at present Lord Maclean, is the titular head of the Queen's Household. However, in practice each of the five departments of the Household is autonomous and their heads — the Comptroller of the Lord Chamberlain's Office, the Private Secretary, the Keeper of the Privy Purse, the Master of the Household and the Crown Equerry — are usually left to their own devices.

The Lord Chamberlain is responsible for the organization of state visits by foreign heads of state for Court ceremonies — such as royal weddings and funerals — and for garden parties. State ceremonials, such as the funeral service of a sovereign (when the Lord Chamberlain breaks his white wand of office over the grave) and the Opening of Parliament, is the province of the Earl Marshal, a hereditary office held by the Duke of Norfolk, who is head of the College of Arms in Queen Victoria Street. This building houses the Kings of Arms, heralds and pursuivants who are to be seen dressed like playing-card people in their tabards on state occasions.

As Lord Chamberlain, Lord Maclean is one of the Great Officers of the Realm. He should not be confused with the Lord Great Chamberlain — an hereditary office connected with the Palace of Westminster which is divided (though not equally) between three families. The Lord Great Chamberlain is the Marquess of Cholmondeley — in the next reign it will be Lord Carrington. The choice of Lord Chamberlain, like that of many other Court appointments used to be political. Until the advent of Ramsay MacDonald and the first Labour Government in 1924, a new Lord Chamberlain was appointed not upon the accession of a new monarch but upon the formation of a new political administration. George V (1910-1936) and MacDonald, however, decided that it would be best to make the Lord Chamberlain a non-political appointment. So it has remained.

Since succeeding Lord Cobbold in 1971, Lord Maclean (a former Chief Scout) has had a busy programme of special ceremonial events on top of his normal Household chores. There was the funeral of the Duke of Windsor in 1972 (when he said goodbye to the Duchess of Windsor at Heathrow, without a bow); Princess Anne's wedding in 1973 (when he played the Queen at the rehearsal);

The Queen's Household

BUCKINGHAM PALACE

Lord Chamberlain	Captain of the Gentlemen at Arms
Lord Steward	Captain of the Yeomen of the Guard
Master of the Horse	Treasurer of the Household
Mistress of the Robes	Comptroller of the Household
Lords-in-Waiting	Vice-Chamberlain of the Household
	Ladies-in-Waiting

PRIVATE SECRETARY'S OFFICE

Private Secretary and Keeper of the Queen's Archives	Press Secretary
	Two Assistant Press Secretaries
Deputy Private Secretary	Assistant Keeper of the Queen's Archives
Assistant Private Secretary	Defence Services Secretary
Chief Clerk	

DEPARTMENT OF THE KEEPER OF THE PRIVY PURSE AND TREASURER TO THE QUEEN

Keeper of the Privy Purse and Treasurer to the Queen	Treasurer's Office, Chief Accountant and Paymaster
Assistant Keeper of the Privy Purse	Establishment Officer
Deputy Treasurer to the Queen	High Almoner
Privy Purse, Chief Accountant	Secretary, Royal Almonry

MASTER OF THE HOUSEHOLD'S DEPARTMENT

Master of the Household
Chief Clerk
Palace Steward and Chief Housekeeper

LORD CHAMBERLAIN'S OFFICE

Comptroller	**Royal Company of Archers**
Assistant Comptroller	Captain General
Secretary	Adjutant
Marshal of the Diplomatic Corps	
Vice Marshal	Clerk of the Closet
Two Assistant Marshals	Deputy Clerk of the Closet
Surveyor of the Queen's Pictures	Dean of the Chapels Royal
Surveyor of the Queen's Works of Art	Sub-Dean of the Chapels Royal
Librarian, Royal Library	Dean of the Chapel Royal in Scotland
Secretary, Central Chancery of the Orders of Knighthood	Physician and Head of the Medical Household
	Serjeant Surgeon
	Apothecary to the Queen
Gentlemen at Arms	
Lieutenant	**Windsor Castle**
Clerk of the Cheque and Adjutant	Constable and Governor
	Superintendent
Yeomen of the Guard	
Lieutenant	**Palace of Holyroodhouse**
Clerk of the Cheque and Adjutant	Hereditary Keeper
	Superintendent

CROWN EQUERRY'S DEPARTMENT

Crown Equerry
Equerry
Superintendent, Royal Mews

RIGHT The duties of the Lord Chamberlain's Office in St James's Palace include the issue of the 1,000 or so Royal Warrants to tradesmen who supply goods to the Queen, the Queen Mother, the Duke of Edinburgh and the Prince of Wales. At the end of each year a list of names of individuals and firms holding 'warrants of appointments' is published in the official organ: the *London Gazette*. The use of the royal arms and insignia for trading purposes is strictly confined to firms holding such warrants; the words 'By Appointment' are placed underneath.

the Silver Jubilee Service of 1977 (this time his wife was the stand-in) and the wedding of the Prince of Wales in 1981 (when he and his Comptroller, Sir Johnny Johnston, were kissed by the Princess at Waterloo Station for their trouble).

The Lord Chamberlain's Office deals with a wide range of responsibilities from the maintenance of the state royal palaces and residences to matters of precedence; from the flying of flags to the care of the Queen's swans. The Lord Chamberlain sees to all appointments in the Household, including the ecclesiastical and medical functionaries, the Marshal of the Diplomatic Corps, the Gentlemen Ushers, the Gentlemen at Arms, the Queen's Bodyguard, the Master of the Queen's Music, the Poet Laureate and the Queen's Bargemaster. The Central Chancery of the Orders of Knighthood and the various experts who look after the royal collections also come under the authority of the Lord Chamberlain. The Puritan legacy of state censorship was relinquished in the late 1960s. Tradesmen who bask under royal patronage receive their warrants from the Lord Chamberlain's Office.

The Private Secretary, now Sir Philip Moore, plays a very important role in constitutional monarchy advising the Queen. The job is largely unsung but it calls for a remarkable range of skills and statesmanship. The Private Secretary has to keep the Queen in touch with news, to arrange tours at home and abroad and to draft her speeches. The latter acquired a more relaxed, humorous vein when Lord Charteris of Amisfield (formerly Sir Martin Charteris) took over as Private Secretary from Lord Adeane (formerly Sir Michael Adeane) in 1972. *The Times* commented that it was engaging to watch Sir Martin laughing immodestly at his own jokes in the royal speeches. 'I think everybody will concede that on this of all days I should begin my speech with the words 'My husband and I', quipped the Queen at the Silver Wedding celebrations the year Charteris took office.

His predecessor, Lord Adeane, was the grandson of a previous Private Secretary Lord Stamfordham, of whom George V said: 'He taught me to be a king'. Edward Adeane, private secretary to the Prince of Wales and son of Lord Adeane, carries on this dynasty of royal service. Perhaps the greatest Private Secretary of all came from another such dynasty; Sir Henry Ponsonby really established the significance of the job in Queen Victoria's time. Under the Private Secretary come the royal archives, the secretariat and the press office.

The Keeper of the Privy Purse looks after the royal accounts (including those of the Duchy of Lancaster); the Crown Equerry after the garages and stables (the Master of the Horse has a ceremonial role); the Master of the Household takes care of the domestic administration of Buckingham Palace. The Queen's Ladies-in-waiting are supervised by the Mistress of the Robes.

In addition to the Queen's Household, the Duke of Edinburgh, the Queen Mother, the Prince and Princess of Wales, Princess Anne, Princess Margaret, Princess Alice, the Duke and Duchess of Gloucester, the Duke and Duchess of Kent, Prince and Princess Michael and Princess Alexandra all have 'Households' of their own, even if in some cases this only runs to a private secretary and a lady-in-waiting.

ABOVE The Queen's Award to Industry was established in 1965. Instituted by Royal Warrant it was awarded to industrial units in recognition of outstanding achievements in exporting goods or services or in technological innovation or both. Then in 1975 the Award was separated (with effect from 1976) into two distinct Awards entitled 'The Queen's Award for Export Achievement' and 'The Queen's Award for Technological Achievement'.

Royal Finance

In 1983 the royal family received £4,515,600 to cover daily 'running costs'; nearly 70 per cent of this Civil List money goes on wages for royal staff. The Queen's current annual allowance from the list is £3,710,400. The Prince of Wales receives nothing; his money comes from the Duchy of Cornwall estates. An 'index-linked' Civil List is under discussion to avoid further controversy.

At the beginning of each reign the monarch surrenders the hereditary revenues from the Crown Estates for the duration of the reign and, in return, is granted a fixed sum of money. This procedure (the 'Civil List') has been followed since the accession of George III (1760-1820). By the Civil List Act of 1952, on the accession of Elizabeth II, Parliament provided a sum of £475,000 a year for the support of the Queen together with annuities for certain members of the royal family. It was anticipated that this annual sum would suffice for the duration of her reign.

However, thanks to inflation, the money proved inadequate and by 1970 total Civil List expenditure had reached £745,000. This meant there was a deficit of £240,000 which had to be met by the Privy Purse. In the words of Prince Philip the monarchy was 'in the red'. Thus in 1971 the Queen was obliged to send a message to the House of Commons asking for additional financial provision for the royal family.

A Select Committee was accordingly appointed and considered a wide range of evidence. For the first time the evidence submitted was published (in November 1971); the *Report* constitutes what one of the committee members, Norman St John-Stevas has rightly called 'a unique and valuable document on the workings of the monarchy in the second half of the twentieth century'. The report was not, however, unanimous. One member of the Committee, William Hamilton — the most vociferous critic of modern monarchy — wanted the Queen to have an annual salary of £100,000, to reduce or abolish the payments to the other members of the royal family and, for good measure, to confiscate the revenues of the Duchies of Lancaster and Cornwall. In the event, the Committee approved by majority an increase in the Civil List of £980,000 a year for the Queen and her Household and increased annuities for other members of the royal family.

The Committee also recommended that the royal trustees should report from time to time ('not less frequently than once every 10 years') and that following receipt of such reports the sums should be charged on the Consolidated Fund and should be increasable by Treasury order. In this way the Committee provided for a means of reviewing the royal finances but avoided the embarrass-

ment of annual inquiries into expenditure. The proposals were subsequently incorporated in the Civil List Act of 1972. In the highly inflationary period since then a number of increases have been necessary.

Royal finance has been a common complaint for centuries. The principal points of controversy today always seem to be the annuities payable to other members of the royal family and the tax exemption of the Queen. Although the Queen pays no income tax, surtax, capital gains or transfer tax and can recover tax, taken away at source, on such items as investments, she does pay local rates, customs and excise and indirect taxes. The Queen's own private fortune, managed by Baring Brothers in the City, remains an unknown quantity though this does not stop gossip columnists describing her as one of the 'richest women in the world', worth about 150 to 200 million pounds.

In fact, the Queen pays a higher proportion

ABOVE The Royal Yacht *Britannia*, in Tunisia in 1980. Built at a cost of £2 million and refitted to the tune of £10 million, it has carried the Queen and Prince Philip nearly three-quarters of a million miles.

BELOW These are the 1983 figures for the Civil List allowances to the royal family.

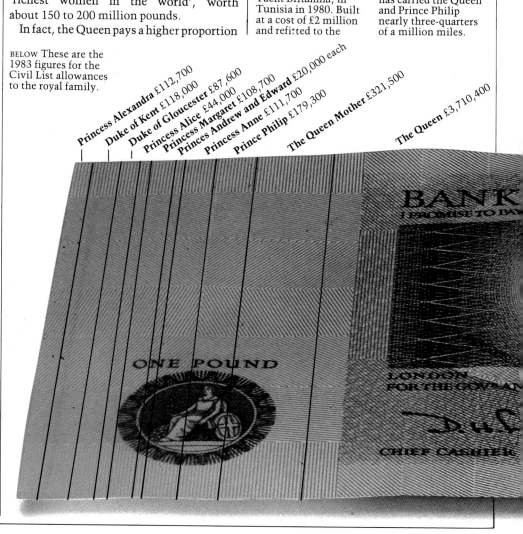

Princess Alexandra £112,700
Duke of Kent £118,000
Duke of Gloucester £87,600
Princess Alice £44,000
Princess Margaret £108,700
Princes Andrew and Edward £20,000 each
Princess Anne £111,700
Prince Philip £179,300
The Queen Mother £321,500
The Queen £3,710,400

of her income to the Exchequer than any other individual in Great Britain, handing over the net revenue of the Crown Lands and a decent contribution of her own money to the Civil List, and it only takes a few elementary sums to establish that the Queen puts in more than she takes out. Moreover, the royal family's value as a major attraction for tourists can hardly be overestimated. Seen against this background, the cost of running the monarchy (and the Civil List is merely the 'expenses' and overheads for a job the Queen and her family do by popular consent) is negligible. For instance, the Queen receives about half what a democratic head of state like, say, the President of West Germany is granted to carry out his duties. The Queen has additional duties in Commonwealth countries for which, typically, she neither asks for nor receives extra pay.

It is also worth stressing the point that the Prince and Princess of Wales and their staff do not cost the public a penny. They live on the income of the Prince's own revenues from the Duchy of Cornwall. Like the Queen, the Prince of Wales does not pay income tax but when he became entitled to the Duchy income (now over half-a-million pounds a year) at the age of 21, the Prince offered half to the Treasury — subject to review by the Consolidated Fund administered by the Exchequer. Faced with rising running expenses after his marriage, the Prince has now revised this to a quarter.

LEFT The Princess of Wales visits the Charlie Chaplin Playground in the comic actor's birthplace of Kennington, South London, December 1982. Kennington is the stronghold of the Duchy of Cornwall, which owns nearly 50 valuable metropolitan areas here, including the Oval cricket ground. The Duchy's other holdings include large tracts of land in the West Country, Dartmoor Prison and parts of the Scilly Isles.

Prince Charles automatically became Duke of Cornwall (in whom the Duchy is vested) on the accession of his mother to the throne in 1952. The title passes, according to Edward III's charter of 1337, to the monarch's 'first begotten son'. Because of his healthy income from the Duchy, the Prince, and his own family, are not included in the Civil List, though he pays back a quarter of the Duchy income to the Treasury as a form of tax.

In 1982 the profits from the royal estates which the Queen handed over to Parliament on her accession in exchange for the Civil List amounted to £14 million.

To avoid the wearisome political row every time an increase is necessary due to inflation, it has been intimated that the Civil List allowances may become 'index-linked'. Such a course could be adopted by the Royal Trustees (the Prime Minister, the Chancellor of the Exchequer and the Keeper of the Privy Purse) who were due to undertake a major review of the royal finances in 1984 — the first for over a decade.

The Royal Roadshow

The busy programme of events carried out by the Queen and other members of the royal family is planned well in advance. In 1982, for instance, the Queen undertook 15 official visits, opening ceremonies and other engagements; attended 73 receptions; presided over 11 meetings of the Privy Council; gave 148 audiences and visited 8 countries.

'There are many engagements both public and private involving visits to local universities, hospitals, factories and units of the Armed Forces...' noted Sir Michael Adeane in his famous Memorandum to the Select Committee of the Civil List in 1971. These engagements, planned well in advance, are frequently in connection with an organization of which the Queen is Patron or President. She will often carry out a series of engagements in one particular county.

The Queen's Flight, taking her from place to place, is based at RAF Benson and consists of some Andovers and Westland helicopters. She does not normally use the latter herself, though an exception was made for her historic visit to Northern Ireland in Silver Jubilee year. The Queen had been determined to go through with the promised visit: 'We said we'd do it and it would be a pity if we didn't'. In August she flew by helicopter from HMS *Fife* in Belfast Lough to Hillsborough Castle, amid intense security arrangements. After being greeted by 200 children and invited guests, she then held an investiture and a garden party. In the evening the Queen received the leaders of the Ulster Peace Movement on board *Britannia*. The following day she visited the New University of Ulster at Coleraine and, in a televised speech, appealed to the people of Northern Ireland to forget the past and work together in a spirit of friendship and forgiveness: 'People everywhere recognize that violence is senseless and wrong and that they do not want it. Their clear message is that it must stop and that is my prayer too'.

On the 'royal roadshow' the Queen, who is not an actress, has to maintain an unflagging interest in what she sees. However, when she drives through a city it is impossible for her to smile the entire time — she would suffer from lockjaw in the endeavour. Yet that one glimpse of her is perhaps the only time one of her subjects will see her in real life. If the Queen is frowning, then her subject will always remember her frowning. The Queen also has the tricky problem of putting the people she meets at their ease; those presented to the sovereign are seldom at their best — either mute with fright or blurting out some inane remark in a nervous attempt to make an impression. In short, it is a tremendously difficult job for a shy person, but the Queen performs all her duties with a dedica-

tion rare in late-20th century Britain. A royalty watcher once aptly described 'that level gaze, so calm in its consciousness of duty fulfilled'.

The rest of the royal family, the 'royal firm', act as the back-up team, carrying out their royal duties throughout the year on the Queen's behalf. 'These functions, you're doing it for the Queen', pointed out the late Princess Alice, Countess of Athlone. 'The Queen can't go and open every little bazaar. Therefore you do it for her as her family'. Actually Princess Alice was talking about her grandmother, Queen Victoria (1837-1901), but this oldest-ever member of the British royal family was still doing her bit for the present Queen as late as 1978 when she made these remarks in a television interview.

MEETING THE PEOPLE
The Queen on her annual visit to the Chelsea Flower Show in the grounds of the Royal Hospital (ABOVE RIGHT). The Queen receives yet another awkward child whom she again manages to put at ease (RIGHT). This particular occasion was the commissioning of HMS *Invincible* at Portsmouth in 1980. The *Invincible* was to play an important part in the Falklands campaign two years later. The Queen visited Winchester College in 1982 (FAR RIGHT), during the celebrations of the school's 600th anniversary. The college was founded by William of Wykeham. Here she is with the school's current headmaster.

LEFT The Princess of Wales, kneeling, in her characteristically natural manner, at the Royal School for the Blind at Leatherhead in Surrey, November 1982. She became Patron of the school earlier that year; this was among her first handful of patronages and presidencies.

ABOVE Prince Philip getting to grips with the manufacture of Land Rovers at the Solihull factory, June 1982.

Foreign and Commonwealth Tours

As well as being Queen of Great Britain, Elizabeth II is also Queen of Australia, the Bahamas, Barbados, Canada, Fiji, Grenada, Jamaica, Mauritius, New Zealand and Papua New Guinea. Her Majesty is also Head of the Commonwealth, now a grouping of 48 countries. She often visits these countries as well as nations outside the Commonwealth.

'Her Majesty is directly involved both in state visits to this country of the Heads of Foreign and Commonwealth States...', Sir Michael Adeane told the Select Committee on the Civil List in 1971, 'and in tours and visits overseas to Commonwealth countries and in state visits to foreign countries. In particular, Her Majesty's programme has increasingly included visits for specific occasions to monarchical countries of the Commonwealth.'

There tend to be two or three state visits to Britain each year. The visitors only ever come once officially, though a new sovereign or president can come from the same country. For instance, Sweden sent King Gustaf VI Adolf in 1954 and then his grandson, King Carl XVI Gustaf, in 1975; King Mahendra of Nepal came in 1960, his son King Birendra 20 years later; Queen Juliana of the Netherlands in 1972, Queen Beatrix 10 years later. In an imaginative gesture, it was arranged that Queen Beatrix and her husband should give a banquet in honour of the Queen and Prince Philip at Hampton Court, the palace where the horse of 'Dutch' William III's (1689-1702) stumbled on a molehill.

ABOVE The night George VI died and the Queen acceded — 5 February 1952 — she and Prince Philip were staying at Treetops in Kenya.

RIGHT The Queen and Prince Philip returned in 1983 to visit Treetops, now a large hotel which has been built near the spot of the original, more modest treehouse.

LEFT The ultimate royal 'walkabout' as the Queen is 'carried' in a bottomless conveyance in India, 1983.
RIGHT During the Commonwealth Summit, 1983, the Queen and Mrs Gandhi talked at length.
BELOW The Queen surrounded by Scouts in Australia, 1982.

ABOVE The Queen and Prince Philip at Owen Roberts airport, Cayman Islands, on their tour of the Americas in February 1983.

ABOVE The Queen in 1981, on one of her frequent visits to Canada.

RIGHT The Queen inspects a guard of honour on her tour of the South Pacific in 1982.

FAR RIGHT On the same tour, she holds her gold Rolleiflex camera in readiness for another snap for her private album.

ABOVE During their tour of Australia and New Zealand in the spring of 1983, the Prince and Princess of Wales broke with precedent by taking their infant son, Prince William of Wales, with them. The baby was not, however, included in this expedition on a tribal canoe at Waitangi, New Zealand.

The Queen has also welcomed such figures as the Shah of Iran, General de Gaulle, the Yang-di-Pertuan Agong of Malaysia and, in 1956, the Russian leaders Khrushchev and Bulganin came to call at Windsor Castle.

Five years later she said: 'How silly I should look if I was scared to visit Ghana and then Khrushchev went a few weeks later and had a good reception'. The decision to go to Ghana in 1961 ranked with her visit to Northern Ireland in 1977 as one of the bravest of many brave decisions she has made during her reign. The republic of Ghana, under the dictatorship of Nkrumah, looked likely to break away from the Commonwealth but the Queen wanted it to remain a member. Only five days before her visit Accra was hit by bombs but she remained resolute in her determination to go. Although there were some bizarre happenings — such as the top table at the State Banquet having several empty places due to the expected guests languishing in gaol — the Queen succeeded in her mission and Ghana still recognizes the Queen as Head of the Commonwealth today.

The Queen's overseas travelling has made royal history. The jet age has made a great difference to the scope of her travels and provides the major contrast between this reign and previous ones. She was the first monarch of any nationality to circumnavigate the globe in her Commonwealth tour during 1953 and 1954, taking in Bermuda, Jamaica, Fiji, Tonga, New Zealand, Australia, Ceylon, Uganda, Libya, Malta and Gibraltar.

During her reign the Queen has put an end to suggestions that she should live for a month or two from time to time in one or other country of the Commonwealth by visiting her subjects overseas so regularly. Either Canada, Australia or New Zealand

LEFT In February 1979 the Queen made a remarkably successful tour of the Gulf States in the Middle East. Here she is seen beneath the Kuwait towers with the Kuwaiti Defence Minister, Salem Sabah. 'I am delighted to be setting foot on Arab soil for the first time', the Queen told Shaikh Jabir III, Emir of Kuwait, when she arrived by Concorde. Her Majesty and Prince Philip went on to Bahrain, Saudi Arabia (where the Queen wore full-length dresses in front of the King), Qatar, Abu Dhabi and the United Arab Emirates.

LEFT High security in Morocco for the Queen's State Visit in October 1980; King Hassan II of Morocco is understandably concerned about such matters: 100 of his guests were killed at a birthday celebration in 1971. Altogether, the Queen's visit was not an easy one, owing to the Moroccan sovereign's somewhat erratic behaviour, particularly in timekeeping. On one notorious occasion, the Queen was kept waiting for what seemed an eternity outside in the blazing sun while the King of Morocco was apparently languishing within his cool caravan. 'QUEEN IN RAGE OVER ROYAL SNUB' and 'BRING OUR QUEEN HOME FROM THIS FLY-BLOWN DESERT KINGDOM', trumpeted the headlines, but, whatever she was really feeling, the Queen managed to see it through with her usual mixture of dignity and determination.

receives visits virtually every year. Each year finds her in some part of the Commonwealth she has not been to before. Today there are 48 countries which recognize the Queen as Head of the Commonwealth. Including the United Kingdom, 11 claim her as their Queen. It is as though her brow must now wear 11 separate crowns, rather than one crown to which all those nations are subject. The 10 other countries which have remained monarchical are Australia, the Commonwealth of the Bahamas, Barbados, Canada, Dominion of Fiji, Grenada, Jamaica, Mauritius, Dominion of New Zealand and Papua New Guinea. In these countries her title varies from that used in the United Kingdom. For example in Mauritius, which became independent in March 1968, she is: 'Elizabeth The Second, Queen of Mauritius and of Her other Realms and Territories, Head of the Commonwealth'. The titles used in South Africa and Pakistan were discontinued on their withdrawal from the Commonwealth in 1961 and 1972 respectively.

The Queen has faced the Canadians and Australians in all political weathers. In 1976 fear was again expressed for the safety of the Queen, when, as Head of State, it was her prerogative to declare open the Montreal Olympic Games. The Queen remained standing, an immobile target in the royal box, for over an hour while all the athletes paraded past, including in their midst Princess Anne, a member of the British Three-Day-Event team. During Silver Jubilee year, the Queen had an extensive travel programme, taking in Western Samoa, Tonga, Fiji, New Zealand, Australia (in the wake of the controversial sacking of Prime Minister Gough Whitlam by her Governor-General Sir John Kerr), Papua New Guinea, Canada, the Bahamas, the Virgin Islands, Antigua, Barbados and Mustique (the celebrated island where her sister Princess Margaret has a house).

The Queen's official state visits to foreign countries outside the Commonwealth have included two to the Vatican (in 1961 and 1980) and several memorable trips to the United States of America. In 1957 she stayed as a guest of President Eisenhower at the White House and addressed a special meeting of the United Nations Assembly.

In 1983, on her tour of the Americas, the plans to sail along the coast of California in the *Britannia* went awry due to the appalling weather conditions; these eventually drove her to stay in a hotel inland. Royalty watchers suspect that the Queen relishes such occasional upsets to the carefully organized royal schedules. In the English blizzards of 1982 she was obliged to shelter in a Cotswold pub and is said to have enjoyed it. At the dinner during the windswept visit to President Reagan's home state of California, the Queen observed that although she knew Britain exported many things to America, she had not been aware that the weather was among them. The President duly reacted as if he had just been pumped full of laughing gas.

LEFT The Queen and Prince Philip pose in the rain at the Reagans' ranch in California during the royal tour of America, March 1983. Whereas the royal couple are attired in British mackintoshes, the First Lady wears red; the President's denim outfit, complete with bootlace tie, recalls some of his earlier roles in cowboy films. This visit by the Queen realized a special ambition of President Reagan who had been much impressed by Her Majesty's 'down-to-earth' manner when he and Mrs Reagan stayed at Windsor the previous year.

Royal Celebrations

The principal celebrations of the Queen's reign have been the Coronation of 1953; the weddings of Princess Margaret, Princess Alexandra and the Duke of Kent in the 1960s; Princess Anne's wedding in 1973; the Queen's Silver Jubilee in 1977; the Queen Mother's 80th birthday in 1980; and the wedding of the Prince and Princess of Wales in 1981.

'Vivat Regina Elizabeth! Vivat! Vivat! Vivat!' shouted the 40 scholars of Westminster School on 2 June 1953 as the Queen came into view in the Abbey for her coronation. It was a moment shared not only by those in the congregation but by some 56 percent of the population (over 20 million people) huddled around television sets and a further 32 percent listening on the wireless as the first great event of the Queen's reign was celebrated amid the drizzle and rain. The BBC had had a difficult job persuading the Archbishop of Canterbury and the Royal Household to permit the television cameras into the Abbey, but the master of ceremonies, the Duke of Norfolk and, above all, the Queen herself were happy to usher in the era of a televised monarchy.

The long-serving writer on royal matters, Dermot Morrah, thought that:

'when the sacring of Queen Elizabeth II was communicated by the revolutionary invention of television to a watching world, there were many who believed themselves aware of a quite new sense of corporate exaltation in the body of the people when they saw the Queen anointed as their supreme representative; it even seemed not altogether fanciful that the look of dedicated joy that shone in her eyes as she sat enthroned was in some way reflected in the hearts of the spectators far away.'

After the 'recognition' whereby the Archbishop of Canterbury presented 'your undoubted Queen' to the congregation, she

ABOVE The fervour that greeted the coronation, on 2 June 1953, could not be marred by the rainy weather. The Gold State Coach takes the Queen back to Buckingham Palace from Westminster Abbey after the ceremony.

BELOW The Queen and the Duke of Edinburgh acknowledge the cheers of the crowd from the balcony of Buckingham Palace. Her Majesty, who was crowned with St Edward's Crown (made for Charles II), is seen here wearing the lighter Imperial State Crown (made for Queen Victoria), with Edward the Confessor's sapphire, the Stuart sapphire and the Black Prince's ruby.

pledged the oath that ensures the sovereign governs according to law. Next, the Archbishop anointed the Queen's hands, breast and head with holy oil under cover of a golden canopy held up by four Garter knights. After the Queen had been given the emblems of sovereignty — the vestments, spurs, jewelled sword, the orb, ring, royal sceptre and the rod of equity and mercy — she was actually crowned. As she sat on the Coronation Chair, which Edward I made to display the Stone of Scone, the Archbishop of Canterbury placed St Edward's Crown on her head. 'God Save the Queen', shouted the princes and princesses, peers and peeresses and kings of arms as they crowned themselves with their own coronets.

The last stage of the coronation ceremony was the homage. Prince Philip duly knelt at her feet before kissing the Queen's left cheek, to be followed by her uncle the Duke of Gloucester, her cousin the Duke of Kent and the senior peers of each degree. The ritual ran with the smooth precision that the late Duke of Norfolk made his hallmark in his years as Earl Marshal. Even that acute observer Cecil Beaton only noticed a few hitches: 'Princess Marie Louise, agonizingly old but still athletic, is obviously very angry with her fatuous lady-in-waiting for making such a balls-up with her train'.

The gargantuan Queen of Tonga stole the show in the procession through the pouring rain by gallantly insisting that the landau she was sharing with the comparatively diminutive Sultan of Kelantan be kept open. The Oceanic Queen beamed infectiously at the cheering crowds as she was soaked to the skin. 'If the people could wait so long in the rain and cold, I quite willingly faced getting wet myself', she said later. History does not record what the wretched Malaysian Sultan thought about it. However, this upstaged passenger was noticed by a friend of Noel Coward who inquired of the 'Master': 'Who's that sitting opposite the Queen of Tonga?' 'Her lunch', said Coward.

The next major royal celebrations in the Queen's reign were a flurry of royal weddings in the early 1960s — Princess Margaret to Antony Armstrong-Jones, the Duke of Kent to Katharine Worsley at York Minster and Princess Alexandra to the Honourable Angus Ogilvy. After Princess Alexandra had signed the register in the Chapel of St Edward the Confessor in Westminster Abbey in 1963, she turned to her chief bridesmaid, Princess Anne, and said 'Your turn next'. Watched on television the world over, Princess Anne married Captain Mark Phillips in the Abbey 10 years later. The marriage register showed the bride as 'Anne Elizabeth Alice Louise Mountbatten-Windsor' which was of particular interest to students of constitutional history because the question of the royal surname had long begged clarification.

In common law, a Queen Regnant is the last of her line; her son inherits his father's name and founds a new line. It seemed likely that Prince Charles would automatically be the first king of the House of Mountbatten. However, the Prime Minister, Winston Churchill, with regard to the Queen, preferred to keep the name of Windsor; one of the first declarations of the Queen's reign therefore established that the House of Windsor would continue under that name ('Her descendants...and their descendants shall bear the name of Windsor'). The Queen is said to have been unhappy about this ruling which, in Dermot Morrah's words 'did less than justice to her husband as the progenitor of the dynasty to come'.

Marriage certificates are one of the few places where the surnames of royal personages are noticed, so the reference to Princess Anne as 'Mountbatten-Windsor' was regarded as a significant pointer to the new dynastic name. The matter seemed likely to be settled by the marriage certificate of

RIGHT The Queen on one of her Silver Jubilee 'walkabouts' in London in 1977. For the first time in these successful celebrations, Her Majesty seemed to have come to terms with the 'walkabout' and there were many nice exchanges overheard:

'We have come here because we love you', said one well-wisher. 'I feel it and it means so much to me', replied the Queen.

'Do you have a mechanical arm to keep waving all the time, the way that you do?' enquired a child. 'I haven't reached that stage yet', said the Queen.

The Queen's Silver Jubilee Trust, under the presidency of the Prince of Wales, raised £16 million 'to help the young to help others'.

the Prince of Wales, but to the confoundment of the constitutional historians the royal bridegroom was merely described as 'Charles, Prince of Wales'.

The Silver Wedding anniversary of the 'Mountbatten-Windsor' marriage itself was celebrated in 1972 and five years later came the jollifications of the Silver Jubilee. On 7 June 1977 the Queen, with Prince Philip, travelled through London in the Gold State Coach for the first time since her coronation, for the Service of Thanksgiving at St Paul's. Afterwards there was one of the most successful 'walkabouts' leading to the Guildhall where the Queen concluded her speech as follows:

'My Lord Mayor, when I was 21, I pledged my life to the service of our people and I asked God's help to make good the vow. Although that vow was made in my salad days when I was green in judgement I do not regret nor retract one word of it.'

Street and village parties that afternoon bore witness to the national affection and gratitude felt for the Queen. Wherever she went she was presented with flowers and, in a pleasing relaxation of protocol, the Queen would smilingly accept these informal tributes before handing them over to a lady-in-waiting to be taken to a hospital ward. The Jubilee Appeal, chaired by the Prince of Wales, raised over £16 million for various youth projects that were initiated 'to help young people help others'.

The Prince of Wales had, for a time, been haunted by a remark he had made to the effect that 30 was a good age to marry, but finally at the age of 32 he married Lady Diana Spencer, who is 12 years his junior. The wedding took place in 1981 not at Westminster Abbey but at St Paul's. Although the Abbey had become the traditional place for royal weddings since the First World War, both the Prince and his bride loved the Cathedral (designed, incidentally, by Christopher Wren, the husband of her fourth cousin nine times removed), with its marvellous musical acoustics. Moreover, the Abbey had unfortunate associations: Lady Diana's divorced parents had been married there and Lord Mountbatten's funeral held there. St Paul's, on the other hand, evoked the joy of the Silver Wedding, the Silver Jubilee and the Queen Mother's 80th birthday celebrations.

'I remember several occasions that were similar, with large crowds: the coronation and Jubilee, and various major national occasions', said the Prince of Wales, recalling the wonder of his marriage on 29 July 1981. 'All of them were special in their own way but our wedding was quite extraordinary as far as we were concerned. It made us both, and we have discussed it several times, extraordinarily proud to be British'.

The day was not only 'quite extraordinary' for the Prince and the new Princess but for the millions who watched them from all over the

ABOVE Princess Elizabeth and the Duke of Edinburgh were married in Westminster Abbey on 20 November 1947. Norman Hartnell's luscious ivory satin bridal gown, which was decorated with garlands of York roses entwined with stars, ears of corn and orange blossom picked out in raised pearls and crystal, was an especially welcome sight in a period of dreary austerity.
BELOW Princess Margaret fingers her engagement ring at Windsor, February 1960, on the announcement of her betrothal to the

photographer Antony Armstrong-Jones, later created Earl of Snowdon. They were married in Westminster Abbey on 6 May 1960, but separated in 1976 and were divorced in 1978.
BELOW RIGHT Princess Anne and Captain Mark Phillips, then a serving officer with the 1st Queen's Dragoon Guards, on the balcony of Buckingham Palace after their wedding in Westminster Abbey on 14 November 1973 (Prince Charles's 25th birthday).

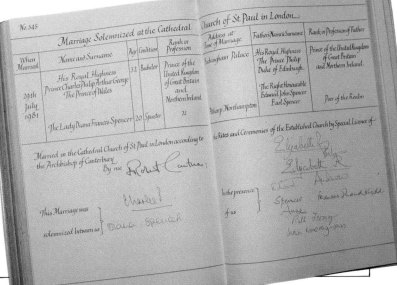

ABOVE The Prince and Princess of Wales, photographed by Patrick Lichfield at Buckingham Palace following their wedding in St Paul's Cathedral on 29 July 1981, with supporters, bridesmaids and pages. The supporters (the royal tradition is to have two 'best men') were Princes Andrew and Edward. The bridesmaids were Lady Sarah Armstrong-Jones (Princess Margaret's daughter), India Hicks (Earl Mountbatten of Burma's granddaughter), Sarah Jane Gaselee (daughter of the Prince of Wales's racehorse trainer), Catherine Cameron (granddaughter of the Marquess of Lothian and of Sir Donald Cameron of Lochiel) and Clementine Hambro (granddaughter of Lord Soames and great-granddaughter of Sir Winston Churchill). The naval pages were Lord Nicholas Windsor (younger son of the Duke of Kent) and Edward van Cutsem (grandson of Bernard van Cutsem, the trainer). The bride's fairytale dress was designed by David and Elizabeth Emanuel.

RIGHT On the lefthand page of the marriage register, the signatures are those of the Archbishop of Canterbury and the Prince and Princess of Wales; on the right hand page the signatures shown include those of the Queen, Prince Philip, and the Queen Mother.

world. The Prince said before the wedding that he wanted everybody to leave St Paul's having enjoyed 'a marvellous musical and emotional experience' and, in the event, it was not just the guests inside the Cathedral who did so. Many surprising and unlikely figures were moved to tears.

Vignettes of the day stay in the mind's eye: Lord Spencer, the bride's father, gamely mounting the steps of St Paul's, his chauffeur at his side; the young Earl of Ulster (son of the Duke and Duchess of Gloucester) waving energetically from his parent's carriage to the packed spectators along the route; the Archbishop of Canterbury in a futuristic-looking silver cope; the bride and bridegroom making a mutual hash of their responses; Kiri te Kanawa singing the Seraphim like a divine bird of paradise. The musical feast was luxuriant: Purcell, Handel, Bach, Holst, Elgar. Vivid memories include that of the Queen trying to control her laughter when an over-enthusiastic choirmaster knocked off a lampshade; the Queen Mother, in her familiar osprey plumes, dabbing away a tear; the *coup de théatre* of the kiss on the Buckingham Palace balcony and, finally, the bunch of blue and silver balloons on the departure landau which conveyed that, for all the splendour and pageantry, it was very much a young people's day.

'We still cannot get over what happened that day', said the Prince of Wales. 'Neither of us can get over the atmosphere; it was electric, I felt, and so did my wife'. Outside his window at Buckingham Palace the noise had been 'almost indescribable'. Since then, the Prince has stood at the same window trying to remember it 'so that I can tell my children what it was like'.

The first of those children was born at St Mary's Hospital, Paddington on 21 June 1982 and christened 'William Arthur Philip Louis' in the Music Room at Buckingham Palace a few weeks later.

JUST MARRIED The bridegroom's supporters, Princes Andrew and Edward, scrawled 'Just Married' on a placard attached to the back of the open landau taking the Prince and Princess of Wales from Buckingham Palace to Waterloo Station for the beginning of their honeymoon at Broadlands.

Three views of the Buckingham Palace balcony on that memorable muggy day are shown here. The public kiss took place after some encouragement from the boisterous Prince Andrew; lip readers claim Prince Charles's initial reaction to his brother's suggestion was that he was not 'going in for that sort of caper'.

The crowd scene captures certain features of the day such as the casual clothing, the periscopes, the St George and Union flags, and also serves as a reminder that a mass of humanity — even one that stretches as far as the eye could see — need not always be an alarming or disorderly mob.

Royalty on and off-duty

In private life, royalty looks to the countryside for its recreations. But what is the public future for the British monarchy? This section sums up the position of the monarchy today and surveys the changes that may come. The question of the Queen's possible abdication in favour of the Prince of Wales is discussed. Such a course is found to be unlikely for the sovereign whose watchword is 'Duty'.

Royal Recreations

The horse is the common denominator in the royal family's leisure pursuits — whether in the context of racing (on the Flat or over the sticks), eventing, hunting, driving or polo. The Queen herself has a remarkable knowledge of bloodstock lines. Recreations of a non-equestrian, even artistic, nature are also enjoyed by the royal family.

'If it were not for my Archbishop of Canterbury', the Queen once said, 'I should be off in my 'plane to Longchamps every Sunday'. Always a keen and highly competent rider, the Queen has developed a passionate interest in racing since inheriting the royal racing stables, with the crown, in 1952. She is not just an enthusiastic owner but a breeder with a sound knowledge of bloodstock lines and a love of conferring the appropriate name on a foal. The Queen has a racing manager, Lord Porchester, and two trainers, Ian Balding and Dick Hern. She has won well over 200 races on the Flat, virtually all with home-bred horses, and has had some notable breeding successes.

Her great horse Aureole won the Derby Trial at Lingfield in 1953; it seemed on the cards that she might win the blue ribbon of racing in her coronation year but Aureole ran second to Pinza in the Derby. Aureole went on to win the King George VI and Queen Elizabeth Stakes at Ascot the following year and then to stand as a stallion at Sandringham.

Royal Ascot for the Queen is not just a col-ourful social occasion but a serious racing week. She has won several major races there with such horses as Alexander, Almeria, Above Suspicion and Magna Carta. Her first 'Classic' winner was Pall Mall who won the Two Thousand Guineas at Newmarket in 1957. The filly Highclere won the One Thousand Guineas in 1974 and also gave the Queen her first Classic victory in France, winning the Prix de Diane. Appropriately enough, her Silver Jubilee year saw the Queen's greatest success to date on the Turf when Dunfermline won both the Oaks and the St Leger, as well as finishing fourth in the Arc de Triomphe.

The Queen began as an owner 'over the sticks' in National Hunt racing, buying Monaveen with her mother thanks to the encouragement of the celebrated amateur rider Lord Mildmay of Flete. But after Monaveen

RIGHT Two royal racegoers, the Queen Mother and the Queen study form for the Derby meeting at Epsom in 1980 . The Derby is the only 'Classic' race to have eluded the Queen as an owner; appropriately enough, her best season was in her Silver Jubilee year of 1977 when Dunfermline won both the Oaks and the St. Leger. The Queen Mother is the *doyenne* of National Hunt racing, with nearly 400 wins to her credit.

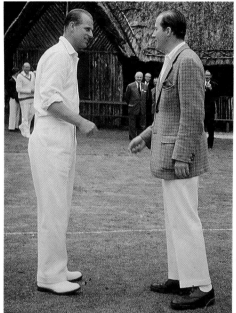

GOOD ALL-ROUNDER Those who associate Prince Philip only with aggressive activity were surprised to see him painting in the revelationary *Royal Family* film in 1969. 'The art world thinks of me as an uncultured polo-playing clot', he once complained. In fact, he is a competent painter, with a taste for landscapes and flowers. 'I don't claim any exceptional interest or knowledge or ability', Prince Philip said about painting. 'It's just average' (ABOVE LEFT).

An all-round sportsman and games player, Prince Philip's varied outdoor pastimes have included sailing and cricket. He sailed in the Cowes Regatta off the Isle of Wight in 1971 (LEFT). At the beginning of a cricket match in the grounds of Highclere Castle in 1958, he is seen tossing a coin with Lord Porchester, who is now the Queen's racing manager, (ABOVE).

PRINCESS AND HORSEWOMAN Princess Anne's equestrianism is a full-scale commitment. In 1971 she was elected the BBC's Sports Personality of the Year. At the Montreal Olympics in 1976, Princess Anne and her husband were both members of the British three-day event team. The Queen, the Prince of Wales, Prince Andrew and Prince Edward came to cheer her on (LEFT). For one of the European championships her team-mates in the British three-day event team were all women. From left to right they are: Princess Anne, Sue Hatherley, Janet Hodgson and Lucinda Prior-Palmer (RIGHT). ABOVE The Princess takes the water on Stevie B. at the Badminton Horse Trials in 1982.

broke his leg at Hurst Park in 1950 and had to be put down, the Queen (then Princess Elizabeth) switched her interest to the Flat. Following Lord Mildmay's own death by drowning in the same year, the Queen Mother bought his horse Manicou and, staying with the 'winter game', went on to become National Hunt racing's greatest patron.

In 1956 her horse Devon Loch, ridden by Dick Francis, inexplicably spreadeagled on the run-in to the finishing post of the Grand National at Aintree with the great race at his mercy. Hiding her shock and disappointment with what one observer described as 'the most perfect display of dignity' that he had ever seen, the Queen Mother said: 'I must go down and comfort those poor people'. She told a tearful Francis: 'Please don't be upset; that's racing'.

So far the Queen Mother has won nearly 350 races under National Hunt rules with horses in training first with Lord Mildmay's friend Peter Cazalet and, after his death, with Fulke Walwyn. The Prince of Wales has inherited his grandmother's love of jump racing and had a couple of horses in training with Walwyn's former assistant, Nick Gaselee. The Prince rode in some races before his marriage but ended up on the ground at Sandown and Cheltenham on the last two occasions.

Prince Charles has been more successful on the polo field, playing for Cambridge and captaining Young England. In this he takes after his father, Prince Philip, whose own interest in racing is not marked. Before taking up four-in-hand driving as his main equestrian pursuit, Prince Philip was a top-class performer on the polo ground at Smith's Lawn and elsewhere, entertaining the crowd

as much with his nautical language as his aggressive play. He has represented Britain in international driving trials.

The Prince of Wales now hunts regularly as does the most famous equestrian in the royal family, Princess Anne. She and her husband, Captain Mark Phillips, are two of the leading figures in three-day eventing. Princess Anne won the European championship at Burghley in 1971 and was a member of the British team at the Montreal Olympics in 1976. Her Gloucestershire neighbour, Princess Michael of Kent, is another member of the royal family to ride (side-saddle in her case) to the hounds of the 'greatest horseman in the kingdom', the Duke of Beaufort.

Shooting and fishing are also popular as recreations among the royal family. The Queen Mother, until recently, was to be seen, rod in hand, wading deep in Scottish

LEFT Prince Charles was photographed after a polo match in 1982. His father, the Duke of Edinburgh (an enthusiastic player until an injury led to him taking up four-in-hand driving) first taught Charles to play at the age of 16 and he was later coached by the Australian, Sinclair Hill (whose son married one of the Princess of Wales's former flatmates). Prince Charles won a half-blue at polo for Cambridge and, particularly since leaving the Navy, he has played to a high representative standard around the world. He has played for various teams, including Guy Wildenstein's Les Diables Bleus. Polo, an exclusive pursuit for which the Prince maintains a string of ponies, is very much a family tradition; his

great-uncle and 'honorary grandfather', Earl Mountbatten of Burma wrote the standard work on the game.

ABOVE Unlike Prince Andrew, Prince Charles has not inherited his father's love of sailing. Here, he is off Cowes on the Isle of Wight in 1979, not in a yacht but windsurfing.

BELOW Prince Charles indulges his old love of go-karting with Prince Edward in 1975.

waters after salmon. Urban-minded critics enjoy pointing out the paradox of the conservationist Prince Philip, so active in the World Wildlife Fund, blasting away at game birds on the Sandringham estate.

Prince Andrew shares his father's love of sailing and Prince Edward has inherited the paternal interest in cricket (Prince Philip is 'Twelfth Man' of the Lord's Taverners). Both Princes also enjoy rugby football. The Princess of Wales is one of several keen skiers in the royal family. The Duke of Kent captained his regimental ski team whereas his brother Prince Michael of Kent won the British bob-sleigh championship in 1972 and used to compete internationally. He is also an experienced rally-driver.

The royal family is sometimes accused of being 'philistine' but people forget that it is perfectly possible to indulge in outdoor activities and yet still be genuinely interested in the arts. Prince Philip paints and collects pictures and the Queen Mother is a connoisseur of the arts. The Prince of Wales is an archaeologist, frustrated actor, cellist, and sometime contributor to *Punch* and *Books and Bookmen*; the Princess, a dancer *manqué*, shares his love of opera and ballet. Even the much criticized Prince Andrew was an enthusiastic potter and actor at school.

Princess Margaret takes a particularly lively interest in the arts, collecting china and modern pictures, singing, playing the piano, going to the theatre and the ballet. Together with the Queen she used to take part in amateur theatricals as a girl. Princess Alice, Duchess of Gloucester paints in watercolours and likes cinematography; her architect son, the present Duke, has published books of his photographs and is know-ledgeable about art. The Duke of Kent is another royal photographer and music-lover; the Duchess is an accomplished pianist and sings with the Bach Choir. Princess Michael of Kent, who runs her own design company, is a keen student of historic buildings. The pleasing Nether Lypiatt in Gloucestershire, where she lives with Prince Michael, is one of the most architecturally distinguished royal residences. Princess Alexandra, like her mother Princess Marina, is also a cultured lady who enjoys and appreciates a wide variety of music and plays the piano.

The young generation of royalty, as represented by Lord Linley, Lady Sarah Armstrong-Jones, Lord St Andrews (a former King's Scholar at Eton), Lady Helen Windsor, James and Marina Ogilvy, are proving to be a bunch of lively individualists with varied hobbies and interests.

LEFT The Princess of Wales chats to famous faces from the world of rock, including some of the Rolling Stones, at a special concert to raise money for the treatment of multiple sclerosis held at the Albert Hall in 1983. Music is a particular interest of the Princess, who once hoped to be a dancer and still attends dancing classes.

BELOW 'The Team', at a charity clay-shooting match in 1982 included (from left to right): Captain Mark Phillips, King Constantine of the Hellenes (a godfather of Prince William of Wales), the Honourable Angus Ogilvy (husband of Princess Alexandra), the Duke of Kent and the Earl of Lichfield, the royal photographer and a cousin of the Queen.

Afterword

The Queen celebrates her 60th birthday in 1986. Stepping down in favour of the Prince of Wales is, however, a most unlikely prospect for this conscientious sovereign. Possibly a form of 'Regency', with the Queen a sort of 'chairperson' and the Prince of Wales in a role analogous to that of a 'managing director', might eventually be worked out.

On 2 June 1983 the Queen celebrated the 30th anniversary of her coronation. She is less than three years away from 'senior citizenship'; the Queen will be 60 on 21 April 1986. Talk of the possibility of her abdication to make way for the Prince of Wales, however, is idle. The monarchy is not, after all, a job, it is a hereditary office. The Queen's strong sense of duty would militate against any idea of stepping down.

As the Prince of Wales himself has said, the longer the Queen is on the throne the better sovereign she becomes. The advantages to the country of having a monarch who can take a long view cannot be emphasized too strongly. In more than 30 years as Queen, Elizabeth II has dealt with eight prime ministers and she has acquired considerable political experience that will stand her in good stead when faced with the constitutional crisis of a 'hung' Parliament — more likely than ever since the advent of the SDP/Liberal alliance — which only she has the power to untangle. Another reason why the Queen's abdication seems remote is that she wants to give the Prince and Princess of Wales a period of relatively carefree family life that was denied to herself and Prince Philip by her father's tragically early death.

It is almost impossible to imagine the Queen ever retiring but, as time goes by, it is to be hoped that the Prince will be brought increasingly into state affairs in the Privy Council. Perhaps, many years hence, some new constitutional stratagem could be worked out whereby the Queen became a 'chairperson' and the Prince of Wales's position was made analogous to a 'managing director', along the lines of a regency. Nobody wants a repetition of what has been called the 'Edward VII situation', with the heir to the throne not having enough to do. There are certainly no signs of inactivity from the Prince who has busied himself since 1978 learning about many aspects of public life. His 'industry programme' has been co-ordinated by the National Economic Development Council and he visits the City and Government departments in addition to a full round of royal engagements.

Suggestions have been made that the Prince should, so to speak, 'go out and govern New South Wales'. However, the Australian Governor-Generalship does not look a likely proposition for the Prince. While Malcolm Fraser's coalition government seemed to favour the idea, the Australian Labour Party remains unconvinced that the job could be kept out of the political fray.

Like the Queen, the Prince of Wales attaches great importance to the Commonwealth. As well as being Queen of the United Kingdom of Great Britain and Northern Ireland, and Head of the Commonwealth, she is also Queen of the following nations: Australia, the Bahamas, Barbados, Canada, Fiji, Grenada, Jamaica, Mauritius, New Zealand and Papua New Guinea. Taking into account her commitment to the Commonwealth, it might be a good idea to see a greater involvement by the Queen and the royal family in European affairs. Britain is now very much part of Europe and the royal family's background could not be more European. This is something that the xenophobic British like to ignore, but it is surely a suitable time to revive the links with the continent which were so strong in 1914.

Less talk of the price of butter and more inspiring education on the wider issues of European unity might eventually lead to the dream of a Federal Europe becoming a reality. If it does, it will be enjoyable to speculate about who might be a suitable Head. A rota system of European monarchs — similar to the Malaysian practice — might be employed; it may be too chauvinistic to suggest that the Queen could be given the job outright. If she were, one theory is that she could then make way for the Prince of Wales on the British throne.

When he becomes King, Prince Charles could find no better example than the recently restored King of Spain. Juan Carlos manages to be both regal and informal. To avoid pomposity on the one hand and yet

RIGHT The Queen is within sight of her 60th birthday; her hair is showing grey at the temples and her spectacles are increasingly in evidence. Here she is reading the Queen's Speech at the State Opening of Parliament in the House of Lords, November 1982. The Prince and Princess of Wales are seated beside the throne.

RIGHT 'We want the Queen!' chanted the crowds, said to number a million, outside Buckingham Palace on 7 June 1977, the high point of the Queen's Silver Jubilee celebrations. In her speech at the Guildhall earlier in the day, the Queen recalled her pledge on her 21st birthday to dedicate her life 'to the service of our people'; she did not 'regret nor retract one word of it!'

LEFT 'In the year I was born', recalled the Queen in her Christmas broadcast of 1983, 'radio communication was barely out of its infancy: there was no television: civil aviation had hardly started and space satellites were still in the realm of science fiction'. With the help of the forward-looking Prince Philip, the Queen has adapted wholeheartedly to the extraordinary changes in travel and communications during her reign. This photograph was taken at Sandringham in 1982 to mark the 30th anniversary of her accession.

bogus informality on the other is one of the problems of modern monarchy. 'Perhaps the most remarkable aspect of our Queen's reign', wrote Lord Mountbatten, 'is how she and her husband and children have succeeded in moving with the times without detracting from the dignity of their duties or sacrificing the royal ceremonial which other countries envy'.

The monarchy symbolizes the nation and somehow the Queen manages to represent Britain's modern aspirations as well as its heritage. To link the past with the present and future is a tricky but vital part of the monarch's function. In an unstable atmosphere the monarchy provides continuity and a necessary reminder that the history of Britain did not begin yesterday. The older an institution is, the better it adapts to change; the monarchy is changing all the time.

There are, however, problems in packaging the monarchy as an idealized middle-class family unit suitable for democratic mass-consumption. This anti-historical approach has had worrying results, including the way people seem to have forgotten that the monarchy is hereditary. However unpalatable this may be in an egalitarian age, it must be faced. If one supports the monarchy one is also supporting the hereditary principle. To defend the hereditary principle — and it is defensible both in theory and practice —

is to risk being considered of unsound mind; to attack the monarchy, on the other hand, can still provoke violent reactions. This conflict spells danger. The more people think of the royal family as being 'just like us', the less they will be inclined to bow the knee. The younger members of the royal family are now expected to chat away in press interviews like footballers or pop stars. A certain divinity still surrounds the Queen herself and most people hope that the day will not dawn when she is asked 'how she feels' about something. The mystique of monarchy needs to be preserved.

To survive, the monarchy needs rational as well as emotional support. Criticism of the monarchy is certainly healthier than the apathy of notional worshippers, but where some modern republicans err is in insulting individuals who cannot answer back. (The personal invective, though, is nothing compared to the lambasting Queen Victoria used to receive 100 years ago.)

The arguments of modern republicans would perhaps be weightier if they concentrated on the institution; as it is they seem a little unimaginative. Philosophical reasoning about monarchy and constructive suggestions as to a replacement are seldom forthcoming. Instead, all their energies are devoted to discussions of the royal finances. Naturally the monarchy is not cheap, but neither is this one extravagant. Very few people would vote to skimp and save over the pomp and ceremony; either one has a splendid show or nothing. In every respect the British monarchy gives magnificent value for the running expenses it receives annually from the state.

The Prince and Princess of Wales and their staff do not cost the public any money at all as their expenses are paid out of the revenues from the Duchy of Cornwall. Looking to the future, it is to be expected that they might move from their home in the Cotswolds, Highgrove, which is an indifferent residence for the heir to the throne, though handily situated. If they do move, the Prince will want to be within reach of good hunting

RIGHT The Queen on another gruelling royal tour, this time in Bangladesh, 1983. The Commonwealth remains a special cause for the Queen, a commitment not altogether shared by some of her British subjects.

BELOW After a day at work at a kindergarten in Pimlico, Lady Diana Spencer tried to hide her face from the press photographers who were hounding her. This was a pose she frequently adopted, giving the impression that she could not cope with the pressure of being in the public eye. However, since her marriage in 1981, the Princess of Wales has emerged as the greatest asset in the 'Royal Firm' of the 1980s. One of the most popular members of the royal family today, she often sets new fashion trends and no longer seems to lack confidence.
In 1983 she carried out 76 public engage-ments, 45 of them without her husband, and in 1984 she made her second 'solo' trip abroad — to Norway as patron of the City of London Ballet. This was one of seven new patronages or presidencies which she took on in 1983 to add to the five she collected in 1982.

LEFT Highgrove, in the favourite royal stamping ground of 'Beaufortshire', has been criticized in some quarters for being inadequate as the residence of the heir to the throne and his family, though the costs involved in a move could prove embarrassing. Many people feel that the Prince and Princess should settle in Wales.

country. A Welsh 'second home' might prove a popular gesture to the principality which the Prince and Princess toured so triumphantly after the royal wedding.

Genealogically the Princess of Wales's ancestry provides a healthy new mix for the royal blood with Irish, Scottish, American and even a dash of something more exotic — her illegitimate great-great-great-great-grandmother was an Armenian living in Bombay — added to the mainstream English aristocratic lines. Thanks to all this, Prince William of Wales will eventually become the most 'British' sovereign since James I with some 58.8 percent British blood (and 4.69 percent American).

The Princess of Wales's style of motherhood will surely set standards for the present generation. She is singularly well qualified for her new role and her former colleagues at the Young England Kindergarten are in no doubt that she will make an excellent mother. Because of the Princess of Wales's youthful 'Sloane-Ranger' persona it is easy to forget that her upbringing conformed to an old-fashioned tradition. Brought up in the nursery wing of the rambling Park House, she was taught in the schoolroom there, with a few other children from the Sandringham estate, by a governess — not a word that one hears much nowadays. The Princess's patronage of the Pre-School Playgroups Association is a pointer to the path she will probably follow with her own children — forming a playgroup at home.

The precedents of the Prince of Wales's pioneering education are not necessarily going to be followed. Hill House (the Knightsbridge day school) and Prince Philip's *alma maters*, Cheam and Gordonstoun, might well, in fact, be avoided. After a prep school not far from home, Eton should be the obvious choice for the young Prince and, in due course, the obligatory stint in the Commonwealth and in the services. Like the monarchy, Eton is a good example of the maxim that the older the institution the better it adapts to change; those establishments such as Gordonstoun where boys wear shorts and shin up mountains now seem oddly dated. Moreover, the Princess of Wales's father and brother are old Etonians. Coeducation will probably not be suitable, despite the Armstrong-Jones children having been at Bedales. It is noticeable that, apart from Eton, Harrow and Winchester, private education is increasingly geared to local patrons; schools close to the family home are sure to be carefully considered.

Security is a key factor in royal education and, apart from anything else, opting for home playgroups and boarding-schools makes the disagreeable sight of an armed motorcade escorting the young Prince to and from school, as happens in Spain, avoidable. It should be borne in mind that one of the factors in favour of Gordonstoun was its distance from Fleet Street.

The intrusiveness of the press is one of the biggest problems for today's royal family and it will not disappear. The hounding of the Princess of Wales in 1981 became so intolerable that the Queen stepped in on her behalf to try to reason with the newspaper editors. The Queen apparently made it clear that she did not want to force the Princess to change her nature so as to conform to royal tradition. It was especially interesting that the Queen herself did not seem to agree with the traditional view that royal duties demand restrictions on personal life. The Queen was intimating that the Princess should be allowed to create a new pattern of royal existence, which might include informal and private excursions when off duty. This can be regarded as a significant pointer to a new style of life for the next generation of royalty. It remains to be seen, though, whether the media can resist the temptation of treating the story of the royal family as a soap opera.

FUTURE KING AND QUEEN The Prince of Wales is being carefully groomed for kingship, studying affairs of state, industry and finance. With Roy Jenkins he is at the headquarters of the European Economic Community in Brussels in 1978 (BOTTOM LEFT) and met Sir Geoffrey Howe, then Chancellor of the Exchequer, at 11 Downing Street in 1982 (BOTTOM RIGHT). His reign still seems a distant prospect but in the meantime he has a chance to enjoy family life. Here he is with the Princess of Wales and their son, Prince William, in the grounds of Kensington Palace, in December 1982 (BELOW). with their son, Prince William, in the grounds of Kensington Palace, in December 1982 (BELOW).

Gazetteer

Featured in the following gazetteer are more than 800 sites, locations, villages, towns and cities in England, Scotland and Wales which have historical or contemporary associations with royalty. Each entry has a page number and grid reference keyed to the comprehensive map section at the back of this book.

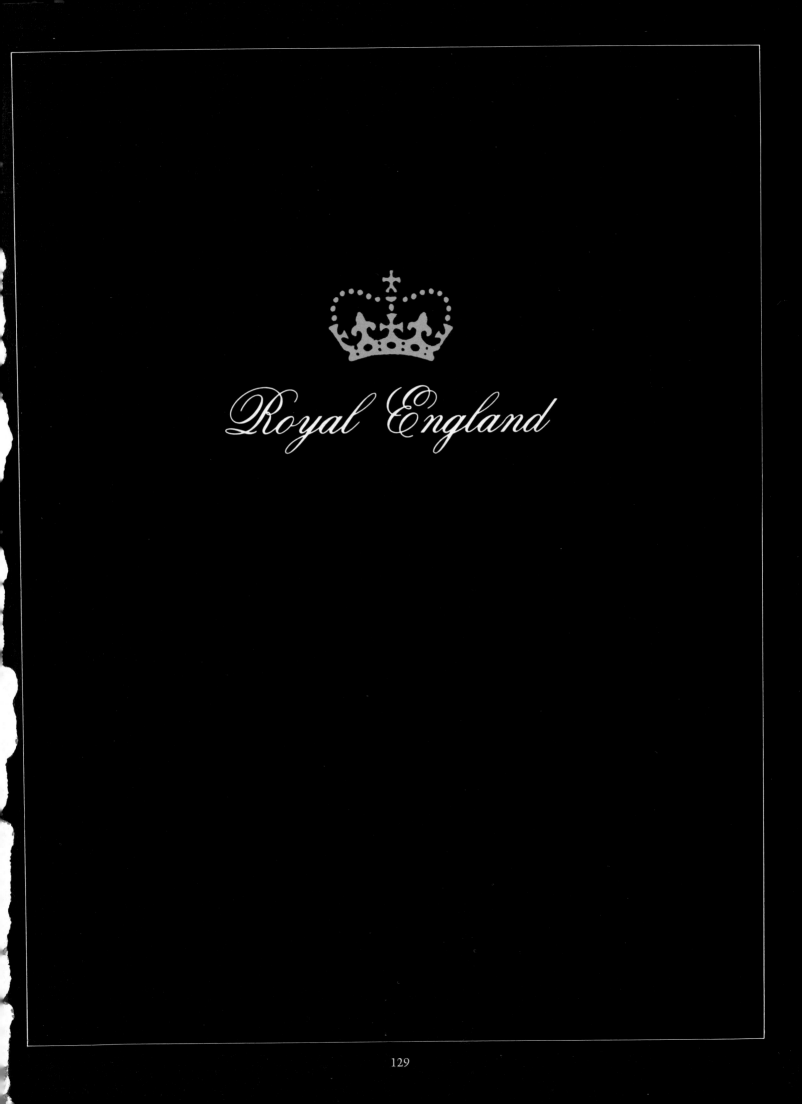

Royal England

Aldborough

North Yorkshire **Map: p241 F2.**
In Roman times this little village was the capital of the Brigantes, one of the most powerful Celtic tribes in Britain. Sections of the walls of a Roman camp can still be seen here.

Alnwick

Northumberland **Map: p243 H3.** *Castle open May to Sept: Sun to Fri afternoons. Closed Sat.*
A mighty castle, seat of the Percy family since 1309, dominates the skyline to the north of the town. It has seen several royal visitors, but few who came in peace. In 1093 — three years before the first stones of the present castle were laid — Malcolm Canmore, King of Scotland (1057-1093), was killed in an ambush near the castle site while harrying the north of England. A cross marks the spot where he fell. In 1174, another Scottish king, William the Lion (1165-1214), was taken prisoner while besieging the castle. A stone commemorating his capture can be seen near Forest Lodge, the main entrance to Alnwick Park.

King John (1199-1216) came to Alnwick three times; on the last occasion in 1215, during his war against the barons, he burned the town. Henry III (1216-1272) was entertained at the castle in 1255. His son Prince Edward successfully laid siege to it 10 years later, after the owner, John de Vescy, who sided with the rebels at the Battle of Evesham, had seized his confiscated fortress by force. In 1462, during the Wars of the Roses, the castle was successfully besieged again, by Queen Margaret, wife of Henry VI (1422-1461).

In 1503, Princess Margaret, daughter of Henry VII (1485-1509), stayed for two days at Alnwick Castle on her way to Berwick and her marriage to James IV of Scotland (1488-1513).

Althorp

Northamptonshire **Map: p238 D5.** *House and garden open Sun, Tue, Thur and Sat afternoons; Tue to Sat afternoons in Aug; public holidays. House closed Sat in July.*
The Spencer family and their ancestors have lived at Althorp since 1508. The house, which was remodelled by the fashionable Whig architect Henry Holland in 1786, is now famous as the family home of the Princess of Wales, formerly Lady Diana Spencer.

Althorp

Anne of Denmark broke her journey here when travelling from Holyrood to London with her son, the young Prince Henry. She was on her way to the coronation of her husband, James I of England (1603-1625).

Two rooms at Althorp have royal associations. The room in which William III (1689-1702) slept in 1695 is still called King William's Room. Queen Mary's room was used by Queen Mary in 1913, when she and George V (1910-1936) stayed at Althorp.

Alton

Hampshire **Map: p234 D4.**
Close by this town, in 1101, the armies of Henry I (1100-1135) and his brother Robert, Duke of Normandy, faced each other ready to fight over the succession. However, the brothers met and were reconciled without a blow being struck.

Amesbury Abbey

Wiltshire **Map: p233 H2.**
The original wicked stepmother, Elfrida, Queen of Edgar (AD 959-975), is said to have founded Amesbury Abbey in AD 980. She did this as penance for arranging the murder at Corfe of her 15-year-old stepson Edward (AD 975-979), to make way for her own child Ethelred the Unready (AD 979-1016). In fact, Elfrida could have refounded an earlier convent, for Queen Guinevere is supposed to have retired to a priory at Amesbury after the death of Arthur.

Eleanor of Provence, wife of Henry III (1216-1272) was a nun at Amesbury for 20 years. The present abbey was built in the 19th century and is a private nursing home.

Ampthill

Bedfordshire **Map: p235 E1.** *Park open daily.*
The park surrounding the 15th-century castle was a favourite hunting ground of Henry VIII (1509-1547), who often brought Anne Boleyn to hunt here. Ironically, it was to this castle that Henry's first Queen, Catherine of Aragon, was banished in 1533. The building was demolished in the 17th century.

Arreton Manor

Isle of Wight **Map: p234 C4.** *Open Easter to Oct: Mon to Sat daily; Sun afternoons.*
This Elizabethan house is one of the most perfectly preserved manor houses in England. The original building was owned by Alfred the Great (AD 871-899), who left it to his younger son Ethelward in a will made between AD 872 and AD 885. A copy of this will is on show in the house. After the Norman Conquest, the manor passed to the Abbey of St Mary at Quarr and remained a church possession until Henry VIII (1509-1547) regained it at the Dissolution of the Monasteries (1536). It remained in royal ownership until Charles I (1625-1649) sold it to settle his debts to the City of London.

James I (1603-1625) often came here to hunt and on one visit reviewed his troops on Arreton Down. In 1628, Charles I held a review here of the Scots

Regiment of Mercenaries, who were stationed on the island. Later royal visitors to the manor were Queen Victoria (1837-1901) with her children and Queen Mary, wife of George V (1910-1936).

Arundel Castle

Arundel Castle

West Sussex **Map: p235 E4.** *Open Apr to Oct: Sun to Fri afternoons only; public holidays.*
Since 1580 this fortress has been the home of the Howard family — Dukes of Norfolk and hereditary Earls Marshal of England. The strategic importance of the site was recognized centuries earlier, set as it is in the cleft cut by the River Arun through the South Downs. Alfred the Great (AD 871-899) had a stronghold here, Harold (1066) owned the land and William the Conqueror (1066-1087) gave it to Roger de Montgomery. He built the first stone fortress on the site, of which the Norman arch and walls of the inner gateway still remain.

Arundel Castle was destroyed in a Parliamentary bombardment during the Civil War and the present castle is largely an 18th- and 19th-century reconstruction.

Queen Victoria (1837-1901) and Prince Albert spent two days at Arundel in 1846.

Ascot

Berkshire **Map: p234 D3.** *Royal Ascot Racecourse open for race meetings.*
Shy by nature, dogged by ill-health, a slave to duty — the picture that historians paint of Queen Anne (1702-1714) is of a homely, rather than a fun-loving queen. So it is a surprise to discover that she had one unexpected passion — she enjoyed going to the races. She kept a string of racehorses in training at Newmarket and in 1711 organized the first race meeting on Ascot Heath and laid out a 2 mile course here. The site she chose is now famous as Royal Ascot Racecourse.

Ashbourne

Derbyshire **Map: p237 H1.** *Hall open daily.*
The last determined attempt of the Jacobites to re-

capture the English throne started at Ashbourne Hall. Bonnie Prince Charlie, grandson of James II (1685-1688), and known as the Young Pretender, stayed here twice in 1745. The first time, the night before his Highland army captured Derby, he still had high hopes of forcing George II (1727-1760) to flee back to Hanover, thus restoring the throne to the Stuarts. The second time, three days later, he was in bitter retreat after his generals had persuaded him to turn back for Scotland against his will.

Ashby-de-la-Zouch

Leicestershire **Map: p237 H1.** *Castle open Mon, Tue, Fri, Sat daily; Sun afternoons.*
James I (1603-1625) frequently enjoyed great hospitality at Ashby-de-la-Zouch Castle with his entire court. However, not all royal visitors had happy memories of Ashby. Mary, Queen of Scots (1542-1567), was briefly imprisoned here twice during her long captivity in England. Charles I (1625-1649) fled to the castle after his defeat at the Battle of Naseby (1645). Originally, the castle was a Norman manor house. Edward IV (1461-1483) gave it to his Lord Chamberlain, William, Lord Hastings, as a reward for his support in the Wars of the Roses, and Hastings later enlarged and strengthened it. He was beheaded by Richard III (1483-1485) for treason, but his son — fighting for Henry Tudor at Bosworth — restored fortune and royal favour to the family.

Ashby St Ledgers

Northamptonshire **Map: p238 C5.** *Plot House not open.*
In 1605, Robert Catesby, lord of the manor of Ashby St Ledgers, and a group of fellow Roman Catholic conspirators met to plan the Gunpowder Plot to blow up the Houses of Parliament. However, one of the conspirators, Francis Tresham, warned a relative, Lord Monteagle, to avoid attending the House of Lords on the crucial day. As a result, the plotters were caught entering the cellars of the Houses of Parliament on 5 November. Catesby, who was not with Guy Fawkes in the cellars, fled back to Ashby St Ledgers but he was killed while resisting arrest. His property was forfeited to the crown.

Ashdown House

Berkshire **Map: p233 H1.** *Open Apr: Wed only; May-Sept: Wed and 1st and 3rd Sat in the month, afternoons only.*
A devoted courtier, Lord Craven, built Ashdown House as a country refuge for a Queen who never lived to see it. The Queen, Elizabeth of Bohemia, sister of Charles I (1625-1649), spent most of her life in exile after her husband was driven from Bohemia during the Thirty Years' War.

Ashford-in-the-Water

Derbyshire **Map: p238 C2.**
This pretty village, which lies 2 miles to the west of Bakewell, was once the home of Edmund Plantagenet, Earl of Kent, stepbrother to Edward II (1307-1327). Some traces of the moat of Edmund's fortified house can still be seen behind Holy Trinity Church. The lower part of the church tower dates from Edmund's time, but the remaining part of the church was extensively rebuilt in 1870.

Ashingdon

Essex **Map: p235 G2.**
In 1016 Danes and Saxons fought by moonlight by the River Crouch near Ashingdon at the end of a day-long battle. Edmund Ironside (1016), King for only six months, had defeated the Danish leader, Canute (1016-1035), four times, but this time he was defeated. The kingdom was afterwards divided, Canute ruling in the north and Edmund in the south. However, Edmund was dead — possibly murdered — a month later.

Ashridge House

Hertfordshire **Map: p234 D2.** *Gardens open Apr to Oct: weekend afternoons only. House open some weekends.*
A 14th-century crypt, a Tudor tithe barn and a 224ft well are all that remain of the old monastery where the children of Henry VIII (1509-1547) spent much of their childhood. The present house was built on the site in the early 19th century and is now Ashridge Management College.
Edward I (1272-1307) spent several weeks at Ashridge in 1290, five years after the monastery was completed. He held his Parliament there the following year. The monastery was later richly endowed by his grandson, Edward, the Black Prince, in 1376.
The last private owners of Ashridge House, Lord and Lady Brownlow, entertained the Shah of Persia there in 1869. Queen Mary, wife of George V (1910-1936), was a frequent guest.

Aston Hall

West Midlands **Map: p237 H2.** *Open to the public.*
In 1642 Sir Thomas Holte, an ardent Royalist, and the owner of the recently built Aston Hall, entertained Charles I (1625-1649) here, just a few days before the King and his Cavaliers defeated a Roundhead army under the Earl of Essex at Edgehill, the first battle of the Civil War.

Athelney

Somerset **Map: p233 F2.**
Alfred the Great (AD 871-899) fled to this stronghold in early January, AD 878. The Danes, led by King Guthrun, had seized his royal fortress at Chippenham and overrun most of his kingdom of Wessex. At that time Athelney was an island in the middle of almost impassable marshes. Alfred and a few of his followers hid here while planning the campaign which was to bring them victory over Guthrun three months later at the Battle of Bratton Down.

Audley End

Essex **Map: p235 F1.** *House open Apr to Sept: Tue to Sun afternoons; public holidays.*
When this mansion was built in the reign of James I (1603-1625) by the Lord High Treasurer, Thomas Howard, Earl of Suffolk, the estimated cost of the house and furniture was £200,000 — more than £8 million in contemporary value. Charles II (1660-1685) bought it in 1669 but the house did not remain long as a royal palace. He and his successors used it only occasionally and in 1701 it reverted to the Suffolk family.
Little remains of Charles's New Palace today.

Ashridge Management College

The great outer courtyard was demolished in 1721, halving the size of the mansion. Since then remodelling, restoration and rebuilding have changed the house considerably. In the saloon, however, the spectacular ceiling and the chimney-piece are both still original, as is the magnificent carved wooden screen in the hall.

Audley End

Avington Park

Hampshire **Map: p234 C4.** *Open May to Sept: weekends and public holidays.*
George Brydges, the owner of Avington Park, was well rewarded by Charles II (1660-1685), when he placed his home at the disposal of the merry monarch's favourite mistress, Nell Gwynne. More than a century later the house served the Prince Regent, later George IV (1820-1830), and his unacknowledged wife, Mrs Fitzherbert, in a similar capacity.

Axbridge

Somerset **Map: p233 F2.** *King John's Hunting Lodge open Apr to Sept: afternoons only.*
The royal forest of Mendip was a hunting ground of Saxon kings before the Norman Conquest, and there was a royal fortress at Axbridge. The pride of the town is King John's Hunting Lodge.

Aylesford

Kent **Map: p235 F3.**
The Downs above this village were the scene of a great battle in AD 455, when the British, led by Vortigern, were defeated by the invading Jutes.

Badminton

Avon **Map: p233 G1.** *House open June to early Sept: occasional Wed afternoons.*
The 5th Earl of Somerset was a staunch Royalist who virtually funded the Royalist campaign during the opening months of the Civil War by giving the impoverished Charles I (1625-1649) more than £120,000 of his personal fortune in 1642. Three years after the Restoration Charles II (1660-1685) and his Queen, Catherine of Braganza, visited Badminton and in 1682, Charles made the 5th Earl's grandson, Henry Somerset, the 1st Duke of Beaufort. It was at about this time

that he began to build the Palladian mansion standing today.

In 1685 James II (1685-1688) visited Badminton while the 2nd Duke, grandson of the 1st Duke, was able to offer princely hospitality to Queen Anne (1702-1714) and her consort, Prince George, soon after her accession.

Badminton is now internationally famous for the three-day event horse trials, which members of the royal family attend each year.

Bamburgh Castle

Northumberland **Map: p243 H3.** *Open May to Sept: Sun to Fri afternoons.*
Celts, Romans and Saxons all fortified the rock on which Bamburgh Castle stands. Rising steeply 150ft above the sea-shore on the eastern side and commanding wide views over the country, it was easily defended. In AD 547, Ida, the Saxon King of Bernicia, made it his capital.

Soon after the Conquest the Normans built a wooden fortress here, which was besieged in 1095 by William Rufus (1087-1100). For the next three centuries Bamburgh provided a strong base for successive English kings in their campaigns against Scotland. In 1164 Henry II (1154-1189) built the massive keep which still stands today; King John (1199-1216) strengthened the defences and appointed a constable; and Henry III (1216-1272) built the King's Hall, which was completely restored in 1900. David II, King of Scotland (1329-1371), was imprisoned here in 1346 after his defeat at Neville's Cross. The castle changed hands several times during the Wars of the Roses, when Margaret of Anjou, Queen of Henry VI (1422-1461), allied herself with the Scots against the Yorkist Edward IV (1461-1483). Finally, Bamburgh became the first English castle to surrender to gunpowder when it fell to Edward's artillery in 1464.

The castle slowly fell into ruins in the 17th century after the crowns of Scotland and England were united, but it was extensively restored in the 18th and 19th centuries.

Banbury

Oxfordshire **Map: p234 C1.**
The original cross mentioned in the nursery rhyme 'Ride a'cock horse to Banbury Cross' was pulled down by Puritans 300 years ago because it was a popish symbol. The present cross was erected in 1860 to commemorate the marriage of Queen Victoria (1837-1901) and Prince Albert. Carved figures of Victoria, Edward VII (1901-1910) and George V (1910-1936) were added in 1914. In the town hall there are portraits of Bonnie Prince Charlie and Prince Rupert.

Barbury Castle

Wiltshire **Map: p233 H1.** *Open all the time.*
Although the battles fought by King Arthur against the Saxons have become the subject of legend, one battle — Mount Badon — is believed to be a historical fact. Fought around AD 500, it checked the Saxon advance into the southwest of England for nearly 50 years. This Iron Age hill fort on the Marlborough Downs, above the prehistoric Ridgeway, has been suggested as a possible site of the two-day conflict, in which Arthur's cavalry is said to have killed thousands of Saxons.

Barking

Essex **Map: p235 F2.**
The abbey at Barking was already 400 years old when William the Conqueror (1066-1087) stayed here while his Tower of London was being built. Founded around AD 666 by Erkenwald, son of Offa, King of the East Angles, its first abbess was Erkenwald's sister, Ethelburga. Both brother and sister became saints. It was one of the richest and most royal religious houses in England but at the Dissolution of the Monasteries (1536) it was demolished. Today, only the Firebell, or Curfew, Gate is left.

Bamburgh Castle

Barnard Castle

Durham **Map: p241 E1.** *Bowes Museum open Mon to Sat daily, Sun afternoons. Closed Christmas, New Year.*

Although bearing the scars of its bombardment by Parliamentary cannon during the Civil War, this castle is still impressive, towering on a crag almost 100ft above the River Tees. Its royal links go back to the time of Richard III (1483-1485), who owned it as a result of his marriage to Anne Nevill, daughter of Warwick the Kingmaker.

The castle was built in 1130 by Bernard Balliol on a site granted to the family by William Rufus (1087-1100). Edward I (1272-1307) made Bernard's descendant, John Balliol, King of Scotland in 1292.

Barnet

Greater London **Map: p235 E2.**
Less than a mile from this north London suburb, the Yorkist army under Edward IV (1461-1483) defeated a far larger Lancastrian force led by Richard Nevill, Earl of Warwick (the Kingmaker) in 1471. An obelisk set up in 1740 on Hadley Green marks the site of the battle.

Barnwell

Northamptonshire **Map: p239 E5.** *Manor House gardens open as advertised.*
The 17th-century manor house of this attractive village is the home of Princess Alice, Duchess of Gloucester, and the present Duke and Duchess of Gloucester. In the grounds are the ruins of 13th-century Barnwell Castle.

Basing House

Hampshire **Map: p234 D3.** *Open Apr and May: weekend and bank holiday Mon afternoons; June to Sept: daily afternoons except Mon and Thur.*
No royal accolade could be sweeter than the remark made to Sir William Paulet, 1st Marquess of Winchester, when he entertained Elizabeth I (1558-1603) at Basing House in 1560: 'By my troth,' the Queen quipped, 'if my Lord were but a young man, I could find it in my heart to love him for a husband before any man in England.' This tribute to the outstanding qualities of the man and the magnificence of his hospitality was well deserved — but Sir William was no stranger to the demands of entertaining a sovereign, having already entertained Henry VIII (1509-1547) and Mary I (1553-1558).

Battle

East Sussex **Map: p235 F4.** *Abbey open daily.*
The battlefield near Hastings, where Harold (1066) drew up his Saxon army to face Duke William's Norman invaders on 14 October 1066, is still open land. Harold, newly crowned, had brought his army in forced marches more than 250 miles from north Yorkshire. There he had defeated another invader, the Norwegian King Harald Hardrada, only three days before William

Bath

Avon **Map: p233 G1.**
A king was once crowned in Bath — one of the few times a coronation has been held outside London or Winchester — but it was arguably the most important crowning in English history. The scatter of stones on Abbey Green mark the site of the Saxon abbey where Edgar (AD 959-975) was crowned on Whit Sunday AD 973. Descendant of Egbert (AD 802-839), Edgar was king of the separate kingdoms of Wessex, Mercia and Northumbria, and so, effectively, ruler of all England. His coronation not only marked the unification of the three kingdoms, but it established a ceremony which has been the basis of all coronations to this very day.

Bath Abbey

Work on the present abbey church, on a site just north of Abbey Green, was started by Oliver King, Bishop of Bath and Wells from 1495 to 1503. It was still unfinished when Elizabeth I (1558-1603) visited the city in 1574, and ordered a national levy to pay for its completion. However, it was not finished until the end of the 19th century.

Royal Circus

From Elizabeth's time onwards Bath was to see more royalty than almost any other place in Britain, apart from London. The principal attraction was the waters, which gush from a hot spring at a rate of half a million gallons each day at a constant temperature of 120°F (49°C). The water was believed to cure almost anything — Anne of Denmark, wife of James I (1603-1625) came here to cure her dropsy; Charles II (1660-1685) was a regular visitor, no doubt seeking recuperation from the rigours of court life; while his brother James II (1685-1688) resorted to the spring for unspecified ailments. His daughter Anne (1702-1714), debilitated by numerous pregnancies and gout, spent much time at the baths.

Under the Hanoverians the city was largely re-built and still survives — despite 20th century depredations — as the most complete and elegant Georgian city in Britain. The four King Georges did not visit Bath, but many of their numerous offspring made constant use of the waters. Queen Charlotte, wife of George III (1760-1820), even maintained a house in Bath, at 93 Sydney Place. This devotion to the waters was understandable. At a time when medicine was as likely to kill as to cure, the waters at least did no harm and, in some cases, provided positive benefits.

Pulteney Bridge

landed at Pevensey. This second battle not only cost Harold his life; it also marked the end of Saxon England.

Soon after his victory William the Conqueror (1066-1087) ordered the building of Battle Abbey, a Benedictine foundation, in fulfilment of a vow and in thanksgiving. William Rufus (1087-1100) attended its consecration in 1094. Henry VIII (1509-1547) dissolved the abbey, giving it to his Master of Horse, Sir Anthony Browne, who built a mansion on the site. Only the ruins of the abbey now survive.

Beaconsfield

Buckinghamshire **Map: p234 D2.**
Elizabeth I (1558-1603) is said to have stayed at the Royal White Hart, a coaching inn here.

Beaminster

Dorset **Map: p233 F3.** *Parnham House open Apr to Oct: Wed and Sun daily; public holiday.*
Parnham House, a beautiful Tudor houses in Dorset, lies 1 mile to the southwest of Beaminster. It is now the John Makepeace Furniture Workshop and School for Craftsmen in Wood, where Viscount Linley, son of Princess Margaret and Lord Snowdon, trained.

Beaulieu Abbey

Hampshire **Map: p233 H3.** *Open daily except Christmas day.*
According to legend King John (1199-1216) gave more than 8,000 acres to the Cistercian monks at Beaulieu. The abbey became a place of sanctuary for fugitives. Years later, during the Wars of the Roses, Margaret of Anjou, wife of Henry VI (1422-1461), and the Countess of Warwick, widow of the celebrated Kingmaker, made their way here after the Battle of Barnet in 1471, where the Earl of Warwick was killed. Another fugitive, Perkin Warbeck, the impostor who claimed to be Richard, the younger of the two Princes in the Tower, fled here after leading a rebellion against Henry VII (1485-1509) in Cornwall in 1495.

The abbey church was pulled down at the Dissolution of the Monasteries (1536) and the Great Gatehouse became the Montagus' home.

Belvoir Castle

Beeston Castle

Cheshire **Map: p238 A3.** *Open Mon to Sat daily, Sun afternoon.*
Richard II (1377-1399) is said to have hidden his royal treasure in the stronghold of Beeston Castle in 1399. The castle belonged to the Earls of Chester but passed to Henry III (1216-1272) in 1264. Today it is an impressive ruin.

Belton House

Lincolnshire **Map: p238 D3.** *Open late Mar to early Oct: daily.*
The King who gave up his crown to marry the woman he loved, Edward VIII (1936), later the Duke of Windsor, was a lifelong friend of the 6th Lord Brownlow, of Belton. The only known portrait of Edward as King was painted there by Frank Salisbury and it still hangs in the house.

Belvoir Castle

Leicestershire **Map: p238 D3.** *Open late Mar to Sept: Tue, Wed, Thur and weekend afternoons; Oct: Sun afternoons; public holidays.*
Part of the Norman keep is all that survives of the medieval fortress, built on a commanding hill. James I (1603-1625) was entertained here by Roger Manners, 5th Earl of Rutland, on his way to London after his accession. Charles I (1625-1649) visited the castle in 1634. Belvoir was, however, demolished in 1649, after the Civil War. The present castle dates from 1801.

Berkeley Castle

Gloucestershire **Map: p234 A2.** *Open Apr, Sept: Tue to Sun afternoons; May to Aug: Tue to Sun daily, Sun afternoons; Oct: Sun afternoons. Gardens open daily and public holidays.*
The oldest inhabited house in England, 12th-century Berkeley Castle was the scene, in 1327, of one of the cruellest murders in English history. The deposed king, Edward II (1307-1327), was murdered here by order of his Queen, Isabella, and her lover Roger Mortimer, in a violent and horrible manner. Unlike most English castles, Berkeley survived the Civil War largely undamaged. It is still possible to stand in Edward's cell in the keep and see the room in which he was killed and where his corpse was displayed by his gaolers, Thomas de Gournay and John Maltravers.

In 1486, Lord William Berkeley, known afterwards as 'Waste-all', gave the castle to Henry VII (1485-1509) in exchange for the title of Earl Marshal. It remained royal property until it was returned to the Berkeley family on the death of Edward VI (1547-1553). Elizabeth I (1558-1603) wanted to give Berkeley Castle to her favourite courtier, the Earl of Leicester, but then discovered it was not hers to give.

Beaulieu Abbey

Berkhamsted

Hertfordshire **Map: p234 D2.** *Open weekdays and Sun afternoons.*

It was at Berkhamsted in 1066, a few weeks after his victory at Hastings, that William the Conqueror (1066-1087) received the homage of the demoralized Anglo-Saxon leaders as he stood poised to march on London. William gave the castle site to his half-brother, Robert, Count of Mortain, and for four centuries the castle was the home of successive princes, queens and nobles.

Thomas à Becket lived at Berkhamsted for 10 years from 1155, and was criticized by Henry II (1154-1189) for his expenditure on the castle. Piers Gaveston, favourite of Edward II (1307-1327), owned the castle briefly in 1309, and in 1336 it was given to Edward, the Black Prince, who had King John of France imprisoned here after capturing him at Poitiers (1356). Little of the original stonework can be seen today.

Berry Pomeroy Castle

Devon **Map: p233 E4.** *Open daily.*

The gatehouse and curtain walls of this 14th-century castle stand on a crag in the middle of a thick wood. The castle was destroyed in a siege during the Civil War. William of Orange, later William III (1689-1702), chose this eerie site — said to be one of the most haunted in Britain — as a stopping-place on his way from Torbay to London in November 1688 to claim the crown.

Berwick-upon-Tweed

Northumberland **Map: p243 G2.** *Castle open Mon to Sat daily, Sun afternoons. Closed public holidays.*

The old town of Berwick-upon-Tweed still crouches behind its defensive walls, just as it did throughout three of the bloodiest centuries in English and Scottish history. During this period it changed hands 13 times before finally coming under the English crown in 1482. The Scots traded Berwick to Henry II (1154-1189) as part of the ransom of their King, William the Lion (1165-1214), in 1174, and Richard I (1189-1199) sold it back to them to raise money for the Third Crusade. It was burned by King John (1199-1216) in 1216. Edward I (1272-1307), the Hammer of the Scots, sacked Berwick in 1296 at the start of a lightning campaign that subdued Scotland in 21 weeks. He returned in triumph to Berwick to receive the homage of the conquered Scots. In his last campaign against Robert Bruce (1306-1329) in 1306, he captured the Countess of Buchan who had crowned Bruce King of Scotland. His successor, Edward II (1307-1327), kept her in a cage in Berwick Castle for six years.

Little is left of the original castle, which was demolished in Victorian times.

Bewdley

Hereford & Worcester **Map: p237 G3.** *Tickenhill House not open to the public.*

The wool trade made Bewdley a prosperous and important town in Tudor times. Tickenhill House was a royal manor house and the home of two ill-fated Princes of Wales: Prince Arthur, son of Henry VII (1485-1509), and, a century later, Prince Henry, the popular and forthright son of James I (1603-1625). Mary I (1553-1558) also lived at Tickenhill, after she had been given her own retinue of courtiers as a future Princess of Wales at the age of 10. During the Civil War the manor was garrisoned for the King.

Bishop Auckland

Durham **Map: p241 F1.** *Bishop's Park open daily.*
Charles I (1625-1649) is known to have visited Auckland Castle three times — once as a child, once as King and once as a prisoner.

Bishop's Waltham

Hampshire **Map: p234 C4.** *Palace open Tue to Sat daily, Sun afternoons; bank holiday Mons.*
The palace, built in the 12th century for the see of Winchester, was the scene of much fund raising for the crusades by both Henry II (1154-1189) and his son Richard I (1189-1199). In 1644, during the Civil War, Roundhead soldiers besieged the palace, which was held by 200 Royalist soldiers. The palace was ruined.

Blackheath

Greater London **Map: p235 F3.** *House open daily.*
Built in the 1680s, largely reconstructed in the 1720s, and enlarged throughout the 18th century, Ranger's House became the residence of Princess Sophia Matilda, Ranger of Greenwich Park in 1814. In 1977, an avenue of lime trees was planted near the house in honour of the Silver Jubilee of Elizabeth II.

Blenheim Palace

Oxfordshire **Map: p234 C2.** *Open mid-Mar to Oct: daily.*
In August 1704 John Churchill, Duke of Marlborough, inflicted a crushing defeat on the army of Louis XIV at Blenheim on the Danube and shattered the French King's dream of controlling the whole of Europe. In gratitude Queen Anne (1702-1714) gave her victorious general the royal

Blenheim Palace

manor of Woodstock. The building of Blenheim Palace, partly paid for by the treasury, was begun in 1704 by Sir John Vanbrugh as 'a monument to the Queen's glory', and lasted 17 years.

The old manor of Woodstock, demolished when work began on the palace, was a royal hunting ground in Saxon times. Henry I (1100-1135) walled it as a deer park. Edward, the Black Prince, son of Edward III (1327-1377), was born here in 1330, and the young Princess Elizabeth was imprisoned here in 1554 by her half-sister Mary I (1553-1558), suspected of plotting treason. The manor was damaged by Parliamentary troops during the Civil War.

Bletchingley

Surrey **Map: p235 E3.** *Place Farm not open.*
Henry VIII (1509-1547) gave his fourth Queen, Anne of Cleves, a manor at Bletchingley when he divorced her in 1540 after only a few months of marriage. She lived at Place Farm, situated a mile north of the village as 'the king's sister', with a comfortable pension, until her death 17 years later. The present house dates mainly from the 18th century.

Blewbury

Oxfordshire **Map: p234 C2.** *Hall Barn not open.*
Some of the houses in this village were already old, possible Saxon, when Henry VIII (1509-1547) first came to hunt in the neighbourhood. He may have used Hall Barn as a hunting lodge.

Blickling Hall

Norfolk **Map: p239 G3.** *Open Apr, May, Oct: Tue, Wed, Fri and weekend afternoons only; June to Sept: daily; public holidays. Gardens open May to Oct: daily.*
Every year since her execution, at midnight on 19 May 1536, the ghost of Anne Boleyn, second wife of Henry VIII (1509-1547), is said to ride up to the door of Blickling Hall in a phantom coach, with her severed head in her lap. The beautiful Jacobean mansion that stands today was never visited by Anne in her lifetime but it is likely that as a child she stayed at an older house that stood on this site, which belonged to her father, Sir Thomas Boleyn.

Blithfield Hall

Staffordshire **Map: p237 G1.** *Open Easter to early Oct: Wed, Thur, Sat daily; Sun afternoons.*
Six centuries have passed since Richard II (1377-1399) enjoyed good hunting in the Forest of Needwood. Elizabeth I (1558-1603) visited the hall with the Earl of Essex 200 years later. The most recent royal visitor, Queen Elizabeth, the Queen Mother, was entertained to luncheon in the Great Hall in 1953, when she opened the reservoir to the southeast of the house.

Bodmin Moor

Cornwall **Map: p232 C4.**
According to legend, Dozmary Pool, a lonely tarn

high on the moor, is where Sir Bedivere flung King Arthur's magic sword, Excalibur. He saw it caught in the air and brandished three times by an arm and hand that rose from the water.

Bognor Regis

West Sussex **Map: p234 D5.**
When society took to sea-bathing in the 18th century Sir Richard Hotham built Dome House and hoped to lure royalty here from Brighton. It was Princess Charlotte, granddaughter of George III (1760-1820), who stayed here and by her visits launched Bognor as a quietly fashionable watering-place. Bognor won the final seal of royal approval — and added Regis (meaning 'of the king') to its name — when George V (1910-1936) convalesced here after a critical illness in 1929.

Bolsover Castle

Derbyshire **Map: p238 C2.** *Open Mon to Sat daily, Sun afternoons. Closed public holidays.*
Lady Shrewsbury, the famous Bess of Hardwick, began the construction of Bolsover, one of five great mansions she built. In 1633 Charles I (1625-1649) and his Queen, Henrietta Maria, were lavishly entertained here by Bess's grandson William Cavendish, Earl of Newcastle, before the building was completed.

Bolton-by-Bowland

North Yorkshire. **Map: p241 E3.**
Even in defeat after the Battle of Hexham (1464) during the Wars of the Roses, Henry VI (1422-1461) found time for his great love — church building. He is said to have designed the tower of the church in this village, while hiding with Sir Ralph Pudsay, the lord of the manor.

Bolton Castle

North Yorkshire **Map: p241 F3.** *Open Tue to Sun daily.*
Mary, Queen of Scots (1542-1567), stayed at the castle in 'honourable custody' for six months. She was allowed to hang her cloth of state (a canopy with a tapestry worked with her coat of arms) in the Great Hall where she dined.

Bolton Castle was built in the 14th century by Richard, 1st Lord Scrope, on the site of his manor house. It was slighted by Parliament in 1647 and the hall itself is now ruined.

Boscobel House

Salop **Map: p237 G2.** *Open Mon to Sat daily, Sun afternoons. Closed Christmas, New Year.*
Charles II (1660-1685) never forgot the days he spent at Boscobel hiding up an oak tree after the Battle of Worcester (1651). It was his favourite story — and one that his courtiers heard almost too often. As he hid there all day, Charles could see Cromwell's soldiers searching the woods. Afterwards he hid in an attic priest-hole in Boscobel House. The King remained ever-grateful to the loyal Penderel family of Boscobel.

Boscobel House was originally a black-and-white timber-framed house, but some time after Charles's stay the outer walls were stuccoed.

Bosham

West Sussex **Map: p234 D4.**
In 1064, Harold Godwinson, later to be King of England, knelt in prayer in Bosham church before embarking on his voyage to Normandy, during which he was shipwrecked and captured by William, Duke of Normandy. To secure his release he swore an oath saying that he would help William to win the throne of England after the death of Edward the Confessor (1042-1066). He was crowned in 1066 but his failure to keep his promise led to the Norman invasion.

The tower and chancel arch of the present church are Saxon. The village of Bosham, set by a tidal creek in Chichester harbour, is claimed to be the place where Canute (1016-1035) demonstrated the foolishness of courtiers who flattered his power, by commanding the tide to ebb.

Bosham

Bosworth Field

Leicestershire **Map: p237 H2.**
When Richard III (1483-1485) fell at Bosworth shouting 'Treason, treason!', he spoke the truth. On that day, 22 August 1485, it was not two armies — those of the houses York and Lancaster — but four that took the field. The Earl of Northumberland, Henry Percy, with his private army, formed Richard's rearguard, and watching from the sidelines stood the 3,000-strong army of the brothers Stanley. Their allegiance to Richard was suspect; during the battle they waited to see how things were going before committing themselves, and the Earl of Northumberland, when called upon to advance, refused to do so until he saw which way the Stanleys swung. Richard staked all on a desperate personal charge against Henry Tudor, later Henry VII (1485-1509). As the King closed in on Henry, Sir William Stanley threw his troops into battle on the rebel side and Richard was surrounded and cut down. He was the last English king to die in battle. This event marked the end of the Plantagenet line.

Bradgate Park

Leicestershire **Map: p238 C4.** *Open all the time.*
The ruins of Bradgate House, birthplace and childhood home of Lady Jane Grey, lie within the 850 acres of this country park and nature reserve. Lady Jane, granddaughter of the sister of Henry VIII (1509-1547), never coveted the throne. It was the scheming ambition of her father-in-law, John Dudley, Duke of Northumberland, that caused her to reign for nine days after the death of Edward VI (1547-1553). Mary I (1553-1558) reluctantly had her executed; Lady Jane was still only 16.

Brading

Isle of Wight **Map: p234 D5.** *Nunwell Manor not open to the public.*
In 1647 Charles I (1625-1649) fled to the Isle of Wight from Hampton Court in fear of assassination. Two days after his arrival he called on Sir John Oglander, a known Royalist, at Nunwell Manor and spent the night here. The Oglanders had lived at Brading for centuries. Henry VII (1485-1509) stayed with the family when he came to the island in 1499 to inspect its defences.

Brampton

Cumbria **Map: p243 F5.**
The house in High Cross Street where Bonnie Prince Charlie, grandson of the deposed James II (1685-1688), stayed in 1745, while his rebel army besieged Carlisle, is now a shoe shop.

Bratton Down

Wiltshire **Map: p233 G2.**
The surprise of the King's sudden appearance in the heart of Wessex with arms and supplies was a vital factor in the defeat by Alfred (AD 871-899) of the Danish King Guthrun on this downland near Salisbury Plain in AD 878. This ended Danish hopes of conquering the whole of England. The huge white horse on Bratton Down was carved in the chalk in 1778. It is thought to be superimposed on an earlier horse cut in the 9th century to celebrate Alfred's victory.

Brenchley

Kent **Map: p235 F3.**
A row of cottages opposite the church is all that remains of the palace of the Dukes of St Albans. The 1st Duke was the illegitimate son of Charles II (1660-1685) by his mistress Nell Gwynne.

Bridgnorth

Salop **Map: p237 F2.** *Castle open daily.*
English history would have taken a different course if an arrow intended for Henry II (1154-1189) had reached its target in 1155, when he was besieging Bridgnorth Castle in the first few months of his reign. Hubert St Clair leapt in front of the king to take the fatal arrow and saved Henry's life. Today the keep of the royal castle

that Henry regained from the rebellious Hugh de Mortimer, leans at an angle of 17° after being undermined in a Civil War siege in 1646.

Ethelred, brother of Athelstan (AD 925-939), is said to have lived as a hermit in one of the sandstone caves on the Cartway — the road which links the low town with the high town.

Bridgwater

Somerset **Map: p233 F2.**
Looking out from the 14th-century tower of St Mary's parish church, James, Duke of Monmouth, illegitimate son of Charles II (1660-1685), would have viewed the royal army camped 3 miles away on Sedgemoor. He later made the fateful decision to attack his enemy by night. In the resulting Battle of Sedgemoor (1685), the seasoned troops of James II (1685-1688) defeated Monmouth's ill-equipped rebel army.

Bridlington

Humberside **Map: p241 H2.**
Henrietta Maria, Queen of Charles I (1625-1649), fled from her bed in a house in Bridlington in the middle of a February night in 1643 and took refuge in a ditch with her ladies. She had arrived in the town on board a ship loaded with munitions and supplies bought on the continent for the Royalist army — pawning some of the crown jewels to pay for them. Today Bridlington is a peaceful resort.

Brighton

See pages 138-139.

Bristol

Avon **Map: p233 F1.** SS *Great Britain open daily. Red Lodge open Mon to Sat daily.*
Bristol's history is one of trade, exploration and innovation and, surprisingly, it has seen few royal visitors. However, Isambard Kingdom Brunel's steam ship, SS *Great Britain* — symbol of Bristol's great sea-going past — is linked with two princes — Albert, Consort of Queen Victoria (1837-1901), and Philip, husband of the present Queen. Albert launched the *Great Britain* on 19 July 1843. In 1970, also on 19 July, Prince Philip was on board the battered hulk of the *Great Britain* as she returned to berth in the Great Western Dock where she had been built 127 years earlier. She had sailed the Atlantic for 43 years before being abandoned on the Falkland Islands in 1886.

Two medieval Kings and a Princess were imprisoned in Bristol Castle, which has long since disappeared. Stephen (1135-1154) was deposed and incarcerated in the castle for seven months in 1141 after being captured at Lincoln by soldiers of his cousin, the Empress Matilda, during their fight over the succession. Matilda proved so harsh a ruler that Stephen was released to be recrowned. King John (1199-1216) left his niece Eleanor, the Maid of Brittany, in close confinement in the castle for the rest of her life, after capturing her and her younger brother in France in 1202.

Edward II (1307-1327) is said to have been brought to Bristol Castle from Corfe in 1327, by the two gaolers who were to murder him. Hearing

Bristol from the Suspension Bridge

of a plot by citizens to rescue the deposed King, they took him away quickly by night to Berkeley Castle. He was never seen alive again. Charles II (1660-1685) slipped through Bristol in fear of arrest, as he made his escape from his defeat at Worcester (1651).

The picturesque Hotwells district of Bristol was once a spa. Henry VIII (1509-1547) visited it and so did Charles II's Queen, Catherine of Braganza. Elizabeth I (1558-1603) visited Bristol in 1547, at the time when the city was growing prosperous with the trade of the New World. Queen Anne (1702-1714) came here in her coronation year. More recent visits by royalty include one by George V (1910-1936) and Queen Mary in 1925, when they officially opened Bristol University. The present Queen opened new council offices on a visit in 1956.

Brixham

Devon **Map: p233 E4.**
Brought by a 'Protestant wind' that blew from the east and kept the English fleet in the Thames estuary, William of Orange, later William III (1689-1702), nephew and son-in-law of James II (1685-1688), crossed the channel with 12,000 men and landed at the little fishing port of Brixham early on 5 November 1688. It was the start of the Glorious Revolution which, without bloodshed, was to depose Catholic James and give the throne to William and his Queen, James's daughter, Mary.

Broadway

Hereford & Worcester **Map: p234 B1.**
The Lygon Arms was an inn during the reign of Henry VIII (1509-1547), when it was called the White Hart — after the badge of Richard II (1377-1399). There is a tradition that Charles I (1625-1649) met friends at this inn while visiting Broadway during the Civil War. Oliver Cromwell is said to have slept here the night before the Battle of Worcester (1651), when he defeated the army raised by Charles II (1660-1685) in his attempt to win back the throne.

Broadwindsor

Dorset **Map: p233 F3.**
Making his escape to France after his defeat at the Battle of Worcester in 1651, Charles II (1660-1685) spent one night at the Castle Inn in this village. A plaque on the wall of a cottage which was once part of the inn near the village centre, commemorates his stay. The cottage is now privately owned and not open to the public.

Brompton Regis

Somerset **Map: p233 E2.**
According to legend this small village was not conquered by William the Conqueror (1066-1087) when the rest of England submitted. Githa, mother of Harold (1066) lived here after escaping from the siege of Exeter in 1068 and refused to surrender her manor to the Normans. William let her live here until her death.

Brough Castle

Cumbria **Map: p241 E1.** *Open Mon to Sat daily, Sun afternoons. Closed public holidays.*
William the Lion of Scotland (1165-1214) destroyed the original 11th-century castle built by William Rufus (1087-1100), when he besieged Brough in 1174. The ruins that can be seen today date from the 12th century.

Brighton

East Sussex **Map: p235 E4.** *Royal Pavilion open daily. Closed Christmas.*

In the summer of 1784, a German pastrycook — with great difficulty, because of his broken and heavily-accented English — succeeded in renting a house on the Steine. His success started a chain of events which transformed an already popular sea-bathing resort into a royal playground and a centre of fashionable society. For the pastrycook, Louis Weltjie, had taken the house for his employer, George, Prince of Wales, later Prince Regent and finally George IV (1820-1830).

The Prince had first visited Brighton in 1783 on the advice of his doctor, who had recommended a course of sea-bathing to treat swollen neck glands. On that occasion he stayed with his uncle, the Duke of Cumberland.

In those days, sea-bathing was not as straightforward as it is today. The 18th-century fashionable male was escorted into the water by an attendant known as a 'bather'. Ladies were attended by 'dippers'. Naturally, the Prince of Wales had the services of the leading bather of the day, Smoaker Miles, who treated his royal client no differently from anyone else and is said to have once led him into the water by the ear.

Whether sea-bathing cured his swollen neck is not known, but George fell in love with Brighton. In 1786, when the lease on the house on the Steine ran out, Weltjie rented a nearby farmhouse, which he had rebuilt as a Palladian mansion to the design of the architect Henry Holland. While the work was in progress, Weltjie bought the freehold, then let the house — which he called the Marine Pavilion — to the Prince on a 21-year lease for

The Seafront

£1,000 a year. To complete his domestic arrangements in Brighton, the Prince leased a nearby villa where he installed Maria Fitzherbert, a twice-widowed lady whom he had secretly married in 1785. Though their marriage was invalid under the terms of the Royal Marriage Act of 1772, the Prince treated Mrs Fitzherbert as his wife and expected everyone else to do the same.

Over the next 10 years the couple spent much of their time together at Brighton — though Maria always maintained her own separate home here. They parted briefly at the time of the Prince's arranged marriage to Princess Caroline of Brunswick in 1795, but within a year they were together again at Brighton.

By this time, Weltjie, who had never obtained regular payment of the rent from his royal tenant, decided to cut his losses and sell the Marine Pavilion to the Prince. This he did for £22,000 around 1797. But he had no more luck in

Brighton Pavilion

collecting the price than he had with the rent, and when he died the debt was still outstanding.

In 1804 the Prince started to extend the Marine Pavilion, building an indoor riding school and stables for 44 horses. The riding school is now known as the Dome and is a concert hall and conference centre. In the same year, Mrs Fitzherbert had a new house built on what is now the Old Steine. It still stands and is now a YMCA hostel. But in 1804 the Prince and Mrs Fitzherbert were seeing less of one another — a succession of new mistresses was taking up more and more of his time — and by 1811 they had parted for good. Mrs Fitzherbert stayed on in her house until her death in 1837. She was buried in the Roman Catholic church of St John the Baptist where her effigy shows her wearing three wedding rings.

However, goodbye to Maria did not mean goodbye to Brighton for the Prince. George still visited his Marine Pavilion and in 1815, when he became Prince Regent and got his hands on more money than ever before in his life, he engaged the architect John Nash to undertake its refurbishment. Seven years and £500,000 later the Pavilion had been transformed into a fantastic oriental palace. Gilt, scarlet lacquer, mirrors; chandeliers, dragons and serpents abound throughout. But in 1820, before his pleasure house was complete, the Prince came to the throne. From then on he rarely visited Brighton and was last at the Pavilion in 1827, three years before he died. William IV (1830-1837) stayed for long periods at the Pavilion and often called on Mrs Fitzherbert. Queen Victoria (1837-1901) did not find the place to her taste and in 1850 sold it to Brighton Corporation for £50,000. Examples of the elegant architectural heritage bequeathed to Brighton by this period of royal favour are to be seen in Royal Crescent, built in 1799, and Regency Square, begun in 1818.

In recent years the Queen has loaned many of the original furnishings to the Pavilion, which once again can be seen in all its royal and exotic splendour and former magnificence.

If George IV is the king who matters most to Brighton, Brighton once mattered very much to one of his predecessors — Charles II (1660-1685). Unlike George, Charles only stayed here one night and never returned. However, there was good reason for his hasty departure — he was being hunted by Cromwell's troops with a price of £1,000 on his head, following his defeat at the Battle of Worcester in 1651. He reached Brighton — then a tiny fishing village known as Brighthelmstone — 41 days after the battle. He stayed overnight at the George Inn before embarking on a coal brig, the *Surprise*, which carried him safely to Fécamp in Normandy. A vivid reminder of Brighton's early days as a fishing port is to be found in The Lanes — a quarter of narrow, twisting streets lined with 17th-century fishermen's cottages, most of which have now been converted to antiques shops.

After the Restoration in 1660, the captain of the *Surprise*, Nicholas Tattersell, renamed his ship the *Escape*, sailed her up the Thames and moored her opposite the royal palace of Whitehall. Charles took the hint and rewarded Tattersell with a pension of £200 a year. But it seems he was no better at paying his debts than George IV, for in 1666 Tattersell returned to London to try and draw his pension. Samuel Pepys, who met him on this occasion, recorded in his diary: 'this poor man hath received no part of his money these four years and is ready to starve, almost'. Tattersell died in 1674 and is buried in the churchyard of St Nicholas, Brighton, where a wordy memorial extols his service to the King.

Churchill Square

Statue of Queen Victoria, Marlborough Place

Broughton Castle

Oxfordshire **Map: p234 C1.** *Open mid-May to mid-Sept: Wed and Sun afternoons; also Thur in July and Aug; public holidays.*

The Tudor mansion of Broughton, built round a 13th-century manor house and islanded by a broad moat, has been in the Fiennes family for six centuries. William Fiennes, 1st Viscount Saye and Sele, was a leading Parliamentarian; and his four sons fought at the Battle of Edgehill (1642), the first, indecisive battle of the Civil War. Afterwards, Royalists besieged and captured Broughton. Lord Saye and Sele in fact opposed the execution of Charles I and retired from political life until the Restoration, when Charles II (1660-1685) appointed him Lord Privy Seal.

Buckden

Cambridgeshire **Map: p239 E5.** *Palace open July to Sept: Sun afternoons.*

The palace of the Bishop of Lincoln at Buckden was the prison of Catherine of Aragon, who was taken here after Henry VIII (1509-1547) divorced her. Today all that stands of the original palace are the massive gatehouse and tower.

Buckingham

Buckinghamshire **Map: p235 D1.** *Manor House not open; Castle House is now offices. Chantry Chapel open as advertised.*

Catherine of Aragon, acting as Regent while Henry VIII (1509-1547) was fighting against the French, is believed to have heard the news of the defeat of the Scots by the English troops at Flodden while staying at Castle House in 1513.

Castle House is now a two-storey, redbrick house, although it still retains part of the older building. Charles I (1625-1649), during a three-day visit in 1644, held a council of war in the old banqueting rooms.

Elizabeth I (1558-1603) stopped for lunch at Manor House, during a progress in 1578. Her half-brother, Edward VI (1547-1553), had earlier endowed the Royal Latin school at Buckingham. Originally a Norman chantry chapel, it was largely rebuilt by Henry VI (1422-1461) who founded the school.

Alfred the Great (AD 871-899) made Buckingham the shire town and his son, Edward the Elder (AD 899-925), while pushing his borders into the Danelaw in AD 915, took Buckingham after a four-week siege and raised fortifications here.

Bures

Essex **Map: p235 G1.**

St Edmund (AD 855-869), last King of East Anglia, who was martyred by the Danes in AD 869 and later canonized, was crowned at the age of 15 on a hill outside this town on Christmas Day, AD 855.

Burgh-by-Sands

Cumbria **Map: p243 F5.**

As he lay dying at Burgh-by-Sands, Edward I (1272-1307) made his son, Edward II (1307-1327), promise not to bury him, but to carry his bones with him on all his campaigns, until he had completely conquered the Scots — so that even after death he could still lead the army to victory. Contrary to his wish, his son had him buried at Westminster Abbey three months later.

Burghley House

Cambridgeshire **Map: p239 E4.** *Open Apr to Sept: daily.*

Few monarchs have ever attended the deathbeds of their faithful courtiers, but Elizabeth I (1558-1603) is one exception. When William Cecil, 1st Lord Burghley, her most trusted adviser, lay dying in 1598, she often visited him.

Lord Burghley started building Burghley House when he retired from public life during the reign of Mary I (1553-1558). One of England's finest Elizabethan mansions, it was only completed in the year of his death. William III (1689-1702) was so overwhelmed by the grandeur of Burghley that he declared it 'too large for a subject'.

The four George rooms were remodelled in 1789 for a visit by the Prince of Wales, later George IV (1820-1830). Queen Victoria (1837-1901) and Prince Albert planted trees here in 1844. More recently, George VI and Queen Elizabeth, the Queen Mother, were entertained at Burghley as Duke and Duchess of York, and their granddaughter, Princess Anne, won the European Championship at the Horse Trials in 1971.

Burley

Leicestershire **Map: p238 D4.** *House not open to the public. Grounds open for the Rutland Show.*

George Villiers, 1st Duke of Buckingham, served an extraordinary dish to Charles I (1625-1649) and his Queen, Henrietta Maria, when they stayed at Burley-on-the-Hill Mansion in 1628. At a ceremonial dinner in their honour, the famous Oakham dwarf, Jeffery Hudson, leapt from a pie to entertain the royal guests. Nine years old, perfectly proportioned and only 18in tall, he had recently joined the Duke's household. The Queen was so fascinated by him that the Duchess gave him to her. James I (1603-1625) visited Burley-on-the-Hill on his way south from Scotland to be crowned King of England, returning 17 years later when the house was owned by his favourite, the 1st Duke of Buckingham. The mansion was destroyed after the Civil War and the present house built between 1694 and 1705.

Bury St Edmunds

Suffolk **Map: p239 G5.**

The size of the abbey gardens and the ruins that cover the site today give visitors some idea of the importance of the abbey which grew up round the shrine of St Edmund (AD 855-869), last King of East Anglia. Edmund was 15 when he was crowned and led a blameless life as King until his death in AD 869 at the hands of invading Danes. He was immediately named a martyr and, 33 years later, after miracles had been reported at his grave at Hoxne, his bones were transferred to the monastery at Bury. The shrine was one of the biggest in medieval England.

Many kings and queens worshipped here. In 1214 the barons gathered to swear a secret oath on the high altar that King John (1199-1216) should be compelled to accept Magna Carta. The last great ceremonial at the shrine was the funeral of the sister of Henry VIII (1509-1547), Mary of France. The abbey was dissolved five years after Mary's funeral, and her body was transferred to the nearby 15th-century church.

In 1881, Queen Victoria (1837-1901) gave the church a painted window, depicting scenes in the life of Mary of France. The marble surrounding the tomb was the gift of Edward VII (1901-1910).

Buxton

Derbyshire **Map: p238 B2.**

When Elizabeth I (1558-1603) heard that George Talbot, Earl of Shrewsbury, her trusted custodian of Mary, Queen of Scots (1542-1567), had taken his royal prisoner to the 'baynes of Buckstones', she reprimanded him for doing so without her leave. The visit must have done the Queen's health and the Earl's gout some good, because they visited the spa, with its warm, mineral springs, on several occasions afterwards.

Cadbury Castle

Somerset **Map: p233 E3.** *Open to the public.*
This Iron Age hill fort, occupying almost 18 acres, is considered to be the most likely site of King Arthur's legendary castle of Camelot. Excavations have shown that the hill was refortified as a stronghold in the 6th century — the time when the British leader, Ambrosius, whose resistance to the Saxon invasion may underlie the legend of King Arthur, was fighting in the southwest.

Calstock

Cornwall **Map: p230 D4.** *Cotehele House open Apr to Oct: daily. Garden open daily.*
A good way to approach Cotehele House is the way George III (1760-1820) did in August 1789 — by water. He embarked with Queen Charlotte and three of their daughters to pay an early morning call on Viscount Mount Edgcumbe. The house, built between 1485 and 1627, has altered little.

Camber Castle

Kent **Map: p235 G4.** *Not open to the public.*
After his break with the Church of Rome, Henry VIII (1509-1547), fearing invasion by French or Spanish forces, strengthened the southern defences of the kingdom with a line of more than 20 forts. Much of the stone used in their construction came from the religious houses demolished during the Dissolution of the Monasteries (1536). The forts were so strongly built that they formed part of the shore defences on the south coast during the Second World War. Unfortunately, Camber Castle is now structurally unsafe and cannot be visited.

Cambridge

See page 142.

Cannock Chase

Staffordshire **Map: p238 B4.** *Open to the public.* Cannock Chase has now shrunk to less than 30 square miles of oak forest, open moorland and Forestry Commission plantations. It was referred to as 'royal' in the Domesday Book and remained a royal hunting ground until it passed into private ownership in the 16th century.

Canterbury

See page 143.

Carisbrooke Castle

Isle of Wight **Map: p234 C4.** *Open Mon to Sat daily, Sun afternoons. Closed Christmas, New Year.*
An elaborate plan to rescue Charles I (1625-1649) from imprisonment at Carisbrooke Castle in 1648 failed when the King became stuck between the bars of his bedroom window. Charles had fled to the Isle of Wight from Hampton Court Palace in November 1647, fearing assassination by the extremists in the Parliamentary army who guarded him. He stayed here for a year, at first enjoying relative freedom. When the Scots invaded England and the secret treaty that Charles had negotiated with them during his stay at Carisbrooke was discovered, the castle became his prison. When he left the island it was to go to London to stand trial. Charles's daughter, Princess Elizabeth, died here aged 14.

The castle was built on the site of a Roman fort soon after the Norman Conquest. In 1597 Elizabeth I (1558-1603) had it refortified. Princess Beatrice, youngest daughter of Queen Victoria (1837-1901), lived in the castle for 55 years and succeeded her husband as governor in 1896. The late Earl Mountbatten of Burma was installed as governor in 1965 by Elizabeth II.

Carisbrooke Castle

Carlisle

Cumbria **Map: p243 F5.** *Castle open Mon to Sat daily, Sun afternoons. Closed Christmas, New Year.*
Carlisle Castle became the last stronghold in English history to succumb to military attack when, in 1745, the Young Pretender's garrison — left behind during the retreat north from Derby — exchanged a few shots with the Duke of Cumberland's soldiers before capitulating. It was the last hostile engagement of this border city.

The Romans and Saxons appreciated this natural defensive site and fortified it. William Rufus (1087-1100) claimed the fort for England in 1092 and began building the present castle, which was continually strengthened throughout the Middle Ages. David I of Scotland (1124-1153) captured Carlisle in 1138 as he marched south in support of his niece, Empress Matilda, daughter of Henry I (1100-1135), in her war against Stephen (1135-1154) for the English crown. After his defeat by English forces at the Battle of the Standard (1138) at Northallerton, he fled back to Carlisle. David died peacefully here in 1153, four years after knighting Matilda's son, the future Henry II (1154-1189). Henry built the walls and keep that still stand today. Edward I (1272-1307), the Hammer of the Scots, used Carlisle as a base during his campaigns against Scotland and held Parliaments here.

Mary, Queen of Scots (1542-1567), was brought to Carlisle after her flight across the Solway to England in 1568. She held court here and was treated as an honoured guest until Elizabeth I (1558-1603) ordered that she be closely guarded. During the Civil War, Carlisle held out for the King. It was besieged by Scottish troops in 1644, and surrendered in 1645.

Castle Acre

Norfolk **Map: p239 F4.** *Open Mon to Sat daily, Sun afternoons; also Apr to Sept: Sun mornings.*
Edward I (1272-1307), desperate for funds for a war with France, threatened to outlaw all the clergy and confiscate their revenues when, in January 1297, church leaders met him at Castle Acre and refused to pay money into his treasury. They acted on a papal bull issued the previous year.

Today Castle Acre reflects both elements of this confrontation. The ruins of the Norman castle and the 12th-century Cluniac priory nearby still dominate the village. The castle fortifications once spread over 15 acres at this key point where the ancient Peddar's Way crosses the River Nar. The 13th-century bailey gateway to the castle, built soon after the Conquest by William de Warenne, son-in-law of William the Conqueror (1066-1087), still stands and the Prior's Lodging close by is now a museum.

Castle Cary

Somerset **Map: p233 G2.**
Charles II (1660-1685) spent a night at Castle Cary Manor disguised as a servant and using the name of William Jackson. He was making his escape from England after his defeat at the Battle of Worcester in 1651. The manor house has since been demolished.

Castle Hedingham

Essex **Map: p235 F1.** *Open May to Sept: Tue to Sun afternoons; bank holiday Mons.*
Built in 1130, this was one of the most formidable castles in England. In the Wars of the Roses, the de Vere family — the owners — supported the House of Lancaster. After years of Yorkist imprisonment in France, the Earl escaped to join Henry Tudor, later Henry VII (1485-1509). He led the vanguard at the Battle of Bosworth (1485).

The 3rd Earl, Robert de Vere, was one of the executors of Magna Carta and his estates were forfeited until after the death of King John (1199-1216). The 9th Earl, Thomas de Vere, was a favourite of Richard II (1377-1399). The 10th Earl, Aubrey de Vere, was appointed a companion for life to the Black Prince in 1367. Matilda of Boulogne, Queen of Stephen (1135-1154), died at Castle Hedingham after a brief illness in 1152.

Castle Rising

Norfolk **Map: p239 F4.** *Open Mon to Sat daily, Sun afternoons. Closed public holidays.*
To enter the 50ft Norman keep of Castle Rising, visitors must cross the 13th-century bridge and climb the flight of worn steps that leads to the castle entrance. It was on this same bridge and steps that Isabella of France, disgraced Queen and widow of Edward II (1307-1327), trod when her young son, Edward III (1327-1377), sent her here after the execution of her lover, Roger Mortimer, in 1333. Isabella had conspired with Mortimer to overthrow and murder her husband.

Castle Rising was built by William d'Albini, who married Henry I's widow, Adeliza of Louvain and later became Earl of Arundel. After Isabella's death the castle belonged to her grandson, Edward, the Black Prince, and then to Richard II (1377-1399).

Cambridge

Cambridgeshire **Map: p239 F5.** *King's College open daily, limited entry mid-May to mid-June. Queen's College open July to Sept: daily; Oct to June: afternoons only. Christ's College open daily. St John's College open mid-June to mid-May: daily. Trinity College opening times shown at Porter's Lodge.*

Five of the ancient colleges of Cambridge were founded by royalty. The oldest 'royal' college is King's College, founded by Henry VI (1422-1461), who laid the first stone himself on 2 April 1441. The Wars of the Roses delayed completion of the chapel until 1515 — hence the many heraldic carvings bearing the arms and badges of the Tudors. A rare combination of the initials of Henry VIII (1509-1547) and Anne Boleyn allows the screen to be accurately dated, since their short-lived marriage only lasted from 1533 to 1536.

Henry VI's Queen, Margaret of Anjou, was the founder of Queen's College in 1448 — possibly in an attempt to emulate her husband's foundation. However, after Henry's deposition by Edward IV (1461-1483) in 1461, Queen's College fell on hard times and the head of the college petitioned Edward's Queen, Elizabeth Woodville, to refound the house, which she did..

Two colleges owe their existence to Margaret Beaufort, Countess of Richmond and Derby and mother of Henry VII (1485-1509). Indeed, had women's rights been what they are today, she would have been Queen, since it was through her royal descent that Henry claimed the throne. Her first foundation was Christ's College, which displays her arms and statue on the gatehouse. The countess spent some time at Cambridge and her rooms in the Master's Lodge have an oriel window looking into the college chapel, through which

The Bridge of Sighs, St John's College

she could join in the services. Work on her other foundation, St John's, did not start until 1511, two years after her death, because her grandson, Henry VIII, tried to divert her endowment for the college to his own use.

It may seem surprising after this, that Henry was the next, and last, monarch to found a Cambridge college. Trinity, which he endowed in 1546, is now the largest college in the university and it was here that his descendant, Prince Charles, spent his years at Cambridge. Henry created Trinity by combining several small, older foundations, including King's Hall, founded by Edward II (1307-1327) in 1317 and extended by his son Edward III (1327-1377) in 1336. Henry's statue looks down from the gatehouse, which also carries the arms of the earlier founders.

Prince Edward has followed Prince Charles by going to Cambridge, where he is reading Archaelogy and Anthropology at Jesus College.

Gonville and Caius College

Canterbury

*Kent **Map**: p235 G3. Cathedral open daily.*

As the spiritual capital of England — and the last staging post on the London to Dover road — Canterbury has seen many royal comings and goings in the last 1,400 years. The most famous royal visit took place on 12 July 1174, when Henry II (1154-1189) entered the city barefoot and wearing penitent's weeds to do penance for the murder of Thomas à Becket. All 70 monks of the cathedral chapter scourged him with rods as he made his way to Becket's tomb where he spent the night in vigil. Whether or not Henry actually uttered the words, 'Who will rid me of this turbulent priest?', he certainly accepted responsibility for the murder, which was carried out by four of his knights following an outburst of temper on his part.

It had taken Henry a long time to get round to making the pilgrimage. Becket was murdered on 29 December 1170 and was canonized two years later, but it was another 18 months before Henry did penance. He was probably prompted by the fact that he was fighting a war on two fronts — in Aquitaine and Northumberland, where the Scots had invaded — and things were not going too well for him. He was soon convinced that he had taken the right decision, for William the Lion, King of Scotland (1165-1214), was captured at Alnwick almost at the very hour that the King finished his penitential vigil.

Curiously enough, the martyrdom of another archbishop, who was also canonized, prompted an earlier royal visit. Archbishop Alphege was killed in 1012 by Danish raiders who were holding him hostage against Danegeld (a tax raised to provide funds for protecting England against the Danes), promised by Ethelred the Unready (AD 979-1016). The Danes had not intended to kill the archbishop, but when he refused to pay his own ransom, drunken warriors pelted him with stones and ox-horns until one, taking pity on the injured archbishop, killed him with an axe-blow to the head. On 15 June 1023, 11 years later, Canute (1016-1035), a Dane himself, had all his court present when Alphege was buried beside the altar in the cathedral.

A happier royal occasion which took place in Canterbury was the marriage on 14 January 1236, of Henry III (1216-1272) to Eleanor of Provence. Many royal weddings have been solemnized by archbishops, before and since, but Archbishop Edmund Rich is the only one to have officiated in his own cathedral. Happier still, no doubt, was Charles I's start to married life. He had married Henrietta Maria, daughter of the King of France, by proxy on 1 May 1625. She crossed to Dover on 13 June where she met the King. They consummated the marriage in the chambers above the Fyndon Gateway to the old abbey of St Augustine.

The most curious royal courtship in English history — which did not end in marriage — was conducted, in part at least, in Canterbury. The unlikely lovers were Elizabeth I (1558-1603) and the Duke of Alençon, younger brother of Charles IX of France. The Duke, who was a dwarf with a face deformed by smallpox, was called by the queen *'ma petite grenouille'* (my little frog). He made several visits to England to see the Queen and on one of those, in 1573, they are said to have spent some time together in the Crown Inn on the High Street. This is now a restaurant called Queen Elizabeth's Guest Chamber. However, they are more likely to have stayed in the accommodation later used by Charles I (1625-1649), which was an official royal residence. Whether Elizabeth used the Duke to keep other suitors at bay is not known, but when he died, in 1584, she declared that she had 'loved him so entirely' that she could not marry another.

There are three royal tombs in the cathedral — those of Edward, the Black Prince, Henry IV (1399-1413) and his Queen, Joan of Navarre. The Black Prince's effigy, in full, gleaming armour, is one of the finest memorials in England. Above it hang replicas of his helmet, gauntlets and other accoutrements. The original items, which had been deteriorating over the tomb for centuries, are now housed in a glass case. Henry IV lies nearby, as if seeking legitimacy from proximity to the man whose son, Richard II (1377-1399), he usurped and possibly murdered. He and his Queen lie dressed in robes of state — another bid for legitimacy, perhaps.

Canterbury Cathedral

Christ Church Gate

Castletown

Isle of Man **Map: p240 A2.** *Castle Rushen open May to Sept: daily; Oct to Apr: Mon to Fri daily, Sat mornings. Closed public holidays.*

For centuries Castletown was the capital of the Isle of Man. It was the seat of the Manx kings from the 6th century until the 9th century, when the island was overrun by the Vikings. When the King of Norway ceded Man to Scotland in 1266, the Manx fought for their independence but were defeated at the Battle of Ronaldsway (1275) near Castletown. After the Battle of Neville's Cross (1346) at Durham, England won Man from Scotland and gained control of the island. Castle Rushen, built in the 14th century, still stands. It was the residence of the English lords who ruled the island until the 18th century.

Chalgrove

Oxfordshire **Map: p234 D2.**

Charles I (1625-1649) is said to have offered the skills of his own surgeon to aid John Hampden the Parliamentary leader, as he lay mortally wounded at Thame after being shot at Chalgrove in 1643. The King appreciated that Hampden had a moderating influence on the Parliamentary zealots.

Chard

Somerset **Map: p231 F3.** *Forde Abbey open May to Sept: Sun, Wed afternoons; public holidays, Easter. Gardens also open Mar, Apr and Oct: Sun afternoons.*

Whether it was a fine or — as some historians hint — a bribe to the infamous Judge Jeffreys, £15,000 was the price that Edmond Prideaux, owner of Forde Abbey near Chard, had to pay to save his life at the Bloody Assizes in 1685. Prideaux, son of Cromwell's Attorney-General, had supported James, the Duke of Monmouth, illegitimate son of Charles II (1660-1685), when he landed in the West Country to instigate a revolt against his uncle, James II (1685-1688). The Protestant Duke, who hoped to drive Roman Catholic James from the throne, was proclaimed King here, but his untried, ill-equipped army of volunteers was soon defeated. The abbey, founded in the 12th century, is a mixture of medieval, Tudor and Jacobean architectural styles.

Charing

Kent **Map: p235 G3.**

Henry VIII (1509-1547) stayed at the Archbishop of Canterbury's palace at Charing on his way to France for the famous meeting with the French King, Francois 1, on the Field of the Cloth of Gold in 1520. The palace was seized from the see of Canterbury at the Dissolution of the Monasteries (1536), and the building fell into decay. A barn near the church is the original great hall and dates from the 14th century.

Charmouth

Dorset **Map: p233 F3.**

Charing

An interfering wife, suspicious of her sailor husband's secretiveness about a voyage he was making one September night in 1651, thwarted Charles II's (1660-1685) plan for escaping to France from the little fishing port of Charmouth. He was on the run after his defeat at the Battle of Worcester. The inn where Charles spent the night waiting for the expected boat, the Queen's Arms, had also housed Catherine of Aragon when she arrived in England in 1501 to marry Arthur, Prince of Wales, elder brother of Henry VIII (1509-1547).

Chastleton

Oxfordshire **Map: p234 C1.** *House open Mon, Tue, Thur, Fri daily, weekend afternoons.*

When Charles I (1625-1649) stepped out onto the black-draped scaffold in Whitehall on 30 January 1649, the only friend with him was William Juxon, Bishop of London. After the King's execution the bishop was deprived of his see and retired to his manor house at Little Compton, near Chastleton House. The Bible which Charles read before his execution can be seen here. The house is virtually unchanged since it was built in 1603.

Chatham

Kent **Map: p235 F3.** *Daily tours of the dockyard.*

Chatham has been a naval base since Tudor times. Henry VIII (1509-1547), building up England's defences against possible invasion by France and Spain, had shipyards here, and Elizabeth I (1558-1603) established the naval dockyard and arsenal. Many of the new ships of faster, more manoeuvrable design, which defeated the Spanish Armada in 1558, were built at Chatham dockyard, and Nelson's flagship at the Battle of Trafalgar (1805), HMS *Victory*, was launched here in 1765.

But Chatham's history is not, however, all glorious. Samuel Pepys, the diarist, then Clerk of the Acts to the Navy Board, described the chaos here in 1667 during the Second Dutch War, when warships blockaded the Thames and sailed up the Medway. The Dutch attacked the dockyard, setting fire to the English fleet moored here, and towed away the finest of the King's ships, the *Royal Charles*.

Chatsworth

Derbyshire **Map: p238 C2.** *Open Apr to Oct: daily. Farmyard also open Apr to Sept: daily.*

At the end of the 17th century, the 6th Duke of Devonshire began to reconstruct Chatsworth, gradually pulling down the Elizabethan mansion which was begun by Sir William Cavendish and finished by his widow, Bess of Hardwick. By 1707 the Duke had completely replaced the older building, except for Queen Mary's Bower. Mary, Queen of Scots (1542-1567), sometimes visited Chatsworth during her imprisonment. Her gaoler was Bess of Hardwick's fourth husband, Sir George Talbot, Earl of Shrewsbury. In 1913 George V (1910-1936) and Queen Mary were entertained at Chatsworth, and members of the present royal family often stay here.

Cheddar Gorge

Somerset **Map: p233 F2.**

While hunting in the Mendips in AD 943 Edmund, King of the English (AD 939-946), had a narrow escape from death. The story goes that he was chasing a stag well ahead of his followers when the beast ran over the edge of the cliffs at Cheddar Gorge. The King's hounds followed it over and Edmund's horse, galloping full tilt, could not be restrained. Edmund is said to have offered a prayer regretting his recent dismissal of the hermit

Dunstan from his court, and at once his horse checked on the very brink of the gorge. Edmund afterwards summoned Dunstan and appointed him abbot of Glastonbury.

Cheltenham

Gloucestershire **Map: p234 B2.**
The alkaline waters of the spa at Cheltenham were considered good for liver disorders, so when George III (1760-1820) suffered from bilious attacks in 1788 his doctors advised him to visit Cheltenham. Although the waters did not help the King, his five-week stay at Bays Hill Lodge had a beneficial effect on the town, for the spa suddenly became fashionable.

Chenies Manor House

Buckinghamshire **Map: p235 E2.** *Open Apr to Oct: Wed and Thur afternoons; public holidays.*
The 1st Earl of Bedford, John Russell, Lord Privy Seal to Henry VIII (1509-1547), added a wing to his manor house at Chenies to accommodate Henry and his retinue on visits. Henry must have been impressed for he engaged the same builders to work on an extension at Hampton Court. Elizabeth 1 (1558-1603) brought her court here in 1570.

Chequers

Buckinghamshire **Map: p234 D2.** *Not open to the public.*
Lady Mary, younger sister of Lady Jane Grey, was banished to Chequers — a Tudor manor house — when Elizabeth I (1558-1603) discovered she had married the Queen's sergeant-porter.

Cheshunt

Hertfordshire **Map: p235 E2.** *Theobalds Park open daily.*
James I (1603-1625) was quick to notice the magnificence of Theobalds, the Elizabethan mansion near Cheshunt. In 1607 the King took a fancy to the house and offered the owner, Robert Cecil, 1st Earl of Salisbury, the Old Palace at Hatfield in exchange. James died here in his favourite residence in 1625. Elizabeth I (1558-1603) had also been entertained here, by Cecil's father, but the mansion fell into decay during the Civil War and Charles II (1660-1685) sold it. Nothing remains of the house today.

Chester

Cheshire **Map: p238 A3.** *King Charles's Tower open Apr to Sept: Mon to Sat daily, Sun afternoons.*
It was at Chester that Charles I (1625-1649) learned of the victory of his nephew, Prince Rupert, in the first skirmish of the Civil War at Powick Bridge, 3 miles west of Worcester, in September 1642. Three years later almost to the day, he saw the Royalist cause finally defeated at the Battle of Rowton Heath, outside the city walls. Charles is said to have viewed the battle from a tower on the northeast corner of the city walls. It is now known as King Charles's Tower and houses a museum of the Civil War.

Chester was a Royalist town from the start of the Civil War and suffered for its loyalty with almost three years of semi-starvation during sieges. The cathedral is built on the site of a 10th-century church which was a shrine to St Warburga, a Princess of Mercia.

Chesterfield

Derbyshire **Map: p238 C2.** *Revolution House open May to Sept: Wed to Sun daily; bank holiday Mons.*
The peaceful revolution which deposed James II in 1688 and put William of Orange (1689-1702) and James's daughter Mary on the throne of England was planned in a room at the Cock and Pynot Inn — now a museum — at Old Whittington, on the outskirts of Chesterfield.

Chichester

West Sussex **Map: p234 D4.** *Fishbourne Palace open Mar to Sept: daily.*
A Roman palace of great splendour was unearthed near Chichester in 1960, on the coast at Fishbourne. It is thought to have been built for Cogidubnus, a British chieftain who welcomed the invading Romans in AD 43. For his support he was made an imperial legate. The palace, which was probably built around AD 70, covered 10 acres but was destroyed by fire in the 3rd century.

In Saxon times the city was the seat of Aella, first king of the south Saxons. His son, Cissa, gave his name to Chichester — Cissa's ceaster.

Chiddingfold

Surrey **Map: p234 D4.**
The medieval Crown Inn at Chiddingfold was a guest house for travellers on the Pilgrim's Way between Winchester and Canterbury. The boy King Edward VI (1547-1553) is believed to have stayed here in 1552.

Chingford

Greater London **Map: p233 E2.** *Queen Elizabeth's Hunting Lodge open Wed to Sun afternoons; public holidays.*
Just to the north of Chingford on the edge of Epping Forest is the Tudor grandstand built by Henry VIII (1509-1547) in 1543. Known then as the Great Standing, huntsmen could gather there to observe or shoot the deer. The staircase inside is wide with shallow steps. Elizabeth I (1558-1603) is said to have ridden her white palfrey up to the top gallery in delight on hearing of the defeat of the Spanish Armada. Now known as Queen Elizabeth's Hunting Lodge, it houses the museum of Epping Forest. In 1882 Queen Victoria (1837-1901) came to Chingford to dedicate her gift of Epping Forest to the people of London.

Chatsworth

Cirencester

Gloucestershire **Map: p234 B2.**
John Holland, Earl of Huntingdon and half-brother of Richard II (1377-1399), and his nephew, Thomas Holland, Earl of Surrey, were involved in a plot to seize Henry IV (1399-1413) and his son and put the deposed Richard back on the throne in 1400. The plan went awry and the conspirators fled to Cirencester. The townsfolk grew suspicious of them and the Hollands were captured and beheaded in the town square.

Cirencester

Claremont

Surrey **Map: p235 E3.** *Open Feb to Nov: first weekend of each month, afternoons only.*
This stately Palladian-style house was built in 1772 by Robert Clive, founder of the empire of British India. It was given to Princess Charlotte by the nation when she married Prince Leopold of Saxe-Coburg-Gotha in 1816. Much depended on this marriage, for the Princess was the only child of the Prince Regent, later George IV (1820-1830) and would eventually be heir to the throne. Tragically Charlotte died the following year aged 21, a few hours after giving birth to a stillborn son. The doctor who attended her, Sir Richard Croft, was so overcome by public criticism that he had mishandled the confinement, that he shot himself three months later.

Queen Victoria (1837-1901), King Leopold's niece, later bought Claremont and presented it to her youngest son, Prince Leopold, when he became Duke of Albany in 1881. The house is now a school and belongs to the National Trust. They have extensively restored the beautiful gardens which are well worth visiting.

Cleobury Mortimer

Salop **Map: p237 G3.**
In 1507 the bier of Arthur, Prince of Wales, elder brother of Henry VIII (1509-1547), was carried through this quiet market town. The Prince's body rested in front of the market cross on its way from Ludlow Castle, where he died, to Worcester Cathedral. A few stones of the cross can still be seen outside the 16th-century Talbot Hotel.

Clipstone

Nottinghamshire **Map: p238 C3.** *Sherwood Forest open all the time.*
While Edward I (1272-1307) held his Parliament at Clipstone in Sherwood Forest in the autumn of 1290, his Queen, Eleanor of Castile, lay dying of a fever a few miles away at Harby. She had gone there to be near the King.

Sherwood Forest spread northwards from Nottingham for nearly 20 miles in the 13th century and part of it was enclosed as a royal deer park by Henry II (1154-1189). The ancient oak beneath which Edward is said to have held his Parliament is still growing in what remains of the forest. The largest oak — the Major Oak — is believed to be 1,000 years old. According to legend Robin Hood and his merry men gathered under it.

Richard I (1189-1199) was in the Sherwood area in 1194, when he returned from the crusades and seized Nottingham Castle from his rebellious brother John.

Cliveden

Buckinghamshire **Map: p234 D2.** *Open Apr to Oct: weekend afternoons. Closed public holidays. Gardens also open Mar to Dec: daily.*
Only the terraces of the earlier 17th-century Cliveden, where Frederick, Prince of Wales, father of George III (1760-1820), lived from 1739 to 1751, can be seen today. The house was demolished in 1850 after two fires had wrecked it. The present imposing mansion was built for the Duke of Sutherland.

Clun

Salop: **Map: p237 F2.**
Caractacus, only surviving son of the great Celtic war-leader Cunobelin (which Shakespeare changed to Cymbeline) held out against the Romans along the Welsh borders during the campaign to subjugate Britain, which followed the Emperor Claudius's brief visit of conquest in AD 43. It is thought that Chapel Lawn, 3 miles southeast of Clun, is where he was finally defeated in AD 50.

Cobham

Kent **Map: p235 E3.** *Cobham Hall open Mar to early Apr: daily; Aug: Wed, Thur, Sun afternoons; summer bank holidays.*
This Elizabethan mansion — now a girls' school — was owned by William Brooke, 7th Lord Cobham, a favourite of Elizabeth I (1558-1603). He entertained the Queen twice at Cobham in 1559 and 1573. His son, however, Henry Brooke, 8th Lord Cobham, spent much of his life in the Tower, having been implicated, with Sir Walter Raleigh, in a plot to depose James I (1603-1625) and put his cousin, Arabella Stuart, on the throne.

Colchester

Essex **Map: p235 G1.** *Castle open Mon to Fri daily, Sat afternoons; Apr to Sept: Sun afternoons also.*

Closed Christmas.
When the Roman emperor Claudius's elephants smashed their way through the defences of Camulodunum, now the site of Colchester, in AD 43, they helped bring about the total surrender of the most important settlement in Britain. It was the royal capital of Cunobelin (Shakespeare's Cymbeline), King of a powerful Celtic tribe, the Catuvellauni. Claudius rode in triumph through the conquered settlement, received the homage of several tribal chieftains and then left Britain, never to return.

The Romans built a temple here in honour of Claudius, which became to the conquered tribes a symbol of their humiliation. When Boudicca, Queen of the Iceni, enraged by the unjust treatment she and her family had received from Rome, looked for revenge in AD 60, Camulodunum was the obvious target. Boudicca led the attack and the Roman settlement was sacked and burnt to the ground. Thick layers of ash from burning Camulodunum still lie under the streets of Colchester.

The large keep of Colchester Castle was built on the site of the temple shortly after the Norman Conquest (1066). King John (1199-1216) besieged and captured the castle in 1216, a few months before his death, when it was held against him by rebel barons. It is now a museum.

Collyweston

Northamptonshire **Map: p238 D4.**
In this village Henry VII (1485-1509) parted from his 13-year-old daughter Margaret in 1503 as she travelled north to marry James IV of Scotland (1488-1513).

Compton Wynyates

Warwickshire **Map: p234 C1.** *Open Apr to Sept: Wed, Sat and bank holiday afternoons; June to Aug: Sun afternoons also.*
The great entrance porch of mellowed pink brick that leads to the inner courtyard of this perfectly preserved Tudor manor house, once rang to the sound of voices greeting Henry VIII (1509-1547) and his Queen, Catherine of Aragon, as they arrived on their many visits. The owner of Compton Wynyates, Sir William Compton, was a lifelong friend of the King, having grown up with him from boyhood. Elizabeth I (1558-1603) maintained the royal friendship with the Compton family. She made William's son, Henry, a baron, and visited Compton Wynyates herself in 1572.

During the Civil War, Compton Wynyates was besieged and captured by Parliamentary troops in 1644. While 400 Roundhead soldiers were billeted in part of the house, which is still known as The Barracks, the Compton family contrived to conceal and tend wounded Royalists elsewhere in the building.

Conisbrough Castle

South Yorkshire **Map: p238 C2.** *Open Mon to Sat daily, Sun afternoons.*
This formidable 12th-century keep is unique in England, being round and supported with buttresses, one of which contains a chapel. King

John (1199-1216) was entertained at Conisbrough in 1201. In the 15th century the castle passed to Richard, Duke of York, father of Edward IV (1461-1483) and Richard III (1483-1485).

Cookham

Berkshire **Map: p234 D2.**
Each year the ceremony of 'swan-upping' is carried out at Cookham. This involves two of London's livery companies — the Dyers and the Vintners — cutting their 'upping' marks on the bills of their swans. The Keeper of the Royal Swans, Mr Tuck of Cookham, then counts the unmarked swans, which belong to the Queen.

Corbridge

Northumberland **Map: p243 G5.** *Corstopitum Museum open Mon to Sat daily, Sun afternoons.*
When the Romans had their large fort at Corstopitum, half a mile from modern Corbridge, life was orderly in the north. It was quite different from the anarchy of the 8th century, when two Saxon kings of Northumbria were murdered by their own courtiers, as rival factions struggled for the crown. Ethelred, who secured his own throne by murdering all possible rivals, including children, was killed at Corbridge in AD 796.

Corbridge's royal history has a stormy reputation. David I of Scotland (1124-1153) captured the town in 1138 and Corbridge was subsequently burned to the ground by three different Scottish invaders: William Wallace in 1296; Robert Bruce (1306-1329), in 1312; and David II (1329-1371) in 1346.

Corfe Castle

Dorset **Map: p233 G3.** *Open Mar to Oct: daily; Nov to Feb: afternoons.*
The 16-year-old Edward, King of the English (AD 975-979), was murdered here on the orders — if not by the hand — of his stepmother Elfrida, so that the throne could pass to her own son, Ethelred the Unready (AD 979-1016). Edward, later styled the Martyr, used to visit his half-

brother at Corfe where he lived with his mother.

The present castle, which was built on the site of the Saxon fortress, dates from the Norman Conquest. The keep was probably built in the 12th century and King John (1199-1216) is known to have improved the fortifications. It was his favourite castle and he used it as a treasure house and a prison. Isabella and Margaret, daughters of William the Lion of Scotland (1165-1214), were imprisoned here in 1209 as hostages for their father's loyalty.

Corfe has a second link with a royal murder; the deposed Edward II (1307-1327) was a prisoner here in the last year of his life, before his transfer to Berkeley Castle where he met a violent death. During the Civil War, the castle withstood two Parliamentary sieges before being slighted. It has stood a ruin ever since.

Coventry

Warwickshire **Map: p237 H2.**
It was at Coventry that Richard II (1377-1399) took the step that was to cost him his throne and eventually plunge England into the Wars of the Roses. He had ordered Henry Bolingbroke, Duke of Hereford, and Thomas Mowbray, Duke of Norfolk, to meet here on 16 September 1398, to undergo trial by battle to determine the truth of Bolingbroke's accusations of treason against Mowbray. The lists were set up at Crofts Green, just outside the city walls, but before battle could commence the King called the contestants before him and commanded them both into exile. Bolingbroke returned from this exile a year later to claim the crown. The next time he visited Coventry, in 1402, he held a Parliament here as Henry IV (1399-1413).

Edward, the Black Prince, was a frequent visitor to the prosperous city of Coventry, where he was lord of the manor of Cheylesmore. It was during this period that the Guildhall of St Mary was built. This is one of the few buildings to have survived the blitz of 1940.

Elizabeth I (1558-1603) was welcomed here on a royal progress in 1565, while Mary, Queen of Scots (1542-1567), arrived as a prisoner four years later and was housed in Caesar's Tower, the armoury attached to the Guildhall.

Cowdray Park

West Sussex **Map: p234 D4.** *Open daily.*
In 1793 Cowdray House was burned to the ground and a week later its owner, Lord Montagu, was drowned. These two events were said to be the result of a curse laid on the Montagu family by a monk of Battle Abbey at the time of the Dissolution of the Monasteries (1536). A Montagu ancestor, Sir Anthony Browne, a trusted courtier and friend of Henry VIII (1509-1547) had been granted the abbey in 1538, and later inherited Cowdray House. He was made a guardian of Prince Edward and Princess Elizabeth who both visited Cowdray.

Today Cowdray House still lies ruined, but the surrounding park has frequent royal visitors. It is famous for its weekend polo matches and both Prince Philip and Prince Charles have played here.

Cowes

Isle of Wight **Map: p234 C5.** *Cowes Castle open Mon to Sat daily, Sun afternoons. Norris Castle open mid-June to Sept: Sat to Tue daily.*
Charles II (1660-1685) was the first member of the royal family to take an interest in sailing for pleasure. However, it was not until 1817, when the Prince Regent, later George IV (1820-1830), joined the recently founded Yacht Club at Cowes, that sailing became fashionable. When he became King in 1820, the club added the prefix 'Royal' and a few years later was renamed the Royal Yacht Squadron. William IV (1830-1837), Queen Victoria (1837-1901) and Prince Albert were all members. In 1909 four reigning monarchs competed in the races during Cowes Week.

The Royal Yacht Squadron, of which the reigning King, or the reigning Queen's husband, is always admiral, is based at West Cowes Castle on the site of an earlier castle, built by Henry VIII (1509-1547). It was one of two he built on either side of the Medina estuary to defend the Solent and his shipyards at East Cowes.

Queen Victoria spent childhood holidays with her mother, the Duchess of Kent, at Norris Castle in East Cowes, built in 1799 by John Nash.

Cranborne Chase

Dorset **Map: p233 G2.** *Gardens open Apr to Oct: first weekend of each month; public holidays.*
One of the largest medieval forests, Cranborne Chase once stretched for more than 100 square miles between Shaftesbury and Salisbury. Within that area only the King, or his warrant-holders, could hunt the beasts of the Chase — deer and wild boar. Other people could only hunt the smaller game with a royal licence. The 17th-century manor house of Cranborne, the Dorset seat of the Cecils, Marquesses of Salisbury, is thought to incorporate an older building, once the hunting-box of King John (1199-1216).

It was on Cranborne Chase that the horse of James, Duke of Monmouth, failed him after two days of desperate galloping from the battlefield of Sedgemoor (1685). The Duke, illegitimate son of Charles II (1660-1685) and pretender to the throne of his uncle, James II (1685-1688), was defeated and on the run. He had to disguise himself as a

Compton Wynyates

farmhand and continue his escape on foot, but was arrested the next day hiding in a ditch.

Cropredy

Oxfordshire **Map: p234 C1.**
This small village was the scene of a Civil War battle in which Charles I (1625-1649) defeated a Parliamentary force in June 1644. The fighting was concentrated around the River Cherwell and Cropredy Bridge.

Croydon

Greater London **Map: p235 E3.** *Old Palace School open when advertised.*
Old Palace School in Croydon is all that is left of the great summer palace of the archbishops of Canterbury, which stood on the site from Norman times until the mid-18th century. Elizabeth I (1558-1603) stayed the night here on several occasions when she came to discuss state business. Her bedroom is on show. The present building is mainly Tudor, but some parts are medieval, including a Norman undercroft.

Dacre Castle

Cumbria. **Map: p240 D1.** *Not open to the public.*
Earthworks between this 13th-century pele tower and its crescent-shaped moat are believed to mark the site of an earlier building, where Athelstan (AD 925-939), King of the West Saxons and Mercia, received the submission of Constantine of Scotland and Eugenius, under-king of the North Welsh, in AD 927. Athelstan had already subdued the northern Danelaw and the royal submissions at Dacre Castle, beside the River Eamont, near Ullswater, made him King of All England.

Danby Castle

North Yorkshire **Map: p241 G1.** *Not open to the public.*
At the time of her marriage to Henry VIII (1509-1547), the reluctant Catherine Parr was the widow of John Nevill, Lord Latimer. As Lady Latimer she lived at Danby Castle, 1 mile southeast of Danby village, in the middle of the North Yorkshire moors. The ruins of the castle now form part of a farmhouse.

Dartington Hall

Devon **Map: p233 E4.** *Open daily.*
One of the most outstanding medieval buildings in England, Dartington Hall was built between 1388 and 1400 by John Holland, half-brother of Richard II (1377-1399).

Dartmouth

Devon **Map: p233 E4.** *Castle open Mon to Sat daily, Sun afternoons. Closed Christmas, New Year.*
An epidemic of mumps and chicken-pox at Dartmouth Royal Naval College in July 1939 brought the present Queen, Elizabeth II, and her future husband, Prince Philip, together for the first time as teenagers. George VI (1936-1952) and his family were then visiting the college with Earl Mountbatten of Burma, the King's cousin. Like the King, he had been a naval cadet at Dartmouth. While the men enjoyed a nostalgic tour, the Princesses Elizabeth and Margaret were removed from any risk of catching mumps or chicken-pox to the home of the officer in charge of the college, Admiral Sir Frederick Dalrymple-Hamilton. While they were there, Prince Philip, Earl Mountbatten's nephew, who was a first-year cadet at the college, was asked to entertain them.

At the age of 12, the youngest naval cadet ever admitted, the future George V (1910-1936), joined the wooden training ship *Britannia* in 1877. Edward VII (1901-1910) laid the foundation stone of the present college which opened in 1905. Other royal cadets include Edward VIII (1936), the present Prince of Wales and his younger brother, Prince Andrew.

Dartmouth was an important seaport in the Middle Ages. Richard I (1189-1199) sailed from here to the crusades in 1190 and, 24 years later, his brother King John (1199-1216) returned to Dartmouth after a crushing defeat in France.

Daventry

Northamptonshire **Map: p238 C5.**
The Wheatsheaf Inn, where Charles I (1625-1649) spent six days before the Battle of Naseby (1645), is little changed since the Civil War. It was here that Charles learned that the New Model Army, led by Sir Thomas Fairfax and Oliver Cromwell, had abandoned the siege of Oxford and was on the move again. Charles's army was then encamped on Borough Hill, north of Daventry.

Deal

Kent **Map: p235 H3.** *Castle open Mon to Sat daily, Sun afternoons. Closed Christmas, New Year.*
Deal Castle, one of the best preserved of the defensive chain of forts ordered by Henry VIII (1509-1547), was built in 1540 in the shape of a Tudor rose. Needing a garrison of only 25 men, its guns could fire red-hot cannon balls 1½ miles.

Deddington

Oxfordshire **Map: p234 C1.** *Castle House not open to the public.*
A visitor to the Jacobean Castle House, Charles I (1625-1649), enjoyed unbroken sleep here the night after his victory over the Roundhead forces of Sir William Waller at Cropredy Bridge in 1644.

Derby

Derbyshire **Map: p237 H1.** *City Museum open Mon to Sat daily, Sun afternoons.*
On 4 December 1745, Derby became the last English town to fall to an invading army when Bonnie Prince Charlie, the Young Pretender, grandson of James II (1685-1688), led his Highlanders into the town without a shot being fired. The Prince stayed in a house in Full Street, near the cathedral — in those days the parish church of All Saints. It was here, after two days of argument, that the Prince gave in to his generals and took the decision to retreat to Scotland. His army set off on the long trek north which was to end in defeat at Culloden.

Ditchling

West Sussex **Map: p235 E4.** *Anne of Cleves's house not open.*
One of the more imposing homes in this attractive village close to the South Downs is the 16th-century house of Anne of Cleves. Henry VIII (1509-1547) gave it to his fourth wife as part of the divorce settlement.

Donnington Castle

Berkshire **Map: p234 C3.** *Open daily.*
Owned by a Parliamentarian, Donnington Castle was seized by the Royalists in 1643 on account of its strategic position close to Oxford, where Charles I (1625-1649) had his wartime royal capital. During a punishing siege in October 1644, 1,000 great shot were thrown against it and three towers and part of a wall reduced to rubble. The castle did not surrender until April 1646.

Donnington was a royal castle in Tudor times. Henry VIII (1509-1547) gave it to the Duke of Suffolk who later married Henry's sister, Mary, Queen of France. Henry visited the castle twice and Edward VI (1547-1553) held a privy council here in 1551. The castle was given to Elizabeth I (1558-1603) when she was a Princess, and she visited it as Queen in 1568, when the castle was put into good repair for the occasion. She gave it to her old friend Sir Charles Howard, Earl of Nottingham, in 1600 in recognition of his services as Lord Admiral during the Armada.

Dorchester

Dorset **Map: p233 G3.**
In a back room of the Antelope Hotel in Dorchester, Judge Jeffreys is believed to have held one of his Bloody Assizes in 1685, following the collapse of the Duke of Monmouth's rebellion. The Protestant duke, illegitimate son of Charles II (1660-1685), had hoped to depose his Roman Catholic uncle, James II (1685-1688), with the help of an army raised in the west of England in 1685. He was defeated at the Battle of Sedgemoor on 5 July 1685.

Dorchester was the tribal capital of the Durotriges and became an important Roman town during the first century of Roman conquest. Part of the 4th-century Roman wall can still be seen in Albert Road. The Norman castle, which King John (1199-1216) may have used as a hunting lodge, was demolished at the end of the 18th century.

Dunchurch

Warwickshire **Map: p238 C5.**
Sir Everard Digby, the Gunpowder Plot conspirator, organized a hunting match at Dunsmore Heath, near Dunchurch, on 5 November 1605 as part of the plot to raise the Roman Catholic gentry in rebellion. Most of those invited to the meeting refused to have anything to do with the conspiracy.

Dover

Kent Map: p235 H3. Castle keep and underground works open Mon to Sat daily, Sun afternoons. Closed Christmas, New Year.

As the gateway to England, Dover has always been strategically important and a fortress of some kind has stood on the site of Dover Castle for more than 2,000 years. The castle itself was garrisoned continuously from Norman times until 1958. The Romans based their British fleet at Dover, building a lighthouse on either side of the harbour entrance. One lighthouse still stands within the castle walls, close to the church of St Mary-in-Castra, which was founded to serve the Saxon fortress. William the Conqueror (1066-1087), appreciating the importance of holding Dover, hurried to secure the town against great Saxon resistance after defeating Harold (1066) at Hastings. Another future king, Charles II (1660-1685), met with a very different reception at Dover when, after years of exile in France, he arrived here to cheering crowds and a cannonade of welcome from the castle guns. He was greeted by the mayor who presented him with a Bible. Charles took it, declaring it to be 'the thing that he loved above all things in the world'.

Stephen (1135-1154), whose reign of continuous anarchy was described as 'the nineteen long winters when God and his saints slept', died suddenly at Dover Priory in 1154. The guest house and refectory of the Benedictine priory are now part of Dover College. The guest house is the school chapel. Henry II (1154-1189) rebuilt the Norman castle, which had been erected on the site of the Saxon fortress shortly after the Conquest. He spent £7,000 — nearly 70% of one year's royal income — on the fortifications. When completed in 1191, it was one of the most impregnable fortresses in England and was soon put to the test.

In 1216, during the barons' wars in King John's reign (1199-1216), it was successfully defended by Hubert de Burgh, the King's Chief Justiciar, against Louis, Dauphin of France, who besieged it in support of the rebel barons. The castle withstood another siege in 1265 during the reign of Henry III (1216-1272) when Henry's sister, Eleanor, Countess of Leicester, held it against her nephew, the Lord Edward, later Edward I (1272-1307). Eleanor was the widow of Simon de Montfort, Earl of Leicester, who had rebelled against Henry and virtually ruled England for 15 months, after defeating the King at the Battle of Lewes (1264). He was himself defeated by the Lord Edward and killed at the Battle of Evesham (1265). Twelve prisoners, who were taken at Lewes and held in Dover Castle, escaped during the siege to help Edward win the castle from his aunt.

King John (1199-1216) did homage at Dover Castle to Pope Innocent III's envoy, Pandulf, in 1213 in a bid to save his kingdom from French invasion. John had been excommunicated and deposed from his throne the previous year by the pope, who had instructed Philip, King of France, to put the order into effect. John promised to make the pope and his successors overlords of England and to send a yearly tribute to Rome. The act of homage was completed on the eve of Ascension Day, confirming a prophesy made by Peter of Pomfret, a hermit of Wakefield, that John's kingly power would pass to another before Ascension Day, 1213. Peter had rashly let his prediction reach the King's ears the previous autumn and had spent the intervening months in a dungeon in Corfe Castle. Ascension Day proved him right, but he was already dead, for John had him taken that very day from Corfe and hanged at Wareham.

Dover has seen many royal arrivals and departures. The future Edward I left Dover for the crusades in 1270. Henry V (1413-1422) returned here after his victory at Agincourt in 1415. Henry VIII (1509-1547) sailed from Dover to another contest with the French in 1520. Then he went with spectacular pomp to vie in opulence with François I, the young King of France, on the Field of the Cloth of Gold. The aim of the meeting was to cement a friendship between the kings, but they parted with mistrust. Henrietta Maria, as a young bride of 15, newly wedded by proxy to Charles I (1625-1649), spent her first night in England at Dover Castle in 1625 after a rough sea-crossing from France. The eager Charles rode from Canterbury early the next morning to meet her here. They parted at Dover, 17 years later, when anti-Catholic feeling ran high in England and the country was moving towards civil war. Fearing for her safety, Charles put his Queen on board a boat for France and sadly watched her sail out of sight from the cliffs above the town. In 1672 his son, the future James II (1685-1688), met his bride, Mary of Modena, at Dover.

It was perhaps the visits of Charles I's youngest child, Henrietta Anne, born at Exeter during the Civil War, which were most diverse. As a child in 1646 she was smuggled through Dover by her governess Lady Dalkeith, to join her mother in France. The three-year-old Henrietta was dressed in a ragged smock and called Peter to mask her lisping use of the word 'princess' when asked her name. Lady Dalkeith, disguised as a valet's wife and carrying Henrietta, caught the regular packet-boat to Calais.

In great contrast was Henrietta's arrival at Dover in June 1670, as Duchess of Orleans. She was the intermediary between Louis XIV of France, her brother-in-law, and Charles II (1660-1685). Charles held court at Dover Castle in her honour, and under cover of the festivities signed the secret Treaty of Dover in which he promised to turn Roman Catholic and support France's ambitious plans for European supremacy, in return for generous financial hand-outs from Louis. Charles parted from his pretty young sister, nicknamed 'Minette', reluctantly. Her health was frail and three weeks later she died at the age of 26. At the time poisoning was suspected, but today it is thought more likely that she died of peritonitis caused by a perforated stomach ulcer. She did leave one memento for her brother. Louise de Kérouälle, one of her maids of honour, had caught the King's roving eye. Minette, however, had refused Charles's request to leave her behind as a token of affection. The next year, though, Louise was invited to the English court, becoming first the King's mistress and later being created Duchess of Portsmouth. Her son by the King was made Duke of Richmond.

Dover Castle

Dunstable

Bedfordshire **Map: p235 E1.** *Priory open to the public.*

Two Queens are associated with the Priory Church of St Peter at Dunstable, part of an Augustinian Priory founded in 1131 by Henry I (1100-1135). The bier of Eleanor of Castile, Queen of Edward I (1272-1307), stood in the priory overnight in November 1290, while being carried from Harby in Nottinghamshire, where she had died, to London. The King followed the cortege south and erected a memorial cross at every stopping-place. A cross was put in the market place at Dunstable, but it has long since gone. The other Queen, one of England's unhappiest, was Catherine of Aragon. It was at this priory that Archbishop Cranmer presided over the court which declared the marriage of Henry VIII (1509-1547) and Catherine invalid in 1533.

Several kings stayed at the priory. Stephen (1135-1154) spent the Christmas of 1137 here, planning his attack on Bedford Castle, which he took from its owner, Miles Beauchamp, to give to one of his favourites. Henry III (1216-1272) and the royal family were welcomed here in 1247.

Dunstanburgh Castle

Northumberland **Map: p243 H3.** *Open Mon to Sat daily, Sun afternoons. Closed Christmas, New Year.*

Margaret of Anjou, Queen of Henry VI (1422-1461), is said to have escaped from a siege of Dunstanburgh Castle in a basket, lowered down the 100ft cliff face to a waiting boat. This story illustrates the spirit of the resolute Queen who, during the Wars of the Roses, led the Lancastrian forces in defence of her husband's throne. Dunstanburgh Castle, built by Thomas, 2nd Earl of Lancaster, was a Lancastrian stronghold and a royal castle. The damage caused during sieges was never repaired, and by the mid-16th century the castle was in ruins.

Dunwich

Suffolk **Map: p239 H5.**

The sea has eaten away the history of Dunwich and all that is left now is a small village. In the 13th century it was a thriving port, which was granted a charter by King John (1199-1216) in the year of his accession. In the 7th century Dunwich was the capital of Sigebert, King of the East Angles, but the site of his royal hall must now lie nearly a mile offshore. A devout Christian, Sigebert established a bishopric and founded a school for boys here.

Durham

Durham **Map: p243 H5.** *Castle open Apr, July to Sept: Mon to Sat daily; Oct to Mar, May, June: Mon, Wed, Sat afternoons.*

With the exception of Henry VI (1422-1461), English monarchs have not been noted for their piety. However, the Danish King Canute (1016-1035) made frequent pilgrimages to Christian shrines. At the start of his reign he walked 6 miles, barefoot, to the newly built cathedral at Durham, bringing with him endowments of land. Monks from Lindisfarne had built the cathedral as a safe resting place for their holiest relic — the body of their 7th-century bishop, St Cuthbert. William the Conqueror (1066-1087) recognized the strategic position of the cathedral and in 1072 he ordered a fortress to be built beside it, to guard the north against Scottish invasion. He later appointed the Bishop of Durham as his representative in the north. Durham Castle was the home of succeeding Bishops of Durham until the 19th century when it became part of the new University of Durham.

Henry VI made a pilgrimage to the shrine of St Cuthbert in 1448. Stephen (1135-1154), came here to make peace with the Scots in 1136 and 1139. Edward III (1327-1377) and his Queen feasted in the Great Hall of the castle in 1334 as guests of Edward's tutor, when he was installed as Prince-Bishop. Princess Margaret, the 13-year-old daughter of Henry VII (1485-1509), on her journey north to marry James IV of Scotland (1488-1513) in 1503, was also entertained at the castle. A century later her great-grandson, James I (1603-1625), stayed at the castle on his way south to be crowned King of England. Charles I (1625-1649) visited Durham twice. In 1633, travelling north to be crowned in Scotland, he stayed at the castle; on his second visit, in 1648, he was a prisoner of Parliament.

Eastbourne

East Sussex **Map: p235 F5.**

Eastbourne's first royal holidaymakers were four children of George III (1760-1820), who enjoyed a summer holiday here in 1780. The resort did not become fashionable until a century later.

The Front, Eastbourne

East Lulworth

Dorset **Map: p233 G3.**

The first Roman Catholic church to be built legally in England after the Reformation can be seen in this pretty village. George III (1760-1820) gave permission for it to be built in 1786.

East Stoke

Nottinghamshire **Map: p238 D3.**

When Henry VII (1485-1509) took the field in 1487 at East Stoke against the supporters of Lambert Simnel, it was the last occasion on which a king of England went personally into battle to defend his title to the throne against a rival claimant. In the bitter three-hour battle at East Stoke, the rebel army was defeated.

Eastwell

Kent **Map: p238 D3.**

A grave on the northern side of ruined Eastwell church is believed to hold the bones of the last Plantagenet. Legend has it that Richard III (1483-1485) had an illegitimate son, also called Richard, who fled from Bosworth (1485) when Henry Tudor, later Henry VII (1485-1509), won the crown there with his victory over the Yorkist army. The young Richard, thought to be about 16, hid himself by becoming a bricklayer on the Eastwell Park estate.

Edgehill

Warwickshire **Map: p234 C1.**

Three kings were present at the Battle of Edgehill, which was fought on 23 October 1642, two months after Charles I (1625-1649) had raised his standard at Nottingham. Charles took the field in person — the first reigning monarch to do so for more than a century — and his two sons, the future Charles II (1660-1685) and James II (1685-1688), aged 12 and 9 respectively, watched the outcome from high ground nearby. The Princes would have seen their cousin Prince Rupert's famous cavalry charge, which was later checked by a troop of Roundheads under Oliver Cromwell. Rupert's return as dusk was falling ended the battle; both sides were exhausted and the fighting ended indecisively.

Elmley Castle

Worcestershire **Map: p234 B1.**

The Norman castle which gave this beautiful village its name has long vanished. It was in ruins when Elizabeth I (1558-1603) visited the village in 1575 to stay with the Savage family in their manor house, built with stones taken from the castle.

Eltham

Greater London **Map: p235 F3.** *Palace open Apr to Oct: Thur to Mon daily; Nov to Mar: Thur to Sun daily.*

Tucked away in the suburbs of south London, at Eltham, is the banqueting hall of one of the most splendid medieval royal palaces. Bishop Anthony Bek of Durham, renowned for his extravagance, built the original castle at Eltham around 1300 — and gave it to the Queen, Margaret, second wife of Edward I (1272-1307). His castle became the favourite palace of successive kings from Edward II (1307-1327) to Henry VIII (1509-1547). Each monarch extended and embellished it.

Ely

Ely

Cambridgeshire Map: p239 F5.

As Canute (1016-1035) and his Queen, Emma, approached Ely by boat to attend a religious festival, the chanting of the monks in the abbey, high above on its hill, was carried to them over the water. The King immediately composed a song in the sheer pleasure of the moment — of which one verse survives:

'Merrily sang the monks in Ely
As Cnut, king, rowed thereby.
Row, men, nearer the shore
Let us hear the song of the monks.'

In the time of Canute (1016-1035) Ely was an island surrounded by water and fens. Etheldreda, Queen of Northumbria and a Princess of East Anglia, had founded the abbey here in AD 673, attracted by its inaccessibility. However, William the Conqueror (1066-1087) discouraged isolated fortresses, religious or otherwise. When Ely became a centre of Saxon resistance under Hereward the Wake in 1071, he drove a 2-mile causeway across the fens to the island, punished the rebels harshly, fined the monastery and built a castle to defend his causeway.

Ely was high in royal esteem in Saxon times. In 1010 Edward the Confessor (1042-1066) went to the King's School here. Later royal visits to Ely concentrated mainly on the now vanished castle, which was besieged by King John (1199-1216), Henry III (1216-1272) and Edward I (1272-1307) as they battled with rebellious barons. Henry III and Prince Edward attended the dedication of the presbytery at Ely Cathedral in 1252.

Etal

Northumberland Map: p243 G3.

The ruins of Etal Castle, which was built in the 14th century by Sir Robert de Manners, stand at the end of the main street of the village. The castle was never rebuilt after its destruction by James IV of Scotland (1488-1513) prior to the Battle of Flodden (1513), when he invaded England in support of Louis XII of France (1498-1515).

Eton College

Berkshire Map: p234 D3. *School yard and cloisters open Mon to Sat afternoons. Chapel open afternoons, mornings also in school holidays. Grounds Mon to Sat daily.*

Henry VI (1422-1461) — a dreamer and a religious man — founded 'King's College of our Lady at Eton beside Windsor' when he was 19, together with King's College, Cambridge, to which he planned his 70 'poor and indigent' scholars would go once their studies were sufficiently advanced. The first building was completed at Eton in 1443; it is now the lower school and still in use. The troubled times of the Wars of the Roses frustrated Henry's plans however, and during the reign of Edward IV (1461-1483) most of the scholars' endowments were withdrawn. The college survived to become one of the most famous schools in the world.

Eton College

Euston

Suffolk Map: p239 G5. *Hall open June to Sept: Thur afternoons.*

In 1670, Charles II (1660-1685) had eyes only for Louise de Kérouälle, a pretty Breton maid of honour in his sister's retinue. She became maid of honour to Catherine of Braganza, Charles's long-suffering Queen and it was not long before Louise was officially installed as the King's mistress — an event which took place at Euston Hall, near Newmarket, the recently completed home of Lord Arlington, a leading politician.

Arlington's daughter later married Charles's illegitimate son by Barbara Villiers; he was later created Duke of Grafton. The house — extensively rebuilt after a fire in 1902 — is owned by their descendant, the present Duke of Grafton.

Evesham

Hereford & Worcester Map: p234 B1.

'May God have mercy on our souls, for our bodies are theirs' — with these words Simon de Montfort, Earl of Leicester, faced the army of his nephew and godson, Prince Edward, at the Battle of Evesham in August 1265. The Earl had defeated Henry III (1216-1272) and the Prince at Lewes (May 1264) and had virtually ruled England since, holding both King and Prince prisoner. However, Edward had escaped two months earlier, raised an army and trapped de Montfort in a loop of the River Avon at Evesham. With brilliant strategy and three forced night marches in four days Edward had defeated de Montfort's son at Kenilworth before turning to attack the father at Evesham. Edward's army outnumbered the Earl's by two to one. A contemporary writer described the battle as 'a murder'. Simon de Montfort was cut down with his eldest son, most of his knights and barons and 4,000 of his soldiers.

Ewelme

Oxfordshire Map: p234 D2. *Manor house not open to the public.*

Wondering just how she should wear her own insignia of the garter at her coronation, Queen Victoria (1837-1901) sent to the village of Ewelme for advice. For here, in the parish church of St Mary, the 15th-century effigy on the tomb of Alice de la Pole, Duchess of Suffolk, shows the garter worn on her left arm, like a bracelet. Henry VIII (1509-1547) honeymooned in 1540 at Ewelme manor house, then a royal palace, with his fifth wife, Catherine Howard.

Exeter

Devon Map: p233 E3. *Guildhall open Mon to Sat daily.*

As a key city in the southwest, Exeter has for centuries served as a stronghold and a haven — and never more so than when William the Conqueror (1066-1087) finally won it two years after his victory at Hastings in 1066. As the Norman King marched triumphantly through the east gate of the Saxon fortress, the last to fall to him in England, Githa, mother of Harold (1066), escaped through the west gate with her household. Exeter was to shelter another royal lady in time of danger six centuries later. Henrietta Maria, Queen of Charles I (1625-1649), fled here in April 1644 when Oxford began to look insecure. She later fled to France.

Exeter had been fortified since pre-Roman times and it was on Celtic earthworks that William the Conqueror personally paced out the dimensions of his Norman castle. Only part of the gatehouse and keep stand today.

William of Orange, later William III (1689-1702), stayed in Exeter in 1688, shortly after his arrival at Brixham, backed by 12,000 troops and supported by leading Protestant politicians. His father-in-law, Roman Catholic James II (1685-1688), fled from London to France as William advanced and the Dutch prince won the throne in a bloodless revolution.

Falmouth

Cornwall Map: p232 B5. *Pendennis Castle open Mon to Sat daily, Sun afternoons. Closed Christmas, New Year.*

Pendennis Castle was built in the 1540s by Henry VIII (1509-1547) to defend the fine natural harbour at Falmouth against invasion from France or Spain. It was the last stronghold in England to surrender to Parliament in 1646, defying a five-month siege by Sir Thomas Fairfax, the Roundhead general.

Henrietta Maria, Queen of Charles I (1625-1649), sheltered for two nights at the castle in 1644, while fleeing from England in bad health after the birth in Exeter of her last child.

Pendennis Castle was a refuge for Henrietta's son, Prince Charles, two years later. He spent nearly three weeks here before sailing for the Scilly Isles to avoid being seized by Parliament. The parish church of King Charles the Martyr in Falmouth was built in the first years of the Restoration and reflected the town's Royalist sympathies.

Farleigh Hungerford Castle

Somerset **Map: p233 G1.** *Open Mon to Sat daily, Sun afternoons. Closed public holidays.*
Margaret, Countess of Salisbury, one of the last Plantagenets, was born at Farleigh Hungerford Castle in 1473. Her father was George, Duke of Clarence, brother of Edward IV (1461-1483) and Richard III (1483-1485). Both Margaret, and her brother Edward, Earl of Warwick, who was born two years later, were to die under the headsman's axe, accused unjustly of treason. Their father was put to death in the Tower of London in 1478 for plotting against Edward — tradition has it that he was drowned in a butt of malmsey wine.

Farnham Castle

Surrey **Map: p234 D3.** *Open Wed afternoons; and by appointment for large parties.*
The only royal visitor who stayed any length of time here was Prince Louis of France, who besieged and captured the castle in 1276, after invading England in support of the rebel barons in the last year of King John's reign (1199-1216). He held the castle for 10 months, surrendering it to the forces of John's successor, Henry III (1216-1272).

As the home of the Bishops of Winchester since the 7th century, the castle would have seen many more peaceful royal guests. It was visited by the Tudor kings and James I (1603-1625) stayed here when he came to hunt nearby. The castle, now a conference centre, has been lived in almost continuously since it was built.

Faversham

Kent **Map: p235 G3.**
James II (1685-1688) was dragged off a customs vessel at Sheerness as it was on the point of sailing for France late at night on 12 December 1688. The King had been trying to escape to the continent in the face of growing support for his Protestant son-in-law William of Orange, who had invaded England a month earlier. The King was not recognized by the fishermen, but was marched to Faversham where they discovered his identity. James was held prisoner at the mayor's house, which no longer exists, for two days until he could get a letter to friends in London to rescue him. He returned to Whitehall and a mixed reception, and then left his kingdom for good.

Flodden

Northumberland **Map: p243 G3.**
To the English their victory at Flodden (1513) was just another battle; to the Scots it was a national disaster. No Scottish army had been stronger or better equipped than the mixed force of 40,000 Highlanders, Lowlanders and Frenchmen that crossed the border at Coldstream on 22 August, led by the Scottish King, James IV (1488-1513). Louis XII of France appealed to the Scots to come to his aid by attacking England, after Henry VIII (1509-1547) had invaded France with the main English army the previous May.

Thomas Howard, Earl of Surrey, was in command of the small army that Henry left behind in England.

In a brilliant, but risky, manoeuvre the English army — outnumbered by two to one — marched round behind the Scottish lines. The Scots were forced to turn northwards, uncertain whether the enemy had moved off to invade Scotland or to do battle. The English opened the attack with an artillery bombardment that stung the Scottish left wing into an ill-disciplined charge downhill. James, commanding the centre, followed only to have his left wing overwhelmed by the English cavalry. At the same time the English archers surprised the Highland right wing on the flank and routed them. Archers and cavalry then encircled the Scottish centre. As night fell, James died fighting on foot, ringed by his nobles and foot soldiers.

Flodden Field

Ford

Northumberland **Map: p243 G3.** *Castle not open.*
Tradition has it that James IV of Scotland (1488-1513) was so captivated by the beauty of the lady of Ford Castle, Lady Heron, that he delayed here with his southward-bound army, allowing the Earl of Surrey to gather a sizeable English army to confront him at Flodden in 1513.

Fotheringay

Northamptonshire **Map: p239 E4.**
On the banks of the River Nene at Fotheringay a few bramble-covered stones surrounded by an iron railing mark the site of the castle where Mary, Queen of Scots (1542-1567) was tried and executed in February 1587. She had been accused of plotting to overthrow her cousin, Elizabeth I (1558-1603), who, after keeping her imprisoned for 20 years, was finally driven to signing the death warrant to safeguard her own throne.

Fotheringay was a stronghold of the Dukes of York — Richard III (1483-1485) was born in the castle. The church was once a much larger building with a 15th-century college choir and cloisters adjoining. Only the foundations of these can now be traced beside the present church. The choir was partly ruined when Elizabeth I visited Fotheringay. She ordered the tombs of the Dukes of York, which were lying there neglected, to be moved into the church.

Framlingham Castle

Suffolk **Map: p239 G5.** *Open Mon to Sat daily, Sun afternoons. Closed public holidays.*
It was to Framlingham Castle that Mary I (1553-1558) fled during the critical days when her rightful accession to the throne seemed threatened by the proclamation of the Protestant Lady Jane Grey as Queen of England, after the death of Edward VI (1547-1553). However, men flocked to Mary's standard as it flew above the battlements of the royal castle. She soon had an army of 13,000 and marched on London. The ambitious Duke of Northumberland, Lady Jane's father-in-law, advanced to meet her but support for Lady Jane dwindled as soon as he left London. Within nine days her reign was over and London welcomed Mary.

Framlingham had seen exciting times before. It was a stronghold of the turbulent rebel baron, Hugh Bigod, Earl of Norfolk, against whom Henry II (1154-1189) battled in the early years of his reign. When Henry razed the castle to the ground in 1175, Hugh's son, Roger, rebuilt it to the strong, new pattern pioneered by Henry himself, and, following family tradition, rebelled against King John (1199-1216). It became one of the most important castles in Suffolk, passing from the Bigods to the Mowbrays and then to the Howards.

Frampton-on-Severn

Gloucestershire **Map: p234 B2.**
Mystery and legend surround Fair Rosamond, the beautiful mistress of Henry II (1154-1189). She is believed to have been born at Frampton-on-Severn and the village green is called Rosamond's Green to this day. She was the daughter of Walter de Clifford, owner of Clifford Castle on the Welsh border, near Hay-on-Wye. Henry is said to have built a secret bower for her at his palace at Woodstock, in the middle of a maze.

Gainsborough

Lincolnshire **Map: p238 D2.** *Old Hall open Mon to Sat daily, Sun afternoons. Closed Christmas, New Year.*
The Old Hall at Gainsborough was probably still being built when Richard III (1483-1485) stayed here with his friend Sir Thomas Burgh in 1484. Today, 500 years later, the great hall and its adjoining kitchen are still intact despite 200 years of mixed commercial and religious use.

Henry VIII (1509-1547) first met his sixth — and last — wife, Catherine Parr, at the Old Hall in 1540, the year he married Anne of Cleves. Sweyn, King of Denmark, father of Canute (1016-1035), made his base at Gainsborough after invading England in June 1013. All the leaders of the north and Midlands paid him homage here without a blow being struck, and he then subdued the rest of the country in a swift campaign. He died suddenly at Gainsborough, eight months later. Alfred the Great (AD 871-899) married here in AD 868.

Gatcombe Park

Gloucestershire **Map: p234 B2.** *Not open.*
Built in the late 18th century for a wealthy clothing merchant and little changed, Gatcombe Park is now the home of Princess Anne and Captain Mark Phillips. A one-day event is held here annually.

Gawsworth Hall

Cheshire **Map: p238 B3.** *Open late Mar to Oct: afternoons.*
This rambling, black-and-white timber-framed manor house was once the home of Mary Fitton, maid of honour to Elizabeth I (1558-1603). It is thought that she may have been the 'dark lady' of Shakespeare's sonnets.

Geddington

Northamptonshire **Map: p238 D5.**
When Eleanor of Castile, Queen of Edward I (1272-1307), died of a fever at Harby in Nottinghamshire in November 1290, the grieving King had her body embalmed and carried to Westminster. He followed the funeral procession most of the way, ordering memorial crosses to be set up at each place where the Queen's coffin rested overnight. Only three of the original crosses still remain, and Geddington's is the best preserved of them all.

Glastonbury

Somerset **Map: p233 F2.** *Abbey open daily.*
A church here, made of wattles, was already old when the Roman missionary Paulinus visited in AD 633, although there are some records of a church on the site of the present abbey ruins from before the 2nd century. King Ine of Wessex (AD

Glastonbury Abbey

688-726) built an additional church next to the ancient wattle one in the year he came to the throne. A great benefactor of churches, it is said he was persuaded to give up his throne and make a pilgrimage to Rome by his wife, Ethelburgh.

Edgar (AD 959-975) held court near Glastonbury. He made generous grants of money for the repair of Viking damage to the abbey and he was buried in front of the high altar.

Glastonbury, however, is linked with a far more ancient King. It has been identified as the probable site of the Isle of Avalon to which, legend relates, the mortally wounded King Arthur was ferried in a barge and later buried in a little, earth-floored chapel. In the 5th century, the period which gave rise to the Arthurian legend, Glastonbury Tor would have been islanded among marshes and lagoons. Queen Guinevere is said to have been buried here beside Arthur.

Glastonbury Abbey was enlarged after the Norman Conquest, but in 1184 a fire destroyed nearly all of it. Henry II (1154-1189) generously supported the rebuilding, but it was not until 1524 that the abbey was completed. It was the wealthiest of all the religious houses that Henry VIII (1509-1547) dissolved.

One of the most ancient traditions of Glastonbury is that Joseph of Arimathea — the man who gave his own tomb for Christ's burial — came here preaching the gospel and brought with him the cup used in the Last Supper. He is supposed to have buried it on Chalice Hill. The cup became the Holy Grail of Arthurian legend, which only the most perfect and sinless knight could find. Joseph is said to have planted his staff on Weary-all Hill where it immediately blossomed. The famous Glastonbury Thorn, which flowers at Christmas time, is said to be rooted from cuttings taken from the original tree, which was cut down on Cromwell's orders. Each Christmas, sprigs of thorn blossom from the abbey tree are sent to the Queen and Queen Mother.

Gloucester

Gloucestershire **Map: p234 B2.**
The tomb of Edward II (1307-1327) near the high altar of the Abbey of St Peter of Gloucester, now Gloucester Cathedral, attracted crowds of pilgrims in succeeding reigns, who saw the murdered king as a royal martyr, if not a saint.

Edward III (1327-1377) encouraged this popular devotion to his father's memory and placed a magnificent alabaster effigy on the tomb.

Saxon kings held councils and courts at Gloucester from the 9th century. Edward the Confessor (1042-1066) made a habit of celebrating Christmas here and it was where Athelstan (AD 925-939) died. It was in council at Gloucester that William the Conqueror devised the Domesday Book, to record just what and how much he had conquered. William Rufus (1087-1100), taken desperately ill at Gloucester in 1093, repented of all the misdeeds of his violent and corrupt reign, vowed to reform his government, recovered, and broke that promise like all the rest. Henry III (1216-1272), when only nine, was hastily crowned at Gloucester after the sudden death of his father, King John (1199-1216). Henry was imprisoned in the Norman castle at Gloucester by Simon de Montfort, Earl of Leicester, 40 years later, after being taken prisoner during the barons' rebellion against him.

During the Civil War Gloucester was besieged by Charles I (1625-1649). The garrison held out and the King, hearing of the approach of the London militia, who had mobilized under the Earl of Essex to march to Gloucester's relief, abandoned the siege. Vindictively, Charles II (1660-1685) ordered the castle to be demolished.

Godalming

Surrey **Map: p235 E4.**
Godalming was once a royal manor. Alfred (AD 871-899) bequeathed it to his nephew, Ethelwald.

Godstow

Oxfordshire **Map: p234 C2.**
The richly decorated tomb before the church altar at Godstow nunnery so offended Bishop Hugh of Lincoln during his inspection in 1191, that he ordered everything to be removed and the lady to be reburied outside the church 'for she was a harlot'. The Bishop might not have dared to be so outspoken two years earlier, for the tomb was that of Rosamond Clifford — the beloved Fair Rosamond, mistress of Henry II (1154-1189). Ruins of the nunnery, dating from the 15th century, can be seen in a meadow at Godstow.

Gatcombe Park

Goodmanham

Humberside **Map: p241 H3.**
After his first meeting with the Roman mission-ary Paulinus in AD 617, it took the pagan King Edwin of Northumbria (AD 616-632) 10 years to become a Christian — he and his court were baptized on Easter Sunday, 12 April AD 627. His high priest, Coifi, borrowed a battle axe from the King and personally demolished his pagan temple at Goodmanham nearby. The Norman church is built on the site of the Saxon shrine that replaced Coifi's temple, making this peaceful village one of the earliest Christian sites in England.

Goodwood

West Sussex **Map: p234 D4.** *House open May to Oct: Sun, Mon afternoons; also Tue, Wed, Thur in Aug; Easter.*
In 1697, the 1st Duke of Richmond, illegitimate son of Charles II (1660-1685) by his mistress Louise de Kérouälle, bought a hunting lodge at Goodwood. This was extended in the late 18th century into the present Goodwood House by the 3rd Duke, who also laid out the racecourse. Among the art treasures in the house are portraits of Charles I (1625-1649) and his family by Van Dyck and a portrait of Charles II by Lely.

The Queen has held Privy Council meetings at Goodwood on several occasions when staying here during race meetings.

Grafton Regis

Northamptonshire **Map: p234 D1.** *Manor house not open to the public.*
In 1464 at Grafton (not yet Regis) Edward IV (1461-1483) secretly married Lady Elizabeth Grey, widowed daughter of the lord of the manor, Sir Richard Woodville. Edward had fallen passionately in love with Elizabeth when she had petitioned him for the restitution of the estates of her first husband, a Lancastrian killed at the second battle of St Albans in 1461. Desperately in love, like many another man he took the one course offered to him — marriage.

In 1524, Henry VIII (1509-1547), grandson of Edward and Elizabeth, was courting a commoner at the manor house, by now a royal property. Once again the girl held out for marriage and got her way, but this time the union ended in tragedy — the bride was Anne Boleyn.

Grantham

Lincolnshire **Map: p238 D3.** *Grantham House open Apr to Sept: Wed, Thur afternoons.*
Grantham lies on Ermine Street, the old Roman road to the north, and among its fine coaching inns is The Angel and Royal Inn — a rare medieval hostelry founded by the Knights Templar. King John (1199-1216) held court here in 1213 in a room now called King John's Chamber.

Grantham House, dating from the 14th century, is set in 27 acres of parkland in the centre of the town. Princess Margaret, daughter of Henry VII (1485-1509), stayed here in 1503 on her way north to marry James IV of Scotland (1488-1513).

Greenwich

Greater London **Map: p235 F3.** *Royal Naval College open Fri to Wed afternoons. Old Royal Observatory open Tue to Sat daily, Sun after-noons. Closed Christmas, New Year. The Queen's House (National Maritime Museum) open Tue to Sat daily, Sun afternoons. Closed Christmas, New Year. Gypsy Moth IV open Mon to Sat daily, Sun afternoons.*
Greenwich has had connections with royalty and sea-faring for centuries. When the present Queen, Elizabeth II, knighted Sir Francis Chichester in the grounds of the Royal Naval College at Green-wich in 1967, on his return from his lone voyage round the world in the 53ft ketch, *Gipsy Moth IV*, she recreated a scene from centuries before. For the college stands on the site of the royal palace of Greenwich where her ancestor, Elizabeth I (1558-1603), stayed when she came to knight Sir Francis Drake on the deck of the *Golden Hind*. Greenwich combined the luxury of court life with serious purpose. Henry VIII (1509-1547) established an armoury here. The craftsmanship of his armourers was renowned, rivalling the best work on the continent. Some of the suits they made at Greenwich are now on show in the Tower of London. Keen to build up a powerful navy to defend his kingdom, Henry also built two great naval dockyards on either side of Greenwich Palace, at Deptford and Woolwich.

The site of the palace had royal connections in Saxon times. Humphrey, Duke of Gloucester, brother of Henry V (1413-1422), built the first castle there, calling it Bella Court. He included a watchtower on the top of the hill, where the Old Royal Observatory now stands, to guard London from invaders approaching along the Dover road. Margaret of Anjou, Queen of Henry VI (1422-1461), seized Bella Court when the Duke, arrested for high treason in 1447, died mysteriously shortly afterwards. She renamed the palace Placentia, the pleasant place, and it became the favourite palace of Henry VII (1485-1509) after the Wars of the Roses. Henry VIII and his two daughters, Mary I (1553-1558) and Elizabeth I, were all born at Greenwich. Henry's only son, Edward VI (1547-1553), died here.

The Stuart kings and queens are responsible

Greenwich Palace

for the fine aspect that Greenwich river front presents today. In 1615 James I (1603-1625) commissioned Inigo Jones to build Queen's House for his wife, Anne of Denmark, on the site of the old gatehouse to the Tudor palace where, it is said, Sir Walter Raleigh once spread his cloak in the mud for Elizabeth I to walk across. Queen's House was not finished when James's Queen died in 1619. It was completed by Charles I (1625-1649) for his wife, Henrietta Maria, in 1635. In February 1642 they spent their last night of peace together here, before Henrietta sailed for France taking their nine-year-old daughter, Mary, to her wedding with Prince William of Orange. They did not meet again until a year later. At the Restoration she returned to live at Queen's House when visiting London.

Charles II (1660-1685) demolished the old Tudor palace at Greenwich, which had been used as a barracks during the Commonwealth, and began building a new palace on the site in 1665. Only the King Charles block and the Observatory were completed, when the King ran out of money. William and Mary (1689-1702) transformed the site — and re-established the royal association with the navy when they appointed Sir Christ-opher Wren to design a hospital for wounded and aged sailors here. It took 50 years to complete, but sailors were being received here from 1704. In 1873 the Royal Hospital for Seamen became the Royal Naval College.

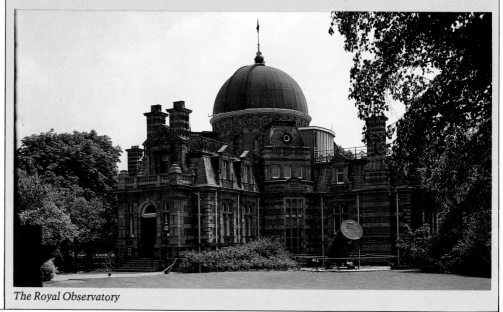

The Royal Observatory

Gravesend

Kent **Map: p235 F3.**
The busy stretch of the Thames at Gravesend has always been the gateway to London. In Tudor times it was the place where important foreign visitors were met to be escorted in state to the city. Henry VIII (1509-1547) met the Emperor Charles V at Gravesend in 1525 when he came to England during the diplomatic negotiations concerning war with France. In 1863 the Danish Princess, Alexandra, coming to Britain to marry the future Edward VII (1901-1910), landed at Gravesend to be met by the Prince, who travelled with her by rail to London. The baby son of James II (1685-1688) — the future Old Pretender — was smuggled out of England by night from Gravesend to Calais when James decided to flee.

Greenstead

Essex **Map: p235 F2.**
The wooden nave of St Andrew's Church at Greenstead, near Ongar, sheltered the coffin of St Edmund in 1013, during the journey from Bury St Edmunds to London. Edmund (AD 855-869), King of East Anglia, was murdered by Danes at Hoxne after refusing to renounce Christianity.

Grimsthorpe Castle

Lincolnshire **Map: p239 E4.** *Open as advertised.*
The core of Grimsthorpe Castle, near Bourne, is a Tudor house built by Charles Brandon, Duke of Suffolk, brother-in-law of Henry VIII (1509-1547). In the 18th century the architect John Vanbrugh was engaged to rebuild the north side, adding an imposing hall more than 100ft long. The castle contains several royal portraits, including one of Charles I (1625-1649) by Van Dyck. There is a collection of royal coronation robes dating from the time of James II (1685-1688) onwards, and other royal relics.

Guildford

Surrey **Map: p235 E2.** *Castle keep open Apr to Sept: daily.*
In 1036 this town, a fording place on the River Way, was the scene of a brutal royal kidnapping. Alfred the youngest son of Ethelred the Unready (AD 979-1016) was set upon here by armed men as he travelled with a troop of Normans to visit his mother at Winchester. His companions were murdered or sold as slaves and Alfred himself was blinded, dying later at Ely. The manor at Guildford was owned by Alfred the Great (AD 871-899), who bequeathed it to his nephew.

Gunby Hall

Lincolnshire **Map: p239 F3.** *Open Apr to Sept: Thur afternoon; Tue, Wed, Fri by written appointment only: J.D. Wrisdale Esq., Gunby Hall, Spilsby, Lincolnshire.*
Miniatures of members of the royal house of Stuart are among the treasures displayed in this 18th-century mansion, not far from Skegness.

Hadleigh

Suffolk **Map: p235 F2.**
Guthrun, the Danish King of East Anglia (AD 880-890), whom Alfred the Great (AD 871-899) defeated at the Battle of Bratton Down (AD 878) and then converted to Christianity, is believed to be buried in the south aisle of St Mary's Church at Hadleigh. The mainly 15th-century church contains a reminder of one of his predecessors — the Saxon king of East Anglia, St Edmund (AD 855-869), who was martyred by Danes at Hoxne.

Hadleigh, however, has its own martyr. Just outside the town, on Aldham Common, stands a memorial to Dr Rowland Taylor, the Protestant vicar of Hadleigh, who was burned at the stake here in 1555, for his faith.

Hadleigh Castle

Essex **Map: p235 G1.** *Ruins open Mon to Sat daily, Sun afternoons.*
The ruins of this late medieval castle, built in the 13th century by Hubert de Burgh, Chief Justiciar to King John (1199-1216) and his son, Henry III (1216-1272), stand on a hill overlooking the Thames estuary near Leigh-on-Sea. Anne of Cleves, fourth wife of Henry VIII (1509-1547), from whom he separated after only six months of marriage in 1540, lived here after their divorce.

Hagley Hall

West Midlands **Map: p237 G2.** *Open Easter to June: public holidays; July to Aug: afternoons.*
The present hall, a stately Palladian mansion set in parkland, was built in the mid-18th century by the 1st Lord Lyttelton. It replaced an earlier house in which two of the Gunpowder Plot conspirators, Robert Winter and Stephen Lyttelton, took refuge three days after the failure of the plot — a Roman Catholic conspiracy — to blow up James I (1603-1625) at the opening of Parliament on 5 November 1605.

Halidon Hill

Northumberland **Map: p243 G2.**
Edward III (1327-1377), pushing the claim of his puppet king, Edward Balliol, to the throne of Scotland in 1333, besieged Berwick and massacred a large Scottish army marching to its relief in the Battle of Halidon Hill on 19 July 1333. After the victory, Balliol, who had been crowned King at Scone during a campaign in Scotland the previous year, ruled as a vassal of Edward.

Halton Castle

Cheshire **Map: p238 A2.** *Ruins open.*
King John (1199-1216) stayed at Halton Castle when he came to hunt in the nearby royal forest of Delamere. During the Civil War it was garrisoned for the King, captured by Parliament and slighted.

Hampton Court

See page 158.

Harbottle Castle

Northumberland **Map: p243 G4.** *Ruins open all the time.*
The ruins of a mighty 12th-century castle dominate Harbottle village. It was here in 1515 that Queen Margaret, widow of James IV of Scotland (1488-1513), gave birth to a daughter eight days after escaping from Scotland. The baby, Margaret Douglas, Countess of Lennox, was the mother of Lord Darnley, Mary Queen of Scots' husband, and grandmother of James I (1603-1625).

Harby

Nottinghamshire **Map: p238 D3.** *Manor house not open.*
For eight days Edward I (1272-1307) sat by the bed-

Guildford Castle

side of his wife, Eleanor of Castile, as she lay dying in the manor house at Harby in November 1290. Edward had been holding a Parliament at nearby Clipstone, when Eleanor was taken ill. She died at the end of November, and on 4 December the slow funeral procession set out for Westminster Abbey, where the Queen was buried on 17 December.

Hardwick Hall

Derbyshire **Map: p238 C3.** *Hall open Apr to Oct: House on Wed, Thur, weekend, public holiday afternoons; Garden on afternoons daily.*

The formidable 'Bess of Hardwick', Countess of Shrewsbury, insisted that one of her daughters marry a great-nephew of Henry VIII (1509-1547), namely Charles Darnley, brother-in-law of Mary, Queen of Scots (1542-1567), when he paid a visit to Hardwick Hall in 1574. Arabella Stuart, the daughter of this match, was thought by many to have a better claim to the throne than James I (1603-1625). Elizabeth I (1558-1603) was so incensed when she learned of the news that she clapped Bess in the Tower for three months for her presumption. Arabella spent some time with her grandmother at Hardwick Hall, visiting for the last time in 1605, when Bess was seriously ill.

Harewood House

West Yorkshire **Map: p238 C1.** *Open Apr to Oct: daily; Feb, Mar: Sun, Tue to Thur daily; limited opening in Nov.*

The Princess Royal, Princess Mary, eldest daughter of George V (1910-1936) and Queen Mary, lived at Harewood House — a magnificent Palladian mansion — until her death here in 1965. She married Henry, Viscount Lascelles, later 6th Earl of Harewood, in 1922. She is buried in the Harewood vault at Harewood parish church. The estate now belongs to her son, the 7th Earl of Harewood, cousin of Elizabeth II.

Harewood House

Harrow

Middlesex. **Map: 235 E2.** *School: viewing by appointment only.*

Founded by John Lyon, yeoman, in 1572, the school later obtained a charter from Elizabeth I (1558-1603).

Hartington

Derbyshire **Map: p238 B3.**

Bonnie Prince Charlie, the Young Pretender, grandson of James II (1685-1688), is believed to have stayed at the early Jacobean Hartington Hall in 1745. He was marching south towards London in his bid to win the crown for his father James, the Old Pretender, and drive George II (1727-1760) from the throne. The hall is now a youth hostel.

Harwich

Essex **Map: p235 G1.**

In Dovercourt Bay, Edward III (1327-1377) gathered his fleet in 1340 before sailing to engage a vastly superior French navy at Sluys on the Flanders coast. In a long battle, Edward trapped the French ships inshore and eventually destroyed the sea-power of France. It was the first sea battle in the Hundred Years' War.

Hastings

Hastings

East Sussex **Map: p235 G4.**

Although the victory of William the Conqueror (1066-1087) over Harold in 1066 is always called the Battle of Hastings, it actually took place 6 miles away. The site has been called Battle ever since. William marshalled his forces at Hastings while Harold (1066) marched 250 miles south from Yorkshire to confront him. William is supposed to have breakfasted at Hastings on the morning of the battle; the Conqueror's stone near the pier is said to have been his table.

Hatfield Forest

Essex **Map: p235 F2.** *Open all the time.*

The wide grassy avenues between the trees of Hatfield Forest are still called 'chases', as they were when Norman and Plantagenet kings galloped along them in pursuit of the royal deer. In those days Hatfield was part of the much larger royal forest of Essex, once owned by Harold (1066), which stretched from the western boundaries of the county as far as Colchester.

Hatfield House

Hertfordshire **Map: p235 E2.** *Open late Mar to early Oct: Tue to Sun afternoons; bank holiday Mons.*

Hatfield House is everyone's idea of Elizabethan splendour, but its foundations were not dug until five years after the death of Elizabeth I (1558-1603). The Hatfield she knew, and where she spent much of her youth, was the Old Palace, of which one wing survives nearby. She was even imprisoned there in 1548, during the trial of her great admirer, Lord Seymour. Only 10 years later, she was sitting, reading, under an oak tree in the grounds — the site is marked by a memorial — when messengers arrived from London in 1558 to tell her that her half-sister, Mary I (1553-1558), was dead and that she was Queen. The Great Hall, where she once watched plays and masques, is still used for entertainment. Now Elizabethan banquets, complete with serving wenches and Tudor revelry, are staged here.

When James I (1603-1625) decided he wanted Theobalds, the Cecil house at Cheshunt, he offered Robert Cecil the Old Palace at Hatfield in exchange — and so the Cecils came to Hatfield and have been here ever since. Robert Cecil built Hatfield House, using the bricks of the Old Palace as a quarry. It was completed in 1612.

Hatfield House contains letters and clothes that belonged to Elizabeth as well as reminders of other monarchs. Letters of Henry VIII (1509-1547), Edward VI (1547-1553) and Mary, Queen of Scots (1542-1567), are here, together with famous portraits and relics of the Tudor monarchs and their successors. The gates to the south courtyard commemorate a visit by Queen Victoria (1837-1901) and Prince Albert.

Hengrave Hall

Suffolk **Map: p239 F5.** *By written appointment only.*

A visit from Elizabeth I (1558-1603) was an honour that most of her subjects prayed to avoid — the financial effect could be crippling. However, when she arrived at Hengrave Hall in 1570, the owner, Sir Thomas Kytson, could only have been delighted: he was one of the wealthiest merchants in London.

Henley-on-Thames

Oxfordshire **Map: p234 D3.** *Speaker's House not open to the public.*

Started in 1839, the annual rowing regatta gained the title 'The Royal Henley Regatta' when Prince Albert, consort of Queen Victoria (1837-1901), gave it his patronage in 1851. However, the town had already received other royal visits. William of Orange, later William III (1689-1702), marching with his army to London in 1688, stopped in Henley to meet a deputation from the House of Lords as support for him grew and James II (1685-1688) prepared to flee to France. During the Civil War Prince Rupert, nephew of Charles I (1625-1649), is said to have hung a Roundhead spy from an elm tree outside the Bell Inn. The inn is now three houses, appropriately called Rupert's Guard, Rupert's Elm and Elm House. Charles and George III (1760-1820) are both said to have stayed at the Red Lion Inn in Henley.

Hereford

Hereford & Worcester **Map: p234 A1.**

In AD 794, a horrible royal murder took place at Hereford, when Ethelbert, the young King of the East Angles, was done to death by his prospective mother-in-law — and all for greed. Offa, King of the Mercians (AD 757-794), and his Queen, Cynethryth, had invited Ethelbert to Hereford to meet and marry their daughter, Aelflaed. Then Cynethryth had the idea of killing him and seizing his kingdom instead. After the murder, Ethelbert's body was transferred to a shrine in Hereford Church and Offa, who was held responsible, made rich endowments to it. The young King was later made patron saint of the cathedral that rose on the site in the 12th and 13th centuries.

Border towns were always dangerous places, and never more so than in times of civil unrest. Athelstan (AD 925-939) met the Welsh princes at Hereford in AD 928 to fix the boundary between England and Wales along the River Wye. When the Welsh sacked the city in 1055 Harold (1066) drove them out, rebuilt the defensive earthworks and then waged a campaign of vengeance in Wales in 1063, using Hereford as a base. When Stephen (1135-1154) attended a cathedral ceremony at Hereford on Whit Monday 1138, supporters of his cousin Matilda, daughter of Henry I (1100-1135), in her claim to the throne, attacked the city and burned it.

Henry III (1216-1272) and his son, Prince Edward, later Edward I (1272-1307) were held prisoner in Hereford Castle by Simon de Montfort, Earl of Leicester, after his victory at Lewes (1264). Little is now left of the castle which was once one of the finest in England.

Herstmonceux

East Sussex **Map: p235 F4.** *Castle grounds only*

Henley-on-Thames

open Easter to Sept: Mon to Fri afternoons, weekends daily; public holidays.

The castle, which was once a fortified manor house, was virtually rebuilt from ruins at the beginning of this century. It is now the home of the Royal Greenwich Observatory which the Queen officially opened in 1967.

Herstmonceux Castle

Hertford Castle

Hertfordshire **Map: p235 E2.** *Open May to Sept: first Sat morning of month; gardens open daily.*

Two ransomed kings spent some time imprisoned in Hertford Castle during the reign of Edward III (1327-1377). David Bruce, King of Scots (1329-1371), had to wait 11 years, until 1357, before his ransom of 100,000 marks was agreed. John II of France, taken prisoner by the Black Prince at Poitiers in 1356, was freed after four years on payment of three million gold crowns.

William the Conqueror (1066-1087) built Hertford Castle at the beginning of his reign on the site of a Saxon fortress to defend a ford on the River Lea. In medieval times it served as both a palace and royal prison. In 1423 another captured king, James I of Scotland (1406-1437), celebrated Christmas at Hertford Castle with Catherine of France, widow of Henry V (1413-1422). The castle remained royal until Charles I (1625-1649) granted it to William Cecil, 2nd Earl of Salisbury.

Today the castle's 15th-century gatehouse is flanked by 18th- and 20th-century buildings which were built in a similar style. These are used as local authority offices.

Hever Castle

Kent **Map: p235 F3.** *Open Apr to Sept: Tue, Wed, Fri, weekends daily; public holidays.*

Romance and tragedy still cling to Hever Castle — the 13th-century moated manor house where Anne Boleyn may have been born and certainly spent her girlhood. Its heyday was the period when Henry VIII (1509-1547) was courting Anne — the girl with black, beautiful eyes, for whom he divorced his Queen, Catherine of Aragon, and changed the religion of his kingdom. He visited often, showering Anne's father, Sir Thomas Boleyn, with honours and grants of land as his romance with his daughter progressed. Anne, who was to be the mother of Elizabeth I (1558-1603), refused to yield to Henry until she knew she would be Queen.

After Anne's execution and her father's death, Henry seized the castle and gave it to his fourth Queen, Anne of Cleves, as part of her divorce settlement. Restorations in the 20th century have preserved the fabric and the romance of Hever.

Hampton Court

Greater London **Map: p235 E3.** *Palace open May to Sept: daily; Oct to Apr: Mon to Sat daily, Sun afternoons. Closed Christmas, New Year.*

Cardinal Wolsey, Lord Chancellor to Henry VIII (1509-1547), built himself a palace so sumptious at Hampton Court, that it could almost be described as a Tudor paradise upon earth. A staff of 500 liveried servants were on call here to attend the cardinal and his guests, for whom 250 lavishly appointed guest rooms always stood ready. Henry and his Queen, Catherine of Aragon, were the first to be entertained here when the palace was completed in 1517. It was then the largest house in England. Unfortunately such well-furnished paradises inevitably have a serpent among the fittings. The opulence of the cardinal's lifestyle eventually roused, first, the King's envy — and then his avarice. When Wolsey fell from power in 1529, he attempted unsuccessfully to save himself by giving Hampton Court and all its contents to Henry. Two years later he died on his way to the Tower, charged with high treason.

Henry made Hampton Court one of his principal palaces. Remote from the danger of plague in London and easily reached by barge on the River Thames, it became one of the most popular of the royal riverside palaces that were built in Tudor times. Henry's last five wives lived here, although his second wife, Anne Boleyn, did not survive to see the queenly suite of rooms that were being built for her. She fell from favour and was executed in 1536 before they were completed. Jane Seymour, her successor, died in the new apartments while giving birth to Edward VI (1547-1553), who was christened in the Chapel Royal here with great pomp in 1537.

Henry courted and publicly acknowledged Catherine Howard as his fifth queen at Hampton Court in 1540, after a secret marriage a week before. She is said to have run screaming through the corridors here a few months later on learning that the King suspected her of adultery, vainly beating on the locked chapel doors behind which Henry was at his devotions. Her shrieking ghost is said to haunt the palace still. Catherine Parr was proclaimed Queen in 1543 in the Great Hall, which Henry built at Hampton Court. She narrowly escaped being tried and executed — for heresy — after arguing with Henry about religion. She was with the King in the gardens at Hampton Court, having been reconciled with him, when an armed guard arrived to arrest her, much to Henry's confusion. For Henry, Hampton Court was a pleasure palace, used for hunting, tournaments and entertaining. He built a tilt-yard here, now laid out as gardens, and the tennis court, which still survives today.

Life was less uncertain at Hampton Court under the Stuart monarchs, who found the charms of the palace just as irresistible. No building work was done during this period — instead Charles I (1625-1649) spent money on works of art to adorn the palace. It even delighted Oliver Cromwell, who use to live here in near regal state as Lord Protector during the Commonwealth. It was not until the reign of William III and Mary (1689-1702) that any great changes were made to Henry's palace. They disliked London and intended to move to Hampton Court. The architect Sir Christopher

The Pond Garden

Wren was engaged to demolish most of the Tudor palace and build new state apartments in Renaissance style. But the first phase was not yet completed when a more modest construction in the park ended Wren's plans. In 1702 William's horse, Sorrel, stumbled over a mole hill, throwing the widower king, who died later at Whitehall. It was left to his sister-in-law, Anne (1702-1714) to complete what he had begun — and all that was added was the small banqueting house overlooking the river. Hampton Court reverted to a summer pleasure palace, and George II (1727-1760) was the last King to use it. His successor, George III (1760-1820), preferred to lead a more simple life at Kew, downriver from Hampton Court.

The Nursery or Prince Edward's Lodgings

Henry VIII's Presence Chamber

Great Hall

The Master Carpenter's Court

Lord Chamberlain's Court

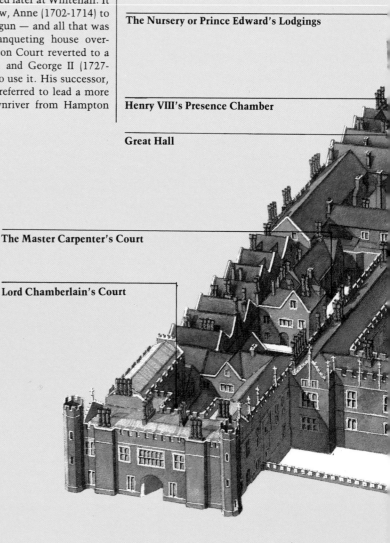

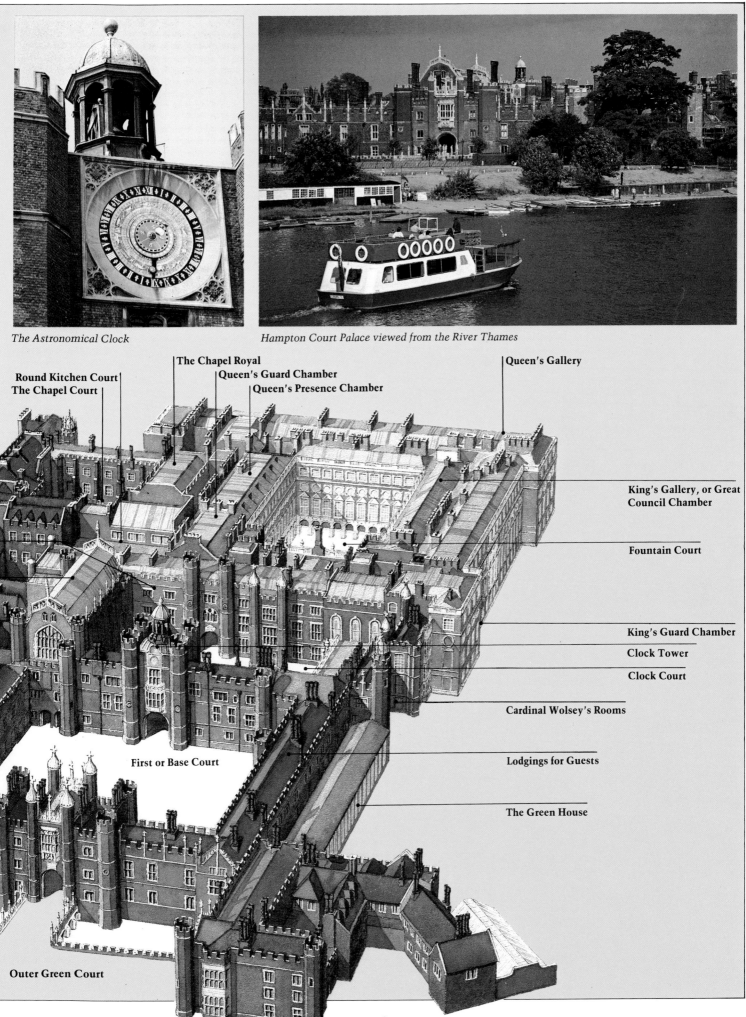

The Astronomical Clock

Hampton Court Palace viewed from the River Thames

Round Kitchen Court
The Chapel Court

The Chapel Royal
Queen's Guard Chamber
Queen's Presence Chamber

Queen's Gallery

King's Gallery, or Great Council Chamber

Fountain Court

King's Guard Chamber

Clock Tower

Clock Court

Cardinal Wolsey's Rooms

First or Base Court

Lodgings for Guests

The Green House

Outer Green Court

Hexham

Northumberland **Map: p243 G5.** *Abbey open daily.*
Hexham Abbey stands on the site of a church built in AD 674 by St Wilfrid. Queen Etheldreda of Northumbria gave the land for the church. St Wilfrid's chair in the chancel is believed to have been used at the crowning of the kings of Northumbria. The Battle of Hexham (1464) sealed the fate of the deposed Henry VI (1422-1461) seven years later.

Highgrove

Gloucestershire **Map: p234 B2.** *Not open.*
Set in 367 acres of parkland, Highgrove, near Tetbury, is the home of the Prince and Princess of Wales. Built between 1796 and 1798, it was sold after being badly damaged by fire in 1893. The new owner extensively rebuilt the mansion and completely redesigned its Georgian interior.

Hoddesdon

Hertfordshire **Map: p235 E2.** *Rye House open weekends and bank holidays in the summer.*
A plan to assassinate Charles II (1660-1685) and his brother, James, Duke of York, later James II (1685-1688), as they rode back from Newmarket to London in April 1683, went awry when a fire, which nearly destroyed Newmarket, made the royal brothers leave the town early. The plot was hatched at Rye House, near Hoddesdon, home of the extremist republican Richard Rumbold.

Holbeche House

West Midlands **Map: p237 G2.** *Not open.*
Relentlessly pursued by the sheriff of Worcestershire and a band of armed horsemen, the Gunpowder Plot conspirators made their last stand at Holbeche House, near Dudley, on 8 November 1605. The house was attacked and caught fire during the fight leaving only one chimney; this was incorporated in the house existing today.

Holdenby House

Northamptonshire **Map: p238 D5.** *Gardens open Apr to Sept: Sun and bank holiday Mon afternoons; also Thur afternoons in July and Aug. House by appointment East Haddon 786 or 241.*
Charles I (1625-1649) spent four relatively relaxed months at Holdenby (or Holmby) House under Parliamentary guard, having been handed over by the Scots in 1647. He was, however, to be more closely guarded when the quarrel between Parliament and its New Model Army grew bitter.

Little is left of the house Charles knew, apart from two arches near the present house.

Honiton

Devon **Map: p233 E3.** *Honiton and All Hallows Museum open Apr to Sept: Mon to Sat daily.*
Lace was produced at Honiton from Elizabethan times until the 19th century, having been introduced to the town by Protestant refugees from Flanders. The wedding dress of Queen Victoria (1837-1901) was made here.

Horncastle

Lincolnshire **Map: p239 E2.** *Scrivelsby Court viewing by written appointment only: Lt Col J L M Dymoke, MBE, DL.*
Since the Norman Conquest the land that lies behind the 'Lion Gate' of Scrivelsby Court, near Horncastle, has been held by the hereditary 'champions' of England. The present owners are the Dymoke family who inherited the manor — and the office of champion — by marriage in 1350. One of the duties of the champion was to ride in full armour into Westminster Hall at the start of the coronation banquet and challenge to mortal combat anyone who dared dispute the monarch's right to the crown. Nowadays the champion has a less spectacular role in the coronation ceremony — he carries the royal standard.

Scrivelsby Court was demolished many years ago and the present champion lives in the Elizabethan gatehouse.

Horsmonden

Kent **Map: p235 F3.**
One man who remained neutral in the Civil War was John Browne, the gunsmith in the village of Horsmonden. He made guns both for Charles I (1625-1649) and for Oliver Cromwell.

Houghton Hall

Norfolk **Map: p239 F3.** *Open Easter to Sept: Thur daily, Sun afternoons; public holidays.*
This grand Palladian mansion was built in the 18th century for Sir Robert Walpole, Prime Minister to George 1 (1714-1727) and George II (1727-1760).

Hovingham

North Yorkshire **Map: p241 G2.** *Hall open early May to Sept: Tue to Thur daily.*
The birthplace and now the family home of the Duchess of Kent, Hovingham Hall dominates the attractive village of golden limestone which clusters round its imposing gateway near the village green. The house was built in the mid-18th century by Sir Thomas Worsley, who was surveyor-general to George III (1760-1820).

Hoxne

Suffolk **Map: p239 G5.** *Hoxne Abbey Farmhouse not open.*
Edmund, King of East Anglia (AD 855-869), gave himself up to the Danes, it is said, to save his people from further slaughter. He was beaten, tied naked to a tree and shot to death with arrows. The Danes cut off his head, tossing it away as they rode off. Edmund's body was brought to Hoxne and buried here. The legend is that the missing head was found in a thicket, guarded by a wolf, after the searchers had been guided to the spot by a voice saying: 'Here! Here!' The wolf is said to have stayed by the graveside until the head was miraculously rejoined to the body.

Edmund's body lay buried in a wooden chapel at Hoxne for more than 30 years. Hoxne Abbey Farmhouse now stands on the site. Miracles were reported and Edmund's remains were transferred to the monastery at Bury. He was later canonized and his shrine became a place of pilgrimage.

Hughenden Manor

Buckinghamshire **Map: p234 D2.** *Open Mar to Nov: weekend afternoons; Apr to Oct: Wed to weekend afternoons; public holidays.*
Queen Victoria (1837-1901) visited Hughenden Manor in 1877 to lunch with her Prime Minister and personal friend, Benjamin Disraeli, Earl of Beaconsfield. The house was his home for 33 years until his death in 1881.

Huntingdon

Cambridgeshire **Map: p239 E5.** *Hinchingbrooke House open Mar to July: Sun afternoons. Cromwell Museum open Tue to Sat daily, Sun afternoons.*
Huntingdon is an ancient town. Edward the Elder (AD 899-925) had a fortress here in AD 915, when he was fighting the Danes, and the earthworks of a castle built by William the Conqueror (1066-1087) are still visible in the park. Henry II (1154-1189) destroyed the castle in 1174. David I of Scotland (1124-1153) founded the hospice of St John the Baptist in Huntingdon and some of his Norman building is contained in the 16th-century grammar school. This is now a museum devoted to a famous old boy — Oliver Cromwell.

Cromwell's birthplace and a centre of Puritanism, Huntingdon was occupied several times by Royalists during the Civil War. Cromwell's grandfather, Sir Henry Cromwell, had entertained Elizabeth I (1558-1603) at Hinchingbrooke House in 1564.

Hurst Castle

Hampshire **Map: p233 H3.** *Open Mon to Sat daily, Sun afternoons. Closed public holidays.*
Time was running out for Charles I (1625-1649) when, on 1 December 1648, he was brought across the Solent to Hurst Castle from the Isle of Wight, where he had been imprisoned at Carisbrooke Castle. Hurst Castle, sited on a two mile spit of shingle, had been built in 1536 as a defensive fort against the threat of French invasion. The King was lodged for 17 days in an upper room the size of a cell. When he left, it was to travel to Windsor Castle, to face trial in London and execution on 30 January 1649.

Inkberrow

Hereford & Worcester **Map: p234 B1.**
Sir Thomas Fairfax and Oliver Cromwell smashed the Royalist cause at the Battle of Naseby in June 1645. It was the decisive battle of the Civil War. Parliament captured the royal baggage train containing the private papers of Charles I (1625-1649), which he had inadvertently left

behind at Inkberrow vicarage, where he had stayed the previous month.

Islip

Oxfordshire **Map: p238 D5.**
In Saxon times there was an important royal palace at Islip, where one of the greatest Saxon kings, Edward the Confessor (1042-1066), was born. There is no trace of the palace today.

Iver

Buckinghamshire **Map: p235 E3.** *Coppins is not open to the public.*
Princess Victoria, the devoted, unmarried daughter of Edward VII (1901-1910) and Queen Alexandra, finally set up her own household at the age of 57, after her mother's death. She bought Coppins, a late-Victorian house at Iver, and lived here until her death in 1935, when she left it to her nephew Prince George, Duke of Kent. Coppins remained a royal residence and the home of the Dukes of Kent until 1972.

Coppins

Kendal

Cumbria **Map: p240 D2.** *Castle open all the time; Town Hall apply to caretaker.*
Catherine Parr, sixth Queen of Henry VIII (1509-1547), was born in Kendal Castle, only part of which still stands, in 1513. Bonnie Prince Charlie, the Young Pretender, grandson of James II (1685-1688), stayed at a house in Kendal, now owned by the YWCA, when marching south with his Highland army in the hope of reaching London and deposing George II (1727-1760) in 1745.

Kenilworth Castle

Kenilworth Castle

Warwickshire **Map: p237 H3.** *Open Mon to Sat daily, Sun afternoons. Closed Christmas, New Year.*
It is hard now to imagine the spectacular scene which Kenilworth Castle must have presented when Elizabeth I (1558-1603) was entertained here by her favourite courtier, Robert Dudley, Earl of Leicester, in 1575. In three weeks of extravagant entertainment, which included feasts, dancing, masques, hunting, bear-baiting and water pageants, the Earl turned his castle into a legendary palace. However, Elizabeth never forgave Leicester for marrying Lettice Knollys in 1578. When he died in 1588 the Queen made his widow sell the contents of Kenilworth to pay off a debt he owed her.

The Elizabethan merry-making at Kenilworth contrasts with earlier, fiercer times. In 1265, the young Edward I (1272-1307), then Prince of Wales, slaughtered the troops of Simon de Montfort's son as they slept encamped around the castle lake, the day before the Battle of Evesham. The following year Edward and his father Henry III (1216-1272) besieged the survivors in Kenilworth for several months. Edward II (1307-1327) was imprisoned at Kenilworth in November 1326, formally deposed in 1327 and later murdered.

During the Civil War Parliamentary troops breached the Norman dam that produced the lake and it has been dry ever since. The castle was slighted to make it unserviceable. However, the gatehouse is still lived in.

Kew

See page 162.

Kimbolton Castle

Cambridgeshire **Map: p239 E5.** *Open mid-July to late Sept: Sun afternoons only; Easter; spring and summer bank holidays.*
The unhappy Catherine of Aragon, the Queen whom Henry VIII (1509-1547) divorced so that he could marry Anne Boleyn, spent the last 19 months of her life at Kimbolton Castle. Although the castle, a fortified Tudor mansion, was reconstructed by Vanbrugh in the 18th century, the Queen's Room, where Catherine died, is part of the original mansion. Her ghost is said to haunt Kimbolton, which is now a school.

Kingsclere

Hampshire **Map: p234 C3.**
In Saxon times this small downland town near Basingstoke was important as a royal manor. It lies close to the Portway, the Roman road linking Salisbury and Silchester.

Kingsettle Hill

Wiltshire **Map: p233 G2.** *Stourhead House open Apr, Oct: Mon, Wed, weekend afternoons; May to Sept: Sat to Thur afternoons. Gardens open daily. Alfred's Tower not open.*
Follies were in fashion in the 18th century, which may have been the reason for the building of Alfred's Tower on Kingsettle Hill by the Hoare family, owners of the Stourhead estate, in 1772. It commemorates the victory of King Alfred (AD 871-899) over the Danish King, Guthrun, at Edington (AD 878).

King's Lynn

Norfolk **Map: p239 F4.** *St George's Guildhall open Mon to Fri daily, Sat mornings.*
It was at King's Lynn in October 1216 that King John (1199-1216) fought his last battle — a successful skirmish against a force of rebel barons. During his stay in the town he sickened with the illness that was to kill him within the month. The town was called Bishop's Lynn until Henry VIII (1509-1547) seized the manor and changed the name.

King's Sutton

Northamptonshire **Map: p234 C1.** *Astrop Park not open.*
St Rumbold, son of a pagan Northumbrian Prince,

Kew

Greater London **Map: p235 E3.** *Houses, museums and gardens open daily. Kew Palace open Apr to Sept: daily.*

For over a century the Hanoverian royal family made Kew very much their own. George II (1727-1760) and Queen Caroline were the first to move here — buying a summer hideaway in the Old Deer Park at Richmond in 1721, rebuilding it and calling it Richmond Lodge. Here Caroline laid out the first royal garden on ground which is now part of the Royal Botanic Gardens at Kew. Caroline's garden was far from botanic, however. Her taste was for landscaping in the romantic manner. She built two Gothic follies to adorn her wild garden — a Hermitage, complete with resident hermit, and Merlin's Cave, which held her library and a set of waxwork effigies of kings and queens. Today nothing remains of Richmond Lodge or her work, except for the less formal aspect of the western half of the present gardens.

It was Caroline's son, Frederick, Prince of Wales, and his wife, Augusta, who really established Kew as a centre for the scientific study of plants, when they leased the White House, now vanished, a mile away in 1730. Both royal households cordially detested each other and the only thing they had in common was an interest in gardening. Frederick and his wife spent most of their time at Kew, planning improvements and working on their pleasure gardens. When Frederick died in 1751 — of pleurisy brought on, some believed, by getting wet while gardening — Augusta solaced herself with yet more gardening and, it is hinted, the close encouragement of John Stuart, 3rd Earl of Bute. Together they enlarged the original botanic garden at White House, established an arboretum and introduced many exotic plants from all over the world, appointing William Aiton as gardener and William Chambers

Kew in spring

as architect. He designed the orangery, the pagoda, the ruined arch and the little temples that still ornament the gardens.

George III (1760-1820), while living at Richmond Lodge during the summer, took over White Lodge on his mother's death in 1772 and joined both estates into one. He later bought the Dutch House, now known as Kew Palace, and as the tally of royal children rose to 15, was driven to farm his family out to other houses nearby. Soon something like a royal colony developed at Kew. In the early years of his reign Kew became a fashionable place to visit and the royal gardens were open to the public. About this time the Queen's Cottage was built as a secluded picnic place among woods. Everything changed, however, when the King went mad for the first time in 1788. He was kept away from his family at the Dutch House, with a strict regime of walks in the gardens. On one such walk he had to be restrained from climbing the 163ft high pagoda.

In the 19th century royal interest in horticulture faded and the houses and gardens at Kew were presented one by one to the nation. The last addition was the Wood Museum and its grounds in 1904.

was born near King's Sutton in the 7th century. It is said he that he only lived three days, but in that time had professed his Christian faith and preached a sermon. It became fashionable in the 18th century to take the spa waters from St Rumbold's Well in Astrop Park.

Kingston Lisle

Oxfordshire **Map: p233 H1.**

The blowing stone at Kingston Lisle once lay on White Horse Hill. Alfred the Great (AD 871-899) is supposed to have summoned his army by blowing through holes in the stone; this produces a strange echoing sound.

Kingston-upon-Hull

Humberside **Map: p239 E1.**

Soon after seeing his Queen, Henrietta Maria, off to safety in France in 1642, as the rift with Parliament grew more dangerous, Charles I (1625-1649) hurried to Hull to take possession of some arms and munitions. On his arrival the gates of the town were shut against him by Sir John Hotham, the governor, who shouted from the walls that he was acting on the orders of Parliament. Charles declared him a traitor. He and his son were, however, put in the Tower accused of treachery by Parliament in 1643. The tables had turned after Sir John changed his mind four times about welcoming the King to Hull. The White Harte Inn, off Silver Street, was Sir John's home.

Kingston-upon-Thames

Greater London **Map: p235 E3.**

Two very different kings are on record as having been crowned at Kingston — Athelstan (AD 925-939) and Ethelred the Unready (AD 979-1016). Athelstan, King of Mercia and Wessex, later ruled the whole of England by conquest. He had been singled out for leadership by his grandfather, Alfred the Great (AD 871-899).

Kirby Hall

Northamptonshire **Map: p238 D4.** *Open Mon to Sat daily, Sun afternoons. Closed Christmas, New Year.*

Although empty and half-ruined, Kirby Hall is still a magnificent Elizabethan house, noted for its carved stonework. James I (1603-1625) is believed to have visited Kirby in its heyday.

Knaresborough Castle

North Yorkshire **Map: p241 F3.** *Open Easter to Sept daily.*

A dungeon and a room called the King's Chamber can still be seen in the ruins of Knaresborough Castle keep, which stands among flower-beds in the town park. The castle was a stronghold of Henry IV (1399-1413), who ordered the deposed Richard II (1377-1399) to be imprisoned here. Richard was, however, soon removed to Pontefract Castle, where he died so mysteriously that rumours that he had escaped and was still alive were current 15 years after his burial.

The Palm House

Knutsford

Cheshire **Map: p238 A2.**
One early visitor here is said to have been Canute (1016-1035), the Dane who became King of England. He is supposed to have forded the stream here and given his name to the crossing around which the town eventually grew.

Lancaster Castle

Lancashire **Map: p240 D3.** *Castle not open.*
Lancaster Castle was one of the strongholds which Richard I (1189-1199), being over-generous, gave to his younger brother King John (1199-1216), making him so powerful that his own throne was threatened when he was out of England on the crusades. John lived here like a king — and plotted to be one. Unlike most ancient castles, Lancaster still has prisoners, for today it holds the county court and gaol.

Little of John's castle remains, however, for it was substantially rebuilt by John of Gaunt, Duke of Lancaster, a son of Edward III (1327-1377), after Robert Bruce (1306-1329) attacked it and burned the town to the ground in 1322. The gatehouse that John of Gaunt built still stands today. Henry I (1100-1135) seized the castle in 1102 when he was crushing the power of the rebel barons at the start of his reign.

Lanercost Priory

Cumbria **Map: p243 F5.** *Open Mon to Sat daily, Sun afternoons. Closed public holidays.*
Edward I (1272-1307) spent some months at Lanercost Priory during the winter of 1306, with his second Queen, Margaret of France. He was recovering from the dysentery that attacked him as he set out to fight Robert Bruce (1306-1329) Most of the priory, founded in the 12th century, is now in ruins, but the nave of the 13th-century priory church is still in use.

Launceston

Cornwall **Map: p232 D3.** *Castle open Mon to Sat daily, Sun afternoons. Closed public holidays.*
Robert of Mortain, half-brother of William the Conqueror (1066-1087), had a stronghold at Launceston, which was mentioned in the Domesday Book. However, the present ruined castle dates from the 12th and 13th centuries. Richard, Earl of Cornwall, brother of Henry III (1216-1272), constructed the round tower and the shell-keep surrounding it, an unusual design in England.

Ledbury

Hereford & Worcester **Map: p234 A1.** *Ledbury Park not open.*
Royalists and Roundheads fought in the streets of Ledbury early on market day, 22 April 1645. The Royalists, headed by Prince Rupert, nephew of Charles I (1625-1649), had surprised the Round-heads in the town, led by Colonel Edward Massey, after marching through the night. After the battle Prince Rupert made Ledbury Park, a half-timbered mansion, his headquarters.

The Biddulph family owned the house from 1680 and Queen Victoria (1837-1901) stayed here as a child.

Leeds

West Yorkshire **Map: p238 C1.** *House open Tue to Sun daily. Closed Mon.*
When Elizabeth I (1558-1603) began her reign, Temple Newsham House near Leeds became the centre of Roman Catholic plots to put Mary, Queen of Scots (1542-1567), and her husband, Henry Stuart, Lord Darnley, on the throne of England. Darnley — a great-nephew of Henry VIII (1509-1547) — was born here in 1545.

The mansion, which stands in a huge park five miles outside Leeds, is mainly Jacobean. It now displays works of art belonging to the city of Leeds.

Leeds Castle

Kent **Map: p235 G3.** *Castle open Apr to Sept daily, except Mons in Apr, May; Oct to Mar: weekends only.*
On 13 October 1321, Isabella of France, Queen of Edward II (1307-1327), was on her way to Canterbury when, on reaching Leeds Castle, she asked if she might stay the night, but was refused admittance. Even Edward, a far from attentive husband, could not ignore such an insult. He raised a large troop of soldiers and besieged the castle which surrendered on 31 October.

A century later two royal ladies passed some time in custody at Leeds Castle, accused of witchcraft. Joan of Navarre, widow of Henry IV (1399-1413), spent the last months of a three-year imprisonment here, until her release in 1422. Eleanor, the 'Lady of Gloucester', mistress, then wife of Humphrey, Duke of Gloucester, uncle of Henry VI (1422-1461), was found guilty of 'necromancy, witchcraft, heresy and treason' and was lucky to escape with her life.

The romantic castle of today is largely a 19th-century reconstruction, although parts of the earlier medieval fortress can still be seen.

Leek

Staffordshire **Map: p238 B3.**
Bonnie Prince Charlie, the Young Pretender, grandson of James II (1685-1688), rode into Leek at the head of his Highland army in 1745 on his way south. He hoped to reach London, depose George II (1727-1760) and give the crown to his father, the Old Pretender. But at Derby his generals persuaded him, against his will, to turn back.

Leicester

Leicestershire **Map: p238 C4.** *Castle gardens open daily.*
Little is left of Leicester's Norman castle, built on the site of a Saxon stronghold, although its central mound can still be seen. The Great Hall of the castle is now contained in the Crown Court building, which dates from the 18th century. Simon de Montfort, Earl of Leicester, leader of the barons' rebellion against Henry III (1216-1272) and often called the father of the Parliamentary system, once held Leicester Castle. In the 14th century it became one of John of Gaunt's strongest fortresses. His son, Henry IV (1399-1413), hearing news of the rising against him led by the Welsh prince, Owain Glyndwr, in 1400, as he returned from a campaign in Scotland gathered a fresh army at Leicester to march against the Welsh.

The church of St Mary de Castro, founded in 1068, was once the castle chapel. Henry VI (1422-1461) would have worshipped here in 1459 when he celebrated Christmas at Leicester.

Lewes

East Sussex **Map: p235 F4.** *Castle open Mon to Sat daily; Apr to Oct: Sun afternoons also. Barbican House (Lewes museum) open Mon to Sat daily.*
An impetuous cavalry charge by Prince Edward, later Edward I (1272-1307), carried him off the field for more than two hours and effectively lost Henry III (1216-1272) the Battle of Lewes in 1264. When the Prince returned from chasing the fleeing enemy's left wing, the fighting was over and his father was a prisoner of Simon de Montfort, Earl of Leicester. The barons, led by de Montfort, were fighting to restore some of the rights granted by the Magna Carta in 1215, but disregarded by Henry. However, the victory at Lewes achieved far more. While he held the King prisoner for the next 15 months de Montfort created a council of barons, knights and burgesses to govern the country. It was the forerunner of Parliamentary government.

Only part of the Norman keep of Lewes Castle, where Edward stayed before the battle, can be seen today. Much of what remains is 19th-century restoration. The medieval priory where Henry camped with the infantry has long vanished, but Anne of Cleves's house in the suburb of Southover, built in the 16th century, was part of the priory of Lewes. After the Dissolution of the Monasteries Henry VIII (1509-1547) gave it to his fourth wife when she agreed to divorce him after six months of marriage. It is now a museum.

Lincoln

Lincoln Cathedral

Lincolnshire **Map: p238 D2.** *Castle open daily. Closed Sun mornings Nov to Mar. Cathedral Treasury open Mon to Sat daily.*

Lincoln has a long and important history. It was a Roman colonial town, *Lindum Colonia*, and the base of the renowned Ninth Legion. The Danes made it one of the five principal boroughs of the Danelaw and in 1068 the Normans built the castle on part of the site of the Roman town. William the Conqueror (1066-1087) appointed the first Norman bishop, Remigius, to the see of Lincoln.

After most of his army had fled at the approach of a much stronger force, Stephen (1135-1154) fought on foot outside the walls of Lincoln Castle in early January 1141, supported by a small band of resolute men. The castle was held for Matilda, Stephen's cousin and rival for the crown. Stephen was eventually defeated, deposed and imprisoned in Bristol Castle. The citizens of Lincoln were massacred for supporting Stephen and Matilda was declared Queen. She proved so ruthless, however, that she was herself deposed within the year and Stephen was recrowned at Canterbury on Christmas Day. Three years later Stephen celebrated Christmas most splendidly at the castle. Prince Louis of France besieged it in 1216 in support of barons rebelling against John (1199-1216), who relieved the siege a month before he died.

Edward I (1272-1307) and his Queen, Eleanor of Castile, are most closely associated with Lincoln. They attended the consecration of the new east end of the cathedral in 1280. Eleanor's body was brought to Lincoln for embalming after her death 10 years later from fever at Harby. In 1301 Edward declared his son, Edward, Prince of Wales at a Parliament held in the chapter house of Lincoln Cathedral. The chair in which he probably sat so long ago is still here.

Lindfield

West Sussex **Map: p235 E4.** *'Old Place' not open.*
Part of the rambling, timber-framed house called Old Place, with its many later additions, is a timber cottage, which is said to have been a hunting lodge of Henry VII (1485-1509).

Littlecote

Wiltshire **Map: p233 H1.** *Open Apr to June: weekend and bank holiday Mon afternoons; July to Sept: all afternoons.*
Henry VIII (1509-1547) is said to have courted Jane Seymour at this great Elizabethan manor house. She married him 11 days after Anne Boleyn's execution in 1536, but died the following year giving birth to Edward VI (1547-1553).

Little Gidding

Cambridgeshire **Map: p239 E5.**
The Ferrar family of Little Gidding paid dearly for their friendship with Charles I (1625-1649). In 1647 their house and the church they had restored here were smashed by Puritan zealots and their small religious community of skilled book-binders was dispersed. The King visited the family twice — in 1633, as he travelled north for his coronation in Scotland, and again 10 years later, when Civil War seemed inevitable.

London

See pages 166-173.

Long Crendon

Buckinghamshire **Map: p234 D2.** *Court House open Apr to Sept: Wed afternoons, weekend afternoons.*
One of the properties given to Catherine of Aragon by Henry VIII (1509-1547) was the fine medieval Court House at Long Crendon.

Longleat House

Wiltshire **Map: p233 G2.** *Open Easter to Sept: daily; Oct to Easter: Mon to Sat daily. Closed Christmas.*
Longleat — the first Renaissance mansion to be built in England — now looks from the outside much as it did when Elizabeth I (1558-1603) visited in 1574. The interior was redecorated in the 19th century in more opulent style; only the Great Hall remains substantially Elizabethan. In 1789 Longleat attracted its first large crowd, when 30,000 local people turned out to cheer George III (1760-1820), Queen Charlotte and three of their daughters, who stayed here for two nights. Now the house and the wildlife park have an average of 250,000 visitors each year.

Long Melford

Suffolk **Map: p235 G1.** *Melford Hall open Apr to Sept: Wed, Thur, Sun afternoons; public holidays.*
Sir William Cordell, a rich lawyer, was Master of the Rolls to both Mary I (1553-1558) and Elizabeth I (1558-1603). He was granted Melford Manor, country home of the abbots of Bury St Edmunds, by Henry VIII (1509-1547) at the Dissolution of the Monasteries (1536).

Loseley House

Surrey **Map: p235 E3.** *Open June to Sept: Wed to Sat afternoons; summer bank holiday Mons.*
Elizabeth I (1558-1603) stayed at Loseley House, near Guildford, on at least three occasions. The owner, Sir William More, was one of her most trusted advisers. James I (1603-1625) and his Queen, Anne of Denmark, visited Loseley in 1603 and 1606 and Charles I (1625-1649) in 1617, as Prince of Wales. Queen Mary, wife of George V (1910-1936), visited the house in 1932.

Lostwithiel

Cornwall **Map: p232 C4.**
Charles I (1625-1649) took so many Roundhead prisoners — about 6,000 — after the Battle of Lostwithiel on 2 September 1644 that he had no choice but to free them after they had promised not to fight again until they reached Portsmouth.

Ludlow

Salop **Map: p237 F3.** *Castle open Mon to Sat daily. Closed Christmas, New Year.*
Ludlow castle, built in the 11th century on a crag overlooking the River Teme, saw its stormiest days during the Middle Ages when it was perpetually garrisoned against the Welsh. In 1310 Roger Mortimer, the lover of Isabella, Queen of Edward II (1307-1327), owned it. Richard, Duke of York, father of Edward IV, inherited it in 1424. During the Wars of the Roses the castle was the scene of much treachery, then in 1472, Edward IV (1461-1483) set up a court of the Marches at Ludlow to administer justice in Wales and sent his two infant sons here as a royal presence. Later they were mysteriously murdered in the Tower.

Arthur, the sickly elder brother of Henry VIII (1509-1547), who married Catherine of Aragon in 1501 when he was 15, died at Ludlow Castle. The

Loseley House

young Princess Mary, later Mary I (1553-1558), daughter of Catherine's second marriage, with Henry VIII, lived at Ludlow from 1525 to 1528. The castle escaped damage during the Civil War when it was held by the Royalists. It started to fall into ruin after the lead was removed from its roof during the reign of George I (1714-1727).

Lullingstone Castle

Kent **Map p235 F3.** *Open Apr to Sept: weekends, bank holiday Mon afternoons. Grounds open Wed, Thur, Fri afternoons also.*
A Tudor gatehouse, built around 1497, leads to a red-brick house of 18th-century aspect, which conceals an essentially Tudor interior. Queen Anne (1702-1714) is said to have visited Lullingstone Castle several times and the early-18th-century alterations to the interior were carried out by her host, Percival Hart, who was a great admirer of the Stuarts and a keen Jacobite.

Lumley Castle

Durham **Map: p243 H5.** *Not open.*
John, Baron Lumley, courtier to Mary I (1553-1558), Elizabeth I (1558-1603) and James I (1603-1625), was so proud of his descent that he erected three monuments with lengthy Latin inscriptions detailing his family tree, in churches in Cheam, where he is buried, Chester-le-Street and at Lumley Castle itself.

Luton Hoo

Bedfordshire **Map: p235 E1.** *Open Apr to mid-Oct: Mon, Wed, Thur, Sat, daily; Sun afternoons.*
The present mansion is less than a century old, but there have been important houses at Luton Hoo for nearly 700 years. It was at a ball here in the winter of 1891 that Prince Albert, Duke of Clarence, the elder son of Edward VII (1901-1910), then Prince of Wales, became engaged to Princess Mary of Teck.

Lutterworth

Leicestershire **Map: p238 C5.** *Stanford Hall open Easter to Sept: Thur, weekend afternoons, public holidays.*
When Henry, Cardinal of York, died in 1807 the royal Stuart male line came to an end. In his will the Cardinal bequeathed the crown jewels, which James II had taken with him to France when he fled from England in 1688, to the Prince Regent, later George IV (1820-1830). Many of his other possessions, including some fine Stuart portraits, can be seen on display at Stanford Hall, which is not far from Lutterworth.

Lydford

Devon **Map: p232 D3.** *Castle open Mon to Sat daily, Sun afternoons.*
A stark, square tower on an artificial mound, Lydford Castle is believed to have been built in the 13th century by Richard, Earl of Cornwall, brother of Henry III (1216-1272). It contains a mouldering dungeon.

Lyme Regis

Lyme Regis

Dorset **Map: p233 F3.**
James, Duke of Monmouth, illegitimate son of Charles II (1660-1685), landed at Lyme in 1685 in the hope of overthrowing his Roman Catholic uncle, James II (1685-1688). The rebellion was quashed a month later.

The suffix Regis (meaning 'of the king') in the town's name dates from the time of Edward I (1272-1307). He sailed from the town's harbour to make war on France in the 13th century.

Maiden Castle

Dorset **Map: p233 G3.** *Open any time.*
The scene at Maiden Castle now is of circles of 125-ft high grassed ramparts, half a mile in length, enclosing an area of 50 acres. It is one of the largest Iron Age earthworks in Europe. Fortified with wooden stockades on every rampart, the castle, near Dorchester, would have been a formidable fortress. Yet it was stormed and taken in AD 44 by soldiers of the 2nd Augustan Legion led by their general, Vespasian, who became emperor of Rome 25 years later.

Maidstone

Kent **Map: p235 F3.** *Castle open afternoons. Manor House Museum open Mon to Sat.*
Rumours of a royal divorce were spreading in 1527 when Henry VIII (1509-1547) visited Allington Castle, near Maidstone, and stayed to meet Cardinal Wolsey. The little, moated, 13th-century castle was the home of the poet Sir Thomas Wyatt, who had been since childhood a friend of Anne Boleyn, Henry's second Queen, and was probably her lover before the King claimed her. The castle has now been extensively restored and is a retreat centre run by the Carmelite order.

Malmesbury

Wiltshire **Map: p233 G1.** *Abbey open daily.*
Malmesbury Abbey grew from a hermitage built on the site in the 7th century. It was built and endowed by Athelstan (AD 925-939), who was brought from Gloucester to be buried here. Only the massive 12th-century nave of the Benedictine

abbey church now remains. The Castle Hotel now stands on the site of a Norman castle.

Malvern

Hereford & Worcester **Map: p234 B1.** *Little Malvern Court open May to Sept: By appointment, Mrs Berrington: Hanley-Swan 310202. Malvern Spa at St Anne's Well open May to Oct: daily.*
The west window in Great Malvern Priory Church was given by Richard III (1483-1485) before he was King. The north transept window, with its brilliant yellows, was presented by the man who defeated Richard and took his crown at Bosworth (1485) — Henry VII (1485-1509). The window was ordered when Henry visited Malvern with his Queen, Elizabeth of York, and sons around 1500. They stayed in rooms over the priory gatehouse. This and the church are all that remain of the Benedictine priory founded in 1085.

Royal health-seekers have concentrated their attention on Malvern Wells, where for centuries springs and wells attracted the sick. In 1831 Queen Victoria (1837-1901) rode on a donkey up to St Ann's Well to sample the waters. Princess Mary of Teck, later Queen of George V (1910-1936), visited in 1891.

Manchester

Lancashire **Map: p238 B2.**
In 1745 the city was occupied by Bonnie Prince Charlie, the Young Pretender, grandson of James II (1685-1688), who was marching south at the head of a 5,000-strong army of Highlanders in the hope of driving George II (1727-1760) from his throne and restoring it to the house of Stuart. Only in Manchester was there any significant English support for his cause.

Manchester Cathedral

Mapledurham House

Oxfordshire **Map: p234 D3.** *Open Easter to Sept: weekend afternoons; public holidays.*
Elizabeth I (1558-1603) was entertained in this fine, pink-brick manor house beside the Thames at Mapledurham. Her host, Sir Michael Blount, built the house between 1581 and 1612; his descendants still live here.

London

Map: p235 E2.

On the evidence of excavation, London was created by the Romans and so, for the first 350 years of its existence, was not a royal but an imperial city. It had the largest forum and basilica north of the Alps. During the 5th and 6th centuries its history is obscure, but the first hint of a royal connection comes in AD 604 when Ethelbert, King of Kent (AD 560-616), with the assent of his nephew, Sebert, ruler of the East Saxons, built a cathedral dedicated to St Paul on the westernmost of the city's twin hills. It is possible that the walls of the Roman fort in the northwest corner of the city may have been adapted for a Saxon palace. Alfred the Great (AD 871-899) ordered the walls of London to be repaired in AD 886 and we know that Edward the Confessor (1042-1046), the last undisputed Saxon ruler, had a residence within the walls of the city of London. He left it in about 1052, moving westwards to live beside the new minster he was building; this, in time, gave its name, Westminster, to a separate city with its own royal connections.

William the Conqueror (1066-1087) was crowned in Edward's Abbey on Christmas Day 1066; though London was not yet the undisputed capital — Winchester, of great importance in Saxon times, was still a rival — Westminster was, without question, a major royal seat, and every one of the 40 monarchs who have reigned — and the 38 who have been crowned since — has had some connection with London, 'the flower of cities all.'

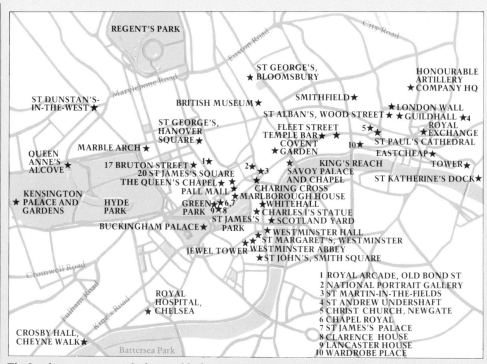

ROYAL ENGLAND

REGENT'S PARK

ST GEORGE'S, ★ BLOOMSBURY

HONOURABLE ARTILLERY ★ COMPANY HQ

ST DUNSTAN'S-IN-THE-WEST ★

BRITISH MUSEUM ★

SMITHFIELD ★

ST ALBAN'S, WOOD STREET ★ ★ LONDON WALL
★ GUILDHALL ★ ★4

ST GEORGE'S, HANOVER SQUARE ★

FLEET STREET
TEMPLE BAR ★ ★ 5 ★ ROYAL ★ EXCHANGE
COVENT 10 ★ ST PAUL'S CATHEDRAL
★ GARDEN EASTCHEAP ★

MARBLE ARCH ★

QUEEN ANNE'S ★ ALCOVE

17 BRUTON STREET ★ 1 ★
20 ST JAMES'S SQUARE
THE QUEEN'S CHAPEL ★ ★
PALL MALL ★

2 ★ ★3 KING'S REACH TOWER ★
SAVOY PALACE
AND CHAPEL ST KATHERINE'S DOCK ★
CHARING CROSS
MARLBOROUGH HOUSE
★ WHITEHALL

KENSINGTON ★ PALACE AND GARDENS

HYDE PARK

GREEN ★ 6,7 ★ CHARLES I'S STATUE
PARK 9 ★ 8 ★ SCOTLAND YARD
ST JAMES'S PARK

BUCKINGHAM PALACE ★

★ ★ WESTMINSTER HALL
★ ★ ST MARGARET'S, WESTMINSTER
JEWEL TOWER WESTMINSTER ABBEY
★ ST JOHN'S, SMITH SQUARE

ROYAL HOSPITAL, ★ CHELSEA

CROSBY HALL, CHEYNE WALK ★

Battersea Park

1 ROYAL ARCADE, OLD BOND ST
2 NATIONAL PORTRAIT GALLERY
3 ST MARTIN-IN-THE-FIELDS
4 ST ANDREW UNDERSHAFT
5 CHRIST CHURCH, NEWGATE
6 CHAPEL ROYAL
7 ST JAMES'S PALACE
8 CLARENCE HOUSE
9 LANCASTER HOUSE
10 WARDROBE PLACE

The London entries are picked out in black

BRITISH MUSEUM

Open Mon to Sat daily, Sun afternoons.

Established by lottery in 1757, the museum first occupied Old Montague House. When George IV (1820-1830) gave it the old Royal Library collection at his succession, the museum had to be rebuilt by Sir Robert Smirke. The books are still housed in the handsome King's Library. The galleries house the Sutton Hoo treasure, the unparalleled grave-goods of a nameless Anglo-Saxon ruler from Essex.

17 BRUTON STREET

Queen Elizabeth II was born here on 21 April 1926. The house had been built by John Shepherd, probably with the help and advice of his brother the architect, Edward Shepherd, in 1742. It was demolished without thought in 1937 and its place taken by Berkeley Square House; a small plaque reminds us of the Queen's birthplace.

BUCKINGHAM PALACE

See pages 80-83.

CHAPEL ROYAL

The Chapel of St James's Palace was built for Henry VIII (1509-1547) during the 1530s. The ceiling is panelled in octagons and crosses with decorations traditionally ascribed to Holbein. Many royal marriages have taken place here including those of Princess Mary, daughter of Charles I (1625-1649), to the Prince of Orange in

1641; Princess Mary, daughter of James II (1685-1688), to William, Prince of Orange in 1677; Princess Anne to Prince George of Denmark in 1683; George III (1760-1820) to Princess Charlotte in 1761; George, Prince of Wales, afterwards George IV (1820-1830), to Caroline of Brunswick in 1795; Queen Victoria (1837-1901) to Prince Albert in 1840; their eldest daughter, the Princess Royal, to the Crown Prince of Prussia in 1858; the Duke of York, afterwards George V (1910-1936), to Princess Mary of Teck in 1893. Another, less exalted marriage took place here in 1676: that of Sir Christopher Wren to his second wife, Jane Fitzwilliam.

CHARING CROSS

Eleanor, Queen of Edward I (1272-1307), died in 1290 on her way to Scotland on a campaign with her husband. Her body was sent back to London for burial in Westminster Abbey, a cross being raised at each place where the funeral cortège

Charing Cross station

rested for the night. Charing Cross was very handsome; costing £650 (Waltham Cross cost £95), the stone was brought from Caen and the best sculptors of the day, William of Ireland and Alexander of Abingdon, worked on the eight figures of the Queen. The cross was destroyed in 1647 by order of Parliament; after the Restoration, a statue of Charles I (1625-1649) was set up on the site. In 1863, the London, Chatham and Dover Railway Company erected a new cross at a cost of £1,800 in the forecourt of its railway terminus.

CHARLES I'S STATUE, WHITEHALL

A bronze equestrian statue of Charles I (1625-1649) sits at the Trafalgar Square end of Whitehall, looking towards the spot outside the Banqueting House where he was executed. The work of Hubert le Sueur, it was concealed during the Commonwealth and brought out in triumph at the Restoration, to be installed on the original Charing Cross site in 1675. On 30 January every year (the anniversary of the King's execution) a short service is held at the statue and wreaths are laid by historical groups.

CHRIST CHURCH, NEWGATE

Only a tower remains of Wren's church that was built to replace the original church of the Franciscans or Grey Friars, destroyed in the Great Fire of London in 1666. Three Queens were buried in the medieval building — Margaret, daughter of Philippe le Hardi, King of France and second wife of Edward I (1272-1307), Isabella, daughter of Philippe le Bel, King of France and wife to Edward II (1307-1327), and Joan, daughter of Edward and Isabella and wife of David Bruce, King of Scots (1329-1371), Robert Bruce's son and successor. Here, too, was buried Roger Mortimer, Earl of March, Isabella's paramour, who was implicated in her husband's death and who was himself executed in 1330 when Edward III (1327-1377), son of Edward II and Isabella, came to power.

CLARENCE HOUSE

Not open.
The house was built by John Nash between 1825 and 1827 for the future William IV (1830-1837) while he was still Duke of Clarence, and is virtually a part of St James's Palace. Now the home of Queen Elizabeth the Queen Mother, it was from here that Lady Diana Spencer went to her wedding in St Paul's Cathedral on 29 July 1981. Clarence House was the London residence of Elizabeth II after her marriage and before her accession, and Princess Anne was born here on 15 August 1950.

Clarence House

COVENT GARDEN

Open daily.
Land formerly belonging to Westminster Abbey was given by Henry VIII (1509-1547) to John, Baron Russell, later the Earl of Bedford, in 1541; a century later, it was developed by his great-grandson, the 4th Earl of Bedford. In 1630 Charles I (1625-1649) granted permission for this on condition that Inigo Jones, the Surveyor of the King's Work, was employed as architect. The land was laid out as London's first square, with St Paul's Covent Garden, 'the noblest barn in Christendom', as the main building. Almost at once, fruit and vegetable stalls assembled in the open space in the centre and the Earl was granted a market charter in 1670 by Charles II (1660-1685). The present buildings were begun in 1830 by the 6th Duke to designs by Charles Fowler. The present Opera House, so often visited by Queen Victoria (1837-1901), was built to designs by E. M. Barry in 1858; the Queen found the blue lamp of Bow Street Police Station too distorting a colour and so it was changed for a white one. The market closed in 1972 and was transferred to Nine Elms. The old buildings have now been retained and transformed into a shopping precinct.

CROSBY HALL, CHEYNE WALK

Originally, this was the Bishopsgate house of Sir John Crosby, an influential city merchant in the 15th century. The Duke of Gloucester was offered the throne there in 1482 and was proclaimed Richard III (1483-1485). In 1908 the old hall, which had been put to many uses over the years, was carefully taken down and re-erected at Chelsea, where today it serves as the headquarters of the Federation of University Women.

EASTCHEAP

The Boar's Head Tavern stood on the south side of Eastcheap. It was claimed to have been the rendezvous of the future Henry V (1413-1422) with Sir John Falstaff and his other drinking companions. All traces of the building vanished when London Bridge was rebuilt in the 1830s.

FLEET STREET

Prince Henry's Room, 17 Fleet Street, open afternoons only.
Number 17 Fleet Street survives from the early 17th century. Originally a tavern, The Prince's Arms, the first-floor room has fine panelling and a handsome plasterwork ceiling, enlivened with flowers and Prince of Wales feathers. Known to Charles Dickens as a waxworks museum in the mid-19th century, it was saved from destruction by the London County Council in 1898.

On the first floor of 143/144 Fleet Street is a stone statue of Mary, Queen of Scots (1542-1567), who, in fact, never visited London. It was placed here by an admirer of the unfortunate Queen, Sir John George Tollemache Sinclair.

GREEN PARK

Open daily.
The park takes its name from the absence of flowers. Along the southern boundary of this triangle of land runs Constitution Hill, where Charles II (1660-1685) loved to walk, whilst its eastern edge is Queen's Walk, laid out for the consort of George II (1727-1760), Caroline of Ansbach. At the Peace of Aix-la-Chapelle (1749), a fireworks display was given in Green Park for which Handel, George's favourite composer, wrote his Fireworks Music. Similar celebrations, to the designs of John Nash, were held in 1814 when it was believed that Napoleon had been safely confined on Elba; in fact he escaped and the wars with France did not end until after the Battle of Waterloo (1815).

GUILDHALL

Great Hall open Mon to Sat daily. Closed public holidays.
The administrative centre of the City of London, the Guildhall was built in 1411; John Croxton was

Covent Garden Market Piazza

The Guildhall

the architect. This Great Hall may be considered the City's equivalent of the King's Great Hall at Westminster, to which alone it is second in size — the Guildhall measures 52ft by 49ft. At intervals during the Middle Ages, and regularly since the time of Charles II (1660-1685), the sovereign has been entertained here by the citizens of London. Charles II feasted here when Sir Robert Vyner was Lord Mayor. The story goes that the company was good and the wine, possibly, even better. When the King rose to leave, the mayor hauled him back from the door, swearing that he should drink another glass with the company. Charles shrugged good-naturedly and, remarking 'He who is drunk is as great as a king', returned to the table and the conviviality. It is now the custom to entertain the sovereign here at the Lord Mayor's banquet in coronation years and on other special occasions.

HONOURABLE ARTILLERY COMPANY'S HEADQUARTERS, CITY ROAD

The HAC is Britain's oldest regiment — its origins can be traced back to the companies of archers in the reign of Edward III (1327-1377) and it was granted a charter by Henry VIII (1509-1547) in 1537. It acquired its present grounds in 1641 and Armoury House was built here in 1735; the embattled gatehouse is Victorian. Milton, Pepys and Wren were all members of the Company, which has the right to march through the City with drums beating, colours flying and bayonets fixed, together with the honour of firing royal salutes from the Tower battery.

HYDE PARK

Open daily.
Known in Saxon times as the manor of Eia (hence Hyde), the land here belonged to Westminster Abbey. In 1536 it passed to the crown. James I (1603-1625) opened it to the public and, in his grandson's day, it became most fashionable to drive around it, seeing and being seen; Pepys, assured by his wife that he 'looked mighty noble', went riding here on May Day 1666 wearing 'painted gloves, very pretty and all the mode'. Rotten Row, along the southern boundary of the park, leads to Kensington Palace; the Serpentine, flowing along the western and southern sides, was diverted on Queen Caroline's orders from the River Westbourne. The Great Exhibition of 1851, brainchild of Prince Albert and Sir Henry Cole, stood just north of the southern carriage drive opposite Prince of Wales Gate; so profitable was the venture that the exhibition committee were able to buy 87 acres of land in Kensington on which, eventually, Imperial College, the Victoria and Albert Museum, the Albert Hall, the Natural History Museum, the Science Museum, the Geological Museum and several other institutions were built. In July 1981, a fireworks display was given in the park on the eve of the forthcoming marriage of the Prince of Wales and Lady Diana Spencer.

JEWEL TOWER

Open Mon to Sat daily.
One of the few morsels of the medieval Palace of

The Queen and King Faisal in Hyde Park during his state visit in 1967

Westminster to have survived the fire of 1834, the Jewel Tower had been built in 1366 to house the state robes and dearest personal possessions of monarchs from Edward III (1327-1377) to Henry VIII (1509-1547). In the inventory made after Henry's death, there is a reference to dolls being stored here, possibly the treasured belongings of his daughters, Mary and Elizabeth, two future Queens. Between 1621 and 1864, the old tower was used to store parliamentary records, and from 1869 until 1938 it served as the Weights and Measures Office. It has now been restored and is open to the public as a historic monument.

KENSINGTON PALACE AND GARDENS

State apartments open Mon to Sat daily, Sun afternoons. Gardens open daily.
Built in the first years of the 17th century, Kensington House was bought by Mary II (1689-1694) from Lord Nottingham in 1689 for £18,000; she hoped that the asthma from which her husband, William III (1689-1702), suffered might be assuaged by the clear air found here. Wren enlarged the little house into a palace for the couple, adding a King's wing and a Queen's wing. Both monarchs died here, Mary cruelly young in 1694, and William in 1702. Queen Anne (1702-1714) commissioned Vanbrugh to build her an orangery, a 'summer supper house', in the grounds, and George I (1714-1727) and George II (1727-1760) remodelled the core of the palace,

providing it with grander state rooms. George I's courtiers, painted by William Kent, still look down from the walls of the King's Staircase. It was here that Queen Victoria (1837-1901) was born and brought up by her widowed mother, the Duchess of Kent; it was also here that she learnt about the death of her uncle, William IV

Kensington Palace

(1830-1837), and realized that she was Queen of England. Princess Mary of Teck, future Consort of George V (1910-1936), grew up here, too. In the southeastern corner of the gardens, long since opened to the public, the Albert Memorial was built for Victoria's beloved husband. Sir Gilbert Scott designed it; the seated statue of the prince is by John Foley; the book in Albert's hand is the catalogue of his beloved Great Exhibition and he gazes across at the Royal Albert Hall. Nearer to the palace, on the Broad Walk facing the Round Pond, is another statue, this time of Victoria herself as a young woman; it is the work of her daughter, Princess Louise, who was a gifted sculptor. Kensington Palace is still a royal home; it is today the London residence of the Prince and Princess of Wales, Princess Margaret, the Duke and Duchess of Gloucester, the Duke and Duchess of Kent and Prince and Princess Michael of Kent.

KING'S REACH

The stretch of the River Thames between London Bridge and Westminster Bridge is called the King's Reach. It was so named in 1935 in commemoration of the 25 years that George V (1910-1936) had been on the throne.

LANCASTER HOUSE

State apartments open Easter to mid-Dec: weekend and bank holiday afternoons.
Built in 1825 by Benjamin Wyatt for the Duke of York, the house was sold to pay the Duke's debts after his death. The residue was used to buy land in Hackney and Poplar which was laid out between 1842 and 1845 by James Pennethorne as Victoria Park, the intention being to provide East London with the equivalent of Regent's Park. The house later became the home of the Duke and Duchess of Sutherland. The Duchess was a close personal friend of Queen Victoria (1837-1901). So magnificent was her house that the Queen used to say, when visiting, 'Now I have come from my house to your palace!' Lancaster House, which at one time housed the London Museum, is used today by government for official meetings and entertainment.

LONDON WALL

Today primarily the name of a street, the walls of London, originally part of the Roman defences, were set in repair on the orders of Alfred the Great (AD 871-899) in AD 886.

MARBLE ARCH

Designed in 1828 by John Nash as a triumphal entrance to Buckingham Palace, it proved to be too small for the state coach and was removed to its present site in 1851. The spot on which it stands is, in fact, the grim site of Tyburn gallows.

MARLBOROUGH HOUSE

Viewing by written appointment.
Built on crown land in 1710 by Wren for Sarah, Duchess of Marlborough, the house — its walls are covered with murals depicting the battles in which the Duke had been engaged — reverted to the crown in 1817. It was given to Princess Charlotte and her husband Leopold, the future King of the Belgians, but the poor Princess died in childbirth before she could occupy it. It has been a home to the widow of William IV (1830-1837),

Marlborough House

kindly Queen Adelaide; also to Edward VII (1901-1910) while he was Prince of Wales, to the future George V (1910-1936), to Queen Alexandra when widowed and to Queen Mary after the death of George V. Three of Queen Alexandra's pet dogs and her rabbit, Benny, have small tombstones in the garden. A wonderful art-nouveau memorial to that beautiful Queen is set in the wall of Marlborough House facing towards St James's Palace. It was installed in 1932 and is the work of Sir Alfred Gilbert, the sculptor of *Eros* in Piccadilly. Today, the house is used for government meetings and entertainment.

NATIONAL PORTRAIT GALLERY

Open Mon to Sat daily; Sun afternoons.
Portraits of all the British monarchs from Richard II (1377-1399) onwards are displayed in this gallery. Holbein's full-sized preliminary drawing for his mural of Henry VIII (1509-1547), which once adorned Whitehall Palace, is worth particular notice.

PALL MALL

This avenue takes its name from the pell mell gallery which Charles II (1660-1685) had laid out beside St James's Palace for the game that resembled croquet. The land on the south side is all crown property with the exception of Number 77 which is freehold. It was Nell Gwynne's house. When provided with a lease of the establishment, she sent it back saying she 'had always conveyed freely under the crown' so the King granted her a freehold. In 1671, John Evelyn confided to his diary how 'I both saw and heard a very familiar discourse between (the King) and Mrs. Nellie as they call'd an impudent comedian, she looking out of her garden on a terrace at the top of the wall and (the King) standing on the greene walke under it. I was heartily sorry at this scene.'

The site of Nell Gwynne's House, Pall Mall

QUEEN ANNE'S ALCOVE

Designed for the Queen at the same time as the orangery, Queen Anne's Alcove originally stood nearer to Kensington Palace. It has now been transferred to the northern end of the Long Water, near Lancaster Gate.

THE QUEEN'S CHAPEL

Open for Sunday services.
Designed in 1626 by Inigo Jones for Henrietta Maria, the French Catholic wife of Charles I (1625-49), this beautiful chapel was originally part of St James's Palace; it is now separated by Marlborough Road which was laid in 1809. Lord Mountbatten's body lay here the night before his funeral in Westminster Abbey in 1979.

REGENT'S PARK

Open daily.
Originally church land, Marylebone Park was appropriated by Henry VIII (1509-1547) and used

for hunting. Edward VI (1547-1553) entertained ambassadors from the King of France here, and Elizabeth I (1558-1603) provided hunting for ambassadors from the Tsar of Russia. Disparked during the Commonwealth, its acres were used as farmland till 1811 when Nash, encouraged and supported by the future George IV (1820-1830), laid them out as Regent's Park. The centre of the Inner Circle used to be occupied by the Royal Botanic Society; when that was dissolved in 1932, it became known as Queen Mary's Rose Garden, due to the great interest that the consort of George V (1910-1936) took in the preservation of the area.

ROYAL ARCADE, OLD BOND STREET

Open daily.
Royal Arcade runs between Old Bond Street and Albemarle Street. Opened in 1879, the shops in the arcade have handsome plate glass windows. It was regularly patronized by Queen Victoria (1837-1901) (hence the 'Royal') who bought her riding shirts, vests and knitting wool from Brettell's.

ROYAL EXCHANGE

Not open.
Established in 1568 by Sir Thomas Gresham as a meeting place for merchants, the Exchange was visited by Elizabeth I (1558-1603) in January 1571 and thereafter was called 'Royal'.

ROYAL HOSPITAL, CHELSEA

Founded by Charles II (1660-1685) in imitation of 'Les Invalides' built by Louis XIV in Paris, the Royal Hospital has provided a place of refuge for old soldiers for nearly three centuries. In 1676, Tobias Rustat presented the King with superb bronze statues by Grinling Gibbons of himself and his brother, James, Duke of York, the future James

II (1685-1688), apparelled in Roman armour. James now stands, a little forlornly, outside the National Gallery, but Charles is cherished in the main or Figure Court of the Royal Hospital. Every year on 29 May, Oak Apple Day, the statue is wreathed in oak boughs; the ceremony commemorates the King's escape from the Roundheads after his defeat at the Battle of Worcester in 1651, when he hid in an oak tree at Boscobel and remained undetected.

ST ALBAN'S, WOOD STREET

The remains of the pre-Conquest foundation of St Alban's, Wood Street, stand in the northwest corner of the City. It is always said to have been the chapel of King Offa's palace — so far there is no certain evidence to deny or confirm the tradition. Sir John Cheke, Greek tutor to Edward VI (1547-1553), was buried here. The medieval church was destroyed in the Great Fire; Wren completed a replacement in 1685, but this was destroyed by bombs in the Blitz. Only the tower remains, standing isolated in the middle of the road.

Chelsea Pensioners at the Royal Hospital

The Royal Hospital

ST ANDREW UNDERSHAFT

Open daily.
This is one of the eight surviving pre-Fire churches. It was rebuilt in the 1520s by the parishioners, every man either giving money or actually helping on site. The flat 16th-century roofs are still in place, and several of the 130 carved bosses in the nave couple the devices of Henry VIII (1509-1547) and Catherine of Aragon — a Tudor rose and a ripe pomegranate.

ST DUNSTAN'S-IN-THE-WEST

Open daily.
With foundations dating from at least the 13th century, the present church dates from the 1830s when it had to be rebuilt in its own churchyard to comply with a road-widening scheme. Designed by John Shaw Senior, it was completed after his death by his son, also John. It is octagonal with a south tower, the parapet of which rises like a stone crown above Fleet Street. When Ludgate was demolished in 1760, statues of Elizabeth I (1558-1603), King Lud and his two sons, which used to adorn the gate, all found refuge in St Dunstan's.

ST GEORGE'S BLOOMSBURY

Open daily.
This church was built between 1716 and 1721 by Nicholas Hawksmoor. The tower which stands apart from the church is topped by a stepped pyramid, modelled on the tomb of Mausolus in Halicarnassus; on the summit of this perches a statue of George I (1714-1727) dressed in a toga and representing St George. The steeple appears in the background to Hogarth's engraving, *Gin Lane*. Horace Walpole said it was 'a masterpiece of absurdity' and wrote a quatrain:
> When Henry VIII left the Pope in the lurch
> The Protestants made him Head of the Church.
> But George's good subjects, the Bloomsbury people,
> Instead of the Church, made him head of the steeple.

ST GEORGE'S, HANOVER SQUARE

Open daily.
The church was built between 1721 and 1724 to designs by John James. On 5 December 1793, a clandestine marriage took place here between Augustus Frederick, Duke of Sussex, and Lady Augusta Murray. Banns had been properly called for three previous Sundays, the young couple having given their names as Mr Frederick and Miss Murray, but the union was promptly annulled under the Royal Marriages Act — the first occasion of it being brought into force. The Duke always considered that he was married, however, and did not remarry until after Lady Augusta's death.

ST JAMES'S PALACE AND PARK

Park open daily.
Henry VIII (1509-1547) acquired the land here in 1532 from the Hospital of St James, a foundation

for the care of 'leprous maidens'. He razed the old building, enclosed the surrounding land and built St James's Palace in its place. Of the original building the Presence Chamber, Chapel Royal and Guard Room still remain, along with the great brick gatehouse — one of the most celebrated landmarks in London. The Armoury and Tapestry rooms, although re-decorated by William Morris in 1866 and 1867, still contain their original Tudor fireplaces. The last changes to the building were effected by Sir Christopher Wren, who enlarged and modernized the palace, in particular adding a magnificent staircase.

Rich with royal associations, the palace has witnessed the births of Charles II (1660-1685), James II (1685-1688), Mary II (1689-1694), Queen Anne (1702-1714), and George IV (1820-1830), as well as housing Edward VI (1547-1553), Mary I (1553-1558), and Elizabeth I (1558-1603). After the Restoration Charles II made the palace his principal residence, and it was under his supervision that St James's Park came into

St Katharine's Dock

St James's Palace

existence. Laid out along the lines of Versailles, it is a modest imitation of the French King's gardens. On its opening, the Russian ambassador presented Charles with a pair of pelicans for his menagerie, after which Birdcage Walk is named. The lake was remodelled for George IV by John Nash, as was The Mall, which now makes a stately approach to Buckingham Palace.

St James's Palace was the location of the drawing rooms of Queen Victoria (1837-1901) until 1865, and royal levées were held here up to the outbreak of World War II. Today it is occupied by the Lord Chamberlain's Department.

20 ST JAMES'S SQUARE

From 1906 until 1920, this was the London home of Lady Elizabeth Bowes-Lyon, the future consort of George VI (1936-1952).

ST JOHN'S, SMITH SQUARE

Open daily.
This building was designed by Thomas Archer and built between 1714 and 1728. The story — almost certainly apocryphal — goes that the architect told Queen Anne (1702-1714) that he was seeking inspiration. She promptly kicked over her footstool and told him to find it there, which accounts for its square shape and four towers.

ST KATHARINE'S DOCK

Just to the east of the Tower, there stood, in the Middle Ages, the Hospital of St Katharine, a charity founded in 1148 by Matilda, Stephen's Queen, and re-founded by Queen Eleanor. Being under the special protection of the queens of England, it escaped the Dissolution of the Monasteries (1536) and good works continued there until 1828, when it was closed and the site excavated for St Katharine's Dock. The dock has now also closed and been redeveloped as a marina and tourist area, with a public house called the Dickens Inn. The Royal foundation of St Katharine is now established in Butcher Row, E14. The chapel there contains some of the original medieval carved stalls depicting the heads of Edward III (1327-1377) and his Queen, Philippa.

ST MARGARET'S, WESTMINSTER

Open daily.
Possibly pre-Conquest, certainly established early in the 12th century, the present church was begun in 1504 and completed by 1523. The east window has royal connections. It was commissioned by the magistrates of Dort to celebrate the marriage of Catherine of Aragon to Arthur, Prince of Wales, eldest son of Henry VII (1475-1509), but by the time the work was finished Arthur was dead and Catherine a widow. The window was an embarrassment. It was sent to Waltham Abbey and, after the Dissolution of the Monasteries (1536), passed into private hands. It was bought in 1758 by the House of Commons and set up in their own church where it may be seen today. St Margaret's has other royal connections. Blanche Parry, nursemaid and faithful personal maid to Elizabeth I (1558-1603), was buried here when she died in 1590 at the age of 82, and Lady Mary Dudley, who served Elizabeth for 40 years, was

buried here when she died in 1605. Effigies of both women adorn their tombs. Another royal servant buried here is Cornelius van Dun, a Dutchman who was Yeoman of the Guard to Henry VIII (1509-1547), Edward VI (1547-1553), Mary I (1553-1558) and Elizabeth; when he died, aged 94 in 1577, he left money to found two small alms-houses for poor widows.

ST MARTIN-IN-THE-FIELDS

Open daily.
Founded in the 12th century, the parish was enlarged on the orders of Henry VIII (1509-1547) so that funerals did not need to pass through his Palace of Whitehall on their way to burial at St Margaret's Westminster. A new church, built in 1544, is where Charles II (1660-1685) was baptized and Nell Gwynne buried; it was rebuilt between 1722 and 1726 by James Gibbs. George I (1714-1727) was asked to be the first church-warden of the new church. Unable to find the time to fulfil the duties involved, however, he gave the church its first organ instead.

ST PAUL'S CATHEDRAL

Open daily.
Founded in AD 604 as a small wooden structure, the later stone medieval building was one of the wonders of Europe. Wren's cathedral replaced this after it was destroyed in the Great Fire in 1660. Two royal weddings have taken place here: Arthur, Prince of Wales, was married to Catherine of Aragon on 14 November 1501 in Old St Paul's, and Charles, Prince of Wales, was married to Lady Diana Spencer on 29 July 1981 in the Wren building. St Paul's is the place of official services of thanksgiving: Queen Anne (1702-1714) came here to give thanks for the victories of the Duke of Marlborough, and George III (1760-1820) also gave thanks here after his recovery from illness in 1789. Queen Elizabeth II came here in 1977 to

St Paul's Cathedral

celebrate the 25th anniversary of her accession; for the occasion, the Bishop of London wore a cope designed and embroidered by Beryl Deane with the spires of all the City of London churches. This magnificent vestment, known as the Jubilee Cope, is now on view in the recently-opened treasury in the Crypt. On 15 July 1980, a service was held here to celebrate the 80th birthday of Queen Elizabeth, the Queen Mother.

SAVOY PALACE AND CHAPEL

Open daily.
A noble house was built here by Peter of Savoy — uncle of Eleanor of Provence, who was the wife of Henry III (1216-1272) — when he came to this country in 1241. From 1351, it served as an honourable prison to John, King of France, who had been made captive by the Black Prince at the Battle of Poitiers (1356). Since his subjects could not afford his ransom, John remained here, save for one brief visit to France, until his death in 1364. By that time, the manor was the property of Blanche, sole heiress of the Lancastrian estates and patroness of Geoffrey Chaucer; at her death,

he composed *The Boke of the Duchesse*. Her widower, John of Gaunt, fled the manor when it was sacked in 1381 by Wat Tyler and his rebels, who virtually destroyed the buildings. At intervals, attempts were made to restore the building as a hospital but they met with little success and most of the buildings disappeared during the construction of Waterloo Bridge. Only the chapel remains. Built early in the 16th century, it suffered a serious fire in 1864. Queen Victoria (1837-1901) paid for its restoration (which was carried out by Sydney Smirke) and it was damaged six times during World War II. In spite of this, it now serves as the chapel for the Royal Victorian Order, a use to which it was appointed in 1937 by George VI (1936-1952).

SCOTLAND YARD

Originally a mansion lying between Whitehall and the river, Scotland Yard was used as a London residence by the Kings of Scotland when they came south to do homage for their English fiefs. Margaret, sister of Henry VIII (1509-1547) and wife of James IV of Scotland (1488-1513), was the

last monarch to use it. When the kingdoms were united under James I and VI (1567-1625), the mansion was turned into offices. Milton lodged here while he was secretary to Cromwell. The old name stuck when the site became the headquarters of the new Metropolitan Police in 1829 and was transferred when they moved to the Norman Shaw building in 1891. The police again took the name when they moved again to Broadway, Westminster, in 1967.

SMITHFIELD

In 1123, land beside the 'Smooth Field' was given by Henry I (1100-1135) to Rahere, who had been inspired by a vision, to found a hospital and a priory here. So valuable did the Londoners find them that, at the Dissolution of the Monasteries (1536), they petitioned Henry VIII (1509-1547) to refound the hospital which he did, giving it a Royal Charter. It still flourishes, the only one of London's medieval hospitals to have survived on its original site.

It was at Smithfield that the child-king, Richard II (1377-1399), had his second meeting with Wat Tyler and his rebels in 1381, which ended in the rebel leader being stabbed to death by the Lord Mayor, Sir William Walworth. It looked as if the crowd would turn violent, but the young King rode forward, declaring that he himself would be their leader, and the immediate trouble was quelled.

TEMPLE BAR

Originally a gateway set across Fleet Street at the entrance to the City, it was taken down in 1760 and rebuilt at Theobalds in Hertfordshire; its site is marked by an obelisk topped by the City griffin. When the monarch enters the City, he or she pauses here to be greeted by the Lord Mayor and be offered the City sword, which must be touched and returned; in this fashion the monarch acknowledges the freedom of the City.

WARDROBE PLACE, WARDROBE TERRACE, EC4

A house in the east of the City, built by Sir John Beauchamp, was purchased after his death by Edward III (1327-1377) and was thereafter used as a branch of the Exchequer dealing with the sovereign's personal expenses. The building vanished in the Great Fire; numbers 3-5 Wardrobe Place are early 18th century.

WESTMINSTER HALL

Open Mon to Sat: mornings only.
Erected between 1095 and 1097 for William II (1087-1100), probably on the site of a wooden Saxon royal hall, the hall, built magnificently in stone, measures 239½ft by 67½ft and was roofed in three spans supported on internal arcades. William boasted that it was 'nothing but a bedchamber' in comparison with what he planned to build, but an arrow in the New Forest ended his ambitions. Three centuries later, Richard II (1377-1399) had the walls raised and a new, single-span hammerbeam roof installed by his master mason, Henry Yeveley, and his master carpenter, Hugh Herland, using 660 tons of oak. The roof was a great technical feat of the time. It was here that Charles I (1625-1649) was tried and condemned

and where George IV (1820-1830) celebrated his coronation banquet — the last at which a Royal Champion threw down the gauntlet and offered battle on his monarch's behalf. Until the coronation of George IV, all coronation processions were marshalled in Westminster Hall; everyone then walked on a raised platform from the hall to the abbey and later returned for the coronation banquet. George V (1910-1936), George VI (1936-1952), Queen Mary and Sir Winston Churchill lay in state here after their deaths. Westminster Hall was one of the three fragments of Westminster Palace to survive the fire of 1834 and Barry's rebuilding of the Houses of Parliament; the other two were St Stephen's Chapel and the Jewel Tower.

WESTMINSTER ABBEY

Open daily.
Tradition asserts that Westminster Abbey was founded in AD 616 by Sebert, King of the East Saxons, and that it was miraculously consecrated by St Peter himself. Certainly a monastery existed here in the time of St Dunstan, who died in AD 960. In 1052, Edward the Confessor (1042-1066) decided to refound the monastery in redemption of an unfulfilled vow to make a pilgrimage to Rome. In order to hasten the work, he moved from the City to Westminster — an action with profound consequences, since it separated king from city, court from commerce and politics from mercantile power. Edward's abbey was completed in 1065; when he died in January the following year, he was buried here. His successor, Harold (1066), was crowned here, and the man whom he himself had named as the next King of England — William of Normandy — was also crowned here, on Christmas Day 1066, thus establishing the abbey as the rightful place for the ceremony. Since then, every monarch, save only Edward V (1483), who was murdered before he could be crowned, and Edward VIII (1936), who abdicated before the ceremony was due to take place, has been crowned here.

Edward the Confessor was canonized in 1161. In 1245 Henry III (1216-1272), who venerated the saint, decided to pull down the Confessor's own abbey and build a more glorious one in his honour. Of the 11th-century building, only the undercroft and the Chapel of the Pyx remain. The new building was a miracle of early English Gothic architecture with the loftiest nave in England — 104ft high. Henry chose to be buried close to Edward's tomb — a privilege reserved thereafter only for the blood royal.

Henry's rebuilding of the abbey stopped in 1265 when only the chancel, transepts and first four bays of the nave were completed. It began again in the mid-14th century; miraculously the architect, Henry Yevele, retained the earlier style. Henry VII (1485-1509) added a new chapel in place of the Lady Chapel, which was originally intended as a resting place for poor murdered Henry VI (1422-1461), a candidate for canonization. The new chapel eventually became a burial place for himself and his wife, Elizabeth of York; they both lie in a tomb by Pietro Torrigiani, the first example of Renaissance art to be created in this country. The architect of the chapel was Robert Vertue; he was responsible for the magnificent fan-vaulting, a counterfoil to the aloof simplicity of the nave. The bronze gates across the nave of the Henry VII Chapel are of particular interest.

Westminster Abbey viewed from the west

They are the work of Thomas Ducheman and are divided into 72 compartments, each filled with a heraldic device relating to the Houses of York and Lancaster, united by Henry's marriage to Elizabeth of York.

In the north chapel lie Henry VII's grand-daughters, Mary and Elizabeth Tudor, who were divided in life by their religious beliefs, but who now share a tomb. Near them is Innocents' Corner, the resting-place of several royal children, including the supposed bones of the little Princes murdered in the Tower, and Mary and Sophia, daughters of James I (1603-1625). Sophia, who lived only a few days, lies snugly in her cradle. In the south chapel, James gave his poor mother, Mary, Queen of Scots (1542-1567), a magnificent tomb. She lies between Lady Margaret Beaufort, Henry VII's mother, from whom James derived his claim to the throne and for whom Torrigiani sculpted a lifelike effigy, and her own mother-in-law, Margaret Douglas, Countess of Lennox, who was renowned for her beauty. On the southern side of the Countess' tomb, her children are shown kneeling; Henry, Lord Darnley, has a crown above his head since he became King Consort of Scotland as husband to Mary, Queen of Scots. George II (1727-1760) was the last monarch to be buried in the abbey; he requested that he should lie beside his wife, Caroline of Ansbach, and that a side should be removed from each coffin so that their dust should mingle, so dearly had they loved each other in life. The same passionate affection had united Richard II (1377-1399) and his first wife, Anne of Bohemia, who also share a tomb; their effigies, prepared in the King's lifetime, originally lay with linked hands, but vandals stole the hands from the figures.

A visit to the museum in the undercroft is essential for all those interested in England's monarchy. Here are preserved the funeral effigies carried on top of royal and noble coffins, clad in clothing worn by the living persons. Several of the heads are taken from death masks.

The building of the abbey was at last completed in 1745 when the western towers, designed by Nicholas Hawksmoor, were added. The edifice had taken five centuries to finish.

WHITEHALL

Banqueting House open Mon to Sat daily, Sun afternoons. Wine cellar viewing by written appointment only.
Originally the London residence of the arch-bishops, York Place was appropriated by Henry VIII (1509-1547) after Cardinal Wolsey's downfall. He made it his chief London seat, renaming it Whitehall. On the walls of the Presence Chamber Holbein, Henry's court painter, executed a magnficent mural, showing the monarch, his parents, Henry VII (1485-1509) and Elizabeth of York, and his third wife, Jane Seymour, the mother of Edward VI (1547-1553). Henry had a large, well-arranged wine cellar which still exists beneath the Ministry of Defence. Among the medley of Tudor apartments, James I (1603-1625) commissioned Inigo Jones to construct the Banqueting House (1619-1622), London's first classical building. Into its ceiling, Charles I (1625-1649) set nine large paintings, the central one representing *The Apotheosis of James I*, by Peter Paul Rubens, as a tribute to his father; it was beneath these paintings that he walked to his death on the scaffold in Whitehall on the bitterly cold afternoon of 30 January 1649. After the Restoration, Charles II (1660-1685), James II (1685-1688) and William (1689-1702) and Mary all occupied Whitehall; Wren constructed a flight of landing steps for Queen Mary which can still be seen behind the Ministry of Defence — they demonstrate how much wider the Thames was before embankment. Whitehall Palace suffered two serious accidental fires in 1691 and 1698; now, only the wine cellar and Banqueting House remain as a reminder of past splendour.

Whitehall viewed from St James's Park in winter

Margate

Kent **Map: p235 H3.**
As the *Prince Royal* sailed for the continent from Margate harbour in the spring of 1613, carrying Princess Elizabeth, daughter of James I (1603-1625), and her 17-year-old husband Prince Frederick, Elector Palatine of the Rhine and head of the German Protestant Union, the future must have looked bright for the newly married couple. However, Elizabeth was not to see England again for 48 years, having suffered for years as a debt-ridden refugee around the courts of Germany and later as a pensioner of the House of Orange.

Market Harborough

Leicestershire **Map: p238 D5.**
Charles I (1625-1649) had his Civil War headquarters at Market Harborough before the Battle of Naseby in 1645.

Maxstoke Castle

Warwickshire **Map: p237 H2.** *Organized parties by written appointment only.*
This red sandstone castle — built more as a home than a fortress — stands in parkland near Coleshill and has been lived in ever since it was built in the 14th century. Richard III (1483- 1485) stayed here on his way to the Battle of Bosworth (1485) and Henry Tudor, later Henry VII (1485-1509), slept here shortly afterwards.

Melksham

Wiltshire **Map: p233 G1.**
This small town was once a village surrounded by royal forest — a favourite hunting ground of the Plantagenet kings.

Melton Mowbray

Leicestershire **Map: p238 D4.**
The stone-built house, now a restaurant, next to the beautiful parish church belonged once, it is believed, to Anne of Cleves, fourth Queen of Henry VIII (1509-1547).

Mere

Wiltshire **Map: p233 G2.**
Charles II (1660-1685), a fugitive with a price of £1,000 on his head after his defeat at the Battle of Worcester (1651), stayed at the Talbot Inn in Mere, disguised as a manservant. He was on his way to find a ship to France.

Meriden

West Midlands **Map: p237 H2.** *Packington Hall and Old Hall not open.*
Jane Lane, the young woman who risked her life to help Charles II (1660-1685) escape to Dorset after the Battle of Worcester (1651), is buried in the estate church at Packington Hall, near Meriden.

The hall, built in the late 17th century in Italianate style, stands in 700 acres of wooded parkland. The Old Hall, sharing the grounds, was built round an older, timber-framed house where Charles I (1625-1649) stayed while on the march to the Battle of Edgehill (1642).

Middleham

North Yorkshire **Map: p241 F2.** *Castle open Mon to Sat daily, Sun afternoons.*
The ruins of one of the great castles of England tower over Middleham. Fortress of Richard Nevill, Earl of Warwick — the Kingmaker — Middleham Castle stands on the edge of the York-shire moors. Edward IV (1461-1483) was imprisoned here briefly by Warwick in 1469, when the Earl, displeased with his waning influence over the King, plotted to depose him in favour of his brother George, Duke of Clarence.

After Warwick's death fighting for the Lancastrians — his former enemies — at the Battle of Barnet (1471), Edward gave Middleham Castle to his brother, Richard, Duke of Gloucester, later Richard III (1483-1485).

Middleton Hall

Warwickshire **Map: p237 H2.** *Not open.*
Elizabeth I (1558-1603) and James I (1603-1625) both stayed at Middleton Hall, now a ruin, on visits to the Midlands.

Milton

Oxfordshire **Map: p234 C2.** *Manor House open Easter to mid-Oct: weekend afternoons; public holidays.*
While William of Orange, later William III (1689-1702), was being entertained at Milton Manor in December 1688, his father-in-law, James II (1685-1688), was making the decision to abandon his kingdom and follow his Queen, Mary of Modena, and baby son to France. It was the birth of this son, and the prospect of a continuing Roman Catholic dynasty, that had brought William to England with 12,000 troops 'in support of the Protestant religion and liberty'.

The tall, central block of Milton Manor is the original house. The side wings, designed by Inigo Jones, were not added until the 18th century.

Milton Abbas

Dorset **Map: p233 G3.** *Milton Abbey open late Mar to mid-Apr: daily; mid-July to late Aug: daily.*
Athelstan (AD 925-939) is said to have had a vision of victory while marching through Milton Abbas to do battle with some unruly lords. The vision proved true and the grateful King returned to found a chapel. St Catherine's Chapel is thought to have been built in Norman times on the site of Athelstan's. In the Middle Ages a great monastery grew up here, but only the 15th-century church and the abbot's Great Hall survives today.

Mortimer's Cross

Hereford & Worcester **Map: p234 A1.**

In the day-long battle on 2 February, 1461 at Mortimer's Cross, 6 miles from Leominster, Edward, later Edward IV (1461-1483), leading the Yorkist forces, defeated the Lancastrians and captured Owen Tudor, grandfather of Henry VII (1485-1509). He had Owen beheaded at Hereford in revenge for the execution of his father, Richard, Duke of York, after the Battle of Wakefield a month before. A monument put up in the 18th century records the battle.

Moseley Old Hall

West Midlands **Map: p237 G2.** *Open Mar and Nov: Wed and Sun afternoons; Apr to Oct: Wed, Thur, weekend afternoons; Easter, spring and summer bank holiday afternoons.*
Charles II (1660-1685) passed some of the most anxious moments of his life crouching cheek-by-jowl with Father John Hudleston in his priest-hole at Moseley Old Hall in 1651. A fugitive from the lost Battle of Worcester, Charles remained indebted to Father John long after the Restoration.

Moseley Old Hall, originally a black-and-white timbered house, was faced with brick in the 19th century, but the inside is little changed.

Much Hadham

Hertfordshire **Map: p235 F1.** *Bishop's Palace now converted into flats.*
The Bishop's Palace, for 800 years the country home of the Bishops of London, lies just off the main street of Much Hadham. It is a long, low, brick-built house noted for its fine Jacobean staircase and panelling. Edmund, son of Catherine of Valois — widow of Henry V (1413-1422) — and a commoner, Owen Tudor, was born here. Edmund's heir became Henry VII (1485-1509).

Much Wenlock

Salop **Map: p237 F2.** *Priory open Mon to Sat daily, Sun afternoons. Closed Christmas, New Year.*
The first priory at Much Wenlock, founded by King Merewald for St Milburga, his daughter, in AD 680, was destroyed by raiding Vikings nearly 200 years later. It was rebuilt for monks in the 11th century by the Saxon Earl Leofric, husband of Lady Godiva, famous for her naked ride through Coventry. The present ruins, of a Cluniac priory founded by Roger de Montgomery, Earl of Shropshire, in 1080, are among the most splendid in the country. The Cluniacs were a wealthy order, noted for the magnificence of their buildings. Part of the priory is early Norman but it mainly dates from the 14th and 15th centuries.

Muncaster Castle

Cumbria **Map: p240 C2.** *Open Apr to Sept: Tue to Thur and Sun afternoons. Grounds and Bird Garden open Apr to Sept: Sat to Thur afternoons.*
For more than a year Henry VI (1422-1461) hid in the north of England after he had narrowly escaped capture at Hexham in 1464. One place where he is said to have stayed is Muncaster Castle, near Ravenglass, the home of Sir John Pennington. His descendants live in a 19th-century mansion that incorporates the ancient tower.

Naseby

Northamptonshire **Map: p238 D5.**
At the Battle of Naseby in June 1645, the untried New Model Army, led by Sir Thomas Fairfax and Oliver Cromwell, defeated a Royalist force half its size. At first the Royalists had the advantage after Prince Rupert, the King's nephew, had driven off the Parliamentary horse on the left wing with a cavalry charge. Then Cromwell took control of the battle. The King's army was wiped out and his baggage train fell into Parliamentary hands. It was the beginning of the end of the Civil War.

Neroche Forest

Somerset **Map: p233 F2.** *Open all the time.*
From the time of the Conquest, Norman kings hunted the roe deer in Neroche Forest on the Black Down Hills. Only the earthworks remain of a castle built 870ft above sea level by Robert of Mortain, half-brother of William the Conqueror (1066-1087). It has a view over six counties.

Neville's Cross

Durham **Map: p243 H5.**
So great a ransom was demanded by Edward III (1327-1377) when David Bruce, King of Scots (1329-1371), was captured after the Battle of Neville's Cross at Durham in October 1346, that it took the Scots 10 years to pay it off.

Newark

Nottinghamshire **Map: p239 E4.** *Castle gardens open daily. Governor's House is now a shop.*
Newark, with its castle set where the Roman Fosse Way crosses the River Trent, was often called the key to the north. In the Civil War it was an important Royalist stronghold. In 1643, Henrietta Maria, Queen of Charles I (1625-1649), stayed here on her way to Oxford with arms and munitions that she had bought on the continent for the Royalist army. The town withstood three Parliamentary sieges. The last, in 1646, only ended when Charles, who had given himself up to the Scottish army besieging Newark, ordered the town to surrender. The 12th-century castle was slighted, but the main gate, west tower and the wall fronting the river still stand.

Under the yawning arch of the main gateway, King John (1199-1216) was carried, in 1216, on a litter, having been taken sick so suddenly that many believed he had been poisoned. John died three days later. Henry VII (1485-1509) stayed in the castle before defeating the supporters of the impostor Lambert Simnel at East Stoke in 1487. More peacefully, James I (1603-1625) came to Newark on his way south from Scotland to be crowned King of England in 1603.

During the present century the castle, which was royal until 1890, has been visited by Edward VII (1901-1910), George V (1910-1936) and Queen Mary. One of the earliest recorded royal visits was that of Edward the Confessor (1042-1066) and his Queen, Edith, who were present when Lady Godiva dedicated her gift of the manor of Newark to the monastery of nearby Stow in 1055.

Newcastle upon Tyne

Tyne & Wear **Map: p243 H5.** *Black Gate Museum: Open Wed to Fri afternoons. Castle Garth: Tue to Sat daily.*
The Norman keep of Newcastle Castle is one of the best preserved in England. When Henry II (1154-1189) built it on the site of a fortress put up in 1080 by the eldest son of William the Conqueror (1066-1087), it was the strongest fortress in the north of England. It needed to be, for Newcastle's position, close to a crossing point on the River Tyne and Hadrian's Wall, has brought it centuries of strife. As Monkchester, its earlier name, the town was destroyed by the Danes in the 9th century and by William the Conqueror in the 11th. William Rufus (1087-1100) besieged and captured the first castle in 1095. It was later seized by David I of Scotland (1124-1153), during Stephen's reign (1135-1154), in support of the Empress Matilda. Edward I (1272-1307) walled the town and it was defended against Scottish attacks on three occasions. Finally, in 1640, a Scottish covenanting army captured and garrisoned the town for almost a year. Charles I (1625-1649) spent nine months imprisoned here before he was 'sold' to the English in 1647.

Newent

Gloucestershire **Map: p234 A1.**
Royalist soldiers who stripped the lead off the parish church roof at Newent in 1644, to make bullets during the Civil War, caused the roof to collapse 30 years later. Charles II (1660-1685) — restored to the throne — gave the market town 60 tons of timber from the Forest of Dean to make good the damage.

New Forest

Hampshire **Map: p233 H3.** *Open all the time.*
When William the Conqueror (1066-1087) created his 'New' Forest as a royal hunting preserve in 1079, the forest area must have looked much as it does today. A mixture of heath and woodland, it covers 145 square miles. King John (1199-1216) particularly liked the New Forest and extended it. The Queen's Bower, not far from Brockenhurst, is supposed to be where Philippa of Hainault, Queen of Edward III (1327-1377), used to rest while hunting. The 19th-century castellated mansion of Rhinefield House nearby is said to be built on the site of a hunting lodge put up by William the Conqueror. William Rufus (1087-1100), the Conqueror's son, was mysteriously killed by an arrow while hunting in the New Forest. Hated for his abuse of authority, the King left few mourners, and his murder has never been solved.

Newmarket

Suffolk **Map: p239 F5.**
Royal interest in horses in the 17th century provided the foundation for Newmarket's present role as the capital of world racing. James I (1603-1625), who was just passing by, discovered that the flat heathland round the tiny village made an ideal setting for coursing and hawking. Soon a palace had been built and horse-racing for its own sake, rather than for chasing game, instituted.

Charles I (1625-1649) spent almost as much time at Newmarket as his father. It was during his reign that the first formal race-meetings — in the spring and autumn — took place. Horse-racing, like many other pastimes, vanished under the Commonwealth, but following the Restoration (1660) Charles II (1660-1685) was back at Newmarket. He improved the royal palace here and in 1664 he established the Newmarket Town Plate, for which he drew up the rules himself. Nell Gwynne stayed in a house in Palace Street — one of the few to survive the fire of 1683 — when she accompanied her royal lover to the races. The 'Rowley' racecourse was named after the King, one of whose nicknames was Old Rowley.

Both William III (1689-1702) and Queen Anne (1702-1714) kept 'running horses' in training at Newmarket in the care of Tregonwell Frampton, the first systematic trainer of racehorses, now recognized as the 'father of the turf'. Anne's Hanoverian successors took little interest in horse-racing until the Prince of Wales, the future George IV (1820-1830), plunged into the sport with an excess of enthusiasm.

The next Prince of Wales, later Edward VII (1901-1910), was an equally enthusiastic patron of the turf. From 1893, when he put his horses into training here, he was a regular visitor, always staying at the Jockey Club.

Newport

Isle of Wight **Map: p234 C4.**
The simple initials E.S., carved on the wall of St Thomas's Church at Newport, were for two centuries the only memorial to a most unhappy Princess. Elizabeth, second daughter of Charles I (1625-1649), died of a fever at Carisbrooke Castle, aged 15, in 1650. She had spent half her life with her brother Prince Henry, separated from the rest of the family in the custody of Parliament during and after the Civil War.

When St Thomas's Church was rebuilt in 1854, Queen Victoria (1837-1901) had a white marble memorial to Elizabeth placed there.

The Old Grammar School at Newport, founded in 1614, is where Charles I negotiated the Treaty of Newport with the Parliamentary commissioners in 1648, after the final defeat of the Royalist cause in the Second Civil War.

Newstead Abbey

Nottinghamshire **Map: p238 C3.** *Open Easter to Sept: afternoons.*
Henry II (1154-1189) is thought to have founded the original Augustinian priory at Newstead to atone for the murder in 1170 of Thomas à Becket, Archbishop of Canterbury, in his cathedral.

Newton Abbot

Devon **Map: p233 E4.** *Forde House is now Council offices, open by appointment.*
William of Orange, later William III (1689-1702), nephew and son-in-law of James II (1685-1688), read the declaration that he had come to England to maintain the Protestant religion and the laws and liberties of the kingdom for the first time at

the market cross in Newton Abbot. He dined at Forde House in the town, the night after he landed at Brixham in November 1688 with his army.

Norham Castle

Northumberland **Map: p243 G3.** *Open Mon to Sat daily, Sun afternoons.*
It was to Norham Castle, set on a bluff overlooking a strategic ford on the River Tweed, that Edward I (1272-1307) came in May 1291 to arbitrate between the claimants to the Scottish crown, who included John Balliol, Robert Bruce and John Hastings. After long, drawn-out legal discussions, John Balliol (1292-1296) was chosen and swore fealty to Edward at Norham on 20 November 1292. Another Scottish king, William the Lion (1165-1214), paid homage to the English King John (1199-1216) at Norham and handed over his two daughters as hostages in 1209.

However, Norham's history is not all about diplomacy. Its strategic position brought it five centuries of battering. David I of Scotland (1124-1153) destroyed the first castle in 1138, while supporting the Empress Matilda's claim to the English throne against her cousin, Stephen (1135-1154). The replacement castle was completed in 1174. Robert Bruce (1306-1329) besieged it several times — once for nearly a year — and finally won it in 1327. During the Wars of the Roses, Norham was unsuccessfully attacked by Henry VI (1422-1461) and his warlike Queen, Margaret of Anjou. It was in 1513 that the castle suffered its most devastating siege when James IV of Scotland (1488-1513) reduced its walls to rubble with the help of Mons Meg, a mighty cannon that now stands in Edinburgh Castle. The accession of James VI of Scotland to the English throne in 1603 brought peace to the borders, but it was then that the castle started to decay.

Northallerton

North Yorkshire **Map: p241 F2.**
Even by medieval standards David I, King of Scotland (1124-1153), overstepped the mark with his campaign of pillage and plunder in the north of England in 1138. The Archbishop of York decided to raise an army in retaliation; with all the fervour of a crusade, 12,000 men joined his standard. The armies met on Cowton Moor, north of Northallerton, on 22 August 1138 and in three fierce hours of fighting the Battle of The Standard, as it came to be called, was won by the English.

Set on the main road between north and south, Northallerton often suffered when the Scots invaded. In 1318 Robert Bruce (1306-1329) burned the town to the ground. Charles I (1625-1649) is said to have stayed at the Porch House, near the church, during the Civil War.

Northampton

Northamptonshire **Map: p238 D5.**
Just as the forces of Henry VI (1422-1461) were about to win the Battle of Northampton on 10 July 1460, the vanguard of the royal army suddenly laid down its arms. As a result of the Yorkist victory, Henry, who had taken no part in the battle — leaving such bloodthirsty work to his Queen, Margaret of Anjou — was captured and taken to London. Richard, Duke of York, was then made Protector of England.

The castle, royal from the time of Henry I (1100-1135) and visited by many medieval kings, has now gone; it was blown up by Charles II (1660-1685) in 1662 to punish Northampton for providing Cromwell's New Model Army with boots. However, when the town was destroyed by fire in 1675 Charles donated 1,000 tons of timber for rebuilding work.

Northiam

East Sussex **Map: p235 G4.** *Brickwall House open late Apr to early July: Wed and Sat afternoons.*
A little pair of green silk-damask shoes on view at Brickwall, a Jacobean mansion at Northiam, were left behind after a royal picnic on the village green. Elizabeth I (1558-1603) is supposed to have stopped at the village on 11 August 1573.

Norton St Philip

Somerset **Map: p233 G1.**
For more than seven centuries The George Inn at Norton St Philip has offered hospitality to travellers, for it was once the guest house of 13th-century Hinton Priory. On 26 June 1687 it sheltered James, Duke of Monmouth, illegitimate son of Charles II (1660-1685). As a Protestant, Monmouth was trying to raise a rebellion against James II (1685-1688), his Roman Catholic uncle. Things did not go well for him and he was defeated 10 days later at the Battle of Sedgemoor.

Norwich

Norfolk **Map: p239 G4.**
The presence of Henry III (1216-1272) was required at Norwich to quell a bloody riot between monks and citizens in August 1272. Henry quashed the riot firmly, executing many of the townsfolk and fining the town 3,000 marks towards the cost of repairing the 12th-century cathedral that had been burnt. Six years later his son, Edward I (1272-1307), was present when the cathedral was reconsecrated.

Norwich Cathedral

Nottingham

Nottinghamshire Map: p238 C3. Castle Museum and Art Gallery open daily.

The original Norman castle at Nottingham, founded in 1068 by William the Conqueror (1066-1087), was once an important royal fortress. It was beginning to decay, however, when, in 1642, Charles I (1625-1649) raised his standard on a hill nearby, now called Standard Hill Street. Only 300 men joined his cause however. Another king who left Nottingham for ultimate defeat was Richard III (1483-1485), who gathered his army at the castle before marching to Leicester and the Battle of Bosworth (1485) where he was killed. In 1212, King John (1199-1216), in a bloodthirsty mood, hanged 24 young Welsh hostages from the ramparts when the Welsh Prince, Llywelyn the Great, broke a truce and captured some of his castles on the Welsh border.

The present castle, which replaced the Norman one demolished by order of Parliament after the Civil War, has also seen violence. Built in 1674, it was burned to the ground in 1831 during riots against the defeat of the Reform Bill. It was rebuilt in 1875 and opened as a museum and art gallery by Edward VII (1901-1910).

Oakham

Leicestershire Map: p238 D4. Castle open Sun and Mon afternoons, Tue to Sat daily. Gardens open daily.

Custom requires that peers of the realm and members of the royal family should present a horseshoe to the lord of the manor at Oakham as they pass through his estates. Today 220 horseshoes hang on the walls of the Norman hall of the castle. Elizabeth I (1558-1603) is believed to have given the oldest, and the present Queen added a shoe to the collection in 1967.

Odiham Castle

Hampshire Map: p234 D3. Open all the time.

The unique octagonal keep which King John (1199-1216) built still stands near Odiham. It was from Odiham Castle, one of his favourite strongholds, that John rode out to sign the barons' Magna Carta in 1215 at Runnymede. In 1216 a garrison of only 13 men held the castle for a fortnight against Prince Louis of France, who had landed with an army to support the rebel barons. David Bruce, King of Scotland (1329-1371), was imprisoned in the castle for part of the 11 years he spent in England as a prisoner of Edward III (1327-1377).

Old Alresford

Hampshire Map: p234 D4.

George IV (1820-1830) lived at the Neo-Classical Grange at Northington, near Old Alresford. The mansion is now being restored.

Old Bolingbroke

Lincolnshire Map: p239 E3.

Two weathered, stone heads which ornament the doorway of the parish church in the village of Old Bolingbroke are believed to represent Edward III (1327-1377) and his Queen, Philippa of Hainault. Close to the church their fourth son, John of Gaunt, Duke of Lancaster, had a castle — the birthplace of Henry Bolingbroke, his son, who usurped the throne of his cousin, Richard II (1377-1399), to become Henry IV (1399-1413). The castle fell into ruins after the Civil War.

Old Sarum

Wiltshire Map: p233 H2.

It took William the Conqueror (1066-1087) four years to subdue England and it was at Old Sarum, a Saxon settlement built on the site of a Roman camp and earlier Iron Age fort, that he disbanded his army and paid off his remaining mercenaries in 1070. The foundations of the cathedral that William's nephew, Bishop Osmund, built at Old Sarum can still be traced in the downland turf.

Orford Castle

Suffolk Map: p235 H1. Open Oct to Mar: Mon to Sat daily, Sun afternoons.

Henry II (1154-1189) built Orford Castle to keep a check on one of his most unruly barons, Hugh Bigod, Earl of Norfolk. When Henry came to the throne he inherited a kingdom in anarchy; for 19 years the nobles had been engaged in pillage and destruction. The key to their power lay in their castles where they could defy authority and sit out a siege for months — far longer, usually, than could the besiegers, whose supply lines often lay in hostile territory. Hugh Bigod had four castles and virtually did as he pleased in East Anglia. Henry confiscated all four at the start of his reign, returning two on payment of a £1,000 fine in 1165.

Henry immediately started building Orford Castle as he had no stronghold in the area. It was well sited for supply, close to the then busy sea port of Orford, and was extremely strong. After completion in 1173, it was immediately in use, as Hugh Bigod joined the rebellion against Henry in support of Henry's second son. Henry crushed the rebellion in East Anglia using Orford Castle as a base, and for the next two centuries it was an important royal stronghold. The 90-foot keep still stands and is very well preserved.

Orleans House

Middlesex. Map: p235 E3. Gallery open Tues to Sun afternoons only.

Orleans House in Twickenham was built in about 1710 by John James for James Johnstone, Secretary of State for Scotland. Some 10 years later, the Octagon Room, now an art gallery, was added for Caroline, Princess of Wales, wife of the future George II (1727-1760). The Octagon Room was saved when much of the rest of the house was demolished in 1926 and 1927.

Osborne House

Isle of Wight Map: p234 C5. Open Easter to Sept; Mon to Sat daily.

Unlike other royal residences — except perhaps

Osborne House

the Royal Pavilion at Brighton — Osborne House is a reflection of the taste of a single monarch. It was built for Queen Victoria (1837-1901) and was never used by her successors, who gave it to the nation in 1904. Designed by Albert to resemble an Italian villa, the house provided a refuge for Victoria and her family. After his death, the Queen allowed no changes to be made, keeping the whole estate as a shrine to his memory. She herself died here on 22 January 1901.

Osmington

Dorset Map: p233 G3.

George III (1760-1820) holidayed frequently at nearby Weymouth in the late 18th century. He is commemorated in the figure on horseback cut out of the chalk downland at Osmington.

Osterley House

Middlesex. Map: p235 E3. Open Tues to Sat afternoons; bank holiday Mons.

Built in the 1560s for Sir Thomas Gresham; Elizabeth I (1558-1603) stayed here in 1578. Robert Adam modernized it in the 18th century.

Oswestry

Salop Map: p237 F1.

A Saxon saint gave his name to Oswestry (Oswald's Tree), for it was here in AD 642 that Oswald, the Christian King of Northumbria, is thought to have been killed fighting Penda, the heathen King of Mercia.

Only the mound of the Norman castle built soon after the Conquest to keep the Welsh in check, is left today. It was the base used by King John (1199-1216) in his war against Llywelyn of Wales, which lasted from 1209 to 1211. As a border castle it often changed hands and was burned down three times. It finally became

English in 1535 under the Act of Union, but most of the townsfolk spoke Welsh.

Oxburgh Hall

Norfolk **Map: p239 F4.** *Open May to Oct: Sat to Wed afternoons; Easter.*

In Tudor times, the Bedingfeld family of Oxburgh Hall were notable royal gaolers. Sir Edmund Bedingfeld had custody of Catherine of Aragon, first Queen of Henry VIII (1509-1547) at Kimbolton Castle, until her death in 1536. His son, Sir Henry, a loyal supporter of Mary I (1553-1558), guarded Princess Elizabeth, later Elizabeth I (1558-1603), first at the Tower and then at Woodstock.

A memento of another royal imprisonment — 100 embroidered wall-hangings done by Mary, Queen of Scots (1542-1567) and the Countess of Shrewsbury, the famous Bess of Hardwick — remains at Oxburgh. The embroidery is dated 1570 — the second year of Mary's imprisonment.

Today the Tudor brickwork of the 15th-century mansion is reflected in the broad moat, just as it must have been in 1497 when Henry VII (1485-1509) visited the house. The Bedingfeld family still live here.

Paradise

Somerset **Map: p233 F2.**

Charles I (1625-1649) named this village Paradise when he stayed nearby in 1643, during the Civil War. He described it as being 'the most delightful spot I have ever seen'.

Parham Park

West Sussex **Map: p235 E4.** *Open Easter to early Oct: weekends, Wed, Thur afternoons; bank holiday Mons.*

Contemporary portraits of Elizabeth I (1558-1603) and some of her famous courtiers hang in the Great Hall of Parham Park, near Pulborough. She is believed to have dined here in 1593. The house, built in 1577, has been sensitively restored.

Penrith

Cumbria **Map: p240 D1.**

It is said that the bones of a huge man — perhaps Owain Caesurius, King of Cumbria (AD 920-937) —, were found when the Giant's Grave in St Andrew's churchyard in Penrith was excavated in the 16th century.

Penhurst Place

Kent **Map: p235 F3.** *Open Apr to Sept: Tue to Sun, public holidays.*

The Great Hall at Penshurst Place, built in 1328, is much the same today as it was in August 1519, when Edward Stafford, 3rd Duke of Buckingham, lavishly entertained Henry VIII (1509-1547) here. The Duke's fortunes were not, however, as enduring as his home — within two years he fell from favour and was beheaded.

Two brothers of Henry V (1413-1422) owned Penshurst in the 15th century and in 1552 Edward

Oxford

Magdalen College

Oxfordshire **Map: p234 C2.** *Christ Church College open afternoons. St John's College open afternoons.*

On the whole, royalty have not fared well at Oxford — from Harold Harefoot (1035-1040), Canute's son, who died here in his early twenties, to Edward VII (1901-1910) who, as Prince of Wales, was sent to study at Christ Church in 1859. Edward's life was not at risk, but he did not have much fun. He was lodged in a large old house in the town under the strict control of a 'governor', instead of living in college with students of his own age. The Prince was not allowed to attend lectures; instead professors came to his house with one or two carefully chosen undergraduates, to coach him in private. There can be little doubt that he was glad to get away, when the following year he was sent on a tour of Canada and the United States.

Several of Edward's ancestors were equally happy to leave Oxford. Just before Christmas 1142, a half-starved Empress Matilda fled in the snow — cloaked in white — through the lines of her cousin Stephen's besieging army, which had penned her in Oxford Castle for three increasingly hungry months. The keep still stands today. Her flight effectively ended her struggle for the throne, though perhaps she felt that in the end she had won, since Stephen (1135-1154) acknowledged her son as his successor. It was this son, Henry II (1154-1189), who is considered to have founded the university at Oxford in 1167 — though that was not his precise intention at the time. Learning that the French had given refuge to his turbulent archbishop of Canterbury, Thomas à Becket, Henry ordered all English students at the University of Paris, as well as those at other continental universities, to return to England. The returning students and scholars gravitated to Oxford, where they established schools and colleges on the continental pattern. Henry himself had built a residence at Oxford. It was known as Beaumont Palace, but was probably used mainly as a hunting lodge. It stood on the present site of Gloucester Green, but in Henry's time it

was outside the city walls.

Two kings were born in Oxford — Henry's sons Richard I (1189-1199), born 1157, and John (1199-1216), born 1167. Oxford was also the birthplace of Parliament — an institution forced upon John's son, Henry III (1216-1272), by Simon de Montfort and his fellow barons after a meeting in the city in 1258. The Provisions of Oxford, which they drew up, obliged Henry to take counsel not only of his barons but also of representatives of the clergy and the commons. The first Parliament met seven years later in Westminster Hall.

Throughout this period the university was growing and royalty were among the benefactors who provided for this growth. One of the most important donations was that of Humphrey, Duke of Gloucester, youngest son of Henry IV (1399-1413). He gave manuscripts and money to provide a home for them — Duke Humphrey's Library — which was completed in 1488 and is now part of the Bodleian Library. A later royal donor to the library was James I (1603-1625), who gave a collection of his own literary efforts. James was the author of 10 published works, including *A Counterblast to Tobacco* and, significantly in view of what was to happen to his son, *An Essay on the Rights of Kings*. Visiting the library in 1614 he declared that, were he not the King, he would

Radcliffe Camera

like to have been 'an Oxford man'.

In fact, James's son, Charles I (1625-1649), did become an Oxford man. After the Battle of Edgehill (1642), Charles set up his headquarters in the city, making his home in Christ Church and establishing a royal mint. He was to remain here for more than three years until, in the last stage of a siege by the Parliamentary army, he fled the city in disguise. At Newark 10 days later he put himself in the hands of the Scottish army who eventually handed him over to Parliament. Charles's stay in Oxford is perhaps best recalled by the bronze statues of himself and his Queen Henrietta Maria, by the sculptor Le Sueur, which stand in the Canterbury Quadrangle of St John's College. Charles II (1660-1685), who was at Oxford with his father during the Civil War, returned several times as King, notably in 1681 when he called on Parliament to meet here because the plague was raging in London.

Penshurst Place

VI (1547-1553) gave it to Sir William Sidney, his former tutor.

James I (1603-1625) called in at Penshurst when it was owned by Sir Robert Sidney, Earl of Leicester. Two of his grandchildren, Princess Elizabeth and Prince Henry, lived here in the care of Sir Philip Sidney for 20 months.

Peterborough

Northamptonshire **Map: p239 E4.** *Museum open May to Sept: Tue to Sat daily; Oct to Apr: Tue to Sat afternoons.*

When Henry VIII (1509-1547) heard that his first wife, Catherine of Aragon, had finally died under guard at Kimbolton Castle, on 7 January 1536, he was so delighted that he danced the next day dressed all in yellow. He did not attend the funeral service in Peterborough Cathedral and refused to let Princess Mary, their daughter, go either.

Half a century later another imprisoned Queen who found release only in death — Mary, Queen of Scots (1542-1567) — was buried at Peterborough after her execution at Fotheringay Castle on 8 February, 1587. The tombs of these two Queens lie on opposite sides of the cathedral's nave, but Mary's is empty; James I (1603-1625) had his mother's coffin transferred to Westminster Abbey in 1612.

Peterborough Cathedral, originally an abbey, was founded in 1117; it is one of the most beautiful Norman buildings in England.

Pevensey

East Sussex **Map: p235 F4.** *Castle open Mon to Sat daily, Sun afternoons. Closed public holidays.*

William the Conqueror (1066-1087) took a bold gamble when he prepared to invade England in 1066 to claim his right to be considered heir to Edward the Confessor (1042-1066). Luck played

its part — on the very day that William sailed for England, Harold (1066), who had been watching the coast all summer, was in Yorkshire fighting his brother and the Norwegian King, Harald Hardrada. When William landed at Pevensey on 28 September 1066 he was unopposed.

William Rufus (1087-1100) besieged the newly fortified Roman castle in 1088, when it was being held in support of Robert, Duke of Normandy, who was claiming the throne. The garrison was starved out, as it was in 1147 when Stephen (1135-1154) besieged the castle during his struggle with the Empress Matilda for the crown.

In the 15th century James I of Scotland (1406-1437) was held at Pevensey for some time. In 1419 Henry V (1413-1422) sent his stepmother, the Queen dowager, Joan of Navarre, to prison here, mysteriously charged with seeking his death by witchcraft. The sea has retreated from Pevensey Castle over the centuries and it now stands more than a mile inland.

Pickering

North Yorkshire **Map: p241 G2.** *Castle open Mon to Sat daily, Sun afternoons. Closed public holidays.*

Set on a hill overlooking the town and the nearby moors, 12th-century Pickering Castle was used more as a hunting-box by medieval kings than as a fortress. It did see action in the reign of Richard II (1377-1399), when it belonged to the Dukes of Lancaster. It was to Pickering that Henry Bolingbroke, later Henry IV (1399-1413), rode to gather an army to attack Richard, after landing at Ravenspur from exile in 1399. Later the deposed King was imprisoned briefly here.

Plymouth

Devon **Map: p232 D4.** *Citadel ramparts open May*

to Sept: organized tours in the afternoons only. Chapel open Sun afternoons.

Charles II (1660-1685) was a forgiving monarch, but he could not forget that Plymouth had withstood two sieges by Royalist forces during the Civil War. In 1670 he ordered the building of the citadel to house troops to keep an eye on the town.

Polesden Lacey

Surrey **Map: p235 E3.** *Open Mar and Nov: weekend afternoons; Apr to Oct: Tue to Thur and weekends daily.*

The future George VI (1936-1952) and Queen Elizabeth honeymooned at Polesden Lacey as the Duke and Duchess of York in 1923.

Pontefract Castle

West Yorkshire **Map: p238 C1.** *Open daily.*

Few prisoners escaped alive from the strong dungeons of Pontefract Castle. In 1399 the deposed Richard II (1377-1399) died here, possibly on 14 February and probably of starvation.

Nearly a century later two protectors of the boy-king, Edward V (1483) — Lord Richard Grey and Sir Thomas Vaughan — were imprisoned and executed at Pontefract after Richard III (1483-1485) had declared that his brother's sons were illegitimate.

Portchester Castle

Hampshire **Map: p234 D5.** *Open Mon to Sat daily, Sun afternoons. Closed public holidays.*

To protect Portsmouth harbour after the Conquest, the Normans built a fortress in one corner of the land enclosed by Roman walls at Portchester. Henry I (1100-1135) used Portchester as a base when his elder brother, Robert, Duke of Normandy, invaded England to dispute the succession in 1101. Henry II (1154-1189) used it as a prison and a treasure store. In the 12th century, a priory was built here. The church still stands today, hardly altered.

In 1396 Richard II (1377-1399) built a palace within the fortress. Henry V (1413-1422) stayed here before sailing with a fleet of 1,500 ships to France and victory at Agincourt in 1415. Margaret of Anjou, newly married by proxy to Henry VI (1422-1461), stepped ashore at Portchester, feeling very sea-sick, on 9 April 1445. In the 18th century French captives from the Napoleonic wars were kept here.

Portsmouth

Hampshire **Map: p234 D5.** *Southsea Castle Military Museum open daily.*

As his 700-ton flagship, the *Mary Rose*, heeled and started to sink on 19 July 1545 while hoisting sail to join battle with invading French warships, Henry VIII (1509-1547) could only watch aghast. Despite immediate attempts to raise the flagship, it was not until 1982 that the spars of the *Mary Rose* broke surface, watched by Prince Charles, the Prince of Wales.

Henry VII (1485-1509) fortified the sea-walls at Portsmouth and built a naval dry dock here in 1495. Henry VIII enlarged it as a royal dockyard in

1540. Now Portsmouth is the chief naval station in England. In 1229, Henry III (1216-1272), was furious when he discovered he only had half the ships needed to transport his army, to a campaign in France. In 1415 Henry V (1413-1422), en route for Agincourt, had the opposite problem. He had so many ships that there was not room for all of them in Portsmouth harbour and the army, gathered at Portchester Castle, were forced to embark at Southampton.

Powerstock

Dorset Map: p233 F3.
Only a grassy mound remains of the Norman castle which King John (1199-1216) used as a hunting lodge when he came to chase the deer in Powerstock Forest.

Preston

Lancashire Map: p238 A1.
Preston is associated with three unsuccessful campaigns in support of the Stuart royal house. In 1648, 20,000 Scots, invading England on behalf of the imprisoned Charles I (1625-1649), were defeated here by Oliver Cromwell in a decisive battle during the abortive Second Civil War.

In 1715 English Jacobites entered the town and proclaimed James Stuart, the Old Pretender, son of James II (1685-1688), as King of England in place of George I (1714-1727). They quickly surrendered Preston on being confronted by government troops. James's son, Bonnie Prince Charlie, the Young Pretender, captured Preston 30 years later, but his hopes of driving George II (1727-1760) from the throne were soon to be dashed by his generals' decision at Derby to turn back for Scotland.

Princes Risborough

Buckinghamshire Map: p234 D2.
Edward, the Black Prince, eldest son of Edward III (1327-1377), had a castle on The Mount here.

Raby Castle

Raby Castle

Durham Map: p241 F1. *Open Easter to June and Oct: Wed and Sun afternoons; July to Sept: Sun to Fri daily; public holidays.*
Lying between Bishop Auckland and Barnard Castle, Raby is one of the finest 14th-century castles in England. It was owned by the Nevill family from early times. Ralph Nevill, the 1st Earl of Westmorland, had 21 children by his two wives. The youngest daughter, Cicely, known as the Rose of Raby, married Richard, Duke of York, and gave birth to two future Kings — Edward IV (1461-1483) and Richard III (1483-1485).

Radway

Warwickshire Map: p234 C1.
The Battle of Edgehill (1642), the first major engagement of the Civil War, was fought just to the west of the village of Radway. Although its outcome was inconclusive, the battle is famous for the cavalry charge led by Prince Rupert, nephew of Charles I (1625-1649).

Ramsey

Isle of Man Map: p240 B2. *Castle Rushen open Mon to Sat daily; also Sun mornings in summer.*
The Isle of Man was under Norwegian suzerainty until after the Battle of Largs (1263), when Alexander III of Scotland (1249-1286) defeated Haakon II. In 1290 Edward I (1272-1307) seized the island, but English control lasted for only 20 years. During his vigorous campaign against the English, Robert Bruce (1306-1329) landed at Ramsey and laid siege to Castle Rushen for five weeks in 1313. On the castle's surrender the island again came under Scots control until it was finally surrendered to England in 1346.

Ramsgate

Kent Map: p235 H3.
Pegwell Bay, near Ramsgate, is supposed to have been the spot at which the Saxon invaders Hengist and Horsa landed, following the departure of the Romans in the 4th century. In AD 596 St Augustine landed at nearby Ebbsfleet on the mission which led to the conversion of the Saxon King, Ethelbert (AD 560-616).

Ravenspur

Humberside Map: p239 E1.
In 1399 Henry Bolingbroke, the future Henry IV (1399-1413), landed at Ravenspur and proceeded to take control of the country with ease. The reigning monarch, Richard II (1377-1399), was captured by the Earl of Northumberland and died in 1400, probably from starvation.

Edward IV (1461-1483) landed at Ravenspur in 1471, but his Yorkist triumph over Henry VI (1422-1461) proved considerably more difficult to achieve. His accession to the throne effectually stopped the Wars of the Roses until his death.

Reading

Berkshire Map: p234 D3. *Abbey open daily.*
Alfred, soon to become King of Wessex (AD 871-899), and his brother Ethelred (AD 866-871) were defeated by invading Danes at Reading in AD 871. Only days later, however, at nearby Ashdown Alfred courageously drove the Danes back to their ships, moored at Reading.

The medieval abbey of Reading was founded in 1121 by Henry I (1100-1135), who was buried here in 1136. The abbey was dissolved by Henry VIII (1509-1547) and subsequently became a royal palace. Royalist during the early stages of the Civil War, the town was forced to surrender to the Parliamentary forces in 1643.

Repton

Derbyshire Map: p237 H1.
By the 7th century Repton had become the capital of the Mercian kings, and it was also the site of the first Mercian abbey, founded in AD 653 by Peada, son of Penda, on the occasion of his marriage to the daughter of Oswy, King of Northumbria.

The abbey was destroyed by the Danes in AD 874, but rebuilt in the last quarter of the 10th century. It fell into neglect after the Dissolution of the Monasteries (1536).

Restormel Castle

Cornwall Map: p230 C4. *Open daily.*
This picturesque castle was first constructed as an earthwork fortification shortly after the Norman Conquest. Transformed into a strong stone building during the next century, it passed into the hands of Richard, Earl of Cornwall, brother of Henry III (1216-1272) in 1270. By 1299 the castle was part of the Duchy of Cornwall and has remained so to this day.

Richmond

Greater London Map: p235 E3. *Park open daily.*
Until 1500 Richmond was called Sheen, but its name was changed by Henry VII (1485-1509), who had been Earl of Richmond (Yorkshire) before becoming King. The palace was frequently used as a royal residence until the 17th century. Edward III (1327-1377) died at Richmond, deserted by friends and courtiers and even by his mistress, Alice Perrers, who fled with the rings she pulled

from the dying man's fingers. Anne of Bohemia, wife of Richard II (1377-1399), died from the plague here in 1394. Henry VIII (1509-1547) gave the palace at Richmond to Cardinal Wolsey in return for Hampton Court, but his daughter, Elizabeth I (1558-1603), resumed royal possession and also died here.

Richmond Park

Richmond

North Yorkshire **Map: p241 F2.** *Castle open daily except Sun mornings: Oct to Mar.*
The castle was built on top of a 100ft crag above the town in 1071 and the keep, with its walls 11ft thick, was added in 1145. William the Lion, King of Scots (1165-1214), was imprisoned here in 1174, after his capture by a party of knights.

The lands belonging to the castle first passed to the Crown shortly after the murder of Arthur of Brittany, grandson of Henry II (1154-1189), in 1203, and were subsequently held by Edmund Tudor, Earl of Richmond and father of Henry VII (1485-1509). Henry's successor, Henry VIII (1509-1547), gave the 'honour of Richmond',

together with a dukedom, to his illegitimate son Henry Fitzroy, and 150 years later Charles II (1660-1685) granted it to Charles Lennox, the son of his mistress Louise de Kérouälle, Duchess of Portsmouth, one of several of the King's paramours to be Lady of the Bedchamber to his Queen, Catherine of Braganza.

Ringwood

Hampshire **Map: p233 H3.**
It was to this quiet town in the New Forest that James, Duke of Monmouth, illegitimate son of Charles II (1660-1685), was taken following his arrest three days after the Battle of Sedgemoor (1685). He had launched a Protestant rebellion against his Roman Catholic uncle James II (1685-1688).

Rochester

Kent **Map: p235 F3.** *Castle open daily except Sun mornings: Oct to Mar.*
Established by the Romans, Rochester occupies a strategic position on the River Medway at Watling Street, which runs between Canterbury and London. In AD 604 St Augustine founded the Cathedral Church of St Andrew at Rochester, built for him by Ethelbert (AD 560-616), the first Saxon King to become a Christian. The church was later partially destroyed by the Danes, but was rebuilt on the orders of William the Conqueror (1066-1087). The impressive castle at Rochester was built for William Rufus (1087-1100). Besieged unsuccessfully by King John (1199-1216) and Simon de Montfort, it was captured by a mob of peasants during the Peasants' Revolt of 1381. All that remains today of the castle is the fine stone keep.

Rochford Hall

Essex **Map: p235 G2.**
This interesting house of several different periods, now a ruin, once belonged to the Boleyn family, and a tradition holds that Anne Boleyn, second wife of Henry VIII (1509-1547), was born here.

Rockingham

Northamptonshire **Map: p235 G2.** *Castle open Easter to Sept: Sun and Thur afternoons; bank holiday Mons.*
The castle at Rockingham was built during the reign of William the Conqueror (1066-1087), on a spur overlooking the River Nene, although the massive twin towers of the gatehouse were not added until 1275.

Rockingham Forest was a favourite hunting ground for medieval English kings, and after King John (1199-1216) had captured the castle, it became a royal hunting lodge. James I (1603-1625) is known to have been entertained here in 1604.

Romsey

Hampshire **Map: p233 H2.** *Abbey open daily. Broadlands open Apr to Sept: Tue to Sun daily; bank holiday Mons.*
Founded in AD 910 by Edward the Elder (AD 899-925), whose daughter, Elfleda, is thought to have been the first abbess, Romsey Abbey was not completed until the 13th century. Today it incorporates fine examples of both Saxon and Norman architecture. The abbey survived the Dissolution of the Monasteries (1536) because it was also used as a parish church by the people living in the area.

Just outside the town stands Broadlands, formerly the home of Lord Palmerston, now belonging to Lord Romsey, son of Countess Mountbatten of Burma. The Queen stayed here on her honeymoon, and the Prince and Princess of Wales spent the first part of their honeymoon here as guests as well.

Rose Castle

Cumbria **Map: p243 F5.** *Not open.*
Edward I (1272-1307) stayed at Rose Castle, the residence of the Bishops of Carlisle, on his way to a campaign in Scotland in 1300.

Rothwell

Northamptonshire **Map: p238 D5.** *Rushton Hall grounds only by appointment in Aug.*
Rushton Hall in Rothwell was the family seat of Francis Tresham, the conspirator in the Gunpowder Plot to blow up James I (1603-1625) and the Houses of Parliament in 1605, who was responsible for its discovery. He sent a letter to his friend, Lord Monteagle, begging him not to appear at the opening of Parliament on 5 November 1605; this aroused suspicion and the plot was discovered.

The peculiar-shaped lodge at Rushton Hall, with its triangular rooms, windows and chimney, was built by Francis's father, Thomas Tresham, as a celebration of the Holy Trinity. The Gunpowder Plot is thought to have been planned within the walls of this architectural folly. Francis Tresham died of natural causes in the Tower of London soon after his arrest and, although he was never tried or even indicted, his body was decapitated and his head placed on show above the main gate of Northampton.

Richmond Castle

Rowton Moor

Cheshire **Map: p238 A3.**
Situated just to the east of the old city of Chester, Rowton Moor was the scene of a Royalist defeat in the late summer of 1644. Charles I (1625-1649) watched the battle from what is now called the King Charles Tower, within the city wall.

Royal Leamington Spa

Warwickshire **Map: p237 H3.**
A popular spa from the 1780s onwards, the prefix 'Royal' was added by Queen Victoria (1837-1901) in 1838, at the height of the resort's popularity.

Royal Tunbridge Wells

Kent **Map: p235 F4.**
The mineral springs which are the reason for Tunbridge Wells's existence were discovered in 1606, and the town quickly became a popular and fashionable spa. Henrietta Maria, Queen of Charles I (1625-1649), came here in 1630 to recuperate after the birth of her son, the future Charles II (1660-1685). Tunbridge Wells was also popular with Queen Anne (1702-1714). Edward VII (1901-1910) bestowed the prefix 'Royal' on the town in 1909.

The Pantiles, Royal Tunbridge Wells

Royston

Hertfordshire **Map: p235 E1.** *Old Palace not open.*
The Old Palace in Royston became the favourite residence outside London of James I (1603-1625). The surrounding country offered excellent hunting and was ideal for horse-racing.

Rufus Castle

Dorset **Map: p233 G4.** *Ruins open.*
Rufus Castle was originally constructed in the late 11th or early 12th century to protect the royal manor of Portland and the passage into Wey-

mouth harbour. Robert, Earl of Gloucester, illegitimate son of Henry I (1100-1135), besieged and captured the castle during the civil wars that troubled Stephen's reign (1135-1154). Robert was the principal supporter of his half-sister, Matilda, in her claim to the throne.

Rufus Stone

Hampshire **Map: p233 H3.**
Standing 4 miles northwest of Lyndhurst in the New Forest, this monument commemorates the spot where the unpopular William Rufus (1087-1100) is supposed to have died, killed by an arrow while out hunting.

Runcorn

Cheshire **Map: p238 A2.** *Castle ruins open all the time.*
In AD 914 a castle or fortification was built at this strategic fording point over the River Mersey by Ethelfleda, ruler of the Mercians and eldest daughter of Alfred the Great (AD 871-899).

Rycote Park

Oxfordshire **Map: p234 D2.** *Chapel open Mon to Sat daily, Sun afternoons.*
Said to be haunted by the ghosts of Sir Thomas More and his youngest brother, the chapel belong to a splendid Tudor house that burned down in 1745, and is supposed to have been visited by Charles I (1625-1649).

St Albans

Hertfordshire **Map: p235 E2.** *Verulamium Roman Theatre open daily; Museum open Mon to Sat daily, Sun afternoons.*
In AD 61 the Roman town of Verulamium was sacked by Boudicca during the revolt of her tribe, the Iceni, against the Romans. Verulamium was later named St Albans after a Roman soldier who was converted to Christianity and subsequently beheaded during a persecution about AD 304.

In AD 793 Offa, King of Mercia (AD 757-796), founded a Benedictine abbey where the shrine of St Alban had previously stood. It was knocked down in 1077 but later rebuilt and rededicated in 1116 at a ceremony attended by Henry I (1100-1135).

Two battles were fought at St Albans during the Wars of the Roses: the first, in 1455, was a victory for Henry VI (1422-1461) and his Queen, Margaret of Anjou, though the King himself was captured; the second was fought in 1461 and ended in victory for the Yorkists.

St Briavels

Gloucestershire **Map: p234 A2.** *Castle now a youth hostel.*
This small castle was first built in 1132 by Milo Fitzwalter, to protect himself against Welsh raids. The present structure dates from around 1276, although the stone keep collapsed in ruins in the 18th century. King John (1199-1216) used the castle as a hunting lodge.

St Michael's Mount

Cornwall **Map: p232 B5.** *Open Apr to May: Mon, Wed, Fri daily; June to Oct: Mon to Fri daily; Nov to Mar: Mon, Wed and Fri by conducted tour only.*
A Benedictine monastery was founded on this tiny island by Edward the Confessor (1042-1066) in 1044 — a copy of the abbey at Mont St Michel in Brittany. The priory was suppressed as an alien foundation in 1425 and the island, which is connected to England by a causeway at low tide, forfeited to the crown.

St Osyth

Essex **Map: p235 G2.** *Priory open mid-May to late Sept: daily; Easter.*
The village is named after the wife of a 7th-century King of Essex, who was probably a nun and was murdered by the Danes. The present abbey was founded for Augustinian canons in the early 12th century, but the remains, including the magnificent 15th-century gatehouse, are mostly of a later date. Dissolved by Henry VIII (1509-1547), it was bought by the D'Arcy family.

St Paul's Walden

Hertfordshire **Map: p235 E1.**
In 1900 the Hon. Elizabeth Bowes-Lyon, now the Queen Mother, was christened in St Paul's Walden Church. Daughter of Lord Glamis, the 14th Earl of Strathmore, she married the Duke of York, later George VI (1936-1952).

Salisbury

Wiltshire **Map: p234 C4.**
Charles II (1660-1685) was compelled to move his court from London to Salisbury in 1665 because of the Great Plague, but only stayed for four months. Salisbury was the farthest that Charles's brother, Roman Catholic James II (1685-1688), advanced against the army of the Protestant William of Orange, later William III (1689-1702), in 1688.

Work on Salisbury Cathedral was begun in the early 13th century and alterations in the 1790s were approved by George III (1760-1820).

Salisbury Hall

Hertfordshire **Map: p235 E2.** *Open Easter to Sept: Sun afternoons and public holidays; July to Sept: Thur afternoons also.*
The house was first built by Sir John Cuttes, treasurer to Henry VIII (1509-1547), in the mid-16th century and modernized towards the end of the 17th century. Charles II (1660-1685) visited here often and is said to have installed Nell Gwynne here for a time.

Salle

Norfolk **Map: p239 G4.**
The magnificent church in this village was made possible by the generosity of Sir Geoffrey Boleyn, Lord Mayor of London, in 1457, and his successors

St Michael's Mount

There is a tradition that his great-granddaughter, Anne Boleyn, second wife of Henry VIII (1509-1547) and mother of Elizabeth I (1558-1603), is buried here.

Sandringham

See pages 88-89. **Map: p239 F3.**

Sandwich

Kent **Map: p235 H3.**
One of the Cinque Ports, Sandwich was perhaps the most important harbour in England until the 16th century, when drifting sand cut it off from the sea. In 1217 Hubert de Burgh, acting for the infant Henry III (1216-1272), sailed from Sandwich to defeat the French fleet which had been summoned by the King's rebellious barons. Richard I (1189-1199) landed here on his return from Europe and the Third Crusade in 1194, as did Edward, the Black Prince, on his return from a French campaign in 1357. Catherine of Braganza, wife of Charles II (1660-1685), is known to have visited in 1672 but refused to step out of her carriage. The best-known visit of all was made by Elizabeth I (1558-1603) in 1573.

Savernake Forest

Wiltshire **Map: p233 H1.** *Open all the time.*
Savernake was a royal forest before the Norman Conquest. Traditionally, on a visit of the reigning monarch, the warden blows a great medieval hunting horn. This ceremony was last performed in 1940, on a visit by George VI (1936-1952). Henry VIII (1509-1547) was a frequent visitor to Wolf Hall, home of the hereditary wardens of Savernake, and in 1536 he married the warden's daughter, Jane Seymour, the day after the execution of his second wife, Anne Boleyn.

Sawston Hall

Cambridgeshire **Map: p239 F5.** *Not open.*
Mary I (1553-1558) spent the first night at Sawston Hall after being informed of the death of her brother, Edward VI (1547-1553). The house is now a language centre.

Scarborough Castle

North Yorkshire **Map: p241 H2.** *Open Mon to Sat daily, Sun afternoons. Closed public holidays.*
The castle at Scarborough was first built in 1136. It was strengthened by Henry II (1154-1189) by the addition, in 1182, of a stone keep. In 1312 Piers Gaveston was besieged in the castle and eventually taken prisoner and beheaded. Gaveston was an arrogant man who had risen from comparatively humble origins to be the favourite and principal advisor of the weak Edward II (1307-1327).

Sedgemoor

Somerset **Map: p234 A4.**
Sedgemoor, near Bridgwater, was the scene of the last battle of any consequence to be fought on English soil. The illegitimate son of Charles II (1660-1685), James, Duke of Monmouth, raised a rebellion against his Catholic uncle but had to flee after losing the battle here in 1685.

Selby

North Yorkshire **Map: p238 C1.**
According to tradition, William the Conqueror (1066-1087) founded a Benedictine abbey at Selby in 1069 to commemorate the birth of his son, Henry, in the town. The Queen handed out the annual Maundy money in Selby Abbey in 1969.

Sevenoaks

Kent **Map: p235 F3.** *Knole open Apr to Nov: Wed to Sat daily, Sun afternoons; bank holiday Mons.*
Knole, the house that dominates Sevenoaks, was begun by Thomas Bourchier, Archbishop of Canterbury, in 1456. Henry VIII (1509-1547) later appropriated the house from another Archbishop, Thomas Cranmer, in 1536. It was in royal hands for 30 years until Elizabeth I (1558-1603) leased it to Thomas Sackville, whose descendants have lived here since.

Knole

Shaftesbury

Dorset **Map: p233 G2.** *Abbey open daily.*
Shaftesbury Abbey contains the grave of St Edward the Martyr (AD 975-979), who had been on the throne of England for only three years before being murdered at Corfe in AD 979, when he was only 16. The abbey, which soon became a centre of pilgrimage, was founded around AD 888 by Alfred the Great (AD 871-899), who appointed his daughter, Ethelgifu, as its first abbess. Canute (1016-1035) died in Shaftesbury in 1035.

Sherborne

Dorset **Map: p233 G2.** *Castle open Easter to May: Thur and weekend afternoons, public holidays; June to Sept: afternoons.*
The ecclesiastical importance of Sherborne dates from the establishment of the see of Western Wessex by St Aldhelm in AD 705. In 1075 the see was transferred to Old Sarum (Salisbury), and the abbey was finally dissolved by Henry VIII (1509-1547), though since it was also a parish church it escaped destruction.

Before 1139 a fine castle was built at Sherborne by the Bishop of Salisbury but it fell into disrepair during the following century. In 1589 the estates were leased to Elizabeth I (1558-1603), and she gave them to Sir Walter Raleigh, who built a new castle here in 1594. By 1625 the lands had passed to the Digby family, who have lived here ever since. During the Civil War the castle held out against siege by Parliamentary forces for three years, until it was taken by General Fairfax in 1645. Once in possession, Fairfax ordered the destruction of its walls.

Sherbourne also has royal connections with education. Alfred the Great (AD 871-899) is supposed to have been taught here. The school was refounded by Edward VI (1547-1553) in 1550.

Sheriff Hutton

North Yorkshire **Map: p241 G2.** *Castle not open.*
Elizabeth of York, eldest daughter of Edward IV (1461-1483), lived at Sheriff Hutton for some years before 1486, when she married Henry VII (1485-1509). The marriage united the Houses of York and Lancaster and prevented any further outbreaks of the Wars of the Roses. In 1525 the castle was given to Henry Fitzroy, illegitimate son of Henry VIII (1509-1547). The castle fell into disrepair in the 17th century.

Sheriff Hutton Church contains the tomb of Edward, Prince of Wales, who died in 1484, aged 10. He was the only child of Richard III (1483-1485).

Shoreham

West Sussex **Map: p235 F3.**
Shoreham was an important port in the Middle Ages. Prince John, later King John (1199-1216), landed here with an army from France in 1199 to assert his claim to the throne. Shoreham was also the scene of a famous departure — that of Charles II (1660-1685) for France after his defeat at the Battle of Worcester in 1651.

Shrewsbury

Salop **Map: p237 F2.** *Castle open Mon to Sat daily; also Sun in summer.*
Shrewsbury Castle was built in about 1080 by Roger de Montgomery, who had arrived in England with William the Conqueror (1066-1087) and been created Earl of Shrewsbury. The Montgomerys lost the earldom only 20 years later, however, after the rebellion of the 3rd Earl, Hugh, against Henry I (1100-1135) in 1102. The castle was besieged and captured by Stephen (1135-1154) in 1138.

Royal visits to Shrewsbury have been frequent, due to the town's proximity to the Welsh border. King John (1199-1216) came here in 1207 and again in 1216. Henry III (1216-1272) visited four times between 1220 and 1241, and again during the war against Simon de Montfort in 1265. In 1283, Edward I (1272-1307) had David, brother of Llywelyn the Last (1246-1282), executed within the walls of Shrewsbury Castle during one of his campaigns against the Welsh. Edward II (1307-1327) visited in 1322 but made himself unpopular by promising his opponents an amnesty and then promptly arresting them.

In 1403.Henry IV (1399-1413) and his son, later Henry V (1413-1422), fought and defeated Sir Henry Percy, known as Hotspur, outside Shrewsbury. The battle forms the climax to Shakespeare's *Henry IV*. Hotspur was later quartered.

Henry VII (1485-1509) stayed at Shrewsbury for two weeks before the Battle of Bosworth (1485). During the Civil War Shrewsbury was in Royalist hands until 1645, when a Parliamentary force took the castle with the loss of two men.

Sidmouth

Devon **Map: p233 E3.**
Queen Victoria (1837-1901) spent a period of her early infancy in this old-fashioned seaside resort, in Woolbrook Cottage, which is now a hotel.

Sissinghurst

Sissinghurst Castle

Kent **Map: p235 F4.** *Castle garden open Apr to mid-Oct: Tue to Fri afternoons, weekends daily.*
Sissinghurst Castle was built in the mid-16th century by the hated Sir John Baker, Attorney-General and a member of the Privy Council of Henry VIII (1509-1547). Mary I (1553-1558), visited him at Sissinghurst. The castle fell into ruins in the 1750s but the garden and gatehouse were beautifully restored in the 1930s.

Sizergh

Cumbria **Map: p240 D2.** *Castle open Apr to Sept: Wed, Thur, Sun and bank holiday Mon afternoons; Aug: Mon afternoons also.*
There has been a castle at Sizergh for many centuries, and the Strickland family have owned it since 1239. The Queen's Room derives its name from Catherine Parr, last wife of Henry VIII (1509-1547), who visited it a few days after the death of her husband.

Slaughter Bridge

Cornwall **Map: p232 C3.**
Not far from Tintagel is Slaughter Bridge, supposedly the site of King Arthur's third battle with his nephew Mordred, during which the latter was finally slain and the King fatally wounded.

Snape Castle

North Yorkshire **Map: p241 F2.** *Part of the castle ruins open.*
For some time Snape was the home of Catherine Parr, sixth and last wife of Henry VIII (1509-1547), who lived here during her previous marriage to John Nevill, Lord Latimer.

Somerton Castle

Lincolnshire **Map: p238 D3.** *Nothing remains of the castle today.*
Two miles west of Boothby Graffoe is where Somerton Castle stood. Built on the site of an old Saxon fortress, the manor house was fortified in 1281 by Bishop Bek, who later gave it to Edward I (1272-1307). Somerton was the home of King John of France from 1359 to 1360, when he was held captive following the Battle of Poitiers (1356).

Southampton

Hampshire **Map: p234 C4.**
For centuries Southampton has been one of the most important ports in England. Canute (1016-1035) was offered the crown here in 1016, on the death of Ethelred the Unready (AD 976-1016) and just over 500 years later Philip of Spain landed at Southampton, surrounded by vast pomp and splendour, on his way to Winchester Cathedral and his marriage to Mary I (1553-1558). Queen Victoria (1837-1901) is known to have stayed in the Dolphin Hotel and the Star Hotel.

Southend on Sea

Essex **Map: p235 G2.**
This seaside resort was made popular by a visit of Princess Caroline, estranged wife of the Prince Regent, later George IV (1820-1830), to nos. 7, 8 and 9 Royal Terrace in 1804.

South Kyme Castle

Lincolnshire **Map: p239 E3.** *Not open.*
Only the grey square keep remains of the old castle of Kyme — the rest was burned down in the 18th century. The castle was once owned by the Dymoke family, who were for many centuries the king's champions.

Southwell

Nottinghamshire **Map: p238 D3.**
Charles I (1625-1649) spent his last hours of freedom at Southwell in May 1646 before going to Newark to surrender up to the Scots.

Southwold

Suffolk **Map: p239 H5.**
The guns that point towards the North Sea on the clifftop near Southwold are supposed to have been captured at Culloden by the Duke of Cumberland, who presented them to the town. Southwold, or more usually Sole Bay, was the site of a British naval victory over the Dutch in 1672. James, Duke of York, later James II (1685-1688), led the English fleet.

Stafford

Staffordshire **Map: p237 G1.** *Stafford Castle open Sun to Fri daily.*

Ethelfleda, Lady of the Mercians, daughter of Alfred the Great (AD 871-899), built a fort at Stafford in AD 913.

There were two castles here, one within and one outside the city walls. Both were built under William the Conqueror (1066-1087), but were in ruins by the 1680s. Many royal visitors have come to Stafford, without dramatic incident, although Prince Rupert, nephew of Charles I (1625-1649), is said to have used the weathercock of St Mary's Church as target practice.

Stamford

Lincolnshire **Map: p238 D4.**
The church of the Friars Minor at Stamford is the burial place of Joan, 'the Fair Maid of Kent', wife of Edward, the Black Prince, who died in 1385. She was the mother of Richard II (1377-1399), who passed from her care on his accession to the throne at the age of 10.

Stamford Bridge

Humberside **Map: p241 G3.**
Only days before the Battle of Hastings Saxon Harold (1066) was engaged in the battle against the invading King of Norway at Stamford Bridge. The invaders were routed and the Norwegian King killed, then Harold's army was forced to march south again to face William the Conqueror.

Sudbury Hall

Derbyshire **Map: p235 G1.** *Open Apr to Oct: Wed to Sun and bank holiday Mon afternoons.*
Queen Adelaide, wife of William IV (1830-1837) often stayed at this fine Jacobean house during her long period of ill health following the death of her husband in 1837.

Sudeley Castle

Gloucestershire **Map: p234 B1.** *Open Mar to Oct: afternoons.*
Sudeley, near Winchcombe, is the burial place of Catherine Parr, last wife of Henry VIII (1509-1547). She died within the castle walls in 1548, aged 36, only a few days after giving birth to a daughter by her fourth husband, Thomas Seymour. A year later, Seymour was beheaded, suspected of poisoning his wife so that he could further his courtship of Princess Elizabeth, later Elizabeth I (1558-1603).

Sutton Cheyney

Leicestershire **Map: p237 H2.**
The Battle of Bosworth, which led to the accession of the Tudor dynasty, was fought near this village in 1485. Richard III (1483-1485) camped close by and is supposed to have drunk from King Richard's Well.

Sutton Hoo

Suffolk **Map: p235 H1.**
The finding of a magnificent ship burial at Sutton Hoo in 1939 has proved to be of outstanding significance, though it is still not known whom it commemorated. The richness of the objects found indicates that he was certainly a mid-7th-century king, but it is not known whether he was Christian or pagan, English or Swedish. Redwald, Ethelhere and Ethelwald are East Saxon royal contenders, and no Swedish name has been put forward with any authority. Whoever it was, his relics are among the most impressive of the British Museum's treasures.

Swanage

Dorset **Map: p233 H3.**
Swanage Bay was the site of the first British naval battle of any consequence, in AD 877. The previous year a Danish army had attacked and taken Wareham. By AD 877 Alfred the Great (AD 871-899) had forced the Danes to retreat, both by land and at sea, finally overtaking the Danish fleet near Swanage and winning a resounding victory.

Swineshead

Lincolnshire **Map: p239 E5.**
According to tradition King John (1199-1216) is believed to have contracted his fatal illness through an over-indulgence of peaches and new ale at the Cistercian abbey at Swineshead. The King was engaged in a civil war at the time and struggled on to Newark, but could go no further and quickly died.

Tamworth

Staffordshire **Map: p237 H2.** *Castle open Mon to Thur daily, Sun afternoons. Closed Christmas, New Year.*
Tamworth was the site of a fortification built by Ethelfleda, Lady of the Mercians and daughter of Alfred the Great (AD 871-899). The keep was built in Norman times but has been much altered since, especially during the 16th century.

Tattershall Castle

Tattershall Castle

Lincolnshire **Map: p239 E3.** *Open Mon to Sat daily, Sun afternoons. Closed Christmas, New Year.*
The 100ft tower that still stands was built by Lord Cromwell, the royal treasurer, in 1445, and is one of the finest examples of medieval brickwork in England. Margaret Beaufort, Countess of Richmond and Derby and mother of Henry VII (1485-1509), lived here for a short time, and in 1520 her grandson, Henry VIII (1509-1547), gave it to Charles Brandon, Duke of Suffolk, who was married to his sister Mary.

Taunton

Somerset **Map: p233 F2.** *Castle open daily.*
Taunton was one of the centres used by the commission which visited the West Country in 1685, under the control of Judge Jeffreys. It was sent to try all those who had taken part in the Protestant rebellion of James, Duke of Monmouth, illegitimate son of Charles II (1660-1685) earlier that year. The trials became known as the Bloody Assizes because the punishments exacted there were so unjust.

Sudeley Castle

Tewkesbury

Gloucestershire **Map: p234 B1.**
After the Battle of Tewkesbury in April 1471, there was no further Lancastrian threat to the throne of England for 12 years, until the death of Edward IV (1461-1483). The Yorkist army was commanded by the King, together with the Duke of Gloucester, later Richard III (1483-1485); the Lancastrians, led by Edward, Prince of Wales, were routed, and the Prince of Wales was killed.

Tewkesbury Abbey

Thornbury

Gloucestershire **Map: p233 G1.**
Edward Stafford, Duke of Buckingham, started building a magnificent castle at Thornbury in 1511 but, as he was executed by Henry VIII (1509-1547) in 1521, he did not finish it. The castle is now a restaurant.

Tickhill

South Yorkshire **Map: p238 C2.** *Castle not open.*
Built soon after the Norman Conquest, Tickhill Castle passed into the hands of Henry I (1100-1135) and remained under royal control until its partial demolition by the Roundhead Colonel Lilburn in 1644.

During the prolonged absence of Richard I (1189-1199) abroad, Tickhill was held for his brother King John (1199-1216). However, on Richard's return from the crusades, the castle's defenders were hanged. In 1254 it formed part of the dowry of Eleanor of Castile, wife of Edward I (1272-1307).

Tilbury

Essex **Map: p235 F3.** *Fort open May to early Aug: Sun afternoons.*

Before they sailed out to attack the Spanish Armada in 1588, Elizabeth I (1558-1603) reviewed her troops at Tilbury, where they were stationed in case the Armada should land. In a famous speech to the assembled company of 20,000 she said: 'I know I have the body of a weak and feeble woman, but I have the heart and stomach of a king, and of a king of England too'.

Tintagel

Cornwall **Map: 232 C3.** *Castle open Mon to Sat daily, Sun afternoons. Closed public holidays.*
Tintagel is famous for its connections with King Arthur and Sir Tristram. According to the 12th-century tales of Geoffrey of Monmouth, Arthur was born here. The historical Arthur, however, was probably a British leader who may have led the British against the Saxons at Mons Badonicus in about AD 500. The ruins visible today are probably of medieval origin.

Titchfield

Hampshire **Map: p234 C4.** *Place House ruins open.*
Henry VI (1422-1461) was married to the 15-year-old Margaret of Anjou in the Abbey of the White Canons at Titchfield in 1445. The abbey was converted into Place House in 1542, following the Dissolution of the Monasteries during the reign of Henry VIII (1509-1547). In 1647, Charles I (1625-1649) escaped from his captivity and rode to Place House where he was welcomed. It was felt that the Isle of Wight would make the best refuge for the King, and so two friends, Ashburnham and Legge, were sent to the governor of the island. He returned to Place House with the envoys and promptly arrested the King.

Towton

North Yorkshire **Map: p238 C1.**
On Palm Sunday 1461 the bloodiest and one of the most decisive battles of the Wars of the Roses was fought. The Battle of Towton established Edward IV (1461-1483) on the throne and deposed Henry VI (1422-1461), temporarily crushing the Lancastrian nobility.

Trematon

Cornwall **Map: p232 D4.** *Castle gardens open as advertised.*
Built by Robert of Mortain, half-brother of William the Conqueror (1066-1087), the keep of Trematon Castle dates from the late 11th century. In 1337 the castle became part of the Duchy of Cornwall created by Edward III (1327-1377) for his son Edward, the Black Prince, then aged seven.

Tutbury

Staffordshire **Map: p238 C4.** *Castle open daily.*
Standing just north of Burton-on-Trent, Tutbury Castle was originally a Saxon fortification, but a castle was built in the 11th century. In 1266, the castle was forfeited to the House of Lancaster, until in 1322, Thomas, Earl of Lancaster, nephew

of Edward I (1272-1307), was hounded northwards from the castle by his cousin, Edward II (1307-1327).

Tutbury Castle acted as a temporary prison for Mary, Queen of Scots (1542-1567), where she was treated more as a guest.

Wakefield

West Yorkshire **Map: p238 C1.** *Sandal Castle ruins open all the time.*
The Battle of Wakefield, on 30 December 1460, was an overwhelming Lancastrian victory. Richard, Duke of York and father of Edward IV (1461-1483), and his son, Edmund, were both killed when they sallied out of Sandal Castle.

Wallingford

Berkshire **Map: p234 D2.**
When William the Conqueror (1066-1087) was marching from Hastings to London in 1066 he was forced to follow the Thames up as far as Wallingford before he could cross. Here he accepted the surrender of Wigod, a Saxon king, and later built a castle to command this important stretch of river. Wallingford Castle was held for the Empress Matilda almost throughout the civil wars of her cousin Stephen's reign (1135-1154), and it was her destination after her dramatic escape from Oxford, through the snow and over the frozen Thames. Both Henry III (1216-1272) and his son Edward, later Edward I (1272-1307), were imprisoned at Wallingford during their struggle against Simon de Montfort and his allies. Wallingford was also the prison used for Margaret of Anjou, widow of Henry VI (1422-1461), after her husband had been murdered in the Tower and her son killed at the Battle of Tewkesbury in 1471. Joan, widow of Edward, the Black Prince, lived at Wallingford for some years towards the end of her life. Little of the abbey survived the Dissolution of the Monasteries (1536), and the castle was destroyed by Cromwell's soldiers.

Walmer Castle

Kent **Map: p235 H3.** *Open Mon to Sat daily, Sun afternoons. Closed Christmas, New Year.*
The castle was built by Henry VIII (1509-1547) as a protection against any possible invasion by Charles V of Spain or François I of France. Together with the castles of Sandown and Deal, it was part of a series of defensive fortifications along the south coast. Since the 18th century, Walmer Castle has been the residence of the Lord Warden of the Cinque Ports, a post whose incumbents have included Pitt, Wellington, Curzon and Churchill. Queen Victoria (1837-1901) visited Wellington here as a young girl. The present Lord Warden is Queen Elizabeth, the Queen Mother, the first woman ever to hold the office.

Walsingham

Norfolk **Map: p239 G3.** *Abbey grounds open Apr: Wed afternoons; May to July and Sept: Wed and weekend afternoons; Aug: Mon, Wed, Fri and weekend afternoons; Easter to Sept: bank holiday Mons.*

The shrine of the Virgin Mary at Walsingham originated in 1061 when the lady of the manor was instructed in a vision of the Virgin to build a replica of the Holy House at Nazareth. The shrine was visited by many medieval kings. The last King to come here was Henry VIII (1509-1547), who ordered its destruction during the Dissolution of the Monasteries (1536).

Waltham Abbey

Essex **Map: p235 F2.**
The abbey was first built by Harold (1066) in the later years of the reign of Edward the Confessor (1042-1066) and was consecrated in 1060. The foundation had been generously endowed with lands and possessions, and Harold visited it often. There is a tradition that his body was brought here after the Battle of Hastings (1066) and buried under the high altar. The abbey was partially destroyed in 1536.

Waltham Cross

Hertfordshire **Map: p235 E2.**
Waltham Cross still has an Eleanor Cross, erected to commemorate the route taken by the funeral procession of Eleanor of Castile, Queen of Edward I (1272-1307), on its way from Lincoln, where she died, to London in 1290.

Walton-on-Thames

Surrey **Map: p235 E3.**
Inscribed on a pillar of Walton Church is a verse attributed to Elizabeth I (1558-1603):

'Christ was the worde and spake it:
He took the bread and brake it:
And what the worde doth make it,
That I believe and take it.'

Wantage

Berkshire **Map: p231 H1.**
Wantage was the birthplace of Alfred the Great (AD 871-899), born in AD 849 in the royal palace built by his father Ethelwulf (AD 839-855). No trace of this palace now remains.

Wareham

Dorset **Map: p233 G3.** *Priory of Lady St Mary gardens open May to Oct: Wed and 3rd Sun of each month.*
Wareham is the burial place of Beorhtric or Brihtric, King of the West Saxons, who died in AD 800. It was during his reign that the Danes first landed, in small numbers, on the south coast, and the town was often ravaged by Danish invasions. Several kings fought battles to defend it, including Alfred the Great (AD 871-899) who drove the invaders out of the town. The ancient nunnery in the town was destroyed in AD 876. The Normans built a keep in the town, which Henry I (1100-1135) used to imprison Robert, Duke of Normandy, eldest son of William the Conqueror (1066-1087). Henry defeated him at Tinchbrai in 1106 and kept the unfortunate Duke in various prisons until his death in 1134.

Warkworth

Northumberland **Map: p243 H4.** *Castle open Mon to Sat daily, Sun afternoons. Closed public holidays.*
Due to its proximity to the Scottish border, Warkworth Castle has had a stormy history. William the Lion (1165-1214) besieged it twice and burned it in 1174, when Henry II (1154-1189) had driven the Scots from Northumbria. By the early 14th century the castle had passed to the Claverings, who held it against Robert Bruce (1306-1329) from 1322 to 1323. Soon after this the Percy family acquired it and held it for many years, although their tenure was often interrupted by forfeiture. Their rebellion in 1405, for example, in alliance with Archbishop Scrope of York, obliged Henry IV (1399-1413) to besiege and take the castle. It was returned by Henry V (1413-1422) but again forfeited during the Wars of the Roses. After 1480 it changed hands several times and was then restored to Sir Thomas Percy by Mary I (1553-1558) in 1557. Sir Thomas held the place for 12 years but lost it again due to his participation in the rising of the North. The castle subsequently fell into decay until its partial restoration in the 19th century.

In 1715 James, the Old Pretender, son of James II (1685-1688), was proclaimed King James III at the market cross of Warkworth.

Warwick

Warwickshire **Map: p237 H3.** *Castle open daily except Christmas day.*
The first fortification at Warwick was built by Ethelfleda, daughter of Alfred the Great (AD 871-899). A stone castle was not built here, however, until after the Norman Conquest, when William the Conqueror (1066-1087) ordered that one be built on the lands of the Saxon thane Thurkel. On Thurkel's death his estates were granted to Henry de Newburgh, who was created Earl of Warwick, though the castle was not given to him as the Earls were made hereditary custodians. In 1264, during the war between Henry III (1216-1272) and Simon de Montfort, the castle was mostly destroyed. The title and the remains of the castle then passed to the Beauchamps, who are responsible for the edifice that can be seen today.

The most famous Earl of Warwick, known as the Kingmaker, inherited the title in the 15th century, but after his Machiavellian career was ended at the Battle of Barnet in 1471, it fell to his son-in-law, George, Duke of Clarence, brother of Edward IV (1461-1483). According to tradition, the Duke drowned in a butt of malmsey wine. The Duke's son Edward was one of the unhappiest victims of the Wars of the Roses: born in Warwick Castle, he was imprisoned from the age of eight,

Warwick Castle

first by his uncle, Richard III (1483-1485), and then by Henry VII (1485-1509), and executed at the age of 24 on a charge of conspiracy.

For 60 years the earldom lapsed, then Henry VIII (1509-1547) granted it to John Dudley, who later became Duke of Northumberland and was executed for his attempts to install the nine-day Queen, Lady Jane Grey, on the throne in place of Mary I (1553-1558). James I (1603-1625) bestowed the castle, but not the title, on Sir Fulke Greville, a cultivated man who restored it to its former splendour. His family was granted the title in the 18th century. Warwick Castle is well preserved.

Wells

Somerset **Map: p233 F2.**
During the Protestant rebellion of James, Duke of Monmouth, illegitimate son of Charles II (1660-1685), in 1685, a number of his hastily raised troops ran amok in Wells and in the cathedral itself. The rowdy levies were no match for the regular army of James's uncle, James II (1685-1688), who defeated them at the Battle of Sedgemoor (1685), and ended the rebellion.

Weybridge

Surrey **Map: p235 E3.**
The Palace of Oatlands in Weybridge was built by Henry VIII (1509-1547), who had long coveted the estate as a useful adjunct to nearby Hampton Court. The palace was intended for his fourth wife, Anne of Cleves, but the 'Flanders Mare' never lived here as the marriage was not consummated and lasted only six months. Henry married Catherine Howard, his fifth wife, at Oatlands on 28 July 1540. By February 1542 Catherine too had been beheaded, for admitted adultery with numerous men both before and after her marriage.

Oatlands was largely destroyed under the Commonwealth, though houses have been built and rebuilt on the site since. It is now a hotel.

Weymouth

Dorset **Map: p233 G3.** *Sandsfoot Castle ruins open to the public.*
Weymouth and Melcombe Regis were once important commercial ports and were both granted privileges by medieval monarchs. Henry VIII (1509-1547) built one of his many defensive forts — Sandsfoot Castle — nearby.

George III (1760-1820) paid the first of several visits here in 1789. The King's belief in the power of sea-bathing to improve his erratic health was to transform several seaside towns into popular holiday resorts.

Wherwell

Hampshire **Map: p234 C4.**
A priory was founded at Wherwell in about AD 986 by Elfrida, stepmother and possible murderess of St Edward the Martyr (AD 975-979). She was the mother of Ethelred the Unready (AD 979-1016), who succeeded Edward. Wherwell Monastery was supposed to have been founded in expiation for Elfrida's guilt. It was destroyed during the Dissolution of the Monasteries (1536).

Whippingham

Isle of Wight **Map: p234 C5.**
It was at St Mildred's Church, Whippingham, that Queen Victoria (1837-1901) and her family worshipped when staying at Osborne House near Cowes. The church was designed by Prince Albert in 1860. Their youngest daughter, Princess Beatrice, was married to Prince Henry of Battenberg in Whippingham Church in 1885 and is buried, together with her husband, in the Battenberg Chapel opposite the royal pew.

Whitchurch

Salop **Map: p238 A3.**
The church of St Alkmund was originally founded by Ethelfleda, Lady of the Mercians, daughter of Alfred the Great (AD 871-899), though it did not last long and has been rebuilt several times. After the Battle of Shrewsbury (1403) Sir Henry Percy, better known as Hotspur, was buried in the village, though he was quickly exhumed due to rumours of his survival, and his corpse was quartered and distributed around the kingdom.

White Ladies Priory

Hereford & Worcester **Map: p234 B1.**
By 1651 the Cistercian priory of White Ladies had long been no more than a yeoman farmhouse. However, it was to this place that Charles II (1660-1685) made his way after his defeat at the Battle of Worcester (1651). It was owned by Charles Gifford, a member of the small group that had escaped with Charles.

Wimborne Minster

Dorset **Map: p233 G3.**
Wimborne nunnery was founded by Cuthburga, sister of Ina, King of the West Saxons. Earlier in her life she had married Aldfrith, King of Northumbria, but soon left him, to the satisfaction of both parties, and retired to a nunnery at Barking. She had founded Wimborne by AD 705 and continued as abbess here until her death.

Wimborne was chosen as the burial place of Ethelred (AD 866-871), who was succeeded by his younger brother, Alfred the Great (AD 871-899). The church was destroyed by the Danes in about 1013, but rebuilt soon after 1066. Edward the Confessor (1042-1066) founded a college of secular canons at Wimborne, which flourished until the Dissolution of the Monasteries (1536).

Winchcombe

Gloucestershire **Map: p234 B1.**
Winchcombe was for some time the principal residence of the Mercian kings. An abbey was founded here by Kenulf, King of Mercia, on the site of a nunnery built 10 years before by Offa (AD 757-796). Kenulf's son and successor, St Kenelm, is supposedly buried here. The abbey was completely destroyed in 1539 by Thomas, Lord Seymour, who had been granted the site by Henry VIII (1509-1547) in 1536.

Winchelsea

East Sussex **Map: p235 G4.** *Court Hall Museum open May to Sept daily.*
Winchelsea was so important as a port that, although the settlement had twice been washed away in storms, Edward I (1272-1307) gave orders that it be rebuilt, placing his treasurer and the Lord Mayor in charge of the project. Today, the sea has retreated and Winchelsea is a quiet village.

Winchelsea parish church contains carved heads believed to represent Edward I (1272-1307) and Edward II (1307-1327), with their respective Queens. The town museum contains a fragment of the canopy carried above James II (1685-1688) at his coronation.

Winchester

Hampshire **Map: p234 C4.** *Castle hall open Apr to Sept: Mon to Sat daily, Sun afternoons.*
The town owes its importance in the Middle Ages to Alfred the Great (AD 871-899), who made it an ecclesiastical and cultural centre, establishing the Royal Mint here and keeping his treasury in the town. This made Winchester the effective capital of Wessex. The cathedral here was largely constructed during the reign of William the Conqueror (1066-1087) near the site of a Saxon church built by Alfred. It became the burialplace of many Saxon kings, and their remains are now enclosed in wooden chests on the top of the choir screen. William Rufus (1087-1100) was also brought to Winchester for burial after his death in the New Forest. It has also been the scene of coronations. Matilda, wife of William the Conqueror (1066-1087), was crowned here on 11 May 1068 in the presence of her husband.

William the Conqueror recognized the city's importance by building a royal palace here as well, but subsequently it was partially destroyed by Oliver Cromwell. Charles II (1660-1685) planned to build another but died before it was finished.

The castle, of which only the Great Hall is still standing — Cromwell's troops destroyed the rest — was begun by William the Conqueror and completed by Henry III (1216-1272) in 1235. This was where the Empress Matilda made her dramatic escape from her cousin Stephen. The Treaty of Winchester in 1153 marked the end of the civil wars that had plagued Stephen's reign.

In the Great Hall hangs King Arthur's Round Table. Measuring 18ft in diameter and weighing 1¼ tons, it dates from the 1350s and in reality has only romantic connections with Arthur.

Windsor Castle

See pages 84-87. **Map: p243 D3.**

Wingfield Manor

Derbyshire **Map: p239 G5.** *Ruins open.*
Wingfield Manor was one of the many houses and castles belonging to the Earl of Shrewsbury during the reign of Elizabeth I (1558-1603). It was in these houses, under the Earl's supervision, that Mary, Queen of Scots (1542-1567), spent her long captivity from 1569 until her execution in 1587.

Winsford

Cheshire **Map: p238 A3.**
The Cistercian Abbey of Vale Royal near Winsford was founded by Edward I (1272-1307) in 1277, and thrived until the Dissolution of 1536. James I (1603-1625) stayed here in 1617, by which time the estate had been sold to the Cholmondeleys, a prominent Royalist family. Parliament plundered and partially destroyed Vale Royal during the Civil War.

Witley

Surrey **Map: p234 D4.**
Witley was a royal manor for many centuries, and before 1066 had belonged to Earl Godwin, father of Harold (1066). It formed part of the dowry of both wives of Edward I (1272-1307) — Eleanor of Castile and Margaret of France. The White Hart pub nearby is said to stand on the site of a hunting lodge that belonged to Richard II (1377-1399).

Woburn

Bedfordshire **Map: p234 D1.** *Abbey open Easter to Oct daily; Feb to Mar and Nov: afternoons.*
Woburn Abbey was a Cistercian foundation before the Dissolution of the Monasteries (1536), when the last abbot was hanged for disagreeing with the actions of Henry VIII (1509-1547). Henry subsequently granted the site to John Russell, 1st Earl of Bedford. It was not until the time of the 4th Earl, a close friend of Charles I (1625-1649), however, that rebuilding began, and Charles is said to have visited the site. The 4th Duke was largely responsible for the 18th-century building standing today.

Wokingham

Berkshire **Map: 240 C1.** *Town hall open by appointment.*
Elizabeth I (1558-1603) provided quantities of mulberry trees for Wokingham and east Berkshire in an effort to encourage the silk industry.

Woodbridge

Suffolk **Map: p235 G1.**
Many of the ships in the fleet of Edward III (1327-1377) were built at Woodbridge, and the great convoy that took the King to Calais first met at the mouth of the River Deben, off Woodbridge.

Worcester

Hereford & Worcester **Map: p234 B1.**
The first know fortification at Worcester was built by Ethelfleda, Lady of the Mercians, and daughter of Alfred the Great (AD 871-899), to combat the Danes. A Norman castle was built here shortly after the Conquest, and played a central role in the civil wars during the reign of Stephen (1135-1154). Its loyalty changed hands from Stephen to his cousin, Empress Matilda, and later to her son Henry II (1154-1189). King John (1199-1216) often visited the city and in the will he dictated on his deathbed desired that he should be 'buried in the Church of the Blessed Virgin and St Wulfstan at Worcester'. His body was duly transported here from Newark in a funeral convoy of armed mercenaries and entombed before St Wulfstan's altar. By this time extensive additions had been made to the castle, including a number of underground dungeons in which John's successor, Henry III (1216-1272), was imprisoned here by Simon de Montfort in December 1264 and January 1265, before de Montfort was defeated and killed by Henry's son, Prince Edward, later Edward I (1272-1307), at the Battle of Evesham (1265).

Worcester is most famous for the Civil War battle between the well-trained Roundhead troops under Oliver Cromwell and the army of Charles II (1660-1685) in 1651, after which the King was forced to hide in the Boscobel Oak and to flee incognito through England to France.

Workington

Cumbria **Map: p234 D3.** *Ruins of Workington Hall in Curwen Park open.*

Mary, Queen of Scots (1542-1567) spent a night at Workington Hall after her defeat at Langside in 1568, and sent a letter from here to her cousin, Elizabeth I (1558-1603), asking for help against the rebels in Scotland. She was taken to Carlisle Castle in semi-captivity soon after.

Worthing

West Sussex **Map: p235 E5.**
Worthing originally became fashionable on account of its popularity with Princess Amelia, the 15th and last child of George III (1760-1820), who was born in 1783. From 1798 onwards the Princess came regularly to Worthing for the sea-bathing.

Wrest Park

Bedfordshire **Map: p235 E1.** *Open Apr to Sept; weekends and bank holiday Mons daily.*
The park was mainly laid out by Henry Grey, 12th Earl and later Duke of Kent, and Lord Chamberlain to Queen Anne (1702-1714). Edward VII (1901-1910) was a regular visitor.

Worcester Cathedral

York

North Yorkshire **Map: p241 G3.** *Clifford Tower open daily.*

In AD 306 Constantius I, Emperor of Rome, died in York, whereupon the army declared his son Constantine emperor. Thus it was at York that one of the most influential periods of Europe's history began, and the new emperor did not forget the city: when calling a council of bishops at Arles in AD 314, he stipulated that one of the British representatives should be the Bishop of York.

After the Romans departed, York's history becomes murky for almost 200 years, although Geoffrey of Monmouth records that King Arthur drove the Saxons from the town. From about AD 592 to AD 876 the independent kingdom of Northumbria had its capital at York. The most famous of its kings is possibly Edwin (AD 616-632), who married a Christian princess and was himself converted by the monk Paulinus, whom he appointed as the first post-Roman bishop. For the next 200 years the kingdom of Northumbria was

governed by Danish or Scandinavian kings such as Eric Bloodaxe. After the Norman Conquest York prospered through its position as county town of the largest county in England. However, it was always liable to raids by the Scots. In 1138 David I (1124-1153), King of Scots, was repelled near Northallerton by Thurstan, Archbishop of York. The Scots who had previously settled in the city were described by a contemporary as 'filthy and treacherous creatures, scarcely human'.

William the Conqueror (1066-1087) had ordered the building of the first castle at York, but it was Henry III (1216-1272) who built the first stone fortifications, between 1244 and 1263. During the 13th and 14th centuries the city continued to prosper as English kings used it as a base for their campaigns against Scotland. At times the city became the effective capital of England: Edward I (1272-1307) kept the exchequer, royal courts and chancery here for seven years, as well as holding several Parliaments in the city.

Almost every king and queen of England visited the city, some more than others: Richard II (1377-1399) came here nine times, and on Good

Lantern Tower, York Minster

Friday 1396 distributed alms to 12,040 paupers in the town. Richard III (1483-1485) was another monarch who favoured the city, granting it, among other things, the right to return four members of Parliament, a privilege shared only by London. On his death, the city fathers recorded that he had been 'piteously slain and murdered, to the great heaviness of this city' — which was not a sentiment shared by all. Henry VIII (1509-1547) only visited the north once, in 1541, with his fifth wife Catherine Howard.

In 1536 York was occupied for a month by what is known as 'the pilgrimage of grace', a peaceful rebellion in defence of the church. No force was necessary to disband the crowds, but the leader of the demonstration was sentenced to hang alive in chains from Clifford Tower until he died. Margaret Clitherow was sentenced to death by 'pressing' for harbouring Catholic priests 50 years later. She was later beatified and her house in the Shambles is now a Roman Catholic shrine.

York City and Minster from the air

St Mary's Abbey

Royal Scotland

Aberchalder

Highland Region **Map: p244 D3.**
The site of Aberchalder Lodge, which was destroyed by fire, is southwest of Fort Augustus, at the foot of Loch Oich. From here, on 27 August 1745, Prince Charles Edward Stuart, better known as Bonnie Prince Charlie, reviewed an army of Highlanders that had grown from seven men to nearly 2,000 in only a month.

Aberdeen

Grampian Region **Map: p245 H3.** *Old Tolbooth open by appointment.*
After the reign of Malcolm Canmore (1057-1093) the power of the Scottish kings was extended over the fertile lands of Moray and it became essential to control Aberdeen, the principal market town and port in the northeast of Scotland. William the Lion (1165-1214) gave the town its first royal charter in 1179, though trading privileges had been allowed by David I (1124-1153).

By petition to the Borgia pope, Alexander VI, James IV (1488-1513) obtained authority to found Scotland's third university at Aberdeen in 1495. The new college included the first faculty of medicine, the first in Britain.

In the city centre is the Old Tolbooth, part of the townhouse since 1868, where Mary, Queen of Scots (1542-1567), was forced by her half-brother, the Earl of Moray, to watch the execution of her admirer, Sir John Gordon.

Abergeldie

Grampian Region **Map: p245 F3.** *Castle not open.*
The lands of Abergeldie were acquired by the 1st Earl of Huntly in 1482 and the first castle was built here by his son, in about 1550. It was the Highland home of the Duchess of Kent, mother of Queen Victoria (1837-1901), and was much enlarged by Victoria's husband, Prince Albert, in the 1850s. At the end of the 19th century it became the Highland home of Albert Edward, Prince of Wales, later Edward VII (1901-1910).

Abernethy

Tayside Region **Map: p243 E1.**
The three tribal centres of the ancient Pictish kingdom (pre-AD 843) were Scone, Dunkeld and Abernethy. Scone was the centre of government, but some of the Pictish kings preferred to hold court at Abernethy, only 8 miles away. Abernethy was the capital of the kingdom when William the Conqueror (1066-1087) invaded Scotland in 1072. His professional army marched unopposed to the Tay, where it was joined by a huge fleet. The Conqueror himself received the homage of Malcolm Canmore (1057-1093) at Abernethy.

Abernyte

Tayside Region **Map: p243 E1.**
So scattered as to be scarcely recognizable as a village, old maps of Abernyte show the remains of the ancient castle of Carquhannan, known locally as Balchoinnie. Nearby is a spring, the King's Well, which is probably named after Edgar (1097-1107), the seventh son of Malcolm Canmore (1057-1093), who was placed on the throne of Scotland with English support.

Aboyne

Grampian Region **Map: p245 G3.** *Castle not open.*
The lands and castle of Aboyne belonged to the Keith family, Earls Marischal of Scotland, before Charles II (1651-1685) created the earldom of Aboyne in 1660 and gave it to Charles Gordon, son of the Marquess of Huntly. The famous Highland Games are held here every September.

Airlie

Tayside Region **Map: p245 F4.** *Castle open as advertised.*
Princess Alexandra's husband, the Hon Angus Ogilvy, is the son of the 9th Earl of Airlie. The Ogilvys have had their family seat at Airlie since 1430 and the earldom was created by Charles I (1625-1649) in 1639. Two years later the old castle was destroyed by the Earl of Argyll, since the Ogilvys remained loyal to the King and refused to sign the national covenant. The Earl then joined Montrose and fought with him throughout 'the year of glory' (1644-1645), during which the Royalist army won numerous victories against the Parliamentarian Covenanters. The castle lay in ruins until 1793, when it was rebuilt.

Airlie Castle

Alloa

Central Region **Map: p243 E2.**
The lands of Alloa were conferred on Sir Robert Erskine in 1360 by David II (1329-1371) and have since remained with his descendants, who became the earls of Mar. Alloa Tower, built by the Earls in the 15th century on an ancient site, still stands in the eastern part of the town. Mary, Queen of Scots (1542-1567), stayed in the tower many times as a child. Her son, James VI (1567-1625), and grandson, Prince Henry, were also visitors here.

Arbroath

Tayside Region **Map: p245 G5.** *Abbey and Abbey Museum open Mon to Sat daily, Sun afternoons.*
The murder of Thomas à Becket at the behest of Henry II (1154-1189) precipitated a rebellion by the English barons, and they were joined by the Scots King, William the Lion (1165-1214). William was captured at Alnwick in 1174, on the same day that Henry suffered the penance of scourging by the monks of Canterbury, and the coincidence of the two events so impressed William that on his return to Scotland he founded a priory at Arbroath dedicated to St Thomas à Becket in 1178.

In 1320 Bernard de Linton, Robert Bruce's secretary and chaplain, was abbot of Arbroath and chancellor of Scotland. It was he who drew up the most important document of Scottish history, the Declaration of Arbroath, which was signed at the abbey by eight Earls and 45 barons in 1320. The declaration was an appeal from the people of Scotland to Pope John XXII, asking for his dispassionate intervention in the bloody quarrel between the Scots and the English.

Ardchattan

Strathclyde Region **Map: p242 B1.** *Priory open daily.*
Ardchattan Priory was founded in 1230 as a house of the strict Vallescaulian order of Benedictines. In 1308 Robert Bruce (1306-1329) held a Parliament here.

Ardtornish

Highland Region **Map: p244 B5.** *Ruins open Apr to Oct: daily.*
Ardtornish castle was built in the 13th century. It was once a seat of the Lords of the Isles.

Ardverikie

Highland Region **Map: p244 D4.** *Ardverikie House not open.*
Lying along the southern shore of Loch Laggan, Ardverikie is one of the greatest of Scotland's deer forests. The estate's connections with royalty stretch back over many centuries to the early kings of Dalriada, who may have hunted here.

Aros

Strathclyde Region **Map: p244 B5.** *Ruins open all the time.*
Like Ardtornish, Aros Castle was held for the Lords of the Isles by the Macleans and guarded the southern part of the Sound of Mull. Little of the castle remains today. During the Wars of Independence Robert Bruce (1306-1329) took the castle from Lame John MacDougall of Lorne, who had sided with the English.

Arran

Strathclyde Region **Map: p242 B3.** *Ruins of Kildonan Castle open all the time.*
At Drumadoon Point near Blackwaterfoot on the western side of the island there are several coastal caves. One of these, the King's Cave, is reputed to have been a hiding place of Robert Bruce (1306-1329) during the winter of 1306-1307. Perhaps it was even the scene of the famous incident in which the despairing King watched a

Arbroath Harbour

spider trying to swing its web into a ledge. He gained the strength to persevere with his campaign when the spider succeeded.

Kildonan Castle in the southwest end of the island may also have been one of the King's hiding-places, and it is likely that he watched from here for the signal to return to the mainland. When the time came, Bruce left Arran from King's Cross, at the southern tip of Lamlash Bay.

Athelstaneford

Lothian Region **Map: p243 F2.**
Tradition has it that Hungus, King of the Picts, defeated an army of Saxon Northumbrians under King Athelstane here.

Ayr

Strathclyde Region **Map: p242 C3.**
William the Lion's (1165-1214) charter creating Ayr a royal burgh in 1203 is the earliest such charter still in existence. He built a castle at the mouth of the River Ayr at the same time.

One of William Wallace's earliest and best known exploits was the burning of the barns of Ayr during which 500 English troops billeted here were killed. In 1307 the castle was captured by Edward I (1272-1307), but Robert Bruce (1306-1329) recaptured it in 1314 and destroyed it, to prevent it falling back into the hands of his enemies. The following year he convened a Parliament in the church of St John at Ayr.

Badenoch

Highland Region **Map: p245 E4.**
The name 'Badenoch' comes from the Gaelic *Baideanach*, 'the drowned land', and it refers to a massive territory in the Central Highlands,

bounded by the Monadhliath, Grampian and Atholl Mountains. Alexander II (1214-1249) granted the area to the Comyns, whose chief was murdered by Robert Bruce (1306-1329) at Dumfries in 1306.

Ballater

Grampian Region **Map: p245 F3.**
In the 19th century a railway was built, connecting Ballater to Aberdeen: Queen Victoria (1837-1901) would allow it to go no further as it would disturb the tranquillity of the area. As the closest station to Balmoral, it was much used by the royal family.

Balmoral Castle

See pages 92-94. **Map: p245 F3.**

Balvenie Castle

Grampian Region **Map: p245 F2.** *Open Mon to Sat daily; Sun afternoons. Closed public holidays.*
Between 1542 and 1550, the Stewarts gave Balvenie — a 13th-century courtyard castle — the shape it still has today. Mary, Queen of Scots (1542-1567), stayed here in 1562.

Banchory

Grampian Region **Map: p245 G3.**
North of Lochton of Leys, in the parish of Banchory, rises the Hill of Fare. This commanding position was taken up by the Earl of Huntly in October 1562 when he confronted the army of Mary, Queen of Scots (1542-1567), at the Battle of Corrichie. The Queen watched the battle from a natural granite seat, still known as 'the

Queen's Chair'. Huntly later died of apoplexy in his armour while surrendering.

Bannockburn

Central Region **Map: p242 D2.** *Bannockburn House not open.*
In 1314 Stirling Castle was held for the English by Sir Philip Mowbray against a siege layed by Edward, brother of Robert Bruce (1306-1329). Mowbray bargained with Edward, saying that if no English army had appeared within 3 miles of the castle by Midsummer's Day he would surrender. Spurred on by the bargain, Edward II (1307-1327) mustered 'the most puissant army England had ever put to the field' and marched north to raise the siege. Bruce chose a position about 2 miles south of the castle and faced the English troops on Midsummer's Eve with a force outnumbered two to one. The Battle of Bannockburn was fought over two days and, mainly due to Bruce's skilful generalship, was a resounding victory for the Scots. Edward II fled to Dunbar and Berwick.

Not far from the battlefield is Bannockburn House, a handsome, late-17th-century mansion. Prince Charles Edward Stuart spent a night here on his march south in 1745, and again made it his headquarters for a time on his return northwards after his victory at the Battle of Falkirk in 1746.

Barra Hill

Grampian Region **Map: 245 G2.**
In 1307, Robert Bruce (1306-1329), wishing to consolidate his position, rode north with 3,000 men to face the Comyn Earl of Buchan who had raised an army to avenge the death of his brother, murdered by Bruce at Dumfries in 1306. Bruce fell sick, however, and had to be carried in a litter; about half his army disbanded, thinking that their leader would die. When Buchan heard of Bruce's illness he advanced boldly towards Slivoch and camped on Barra Hill nearby. Tradition has it that Bruce, on hearing that his enemy had been boasting of the slaughter of one of his patrols, rose from the litter and led 700 men to Buchan's camp. They attacked on Christmas Eve and routed Buchan's army.

Bass Rock

Lothian Region **Map: p243 F2.** *Boat trips around the rock.*
A massive volcanic plug rising 320ft out of the Firth of Forth, the Bass Rock was for many years a prison. James, youngest son of Robert III (1390-1406) later James I (1406-1437), was taken to the Bass Rock in 1406, when he was 11 years old. His escort, however, was killed and the young Prince was stranded on the island for a month. At last a ship bound for Danzig rescued him, but it was captured by pirates and the boy was delivered to the English King, Henry IV (1399-1413), who held him prisoner for 18 years.

Ben Alder

Highland Region **Map: p244 D4.**
Situated to the east of Fort William, Ben Alder is

one of the wildest mountains in a wild region. This area is known as Macpherson country, and after the Battle of Culloden in 1746, the chief of that clan, Ewan Macpherson of Cluny, a keen Jacobite, lived in a thicket on the side of Ben Alder in a hut called 'Cluny's Cage'. The 'cage' could house six or seven people and Cluny lived secretly inside it for 10 years, and between 2 and 13 September 1745 he was joined by Prince Charles Edward Stuart.

Birgham

Borders Region **Map: p243 G3.**
In 1018 Birgham was the site of a vicious battle between Malcolm II (1005-1034) and the Anglo-Danes of Northumbria. During the 12th and 13th centuries, Birgham was used as a meeting-place by representatives of Scotland and England, and it was here in 1290 that the Treaty of Birgham was finally agreed. By this, Margaret, the Maid of Norway and infant Queen of Scotland (1286-1290), was to marry Prince Edward of England, later Edward II (1307-1327). The young bride died within three months of the treaty being signed. The bitter dispute about the succession that followed led to the Wars of Independence.

Birnam

Tayside Region **Map: p245 F5.**
The moving of Birnam Wood, near Perth, to Dunsinane, some 12 miles to the southwest, would spell the end for Macbeth (1040-1057), according to Shakespeare. In fact, the Battle of Lumphana between Macbeth and Malcolm, the future Malcolm III (1057-1093), was fought in Aberdeenshire. On the southeast side of Birnam

Blair Castle

hill the marks of a round fort known as 'Duncan's Camp' where Duncan I (1034-1040) is reputed to have held court here.

Blackford

Tayside Region **Map: p243 E1.**
The village of Blackford is close to an early fording place on the River Allan. According to legend, an early Caledonian King lost his wife, Helen, here while she was crossing the river in spate. The King was so distraught that he drained the whole strath to recover her body, and Helen's burial place is identified by a solitary knoll on the river bank.

Blackford was famous for its brewery and following his coronation at Scone in 1488, James IV (1488-1513) stopped here to sample the ale.

Blackness

Lothian Region **Map: p243 E2.** *Castle open Mon to Sat daily, Sun afternoons.*
Blackness served as the port for Linlithgow, the palace of the kings, and was therefore one of the principal harbours on the Forth. Built in the 15th century, Blackness Castle was the scene of a meeting between James III (1460-1488) and his rebellious nobles.

Blair Atholl

Tayside Region **Map: p245 E4.** *Blair Castle open May to early Oct: Mon to Sat daily, Sun afternoons; Apr: Sun and Mon; Easter week.*
The village of Blair Atholl has grown up around Blair Castle, ancient seat of the Murrays, Dukes of Atholl. Edward III (1327-1377) visited Blair Atholl in 1336, and Mary, Queen of Scots (1542-1567), came in 1564. Montrose garrisoned the castle in 1644 and during the Civil War it was stormed by Cromwell in 1652. Prior to the Battle of Killicrankie in 1689, the castle was occupied for James II (1685-1688).

The Duke of Atholl was exiled for supporting the Old Pretender, son of James II, in the 1715 rebellion, but he returned with the Young Pretender, Bonnie Prince Charlie, 30 years later. He and the Prince stayed at Blair Castle in September 1745 and reviewed their growing army. The following year the castle was captured and unsuccessfully besieged by the Highland army under Lord George Murray, the Duke of Atholl's brother. This was the last time in British history that a castle was besieged.

Borrodale

Highland Region **Map: p244 C4.** *The farmhouse of Borrodale not open.*
The farmhouse of Borrodale is where Prince Charles Edward Stuart landed in August 1745. He spent several days here and won the allegiance of Donald Cameron of Lochiel, one of the most important leaders in the west.

Borthwick

Lothian Region **Map: p243 F2.** *Castle not open.*
Borthwick Castle was built in 1430 for the 1st Lord Borthwick. Mary, Queen of Scots (1542-1567), stayed here in June 1567 but was forced to escape disguised as a page when the castle was surrounded by nobles who did not approve of her marriage to the Earl of Bothwell.

Braemore

Highland Region **Map: p247 F2.**
At Eagle Rock, just above Braemore, is a monument to the Duke of Kent, son of George V (1910-1936), who was killed when his aeroplane crashed here on 25 August 1942.

Brechin

Tayside Region **Map: p245 G4.** *Round tower open.*
Brechin was 'given to the Lord' in AD 990, and the round tower of the cathedral may date from that time, although the main part of the building dates from the 13th century. It was completely rebuilt during the 19th century.

Between March and July 1296 Edward I (1272-1307) devastated the kingdom of Scotland, and at Perth on 2 July he received an abject letter of submission from John Balliol (1292-1296). John was required to surrender to the Bishop of Durham at Brechin Castle, and when he did so the red and gold arms of his humbled kingdom were ripped from his tunic. From that day the unfortunate King was known as 'Toom Tabard' — the Empty Coat — and he and his son were sent into captivity in England.

Brodick

Strathclyde Region **Map: p242 C3.** *Castle open*

Brodick Castle

Apr: Mon, Wed and Sat afternoons only; May to Sept: afternoons only. Country Park and Garden: open daily.

Brodick Castle occupies an impressive site overlooking the safe anchorage of Brodick Bay, on the east coast of the Isle of Arran. It was the ancient seat of the Dukes of Hamilton and passed from them by marriage to the Dukes of Montrose.

A Viking fort on the site had been expanded into a tower by the 14th century, when Sir James Douglas stormed it in the name of Robert Bruce (1306-1329). The whole building was levelled by Donald Balloch of Isla in 1455, in support of the Douglas cause against James II (1437-1460). Shortly after he had destroyed Brodick Castle the political wind turned against him and his expedition petered out. The castle was again destroyed in 1544 as part of the 'rough wooing' by Henry VIII (1509-1547) of Mary, Queen of Scots (1542-1567), whose childish hand he wanted for his son Edward, later Edward VI (1547-1553).

Today the oldest parts of Brodick Castle date from 1558; further additions were made in 1650 and during the 19th century.

Burntisland

Fife Region **Map: p243 E2.**

Burntisland, on the Forth, was used as a harbour by Agricola in AD 83. The town grew up around the harbour and was developed by monks until, in 1541, it became a royal burgh with a charter dated 1586. The General Assembly of the Church of Scotland met here in the presence of James VI (1567-1625) in 1601 and laid its plans for *The Authorized Version of the Bible* before the King.

Cadzow

Strathclyde Region **Map: p242 D3.** *Ruins not open.*

Now a picturesque ruin standing above the River Avan, Cadzow Castle was formerly the seat of the Hamilton family, who gave their name to the nearby town. Prior to that it was a royal residence, and the old oak trees in the park are said to have been planted by David I (1124-1153).

The Hamiltons received the grant of Cadzow from Robert Bruce (1306-1329) after the Battle of Bannockburn in 1314, and maintained the castle until the mid-16th century. After defeating Mary, Queen of Scots (1542-1567), at the Battle of Langside in 1568, the Regent of Scotland, the Earl of Moray, destroyed Cadzow Castle to punish Archbishop Hamilton of St Andrews, a loyal supporter of the Queen.

Caerlaverock Castle

Dumfries & Galloway Region **Map: p243 E5.** *Open Mon to Sat daily, Sun afternoons; closed Tues and alternate Weds in winter.*

This great triangular moated fortress is of unusual size and splendour for a border castle. In 1300 Caerlaverock was the scene of a famous siege by Edward I (1272-1307). From the 14th century the castle was the home of the Earls of Nithsdale, but since it was a key stronghold in controlling the western marches of Scotland, it changed hands several times. In 1644, the castle was largely destroyed by Covenanters.

Cakemuir

Lothian Region **Map: p243 F2.** *Castle open by appointment only.*

After her escape by night from Borthwick Castle, Mary, Queen of Scots (1542-1567) made her way to the nearby Black Castle in Cakemuir. She was found by her husband, the Earl of Bothwell, wandering in the garden, dazed after her ordeal, and was taken to Bothwell's castle at Dunbar.

Callander

Central Region **Map: p242 D1.**

Together with Crieff and Pitlochry, Callander is described as one of the natural gateways to the Highlands. The manse of the parish church of St Kessog, named after the 6th-century Columban missionary Kessog, is built on the site of the old castle of Callander. This was granted to the Livingstone family, later Earls of Callander and of Linlithgow, by Robert Bruce (1306-1329). The 1st Earl was a close friend of James VI (1567-1625) and when James became King of England in 1603, he entrusted Livingstone with the safe keeping of his daughter, the Princess Elizabeth. In later life Elizabeth, grandmother of George I (1714-1727), was married to Frederick, Elector of Palatine, who was briefly King of Bohemia.

Cambuskenneth Abbey

Central Region **Map: p242 D2.** *Open Apr to Sept: Mon to Sat daily, Sun afternoons.*

Lying within a loop of the Forth across the river from Stirling, Cambuskenneth is named after Kenneth McAlpin (AD 843-858), who defeated the Picts at the Battle of Logie in about AD 845, and thus united the thrones of the Picts and the Scots.

The abbey, little of which remains today, was founded by David I (1124-1153) in 1147 for a colony of Augustinian monks from France; it became both wealthy and strategically important. Robert Bruce (1306-1329) kept his reserves of arms here during the Battle of Bannockburn (1314), and in 1326 he held a Parliament here, the first at which representatives of the burghs are recorded as appearing. Bruce's sister married Andrew Moray of Bothwell in the abbey church.

James III (1460-1488), who was cruelly murdered by a man disguised as a priest after the Battle of Sauchieburn, near Stirling, and his Queen were secretly buried at Cambuskenneth. Their tomb under a blue marble slab before the high altar was not discovered until 1864; Queen Victoria (1837-1901) ordered that a monument be erected to them here.

Campbeltown

Strathclyde Region **Map: p242 B3.**

Campbeltown is claimed to be the first settlement of the Dalriadan sovereigns on their arrival from Ireland in the 5th century. In the 6th century St Kiaran set up his headquarters on an islet near Davarr Island, off Campbeltown.

The present name comes from the Campbells of Argyll, to whom the town was transferred by James V (1513-1542) in an attempt to break the power of the Macdonald Lords of the Isles. James's father, James IV (1488-1513), had also tried to curb the western clans, and to this end built a castle called Kilkerran above the town in 1498. The King held court here in the summer of that year. The exact site of Kilkerran Castle is uncertain, for nothing of it remains today.

Carberry

Lothian Region. **Map: p243 F2.** *Tower not open.*

Carberry Hill is 8 miles east of Edinburgh, close to Pinkie. It was here, on 15 June 1567, that Bothwell took up his position with his wife Mary, Queen of Scots (1542-1567), and a small royal army, to face the Confederate lords who were demanding his execution. Neither army was keen to commence the fight and by the end of the day many of the Queen's soldiers had slipped away. Bothwell, realizing that a fight would then be hopeless, said farewell to his wife, whom he had married only four weeks earlier, and rode to Dunbar, and thence to Denmark. Mary was taken prisoner by the Confederate lords.

Cardross

Strathclyde Region **Map: p242 C2.**
Lying 3 miles east of the modern village of Cardross is the site of the Palace of Cardross Castle, where Robert Bruce (1306-1329) died.

Castle of Mey

Highland Region **Map: p246 G1.** *Gardens open in July and Aug as advertised.*
Formerly called Barrogill, a house was built here, first for the Bishops of Caithness and, after the Reformation, for the Sinclair earls of Caithness. From 1650 Macleod of Assynt was held prisoner at Barrogill for many years by the 4th Earl of Caithness for betraying Montrose to his death after the Battle of Carbisdale. Queen Elizabeth, the Queen Mother, acquired the house as a private residence in the Highlands shortly after the death of her husband, George VI (1936-1952). It took her three years to renovate the castle.

Castle Stalker

Strathclyde Region **Map: p244 C5.** *Not open.*
Situated on an islet in Loch Laich, Castle Stalker was built in the 15th century to receive James IV (1488-1513). For many years it was a favourite hunting lodge for successive kings, and thereafter it was the seat of the Stewarts of Appin.

Cawdor

Highland Region **Map: p245 E2.** *Castle open May to Sept: daily.*
Cawdor was originally named 'Calder', after the Calders who were descended from the brother of Macbeth (1040-1057), to whom Macbeth resigned the thanedom when he assumed the crown. The castle is still the home of the Earls.

Cluny Castle

Highland Region **Map: p245 E3.** *Ruins open.*
After the '45 Rising, Cluny Castle was burned by government troops while its owner, Sir Ewan Macpherson of Cluny, hid in his 'cage' above the castle on the slopes of Ben Alder. The mansion house that replaced the old castle was designed by Robert Adam in the later years of the 18th century. It is regarded as one of his less successful buildings, though Queen Victoria (1837-1901) considered it as a possible Highland residence before settling in Deeside.

Coldingham

Borders Region **Map: p243 G2.**
The village of Coldingham grew up around the remains of a 13th-century priory, successor to a nunnery founded by the Northumbrian Princess Ebba in the 7th century, on nearby St Abbs Head. King John of England (1199-1216) plundered and burned the priory in 1216, while fighting William the Lion, King of Scots (1165-1214). It was partly burned again in 1544 by an English raiding party. In 1662 the priory was reconstructed and further work was carried out in 1854 and in 1955. Today the church is one of the oldest in Scotland to be still in use.

Coldstream

Borders Region **Map: p243 G3.**
Due to its position on the border, Coldstream has been a military fording place since earliest times. Edward I, the 'Hammer of the Scots' (1272-1307), crossed here on his punitive northern expedition of 1296, and Robert Bruce (1306-1329) used the ford several times in his fight against Edward II (1307-1327). James IV (1488-1513) led the flower of Scottish chivalry over the burn en route to their death at Flodden only 3 miles away, in 1513.

In 1640 General Leslie led the Covenanting army through Coldstream against Charles I (1625-1649), who was at Berwick, and 20 years later the Parliamentarian General Monck brought his experienced army down from the north, through Coldstream, on his way to London to bring about the restoration of Charles II (1660-1685). The Coldstream Guards were raised by Monck on his way through Coldstream by combining Fenwick's and Hessellrigg's regiments, and the regimental headquarters was established here in 1659.

Craigmillar Castle

Lothian Region **Map: p243 F2.** *Open Mon to Sat daily, Sun afternoons.*
A large L-plan tower built some 3 miles from Edinburgh, just south of the village of Duddingston, in about 1374, Craigmillar Castle stands in ruins in a modern housing development. James III (1460-1488) imprisoned his younger brother John, Earl of Mar, here in about 1475 in the belief that he was conspiring against him.

Craigmillar is best known as the favourite residence of Mary, Queen of Scots (1542-1567); the country around reminded her of happier days, and she called it 'Little France', by which name it is still known today. It was at Craigmillar that Mary heard the proposals of her cousin, Elizabeth I (1558-1603), for her marriage in 1564. Five years later, at the Craigmillar Conference, she listened to proposals for her separation from her husband, Lord Darnley, which were put to her by a group of leading noblemen. The Queen left the matter up to them, little thinking that the result would be murder and the nobles signed a pact — the 'Craigmillar Bond' — to remove Darnley.

Craignethan Castle

Strathclyde Region **Map: p243 E3.** *Open Sat to Wed daily, Thur morning.*
Craignethan Castle was built in the 16th century by Sir James Hamilton of Finart, bastard son of the Earl of Arran. A favoured royal architect, he did much to improve Falkland, Linlithgow, Stirling and Edinburgh castles. He was beheaded by James V (1513-1542) in 1540, on a doubtful charge of intended regicide, and it was said that the King wished to acquire his estates.

The Hamiltons were staunch supporters of Mary, Queen of Scots (1542-1567), and there is a

Craigmillar Castle

Cramond

large vaulted hall within the castle, where the Queen stayed. The castle was largely dismantled by her opponents, but a new house was built by the Hay family in 1665 on the site.

Cramond

Lothian Region **Map: p243 E2.**
Situated at the mouth of the River Almond on the southern shore of the Forth, Cramond was of considerable importance in Roman times. It was from here that Roman galleys made the first circumnavigation of Britain.

Cramond Bridge was built in 1619 and stands on the site of an earlier, wooden structure which was the scene of an attack by gypsies on James V (1513-1542), who was disguised as a commoner. Saved by a miller, who attended to the King's bruises, a tradition remains that whenever a monarch crosses the bridge, the miller's descendants should stand ready with a ewer of water and a basin to present to the sovereign. In 1952, Elizabeth II crossed the bridge and the obligation was fulfilled.

Crathie

Grampian Region **Map: p245 E3.**
Crathie Church, built in 1895 close to Balmoral, is the worshipping place of the royal family while they are staying on Deeside. The building itself contains many royal memorials, and John Brown, trusty gillie and Highland companion of Queen Victoria (1837-1901), is buried in the churchyard.

Crawford Castle

Strathclyde Region **Map: p243 E3.** *Castle open.*
The 1st Earl of Crawford was Sir David Lindsay of Glenesk (1365-1407), and the title, still in the Lindsay family, is the oldest, continually held earldom in Scotland. Sir David and his men fought on the field of Otterburn in 1388 and were commemorated by the unknown author of the *Ballad*

of Otterburn as 'the Lindsays light and gay'. He married the Princess Elizabeth, daughter of Robert II (1371-1390).

In 1449 the 4th Earl, known as 'the Tiger Earl of Crawford', allied himself with the Douglas opposition to James II (1437-1460), and besieged the King in Perth, but his son supported James III (1460-1488) and as a result was created Duke of Montrose, the first Scot of non-royal birth to be elevated to a dukedom. The title died with him in 1495. In the same year, Crawford Castle passed to the Douglas family and in the 1520s they handed it over to James V (1513-1542), who used it as a hunting lodge. The hunting in the area was especially good and James used Crawford to entertain foreign ambassadors. The story goes that on days when the hunting was disappointing, the King would give his foreign guests gold pieces, mined from Leadhills and minted with an image of the King wearing a hunting bonnet.

The Douglas lairds reconstructed the castle in the late 16th and early 17th centuries.

Crichton Castle

Lothian Region **Map: p243 F2.** *Open Mon to Sat daily; Sun afternoons. Closed Oct to May: Fri; public holidays.*
Crichton grew from a plain 14th-century tower into an elegant mansion house noted for its elaborate 16th-century Italianate decorations. Turstan of Crichton had held lands under David I (1124-1153), but the castle itself was originally owned by Sir William Crichton. By the 15th century it had passed to the Earls of Bothwell, and it was from here in 1513 that the 2nd Earl marched out to his death with all his retainers on the battlefield of Flodden.

Crichton Castle features several times during the troubled reign of Mary, Queen of Scots (1542-1567). She first came here in 1562, with her 'four Maries', as a guest at the wedding of her half-brother, James Stewart, Earl of Moray. The second time was in 1565 during her honeymoon with Lord Darnley, who was immensely unpopular with the Scottish nobility. By 1567 he had,

however, been blown up and the Earl of Bothwell accused as his principal murderer. The Earl, meanwhile, insinuated himself into the Queen's favour and gently abducted her and brought her to Crichton. It is claimed that he raped her here so that the Queen could not but marry him. They were married in Edinburgh a month later, but within a month of the marriage both were fugitives and they never met again.

Crieff

Tayside Region **Map: p245 E5.**
Standing at the gateway to the Highlands by way of the Sma' Glen, Crieff was thoroughly burned by the Jacobites in 1715 and again in 1745. In the central square of the town is the Drummond Arms Hotel, built on the site of an earlier hostelry of the same name where Prince Charles Edward Stuart, Bonnie Prince Charlie, spent three nights from 2 February 1746.

Cromdale

Highland Region **Map: p245 F2.**
The village of Cromdale stands on the east bank of the River Spey in the fertile Haughs of Cromdale. In 1609 the village was acquired by the Laird of Grant, who persuaded James VI (1567-1625) to make it into a burgh of barony, with a gaol and court-house. Almost immediately after the accession of William and Mary (1689-1702) to the throne of England in February 1689, a Jacobite and episcopalian rebellion broke out in Scotland. On 1 May 1690 the final battle of the rebellion was fought on the Haughs of Cromdale, when General Livingstone's dragoons surprised the sleeping Highland army, killing over 300 and extinguishing the Jacobite cause for 25 years.

Crookston Castle

Strathclyde Region **Map: p242 D2.** *Open Mon to Sat daily, Sun afternoons.*
There has been a castle at Crookston since 1130, but all traces of the earlier building have disappeared and the present castle, built in the early 14th century, is now a ruin.

In 1330 the lands were granted to Stewart of Darnley. A later Darnley, Earl of Lennox, took part in a revolt against James IV (1488-1513) in 1489. The 16-year-old King led the siege of Crookston, bringing with him the famous siege gun 'Mons Meg' from Edinburgh Castle.

The son of the fourth Earl of Lennox was Lord Darnley, who married Mary, Queen of Scots (1542-1567) and was murdered in Edinburgh in 1567. Legend, probably unfounded, has it that the couple courted at Crookston.

Culloden

Highland Region **Map: p245 E2.**
By the spring of 1746 Britain had recalled several seasoned regiments from France to defend the country against Prince Charles Edward Stuart's invasion. These marched north to Inverness under the Duke of Cumberland, third son of George II (1727-1760), to confront the ragged remains of the Jacobite army.

At dawn on 16 April, less than 5,000 exhausted clansmen limped into line of battle on a bleak moor above Culloden House. They had spent the night marching to Nairn and back in a snowstorm and had not eaten for several days. The position they had chosen favoured the enemy and they were outnumbered almost two to one. The last battle fought on British soil turned into a rout for the Young Pretender and ended forever any hopes of a Stuart succession.

A cairn raised in 1881 on the north side of the road through this lonely place to Inverness commemorates the fallen, and on both sides of the road scattered stones marked with the names of the clans show the graves of the Highlanders.

Culross

Fife Region **Map: p243 E2.** *Palace open Mon to Sat daily, Sun afternoons. Closed Christmas, New Year.*

St Kentigern, the founder of Glasgow Cathedral and patron saint of that city, was born at Culross in about AD 520. Legend has it that Kentigern's mother, Theneu (also known as St Enoch), secretly married the Christian King, Owen of Lothian. Her family were pagans and when her father discovered her marriage she had to flee across the Forth alone in a small boat. The boat was driven ashore at Culross and her son was born on the beach. He was taken in and educated by St Serf, who had founded a religious community in the village.

During the 16th and 17th centuries Culross was a thriving business community, trading principally in coal and salt. James VI (1567-1625) visited the salt pans and coal mines in 1592, after he had elevated the town to a royal burgh; he visited again in 1617. The abbey, founded for Cistercians in 1215, was rebuilt by James IV (1488-1513).

Dalkeith Palace

Lothian Region **Map: p243 F2.** *Park open late Mar to Oct: daily; Nov: Sat and Sun.*

Within the present building of Dalkeith Palace are the remains of the original 12th-century castle, a Graham stronghold granted by David I (1124-1153) in 1128. The property passed by marriage to the Douglases in 1328, and it was the Douglas Earl of Morton, Regent of Scotland during the minority of James VI (1567-1625), who began the conversion from castle into palace. Morton had been an accessory to the murder of David Rizzio, favourite of Mary, Queen of Scots (1542-1567), and to the murder of Mary's husband, Lord Darnley. He was executed for the latter's murder by Mary's son, James VI in 1581.

The property passed to the Dukes of Buccleuch in the 17th century and they employed John Smith, clerk of works to Charles II (1660-1685), to complete the work of aggrandisement to designs by Sir John Vanbrugh. The palace was given as a gift to Anne, Duchess of Buccleuch and Monmouth, formerly the wife of the ill-fated Duke of Monmouth, illegitimate son of Charles II, who had raised a rebellion against his uncle, James II (1685-1688).

In 1822 the 5th Duke of Buccleuch entertained George IV (1820-1830) here, and in 1842 Queen Victoria (1837-1901) visited the palace.

Dalwhinnie

Highland Region **Map: p245 E4.**

This wild area was a favourite rallying place of the clans in the Central Highlands. Cromwell's Ironsides were checked by the men of Atholl here in 1650, and in the summer of 1745 General Cope refused to face Prince Charles Edward Stuart's growing Highland army in their native stronghold. He retired to Inverness, leaving the road to Edinburgh open to the Prince.

Queen Victoria (1837-1901) and Prince Albert stayed incognito at the Dalwhinnie Hotel in 1861.

Dingwall

Highland Region **Map: p244 D2.**

Dingwall derives its name from a corruption of 'Thing Vollr', Scandinavian for a meeting place of Parliament. The Vikings were driven out in the 12th century by William the Lion (1165-1214), who built a royal castle in the town. The castle was maintained until the 17th century, but by the mid-18th century it was in ruins.

Doune Castle

Tayside Region **Map: p242 D1.** *Open Apr to Oct daily, except Thur in Apr and Oct.*

Robert, Duke of Albany, became Regent of Scotland on the death of his brother Robert III (1390-1406), since his nephew, James I (1406-1437) was a prisoner in England. Robert persuaded the Privy Council to nominate his son Murdoch as his successor, but the inept Murdoch was seized and executed on a charge of treason on James's return in 1422. The castle of Doune was forfeited to the crown.

Margaret Tudor, Queen of James IV (1488-1513), remarried twice after the King was slain at Flodden. On the second occasion her husband was Henry Stewart, Lord Methven, whose family had been given the hereditary office of Constable of Doune Castle. In 1570 James V (1513-1542) created Sir James Stewart Lord of Doune, and by the marriage of his son to the heiress of the Regent Moray, the castle and title passed to the Earls of Moray in about 1610. During the Jacobite Rising of 1745 the castle was held for Prince Charles Edward Stuart and prisoners captured at the Battle of Falkirk in January 1746 were confined here.

By the end of the 18th century the castle was a roofless ruin and it remained so until 1883, when the 14th Earl of Moray restored it.

Duddingston

Lothian Region **Map: p243 F2.**

Duddingston village lies on the shore of Duddingston Loch at the back of Arthur's Seat, the mountain in the middle of Edinburgh. The village boasts the oldest licensed premises in Scotland, The Sheep's Heid Inn, which was visited by Mary, Queen of Scots (1542-1567) and James VI (1567-1625). There is also a 17th-century house where Prince Charles Edward Stuart stayed before his victory at Prestonpans. The Jacobite army camped near the village for six weeks at the same time.

Dumbarton

Strathclyde Region **Map: p242 C2.** *Castle open Mon to Sat daily, Sun afternoons.*

Dumbarton Rock, a 240-ft high volcanic plug of basalt washed by the Rivers Clyde and Leven, is the oldest stronghold in the British Isles. A fortress was built here in very early times and from the 4th to the 11th centuries it was the royal capital of the British kingdom of Strathclyde.

In 1026 Malcolm II, King of Scots (1005-1034) allied himself with the King of Strathclyde. When the Strathclyde King died, Malcolm set his grandson, Duncan, upon it, naming him as his successor to the throne of all Scotland. Dumbarton continued as a royal castle under a governor but was rarely used by succeeding monarchs.

When James V (1513-1542) died in 1542 he left an heir, Mary, who was only six days old. Immediately, rival factions amongst the nobility were formed; some favoured alliance with England and marriage of the baby Queen to Edward, later Edward VI (1547-1553), son of Henry VIII (1509-1547), while others favoured alliance with France and marriage to the Dauphin. The latter course was decided upon and the country was ravaged by Henry's 'rough wooing'. The five-year-old Queen was brought to Dumbarton for safety, and in July 1548 the King of France's own galley, accompanied by a small fleet, sailed up the Clyde and Mary embarked for France where she stayed for 13 years.

During the minority of James VI (1567-1625), Scotland was again plunged into internecine war between rival noble factions. Dumbarton Castle was held for the Hamiltons against the Regent, the Earl of Moray, and withstood siege for longer than any other castle except Edinburgh. In 1570 the Regent was shot and killed.

Dumfries

Dumfries & Galloway Region **Map: p243 E5.**

Dumfries has been a provincial capital from early times and it was created a royal burgh by William the Lion (1165-1214) in 1186. William also built a castle in the town, although nothing of it remains today. When Edward I, the 'Hammer of the Scots' (1272-1307), occupied Dumfries in 1300 he enlarged it and installed an English garrison. In February 1306 Robert Bruce (1306-1329) had his fateful meeting with John Comyn, known as the Red Comyn, in the church of the Gray Friars at Dumfries. It seems likely that Bruce's murder of Comyn was not premeditated, but once committed Bruce knew that the wrath of the Hammer of the Scots would fall upon him. He immediately seized Dumfries Castle, unseating the English justices while they were in session; with this event the war that would win Scotland her independence was begun.

At the end of December 1745 Prince Charles Edward Stuart stayed at Dumfries for three days.

Dunadd

Strathclyde Region **Map: p242 B2.**

The dramatic volcanic outcrop of Dunadd rises steeply for 176ft out of flat fields beside the sea, close to the village of Kilmichael Glassary. It was from here that the Scots kingdom of Dalriada was ruled. Tradition has it that the fortress was first built by Fergus, Loarn and Angus, the three sons of Erc, King of Dalriada in Ulster, when they arrived to colonize the west of Scotland in the 5th century. They came as colonists not conquerors, and skilful negotiation and intermarriage with the indigenous Pictish tribes allowed them to gain a firm foothold. The assistance of the new religion, Christianity, boosted by the arrival of St Columba in AD 563, made it possible for the newcomers to expand their influence, so that by AD 863 their tribal name was applied to the whole country — Scotland — and their King, Kenneth McAlpin (AD 843-858) was King of the Picts as well as the Scots.

Fergus brought the Stone of Destiny from Ireland, and this was kept at Dunadd for many years before it was moved to Dunstaffnage and thence to Scone.

Dunaverty

Strathclyde Region **Map: p242 B4.**
The steep rock in South Kintyre on which Dunaverty Castle was built, was the site of a prehistoric fort. All that remains today are a few fragments of masonry from the curtain walls of what was formerly one of the most important strongholds of the Lords of the Isles. It was here that Robert Bruce (1306-1329) was sheltered by Angus Og MacDonald, 'King of the Isles', in the winter of 1306, during which time Angus offered Bruce the crucial support of his Macdonald clansmen. On the collapse of the Lordship of the Isles in 1494, James IV (1488-1513) besieged the castle, captured it and installed a garrison. John of the Isles was furious, and as the King was leaving with his fleet, he recaptured Dunaverty and hanged the governor from the castle walls, in sight of James and his fleet. The King had his revenge next year, however, and John was caught, brought to Edinburgh and hanged with his four sons for high treason.

Dunaverty held out for the Royalist cause during the Civil War. The Covenanting general besieged and captured the castle in 1647, massacred the garrison and demolished the fort.

Dunbar

Lothian Region **Map: p243 F2.** *Castle ruins open.*
Dunbar, or March, and Carrick are the only two original earldoms in the south of Scotland. The position of Dunbar Castle on the coast 25 miles to the east of Edinburgh made it important for any invading army to take.

Edward I (1272-1307) was determined that the Scots King, John Balliol (1292-1296), should be his vassal. He had backed Balliol's claim to the crown on condition that he swear fealty to the English throne. The conditions imposed were humiliating and when Balliol was persuaded by his barons to rebel, Edward led a punitive expedition north, in 1296, to impose his will. At Dunbar he met the Scots army under John Comyn, persuaded them to leave their strong position on high ground and annihilated about 10,000 of them in battle.

On the night that David Rizzio, favourite of Mary, Queen of Scots (1542-1567), was murdered, in March 1566, Mary and her husband Darnley escaped to Dunbar Castle. While she was here she

gave the wardenship of the castle to Lord Bothwell, as the previous warden had been complicit in the murder, and from here she rallied support, so that nine days later she rode into Edinburgh at the head of an army of 8,000 men.

A year later Mary was back at Dunbar as the 'prisoner' of its warden. Bothwell had abducted her while she was riding from Edinburgh to Stirling, although she willingly came with him to Crichton and then to Dunbar. The last time Mary visited Dunbar Castle was on 5 June 1567, when she had escaped from Borthwick Castle and been reunited with Bothwell, now her husband.

Dunblane

Central Region **Map: p242 D1.**
In 1140, after the reduction of the Celtic Church at the instigation of the sainted Queen Margaret, wife of Malcolm III (1057-1093), her son David I (1124-1153) created a bishopric of Dunblane, and the present cathedral was started by Bishop Clement a century later. Under three blue slabs in the cathedral lie the remains of Margaret Drummond and her two sisters, daughters of the 1st Lord Drummond. They were poisoned at breakfast to make sure that James IV (1488-1513) did not marry Margaret in place of Margaret Tudor, sister of Henry VIII (1509-1547).

Dundee

Tayside Region **Map: p243 F1.**
The large number of Pictish symbol stones and

Celtic cross slabs in the neighbourhood of Dundee are an indication of the importance of the area during the Dark Ages.

Dundee was made a royal burgh about 1190 by William the Lion (1165-1214) and it quickly became one of the chief towns in Scotland. William Wallace was brought up here and made it his base in the early stages of the Wars of Independence: as a result Edward I (1272-1307) destroyed both the town and its castle twice.

A friary was founded in Dundee before 1289 by Devorguilla, mother of John Balliol (1292-1296). It was here in 1209, 11 years before the Declaration of Arbroath, that the Scottish clergy declared their support for Robert Bruce (1306-1329). Early in the reign of Mary, Queen of Scots (1542-1567), the town had been bombarded by the fleet of Henry VIII (1509-1547), as part of his 'rough wooing'.

James VIII, the Old Pretender, was proclaimed King at the Mercat Cross in Dundee on 7 January 1716, and spent a night in the town on his way to Scone for his coronation.

Dundonald

Strathclyde Region **Map: p242 C3.** *Castle ruins not open.*
An ivy-covered ruin in the village of the same name, Dundonald Castle was held during the 13th and 14th centuries by the Fitzalan (Stewart) family, one of whom married the daughter of Robert Bruce (1306-1329) and was the father of Robert II (1371-1390). Both Robert II and Robert III (1390-1406) died here.

Dunfermline

Fife Region **Map: p243 E2.** *Abbey open Mon to Sat.*
Malcolm III (1057-1093) became King of Scots by defeating Macbeth (1040-1057) at the Battle of Lumphanan. He was known as Malcolm Canmore and through his marriage to the Princess Margaret of England, the sister of Edgar the Atheling, introduced European ways into Scotland. While Malcolm removed the royal capital from Scone and Dunkeld to Dunfermline, building a 'palace' in what is now Pittencrieff Park, Margaret set about building an abbey and introducing Benedictine monks owing allegiance to the Archbishop of Canterbury, in the hope that Dunfermline would become the episcopal centre of the kingdom. When they died within three days of one another in 1093, Malcolm and Margaret were buried in their new abbey rather than at Iona. Their descendants continued to use Dunfermline as their capital.

David I (1124-1153) enlarged his mother's church into a great monastery in the middle years of the 12th century, and in 1210 William the Lion (1165-1214) was persuaded not to invade England by a divine warning that came to him while he slept beside Queen Margaret's tomb.

Additions during the following century were so extensive that the pope had to rule whether or not the church should be reconsecrated in 1249, and the following year Queen Margaret's shrine was given greater status by her canonization. It was while on his way to visit his new queen at Dunfermline that Alexander III (1249-1286) died.

In 1303 Edward I (1272-1307) set up court in

The Old Abbey

Dunfermline during his second invasion of Scotland, and on his departure he burned the abbey, though not to the ground, for it was repaired by Robert Bruce (1306-1329), who was in turn buried here.

The medieval *Ballad of Sir Patrick Spens* narrates that 'The King sits in Dunfermline toun, drinking the bluid red wine': with the accession of the Stuart kings at the end of the 14th century, the centre of government was moved to Edinburgh, and the royal palaces to Linlithgow, Falkland, Stirling and Holyrood. The palace at Dunfermline was still maintained, however, and used sporadically. Charles I (1625-1649) was born here in 1600 and his son, Charles II (1660-1685) stayed here for a short period in 1650. In all, Dunfermline has seen the birth of seven kings, one queen mother, four princes and an empress, and is the final resting-place of nine kings, five queens, six princes and two princesses.

Dundrennan Abbey

Dumfries & Galloway Region **Map: p242 D5.**
The Cistercian abbey of Dundrennan was founded by David I (1124-1153) and Fergus, Lord of Galloway, in 1142, but was not completed until 1180. The ruins that exist today consist of Norman transitional work and a chapter house dating from the 13th century.

Mary, Queen of Scots (1542-1567) spent her last night in Scotland at Dundrennan, on 15 May 1568. From the abbey she wrote again to her cousin Elizabeth I (1558-1603) asking for sanctuary, but did not wait for a reply. The following afternoon she went down to the little harbour at the mouth of the abbey burn, known today as Port Mary, and boarded a fishing boat for England. She was executed 20 years later.

Dunkeld

Tayside Region **Map: p245 F5.** *Cathedral open Mon to Sat daily, Sun afternoons.*
Dunkeld is claimed to be built on the site of Orrea, one of the five original Pictish centres. The fort ('dun') from which the town derives its name, was perched on top of the isolated hillock of King's Seat, which is now in the grounds of the Dunkeld House Hotel. Kenneth McAlpin (AD 843-858), who united the thrones of the Picts and Scots in AD 844, made Dunkeld and Scone his joint capitals.

One of the later lay abbots of Dunkeld Abbey was Crinan the Seneschal, who married Bethoc, daughter of Malcolm II (1005-1034), and whose son, Duncan I (1034-1040), was killed by Macbeth (AD 1040-1057).

Prince Charles Edward Stuart arrived in Dunkeld on 3 September 1745, and dined at Nairne House, home of Lady Nairne, between Dunkeld and Perth.

Dunnichen

Tayside Region **Map: p245 G5.**
The invading Northumbrian Angles and the Picts under King Brude confronted one another at Dunnichen in May AD 685. After decades of fighting the Angles were routed and the Picts regained all the territory north of the Forth.

Dunolly

Strathclyde Region **Map: p242 B1.** *Castle ruins open all the time.*
Dunolly Castle has been a MacDougall stronghold since the 13th century. The MacDougalls are descended from the Norse-Celt Dougall, King of the South Isles.

In the 14th century the MacDougalls were the most powerful clan in the west. Their chief, Lame John MacDougall of Lorne, was resolutely opposed to Robert Bruce (1306-1329). After his defeat at Methven in 1306, Bruce and his family, together with a group of followers, had to flee into Argyll. Here they were pursued by Lame John and his clansmen, who caught up with them at Dalrigh in the mountains south of Rannoch Moor and scattered Bruce's companions. As the future King of Scots was fleeing from the field he was stopped by a group of MacDougalls and escaped only by unfastening his cloak and riding on in his shirt. The brooch that buckled his cloak is the famous Brooch of Lorne, which is still kept by the chief of clan Dougall at Dunolly House, built in 1747 near the ruin of Dunolly Castle.

Dunoon

Strathclyde Region **Map: p242 C2.**
There has long been a castle on the hill commanding the town of Dunoon, and the present ruins date from the early 13th century. At the beginning of the Wars of Independence Dunoon was taken by Edward I (1272-1307) but after Bannockburn it was given by Robert Bruce (1306-1329) to Walter, the High Steward, who married Bruce's sister Marjorie and founded the Stuart dynasty.

In 1332 the castle was surrendered to Edward Balliol, during the civil war that followed Bruce's death, but it was retaken by Robert Stuart, who later became Robert II (1371-1390). It has remained a royal possession ever since. In 1471 James III (1460-1488) made the Earl of Argyll and his heirs hereditary keepers of Dunoon, on the condition that they should present a red rose to the sovereign whenever it be demanded. The most recent such occasion was in 1958.

In 1685 the castle was demolished by the men of Atholl and never rebuilt.

Dunottar Castle

Grampian Region **Map: p245 H4.** *Open daily Mon to Sat, Sun afternoons. Closed Nov to Mar.*
On 8 July 1650 Charles II (1660-1685) was entertained at Dunnottar by the Earl Marischal of Scotland, prior to the King's abortive attempt to recover his father's throne. Charles was crowned King of Scotland at Scone on New Year's Day 1651 and after the coronation the regalia of Scotland were taken to Dunnottar for safety, along with some private papers belonging to the King. Knowing this, an English army besieged the castle for eight months. In the meantime the castle's governor, Sir George Ogilvy, had had the papers stitched into a belt and smuggled out by his wife's kinswoman, Anne Lindsay. The crown, which had been made for Robert Bruce, the sword of state and the sceptre of Scotland were smuggled out by the wife of a local minister and were hidden under the pulpit of the church at Kinneff.

Dunsinane

Tayside Region **Map: p243 E1.**
This conspicuous conical hill rising for 1,000ft above sea-level in the Sidlaw Mountains, 12 miles to the east of Birnam Wood, is traditionally the site of a castle belonging to Macbeth (1040-1057). The remains of a prehistoric fort can be seen.

Dunstaffnage Castle

Strathclyde Region **Map: p244 C5.** *Open Apr to Sept: Sat to Wed daily.*
One of the most important castles in the west, Dunstaffnage rises from a rocky promontory guarding the entrance to Loch Etive, 4 miles north of Oban. The present building was erected in the 13th century for Alexander II (1214-1249) and was intended to be a base from which to attack the Norse rulers of the Hebrides. There had long been a fortress on the site which, in early medieval times, was the seat of the kings of Dalriada and the home of the Stone of Destiny.

The MacDougall Lords of Lorne held the castle until after Bannockburn when their lands were forfeited on account of their opposition to Robert Bruce (1306-1329). The King appointed a royal constable to hold Dunstaffnage for the crown, and then, in 1470, James III (1460-1488) gave it to the Campbell Earl of Argyll, who appointed a kinsman to hold it for him with the title of 'The Captain of Dunstaffnage'. The present owner of the castle still holds this title.

Dupplin Moor

Tayside Region **Map: p243 E1.**
On his death in 1329, Robert Bruce (1306-1329) left a five-year-old son, in the charge of Regents, to govern his unruly country. Edward Balliol, son of John Balliol (1292-1296) whom Bruce deposed, pressed his claim to the throne with the help of a large English army in the summer of 1332, sailing from the Humber with a fleet of 88 ships. They landed at Fife, marched towards Perth and defeated the royal army at Dupplin Moor. Six weeks later Edward was crowned King at Scone.

Edinburgh

See pages 202-207.

Edzell Castle

Tayside Region **Map: p245 G4.** *Open daily Mon, Wed, Fri, Sat; Thur and Sun afternoons. Closed Christmas, New Year.*
Parts of the ruined tower house of Edzell date from the early 16th century. It was originally the seat of the Stirling family, and passed from them to the Lindsays of Glenesk, who added to the original building and transformed the castle into 'the most splendid house in Angus'. In 1562 Mary, Queen of Scots (1542-1567), was a guest in the castle while on her way to Aberdeen to curb the power of the Earl of Huntly. Mary's son, James VI (1567-1625), also visited Edzell.

Elgin

Grampian Region **Map: p245 F2.**
Elgin had been created a royal burgh by 1136, and from early times was a market town and administrative centre for a wide area. David I (1124-1153) built a royal castle here, in about 1130. The castle was occupied by Edward I (1272-1307) in 1296 and marked the northern limit of his punitive expedition into Scotland. Having returned to the crown, it was popular with the early Stuart kings, particularly James II (1437-1460), who used it as a royal residence. The castle was destroyed in the 15th century, and today only fragments remain.

Elgin Cathedral, 'the Lantern of the North', was the third largest cathedral in Scotland. It was founded in 1224 and completed by the end of the

Elgin Cathedral

13th century. In May 1390 Alexander, Earl of Buchan, known as 'the Wolf of Badenoch', son of Robert II (1371-1390), was so enraged at being reprimanded by the Bishop of Moray for deserting his wife, that he plundered Elgin and burned its churches, hospices and cathedral. The cathedral was rebuilt, but it fell into disuse at the Reformation.

Between 11 and 20 March 1746 Prince Charles Edward Stuart lived in Thunderton House, now a hotel, in Thunderton Place off the High Street. It was the most splendid mansion in the city.

Eriskay

Western Isles Islands Area **Map: p246 A5.**
Prince Charles Edward Stuart arrived in the Outer Hebrides from France on 22 July 1745. His first landfall was the island of Barra; they did not land there but sailed on to anchor on the west side of Eriskay, between Barra and South Uist. The place is still known as 'the Prince's Shore'.

Ettrick Forest

Borders Region **Map: p243 F3.**
Ettrick Forest at one time covered most of Selkirkshire and much of Peebleshire. Robert Bruce (1306-1329) gave this area of wild country to Sir James Douglas, his loyal companion, and it remained in the possession of the Douglases until 1455 when the lands were forfeited. Thereafter it became a royal hunting ground.

James V (1513-1542) was determined to enforce rule in the lawless borders. In 1529 he summoned the leaders of the principal families in the neighbourhood, took assurances from them, and when they broke their assurances the following year, imprisoned or executed the ring leaders. The most notorious brigand of all, however, could not be so easily caught; 'Black Jock' Armstrong and his clan were the most powerful and troublesome of all. In the spring of 1630 James summoned his nobles to Edinburgh telling them to bring their men-at-arms and supplies for a month. With an army of between 10,000 and 12,000 men he descended on Ettrick. The brigand chief was tricked into giving himself up and was later executed without trial.

Falkirk

Central Region **Map: p243 E2.**
In July 1298 William Wallace was encamped at Callendar Wood, close to Falkirk. Hearing of this as he was preparing to fall back to Edinburgh, Edward I (1272-1307) resolved to lead his mutinous and hungry army straight there. While his men were resting on the night before the battle, Edward, who could not sleep, fell from his horse and broke two ribs, but he hid his injury and led his men up to Falkirk in the dawn of 22 July. Wallace's small army was utterly destroyed though the leader escaped.

In January 1746, on his return from England, Prince Charles Edward Stuart and his army had taken the town of Stirling. General Henry Hawley, the commander of the Hanoverian forces in Scotland and a seasoned campaigner, led his army out of Edinburgh to relieve Stirling but he was surprised by the Jacobites at Falkirk Muir, just south of the town, and his army was routed.

Falkland

Fife Region **Map: p243 E1.** *Palace open Apr to Oct: daily Mon to Sat, Sun afternoons.*
Falkland was the principal hunting seat of the kings of Scotland from the 12th century, and even before this the MacDuff 'kings' and thanes of Fife had had a castle here. In 1371 Robert II (1371-1390) granted the castle to his son, the Duke of Albany, who was governor of Scotland during the last two years of his father's reign. He was relieved of this position by his brother Robert III (1390-1406), but this King proved so inept that the General Council appointed his son and heir, David, Duke of Rothesay, as governor. Albany invited Rothesay, his nephew, to Falkland and starved him to death here in 1402. In 1425 Albany's son and grandsons were all executed by James I (1406-1437) and the castle became royal property.

The Palace of Falkland was begun by James IV (1488-1513) before 1500, and enlarged by his son, James V (1513-1542), who added Renaissance decorations to the courtyard facades on the occasion of his marriage to Madeleine, daughter of Francois I of France. After her death he further embellished the palace for his second wife, Mary of Lorraine. It was certainly the King's favourite residence, and it was to Falkland that he came to die, supposedly of a broken heart caused by the news of his army's defeat at Solway Moss in 1542. On his deathbed he was told that his wife had given birth to a female child, Mary, who was to become Queen of Scots (1542-1567).

The next three generations of monarchs, Mary, James VI (1567-1625) and Charles I (1625-1649) all enjoyed the hunting at Falkland. The royal tennis court, built by James V in 1539, and the 'lang butts' where the monarchs were accustomed to practice archery still exist.

Falkland Palace

Fassifern

Highland Region **Map: p244 C4.** *Fassifern House not open.*
Prince Charles Edward Stuart spent the night of 23 August 1745 at Fassifern House, by Loch Eil. He had raised his standard at Glenfinnan only four days before and his growing army was headed for Perth. In the garden here the Prince picked a white rose as the badge of the Jacobites.

Fast Castle

Borders Region **Map: p243 G2.**
The remains of Fast Castle are situated on the coast some 3 miles north of St Abbs Head. At one time the castle was of considerable importance, being virtually impregnable and providing a secure base from which to launch sea attacks. In 1510 the Marshal of Berwick needed 2,000 men to wrest the castle from its 10 inhabitants.

In the Middle Ages the castle was a stronghold of the Home family, and Margaret of England, daughter of Henry VII (1485-1509) stayed here on the way north to her marriage to James IV (1488-1513). By 1600 it was owned by Sir Robert Logan of Restalrig, who forfeited it for his part in the Gowrie conspiracy to kidnap James VI (1567-1625).

Fettercairn

Grampian Region **Map: p245 G4.**
The royal arch at the entrance to the village of Fettercairn is of Rhenish Gothic design and was erected in 1864 to commemorate an 'incognito' visit to the village by Prince Albert and Queen Victoria (1837-1901) in 1861.

Findochty

Grampian Region **Map: p245 G1.**
The Muir of Findochty, which lies above the township of the same name, has now been largely reclaimed and converted into farmland. On it stands the King's Cairn, a monument to the Pictish King Indulf (AD 954-962).

Fingask

Tayside Region **Map: p243 E1.** *Castle open by appointment only.*
Despite many vicisssitudes the late 16th-century castle of Fingask stands today almost as it did when the Threipland family bought it from the Bruces in the 17th century.

In 1715 Sir David Threipland was one of the first to proclaim the Old Pretender as James VIII and join the Jacobite Earl of Mar. Twice during his visit to Scotland the Pretender stayed at Fingask. After the collapse of the rising, the lands and castle were forfeited to the crown. Lady Threipland managed to lease the castle back but it was again forfeited after the '45 Rising, during which both her sons supported Bonnie Prince Charlie. The younger son, Sir Stewart Threipland, managed to buy his estate back in 1783, however, and the baronetcy was restored to his son in 1826.

Edinburgh

Lothian Region **Map: p243 E2.**

The shape of the old capital of Scotland resembles that of a fish skeleton, with the castle as its head and Holyrood Palace as its tail. Its mile-long spine is the Royal Mile, Edinburgh's high street, and its bones are the numerous wynds (passages and narrow thoroughfares) and closes (alleyways leading to courtyards) running at right angles to the spine along its length. The city proper finished about half-way down the Royal Mile at the Nether Bow Gate. The area beyond this, between the gate and Holyrood, is the Canongate, a 'suburb' with its own customs and administration.

Towards the end of the 15th century the 'belly' of the fish began to swell. Houses and churches were built outside the city wall to the south, and after the disaster of the Flodden (1513) the walls were quickly extended to bring them within the fortifications. For more than 250 years the boundary of the town remained the same and the houses piled up within the walls, 'close and massy, deep and high', into steep tenement 'lands' soaring cliff-like up to 10 storeys.

The old town can be divided into four principal areas: Edinburgh Castle, the Royal Mile, the South Side and Holyrood Palace. The earliest citizens of Edinburgh lived on castle rock and grazed their animals on its shoulders, but even before AD 1000 houses and churches were built along the ridge which slopes away from the rocky eminence. The existing Church of St Giles was referred to in the 9th century, and may be older.

However, it seems that the most desirable place to live was within the castle walls, and Robert II (1371-1390) granted the privilege of building houses here to the principal citizens of the town. As early as 1124 David I (1124-1153) had established the Abbey of Holyrood, and by the early 15th century there were several religious and monastic houses 'in the shadow of the castle' — white, grey and black friars of Augustinian, Franciscan and Dominican foundations. Merchants began to build around the gardens and orchards of these establishments, further expanding the town beyond the castle walls. The canons of Holyrood had been granted the right to build along the road between the abbey and the castle and this gradually grew into the burgh of Canongate. Nobility attending court preferred to lodge in the monasteries until Holyrood Palace was built, when many had their own fine houses built in the Canongate. The royal household itself often moved from the cramped castle to enjoy the hospitality of the monks of Holyrood long before the palace existed.

The first city wall was built in 1437 and 1438, describing a narrow oval with the castle at one end and the Nether Bow, one of the city's gates, at the other. To the south the wall ran along the southern slope of the ridge, between the High Street and the valley of the Cowgate, and to the north the town was contained by the Nor'Loch, a substantial stagnant pond which was drained about 150 years later. However, the south walls were soon outstripped and on both sides of the Cowgate houses and gardens began to appear, built largely by the nobility, well-to-do merchants and prosperous clergy, so that it became known as 'a street of palaces'. Today much of the Cowgate is slum property.

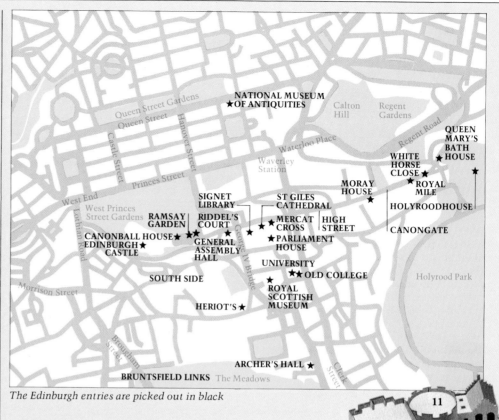

The Edinburgh entries are picked out in black

Both before and after the building of Holyrood Palace royalty moved freely about Edinburgh without pomp and massive companies of attendants. Sadly, most of the buildings that witnessed these progresses have disappeared but the shape of the old town is much the same as it was in the past.

1 Esplanade
2 Statue of Robert the Bruce
3 Statue of William Wallace
4 Gatehouse
5 Gateway to the Castle
6 Portcullis Gateway
7 Disused stables
8 Forewall Battery
9 Lang Stairs
10 Saint Margaret's Chapel
11 Water reservoirs
12 Foog's Gate
13 Scottish United Services Museum
14 Dury's Battery
15 Vaults/French Prisons
16 Great Vault/Mons Meg
17 Great Hall
18 Palace
19 Half Moon Battery
20 Twentieth-century Naafi building
21 Seventeenth-century ditch
22 Crown Square
23 Scottish National War Memorial
24 The Well

ARCHER'S HALL

Not open.
First built in 1776 and situated just south of George Square, Archer's Hall is the headquarters of the Royal Company of Archers, the monarch's bodyguard in Scotland. The Company of Archers was constituted in 1676, chartered under Queen Anne (1702-1714) in 1704, and formally appointed to its present position by George IV (1820-1830) in 1822. It has high rights of precedence and consists of 500 noblemen and gentlemen of distinction under the command of a captain-general who is usually a high ranking Scottish peer. Whenever the monarch holds court in Edinburgh the archers serve as escorts, guards and gentlemen-in-waiting, wearing distinctive and elaborate dark green uniforms and carrying short swords and bows. The ancient art of archery is kept alive by several annual archery competitions.

THE BRUNTSFIELD LINKS

Together with the adjoining meadows, just outside the city wall, the Bruntsfield Links formed the Burgh Muir until modern times. Here it was customary to marshal national armies prior to a campaign, and many kings up to the time of Cromwell reviewed their troops here.

The game of golf was first played on these links, and it is said that James IV (1488-1513) was an early enthusiast of the sport. The Royal Burgess Golf Club, the oldest golf club in the world, originated here.

CANONBALL HOUSE

Not open.
Situated on the edge of the Castle Esplanade, Canonball House was built in about 1630. It is named after the cannonball lodged in the westerly gable of the house, which tradition claims was fired from the castle in 1745. It was probably aimed at Holyrood Palace, which at that time was in the possession of Prince Charles Edward Stuart.

THE CANONGATE

Canongate church open Mon to Sat daily.
David I (1124-1153) gave the Augustinian canons of the castle permission to found an abbey at Holyrood in 1128, and in the same year allowed them to found their own burgh on either side of the road, or 'gait', between their abbey and the town. Until 1636 this was an entirely separate town from Edinburgh; in fact, it did not come under the aegis of Edinburgh Town Council until 1856. With the building of Holyrood Palace the area was adopted by the gentry who wished to retain town houses close to the court, and since there was not the restriction of having to build within the city walls, the houses were often spacious, with elegant gardens.

The Canongate church was built in 1688 as a parish church for those who had been evicted from the Abbey Church of Holyrood by James VII and II (1685-1688). In the southeast corner of the church the remains of David Rizzio, favourite of Mary, Queen of Scots (1542-1567), who was murdered in 1566 by Mary's husband, Lord Darnley, and others, are supposed to be entombed.

Near the head of St John Street is a plaque marking the spot where Charles I (1625-1649) knighted the Lord Provost of Edinburgh, who greeted him on his entry to the city. After the Treaty of Union in 1707 the Canongate fell into disrepair and later into squalor. In 1753 it was remarked: 'The Canongate has suffered more by the union of the Kingdoms than any other part of Scotland; for having, before that period, been the residence of the chief of the Scottish nobility, it was then in a flourishing condition, but being deserted by them, many of their houses are fallen down, and others in a ruinous condition: it is a perilous case'.

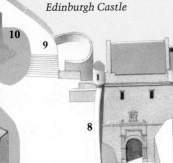

Edinburgh Castle

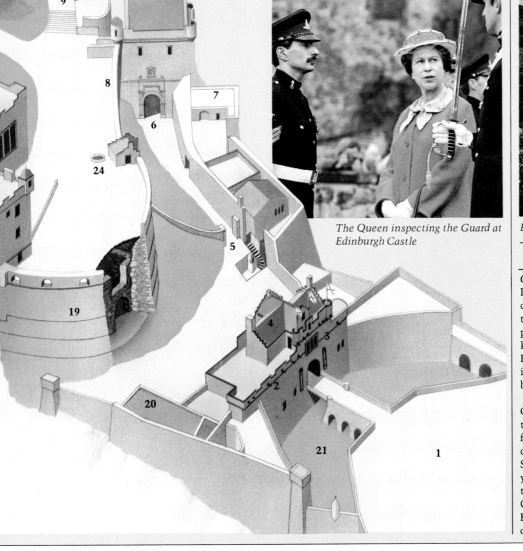

The Queen inspecting the Guard at Edinburgh Castle

Edinburgh Castle

EDINBURGH CASTLE

Open weekdays, Sun.
Legend refers to an early fort on the summit of castle rock being known as *Castrum Puellarum*, the castle of the maids, because it was used as a place of safe retreat for daughters of the Pictish kings. Since Pictland began north of the Firth of Forth, however, this seems unlikely, although it is an indication of how long the rocky hilltop had been used as a place of refuge.

It is more likely that the fort here was British. One of the earliest British poems, *The Gododdin*, tells how Mynydog the Wealthy, the British King, feasted the 300 heroes of the Gododdin (a confederation of Welsh, Cumbrian and southern Scottish tribes) in his great hall at Dun Eidyn for a year before leading them to their destruction by the Northumbrian Angles at the Battle of Catraetn (Catterick) in about AD 600. After this, King Edwin of Northumbria occupied the hill-fort on the rock, and it is said that the later name of

'Edwin's Burgh' was derived from him.

For over 300 years the fort marked the northern stronghold of the kingdom of Northumbria, then, in AD 973 Edgar, King of the English (AD 959-975), gave Kenneth II, King of Scots (AD 971-995), all the land betweeen the Forth and the Tweed in return for an acknowledgement of superiority. Kenneth strengthened the fort at Edinburgh, but the actual dramas of the early Scots kings occurred in the heartland of their kingdom, north of the Forth, and the castle was not significant until almost 100 years had passed.

After the Battle of Hastings in 1066, Edgar Atheling, king-elect of England, and his sister Margaret, sought refuge at the court of Malcolm III (1057-1093). Four years later the Saxon Princess married the Scots King and resolutely set about the Anglicization of her adopted kingdom.

The highest part of the rock was surrounded by a stockade, and within this was built a wooden palace and a tiny stone chapel, the oldest ecclesiastical building still standing in Scotland. Queen Margaret adorned her hall with luxuries unknown in Scotland before that date, and it was said that her own chamber was the most sumptuous in all the land. She died here on 16 November 1093, on hearing of the death of her husband and son in a fight with the English at Alnwick, and was later canonized for her piety. The succession was contested by her husband's brother, Donald Bane, known to history as 'that incorrigible old Celt', and her body had to be smuggled out of the castle and through the besieging army before she could be laid to rest at Dunfermline.

During the next 200 years, Edinburgh Castle became increasingly popular with Scots kings as both a residence and an administrative centre. Margaret's youngest son, David I (1124-1153), adopted the castle as his principal residence, and his example was followed by his successors until the Wars of Independence at the end of the 13th century. Alexander II (1214-1249) held the first Parliament here in 1215, and his son, Alexander III (1249-1286), held judicial courts and stored the principal records and regalia of the kingdom in the castle. He also stored his wife, Queen Margaret, a daughter of Henry III of England (1216-1272) here; she described the castle as 'a sad and solitary place, without verdure, and by reason of its vicinity to the sea, unwholesome'.

In June 1291 the castle surrendered to Edward I (1272-1307) after a 15-day siege, and five years later the English King received the submission of many Scots magnates within its walls. However, late in 1312 a former member of the Scots garrison led a band of besiegers up the precipitous cliffs of the castle rock. They scaled the walls and took the fortress. Robert Bruce (1306-1329) ordered it to be destroyed, apart from St Margaret's Chapel, to prevent it being of any further use to the enemy.

On his return from captivity in England, Robert Bruce's son, David II (1329-1371), set about rebuilding the castle by constructing a strong, 60ft tower on the site of what is now the half-moon battery. He died in the castle before his tower was completed, but his successors continued to strengthen the castle defences, and in 1430 James I (1406-1437) built a new palace adjacent to David's Tower.

After the assassination of James I (1406-1437) at Perth in 1437, the safety and strength of Edinburgh Castle played an increasingly important role in the decisions of Scottish sovereigns and their guardians. The young James II (1437-1460) was held captive by the governor of Edinburgh Castle for two years, until his mother managed to smuggle him out in a box. Two years later this same governor and others held the notorious 'black dinner' in the castle, during which the 16-year-old Earl of Douglas and his brother were executed, despite the tears and entreaties of the young King.

James III (1460-1488) so feared his brothers seizing the throne that in 1479 he imprisoned them in David's Tower. John, Earl of Mar, died from an overzealous bleeding, but Alexander, Duke of Albany, managed to escape by drugging his guards' wine and setting them on fire before abseiling down the castle cliff on a rope of sheets. Ironically, the King himself was imprisoned in the Tower three years later and was only released on Albany's intervention.

By the late 15th century and the time of James IV (1488-1513), Holyrood Palace had become the principal royal residence. Nevertheless both he and his successor embarked on an ambitious building project, constructing the Great Hall and modernizing the residential quarters. The castle also became important as an arsenal; artillery was cast here and powder stored. In 1517 James V (1513-1542) was brought here for safety, and his Queen, Mary of Guise, died here in 1560. Their daughter, Mary, Queen of Scots (1542-1567) gave birth to James VI and I (1567-1625) in a tiny room in the castle, and there is a story that she lowered the baby in a basket to retainers below, so that he could be carried off to Stirling and baptized a Catholic. When Mary went into exile the Regent Moray appointed Sir William Kirkaldy of Grange to be Captain of the castle. On Moray's death Grange held the castle for the Queen's party and endured a siege and bombardment for three years.

The Regent Morton began an extensive rebuilding programme which continued through much of James IV's reign, though the King himself rarely visited the place. Charles I (1625-1649) feasted in the Banqueting Hall during his visit to Edinburgh in 1633, and slept in the palace the night before his coronation on 18 June. Apart from a brief visit by his son Charles II (1660-1685), no other king entered the castle until George IV (1820-1830) in 1822.

THE GENERAL ASSEMBLY HALL OF THE CHURCH OF SCOTLAND

Not open.

Backing onto Castlehill, close to Ramsay Garden, is the hall in which sits the General Assembly of the Church of Scotland, the governing body of the national church. This was built in 1861, on the site of the 'palace' of Queen Mary of Guise, wife of James V (1513-1542) and mother of Mary, Queen of Scots (1542-1567), who was Regent of Scotland between 1554 and 1560. A courageous and charming woman, Mary had to steer a political path through the troubled early years of the Scottish Reformation and the brutality of the 'rough wooing' by Henry VIII (1509-1547) of her daughter.

Her 'palace' had little to distinguish it from the houses of the common people, though the building was better decorated than most, both inside and out. Its door was in no way different from the access to a common stair and its apartments were dark and cramped.

Heriots

HERIOT'S

George Heriot, known as 'Jingling Geordie', was jeweller to James VI and I (1567-1625), and on his death endowed the school for boys which stands today on Lauriston Place, with the Flodden Wall as its western boundary. Heriot's shop was close to St Giles, on the site of what is now the Advocates Library, and although it measured only 7ft square, the King would visit him there. On one occasion Heriot was visiting the King at Holyrood and remarked upon a sweet-smelling fire that was burning in the room. The King told him it was quite as costly as it was sweet-smelling, whereupon the jeweller said that next time the King came to his shop he would show an even more costly fire. When the King arrived at the shop he found only a dull fire. 'Is this your fine fire, then?' he asked. 'Wait until I fetch my fuel', replied Heriot, and so saying took out a bond for £2,000, which he had lent to the King, and laid it on the fire. 'Now, whether is your Majesty's fire or mine most expensive?'

Heriot's Hospital is one of the most striking buildings in Edinburgh. Designed by William Wallace, royal master mason, it was finished by William Aytoun and decorated by Inigo Jones. In November 1650, after the troops had accidentally burned down Holyrood Palace where they had been billeted, Cromwell moved his soldiers into the unfinished building of Heriot's School, and it was only with great difficulty that General Monck was later persuaded to give it up again.

THE HIGH STREET

The High Street has been romantically referred to as 'the battlefield of Scotland, whereon private and party feuds, the jealousies of the nobles and burghers and not a few of the contests between the crown and the people were settled at the point of the sword'. The most famous fray, fought between St Giles and the Nether Bow, was the pitched battle between supporters of the House of

Hamilton and those of the House of Douglas in April 1520, known as 'Cleanse the Causeway'. The citizens of Edinburgh took the side of the Earl of Angus (a Douglas) and in reply the Earl of Arran (a Hamilton) raised an army of supporters big enough to outnumber the 400 Douglas spearmen already in the town. The brawl covered the cobbles with blood and claimed many victims; in the end Arran and his son had to flee across the Nor'Loch clinging to a collier's horse.

John Knox, the religious reformer who founded Scottish Presbyterianism and who served briefly as a royal chaplain, may have lived in a house in the High Street between 1561 and 1572.

HOLYROODHOUSE

See pages 90-91.

THE MERCAT CROSS

Open Mon to Fri daily, Sat mornings.
The Mercat Cross, a small octagonal building surmounted by a column bearing the unicorn of Scotland, was a centre of interest in days gone by. It stands close to the east end of St Giles Cathedral and is the place where royal proclamations were made and where notable criminals were executed. The building seen today is a 19th-century copy of the 16th-century original.

MORAY HOUSE

Not open.
Built for the Earls of Moray in 1628, Moray House was famous for its garden — 'of such elegance, and cultivated with so much care, as to vie with those of warmer countries, and perhaps even of England itself.' Charles I (1625-1649) is reputed to have stayed in the house during his visit to Edinburgh in 1633; Oliver Cromwell made the house his headquarters in the summer of 1648 and held secret meetings with the leaders of the anti-monarchist party here.

Tradition has it that the Treaty of Union (1707) with England was secretly arranged in a summer house in the garden of Moray House, though for the actual signing the Commissioners are said to have gone to a cellar underneath Number 179 High Street to avoid the angry mob.

NATIONAL MUSEUM OF ANTIQUITIES

Open Mon to Sat daily, Sun afternoons.
Located at the east end of Queen Street in the new town, the National Museum of Antiquities grew out of the Society of Antiquarians of Scotland which was founded in 1780 and moved to its present building in 1892. The collection covers every aspect of Scottish history from early times to the present day and includes several personal items associated with Mary, Queen of Scots (1542-1567), and Prince Charles Edward Stuart.

OLD COLLEGE

The central building of the University of Edinburgh, the Old College was designed in the Classical style by Robert Adam in 1789 and completed by W.H. Playfair in 1834. It is one of the finest examples of these architects' work.

The building stands on the site once occupied by the ancient church of St Mary-in-the-Fields, known as Kirk o'Field, which was the scene of the murder of Lord Darnley, husband of Mary, Queen of Scots (1542-1567) and self-styled king of Scotland. Darnley was convalescing in the house of the provost of Kirk o'Fields from an illness which is believed to have been syphilis. The Queen visited her husband on the night of his murder, 9 February 1567, with the Earls Bothwell, Argyll, Huntley and Cassilis, one or more of whom may have been involved in the plot. They left at about 10 o'clock and at about 2 am the whole city was awoken by an explosion. The house had been destroyed 'to the very grund stone' and when the bodies of the 'king' and his manservant were examined it was discovered that they had also been strangled. Many were blamed for the murder, but responsibility has never been finally and doubtlessly allocated.

PARLIAMENT HOUSE

Open Tue to Fri daily.
In medieval times the High Court of Parliament had no fixed meeting place, but by the time Edinburgh had become the capital it was meeting regularly, first in the castle or in Holyrood Palace, and later in the Tolbooth (now demolished), close to St Giles Cathedral. Parliament House was begun in 1632, on the orders of Charles I (1625-1649), in order to provide both a home for the Court of Session, the High Court of Scotland, and a Parliamentary chamber. The building was completed in 1639, and from that date until the Act of Union in 1707 the Scottish Parliament sat here regularly.

Today the Parliament Hall itself is little changed and displays a magnificent hammer-beam ceiling and a large stained-glass window depicting the inauguration of the Court of Session by James V (1513-1542) in 1532, both of which are original. It is used by advocates today as a Beneath it is the vaulted Laigh Hall (Low Hall), which was used as both an auxiliary chamber and a stable by Oliver Cromwell in 1650. In front of Parliament House stands an equestrian statue of Charles II (1660-1685); made in 1685 it is the oldest lead equestrian statue in Britain. Ironically, it stands upon the only known grave in the ancient graveyard of St Giles, which formerly occupied the square — that of John Knox, the anti-monarchist religious reformer.

QUEEN MARY'S BATH HOUSE

Not open.
Standing on the very edge of the grounds of Holyrood Palace, this quaint little building has been associated with Mary, Queen of Scots (1542-1567), for many centuries. It is said that the Queen bathed herself in white wine here to preserve her beauty. At the end of the 18th century a richly inlaid dagger was found under the slates of the roof and it is supposed, with some reason, that this may have belonged to one of the murderers of the Queen's favourite, David Rizzio.

RAMSAY GARDEN

On the north side of Castlehill is a group of houses with pan-tiled roofs surrounding a small garden. The westernmost of these houses was built in the mid-18th century by the pastoral poet Allan Ramsay; three more were added by his son, also Allan Ramsay, a portrait painter to George III (1760-1820). The others were designed around the earlier group at the end of the 19th century by Sir Patrick Geddes.

Ramsay Garden

RIDDEL'S COURT

The Lawnmarket was the original 'agora' or market-place of the old town. Here a variety of produce and food was displayed in stalls, except on Wednesdays when a special sale of linen and woollen cloth was conducted. Off the Lawnmarket to the south is Riddel's Court, in which stands the house of Baillie Macmoran, a rich

Riddel's Court

The Main Hall at the Royal Scottish Museum

merchant in the reign of James VI and I (1567-1625). His house was so grand that the city used it to hold two royal banquets in 1598, both of which the King and Queen attended. Baillie Macmoran was accidentally killed by a group of schoolboys who had barricaded themselves into their school as a protest against short holidays. His actual murderer escaped justice and became Sir William Sinclair of Mey, the ancestor of the Earls of Seaforth.

THE ROYAL MILE

The Royal Mile connects the castle with Holyrood Palace. Slightly sloping to the east, it is made up of four sections: Castlehill, the Lawnmarket, the High Street and the Canongate. Each has many royal associations.

ROYAL SCOTTISH MUSEUM

Open Mon to Sat daily, Sun afternoons.
The museum was established on Chambers Street in 1854, though the foundation stone was laid by Prince Albert, husband of Queen Victoria (1837-1901), in 1861. It has many important objects with royal associations in its collection, including the exquisite Lennoxlove toilet service given by Charles II (1660-1685) to his mistress, Frances, Duchess of Lennox and Richmond, a great beauty who was known as 'La Belle Stuart'.

ST GILES CATHEDRAL

Open Mon to Fri daily, Sat mornings.
St Giles was in fact only a 'cathedral' for the five years following the introduction of bishops into

St Giles Cathedral

the Presbyterian Church of Scotland by Charles I (1625-1649) in 1635. It is more properly referred to as 'The High Kirk of Edinburgh'. There was a parish church of St Giles on the site of the present building in the 9th century and a Norman edifice, built by Alexander I (1107-1124), replaced it in 1120. This church was destroyed by Richard II (1377-1399) in 1385, when an invading English army occupied the town for five days and razed it to the ground. Only the four central columns and one or two other features survived, but have since disappeared.

The present Gothic church grew throughout the 15th and 16th centuries; the King's Pillar was erected as a memorial to James II (1437-1460) in 1460 and the crown spire was completed in 1485. As the town became more prosperous, altars and chapels were endowed by the citizens, including the Chepman Aisle, dedicated in 1513 to the memory of James IV (1488-1513). During the Reformation, the church was badly damaged when it was stripped of 44 altars and its ancient statue of St Giles. The saint had been dipped in the Nor'Lock as an adulterer and then burned as a heretic. John Knox, Scotland's greatest reformer, was minister here between 1559 and 1572, a period during which he frequently enjoyed religious debates with Mary, Queen of Scots (1542-1567).

Charles I (1625-1649) was crowned at Holyrood in 1633, and the following Sunday went to an Anglican service at St Giles, conducted by Archbishop Laud's chaplains. Four years later a market woman, Jenny Geddes, hurled her stool at the minister when he attempted to read from the Archbishop's prayer-book, striking the first blow

White Horse Close

for the Covenanters.

The Chapel of the Order of the Thistle, Scotland's highest order of chivalry, was added to St Giles in 1911, and the church also contains the flags of many Scottish regiments, including the craftsman's banner presented to the guild by James III (1460-1488). Known as 'The Blue Blanket', it was carried at Flodden.

THE SIGNET LIBRARY

Open Mon to Fri daily, Sat mornings.
The Society of Writers to HM Signet has its origin in the office of the king's secretary which attended to the public and private correspondence of the monarch from the middle of the 14th century. With the foundation of the College of Justice and the Court of Session by James V (1513-1542) in 1532, many 'writers' transacted business on behalf of litigants before the new courts and in legal matters generally. They also had the privilege of preparing all writs pertaining to the supreme court. In the latter part of the 17th century, the Society acquired premises on the north side of the Lawnmarket, and in 1815 a spacious library was provided for it adjacent to Parliament House. In 1826 the Society acquired a further hall above the 'lower library', a library which had formerly belonged to the Faculty of Advocates and which George IV (1820-1830) described as 'the most beautiful room in Scotland'.

THE SOUTH SIDE

When the terrible news of disaster at Flodden Field reached Edinburgh on 10 September 1513

the town was thrown into panic. It was fully expected that the victorious English army would march on Edinburgh and sack the town, as had happened so many times before, and those living on the South Side, outside the city walls, were particularly vulnerable. The inhabitants immediately set about extending their defences. Farmers from the Lothians lent their labourers and horses to the great work, and in an incredibly short time walls, ports, battlements and towers had been thrown around the exposed southern part of the city. Fortunately Henry VIII (1509-1547) was too engrossed in a war with France to press his advantage. The Flodden Wall remained the boundary of the city for over 250 years and parts of it still exist.

THE UNIVERSITY

In 1566 the city authorities granted the Kirk o'Field site for 'the toun's college', and when James VI and I (1567-1625) extended his patronage to it by granting a charter in 1582, it became known as the College of King James. It is the fourth oldest university in Scotland.

WHITE HORSE CLOSE

Standing at the foot of the Canongate, White Horse Close is believed to have been named after the white palfrey belonging to Mary, Queen of Scots (1542-1567), which may have been stabled here. The close dates from the early 17th century and was once a coaching station with a tavern, The White Horse Inn, which was very popular with Cavaliers during the reign of Charles II (1660-1685).

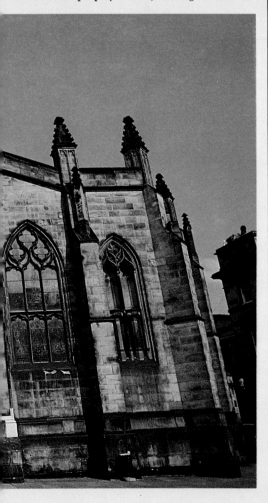

Finlaggan

Strathclyde Region **Map: p242 A2.** *Ruins open .*
Eilean Mhor, an island close to the northwest edge of Loch Finlaggan, was the principal seat of the Lords of the Isles, whose antecedents had been the Kings of the Isles and of Man. Accounts of the place tell of a great palace with round towers and turrets. Only fragments are visible today.

Forfar

Tayside Region **Map: p245 G5.**
Forfar is said to have been the site of one of the last battles between the Picts and the Scots before the two kingdoms were united under Kenneth McAlpin (AD 843-858). After defeating Macbeth (1040-1057), Malcolm III (1057-1093) held a Parliament in Forfar at which he granted surnames and titles to the Scots nobility.

It is likely that a royal residence existed on Castlehill at the northeastern corner of the town, and Malcolm's Queen, Margaret, had a residence on a small island in Forfar Loch.

Forres

Highland Region **Map: p245 F2.** *Tours of Earl Randolf's Hall and the castle estate available by appointment.*
Forres is a very ancient royal burgh and was used as a royal seat in the Dark Ages. Later, Donald II (AD 889-900) was killed here, and his son Malcolm I (AD 942-954) may have been murdered 'by the men of Moray' at Blervie Castle, 4 miles to the southeast of the town. Duncan I (1034-1040), whom Macbeth (1040-1057) overthrew, held court at Forres, although it is uncertain whether his successor murdered him here or at Inverness.

After the foundation of the bishopric of Elgin in 1150 Forres declined in importance, although there continued to be a royal residence here. Mary, Queen of Scots (1542-1567), held court in Earl Randolph's Hall at Darnaway Castle, to the south of Forres, in 1564.

Forteviot

Tayside Region **Map: p243 E1.**
Forteviot was the residence of the kings of Pictland and Alba, and the capital of the Pictish province of Fortrenn. It is possible that the first 'palace' built here was erected by Angus MacFergus (AD 731-761), and a succession of kings, including Malcolm III (1057-1093), used the place. Kenneth McAlpin (AD 843-858), the first king to rule after the union of the Picts and the Scots, died at Forteviot. The castle or palace stood on Halyhill to the northwest of the present village, but there are no traces of it today.

Garmouth

Highland Region **Map: p245 F2.**
Now a small village, Garmouth was once a busy port, and it was here that Charles II (1651-1685) landed from Holland on 23 June 1650. The Scottish Covenanters were appalled by the execution of Charles I (1625-1649) in January 1649, and on 5 February proclaimed Charles, Prince of Wales, King of Scotland on condition that he sign the Solemn League and Covenant and uphold Presbyterianism. He was made to sign immediately upon landing at Garmouth.

Gask

Tayside Region **Map: p243 E1.**
Today Gask exists as a combination of the parishes of Findo-Gask and Trinity Gask, with the village of Clathy in the middle. Robert Bruce (1306-1329) granted the lands and the title Lord of Gasknes and Aberdalgie to Sir William Oliphant for services rendered during the Wars of Independence. The succeeding Oliphant lairds were ardent Jacobites and Prince Charles Edward Stuart breakfasted at the House of Gask on 11 September 1745. The following year the house was ransacked and burnt by Hanoverian troops.

Glamis

Glamis Castle

Tayside Region **Map: p245 F5.** *Castle open May to Sept: daily except Sats; Easter.*
There has been a building on the site of Glamis Castle since very early times. It was here that Malcolm II (1005-1034) was murdered. Robert II (1371-1390) granted the lands of Glamis to his son-in-law, John Lyon, in 1372, and the lands have remained in the same family. In 1537 Lady Glamis was burned for witchcraft and conspiring to murder James V (1513-1542) and the lands were forfeited to the crown. After her death her innocence was established, however, and the lands and titles of Glamis were returned to her son, whose descendant, Patrick Lyon, became Earl of Strathmore in 1677. He added the clusters of turrets and battlemented parapets that give the castle its present aspect. In 1715 the Old Pretender stayed at Glamis and held court here.

Queen Elizabeth, the Queen Mother, is the daughter of the 14th Earl of Strathmore and spent some of her childhood at Glamis. Her daughter Princess Margaret was born in the castle in 1930.

Glasgow

Strathclyde Region **Map: p242 D2.** *Provand's Lordship open daily, Apr to Sept, except Sun.*
The city of Glasgow is thought to have grown out of a cluster of huts surrounding a church established by St Kentigern (also known as St Mungo) in the sixth century. The great medieval cathedral of Glasgow was begun in the 12th century on the same site as Kentigern's church.

In the 12th century there was a castle in Glasgow, and Alexander III (1249-1286) made it a royal castle, though there are few records of it having been used by the monarch. After a time it was adopted as the bishop's residence, and remained so until the late 17th century when it became a prison. In 1791 it was demolished to make way for the Royal Infirmary.

Close to the Infirmary is Provand's Lordship, the oldest existing house in the city, which dates from 1471 and was the town house of the prebendaries of Barlanark. Mary, Queen of Scots (1542-1567), stayed here in January 1567 when she journeyed through Glasgow to persuade her husband, Lord Darnley, to return to Edinburgh. It has been suggested that some of the 'casket letters' supposedly written by the queen, which were used to incriminate her in the murder of Darnley a month later, were written while she was in Glasgow.

Prince Charles Edward Stuart came to Glasgow for a week in January 1746, on his return from Derby. He found few friends here, for the town provided only 60 recruits for his cause, whereas it had raised 1,200 men at its own expense for the suppression of his rising. He reviewed his army on Glasgow Green on 3 January, but although his men were newly equipped with coats, shirts and stockings provided by the town, he was melancholy, according to observers.

George Square, Glasgow

Glenfinnan

Highland Region **Map: p244 C4.**
Glenfinnan, at the head of Loch Sheil, where the River Finnan flows into the loch, is a narrow valley flanked by high mountains. Here Prince Charles Edward Stuart waited with his small band of followers for the arrival of Donald Cameron of Lochiel and Alexander Macdonald of Keppoch and

their clansmen, on 19 August 1745. They arrived with about 1,000 men. The royal standard was raised, proclaiming the Old Pretender as James VIII and his son, Prince Charles, as Regent. Today there is a monument on the spot.

Glenluce Abbey

Dumfries & Galloway Region **Map: p242 C5.**
The remains of Glenluce Abbey are situated 2 miles northwest of the village of Glenluce on the east bank of the Water of Luce. It was founded in 1192 by Roland, Lord of Galloway, as a Cistercian house, and although only the vaulted chapter house remains intact, the place is of considerable architectural interest. James IV (1488-1513) and Mary, Queen of Scots (1542-1567), both visited the abbey while on pilgrimage.

Glenmoriston

Highland Region **Map: p244 D3.**
The wooded slopes of Glenmoriston climb above the village of Invermoriston to the north of Fort Augustus. At the roadside is a cairn to the memory of Roderick MacKenzie, a Jacobite officer who allowed himself to be identified as Prince Charles Edward Stuart in July 1746, thus drawing the red-coats off the Prince's trail.

Glenmuick

Grampian Region **Map: p245 F3.** *Birkhall not open.*
Glenmuick lies just outside Ballater, close to Balmoral, and has many associations with Queen Victoria (1837-1901). On the west bank of the River Muick, which runs through the glen, is the mansion of Birkhall which was built in 1715 and bought by Prince Albert, the Prince Consort. Birkhall is now the Scottish home of Queen Elizabeth, the Queen Mother.

Glenshiel

Highland Region **Map: p244 C3.** *Eilean Donan Castle open Apr to Sept: daily.*
On 10 June 1719 an army of Spanish mercenaries, Highlanders and Jacobite exiles under the command of the Marquis of Tullibardine met a Hanoverian force under Major-General Wightman of Glenshiel, near Eilean Donan Castle, on Loch Alsh. The castle, which was built by Alexander II, King of Scotland (1214-1249), in 1220, was bombarded during the fighting by the English warship *Worcester*, although it has since been rebuilt. This was the only engagement of the futile second attempt by the Old Pretender to claim the throne, and the Jacobites were routed.

Glen Trool

Dumfries & Galloway Region **Map: p242 C4.**
Robert Bruce (1306-1329) came out of hiding in the west in February 1307 and with a small force embarked upon a campaign of guerilla warfare against the English in Galloway and Ayrshire. At the east end of Loch Trool a monument was erected in 1929, to mark the 600th anniversary of Bruce's death. A boulder was inscribed with the words: 'In loyal remembrance of Robert the Bruce, King of Scots, whose victory in this glen over an English force in March 1307 opened the campaign of independence which he brought to a decisive close at Bannockburn on 24th June 1314'.

Gordonstoun

Grampian Region **Map: p245 G2.** *By appointment only.*
The 300-acre estate of Gordonstoun was formerly known as 'the Bog of Plewlands'. The towerhouse dates from the 15th century and still stands among later buildings. The name was changed to Gordonstoun by Sir Robert Gordon, the 3rd Bt, who bought the house in 1638 and set about giving the building a symmetrical frontage. Another Sir Robert Gordon, known as the 'Warlock Laird', built the Round Square, which is said to have magic proportions.

In 1934 a private school was established on the estate by Kurt Hahn. The Round Square now houses dormitories, classrooms and a library. Prince Philip, Duke of Edinburgh, the Prince of Wales, Prince Andrew and Prince Edward all attended the school.

Haddington

Lothian Region **Map: p243 F2.** *Town House open.*
Haddington has been the market town for the 'rich red lands' of East Lothian since the 12th century, and was an important monastic centre in the Middle Ages. A Cistercian nunnery was founded here by Ada, mother of Malcolm IV (1153-1165), before 1159. It was burned by the English in 1336 and again in 1544-1545, during Henry VIII's 'rough wooing' of Mary, Queen of Scots (1542-1567).

The Duke of Somerset, self-styled Protector of England, led a strong army north in September in 1547 and, having routed the Scots at the Battle of Pinkie, garrisoned Haddington and set up his headquarters here. A formidable French army arrived in July 1548, joining the Scots army which was ineffectually besieging Haddington. The Treaty of Haddington was concluded, by which the French promised help if the young Queen was sent to France as a bride for the Dauphin, later François II, as soon as both were old enough.

In the Middle Ages there were several 'hospitals' or almshouses in the town. One of them, St Lawrence's, which had been founded before 1312 and functioned as a leper house, was suppressed by the pope in 1511 on the petition of James IV (1488-1513) so that an Augustinian friary could be erected in its place. The Battle of Flodden occurred two years later and the order never took possession of their friary.

There had been a Franciscan friary in the town since before 1242; this was burned by the English in 1355 and again in 1544. After the former occasion, it became known as 'the Lamp of Lothian'. The Episcopal church is built on its site.

Hailes Castle

Lothian Region **Map: p243 F2.** *Open Mon to Sat daily, Sun afternoons.*
The oldest parts of Hailes Castle, 2 miles south-west of East Linton, pre-date the Wars of Independence. The 4th Earl, husband of Mary, Queen of Scots (1542-1567), brought the Queen to Hailes after their escape from Borthwick Castle in April 1567. Oliver Cromwell dismantled part of the castle in 1650, though much of it remains.

Hamilton

Strathclyde Region **Map: p242 D3.**
On her escape from Loch Leven on 2 May 1568, Mary, Queen of Scots (1542-1567), made her way to Hamilton to raise support for her cause in the west. On 13 May the army mustered at Hamilton met that of the Regent Moray at Langside, but was defeated, forcing the Queen to flee to England.

Hawthornden

Lothian Region **Map: p243 F2.**
Beneath Hawthornden Castle are several man-made caves and tunnels of unknown origin and great antiquity. Three of the caves are traditionally associated with the Wars of Independence and are known as the King's Gallery, the King's Bedchamber and the King's Dining Room, since Robert Bruce (1306-1329) is believed to have gone to ground here in 1307. The caves were certainly used 30 years later as a retreat from the English by Sir Alexander Ramsay of Dalhousie and his men.

Hermitage Castle

Borders Region **Map: p243 F4.** *Open daily Mon to Sat, Sun afternoons. Closed Tue and alternate Weds in winter.*
Hermitage Castle was built in the 13th century by the de Soules family and is one of the best preserved of the border keeps. Nicholas de Soules was a descendant of the illegitimate daughter of Alexander II (1214-1249), and as such was one of the 13 'competitors' for the throne of Scotland on the death of the Maid of Norway in 1290, along with Robert Bruce (1306-1329) and John Balliol (1292-1296). De Soules' great nephew, William, forfeited the castle in 1320 for having conspired against Bruce and was condemned to perpetual imprisonment. In 1341 the Douglases acquired the castle, but exchanged it for another with the Earls of Bothwell in 1492.

In October 1566 Mary, Queen of Scots (1542-1567), rode 100 miles to Hermitage and back in a day on hearing of the wounding of her lieutenant in the borders, Bothwell. Since they were married seven months later, it has often been suggested that the Queen's compassionate visit may have had romantic overtones.

Hopetoun House

Lothian Region **Map: p243 E2.** *Open Apr to mid-Sept: daily; Easter.*
Hopetoun House is one of Scotland's finest classical mansions, and is perhaps the best example of the genius of the Adams, father and son, who rebuilt and enlarged the original structure of 1703 between 1721 and 1754. In 1824 George IV (1820-1830) held a levée in the Red Drawing-room at Hopetoun, during which he

Hopetoun House

knighted several distinguished Scots, including Henry Raeburn, the painter and architect. Today it is the seat of the Marquess of Linlithgow.

Huntingtower

Tayside Region **Map: p243 E1.** *Castle open Mon to Sat daily, Sun afternoons.*

Huntingtower was formerly called Ruthven Castle and belonged to the Ruthven family, Earls of Gowrie. In August 1582, when James VI (1567-1625) was 15, he was abducted and brought to Ruthven Castle by the Earls of Gowrie, Mar and Glencairn. For 10 months he was held captive while his kidnappers ruled the country with the support of the Church, but when he escaped he reasserted his authority and executed Gowrie.

In August 1600, 18 years later, the sons of the executed Earl of Gowrie lured the King from Falkland to their house in Perth with a tale about an old man who had discovered a pot of gold. After dinner, a brawl ensued and the Ruthvens of Gowrie were killed.

Inchcolm

Fife Region **Map: p243 E2.**

The tiny island of Inchcolm, which lies 1½ miles off Aberdour, derives its name from the Gaelic 'Columba's Isle' and in the 12th century a Columban hermit lived here. Alexander I (1107-1124) was stormbound on the island in 1123 and might have perished had it not been for the hermit's kind attentions. In gratitude the King vowed that he would endow and build an abbey on the island, but he died the following year and it was left to his successor, David I (1124-1153), to carry out his vow. The abbey still stands today.

Inchgarvie

Fife Region **Map: p243 E2.**

The island of Inchgarvie now supports one of the legs of the Forth Railway Bridge. It is said that Mary, Queen of Scots (1542-1567), sheltered on the island while crossing the Forth in a storm.

Inchmahome

Central Region **Map: p242 D1.**

The Augustinian priory of Inchmahome in the Lake of Menteith was founded in 1238 by Walter Comyn, Earl of Menteith. The remaining buildings are still in excellent condition. David II (1329-1371), son of Robert Bruce (1306-1329), married Margaret Logie in the abbey church in February 1364. After the Scots' rout at the Battle of Pinkie in 1547 Mary, Queen of Scots (1542-1567), retreated to Inchmahome and begged for help from France.

Inveraray

Strathclyde Region **Map: p242 C1.** *Castle open Apr to early Oct: daily Mon to Thur and Sat; Sun afternoons.*

Archibald Campbell, 4th Earl of Argyll, was appointed Royal Lieutenant in the Isles by James V (1513-1542) in 1528. Argyll, however, abused his position of authority for his own gain; eventually James summoned him and imprisoned him . In September 1532 the King himself went to Inveraray, Argyll's seat, and held a council to win over the island chiefs; he returned to Inveraray in September and October 1534, and so kept the western isles in 'a more complete state of obedience to the crown than at any former period'.

Queen Victoria (1837-1901) and Prince Albert visited Inveraray Castle in 1847.

Invergarry

Highland Region **Map: p244 D3.**

Today it stands in ruins on the shores of Loch Oich, but for centuries, Invergarry Castle was the seat of the Macdonalds (or Macdonnells) of Glengarry, and suffered repeatedly for the family's support of the Stuart cause.

The first castle was destroyed by Cromwell's Governor of Scotland, General Monck, in 1654 to punish Glengarry's support for Charles I (1625-1649). It was rebuilt, but again burned in 1689, this time by the Earl of Argyll, acting as Royal Lieutenant, in retaliation for Glengarry having supported James Graham of Claverhouse, 'Bonnie Dundee', for the Jacobite cause against the recently crowned William and Mary (1689-1702). Invergarry was rebuilt a second time, and a third time destroyed, this time by the Duke of Cumberland to revenge Glengarry's involvement in the '45 Rising. Prince Charles Edward Stuart stayed the night of 25 August 1745 at Invergarry.

Inverlaidnan House

Highland Region **Map: p245 E2.** *Open all the time.* The ruins of Inverlaidnan House are situated in the small ski-resort of Carr Bridge. Prince Charles Edward Stuart spent the night of 15 February 1746 here on his way north to Culloden.

Inverness

Highland Region **Map: p245 E2.** *Castle not open.* During the Wars of Independence Inverness was occupied by the English on three occasions, and when Robert Bruce (1306-1329) recaptured it in 1307 he destroyed the castle. In 1428 James I (1406-1437) summoned over 40 Highland chiefs

Inverary Castle

to a Parliament at Inverness under the pretence of 'binding them to him'. As each appeared before the throne he was seized and thrown into prison. Three chiefs were hanged, the rest being released after a time. Alexander of the Isles, the most powerful of the chiefs thus treated, returned the next year and sacked Inverness in revenge. Again the castle was rebuilt and placed under the guardianship of the chiefs of MacKintosh, and later the Earls of Huntly, as sheriffs of the town.

In 1562 the governor of the castle was Alexander Gordon, son of the Earl of Huntly, against whom Mary, Queen of Scots (1542-1567), was campaigning. Gordon refused the Queen admission to the town, but on hearing that the rest of the country was supporting her, Huntly ordered his son to allow her entry.

In 1715, and again in 1745, Inverness was occupied by the Jacobites. Prince Charles Edward Stuart blew up the castle before he left to make sure it could not be used by his enemies, and the site of it was cleared in 1834 to make way for the present building.

Inverness Castle

Iona

Strathclyde Region **Map: p242 A1.**
St Columba landed on this tiny island in AD 563 and used it as a base from which to convert Pictland to Christianity. Stone structures from the 14th century are still standing; these include the abbey church which has been well restored.

Iona became the burial place of the kings of Dalriada, and later of Scotland, Ireland, Norway and, it is claimed, France. There are 48 Scottish kings buried on the island, the last being Duncan I (1034-1040).

Irvine

Strathclyde Region **Map:p242 C3.**
Irvine's origins date back to its importance as a port in the 13th century. A burgh of barony was created here by Alexander II (1214-1249) and the town was made a royal burgh by Robert II (1371-1390) in 1372.

During her progress to the southwest in the summer of 1563, Mary, Queen of Scots (1542-1567), visited the town and was entertained in the

13th-century Seagate Castle. Her visit is commemorated by the town each August, with Marymass, a week of festivity.

Jedburgh

Borders Region **Map: p243 F3.** *Queen Mary's House open Apr to Sept: Mon to Sat daily, Sun afternoons.*
Jedburgh Castle was one of the five fortresses handed over to England under the Treaty of Falaise in 1174, which provided security for the ransom of William the Lion (1165-1214) who had been captured by Henry II (1154-1189) some months before. It subsequently became a favourite royal residence. Malcolm IV (1153-1165) died here. In 1285, while celebrating his marriage, a ghost appeared before Alexander III (1249-1286), warning him of his impending death. Six months later Alexander was killed when he fell from his horse over a cliff at Kinghorn. The castle was demolished by request of the town's magistrates in 1409, to put a stop to English attacks.

On 9 October 1566 Mary, Queen of Scots (1542-1567), arrived in Jedburgh to preside at the assizes in the Tolbooth. She stayed in the 'bastel house', a fortified dwelling, in the main street, which is known today as 'Queen Mary's House'.

Kelso

Borders Region **Map: p243 G3.**
In the 12th century Kelso was known as 'Calkou' (chalk hill) and it was never fortified, relying on its status as an abbey town and on the strength of the nearby castle of Roxburgh. The Earl David, who became David I (1124-1153), founded the abbey, originally at Selkirk, in about 1113. It moved to Kelso in 1128 and for several centuries it enjoyed great prestige and influence.

James III (1460-1488) was crowned in the abbey in 1460 after the death of his father James II (1437-1460), at the siege of Roxburgh. When the Earl of Hertford, appointed lieutenant in Scotland by Henry VIII (1509-1547), found the abbey garrisoned in 1544, he slaughtered its 100 defenders and destroyed the abbey buildings.

The town was a traditional rallying place for Scottish armies on their way south, and was frequently visited with violence by English armies on their way north. In 1715 the Old Pretender was proclaimed King at the Mercat Cross, and in November 1745 his son, Prince Charles Edward Stuart, spent two nights in the town on his triumphant march into England.

Kenmore

Tayside Region **Map: p245 E5.**
The island lying close to Kenmore in Loch Tay is called Eilean nan Bannoamh, the Isle of the Female Saints. According to tradition, Queen Sibilla, illegitimate daughter of Henry I of England (1100-1135) and wife of Alexander I of Scotland (1107-1124), died here in 1124, and was buried on the islet.

Kenmure Castle

Dumfries & Galloway Region **Map: p242 D4.** *Not*

open.
Kenmure Castle stands to the south of New Galloway at the north of Loch Ken. Mary, Queen of Scots (1542-1567), stayed at the castle while on her western progress in 1563.

Kerrera

Strathclyde Region **Map: p242 B1.** *Ruins of Gylen Castle open.*
Alexander II (1214-1249) died at Gylen Castle on the island of Kerrera, close to Oban, during an expedition to wrest the western isles from the control of Norway, though the castle that now stands on this site is of a much later date.

Kildrummy Castle

Grampian Region **Map: p245 H3.** *Castle open Apr to Oct: daily. The Mansion House is now a hotel.*
The impressive castle of Kildrummy was founded in the 13th century on the instructions of Alexander II (1214-1249), and was owned by the Earls of Mar until it came into the hands of Robert Bruce (1306-1329).

Later in the Wars of Independence it fell to Edward I of England (1272-1307), who visited it in person in 1296 and 1303, installed a garrison and made substantial alterations to the building. Again the castle changed hands and in 1306, after the Battle of Methven, Sir Nigel Bruce, Robert Bruce's brother, escorted the King's wife and children to Kildrummy for safe keeping while the King fled to Rathlin Island, off the north coast of Northern Ireland. The castle was besieged by Prince Edward of Caernarvon, later Edward II (1307-1327), and eventually surrendered. Sir Nigel was executed and the castle garrison drawn and quartered. Bruce's wife and children escaped to Tain, where they were later captured.

After the failure of the 1715 Rising the lands were forfeited and the castle largely dismantled.

Killiecrankie

Tayside Region **Map: p245 E4.**
William and Mary (1689-1702) were crowned in April 1689. A month before the coronation, James Graham of Claverhouse, Viscount Dundee, had raised the Jacobite banner outside the city of his title and had gone to raise an army. In July he emerged with about 2,000 Highlanders and met a veteran army twice as large under the command of General Mackay, the Williamite commander in Scotland, at the Pass of Killiecrankie. 'Bonnie Dundee' was killed in the battle, and since there was nobody else to lead the clansmen, the rebellion soon petered out.

Kilravock Castle

Highland Region **Map: p245 E2.** *Kilravock now run as a guest house.*
Kilravock castle (pronounced 'Kilrawk') is the ancestral home of the Rose family and has been occupied by them since 1460, the present owner being the 25th of the line. It was built in 1460 and the present castle incorporates the original tall keep within a 17th-century manor house.

Mary, Queen of Scots (1542-1567), visited the

castle in 1562, during her campaign against the rebel Earl of Huntly.

Kindrochit Castle

Grampian Region **Map: p245 F3.** *Ruins open all the time.*

Kindrochit Castle is today a neglected fragment beside the car park by the Cluny Bridge in Braemar. The name means 'head of the bridge' and at one time the castle commanded all the glens converging on the town. A castle on the same site is thought to have been occupied by Malcolm III (1057-1093) in the 11th century, but the ruins visible today date from a hunting lodge built by Robert II (1371-1390).

Kinghorn

Fife Region **Map: p243 E2.**

David I (1124-1153) made Kinghorn a royal burgh in the early 12th century, and it was a popular resort with royalty and the nobility at that time, being so close to the palace at Dunfermline.

While out riding in 1286, Alexander III (1249-1286) stumbled and fell to his death over a cliff at Kinghorn Ness. On the road to Pettycur, outside the town, a Celtic cross from the Jacobite Earl of Mar marks the spot where the King fell.

Kinlochmoidart

Highland Region **Map: p243 C4.**

While Prince Charles Edward Stuart was at Borrodale in the days immediately after his arrival in Scotland, his few attendants — 'the Seven Men of Moidart', as they have become known — stayed at Kinlochmoidart. The Prince later joined them.

Kinloss

Grampian Region **Map: p245 F2.**

Kinloss Abbey, situated 3 miles northeast of Forres, is today a creeper-clad ruin. It was established by David I (1124-1153), who chose the site because he was guided to it by a white dove when he was lost in the wood.

Kirkcudbright

MacLellan's Castle

Dumfries & Galloway Region **Map: p242 D5.** *MacLellan's Castle open Mon to Sat daily, Sun afternoons.*

Kirkcudbright may have been a small royal burgh in the 14th century, but the Douglases became its feudal superiors until their fall in 1455, when it certainly became a royal burgh. All that remains of the 13th-century town are some fragments of MacLellan's Castle. Edward I (1272-1307) stayed in the castle in 1300, having captured it, as did James II (1437-1460).

Kirkpatrick Fleming

Dumfries & Galloway Region **Map: p243 E5.**

In a cliff near Kirkpatrick Fleming is a cave which was cut by Stone Age men. Robert Bruce (1306-1329) hid here for about three months during the winter of 1306 and 1307 when he was a hunted fugitive. The cave itself was accessible only by swinging down over the cliff by rope, although now there is a path to it.

It is claimed that in this cave Bruce watched a spider weave its web up to an impossibly difficult ledge, and thus gained hope that his own goals might eventually be achieved.

Kirkwall

Orkney Islands Area **Map: p247 H2.** *Bishop's Palace open Mon to Sat daily, Sun afternoons.*

Orkney belonged to the Norwegian crown until 1472, and in the early Middle Ages the islands, with their fine harbour at Kirkwall, provided an important base from which the Jarls (Earls) of Orkney, who were in effect petty kings, could mount Viking raids on the coast of Britain.

King Haakon the Old died in the Bishop's Palace attached to the 12th-century cathedral at Kirkwall in 1263, after his defeat at the Battle of Largs. Margaret, the Maid of Norway (1283-1290), also died here. Her mother was the daughter of Alexander III (1249-1286). Her untimely death, having been proclaimed Queen of Scots on her grandfather's death, precipitated the wrangle over the succession which was to lead to the Wars of Independence.

Another Margaret, daughter of King Christian I of Denmark, married James III (1460-1488), and when her dowry was not paid, her husband annexed Orkney to the Scottish crown and made Kirkwall a royal burgh. James's grandson, James V (1513-1542), held a Council at Parliament Close in Kirkwall, the site of which is today occupied by the Commercial Bank.

Ladykirk

Borders Region **Map: p243 G3.**

The kirk of Ladykirk was built by James IV (1488-1513) in 1500, in thanksgiving for his narrow escape from drowning when he fell into the river the previous year.

Langside

Strathclyde Region **Map: p242 D2.**

By 13 May 1568, 11 days after her escape from Loch Leven, Mary, Queen of Scots (1542-1567), had gathered about her a force of between 3,000

and 5,000 supporters, notably the forces of the Earls of Argyll and Hamilton. She determined to march to the secure stronghold of Dumbarton, but on the way passed close to the Regent Moray's smaller army, camped outside Langside. The royal vanguard stormed into the village, hoping for a quick victory, but the main body of the army, under Argyll, failed to follow up. By the end of the day she had lost her army; very few were killed, but the others had dispersed. Her hopes of regaining her crown also disappeared.

Largs

Strathclyde Region **Map: p242 C3.**

Alexander II (1214-1249) and Alexander III (1249-1286) had both tried to wrest the western isles from Norway, with both money and might, and in 1263 Haakon the Old determined that he would make sure of his possessions for all time and sailed with a fleet of 120 galleys to Scotland. On the last day of September a gale scattered the Norse fleet and drove some of the galleys ashore at Largs, including Haakon's own ship. After two days, Haakon withdrew, with only a fragment of his fleet. He died a year later, in Orkney, and his successor surrendered the isles to Scotland at the Treaty of Perth.

Lauder

Borders Region **Map: 243 F3.**

James III (1460-1488) was an unpopular king. When he went to war with England in 1482 he was supported very reluctantly by his barons. He called them to Lauder, close to the border, and formed a council of war with his favourites. The nobles were in no mood to fight and their dignity was offended by the King's attention to low-born favourites. According to legend, they met in Lauder kirk to fulminate against their sovereign, none of them willing to face him, until the young Earl of Angus, Archibald Douglas, announced that he would 'bell the cat' and went to the royal tent. When James refused to dismiss his favourites, the barons seized six of them and hanged them from the bridge above the Leader Water.

Leith

Lothian Region **Map: 253 E2.** *Lamb's House is now a home for the elderly.*

The first mention of Leith, the harbour for Edinburgh, is in 1134, when David I (1124-1153) gave the fisheries to the Canongate canons, and in 1313 it is recorded that Edward II (1307-1327) burned all the ships in the harbour, but he returned the following year and set up camp here before the Battle of Bannockburn. A village was not established here until 1329 when Robert Bruce (1306-1329) included Leith in his charter for Edinburgh, and as it grew Logan of Restalrig was allowed to set the village up as a burgh of barony. Mary of Guise, Queen of James V (1513-1542), bought part of the town, and during her struggle against the Protestant Lords of Convention while she was Regent she made her headquarters in Water Street.

When Mary, Queen of Scots (1542-1567), returned to Scotland in 1562 she landed at Leith and was entertained by a local merchant, Andrew

Lamb, in what is still known as Lamb's House in Burgess Street. Her son, James VI (1567-1625), was also no stranger to the town, and it was from the port that he sailed in 1589 to fetch his bride, Anne of Denmark, returning with her to the same port later in the year. In 1614 the King founded the King James Hospital, Kirkgate.

Lennoxlove

Lothian Region **Map: p243 F2.** *House open Apr to Sept: Wed, Sat and Sun afternoons. By appointment at other times.*

Lennoxlove House, near Haddington, belonged to the Maitland family from the 14th century until 1682 when the house was sold to Frances, Duchess of Lennox and Richmond, 'La Belle Stuart'. She was the mistress of Charles II (1660-1685) and the model for 'Britannia', featured on coins and medals. Early in the 18th century the house again changed hands, and in 1704 its name was changed to Lennoxlove in remembrance of the Duchess's royal lover. The house now belongs to the Dukes of Hamilton.

Lincluden Abbey

Dumfries & Galloway Region **Map: p243 E5.** *Open Sat to Thur morning.*

Lincluden Abbey was founded in 1164 by Uchtred, Lord of Galloway, for Benedictine nuns. The remains visible today include the canopied tomb of Princess Margaret, daughter of Robert III (1390-1406), and widow of the Earl of Douglas. In 1460, Queen Margaret, wife of Henry VI (1422-1461), and the Prince of Wales were received at Lincluden by the recently widowed Queen of James II (1437-1460).

Lindores

Fife Region **Map: 243 E1.**

David, Earl of Huntingdon — the 'Sir Kenneth' of Sir Walter Scott's *Talisman* — founded Lindores Abbey for the Benedictine order on his return from Palestine in 1178, and until its secularization in 1600 it formed one of the great religious communities in Fife. Prince Alexander, elder son of Alexander III (1249-1286), died within its walls in 1284, and Edward I of England (1272-1307) summoned all classes to swear allegiance before him at Lindores in 1297.

In 1402 David, Duke of Rothesay, son of Robert III (1390-1406) and heir to the throne, was buried in the abbey after he had been starved to death by his uncle, the Duke of Albany. His tomb was said to be a source of miracles until his brother, James I (1406-1437), avenged his death by executing Albany's son and grandsons in 1425.

Little France

Lothian Region **Map: p243 E2.** *Craigmillar Castle open Mon to Sat daily, Sun afternoons.*

Half a mile to the south of Craigmillar Castle is a small group of cottages; they were the home of some of Mary, Queen of Scots' (1542-1567) French attendants. The countryside round about reminded Mary of happy years in France and the whole area came to be known as 'Little France'.

Linlithgow

Central Region **Map: p243 E2.** *Palace open daily Mon to Sat; Sun afternoons. Closed Christmas, New Year.*

Linlithgow means 'the lock of the wet valley', and it was on a promontory into this loch that David I (1124-1153) built a timber manor house from which to administer the royal lordship of Linlithgow and the central belt of Scotland. From his reign onwards it became customary to settle the rents of the lordship of Linlithgow on the queen as a jointure or dowry.

During the Wars of Independence, Linlithgow became a centre of military activity. Edward I (1272-1307) occupied the royal manor, demolished it and built a stronger and larger tower and palisade on the promontory. He used his new fort as a base of operations against Stirling Castle in 1303 and 1304, building siege engines here and amassing stores. In 1313 a local farmer, William Binnock, overpowered the English garrison of the fort with a force of eight men hidden under hay on a wagon. Robert Bruce (1306-1329) then took possession of it and destroyed it.

Bruce's son, David II (1329-1371), rebuilt the royal manor at Linlithgow, but his building, along with much of the town that had grown up in the shadow of the manor's walls, was destroyed by fire in 1424. James I (1406-1437) returned from his 18-year-long captivity in England the same year and at once set about planning and building a great palace on the promontory, and building work continued intermittently for the next 100 years.

The new palace was a favourite residence of most of the Stuart kings, many of whom made additions and improvements to the massive structure. Early in the reign of James III (1460-1488) the palace was the residence of Henry VI of England (1422-1461) and his Queen, who fled here after defeat at the Battle of Towton in March 1461 and lived here for a year.

James IV (1488-1513) gave the palace to his young Queen, Margaret, daughter of Henry VII (1485-1509), and she lived here for most of her married life, giving birth to James V (1513-1542) here in 1512. Tradition has it that shortly before her husband's disastrous invasion of England in 1513 she contrived that he be approached by St John in the chapel at Linlithgow, who warned him not to go to war. It was in her favourite chamber in the northwest tower of the palace that Margaret heard the news of her husband's death and the Scots' rout at Flodden.

As his father had done, James V brought his Queen, Mary of Guise, to Linlithgow: she declared that she had never seen so princely a place, and in 1542 their daughter, Mary, Queen of Scots (1542-1567) was born here, six days before her father's death. During her minority and absence in France, the Queen Dowager came to Linlithgow many times, holding Privy Councils here, and even the Court of Session sat here at times while the plague raged in Edinburgh. Queen Mary visited Linlithgow only rarely on her return to Scotland in 1561, but her son, James VI (1567-1625) continued the building programme started by his forebears.

After the union of the crowns James did not return to Scotland, though he had said he would, and the Palace of Linlithgow fell into disrepair. In 1605 the King was warned that disaster was imminent unless something was done. Two years later, the Earl of Linlithgow reported that 'betuixt thre and four in the morning, the north quarter of your Majesties' Palace of Linlythgow is fallin, rufe and all within the wallis, to the ground; but the wallis ar standing yit, bot lukis euerie moment when the inner wall sall fall, and brek your Majesties' fontan'. Some repairs were carried out, and although Charles I (1625-1649) spent one night here in July 1633, and James II (1685-1688) lived here for a short time before his accession to the throne, no other monarch slept in the palace.

The end of the Palace of Linlithgow came by accident on 31 January 1746 when the Duke of Cumberland's army bivouacked here after the Battle of Falkirk. When they left the palace the following day they omitted to smother properly the fires they had kindled the night before: within a short time their bedding straw caught fire, and soon the great building was ablaze. Although roofless, Linlithgow Palace still has the presence of which Sir David Lindsay of the Mount wrote:

'Adieu Linlithgow, whose palayce of plesance might be ane pattern in Portugal & France.'

George V (1910-1936) and Queen Mary held a court in the Lyon Hall here on 11 July 1914, and 40 years later, their granddaughter, Elizabeth II, held a reception here.

Linlithgow Palace

Loch Leven

Tayside Region **Map: p243 E1.** *Castle open May to early Oct: Mon to Sat daily; Sun afternoons.*
Loch Leven is famous for its peculiar breed of trout and its seven islands. On one of these, St Serf's Island, are the ruins of an ancient priory dating from Celtic times. David I (1124-1153) visited the island in 1150 and transferred the property to the Augustinian canons of St Andrews, who built the buildings seen today.

On another island, Castle Island, Mary, Queen of Scots (1542-1567), was imprisoned. She was brought here after her defeat at Carberry Hill.

In spite of being closely guarded, Mary made more that one attempt to escape. On one occasion she disguised herself as a washerwoman, until the boatman noticed her pale hands. In the end she was aided by her gaoler's son, who rowed her across the loch to her waiting friends, Lord Seton and Sir James Hamilton

Loch Lomond

Central/Strathclyde Region **Map: p242 C2.**
Loch Lomond is the largest inland water in Britain, being 24 miles long. Magnus, King of Man and son-in-law of Haakon the Old, King of Norway, dragged his galleys across the narrow isthmus between Arrochar on Loch Long and Tarbet on Loch Lomondside in 1263, while his father-in-law was attacking the mainland further south, prior to his defeat at the Battle of Largs.

Lochmaben

Dumfries & Galloway Region **Map: p243 E4.**
Castle ruins open at all times.
Lochmaben was traditionally given its charter by Robert Bruce (1306-1329), and was certainly the centre of the Bruce power in Annandale from about 1200. On the edge of the present burgh is the motte of a Bruce castle which was erected about 1130, and it is claimed that Bruce was born here, though Turnberry also claims the honour.

On 22 July 1484, the Duke of Albany, brother of James III (1460-1488), who tried to depose the King and have himself crowned on more than one occasion, made his last attempt to achieve recognition by riding across the Solway to Lochmaben with a company of horsemen. The citizens of the town and some of the local lairds drove him back into England.

A stone castle had been built in the town by the beginning of the 14th century, and it became a favourite residence of James IV (1488-1513). His son, James V (1513-1542) also used it, and came here on 22 November 1542 before his proposed invasion of England. His army was routed two days later at the bloody Battle of Solway Moss.

Loch nan Uamh

Highland Region **Map: p244 B4.**
On 25 July 1745, Prince Charles Edward Stuart landed on the Scottish mainland from Loch nan Uamh, a sea loch. On 19 September 1746, 13 months later, after the collapse of all his hopes and the defeat of his army at Culloden, the Prince again came down to the shore of Loch nan Uamh, to board the frigate *L'Heureux*, which was to take him to France, never to return.

Loch Lomond

The Long Island

Western Isles Islands Area **Map: p246 B2.**
After his Rising had failed, Prince Charles Edward Stuart landed 'at peep of day' at Rossinish, in Benbecula, on 27 April 1746, and two days later proceeded north towards Stornoway in Lewis, in the hope of escaping to Orkney and then Norway. He endured terrible hardships in the wilds as he dodged his pursuers. Some months later, on 21 June, a chance meeting with Flora Macdonald resulted in escape. She managed to obtain passports for herself, a man-servant and a maid, 'Betty Burke', to travel to Skye. 'Betty Burke' himself hid under a rock in Benbecula for the next week until the coast was clear, and on the night of 28 June, they sailed 'over the sea to Skye'.

Loudon Hill

Strathclyde Region **Map: p242 D3.**
The first proper battle of the Wars of Independence after Robert Bruce (1306-1329) came out of hiding was fought on 10 May 1307, when he challenged an English army at Loudon Hill, east of Kilmarnock. Bruce probably had less than 1,000 men, mostly armed with long spears, but he deployed them skilfully across the hillside. The English outnumbered his army by three to one, but they suffered considerable losses. After a long day's fighting they turned and fled down the slope.

Lumphanan

Grampian Region **Map: p245 G3.**
Tradition has it that Macbeth (1040-1057) was killed while leading his bodyguard in a charge against Malcolm — later Malcolm III (1057-1093) — at Lumphanan. To the north of the village is Macbeth's Cairn, marked by a small ring of trees, which is the place where he was finally cut down.

Luncarty

Tayside Region **Map: p243 E1.**
On the north side of Luncarty is Denmarkfield, where in AD 990, Kenneth II (AD 971-995) attacked an invading army of Danes. Tradition has it that the battle was not going well for the Scots when a peasant, who had been ploughing his nearby fields with his two sons, seized the yoke of his oxen and rushed into the fray, so cheering the Scots that they drove the Danes from the field. The peasant's name was Hay or Haya, the progenitor of the Hay family who became Earls of Errol, hereditary High Constables of Scotland.

Melrose Abbey

Borders Region **Map: p243 F3.** *Open daily Mon to Sat; Sun afternoons. Closed Tue and alternate Weds in winter.*
An early monastery was established at Old Melrose by St Aidan in about AD 635, and two of its earliest priors were St Boisil (St Boswell) and St Cuthbert. It was succeeded in 1136 by a Cistercian abbey, built by David I (1124-1153). Lying so close to England, the abbey was repeatedly burned. Damage was severe in 1322, but Robert Bruce (1306-1329) rebuilt it four years later. His heart was buried in Melrose Abbey.

The abbey was again sacked in 1385, and in 1545 it was destroyed completely at the behest of Henry VIII (1509-1547). Little remains today of the once proud edifice.

Melville Castle

Lothian Region **Map: p243 F1.**
Melville Castle was built outside Lasswade for Henry Dundas, 1st Viscount Melville, the most powerful man in Scotland from 1775 to 1805.

Both George IV (1820-1830) and Queen Victoria (1837-1901) visited the castle, which was sold in 1983 and turned into a hotel.

Methven

Tayside Region **Map: p243 E1.**
During the weeks following the murder of the Red Comyn in Greyfriars Church, Dumfries, in February 1306, Robert Bruce (1306-1329) moved fast. Dumfries Castle was seized, the support of the Bishop of Glasgow obtained and a coronation arranged at Scone for Palm Sunday. Edward I (1272-1307) gathered an army to crush him and routed Bruce's small force.

Moy

Highland Region **Map: p244 D4.** *Moy Hall open by appointment only.*
On Sunday 16 February 1746, Prince Charles Edward Stuart and part of his army reached Moy Hall, 8 miles southwest of Inverness, the seat of the Laird of Mackintosh. The Laird himself was absent in the Hanoverian army, but the Prince was entertained by his wife, 'La Belle Rebelle' as she has been nicknamed. The Hanoverian commander in Inverness, Lord Loudon, heard that Charles was at Moy with only a few attendants and resolved to capture him. Lady Mackintosh, cautious for her guests' safety, sent out four of her servants and a blacksmith, Donald Fraser, to scout some 2 miles beyond the sentries. They surprised Loudon's force in the darkness, made a terrific noise and shot some of the Hanoverian troops. The Hanoverians fled back to Inverness and the event became known as 'the rout of Moy'.

George V (1910-1936) was a friend of the Laird of Mackintosh and used to stay at Moy Hall.

Nairn

Highland Region **Map: p245 E2.**
There is said to have been a royal castle at Nairn in early times, with the Thanes of Cawdor as its governors. Certainly a castle was built here by William the Lion (1165-1214), on the site of what is today the Constabulary Garden, but this was 'cast doun' in 1581. The town itself was probably made a royal burgh by Alexander I (1107-1124), and the town charter was confirmed by James VI (1567-1625) in 1589, who said of Nairn that the inhabitants of one end did not understand the language of those at the other end.

Newbattle Abbey

Lothian Region **Map: p243 F2.** *By appointment only.*
Newbattle Abbey, which is situated a mile southeast of Dalkeith, was originally a 12th-century Cistercian foundation, but became the family seat of the Kerrs, Marquesses of Lothian. David II (1329-1371), the son and heir of Robert Bruce (1306-1329), buried a murdered mistress here, and James IV (1488-1513) first met his bride Princess Margaret of England, in the abbey. Several subsequent sovereigns visited the place, including Queen Victoria (1837-1901) in 1842.

Niddry Castle

Lothian Region **Map: p243 E2.** *Ruins open.*
Set against the grim background of the nearby mining village of Winchburgh stands the roofless ruin of the tower of Niddry Castle, built in the reign of James IV (1488-1513) by the Seton family. George, 5th Lord Seton, whose daughter was one of the 'four Maries' of Mary, Queen of Scots (1542-1567), was himself a passionate supporter of the Queen. It was he who waited for her on the shores of Loch Leven in May 1568, and rode with her pell-mell to Niddry Castle.

Paisley

Strathclyde Region **Map: p242 D2.** *The Palace of Paisley open by appointment only.*
Walter FitzAllan, the first High Steward of Scotland, founded an abbey in 1163 for Cluniac monks. The tomb of Marjorie, daughter of Robert Bruce (1306-1329) and mother of Robert II (1371-1390), the first Stuart King, is in the St Mirren Chapel. The second Stuart King, Robert III (1390-1406), is buried in front of the high altar, hence the abbey is often referred to as 'the cradle of the Stuart kings'.

The original buildings were destroyed by the English in 1307, but a more splendid abbey replaced them in 1484. After the Reformation the building was badly neglected, but restoration work was undertaken in 1788 and 1859.

Peebles

Borders Region **Map: p243 E3.**
Peebles started as a county town under the shelter of a castle built by David I (1124-1153), and was granted a royal charter by David II (1329-1371) in 1367. The castle existed until about 1685, and was then used as a quarry for building material, a church being built on its site. Another church, Cross Kirk, now in ruins, was founded by Alexander III (1249-1286) in 1261.

The great Celtic/Druidic feast of Beltane, on 1 May, is still celebrated with vigour in Peebles, though the festival is now held in June.

Perth

Tayside Region **Map: p243 E1.**
After Kenneth McAlpin (AD 843-858) had united the kingdoms of the Picts and Scots he moved his capital to Scone, which had previously been a Pictish provincial centre, about a mile from Perth. This gave the town some importance, and situated where it was, among fertile lands and with a navigable river running through it, Perth soon began to prosper.

Edward I of England (1272-1307) captured the town in 1298, improved its fortifications and installed a garrison. His son, Edward II (1307-1327), sent his favourite, Piers Gaveston, to reinforce the town in 1310, but the following year Robert Bruce (1306-1329) took the town.

James I (1406-1437), was murdered in the garden of Black Friars Monastery. He had favoured Perth above all other places in his kingdom and held several Councils and Parliaments here, in Parliament Close off the High Street. His son, James II (1437-1460) continued to hold Parliaments here, but the building in which they sat was demolished in 1818. It was to Perth that James VI (1567-1625) was lured to his near death in 1600.

During both the '15 and '45 Risings, Perth was a Jacobite stronghold. James Drummond, 4th Earl of Perth, was created Duke by the Old Pretender, the first Jacobite peerage. His son, James, who became the 2nd Duke of Perth, commanded the Jacobite cavalry at the Battle of Sheriffmuir (1715), and his son, the 3rd Duke, landed with Prince Charles Edward Stuart from France in 1745. When the Prince reached Perth, the Duke was made joint commander of the Jacobite army with Lord George Murray. The Duke led the left wing at the Battle of Culloden (1746).

Pinkie

Lothian Region **Map: p243 F2.**
The great English army that came north by land and sea under the Duke of Somerset, self-styled 'Protector of England', on the death of Henry VIII (1509-1547), was trying to secure the hand of the child-queen, Mary (1542-1567), for the boy-king Edward VI (1547-1553). They were met by an even larger, though badly equipped, Scots army on 10 September at Pinkie, 6 miles east of Edinburgh. Cannonade and methodical tactics were too much for the Scots; the Highland contingent fled the field, and a rout quickly ensued. The Scots' dead were estimated at over 10,000.

Pitcaple Castle

Grampian Region **Map: p245 G3.** *Open May to Sept as advertised.*
Situated 4 miles northwest of Inverurie, Pitcaple Castle was built in the 15th century and has been continuously inhabited since. James IV (1488-1513) visited the place, and his granddaughter, Mary, Queen of Scots (1542-1567), dined here and spent the night of 16 September 1562, while on her northern progress.

Portree

Highland Region **Map: p244 B2.**
Throughout James V's reign (1513-1542) the island chiefs refused to honour the authority of the King. Finally, in May 1539, James himself sailed to the isles with a fleet of 12 ships. When the local chiefs came aboard to speak to their monarch they were clapped in irons and taken back to Edinburgh to agree terms.

Prince Charles Edward Stuart arrived in Skye on 29 June 1746 in the company of Flora Macdonald, and made his way to Portree the following day. At the inn (now the Royal Hotel) he bade farewell to the loyal Flora. They never met again, and Flora was captured on her way home and sent to the Tower of London.

Prestonpans

Lothian Region **Map: p243 E2.**
Edinburgh had fallen to Prince Charles Edward Stuart on 17 September 1745, and Sir John Cope marched to retake it. He drew up his army in a good position and prepared for battle. The Highlanders, however, surprised Cope by traversing a large bog between the armies at night. The Battle of Prestonpans, on 20 September, lasted just 10 minutes before the Hanoverians fled.

Prestwick

Strathclyde Region **Map: p242 C3.**
Tradition has it that when Robert Bruce (1306-1329) visited Prestwick, sick with leprosy, he sat down at the place now known as 'Bruce's Well' and drove his spear into the ground. Water immediately welled up and after drinking it, the King felt much restored. He went on to endow a leper hospital near the ruined chapel of St Ninian in the town.

Queensferry

Fife/Lothian Regions **Map: p243 E2.**
The crossing over the Forth at Queensferry has a recorded history of over 1,000 years. It is likely that the Romans used the passage, but the name derives from Queen Margaret, wife of Malcolm III (1057-1093), who frequently used the crossing when travelling to her favourite palace at Dunfermline. Margaret gave the inhabitants of North Queensferry the exclusive right of ferrying, but her son, David I (1124-1153), founded a regular ferry service, to be operated by the abbot of Dunfermline. By 1275 the Church found the running of the ferry service irksome, and leased the right back to the inhabitants of North Queensferry.

Raasay

Highland Region **Map: p244 B2.**
Prince Charles Edward Stuart reached Raasay at daybreak on 1 July 1746. Since Macleod of Raasay and one of his sons had fought for the Prince during the '45 Rising, the island had been terribly devastated by government troops. After staying the night it was felt that it would be much safer for the Prince if he returned to Skye.

Ravenscraig Castle

Fife Region **Map: p243 E2.** *Open Mon to Sat daily; Sun afternoons. Closed public holidays.*
Ravenscraig Castle, to the north of Kirkaldy, was begun by James II (1437-1460) in 1460. It was the first castle in Britain to be purpose built for defence by and against firearms. In 1470 James III (1460-1488) gave the castle to William Sinclair, Earl of Orkney.

Red Castle

Tayside Region **Map: p238 A3.** *Ruins open.*
This stark red sandstone ruin overlooks Lunan

Bay and was built in the 13th century by William the Lion (1165-1214). It probably replaces an earlier royal stronghold on the same site. William used the castle as a defence against the depradations of Danish pirates. In 1328 Robert Bruce (1306-1329) gave the castle to his son-in-law Hugh, 6th Earl of Ross.

Renfrew

Strathclyde Region **Map: p242 D2.**
The burgh and barony of Renfrew were granted by David I (1124-1153) to Walter, the High Steward, ancestor of the Royal House of Scotland. Either David or Walter himself built a motte and bailey castle in the town, and it was while camped before this that Somerled, King of the Isles, died in 1164. Somerled had declared war on Malcolm IV (1153-1165) and invaded the mainland of Scotland with a large fleet, sailing up the Clyde and attacking Renfrew. Tradition has it that the island King was assassinated in his tent and that without their leader the islesmen withdrew back to the west. Today Baron Renfrew is still one of the titles adopted by the eldest son of the Scots monarch.

Restenneth Priory

Fife Region **Map: p245 G4.** *Open as advertised.*
Restenneth Priory, 1½ miles northeast of Forfar, is believed to have been founded in AD 710 by the Pictish King Nechtan, for St Boniface, who converted him to Christianity. It was refounded in 1154 by Malcolm IV (1153-1165) for Augustinian monks from Jedburgh. In 1296 the priory was burned by Edward I (1272-1307), but recovered largely due to the encouragement of Robert Bruce (1306-1329), who visited the place.

Although ruined today, the tower of the priory church is a fine example of Norman stonework.

Rossend Castle

Fife Region **Map: p243 E2.** *Not open.*
Rossend Castle was built in the 12th century and added to in the 14th and 16th centuries. It was formerly the residence of the abbots of Dunfermline but later became a private residence. Mary, Queen of Scots (1542-1567), stayed in the castle in January 1562, while on a progress to St Andrews.

Rosslyn

Lothian Region **Map: p243 F2.** *Castle not open. Chapel open daily.*
According to tradition, the lands of Roslin, or Rosslyn, were won by Sir William St Clair from Robert Bruce (1306-1329). William's descendant, Henry St Clair, became Earl (or Prince) of Orkney in 1379 and built a great castle at Rosslyn in about 1390. His son, also Henry, was Admiral of Scotland, and as such took Prince James, later James I (1406-1437), to France in 1406. On the voyage, the ship was captured by an English fleet, and James was taken to gentle imprisonment in England for 18 years.

The last Prince of Orkney, Henry's son William, was also Admiral of Scotland and captained the ship that took James's daughter Margaret to marry the Dauphin of France,

narrowly escaping English pirates on the way. William was renowned for his wealth and intelligence, and for the fact that he faithfully served the first three King Jameses (between 1406 and 1488). In 1446 he determined to build a church in thanksgiving for the beneficence that God had showered on him.

Rothesay Castle

Strathclyde Region **Map: p242 C2.** *Castle open Mon to Sat daily, Sun afternoons.*
Rothesay Castle, which is noted for its round keep, dates from 1097. It was stormed and captured by Norsemen in 1230 and again in 1263, prior to the Battle of Largs (1263). Robert Bruce (1306-1329) took the castle in 1313 and from then on it was held by the crown. Bruce's grandson, Robert II (1371-1390) and great-grandson, Robert III (1390-1406), were both visitors here, and the latter died in the castle. Robert III created his eldest son, David, Duke of Rothesay, the first dukedom bestowed in Scotland, and the title is borne to this day by the heir to the throne of Scotland. The Prince of Wales is known by this title in Scotland.

James IV (1488-1513) and James V (1513-1542) both used the castle as a base for operations against the Lords of the Isles.

Roxburgh

Borders Region **Map: p243 F3.**
In the reign of David I (1124-1153) Roxburgh was one of the four royal burghs of Scotland, the others being Edinburgh, Stirling and Berwick. It relied on its castle, some 2 miles away between the Rivers Tweed and Teviot, for protection, but both town and castle fell so frequently into the hands of the English that the former could not prosper.

In the early Middle Ages it had been a royal residence: Alexander II (1214-1249) was married here, and his son, Alexander III (1249-1286) was born here. The castle was captured by the English in 1330, and was not recaptured until 1460. During the final siege James II (1437-1460) had brought a great cannon called The Lion to reduce the stronghold. While training it on the castle in person, it exploded and killed him. The spot is marked today by a holly tree. His eight-year-old son was crowned James III (1460-1488) in nearby Kelso Abbey, and his widowed Queen urged her husband's army on to take Roxburgh, and when they had done so, to reduce it to ruin.

St Monance

Fife Region **Map: p243 F1.**
Lying to the southeast of the ancient boat-building village of the same name is the church of St Monan, believed to have been founded by Irish monks fleeing to Scotland in the 9th century, who brought with them the relics of St Moinenn. David II (1329-1371) came to the shrine in 1362 after he had received a supposedly mortal wound from an arrow at the Battle of Durham. His physicians could not heal him, but as he prayed, the barb was miraculously plucked from him and the wound healed. He refounded the church as a result, and the exchequer rolls show that the cost of the new building was £600.

St Andrews

Fife Region **Map: p243 F1.** *Castle, Cathedral &* *Priory open daily except public holidays.*

St Regulus dreamed that he must take the relics of St Andrew to the westernmost island in the world, and was shipwrecked on the coast of Fife, near St Andrews. When Angus, King of the Picts, came down to the shore to seize what he could from the wreck, he was dramatically converted to Christianity and founded a chapel on the spot dedicated to St Andrew. It is certain that there was an early Culdee settlement, the 'servants of God' of the Celtic Church, close to the cathedral precinct, and when it became a bishopric at the beginning of the 10th century, it superseded Abernethy in importance.

A cathedral was built in the town in the 11th century, dedicated to St Regulus, and its tower still stands. Around it was built the medieval cathedral, begun in 1160 and consecrated with great pomp in 1318 by Robert Bruce (1306-1329) in a service giving thanks for his victory at Bannockburn (1314). It is by far the largest cathedral in Scotland, though it is now in ruins. The castle was begun in 1200 as the episcopal residence, and in 1472 the see became an archbishopric. It was taken and held by Edward I (1272-1307) and by Edward III (1327-1377), both of whom stayed here briefly.

The town has a long history of education. The first university to be founded in Scotland — the second in Britain — was established here by papal bull in 1413, and both James I (1406-1437) and James II (1437-1460) were educated in the town by Bishops Wardlaw and Kennedy respectively. Bishop Kennedy was a grandson of Robert III (1390-1406) and taught the King how to break a bundle of arrows by separating them and snapping them one by one, a lesson he was later to apply to his troublesome barons. Kennedy had a very beautiful niece, Katherine, and gave a bell named after her to the new university: it is rung at the end of wars. Each spring the students of the university

The Old Harbour and Cathedral

mount a great pageant through the streets of the town, the Kate Kennedy Procession, and Kate herself is the centre of attraction.

In 1538 Mary of Guise was married to James V (1513-1542) in the cathedral. The night before her wedding she watched a performance of Sir David Lindsay of the Mount's *Satire of the Thrie Estaits*. Her daughter, Mary, Queen of Scots (1542-1567) made a royal progress to St Andrews in February 1562 and was molested by an admirer called Châtelard, who was executed for his pains at the Mercat Cross. Mary returned to St Andrews several times during her reign and stayed in the house of a local merchant, Henry Scrymgeour, to escape from the pressures of the court. The house is now called Queen Mary's House. The Queen also planted a thorn bush outside St Mary's College, the divinity school of the university.

At the beginning of the Scottish Reformation, John Knox delivered his famous sermon on the 'cleansing of the temple' four times in the cathedral on four consecutive days in 1559. This led to the destruction of images and popish ornaments. Neglect had reduced the building to a ruinous state by 1649 when Cromwell authorized that it be used as a quarry. Three years previously a Parliament had been called in the Parliament Hall, within the university, to debate the fate of Royalists in Scotland.

Sauchieburn

Central Region **Map: 245 G4.**

By his avarice and his fondness for favourites, James III (1460-1488) alienated himself from his nobles. In the end they banded together and went to war against him in the name of his son, the Duke of Rothesay. The barons met the royal army on 11 June 1488 at Sauchieburn on the Stirling Plain and defeated it. While fleeing from the battlefield, the King was thrown from his horse near Beaton's Mill. He asked for a priest to be sent to him, but the man that came to give him absolution drew a knife and stabbed him to the heart. The Duke of Rothesay became James IV (1488-1513), and throughout his life wore a chain next to his skin to expiate the guilt he felt for having caused his father's death.

Scone

Tayside Region **Map: p243 E1.** *Palace open Apr to early Oct: daily Mon to Sat; Sun afternoon (all day in July and Aug).*

When Fergus MacErc came from Ireland in about AD 500 to establish the kingdom of Dalriada he brought the Stone of Destiny with him and the kings of Dalriada, and later the kings of Scotland, always stood upon it during their coronations. The accession of Kenneth McAlpin (AD 834-858) united the Pictish and Scottish crowns, and Kenneth brought the Stone of Destiny to Scone from Dunstaffnage. Edward I (1272-1307) took it to Westminster Abbey in 1296. Today it is under the Coronation Chair there and kings and queens of Great Britain continue to 'stand' upon it at their coronation.

At Scone the coronation ceremony itself was conducted on the ancient Moot Hill, the Stone of Destiny being carried here for each occasion. Even after the stone was lost, kings continued to be crowned here until James I (1406-1437).

A parish church was built here in 1620, and Charles II (1651-1685) was crowned here on 1 January 1651. The church has been replaced by a mausoleum for the Earls of Mansfield. A priory was founded at Scone by Alexander I (1107-1124), and an abbey in 1164. It was pillaged by Edward I in 1298 but repaired. A Parliament met in the abbey in 1373 to solemnly declare Robert II (1371-1390) and his heirs to be the successors to the throne, thus confirming the Stuart line. Robert II was buried in the abbey.

By 1650 the abbey had been destroyed. The Old Pretender held court in the house built on the site in 1715, and his son did the same in September 1745. The original house was replaced between 1803 and 1808 by the present 'palace'.

Seton

Lothian Region **Map: p243 F2.** *Castle open daily.*

The 'villa' of Seton was granted by Robert Bruce (1306-1329) to Sir Alexander Seton, who had deserted Edward II (1307-1327) on the eve of the Battle of Bannockburn (1314). Whatever castle was built here was destroyed by the English in 1544. It was rebuilt shortly after, however, and Mary, Queen of Scots (1542-1567), was a frequent visitor. By the early 17th century the castle had

The Quadrangle, St Saviour's College

been enlarged into a 'palace' and was frequently visited by royalty. The palace was damaged by government forces during the 1715 Rising.

Skye

Highland Region **Map: p246 C4.**
Prince Charles Edward Stuart landed in Skye with Flora Macdonald and five boatmen on the afternoon of 29 June 1746. The Prince, escaping Hanoverian search parties, was dressed as a woman and addressed as Betty Burke.

Solway Moss

Cumbria/Dumfries & Galloway Region **Map: p243 F5.**
The hated James V (1513-1542), preparing to confront Henry VIII (1509-1547) and an invading English army, was taken by surprise at Solway Moss while waiting for the tide to ebb before crossing the sands. The Scottish fight was half-hearted, and 12,000 prisoners were taken by the English. James fled back to Edinburgh and died a month later at Falkland.

Tain

Highland Region **Map: p245 E1.**
St Duthac, one of the last great saints of the Celtic Church, was born at Tain in about AD 1000. He died in Northern Ireland in 1065, and when his body was brought back to Tain in 1253, the shrine became a place of pilgrimage. Queen Elizabeth de Burgh, wife of Robert Bruce (1306-1329), fled to Tain in 1306, and it was here that she and her children were betrayed by the Earl of Ross.

James IV (1488-1513) made a pilgrimage to Tain every year between 1493 and 1513, in expiation of his guilt over his father's death.

Tantallon Castle

Lothian Region **Map: p243 F2.** *Open daily Mon to Sat; Sun afternoons. Closed Tues and alternate Weds in winter.*
This famous Douglas stronghold is today a massive red sandstone ruin on a cliff promontory with a sheer drop to the sea on three sides. It is uncertain when Tantallon was built, but its walls were already venerable when James IV (1488-1513) laid siege to them in 1491. He was waiting for his over-mighty vassal, Archibald Douglas, 5th Earl of Angus, known as 'Bell-the-

Tantallon Castle

Cat', to surrender. After some weeks they made their peace and James raised the siege.

A similarly aggressive relationship continued between the Douglases and James V (1513-1542). When the 6th Earl assumed the role of Regent, the young James gathered his forces and besieged Tantallon with the great cannon 'Mons Meg', now in Edinburgh Castle. However, no impression was made on the walls of the castle, and after 20 days the siege was raised. The castle was not taken until 1651 when it was besieged by Cromwell's forces. It subsequently fell into a state of decay.

Tibbers Castle

Dumfries & Galloway Region **Map: p243 E4.**
Only vestiges remain of this castle, which was reputed to have been built by the Romans and named after the Emperor Tiberius. During the Wars of Independence it was garrisoned by the English but taken by William Wallace, and later by Robert Bruce (1306-1329), who destroyed it.

Traquair House

Borders Region **Map: p243 F3.** *Open Apr to June and mid-Sept to late Oct: afternoons; July to mid-Sept: daily.*
The Stuart stronghold of Traquair claims to be the oldest continuously inhabited house in Scotland. Certainly, there was a royal hunting lodge here in the 12th century. It is said that 12 successive kings used the place, and it was particularly popular with Alexander I (1107-1124).

Turnberry

Strathclyde Region **Map: p242 C4.**

Turnberry lighthouse stands in what was once the courtyard of Turnberry Castle, but only a few fragments of the rest of the building remain. Situated in a commanding position overlooking the whole of the Firth of Clyde, there has been a fort here since earliest times. When Margaret, a descendant of Fergus of Galloway, married Robert de Brus in 1271, she brought Turnberry Castle with her as a dowry. It is claimed by many that Margaret's son, Robert Bruce (1306-1329), was born at Turnberry in 1274, and it is certain that he spent much of his childhood here. In September 1286 the castle was the meeting-place of the Scottish barons who supported Robert's claim to the throne, and it was the fires lit at Turnberry that signalled to the King, who was in hiding in Arran, to return to the mainland. He did so in February 1307, to begin the liberation of Scotland.

Wemyss Castle

Fife Region **Map: p243 F1.** *Castle not open*
Wemyss Castle stands half a mile from the village of East Wemyss on the northern shore of the Forth and dates in part from the 13th century, although it was much enlarged and altered in the 16th century. It was here that Mary, Queen of Scots (1542-1567), first met her future husband, Lord Darnley, on 17 February 1565.

Whithorn

Dumfries & Galloway Region **Map: p240 B1.**
From early times St Ninian's shrine at Whithorn was an important focus for pilgrims, and many kings of Scotland came here, including Robert Bruce (1306-1329) in the last year of his life, James II (1437-1460), James III (1460-1488), James IV (1488-1513), James V (1513-1542). and Mary, Queen of Scots (1542-1567).

Stirling

Stirling Castle

Central Region **Map: p242 D1.** *Castle open daily Mon to Sat; Sun afternoons.*

It is thought that the Romans may have had an encampment on the rugged volcanic plug which supports Stirling Castle, and there is a legend that two or three centuries later the Saxon fort which succeeded the Roman camp was taken by the English King Arthur.

The castle receives its first reliable mention as the place where Alexander I (1107-1124) died, and as a frequent resting-place of his brother, David I (1124-1153). Situated in the heart of Scotland, sentinel over the fords across the river Forth and dominating the passage to the north of the country, it was recognized as one of the most important castles in the realm, and was named as such by the Treaty of Falaise, when it was handed over to the English as part of the ransom for William the Lion (1165-1214) in 1174.

At this time the castle would have been mainly of timber, with ditches and palisades, but this did not prevent it being acknowledged as the strongest fortress in the realm at the time of the invasion by Edward I (1272-1307) in 1296. The Battle of Stirling Bridge gave the castle back to the Scots the following year, but on his return in 1304 Edward besieged the place with every known siege-engine, including a formidable machine called 'the War-Wolf'. When the castle finally surrendered after three months, there were only 150 starving defenders left.

For 10 years the castle was a symbol of English authority and prevented intercourse between north and south. In 1313 Robert Bruce (1306-1329) blockaded the town, however, and the English governor agreed to surrender if no force came to relieve him before 24 June 1314. The force that came north under Edward II (1307-1327), met the Scots at Bannockburn, within sight of the beleaguered castle. Bruce demolished much of the castle, but by the end of the 14th century it had been repaired and fortified. Robert II (1371-1390) appointed his son, the Duke of Albany, as governor of the castle, and he was succeeded by his son. On the return of James I (1406-1437) from exile in England, Albany's son was beheaded at Stirling, after a perfunctory trial, as being an over-mighty vassal.

James's harsh treatment of his barons led to his own murder at Perth. His murderer, Sir James Graham, was tortured to death at Stirling. James II (1437-1460) made Stirling Castle a dower-house for his Queen, Mary of Gueldres, and frequently used it as a residence, holding great knightly tournaments on the plain below the castle rock. It was here that he murdered the Earl of Douglas with his own hands in 1452, and it was to Stirling that the Earl's brother brought an avenging force the following year, doing much damage to the town, though he could not take the castle.

James III (1460-1488) was born at Stirling in 1451, and throughout his life 'he tuik sic pleasour to duall thair that he left all other castellis and touns in Scotland'. It was he who gave the castle its present shape, erecting the Great Hall, in which Parliament sat, the Gatehouse or 'portcullis' and the original Chapel Royal, as well as dramatically improving the curtain walls and flanking towers. Robert Cochrane, the King's architect and one of his favourites, was hanged by 'Bell-the-Cat' Douglas at Lauder Brigg. James III himself was murdered after the Battle of Sauchieburn (1488) on the Stirling Plain, and his son, James IV (1488-1513), blamed himself for his father's death throughout his life, 'daylie passing to the Chapell Royall' in repentance while he was at Stirling.

After the Battle of Flodden (1513), the castle passed to James IV's widow, and just as his father had done, the boy-king James V (1513-1542) spent much of his childhood here. Later he improved the defences of the fortress and installed 'artaillye and harneis witht powder and bullat'. He also built the Palace of Stirling within the ramparts, enclosing a courtyard known as 'the Lion's Den' which was reputed to hold living counterparts of the lion rampant depicted on the royal coat of arms. James V would wander abroad disguised as a commoner, in order to better understand his subjects. When disguised he was known as 'the Gudeman of Ballengeich', after a hamlet close to the castle.

Mary, Queen of Scots (1542-1567), was crowned in the Church of the Holy Rood at Stirling, at the age of nine months, and spent the first four years of her reign here. After the Battle of Pinkie (1547), even Stirling was thought unsafe, and she was removed to Inchmahome and then Dumbarton and so to France. On her return she used the castle as a temporary residence when journeying north, and one night nearly fulfilled an old prophecy of a queen being burned to death the castle, when her bed hangings caught fire. During 1565, when she was infatuated with Lord Darnley, she spent several months nursing him in the castle, and the following year her infant son was christened here.

On his mother's abdication, James VI (1567-1625) was crowned in Stirling, and remained here during the regency of the Earls of Mar and Morton, receiving tuition from George Buchanan, the famous scholar and author of *The History of Scotland*, in the Prince's Tower of the Palace. It was from Stirling that the young King was abducted by the Earls of Gowrie, Mar and Glencairn in August 1582, and 12 years later James's son and heir, Henry, Duke of Rothesay and later Prince of Wales, was baptized in the Chapel Royal within the castle.

Prince Henry was the last Prince to be brought up at Stirling: after the union of the crowns in 1603 it ceased to be a royal residence, although James VI returned twice, and Charles I (1625-1649) and Charles II (1651-1685) both stayed here for short periods. Stirling Castle is still inhabited and is today the headquarters of the Argyll and Sutherland Highlanders.

Statue of Robert Burns

The Carse of Forth and Stirling Castle

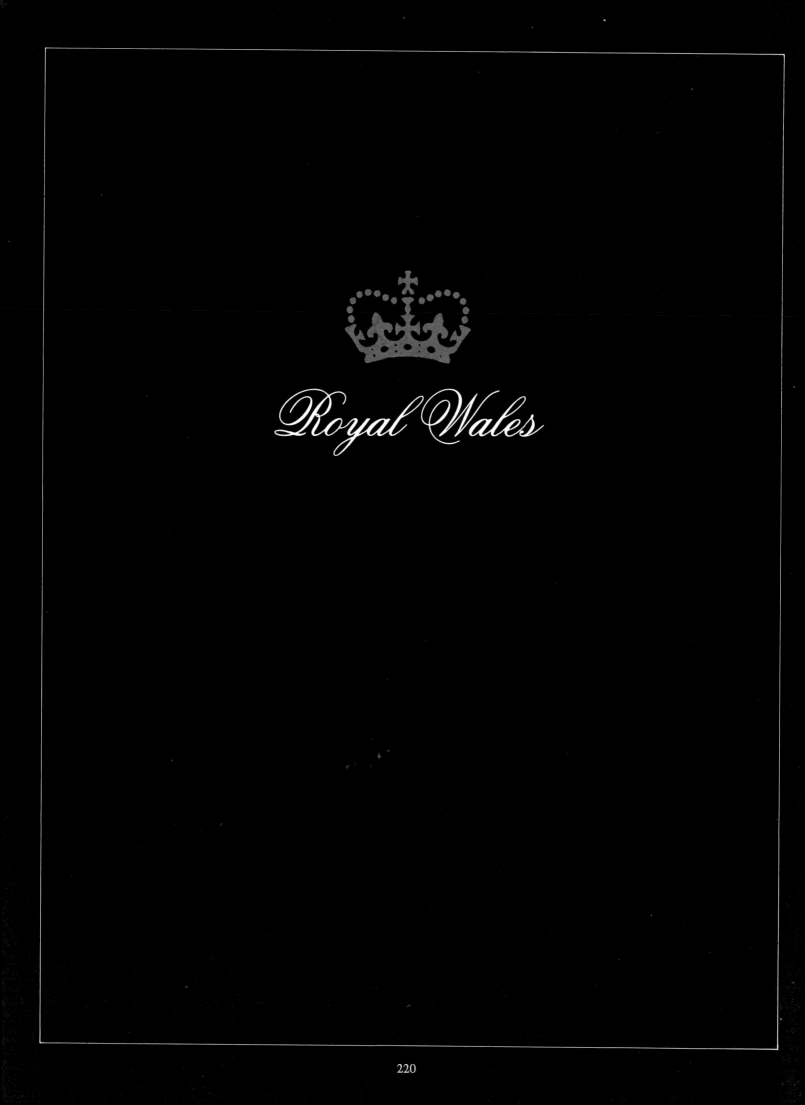

Royal Wales

Abbey Cwm Hir

Powys **Map: p237 E3.**
The scanty remains of this 12th-century abbey overlook a memorial to Llywelyn ap Gruffydd (1246-1282), the last undisputed native Prince of Wales. His decapitated corpse was buried here a few days after he had been killed by an English soldier at Cilmery, west of Builth Wells, on 11 December 1282. The head was displayed outside the Tower of London.

The abbey was founded in 1143 by a cousin of Rhys ap Gruffydd (1153-1197). The most powerful Welshman of his time, 'Lord Rhys' was Prince of Deheubarth, a region similar to the modern county of Dyfed. Owain Glyndwr (1404-1408) sacked the abbey in 1401 or 1402.

Aber

Gwynedd **Map: p240 B5.**
The little village of Aber was a seat of the rulers of North Wales in the 13th century. A small mound is all that remains of the castle built by Llywelyn ab Iorwerth (1194-1240) — generally known as Llywelyn the Great — to guard the route over the tide-swept Lavan Sands to Anglesey. It was here that Llywelyn discovered his wife Joan, illegitimate daughter of King John (1199-1216), in bed with William de Breos, a powerful Norman baron. De Breos was hanged at Aber on 2 May 1230. Joan was kept in prison until 1231, and she died in the castle six years later. Her son David married Isabella, daughter of de Breos, and died at Aber in 1246, leaving no children.

At Aber, Llywelyn ap Gruffydd (1246-1282), grandson of Llewellyn the Great, made his fateful decision not to visit London to pay homage to Edward I (1272-1307). It was one of several defiant gestures which eventually obliged the English King to crush the Welsh rulers.

Aberdaron

Gwynedd **Map: p236 C1.**
Gruffydd ap Rhys, Prince of South Wales (*d.* 1137), sought refuge in the Aberdaron church in the 12th century. He was fleeing from enemies who intended handing him over to Henry I of England (1100-1135). Troops sent to capture him dared not violate holy ground. The prince escaped by night.

Aberdyfi

Gwynedd **Map: p236 D2.**
Aberdyfi was the scene of a diplomatic triumph by Llywelyn the Great (1194-1240) in 1216. He assembled what is generally accepted as the first Welsh Parliament, to sort out territorial claims being made by the many chiefs and minor princes.

Aberedw

Powys **Map: p237 E3.**
The tranquil little village of Aberedw has links with the final days of Llywelyn ap Gruffydd (1246-1282), the last undisputed native Prince of Wales, who had a small castle here. Hoping to raise support for his war with England, Llywelyn is said to have ridden to Aberedw from Builth Wells to meet local chiefs. They failed to make the rendezvous, so the prince and his squire sheltered overnight in a small cave about half a mile southeast of the village church. The prince was killed a day or two later at Cilmery.

Aberffraw

Gwynedd **Map: p240 A5.**
Aberffraw was the capital of Gwynedd for some 600 years before Edward I of England (1272-1307) completed his conquest of Wales. No traces remain of the royal palace, Llys Aberffraw, which was probably a timber building where rulers, including Llywelyn the Great (1194-1240) and Llywelyn the Last (1246-1282), held court.

Other rulers whose names are associated with Aberffraw include King Cadfan of Gwynedd (d AD 625) and Rhodri Mawr (AD 844-878), who died in battle against the English in AD 878. Rhodri the Great, as he is known, ruled as King of Gwynedd, Powys and Ceredigion.

Abergavenny

Gwent **Map: p237 F4.** *Castle open daily.*
Founded in the 11th century, Abergavenny Castle was the setting for one of the most infamous deeds in Welsh history. In 1177 it was held by a Norman baron, William de Breos, who invited the local chiefs and princes to dine with him at Christmas. While feasting, the guests were set upon and murdered by their host's soldiers. De Breos eventually fell foul of King John (1199-1216) and was hanged a penniless beggar.

In 1215 the castle was captured by Llywelyn the Great (1194-1240) during one of his many campaigns against the English. Owain Glyndwr (1404-1408) burned the castle and the town in 1403 during the rebellion in which he was proclaimed Prince of Wales.

Charles I (1625-1649) retreating westwards after his defeat at Naseby in 1645, visited Abergavenny to meet the Commissioners of counties in South Wales. But the support promised to him failed to materialize.

Abermule

Powys **Map: p237 E2.** *Castell Dolforwyn open daily.*
This village is overlooked from the west by the hilltop site of Castell Dolforwyn which was built by Llywelyn the Last (1246-1282) to defy the English fortress at nearby Montgomery.

Aberystwyth

Dyfed **Map: p236 D2.** *Castle site is now public gardens. Open daily.*
Aberystwyth Castle has a unique distinction — in 1407 its possession was contested by two Princes of Wales. One, the future Henry V (1413-1422), had been invested eight years earlier, while his rival, Owain Glyndwr (1404-1408), had claimed the title in 1404 during his rebellion against Henry's father, Henry IV (1399-1413).

Glyndwr captured the stronghold at Aberystwyth in 1403 and it was here, two years later, that his treaty with the French was ratified and signed. Prince Henry attacked the fortress in the summer of 1407. The garrison's commander was on the brink of surrender when Glyndwr arrived to bolster morale. Prince Henry was obliged to fall back to England but he returned to Aberystwyth the following year and, during Glyndwr's absence, the castle at last fell.

Work was first started on the castle in 1277 by Edmund of Lancaster, brother of Edward I (1272-1307). It was demolished in 1647, during the Civil War, but fragmentary remains survive on the university town's sea front.

Prince Charles, Prince of Wales, spent a term at the University College of Wales in Aberyswyth, learning Welsh before his investiture as Prince of Wales at Caernarvon Castle in 1969.

Bangor

The Menai Strait near Bangor

Gwynedd **Map: p240 B5.**
Bangor's ancient cathedral, rebuilt in the 15th century, was the burial place of Owain Gwynedd (1137-1170). He and his brother Cadwallon (killed 1132) had done much to restore the kingdom's fortunes and had expanded their aged father's domain to the east and southeast.

Basingwerk Abbey

Clwyd **Map: p240 D5.**
It was near this 12th-century abbey that Owain Gwynedd (1137-1170) and his sons set a trap for Henry II (1154-1189) when the English King invaded North Wales in 1157. Henry's army was ambushed, but the encounter did not produce a decisive Welsh victory. Owain later handed two of his eastern provinces over to Henry and agreed to change his title from king to the more humble one of prince. Eight years later Owain's domain was again extended right across North Wales and he captured and destroyed Basingwerk Castle.

Cenwulf, King of Mercia, died at Basingwerk in AD 821 during a war with Merfyn the Freckled, King of Gwynedd.

Beddgelert

Gwynedd **Map: p236 D1.**
Beddgelert has long been linked with the name of Llywelyn the Great (1194-1240). The story tells how Llywelyn, Prince of Aberffraw and Lord of Snowdon, went out hunting while leaving his

dog, Gelert, to guard his baby son. He returned to find the animal covered in blood and, thinking it had eaten the boy, slew Gelert before realizing that the dog had actually saved the young prince's life by killing a wolf.

Berwyn Mountains

Clwyd and Gwynedd **Map: p237 E1.**
The mountains which run southwest from Llangollen are crossed by an ancient track known as Ffordd y Saeson or the English Road. Its name recalls the summer of 1164 when Henry II (1154-1189) marched from Oswestry over the mountains with a great host of soldiers. His plan was to attack the Welsh army camped at Corwen and commanded by Owain Gwynedd (1137-1170), King of North Wales. Henry was thwarted by storms and forced back to Oswestry. He sought revenge by ordering the mutilation of 22 hostages. Owain Gwynedd's sons, Rhys and Cadwaladr, were among those whose eyes were plucked out.

Borth

Dyfed **Map: p236 D2.**
Borth's beach, backed by shingle and dunes, runs northwards to the mouth of the River Dyfi, then sweeps round to meet the tidal sands of Traeth Maelgwn. According to legend it is where Maelgwn Gwynedd made his successful bid to become ruler of North Wales in the sixth century. He and his rivals agreed that the crown would go to the man who defied the incoming sea longest. Maelgwn won the contest by building himself a chair which floated on the waves.

Brawdy

Dyfed **Map: p236 B4.**
Some authorities claim that Trefgarne Owen, a tiny hamlet in the parish of Brawdy, is where Owain Glyndwr (1404-1408), the champion of Welsh independence, was born in about 1359.

Brecon

Brecon Cathedral

Powys **Map: p237 E4.**
Known in Welsh as Aberhonddu, Brecon commands one of the main routes across South

Beaumaris

Gwynedd **Map: p240 B5.** *Castle open mid-Mar to mid-Oct: daily; mid-Oct to mid-Mar: weekdays, Sun afternoons. Closed Christmas, New Year.*
The name of this delightful little seaside resort is derived from the Norman-English for 'beautiful marsh'. It refers to the site chosen by Edward I (1272-1307) for the last of the eight castles he had built in North Wales after the death of Llywelyn the Last (1246-1282). The English King visited Beaumaris for three or four days in the summer of

Beaumaris Castle

Wales and featured prominently in the wars of Llywelyn the Great (1194-1240) and Llywelyn the Last (1246-1282). The 11th-century castle, whose scanty remains still stand above the confluence of the Rivers Honddu and Usk, was attacked on six occasions between 1215 and 1273. It was attacked again in 1403 by Welsh troops fighting for Owain Glyndwr (1404-1408), who claimed the title of Prince of Wales during his war with England. The garrison held out, but the size of the Welsh army caused panic to race through the royalist forces in southern and central Wales. Glyndwr himself raided Brecon in 1404.

Builth Wells

Powys **Map: p237 E3.**
Strategically sited on the River Wye, in the heart of Wales, Builth Wells was the site chosen by Edward I (1272-1307) for the first of his Welsh castles. Work started in 1277, a few months after the King declared war on Llywelyn the Last (1246-1282). The castle had several owners, but reverted to the crown during the reign of Edward IV (1461-1483). It was probably demolished towards the end of the 16th century.

Caerphilly

Mid Glamorgan **Map: p233 E1.** *Castle open mid-Mar to mid-Oct: daily; mid-Oct to mid-Mar: weekdays, Sun afternoons. Closed Christmas, New Year.*
Caerphilly's focal point is a huge, moated castle

1283, but work on the castle did not start until 1295, soon after Madog ap Gruffydd's revolt.

Early in 1296 the architect sent a letter to the King's ministers with the news that 1,000 men were working at Beaumaris — the total labour force later reached nearly 3,000.

The 'new town' which grew up around the castle soon outgrew the nearby village of Llanfaes, where Llywelyn the Great (1194-1240) had founded a Franciscan friary in 1237. It was also the burial place of his wife Joan, illegitimate daughter of King John (1199-1216). Joan's stone coffin, used for many years as a drinking trough for horses, now rests in the porch of Beaumaris Church.

which covers 30 acres and is the largest in Britain apart from Windsor. Work on the fortress was started in 1268 by Gilbert de Clare, Earl of Gloucester and Lord of Glamorgan, after he had defeated the local ruler, Gruffydd ap Rhys. Two years later the preliminary defences were destroyed by Llewelyn the Last (1246-1282), but de Clare eventually completed the castle which epitomizes the power of the Norman barons.

De Clare's daughter married Hugh Despenser, the unpopular favourite of Edward II (1307-1327). In 1326 Edward's Queen, Isabella, sailed to France and asked several exiled nobles to help her get rid of the King's favourite. Learning of the plot and fearing for his own safety, Edward fled to Wales where Caerphilly Castle became his headquarters for several days. He then headed west, but was captured near Llantrisant in November and later murdered. Queen Isabella and her supporters captured Caerphilly Castle and had Hugh Despenser dragged through the streets of Hereford on a hurdle before being hanged and quartered. His elder brother, the Earl of Winchester, was hanged and decapitated in Gloucester.

Cardigan

Dyfed **Map: p236 C3.**
The castle, whose remains overlook the River Teifi in Cardigan, is a reminder of Rhys ap Gruffyd, Prince of Deheubarth (1153-1197). It was one of the fortresses from which the Lord Rhys, as he is generally called, ruled most of South Wales and emerged as the most important Welsh leader after the death of Owain Gwynedd (1137-1170).

Caernarvon

Two views of Caernarvon Castle

Gwynedd **Map: p240 B5.** *Castle open mid-Mar to mid-Oct: daily; mid-Oct to mid-Mar: weekdays, Sun afternoons. Closed Christmas, New Year.*
The majestic walls and towers of Caernarvon Castle symbolize the royal status of this bustling, history-steeped town on the Menai Strait where Prince Charles Philip Arthur George was invested as the 21st Prince of Wales in 1969. The great building which provided such a romantic setting had been used for a similar ceremony in 1911.

Edward I (1272-1307) ordered work to start on the castle in 1283, the year after the death of Llywelyn the Last (1246-1282) near Builth Wells ended the days of the native princes. It was destined to become the greatest of all the fortresses built by Edward to pacify the Welsh, and cost more than £20 million in today's money. Tradition pinpoints the Eagle Tower as the place where Edward's wife, Queen Eleanor, gave birth to their son, the future Edward II (1307-1327). But the event almost certainly took place in a timber-framed building erected for the royal visitors while work on the castle itself was still in the early stages. Tradition also maintains that the baby's father summoned the Welsh leaders to Caernarvon and presented them with a prince born in Wales who could not speak a single word of English. His son was, of course, too young to speak a single word of any language. Edward of Caernarvon, as he became known, was officially created Prince of Wales in 1301 and held the title until he became King on his father's death, six years later. He was eventually murdered in Berkeley Castle. Edward I's visit to Caernarvon in 1295, during his final journey through Wales, was the last by a ruling monarch until Richard II

(1377-1399) spent a night in the castle in 1399, sleeping on nothing more regal than a straw-covered floor. It may have lacked regal trappings, but the fortress proved strong enough to defy the efforts of Owain Glyndwr (1404-1408) during the next decade. Glyndwr, proclaimed Prince of Wales by his followers, attacked in 1401 and withdrew after losing about 300 men.

The official Princes of Wales had all been invested in London, York or Windsor until Caernarvon's logical and long-standing claims were successfully promoted by David Lloyd George, Constable of Caernarvon Castle, Chancellor of the Exchequer and the local Member of Parliament. The investiture of 17-year-old Prince Edward Albert Christian George Andrew Patrick David, son of George V (1910-1936) and Queen Mary, in 1911 was the first time that a Prince of Wales had been invested in the principality and formally presented to the Welsh people. The Prince was destined to become Edward VIII (1936), the uncrowned King.

At his investiture in the summer of 1969 — hailed as Britain's greatest royal event since the coronation of Elizabeth II in 1953 — Prince Charles, kneeling with his back to the Eagle Tower, was officially invested with the title granted to him 11 years earlier. The ceremony took place beneath a transparent canopy bearing the crest of three ostrich feathers which Edward, the Black Prince, son of Edward III (1327-1377), is said to have adopted after the Battle of Crécy in 1346, where the emblem had been used by the blind King of Bohemia. Edward, the second non-Welsh Prince of Wales, held the title from 1343 until his death in 1376. He never visited Wales.

Cardiff

South Glamorgan **Map: p233 F1.** *Castle open daily.*
On 26 July 1958, Cardiff Arms Park was the scene of the closing ceremony of the sixth British Empire and Commonwealth Games. Unable to attend because of an illness, Elizabeth II had recorded a special message to be broadcast over the loudspeakers: 'I intend to create my son, Charles, Prince of Wales today. When he is grown up I will present him to you at Caernarvon.' The 10-year-old Prince visited Wales a few weeks later, but was not officially invested as Prince of Wales until 1969. Cardiff also remembers Elizabeth II as the ruler who, in 1955, decreed that it should be the first official capital of Wales.

The city's recorded links with royalty go back to 1126, when Robert, Duke of Normandy, became a prisoner in Cardiff Castle. The eldest son of William the Conqueror (1066-1087), he would probably have become king after the death of his brother, William Rufus (1087-1100), had he not been crusading in the Holy Land. The crown passed to his youngest brother, Henry I (1100-1135), who defeated Robert in 1106. The last 28 years of the Duke's life were spent as a captive in Bristol and Cardiff castles. He is said to have had his eyes gouged out after attempting to escape from the Welsh fortress.

In 1404 the castle was captured by Owain Glyndwr (1404-1408) during the revolt in which he was proclaimed Prince of Wales. Its walls were breached and the garrison was put to the sword.

Glyndwr also burned the town of Cardiff. The castle later passed into the hands of Richard, Duke of Gloucester, the future Richard III (1483-1485).

Charles I (1625-1649) visited Cardiff in July 1645, hoping to rally support after his defeat at Naseby and march to relieve the siege of Hereford. He was in the castle when news came through

that Bridgwater, one of the most important Royalist centres in the West Country, had fallen to the Parliamentarians. Four thousand men met the King at St Fagan's, just outside the city, but they were more interested in voicing complaints about their commander than helping the Royalist cause at Hereford.

The City Hall

Carew

Dyfed **Map: p236 C5.** *Castle open to the public.*
Carew Castle, now a romantic, ivy-clad ruin on a reedy inlet near Pembroke, was the home of Nest, a woman of great beauty. Her father, Rhys ap Tewdwr, was Prince of Deheubarth, and he included the castle in her dowry when Nest married Gerald de Windsor, a Norman baron, in 1095. Fourteen years later, Nest was abducted by Owain ap Cadwgan, Prince of Powys and the outrage triggered a series of major feuds between the Welsh and Normans.

Carmarthen

Dyfed **Map: p236 D4.** *Castle open to the public.*
Carmarthen was granted a charter by King John (1199-1216) in 1201 and featured prominently in the wars which ravaged Wales until the early years of the 15th century. In 1215, after 70 years in English hands, it fell to Llywelyn the Great (1194-1240).

In 1403 the castle was captured and the town burned by Owain Glyndwr (1404-1408) during the revolt in which he was proclaimed the true Prince of Wales in defiance of the title's 'official' holder, Henry of Monmouth, later Henry V (1413-1422). Carmarthen was regained by the English, but Glyndwr captured the castle again in 1405 after his army had been reinforced by French allies.

Edmund Tudor, Earl of Richmond and father of Henry VII (1485-1509), was buried in the friary in Carmarthen in 1456 a few months before the birth of his son.

Carreg Cennen Castle

Dyfed **Map: p236 D2.** *Open daily except public holidays.*
This castle was once a stronghold of the mighty Rhys ap Gruffydd (1153-1197), Prince of Deheubarth. In 1403 Carreg Cennen fell to Owain Glyndwr (1404-1408) after a lengthy siege. It was later recaptured by the English and then became a royal stronghold.

Castell-y-Bere

Gwynedd **Map: p236 C2.** *Castle ruins open daily.*
Castell-y-Bere is where the troops of Edward I (1272-1307) completed their conquest of North Wales in 1283. Demoralized after the death of Llywelyn the Last (1246-1282) near Builth Wells, five months earlier, the castle's 49-man garrison surrendered after a 10-day siege. Llywelyn's brother, David, fled before the castle fell, but was captured and taken to Shrewsbury where he was hanged, drawn and quartered.

Unlike most of the castles in North Wales, which were built by Edward I to consolidate his victory, Castell-y-Bere was a native fortress. It dates from 1221 and was built by Llywelyn the Great (1194-1240). Edward I ordered Castell-y-Bere to be repaired and tried to make it the focal point of a 'new town' development. But the castle was attacked again in 1294, during Madog ap Llywelyn's revolt.

Cilgerran

Dyfed **Map: p236 C3.** *Castle open Mon to Sat; Sun afternoons. Closed Christmas, New Year.*
Cilgerran Castle, high above the River Teifi's wooded gorge, is often pinpointed as the place from which Nest, daughter of Rhys ap Tewdwr, Prince of Deheubarth, was abducted by Owain ap Cadwgan, Prince of Powys, in 1109.

Cilgerran was one of the many castles held by Rhys ap Gruffydd (1153-1197), Prince of Deheubarth, during his years as ruler of most of southwest Wales. His feuding sons lost the fortress to the Normans, but it was captured by Llywelyn the Great (1194-1240) during a brilliant campaign in 1215.

Cilmery

Powys **Map: p237 E3.**
A grassy mound topped with a great spearhead of granite stands beside the A483 near Cilmery as a memorial to Llywelyn ap Gruffydd (1246-1282), the first and last Welshman whose right to be called Prince of Wales was acknowledged by the rulers of England. Llywelyn was killed nearby on 11 December 1282, and his death effectively marked the end of Welsh independence.

Conwy

Gwynedd **Map: p240 C5.** *Castle open mid-Mar to mid-Oct: daily; mid-Oct to mid-Mar: weekdays, Sun afternoons. Closed Christmas, New Year.*
Although its walls and magnificent castle date from the time of Edward I (1272-1307), Conwy grew up around a Cistercian abbey richly endowed by Llywelyn the Great (1194-1240). It was here that he died and was buried. His son, David, died after ruling the ancient kingdom of Gwynedd for only six years, and was also buried at Conwy.

In 1277 the town gave its name to the treaty reluctantly signed by Llywelyn's grandson, Llywelyn the Last (1246-1282), after Edward I had invaded North Wales. Llywelyn kept his Prince of Wales title, but gave up many of his lands and agreed to pay homage to the King in London that Christmas. In return, Edward promised that the Welshman's intended bride, the daughter of Simon de Montfort, would be released from prison.

Criccieth

Gwynedd **Map: p236 D1.** *Castle open mid-Mar to mid-Oct: daily; mid-Oct to mid-Mar: weekdays, Sun afternoons. Closed Christmas, New Year.*
Criccieth Castle was built by Llywelyn the Great (1194-1240) about 10 years before his death. In 1239 its walls imprisoned his eldest son Gruffydd, and Gruffydd's son, who became Llywelyn the Last (1246-1282). They had been made captives after refusing to acknowledge the supremacy of the English crown. Edward I (1272-1307) made alterations to the castle and visited Criccieth in 1283 and 1284. The town's military importance ended in 1404, when the castle was captured and then partly demolished by Owain Glyndwr (1404-1408).

Dale

Dyfed **Map: p236 B4.**
Mill Bay was the starting point for the brief but spectacular campaign which swept Richard III (1483-1485) from the throne of England and established the glittering Tudor dynasty. Henry Tudor, later Henry VII (1485-1509), landed here in August 1485 with about 2,000 men after sailing from exile in France.

Deganwy

Gwynedd **Map: p240 C5.**
The hill which rises steeply behind Deganwy reveals only a few traces of a castle originally established by King Maelgwn of Gwynedd, who died in AD 547. He ruled a large area of North Wales from this base.

The natural defences of Maelgwn's site were acknowledged by Hugh Lupus, Earl of Chester, when he built a new castle on the hilltop, in 1088. It was destroyed by Llywelyn the Great (1194-1240), rebuilt and finally demolished by his grandson, Llywelyn the Last (1246-1282), in 1263.

Denbigh

Clwyd **Map: p240 C5.** *Castle open daily except public holidays.*
Denbigh Castle dates from 1282 when the site was granted to Henry de Lacy, Earl of Hereford by Edward I (1272-1307). He was staying in Denbigh and contributed the equivalent of about £15,000 to the project. Charles I (1625-1649) visited the castle during the Civil War, shortly before it was captured by the Parliamentarians.

Dolgellau

Gwynedd **Map: p236 D2.**
Owain Glyndwr (1404-1408), the soldier and statesman who fought the English and ruled as the 'unofficial' Prince of Wales during the first few years of the 15th century, held his last Parliament in Dolgellau in 1404.

Dolwyddelan

Gwynedd **Map: p236 D1.** *Castle open daily.*
Set in the majestic heart of Snowdonia, Dolwyddelan's crag-perched castle is generally believed to be the birthplace of Llywelyn the Great (1194-1240) one of the most accomplished of all the native rulers of Wales. Born in about 1173, he was responsible for uniting Wales but never used the title of Prince of Wales.

Dryslwyn Castle

Dyfed **Map: p236 D3.** *Ruins open all the time.*
Perched on a grassy mound in the Vale of Tywi, between Carmarthen and Llandeilo, stand the ruins of the castle held by Rhys ap Mareddud towards the end of the 13th century. He sided with Edward I (1272-1307) against Llywelyn the Last (1246-1282), but the victorious King 'rewarded'

Rhys by depriving him of all his lands apart from the castle. Rhys rebelled in 1287 but was captured three years later and decapitated.

Elan Valley

Powys **Map: p237 E3.**
Edward VII (1901-1910) was the guest of honour when the first of the Elan Valley's dams — built to provide water for Birmingham — was officially inaugurated in 1904.

Flint

Clwyd **Map: p240 D5.** *Castle open daily except public holidays.*
Flint Castle was the first of the fortresses built overlooking one of the first 'new' Anglicized towns in North Wales by Edward I (1272-1307). The site provided a base from which the King and his army, accompanied by the ships of the Cinque Ports, went to confront Llywelyn the Last (1246-1282) in the war of 1277.

Edward II (1307-1327) welcomed his favourite, Piers Gaveston, back from Ireland here in 1311. Flint is also the place where the unhappy reign of Richard II (1377-1399) ended in 1399. He was taken prisoner by Henry Bolingbroke, Duke of Lancaster and the future Henry IV (1399-1413).

Glyndyfrdwy

Clwyd **Map: p237 E1.**
Owain Glyndwr (1404-1408), the most charismatic of all Welsh heroes, is believed to have been born near this little village where the Berwyn Mountains plunge down to the River Dee. The exact date of his birth is not known, but it was probably 1359.

Goodwick

Dyfed **Map: p236 C4.**
Goodwick's sandy beach, on the western side of Fishguard Bay, is backed by a valley where rival rulers did battle in 1078. The local champion, Rhys ab Owain, Prince of Deheubarth, was defeated by Trahaearn ap Caradog, King of Gwynedd (1075-1081).

Grosmont

Gwent **Map: p234 A2.** *Castle ruins open daily.*
Grosmont's ruined castle stands on a hill above the meandering River Monnow, which marks the border between Wales and England. It was here that Llywelyn the Great (1194-1240) nearly captured Henry III (1216-1272) shortly after Hubert de Burgh had finished rebuilding the fortress in 1232.

Now an attractive little village, Grosmont was a fully fledged borough in 1405 when it was sacked by an army fighting for Welsh independence under Owain Glyndwr (1404-1408). Buildings were blazing when Henry, Prince of Wales, the future Henry V (1413-1422), swept down on the rebels. He eventually fell back to Monmouth, but about 1,000 Welshmen had been killed and Grosmont proved to be Glyndwr's greatest defeat.

Hanmer

Clwyd **Map: p237 F1.**
This tranquil village overlooks a reed-fringed lake and is where Owain Glyndwr, the 'unofficial' Prince of Wales, married Margaret Hanmer in around 1383.

Harlech

Gwynedd **Map: p236 D1.** *Castle open mid-Mar to mid-Oct: daily; mid-Oct to mid-Mar: weekdays, Sun afternoons. Closed Christmas, New Year.*
Harlech's spectacular castle, perched on a crag with superb views of Snowdonia and the Lleyn peninsula, is one of the ring of fortresses built by Edward I (1272-1307) to confirm his conquest of North Wales. It was completed in 1290 at a cost of £8,000 (more than £5 million in today's money).

Capturing the castle in 1404 gave Owain Glyndwr (1404-1408) a mighty base for his rebellion against Henry IV (1399-1413). It was here that he was proclaimed the rightful Prince of Wales in a ceremony attended by envoys from Scotland, France and Castile. The banner of the ancient kingdom of Gwynedd — four rampant lions — flew from Harlech's highest tower, and Glyndwr held Parliaments in the castle. Together with his allies, Edmund Mortimer and the Earl of Northumberland, he planned to divide England and Wales into three parts with Glyndwr himself ruling an area which extended many miles east of Offa's Dyke with the River Mersey as its northern frontier. Mortimer, a former enemy who had married one of Glyndwr's daughters, died while Harlech was under siege in 1408. Glyndwr escaped before the castle fell, but its loss heralded the eventual collapse of his revolt.

In 1461, during the Wars of the Roses, Harlech became the headquarters of Jasper Tudor, Earl of Pembroke, before his flight to France. He was a half-brother to Henry VI (1422-1461) and the uncle of Henry VII (1485-1509). Harlech's formidable strength and remote location made it the last castle to hold out for Charles I (1625-1649) during the Civil War. The commander surrendered to Cromwell's brother-in-law in 1647.

Haverfordwest

Dyfed **Map: p236 C4.** *Castle museum open daily except Sun.*
Henry VIII (1509-1547) acknowledged Haverfordwest's old-established status as a port, administrative centre and stronghold by making the town a county within what was then called Pembrokeshire. The castle stands on a steep hill above the Western Cleddau river and was captured when Llywelyn the Great (1194-1240) burned the town in 1220. In 1405 the fortress held out while the town itself was sacked by Owain Glyndwr (1404-1408).

Hawarden

Clwyd **Map: p240 D5.** *Castle open weekend afternoons only.*
Hawarden's ruined castle, close to the English border, recalls a dramatic event which signalled the end of Welsh rule in North Wales. On Palm Sunday 1282 it was attacked and captured by David, brother of Llywelyn the Last (1246-1282), the last of the native princes. Llywelyn had been forced to come to terms with Edward I (1272-1307) five years earlier after previously refusing to pay homage to the King. David's assault on Hawarden, which ended with the entire garrison being slaughtered, triggered a second war which ended when Llywelyn was killed at Cilmery, near Builth Wells, at the end of the year. David was eventually captured and executed.

Laugharne

Dyfed **Map: p236 C4.** *Castle open by appointment.*
Laugharne's tide-lapped castle was one of the strongholds of the powerful Rhys ap Gruffydd (1153-1197) in the 12th century. He was a shrewd warrior and diplomat who ruled most of southwest Wales until his death in 1197.

Elizabeth I (1558-1603) leased the castle to Sir John Perrot, who turned the stark old fortress into a palatial Tudor residence. Destined to die in the Tower of London, Sir John was said to be an illegitimate son of Henry VIII (1509-1547).

Llanberis

Gwynedd **Map: p240 B5.** *Dolbadarn Castle open daily, except Sun mornings Oct to Mar.*
A five-minute walk from this small town in the heart of Snowdonia leads to ruined Dolbadarn Castle, which was almost certainly built by Llywelyn the Great (1194-1240) during the period when his rule extended over most of Wales. Llywelyn the Last (1246-1282) had one of his brothers, Owain the Red, held prisoner there for 23 years. Dolbadarn was also used as a prison by Owain Glyndwr (1404-1408) after he had captured Lord Grey de Ruthin and was awaiting payment of a huge ransom. It was a dispute with Lord Grey which triggered the revolt that made Glyndwr the 'unofficial' Prince of Wales after he took Harlech Castle in 1404.

Llandeilo

Dyfed **Map: p236 D4.** *Dinefwr Castle not open.*
The ivy-clad ruins of Dinefwr Castle overlook the River Twyi from a private estate to the west of this small, ancient town. For several hundred years Dinefwr was the main seat of power in Deheubarth, a region embracing most of western and southern Wales. The first castle is believed to have been built by Rhodri the Great (AD 844-878), a soldier and statesman who united most of Wales. The task had been started by his father, Merfyn the Freckled, King of Gwynedd, when he married the daughter of Cadell ap Brochwel, King of Powys. Rhodri's stronghold at Llandeilo was later used by one of his grandsons, Hywel the Good (AD 916-950), who had brought most of Wales under his leadership by AD 942.

Llandeilo and its castle later became the 'capital' of Rhys ap Gruffydd (1153-1197), Lord of Deheubarth and Prince of South Wales. The Lord Rhys, as he was known, died in 1197. An English army attacking Dinefwr 60 years later was routed by Llywelyn the Last (1246-1282).

Llandovery

Dyfed **Map: p237 E4.**
The old market town of Llandovery is where Henry IV (1399-1413) and his young son, the future Henry V (1413-1422), witnessed the execution of Llywelyn ap Gruffydd Fychan in October 1401. Llywelyn, a wealthy local landowner, had volunteered to help the English King and his army track down Owain Glyndwr (1404-1408). But the guide had two sons fighting for Glyndwr and spent several days leading Henry in the wrong direction. When the deception was revealed, Llywelyn was taken to Llandovery, hanged, beheaded and quartered.

Llangadwaladr

Gwynedd **Map: p240 B5.**
Two miles inland from Abberffraw, where the rulers of Gwynedd held court for 900 years, the tiny village of Llangadwaladr has a medieval church dedicated to St Cadwaladr the Blessed, King of North Wales, who died during the great plague of AD 664. A gravestone in the church commemorates his grandfather, Cadfan of Gwynedd, who died about AD 625. Cadfan's son, Cadwallon, married the daughter of King Pibba of Mercia, but was slain near Hexham in a battle with Oswald, King of Northumbria, in AD 634.

Llangollen

Clywd **Map: p237 E1.** *Valle Crucis Abbey open daily except Sun mornings Oct to Mar.*
Two miles from the centre of Llangollen, a town famous for its annual international eisteddfod, the road to Ruthin passes ruined Valle Crucis Abbey, founded by Madoc ap Gruffydd Maelor, King of Powys (1191-1236), who is buried here. A few hundred yards beyond the abbey is Eliseg's Pillar, which commemorates Eliseg of Powys, who died in AD 854 while on a pilgrimage to Rome. He was the last of a line of kings who had ruled Powys for 250 years.

Llanrhos

Gwynedd **Map: p240 C5.**
The ancient church in this small, scattered place on the inland road from Deganwy to Llandudno is said to have been the burial place of Maelgwyn the Tall, King of Gwynedd. He is said to have been a victim of the Yellow Plague of AD 547.

Llantrisant

Mid Glamorgan **Map: p233 E1.**
A band of archers, known as the Black Army of Llantrisant, served with Edward, the Black Prince, during his campaigns in France, which included the great victory at Poitiers in 1356. The Black Prince's grandfather, Edward II (1307-1327), was captured at or near Llantrisant in 1326 while trying to escape to Ireland from a rebel army raised by his wife, Queen Isabella. The King was later murdered in Berkeley Castle a few months after his son had been proclaimed king.

Llanrwst

Gwynedd **Map: p240 C5.** *Gwydir Castle open Easter to mid-Oct: Sun to Fri daily.*
Llywelyn the Great (1194-1240) was buried in Aberconwy Abbey, but his empty coffin, carved from pale stone, now lies in the Gwydir Chapel near Llanrwst.

Lleiniog

Gwynedd **Map: p240 B5.**
Now little more than a name on the coast of Anglesey, between Beaumaris and Penmon, Lleiniog was the site of a motte-and-bailey castle built by Hugh the Wolf, Earl of Chester, when the Normans were struggling to establish a foothold in North Wales at the end of the 11th century. It was here that King Magnus of Norway added a brief but dramatic footnote to Welsh history in 1098, when his Viking fleet sailed up the Menai Strait, beached its longships and fought alongside the Welsh against the Normans. Lleiniog castle fell to the Welsh.

Machynlleth

Powys **Map: p236 D2.**
This small town near the head of the River Dyfi's estuary has strong links with Owain Glyndwr (1404-1408), the charismatic leader who united most of Wales in a struggle for independence against the English. A stone-walled building in Maengwyn Street, which houses an exhibition relating to his life, is where Glyndwr held his first Parliament in 1404.

Moel Fammau

Clwyd **Map: p240 C5.**
The ancient earthworks on the 1,676ft summit of this hill in the Clwydian range between Mold and Ruthin are said to have been the stronghold of Benlli, King of Powys, in the 5th century. Ancient chronicles describe him as a tyrannical ruler who ordered the murder of Christians in the area.

Mold

Clwyd **Map: p240 D5.**
Llywelyn the Great (1194-1240) captured Mold in 1199 during one of his many campaigns. One of the most able of all Welsh rulers, Llywelyn was one of the leaders who compelled King John (1199-1216) to sign the Magna Carta in 1215. Llywelyn eventually controlled most of Wales, and in 1234 negotiated the Pact of Myddle with Henry III (1327-1377) to secure independence for himself and his people.

Monmouth

Gwent **Map: p234 A2.** *Castle Hill House open by appointment.*
Immortalized by Shakespeare and particularly famous for his astonishing victory over the French at the Battle of Agincourt (1415), Henry V (1413-1422) was born in Monmouth Castle on 9 August 1387.

Montgomery

Powys **Map: p237 F2.** *Castle open daily.*
This tiny border town, overlooked from a rocky ridge by the ruins of a Norman castle, gave its name to the agreement of 1267 whereby Henry III (1216-1272) accepted the right of Llywelyn ap Gruffydd (1246-1282) to be entitled Prince of Wales. Llywelyn was the first and last Welshman to hold the title.

Mynydd Carn

Dyfed **Map: p236 C4.**
Mynydd Carn, where a great battle was fought in 1081, is believed to be one of the hills which rise steeply above the rocky coast between Fishguard and Newport. The battle resulted in the death of Trahaearn ap Caradog (1075-1081), a very forceful and ambitious prince of Arwystli, who became King of Gwynedd.

At the Battle of Mynydd Carn, Trahaearn was challenged by the rightful heir to Deheubarth, Rhys ap Tewdwr, and his ally Gruffydd ap Cynan (1081-1137), who became King of Gwynedd. Gruffydd was the son of Prince Cynan of Gwynedd, who had fled to Ireland and married the daughter of King Olaf, the Viking ruler of Dublin. Norsemen fought alongside Welshmen in the allies' victorious army.

Gruffyd died peacefully at the age of 82, while Rhys, now King of Deheubarth, was killed fighting the Normans at Brecon 12 years after the Battle of Mynydd Carn.

Narberth

Dyfed **Map: p236 C4.**
Few traces now remain of the castle which was captured in 1116 by Gruffydd ap Rhys, King of Deheubarth (1093-1137). The castle was later held by Roger Mortimer, the lover of Queen Isabella, who led the revolt which deposed her husband, Edward II (1307-1327).

Nefyn

Gwynedd **Map: p236 C1.**
This small town on the Lleyn peninsula's northern coast is where Edward I (1272-1307) held a great tournament in 1284 to celebrate his conquest of Wales. Nefyn was later made a royal borough by Edward III (1327-1377).

New Radnor

Powys **Map: p237 E3.**
New Radnor is believed to have been founded by Harold Godwinson, Earl of Hereford, whose brief reign as Harold of England (1066) ended at the Battle of Hastings. The little town, now just a sleepy village, was established to replace Old Radnor as a strongpoint guarding one of the most important natural gateways to central Wales. Grassy banks and ditches behind the church are all that remain of the castle built by the Normans.

In 1195 the castle fell to the Welsh under Llywelyn the Great (1194-1240) and was held by them until King John (1199-1216) stormed New Radnor in the last year of his reign. The castle returned briefly to Llywelyn 14 years later. His grandson, Llywelyn the Last (1246-1282), captured the castle and destroyed the town in 1265, but both were rebuilt during the reign of Edward I (1272-1307). In 1401 the castle fell to Owain Glyndwr (1404-1408) during the rebellion in which he was proclaimed as the true Prince of Wales. The stronghold's 60 defenders were hanged from the ramparts.

Offa's Dyke

Clwyd/Powys/Gwent.
This great earthwork, some 80 miles of which can still be seen after 1,200 years, was built by Offa, King of Mercia (AD 757-796), to mark the border between Wales and his Anglo-Saxon realm, whose capital was Tamworth.

Old Radnor

Powys **Map: p237 F3.**
Old Radnor played host to Charles I (1626-1649) during the Civil War when he visited Wales hoping to raise fresh support after being defeated at the Battle of Naseby. The King dined in a yeoman's house on the night of 6 August 1645.

Painscastle

Powys **Map: p237 E3.** *Castle ruins not open.*
Henry III (1216-1272) spent two months at Painscastle in the late summer of 1231, when the original wooden castle was being replaced by a stronger fortification of stone. This was during the troubled time when Llywelyn the Great (1194-1240) and his army were sweeping through central and southern Wales.

Pencader

Dyfed **Map: p236 D4.**
Pencader, a small village in the hills between Carmarthen and Lampeter, is where Gruffydd ap Llywelyn, King of Gywnedd (1039-1063), defeated a local prince in 1041 and made off with his beautiful wife.

Penmynydd

Gywnedd **Map: p240 B5.** *Alms Houses open by appointment.*
Penmynydd was probably the birthplace and certainly the childhood home of Owen Tudor, a member of Henry V's court. One of the children of his marriage to Catherine of Valois, widow of Henry V (1413-1422), was Edmund, Earl of Richmond and half-brother to Henry VI (1422-1461).

Penrhyn Castle

Gwynedd **Map: p240 B5.** *Open June to Sept: daily; Apr, May and Oct: afternoons; all bank holiday*

Pembroke Castle

Dyfed **Map: p236 C5.** *Open Easter to Sept: daily.*
This mighty castle on one of Milford Haven's many tidal creeks is where Henry Tudor, later Henry VII (1485-1509), was born on 28 January 1457. His father, Edmund Tudor, Earl of Richmond, had died at Carmarthen three months earlier, but his widow had been welcomed to the castle by her brother-in-law Jasper Tudor, Earl of Pembroke. Realizing that Henry's slender claim to the English throne put his life in danger during the Wars of the Roses, Jasper Tudor spirited the boy away to the safety of exile in France 14 years later. (Henry Tudor's claim to the throne

Pembroke Castle

stemmed from his mother, Margaret Beaufort, who was descended from John of Gaunt, son of Edward III (1327-1377).) Uncle and nephew returned in 1485, landed at the seaward end of Milford Haven and, gathering strength day by day, marched to defeat Richard III (1483-1485) at the Battle of Bosworth.

The original Pembroke Castle was built at the end of the 12th century, after the death of Rhys ap Tewdwr of Deheubarth in battle at Brecon in 1093 had cleared the way for the Norman invasion of west Wales. Stephen (1135-1154) later granted the fortress to Gilbert de Clare and made him the first Earl of Pembroke. De Clare's son, Richard Strongbow, used the castle as his base for the invasion of Ireland. In 1172 it was visited by Henry II (1154-1189).

weekends: daily.
Although medieval in aspect, Penrhyn Castle dates from the first half of the 19th century. It was built by Thomas Hopper for the Dawkins Pennant family. Now owned by the National Trust, the castle's many treasures include the elaborate King's Bed which was made for a visit in 1894 by Edward VII (1901-1910), the longest-serving Prince of Wales, who held the title for 59 years. Queen Victoria (1837-1901) spent a night in the great state bed, designed by Hopper, when she visited Penrhyn in 1859.

Penrhyn Castle

Pilleth

Powys **Map: p237 F3.**
Pilleth is the site of one of the bloodiest battles in Welsh history. It was fought on 22 June 1402, two years after Owain Glyndwr (1404-1408) started his revolt, and was a triumph for the rebels.

It is not known if Glyndwr was present at the Battle of Pilleth — the Welsh are generally said to have fought under Rhys ap Gethin — but the victory certainly added an immense amount of credibility to his cause, and was a severe setback for Henry IV (1399-1413). It encouraged Welshmen who had previously been half-hearted about the new leader to join the army on a dramatic sweep southwards. Edmund Mortimer commanded the army which charged up Bryn Glas hill to attack Glydwr's supporters. It was a powerful force, but Rhys ap Gethin's strong position on the steep slopes became even stronger when many of Mortimer's troops, Welshmen from the borderlands, changed sides and fought for their compatriots. The rebels slew more than 1,000 of the English troops. Mortimer, whose nephew Edmund, son of Roger Mortimer, Earl of March, was the rightful heir to the English throne, was the most prized of many prisoners. The King refused to pay his ransom — possibly because he realized that a potential rival to the throne was now out of contention — and the captive eventually married Glyndwr's daughter Catherine. He died in Harlech Castle shortly before it was recaptured by the English.

In military terms the Battle of Pilleth ranked among the greatest triumphs of Glyndwr's rebellion. It added to King Henry IV's problems by underlining the fact that Glyndwr's troops, previously noted for hit-and-run tactics, could also stand and fight. Pilleth farmers who planned to cultivate land on Bryn Glas in the 1870s uncovered what was obviously a mass grave dug in 1402. They stopped ploughing and planted a grove of trees to commemorate the dead.

Plynlimon

Dyfed/Powys **Map: p237 E2.**
The western slopes of 2,468ft-high Plynlimon sweep down to the Nant-y-moch reservoir whose dam is overlooked by a small monument. It commemorates a battle fought on nearby high ground above the River Hyddgen in 1401. The victor was Owain Glyndwr (1404-1408), the wealthy landowner who rebelled against Henry IV (1399-1433) and was hailed by his followers as the true Prince of Wales.

Portmeirion

Gwynedd **Map: p236 D1.**
The Italianate village of Portmeirion was created by Sir Clough Williams-Ellis, architect and planner whose ancestors included Gruffyd ap Cynan, King of Gwynedd (1081-1137) and one of the most able of all Welsh rulers. The village's slender campanile, built by Sir Clough, was made with stones from the site of one of the King's castles which stood nearby until it was razed in the 19th century. The many visitors enchanted by Portmeirion's unique magic have included Edward VIII (1936), later the Duke of Windsor, and the exiled King Zog of Albania.

Portmeirion

Powis Castle

Powys **Map: p237 F2.** *Open May, June and Sept: Wed to Sun afternoons only: July and Aug: Tue to Sun afternoons only; bank holidays.*
Powis Castle, now a National Trust property, has been inhabited for more than 700 years. It is entered through a lofty gatehouse believed to have been built by Owain, the last Prince of Powys, who died in 1293. His family had previously adopted the Norman surname of de la Pole. In 1587 the castle was bought by Sir Edward Herbert whose grandson, a staunch Royalist supporter during the Civil War, went into exile with Charles II (1660-1685).

History repeated itself in 1688, when the first Marquess of Powis joined James II (1685-1688) after his abdication. His wife, Lady of the Bedchamber to James's wife, Mary, had been present when the Stuart heir, James Francis Edward, was born in St James's Palace, London, on 10 June 1688. She later helped smuggle the baby to France. Appointed Prince of Wales less than a month after his birth, James lost the title when his father gave up the throne at the end of 1688. He was known as the Old Pretender, and dreamed of becoming king of England. He was the father of Prince Charles Edward Stuart, the Young Pretender.

The castle has a link with the Stuart dynasty — an elaborate state bed bearing the monogram of Charles II (1660-1685). It is believed to have been built specially for a royal visit, but in fact Charles never went to the castle.

Between 1688 and 1722 Powis was the home of William van Zuylesteyn, a Dutchman descended from an illegitimate branch of the House of Orange. He was created Earl of Rochford by William III (1689-1702).

Prince's Oak

Powys **Map: p238 A4.**
Surrounded by iron railings and a low sandstone wall, this withered oak stands beside the road a mile west of the Shropshire village of Alberbury. It marks the point where George IV (1820-1830) first set foot in Wales, on 9 September 1806. He had then been Prince of Wales for 44 years and was destined to hold the title until the death of his father, George III (1760-1820), in 1820. The Prince was visiting nearby Loton Park, the home of Sir Robert Leighton, when his host suggested a short trip to the border. His formal escort was Sir Richard Puleston, a Flintshire landowner and the only Welshman in the house party. A brass plaque commemorating the visit was restored at the time of the coronation of George VI (1936-1952).

Raglan Castle

Gwent **Map: p234 A7.** *Open daily except public holidays.*
This great 15th-century castle was a Royalist stronghold during the Civil War. In 1642, shortly before the Battle of Edgehill, it was visited by the 13-year-old Prince of Wales, later Charles II (1660-1685), who had been sent to Wales on a recruiting drive by his father.

Charles I (1625-1649) followed in his son's footsteps three years later, hoping to raise fresh support after his army's defeat at the Battle of Naseby, but he met with little success.

Rhuddlan

Clwyd **Map: p240 C5.** *Castle open mid-Mar to mid-Oct: daily; mid-Oct to mid-Mar: weekdays, Sun afternoons. Closed Christmas, New Year.*
For more than 200 years, Rhuddlan was a focal point in the endless wars between the native princes and their foes from across the border. The castle was a base for Gruffydd ap Llywelyn, King of Gwynedd (1039-1063), who controlled most of Wales during the 11th century, but it fell to Harold Godwinson, later King Harold (1066), four years before the Saxon king's brief reign ended at the Battle of Hastings.

Norman invaders followed in Harold's footsteps, but in 1075 their castle at Rhuddlan was captured by Gruffydd ap Cynan, King of Gwynedd (1081-1137). Rhuddlan later reverted to the Normans, but fell to Owain Gwynedd (1137-1170) after a three-month siege in 1075, when Henry II (1154-1189) was in France and unable to relieve the garrison. Rhuddlan's capture was probably Owain's greatest triumph.

Rhuddlan's strategic importance was swiftly appreciated by Edward I (1272-1307) when he advanced along the coast from Chester in 1277 during the first of his two campaigns against Llywelyn the Last (1246-1282). The King realized that direct links with the sea were a key to success in a country whose mountains formed a formidable natural barrier. He therefore ordered his engineers to canalize the lower reaches of the Clwyd so that ships could sail right up to a new castle on the eastern bank.

The castle was completed in 1280, two years before Llywelyn's fiery brother, David, launched a series of attacks which plunged North Wales back into another war with Edward. The King made Rhuddlan his base in July 1282 and remained here until March 1283, when he moved his headquarters westwards to Conwy. It was to Rhuddlan that Llywelyn's head was brought as proof that the Welsh prince was indeed dead. David was also sent to Edward before being executed in Shrewsbury.

In 1284 Edward drew up the Statute of Rhuddlan, which established the framework for Norman rule in North Wales. Its provisions included the creation of four counties — Anglesey, Caernarvonshire, Merionethshire and Flintshire — which survived until Britain's local government was reorganized in 1974.

Gwernigron, now little more than a name on the map 2 miles south of Rhuddlan, is where Prince David of Gwynedd (1240-1246), son of Llywelyn the Great (1194-1240), surrendered to Henry III (1216-1272) in 1241. He was forced to surrender much of the territory secured by his father's military and diplomatic skills, and also obliged to hand his illegitimate brother, Gruffydd, father of Llywelyn the Last, over to the English. Gruffydd was taken to the Tower of London where he died in 1244, attempting to escape down a rope of knotted sheets which parted under his weight.

Roch Castle

Dyfed **Map: p236 B4.** *Not open to the public.*
Built in the 13th century on an isolated rocky outcrop near the coast between Haverfordwest and St David's, Roch Castle passed into the hands of the Walter family in 1601. About 29 years later it was the birthplace of Lucy Walter, who met the future Charles II (1660-1685) when he was an exile in Holland. She became the first of the Prince's many mistresses and was the mother of his first and favourite son James, the illegitimate Duke of Monmouth. Born in Rotterdam in 1649 the Duke was executed 36 years later after his attempt to wrest the crown from his uncle, James I (1685-1688), was crushed at the Battle of Sedgemoor. Lucy Walter — described by the diarist John Evelyn as 'a bold, brown, beautiful but insipid creature' — died in Paris in 1658.

Ruthin

Clwyd **Map: p237 E1.**
This attractive hilltop town, notable for its many timber-framed buildings, witnessed the start of the last great bid for Welsh independence. On 21 September 1400, when the people of Ruthin were preparing for the annual St Matthew's Day fair,

Owain Glyndwr (1404-1408) swept down from the hills, attacked the town and left it in flames. His jubilant followers hailed their leader as the true Prince of Wales and went on to attack Denbigh, Flint, Hawarden, Holt, Oswestry and Welshpool. It was the start of a rebellion which lasted from some 10 years and reached its zenith when Glyndwr captured the mighty fortress of Harlech in 1404.

Glyndwr was a wealthy, educated man who owned considerable estates in his native north Wales. But he fell foul of his neighbour, Lord Grey de Ruthin, a powerful and devious man who enjoyed the support of Henry VI (1399-1413). Convinced that right was on his side, but unable to secure justice by conventional means, Glyndwr eventually decided to settle the quarrel by attacking Grey's stronghold. Grey escaped, but was ambushed in 1402 and held prisoner inn Dolbadarn Castle at Llanberis until a huge ransom was paid.

St Peter's Church in Ruthin dates from the 14th century. Its elaborate oak ceiling is said to have been presented by Henry VII (1485-1509) to thank the many Welshmen who supported his campaign to wrest the crown from Richard III (1483-1485) at the Battle of Bosworth.

Snowdon

Gwynedd **Map: p236 D1.**
Like many other parts of Wales, Snowdon has legends relating to King Arthur and his exploits in the sixth century. One tells that he was mortally wounded in a battle at Bwlchysaethau, the Pass of the Arrows, near the mountain's 3,560ft-high summit. A nearby cave is said to be where the King and his knights rest in an enchanted sleep, awaiting the call to save Britain from disaster. Arthur is also credited with killing Rhita Fawr, a giant who lived on Snowdon, slew kings and wore clothing made from their beards.

Strata Florida

Dyfed **Map: p236 D3.** *Abbey open Mon to Sat daily; Sun afternoons.*
Now a picturesque ruin set amid high hills some 14 miles southeast of Aberystwyth, St Mary's Abbey at Strata Florida was regarded as the 'Westminster of Wales' during the Middle Ages. It was founded in 1164 by one of the greatest Welshmen of his time, Rhys ap Gruffydd, Lord of Deheubarth and Prince of South Wales (1153-1197), who was buried here before being taken to St David's when the abbey was closed at the Dissolution of the Monasteries (1536).

In 1238 many Welsh rulers assembled at Strata Florida and vowed to Llywelyn the Great (1194-1240) that they would support his legitimate but younger son, David (1240-1246). David's mother was Joan, illegitimate daughter of King John of England (1199-1216). The abbey's reputation as a centre of Welsh nationalism resulted in it being burned down by Edward I (1272-1307) during a bloody revolt in 1294.

Talley Abbey

Dyfed **Map: p236 D4.** *Ruins open all the time.*
Talley Abbey was founded towards the end of the

St David's

Dyfed **Map: p236 B4.**
The present St David's Cathedral dates from 1180, but links with the patron saint of Wales have made Britain's smallest city — it is little more than a village — a place of pilgrimage since the Dark Ages. In 1081 it was visited by William the Conqueror (1066-1087) on his only journey to Wales. Riding west at the head of an army, he combined his pilgrimage with a show of force to impress Rhys ap Tewdwr, King of Deheubarth, who had reclaimed his birthright that same year at the Battle of Mynydd Carn, on the hills near Fishguard.

Henry II (1154-1189) walked the last few miles to the cathedral when he visited St David's before sailing to Ireland in 1172. The King was trying to make public amends for his part in the murder of Thomas à Becket, Archbishop of Canterbury, two years earlier.

Among those buried in the cathedral are Edmund Tudor, Earl of Richmond and father of Henry VII (1485-1509). Edmund died at Carmarthen, shortly before his son's birth in 1457, but his body was taken to St David's 80 years later. The cathedral also shelters the tomb of Rhys ap Gruffydd, Lord of Deheubarth, Prince of South Wales (1153-1197), the most influential ruler of 12th-century Wales after the death of Owain Gwynedd (1137-1170). The Lord Rhys, as he was known, was about 65 when he died in 1197. His original burial place was the abbey of Strata Florida, in the heart of Wales.

12th century by Rhys ap Gruffydd, Lord of Deheubarth and Prince of South Wales (1153-1197). In 1277 the abbey passed into the hands of Edward I (1272-1307), who regarded monastic settlements as hotbeds of Welsh nationalism and endeavoured to make the monks more sympathetic towards the English.

Tenby

Dyfed **Map: p236 C5.**
Medieval town walls and the scanty ruins of a castle are reminders that this seaside resort once played its part in the military affairs of West Wales. In 1405 it seemed doomed to fall to Owain Glyndwr (1404-1408) and his French allies who had landed at Milford Haven, but the French lost heart when an English fleet sank 15 of their ships.

In 1471, 66 years later, Tenby was the port from which Jasper Tudor, Earl of Pembroke, sailed to exile in France with his nephew Henry Tudor. The 14-year-old boy returned to Wales in 1485, marched to victory against Richard III (1483-1485) at the Battle of Bosworth and was later crowned Henry VII (1485-1509).

Tomen-y-Mur

Gwynedd **Map: p236 D1.**
Also known as Mur-y-Castell, this medieval earthwork on the site of a Roman fort stands at the end of a short narrow lane 2 miles north of Trawsfynydd. Here Henry I (1100-1135) mustered his army to challenge the growing power of

The Queen at the Maundy Service, 1982

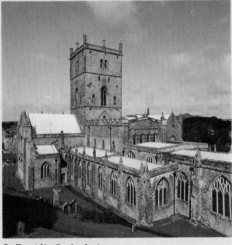
St David's Cathedral

Gryffydd ap Cynan, King of Gwynedd (1081-1137) and one of the most able rulers of North Wales. (1081-1137). Gruffydd, heavily outnumbered by a foe whose army included Scottish allies, opted for negotiations rather than battle, and paid homage to Henry.

Whitland

Dyfed **Map: p236 C4.**
This small town on the road between Carmarthen and Haverfordwest is where Hywel the Good (AD 916-950), ruler of all but the southeastern region of Wales, held a six-week meeting in AD 930. Representatives were summoned from all over Wales to codify the laws of the land. The King is believed to have modelled himself on Alfred the Great (AD 871-899).

Wrexham

Clwyd **Map: p237 F1.**
The 'capital' of northeastern Wales was visited by Charles I (1625-1649) and his son, the future Charles II (1660-1685), a month after the raising of the royal standard at Nottingham had heralded the start of the Civil War in 1642. On their way from Chester to Shrewsbury, the King and Prince were guests of Richard Lloyd, Attorney-General for North Wales, who was knighted at the end of the visit Hoping to rally support for his cause, the King told Wrexham's inhabitants: 'My confidence is in the protection of Almighty God and the affection of my good people'.

Section

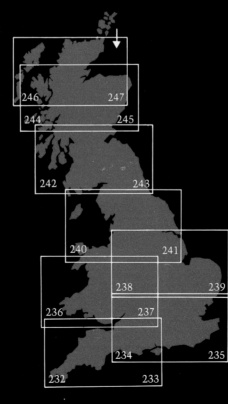

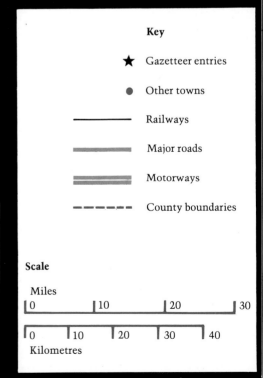

Key

★ Gazetteer entries

● Other towns

—— Railways

━━ Major roads

━━ Motorways

- - - - County boundaries

Scale

Miles

| 0 | | 10 | | 20 | | 30 |

| 0 | 10 | 20 | 30 | 40 |

Kilometres

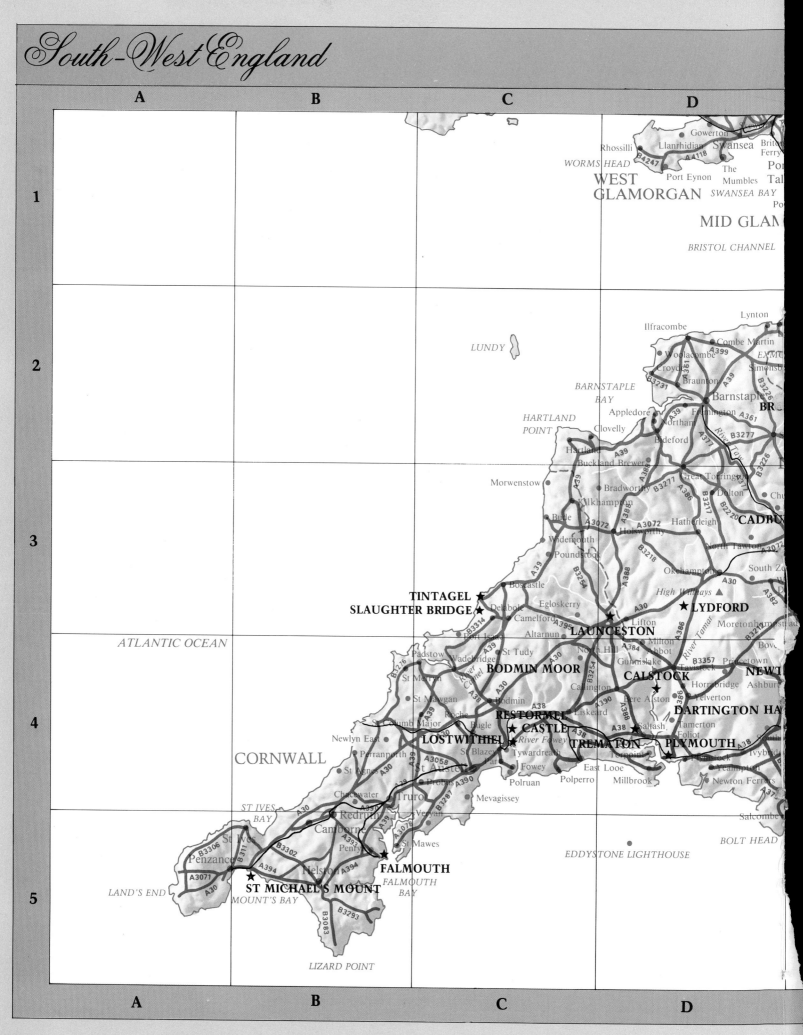

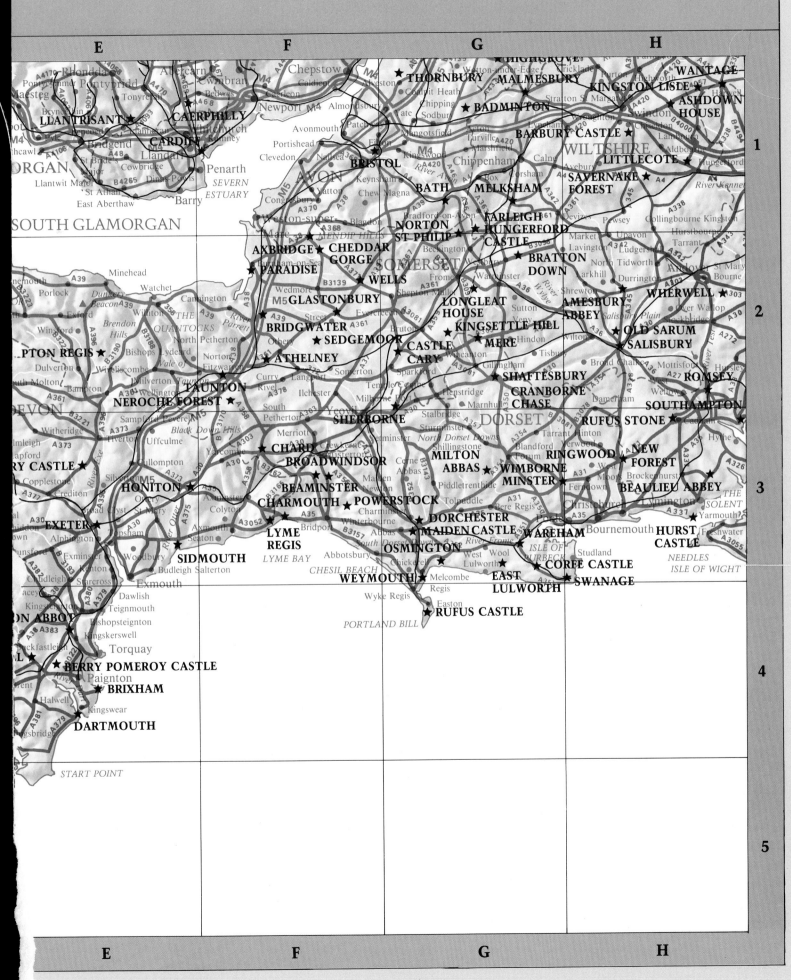

A   B   C   D

1

MORTIMER'S CROSS
WORCESTER • INKBERROW • Studley Wooton Wawen • Cotham • A425 • DAVENTRY • NORTHAMPTON
Stratford-on-Avon
WHITE LADIES PRIORY • EDGEHILL • CROPREDY • GRAFTON REGIS
MALVERN • EVESHAM • COMPTON WYNYATES • RADWAY
HEREFORD • LEDBURY • ELMLEY CASTLE • BROADWAY • BANBURY • KING'S SUTTON
VALE OF EVESHAM • BROUGHTON CASTLE • BUCKINGHAM • WOBURN
TEWKESBURY • CHASTLETON • DEDDINGTON
NEWENT • WINCHCOMBE • SUDELEY CASTLE • DUNSTABLE
GROSMONT • CHELTENHAM • GLOUCESTER • BLENHEIM PALACE • OXFORDSHIRE • BUCKINGHAMSHIRE
MONMOUTH • Forest of Dean • ASHRIDGE HOUSE

2

RAGLAN CASTLE • FRAMPTON-ON-SEVERN • GODSTOW • LONG CRENDON • AYLESBURY • BERKHAMSTED
ST BRIAVELS • GLOUCESTERSHIRE • CIRENCESTER • OXFORD • RYCOTE PARK • CHEQUERS
BERKELEY CASTLE • GATCOMBE PARK • PRINCES RISBOROUGH • CHALGROVE • HUGHENDEN MANOR
HIGHGROVE • MILTON • EWELME • WALLINGFORD
THORNBURY • MALMESBURY • WANTAGE • BLEWBURY
KINGSTON LISLE • ASHDOWN HOUSE • HENLEY-ON-THAMES • COOKHAM

3

BADMINTON • BARBURY CASTLE • MAPLEDURHAM HOUSE • ETON COLLEGE
WILTSHIRE • LITTLECOTE • DONNINGTON CASTLE • WINDSOR CASTLE • READING
BRISTOL • BATH • MELKSHAM • SAVERNAKE FOREST • WOKINGHAM • HAMPTON
BERKSHIRE
FARLEIGH HUNGERFORD CASTLE • KINGSCLERE • ODIHAM CASTLE
NORTON ST PHILIP • BASING HOUSE • GUILDFORD
AXBRIDGE • CHEDDAR GORGE • BRATTON DOWN • BASINGSTOKE • FARNHAM CASTLE
PARADISE • HAMPSHIRE • ALTON

4

WELLS • LONGLEAT HOUSE • WHERWELL • OLD ALRESFORD
GLASTONBURY • AMESBURY ABBEY
BRIDGWATER • KINGSETTLE HILL • OLD SARUM • AVINGTON PARK
SEDGEMOOR • CASTLE CARY • MERE • SALISBURY • WINCHESTER • WEST SUSSEX
ATHELNEY • ROMSEY • BISHOP'S WALTHAM • COWDRAY PARK
SHAFTESBURY • CRANBORNE CHASE • SOUTHAMPTON • GOODWOOD
SHERBORNE • DORSET • RUFUS STONE • TITCHFIELD • BOSHAM

5

CHARD • BROADWINDSOR • MILTON ABBAS • RINGWOOD • NEW FOREST • PORTCHESTER CASTLE • CHICHESTER
BEAMINSTER • WIMBORNE MINSTER • PORTSMOUTH • BOGNOR REGIS
CHARMOUTH • POWERSTOCK • BEAULIEU ABBEY • SPITHEAD • SELSEY BILL
LYME REGIS • DORCHESTER • HURST CASTLE
MAIDEN CASTLE • WAREHAM • NEEDLES ISLE OF WIGHT • NEWPORT
OSMINGTON • CORFE CASTLE
WEYMOUTH • EAST LULWORTH • SWANAGE
RUFUS CASTLE • ST CATHERINE'S POINT • PORTLAND BILL

1 COWES
2 OSBORNE HOUSE
3 WHIPPINGHAM
4 NEWPORT

A   B   C   D

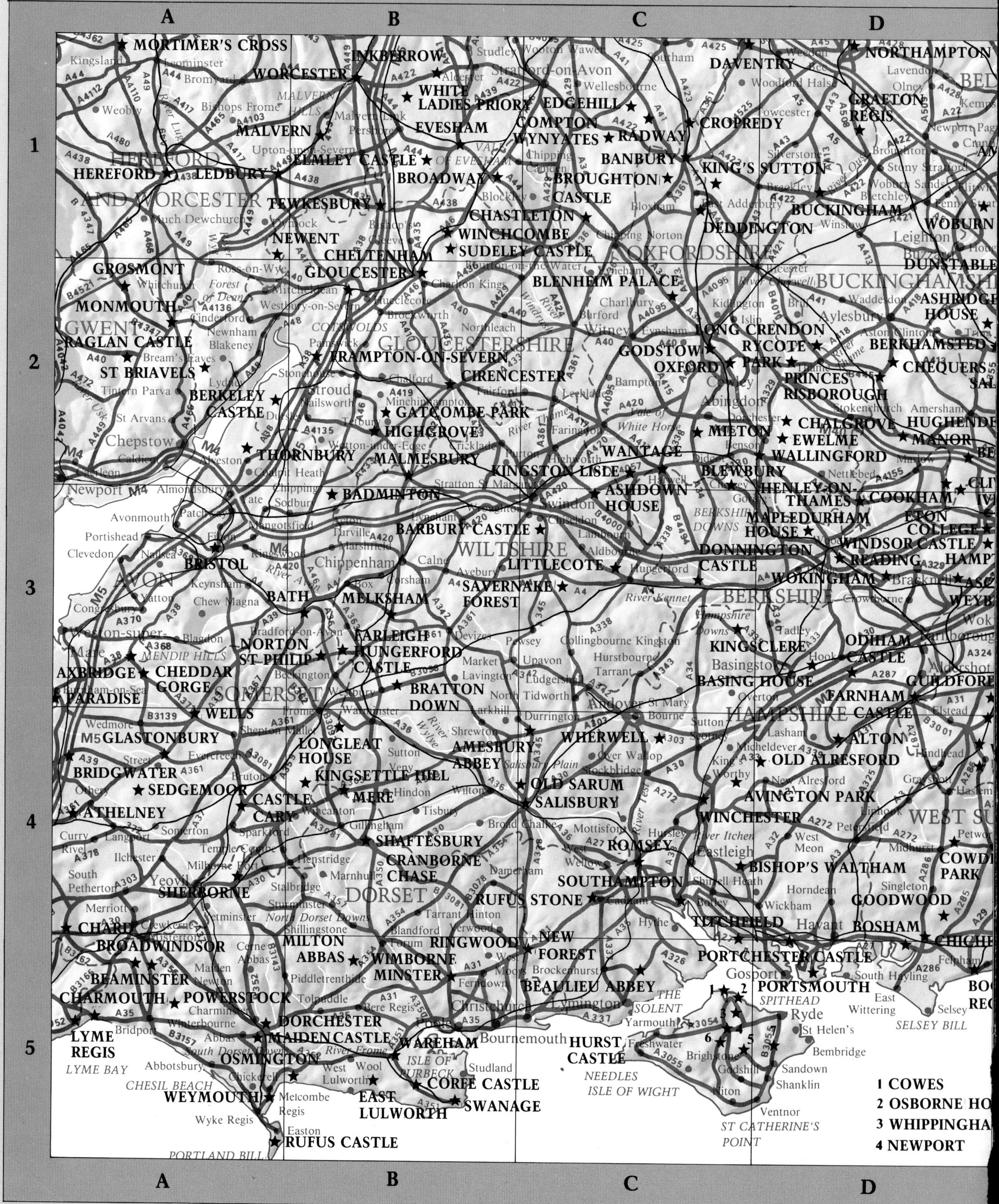

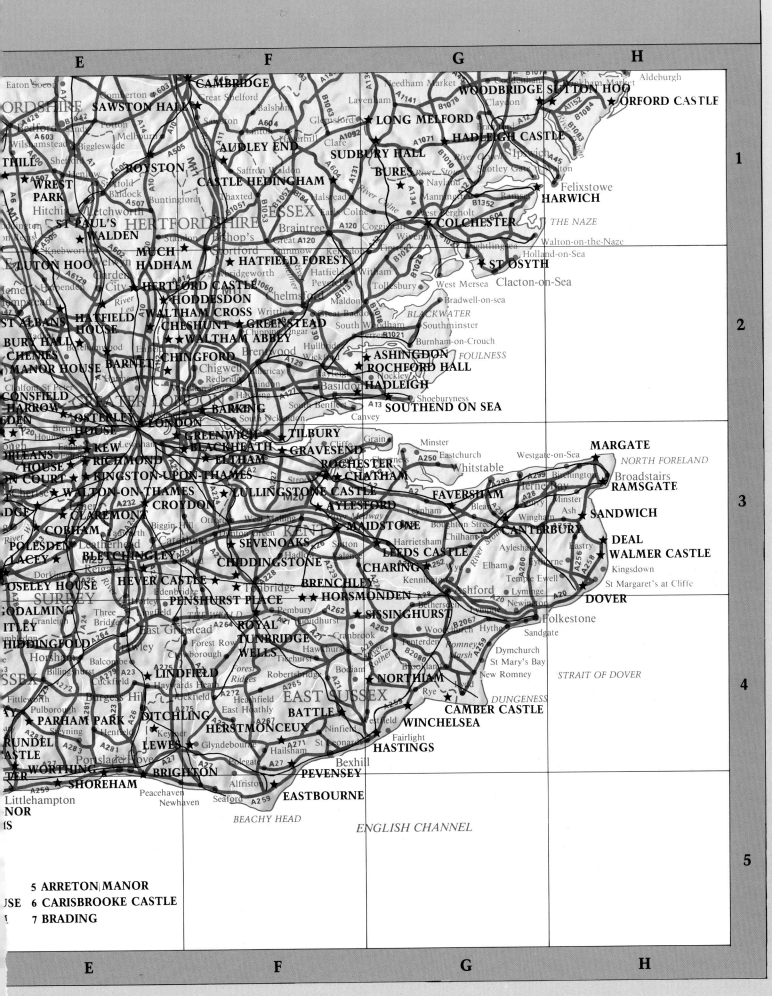

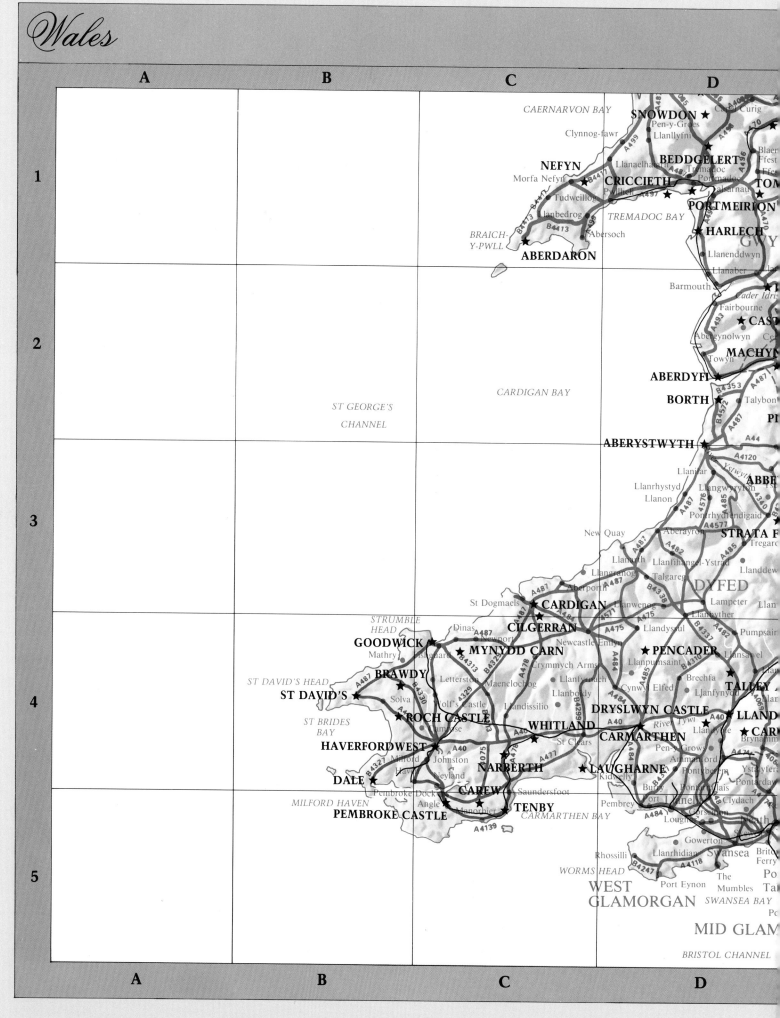

	A	B	C	D

1

CAERNARVON BAY

SNOWDON ★

Clynnog-fawr

Pen-y-Groes
Llanllyfni

NEFYN

Morfa Nefyn
Llanaelhaearn · Tremadoc

BEDDGELERT ★

Blaen
Ffest
Effe

Tudweiliog · CRICCIETH
Pwllheli
Porthmadog

Llanbedrog

PORTMEIRION ★

TO

TREMADOC BAY

HARLECH ★

BRAICH-
Y-PWLL ★

Abersoch

GWY

ABERDARON ★

Llanenddwyn

Llanaber

2

Barmouth

Cader Idris
Fairbourne

Abergynolwyn

CAST

CARDIGAN BAY

Towyn

MACHYN

*ST GEORGE'S
CHANNEL*

ABERDYFI ★

BORTH ★
Talybont

PI

ABERYSTWYTH ★

A44

A4120

Llaniar

Llanrhystyd
Langwyryfon

ABB

Llanon

3

Pontrhydfendigaid

A4577

New Quay
Aberayron

STRATA F ★

Llanarth

Tregaro

Llanfihangel-Ystrad

Llanddew

Talgareg

DYFED

Aberporth

Lampeter

Llan

St Dogmaels

CARDIGAN ★

Llanwenog

Llanbyther

*STRUMBLE
HEAD*

Dinas

CILGERRAN ★

Llandysul

B4337
Pumpsain

4

GOODWICK ★
Mathry · Fishguard

Newport

Newcastle Emlyn

A475

PENCADER ★

Llansawel

MYNYDD CARN ★

Crymmych Arms

Llanpumsaint

ST DAVID'S HEAD

BRAWDY ★
Letterston

Maenclochog

Llanfynach

Brechfa

TALLEY ★

ST DAVID'S ★

Solva

Wolf's Castle

Landissilio

Cynwl Elfed
Llanfynydd

LLAND

ROCH CASTLE ★

Llanboidy

DRYSLWYN CASTLE ★

Llangadog

*ST BRIDES
BAY*

WHITLAND ★

River Tywi

CARM ★

HAVERFORDWEST ★

A40

St Clears

CARMARTHEN ★

Llangadog

Milford

Johnston

Pen-y-Groes

Brynamman

DALE ★

Neyland

NARBERTH ★

LAUGHARNE ★
Kidwelly

Ystalyfera

Pontarddulais

MILFORD HAVEN

CAREW ★

Saundersfoot

Pembrey

Clydach

PEMBROKE CASTLE ★
Angle · Manorbier

TENBY ★

CARMARTHEN BAY

A484

Gowerton

5

Rhossili
Llanrhidian · Swansea

Brit
Ferry

WORMS HEAD

B4247

Port Eynon

The
Mumbles
Ta

WEST
GLAMORGAN

SWANSEA BAY

Po

MID GLAM

BRISTOL CHANNEL

	A	B	C	D

A **B** **C** **D**

LANCASHIRE
Clitheroe
Whalley
Nelson
Colne
Bingley
Guiseley
★ HAREWOOD HOUSE
★ TOWTON
GOODMANHAM
Keighley
Shipley
Bradford
WEST YORKSHIRE
LEEDS
SELBY
HUMBERSIDE
KINGSTON-UPON-
PRESTON
Blackburn
Todmorden
Halifax
Huddersfield
Dewsbury
★ PONTEFRACT CASTLE
WAKEFIELD
Lytham
Rawtenstall
Bacup
Rochdale
Holmfirth
Penistone
Doncaster
★ CONISBROUGH CASTLE
GAINSBOROUGH
MANCHESTER
Stockport
Glossop
Sheffield
SOUTH YORKSHIRE
★ TICKHILL
East Retford
RUNCORN
KNUTSFORD
BUXTON
CHESTERFIELD
NOTTINGHAMSHIRE
HALTON CASTLE
Macclesfield
★ ASHFORD-IN-THE-WATER
★ BOLSOVER CASTLE
CHESTER
WINSFORD
★ GAWSWORTH HALL
CHATSWORTH
★ CLIPSTONE
ROWTON MOOR
HARTINGTON
HARDWICK HALL
Mansfield
SOMERTON CASTLE
BEESTON CASTLE
★ LEEK
Matlock
★ NEWSTEAD ABBEY
Nantwich
ASHBOURNE
SOUTHWELL
EAST STOKE
WREXHAM
CHESHIRE
DERBYSHIRE
NOTTINGHAM
HANMER
★ WHITCHURCH
Newcastle under Lyme
Stoke-on-Trent
BELT
GRANTHAM
★ RED CASTLE
STAFFORDSHIRE
Uttoxeter
DERBY
TUTBURY
★ BELVOIR CASTLE
Repton
EASTWELL
STAFFORD
★ BLITHFIELD HALL
Burton-upon-Trent
HARBY
SHREWSBURY
CANNOCK CHASE
ASHBY-DE-LA-ZOUCH
MELTON MOWBRAY
BOSCOBEL HOUSE
Cannock
TAMWORTH
BRADGATE PARK
BURLEY
MUCH WENLOCK
MOSELEY OLD HALL
MIDDLETON HALL
SUTTON CHEYNEY
LEICESTERSHIRE
OAKHAM
Wolverhampton
LEICESTER
COLLYWESTON
BRIDGNORTH
HOLBECHE HOUSE
BOSWORTH FIELD
Hinckley
ROCKINGHAM
KIRBY HALL
ASTON HALL
Birmingham
MAXSTOKE CASTLE
MARKET HARBOROUGH
GEDDINGTON
CLEOBURY MORTIMER
HAGLEY HALL
MERIDEN
LUTTERWORTH
ROTHWELL
BEWDLEY
COVENTRY
NASEBY
LUDLOW
KENILWORTH CASTLE
DUNCHURCH
KIMBOLTON CASTLE
ASHBY ST LEDGERS
DROITWICH
ROYAL LEAMINGTON SPA
HOLDENBY HOUSE
WARWICK
ALTHORP
NORTHAMPTON
MORTIMER'S CROSS
INKBERROW
WORCESTER
Stratford-on-Avon
DAVENTRY

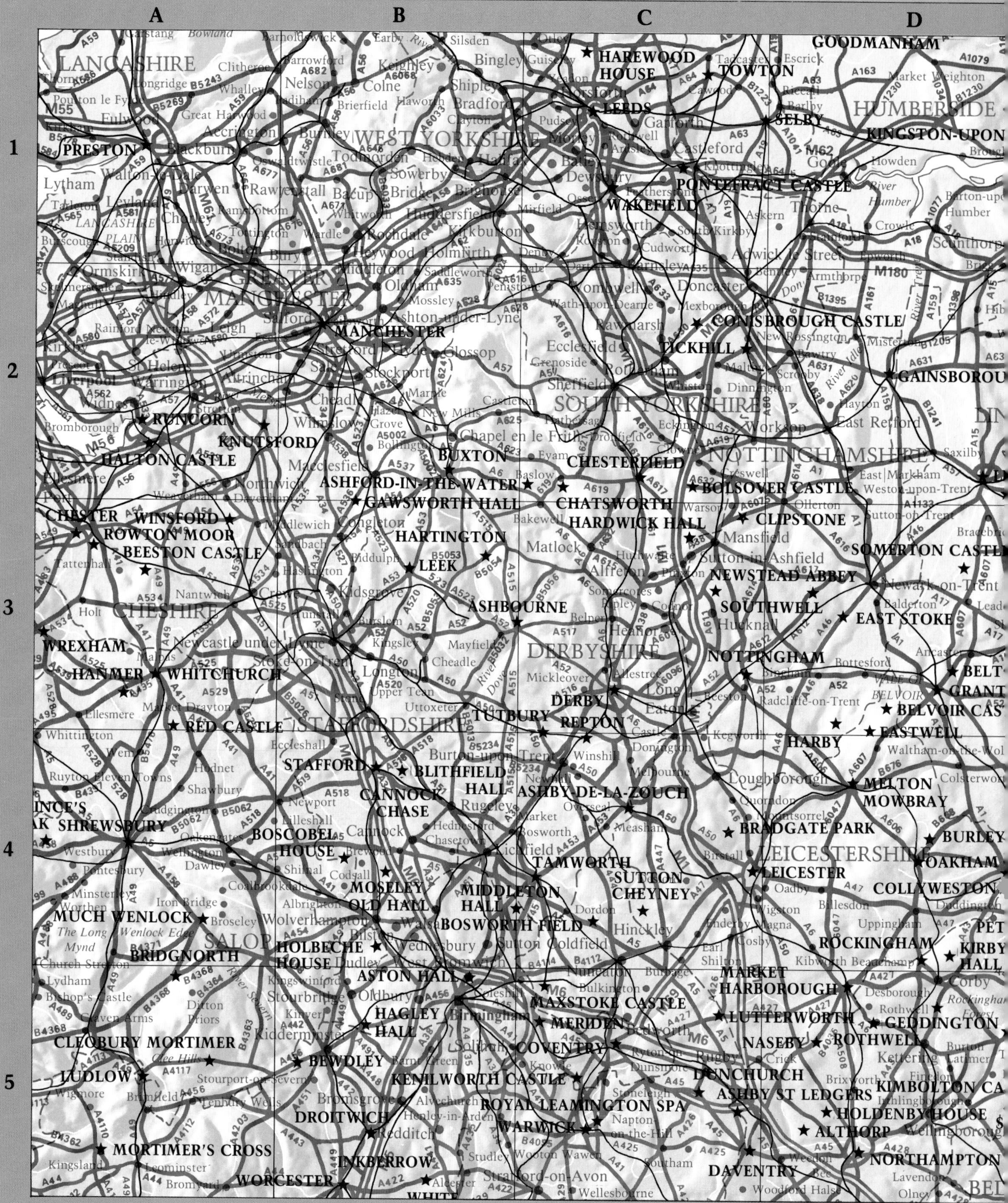

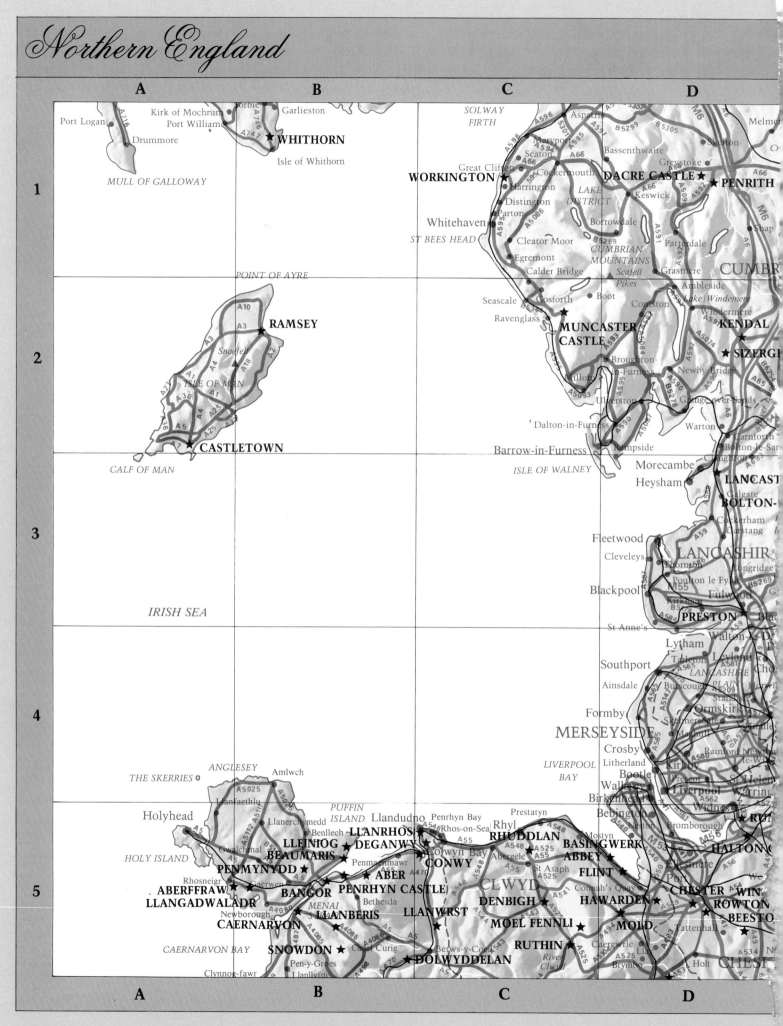

	A	B	C	D

A — **B** — **C** — **D**

Port Logan
Kirk of Mochrum
Port William
Drummore
Sorbie
Garlieston
WHITHORN ★
Isle of Whithorn
MULL OF GALLOWAY

SOLWAY FIRTH
Aspatria
Maryport
Seaton
Great Clifton
WORKINGTON ★
Harrington
Distington
Parton
Whitehaven
ST BEES HEAD
Cleator Moor
Egremont
Calder Bridge
Bassenthwaite
Cockermouth
LAKE DISTRICT
Keswick
Borrowdale
CUMBRIAN MOUNTAINS
Scafell Pikes
DACRE CASTLE ★
Greystoke
Patterdale
Grasmere
PENRITH ★
Skelton
Melmer
Shap
CUMBR

POINT OF AYRE
RAMSEY ★
Snaefell
ISLE OF MAN
CASTLETOWN ★
CALF OF MAN

Seascale
Ravenglass
Gosforth
Boot
MUNCASTER CASTLE ★
Broughton-in-Furness
Millom
Newby Bridge
Coniston
Lake Windemere
Ambleside
Windermere
KENDAL ★
SIZERGH ★

Ulverston
Dalton-in-Furness
Barrow-in-Furness
Rampside
ISLE OF WALNEY
Grange-over-Sands
Warton
Carnforth
Bolton-le-Sands
LANCAST
BOLTON-
Galgate
Cockerham
Garstang
Morecambe
Heysham

IRISH SEA

Fleetwood
Cleveleys
Blackpool
Thornton
Poulton le Fylde
Kirkham
St Anne's
Lytham
LANCASHIRE
Longridge
Fulwood
PRESTON ★
Walton-le-D
Leyland
LANCASHIRE PLAIN

Southport
Ainsdale
Formby
Burscough
Ormskirk
Skelmersdale
MERSEYSIDE
Crosby
Litherland
Bootle
Wallasey
LIVERPOOL BAY
Kirkby
Prescot
St Helen
Liverpool
Warring
Birkenhead
Widnes

THE SKERRIES
ANGLESEY
Amlwch
Llanfaethlu
Holyhead
HOLY ISLAND
Llanerchymedd
Benllech
Gwalchmai
Rhosneigr
PUFFIN ISLAND
Llandudno
Penrhyn Bay
Rhos-on-Sea
Colwyn Bay
Prestatyn
Rhyl
Abergele
St Asaph
Mostyn
RHUDDLAN ★
BASINGWERK ABBEY ★
Neston
Bromborough
Bebington
HALTON
ROW

LLANRHOS
DEGANWY ★
LLEINIOG ★
BEAUMARIS ★
PENMYNYDD ★
Penmaenmawr
ABER ★
CONWY ★
FLINT ★
Caerwen
ABERFFRAW ★
LLANGADWALADR
BANGOR ★
PENRHYN CASTLE ★
Bethesda
Newborough
CAERNARVON
LLANBERIS ★
LLANWRST
DENBIGH ★
MOEL FENNLI ★
CLWYD
Caergwrle
Connah's Quay
HAWARDEN ★
MOLD ★
CHESTER
ROWTON
BEESTO
Tattenhall
CAERNARVON BAY
SNOWDON ★
Capel Curig
Betws-y-Coed
RUTHIN ★
DOLWYDDELAN ★
River Clwyd
Holt
CHES
Pen-y-Groes
Clynnog-fawr
Llanllyfni

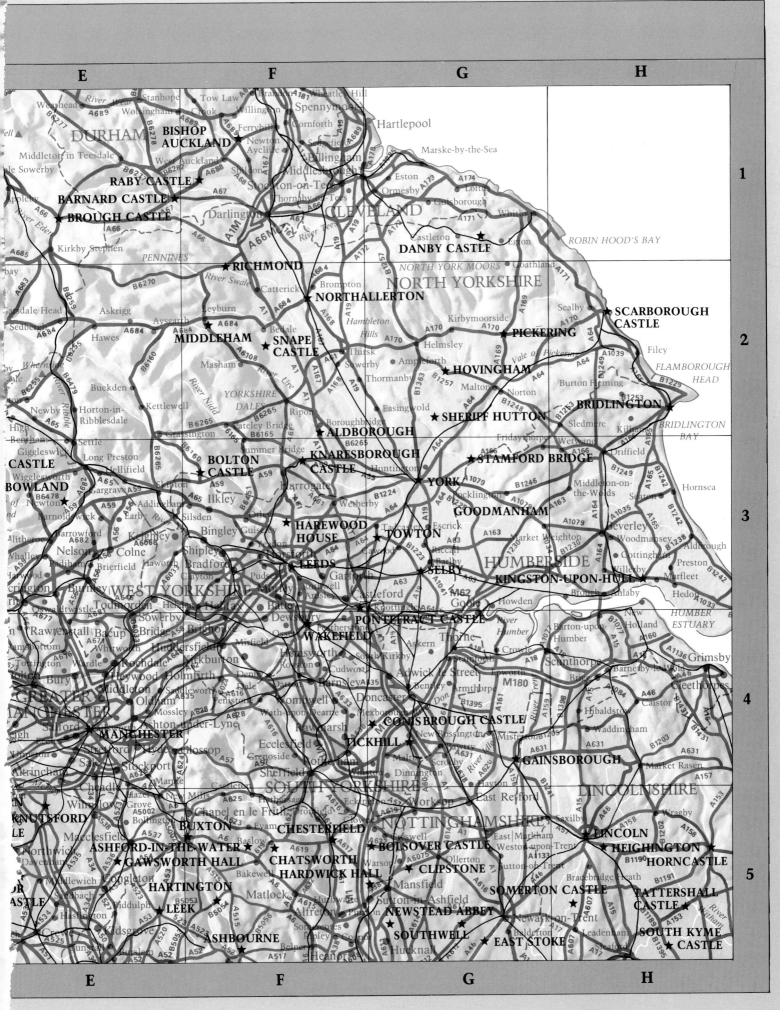

DURHAM

BISHOP AUCKLAND

RABY CASTLE ★

BARNARD CASTLE ★

★ BROUGH CASTLE

Hartlepool

Marske-by-the-Sea

CLEVELAND

ROBIN HOOD'S BAY

DANBY CASTLE

PENNINES

NORTH YORK MOORS

NORTH YORKSHIRE

★ RICHMOND

★ NORTHALLERTON

★ SCARBOROUGH CASTLE

MIDDLEHAM ★

SNAPE CASTLE

★ PICKERING

FLAMBOROUGH HEAD

★ HOVINGHAM

YORKSHIRE DALES

★ SHERIFF HUTTON

★ BRIDLINGTON

BRIDLINGTON BAY

★ ALDBOROUGH

CASTLE

BOWLAND

BOLTON CASTLE ★

KNARESBOROUGH CASTLE

★ STAMFORD BRIDGE

★ YORK

GOODMANHAM

HAREWOOD HOUSE ★

★ TOWTON

HUMBERSIDE

★ LEEDS

★ SELBY

KINGSTON-UPON-HULL

WEST YORKSHIRE

HUMBER ESTUARY

PONTEFRACT CASTLE

WAKEFIELD

GREATER MANCHESTER

★ MANCHESTER

★ CONISBROUGH CASTLE

Grimsby

★ TICKHILL

★ GAINSBOROUGH

SOUTH YORKSHIRE

LINCOLNSHIRE

NOTTINGHAMSHIRE

BUXTON

CHESTERFIELD

★ LINCOLN

ASHFORD-IN-THE-WATER ★

★ BOLSOVER CASTLE

★ HEIGHINGTON

★ GAWSWORTH HALL

CHATSWORTH

HORNCASTLE

HARDWICK HALL

★ CLIPSTONE

HARTINGTON

SOMERTON CASTLE

TATTERSHALL CASTLE

★ LEEK

NEWSTEAD ABBEY

★ SOUTHWELL

★ EAST STOKE

SOUTH KYME CASTLE

ASHBOURNE

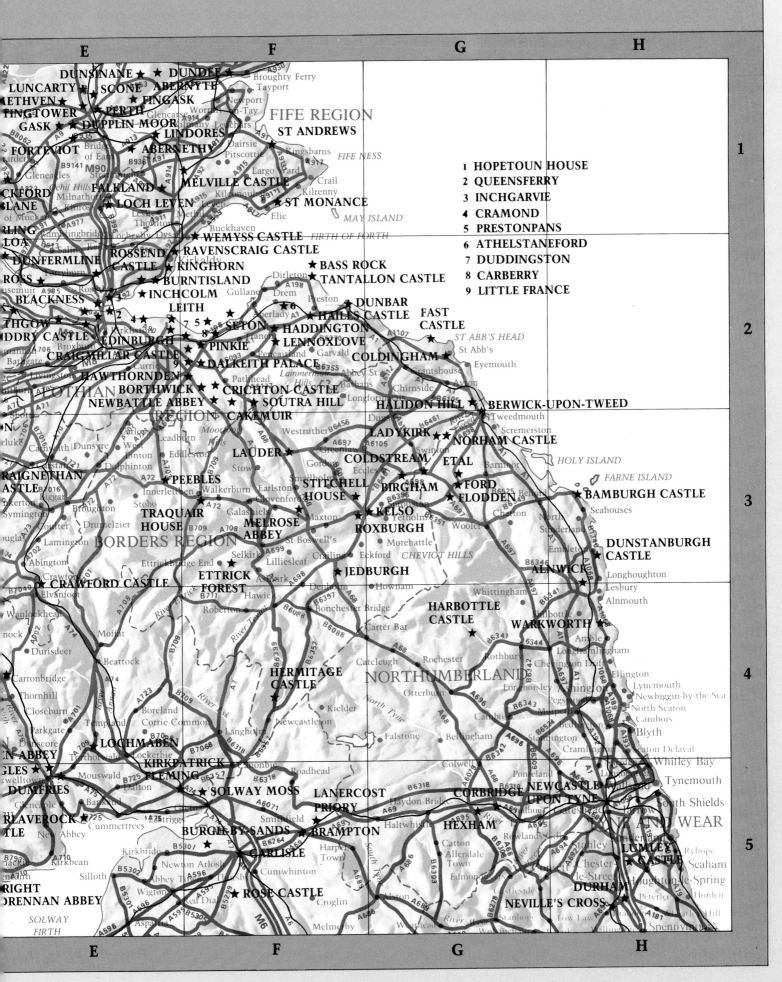

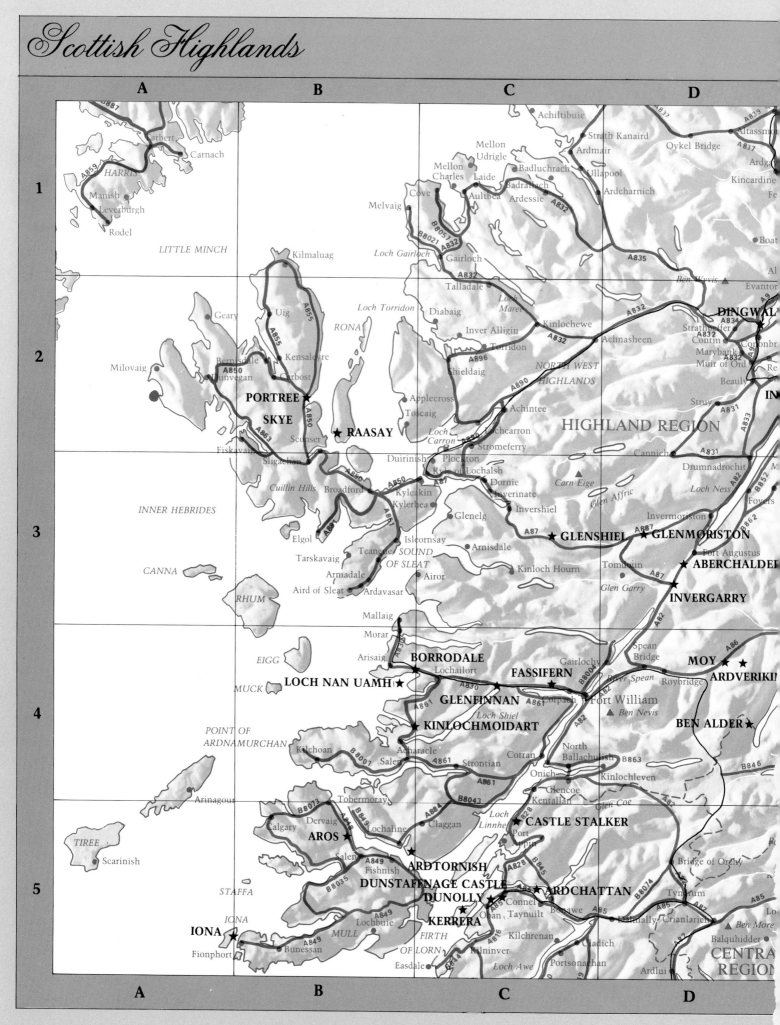

A   B   C   D

1

2

3

4

5

A   B   C   D

HARRIS
Carbert
Carnach
Manish
Leverburgh
Rodel
LITTLE MINCH
Milovaig
Geary
Uig
Kilmaluag
RONA
Kensaleyre
Bernisdale
Dunvegan
Carbost
PORTREE
SKYE
RAASAY
Sconser
Fiskavaig
Sligachan
Cuillin Hills
Broadford
INNER HEBRIDES
Elgol
Tarskavaig
Teangue
SOUND
OF SLEAT
Armadale
Aird of Sleat
Ardvasar
CANNA
RHUM
Mallaig
Morar
EIGG
Arisaig
BORRODALE
Lochailort
MUCK
LOCH NAN UAMH
GLENFINNAN
KINLOCHMOIDART
Loch Shiel
POINT OF
ARDNAMURCHAN
Kilchoan
Acharacle
Salen
Strontian
Arinagour
Tobermoray
TIREE
Scarinish
Calgary
Dervaig
AROS
Lochaline
Claggan
Fishnish
ARDTORNISH
DUNSTAFFNAGE CASTLE
DUNOLLY
ARDCHATTAN
KERRERA
Oban
Connel
Taynuilt
Bonawe
IONA
Fionphort
Bunessan
MULL
FIRTH
OF LORN
Lochbuie
Kilninver
Easdale
Loch Awe
Kilchrenan
Cladich
Portsonachan
STAFFA
Kilmelford

Achiltibuie
Strath Kanaird
Mellon
Udrigle
Ardmair
Oykel Bridge
Altassm
Mellon
Charles
Laide
Badluchrach
Ullapool
Ardg
Cove
Badrallach
Ardessie
Kincardine
Ardcharnich
Fe
Melvaig
Aultbea
Ben Wyvis
Evantor
Loch Gairloch
Gairloch
A832
Al
Boat
Talladale
A835
Loch
Maree
DINGWAL
Diabaig
Kinlochewe
Strathpeffer
A834
Inver Alligin
Achnasheen
Contin
Conon br
Torridon
Marybank
Muir of Ord
Shieldaig
NORTH WEST
HIGHLANDS
Beauly
Applecross
Achintee
HIGHLAND REGION
Struy
IN
Toscaig
Lochcarron
Stromeferry
Cannich
Plockton
Duirinish
Kyle of Lochalsh
Drumnadrochit
Dornie
Carn Eige
Loch Ness
Kyleakin
Inverinate
Glen Affric
Fov
Kylerhea
Invershiel
Invermoriston
Glenelg
GLENSHIEL
GLENMORISTON
Isleornsay
Arnisdale
Fort Augustus
Airor
Kinloch Hourn
Tomdoun
ABERCHALDE
Glen Garry
INVERGARRY
Spean
Bridge
MOY
ARDVERIKI
Gairlochy
FASSIFERN
River Spean
Roybridge
BEN ALDER
Corpach
Fort William
Ben Nevis
North
Ballachulish
Corran
Onich
Kinlochleven
Glencoe
Kentallan
Glen Coe
Loch
Linnhe
CASTLE STALKER
Port
Appin
Bridge of Orchy
Tyndrum
Dalmally
Crianlarich
Ben More
Balquhidder
CENTRA
REGION
Ardlui

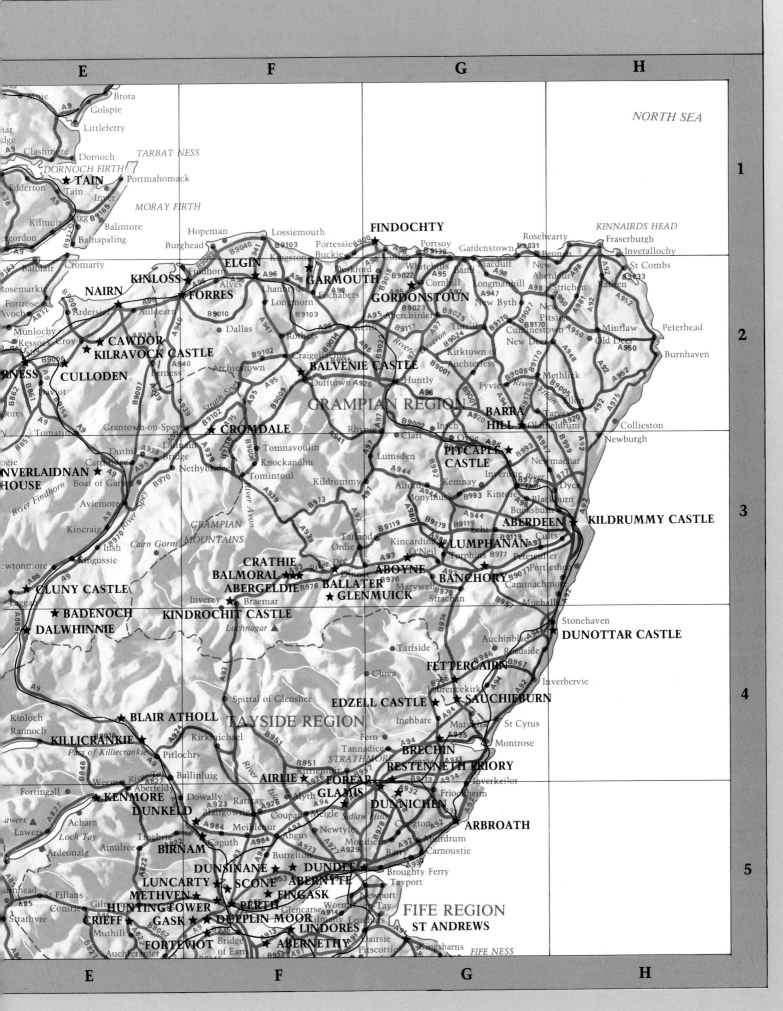

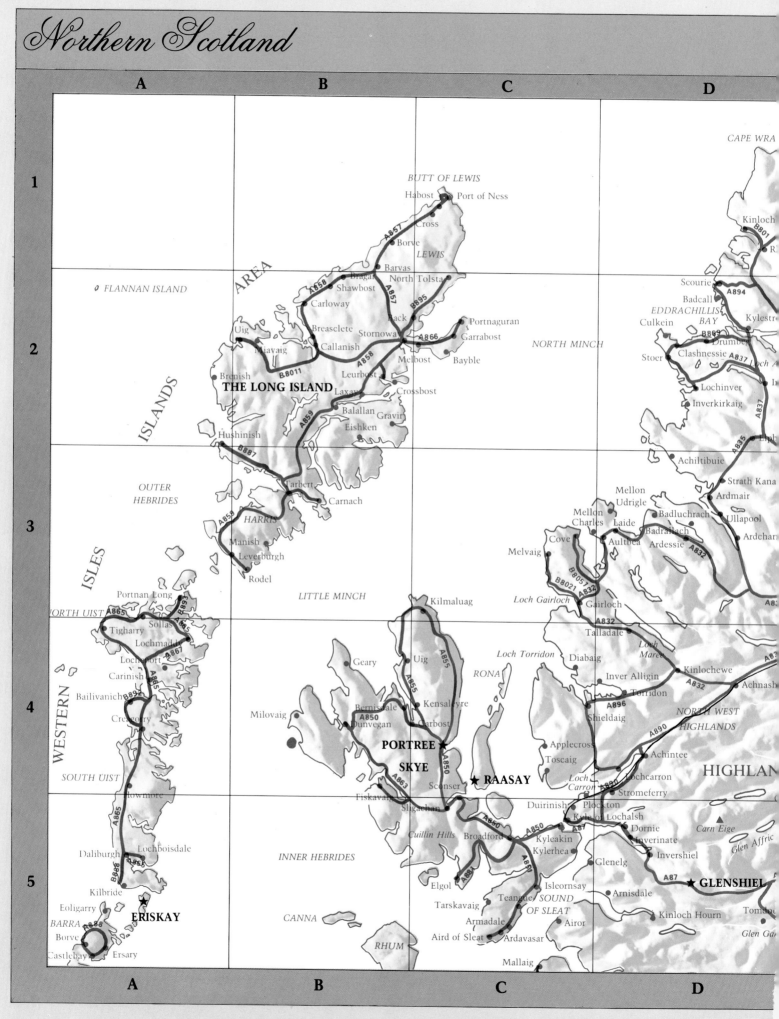

A   B   C   D

1

2

3

4

5

CAPE WRA

BUTT OF LEWIS

Habost   Port of Ness

Cross

Borve

LEWIS

Barvas

Bragar   North Tolsta

Shawbost

AREA

Carloway

Breasclete

Callanish

Back

Stornoway

Portnaguran

Garrabost

Melbost   Bayble

NORTH MINCH

Uig

Miavaig

Leurbost

THE LONG ISLAND

Brenish

Laxay   Crossbost

ISLANDS

Balallan   Gravir

Eishken

FLANNAN ISLAND

Scourie

Badcall

EDDRACHILLIS

BAY

Culkein

Kylestr

Drumbe

Clashnessie

Stoer

Lochinver

Inverkirkaig

Hushinish

OUTER

HEBRIDES

Tarbert

Carnach

Achiltibuie

Strath Kana

Ardmair

Ullapool

Ardchar

HARRIS

Manish

Leverburgh

Rodel

LITTLE MINCH

Mellon

Udrigle

Mellon

Charles   Laide

Cove   Aultbea

Badluchrach

Badrallach

Ardessie

ISLES

Melvaig

Portnan Long

NORTH UIST

Kilmaluag

Loch Gairloch   Gairloch

Tigharry

Sollas

Lochmaddy

Lochport

Carinish

Bailivanich

Creagorry

WESTERN

SOUTH UIST

Milovaig

Geary

Uig

RONA

Loch Torridon

Diabaig

Talladale

Loch

Maree

Kinlochewe

Achnash

Inver Alligin

Torridon

NORTH WEST

HIGHLANDS

Bernisdale

Kensaleyre

Dunvegan

Carbost

Shieldaig

PORTREE

SKYE

RAASAY

Applecross

Toscaig

Achintee

HIGHLAN

Sconser

Fiskavaig

Duirinish   Plockton

Lochcarron

Stromeferry

Sligachan

Loch

Carron

Cuillin Hills

Broadford

Kyle of Lochalsh

Dornie

Carn Eige

Glen Affric

INNER HEBRIDES

Kyleakin

Kylerhea

Glenelg

Invershiel

Inverinate

Elgol

Isleornsay

Arnisdale

GLENSHIEL

Tarskavaig

Teangue

SOUND

OF SLEAT

Airor

Kinloch Hourn

Tomdou

CANNA

BARRA

Borve

Castlebay   Ersary

Eoligarry

Kilbride

ERISKAY

Daliburgh

Lochboisdale

Howmore

Armadale

Aird of Sleat   Ardvasar

RHUM

Mallaig

Glen Ga

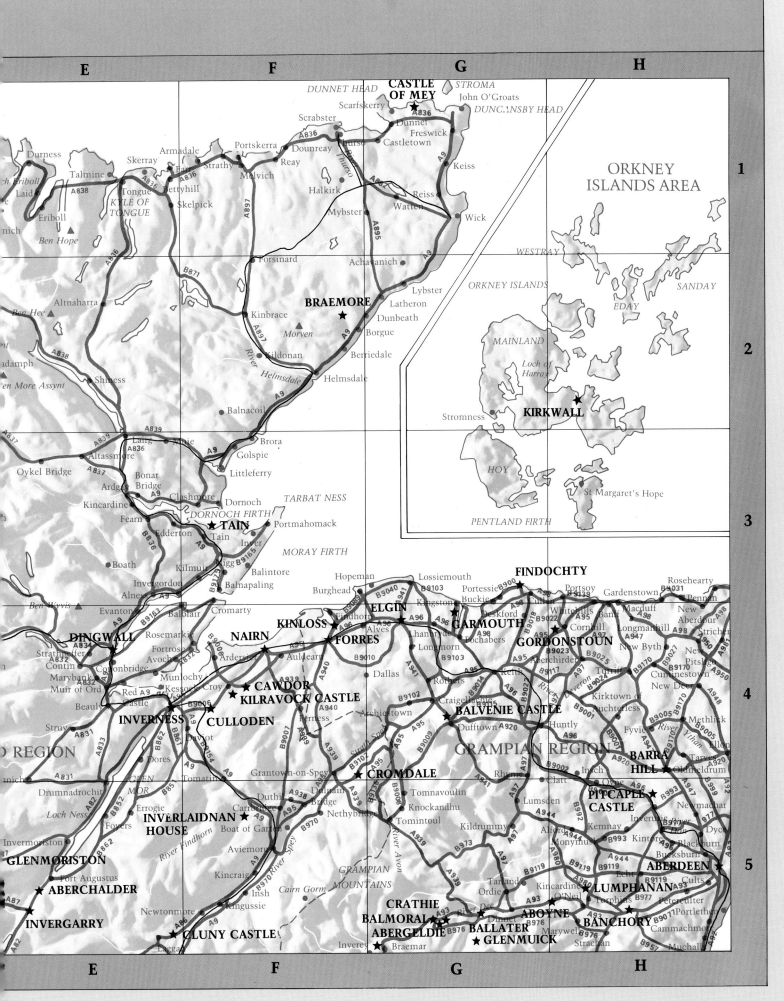

DUNNET HEAD   **CASTLE OF MEY**   *STROMA*

John O'Groats

Scarfskerry   *DUNCANSBY HEAD*

Scrabster   Dunnet

Portskerra   Dounreay   Freswick

Armadale   Strathy   Reay   Castletown

Skerray   Melvich   Keiss

Durness

Talmine   Bettyhill

Laid   Tongue   Skelpick   Halkirk   Reiss

KYLE OF TONGUE   Thurso   Watten

Eriboll   Mybster   Wick

Ben Hope   Wick

ORKNEY ISLANDS AREA

WESTRAY

Altnaharra   Forsinard   Achavanich

Ben Hee   *ORKNEY ISLANDS*   *SANDAY*

BRAEMORE   Lybster   *EDAY*

Kinbrace   Latheron

adamph   *Morven*   Dunbeath

en More Assynt   Kildonan   Borgue   *MAINLAND*

Shiness   Berriedale   *Loch of Harray*

Helmsdale   Helmsdale

Balnacoil   Stromness

Laing   **KIRKWALL**

Altassmore   Muie   Brora

Oykel Bridge   Bonar Bridge   Golspie

Ardgay   Littleferry   *HOY*

Kincardine   Clashmore   Dornoch   *TARBAT NESS*   St Margaret's Hope

Fearn   *DORNOCH FIRTH*   Portmahomack

Boath   **TAIN**   *PENTLAND FIRTH*

Edderton   Tain   Inver

Kilmuir   Nigg   Balintore   *MORAY FIRTH*

Invergordon   Balnapaling   Hopeman   Lossiemouth

Alness   Burghead   Portessie   **FINDOCHTY**   Rosehearty

Ben Wyvis   Evanton   Cromarty   Portsoy   Gardenstown   Pennan

Balblair   Findhorn   Buckie   New Aberdour

DINGWALL   Rosemarkie   **ELGIN**   Kingston   Deskford   Whitehills   Banff   Macduff

Strathpeffer   Fortrose   **KINLOSS**   Alves   **GARMOUTH**   Cornhill   Longmanhill

Contin   Avoch   **NAIRN**   **FORRES**   Lhanbryde   Fochabers   **GORDONSTOUN**   New Byth

Marybank   Ardersier   Auldearn   Longmorn   Aberchirder   Turriff   New Deer

Muir of Ord   Munlochy   Dallas   Rothes   Keith

Beauly   Croy   **CAWDOR**   Craigellachie   **BALVENIE CASTLE**   Methlick

Red Castle   **KILRAVOCK CASTLE**   Archiestown   Huntly   Fyvie   Ellon

INVERNESS   **CULLODEN**   Daviot   Furness   Dufftown   **BARRA HILL**

Struy   Dores   **GRAMPIAN REGION**   Oldmeldrum

O REGION   Tomatin   Grantown-on-Spey   **CROMDALE**   Rhynie   Insch   Oyne   **PITCAPLE CASTLE**

Drumnadrochit   Duthil   Dulnain Bridge   Clatt   Lumsden   Inverurie   Newmachar

Loch Ness   Errogie   Carrbridge   Nethybridge   Kildrummy   Kemnay   Kintore   Dyce

Foyers   **INVERLAIDNAN HOUSE**   Knockandhu   Alford   Monymusk   Blackburn

Invermoriston   Boat of Garten   Tomintoul   Bucksburn

GLENMORISTON   Fort Augustus   Aviemore   *River Avon*   Tarland   Echt   **ABERDEEN**

ABERCHALDER   Kincraig   *CAIRN GORM*   Ordie   Kincardine O'Neil   **LUMPHANAN**   Cults

INVERGARRY   Newtonmore   Insh   *GRAMPIAN MOUNTAINS*   Torphins   Peterculter

Kingussie   **CRATHIE**   **ABOYNE**   Portlethen

CLUNY CASTLE   **BALMORAL**   *River Dee*   **BANCHORY**

Laggan   **ABERGELDIE**   **BALLATER**   Marywell   Cammachmore

Inverey   Braemar   **GLENMUICK**   Strachan   Muchals

Index